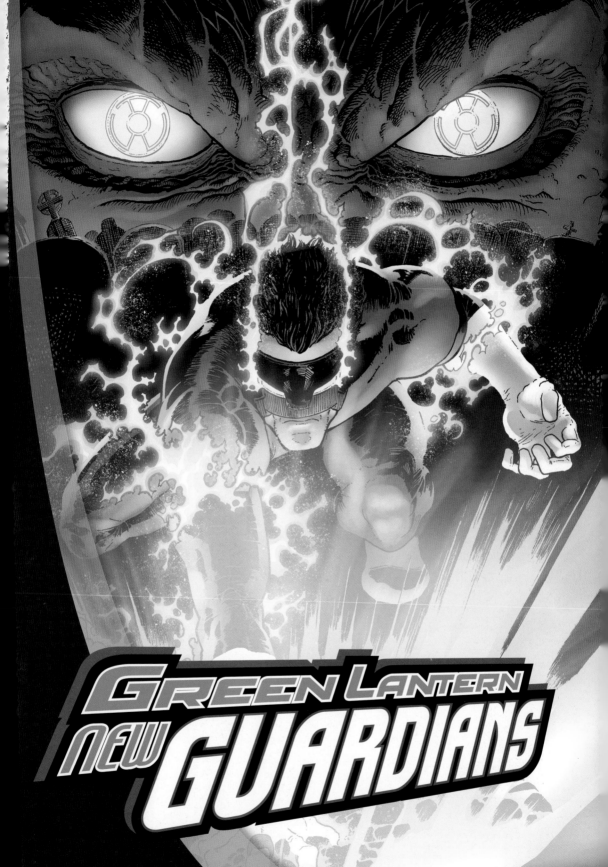

GREEN LANTERN
NEW GUARDIANS

VOLUME 3   LOVE AND DEATH

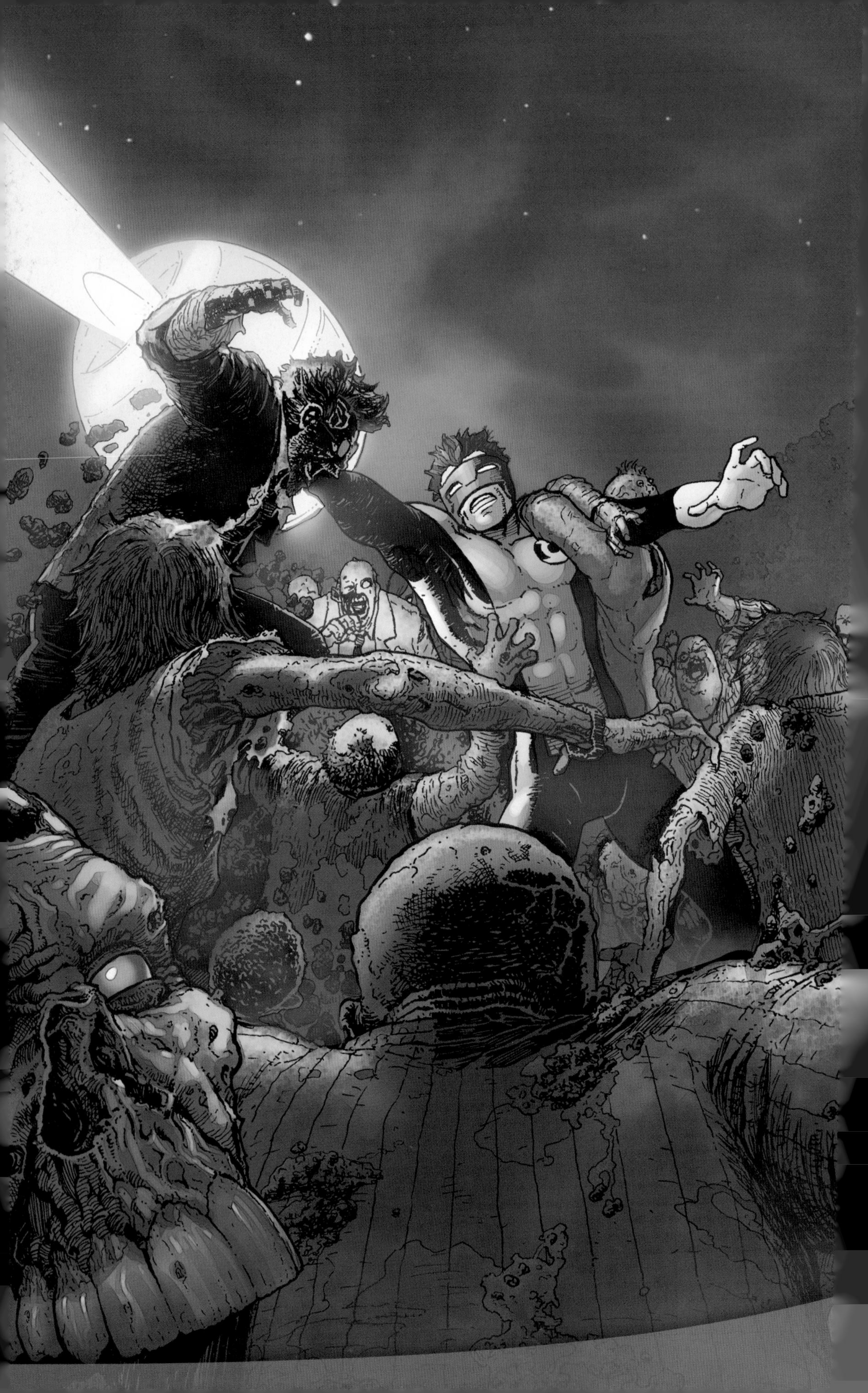

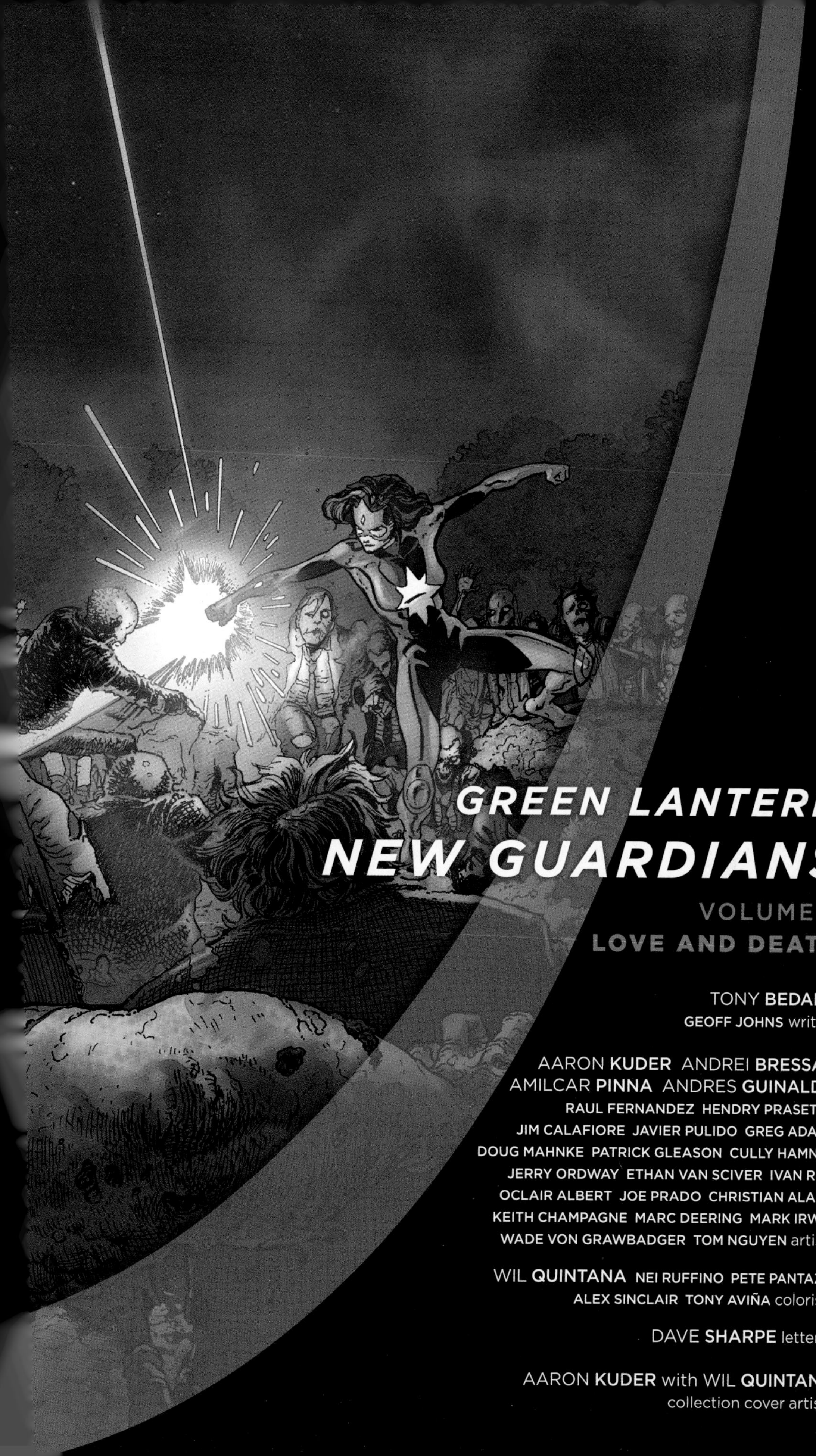

GREEN LANTERN
NEW GUARDIANS

VOLUME 3
LOVE AND DEATH

TONY **BEDARD**
GEOFF JOHNS writers

AARON **KUDER** ANDREI **BRESSAN**
AMILCAR **PINNA** ANDRES **GUINALDO**
RAUL FERNANDEZ **HENDRY PRASETYO**
JIM CALAFIORE **JAVIER PULIDO** **GREG ADAMS**
DOUG MAHNKE **PATRICK GLEASON** **CULLY HAMNER**
JERRY ORDWAY **ETHAN VAN SCIVER** **IVAN REIS**
OCLAIR ALBERT **JOE PRADO** **CHRISTIAN ALAMY**
KEITH CHAMPAGNE **MARC DEERING** **MARK IRWIN**
WADE VON GRAWBADGER **TOM NGUYEN** artists

WIL **QUINTANA** **NEI RUFFINO** **PETE PANTAZIS**
ALEX SINCLAIR **TONY AVIÑA** colorists

DAVE **SHARPE** letterer

AARON **KUDER** with WIL **QUINTANA**
collection cover artists

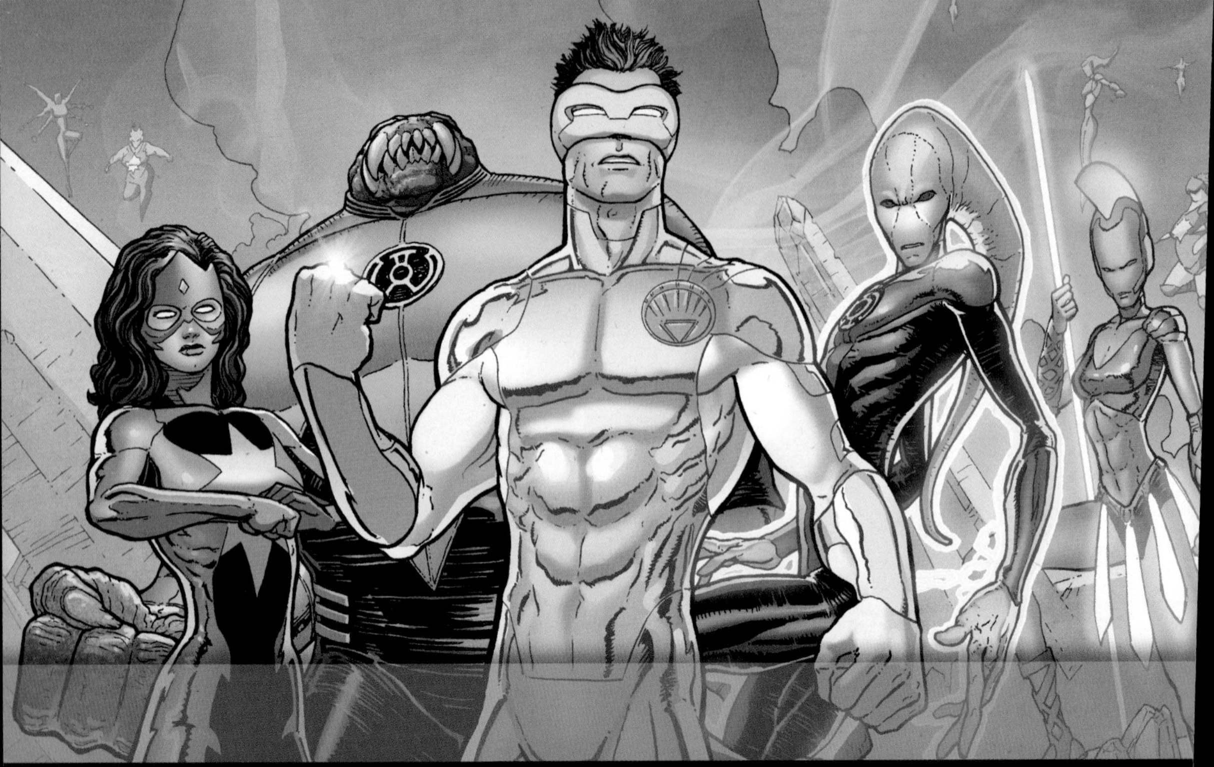

MATT IDELSON PAT MCCALLUM WIL MOSS Editors - Original Series CHRIS CONROY Associate Editor - Original Series
SEAN MACKIEWICZ KATE STEWART Assistant Editors - Original Series
PETER HAMBOUSSI Editor RACHEL PINNELAS Assistant Editor
ROBBIN BROSTERMAN Design Director - Books ROBBIE BIEDERMAN Publication Design

BOB HARRAS Senior VP - Editor-in-Chief, DC Comics

DIANE NELSON President DAN DIDIO and JIM LEE Co-Publishers
GEOFF JOHNS Chief Creative Officer
JOHN ROOD Executive VP - Sales, Marketing and Business Development
AMY GENKINS Senior VP - Business and Legal Affairs NAIRI GARDINER Senior VP - Finance
JEFF BOISON VP - Publishing Planning MARK CHIARELLO VP - Art Direction and Design
JOHN CUNNINGHAM VP - Marketing TERRI CUNNINGHAM VP - Editorial Administration
ALISON GILL Senior VP - Manufacturing and Operations HANK KANALZ Senior VP - Vertigo and Integrated Publishing
JAY KOGAN VP - Business and Legal Affairs, Publishing JACK MAHAN VP - Business Affairs, Talent
NICK NAPOLITANO VP - Manufacturing Administration SUE POHJA VP - Book Sales
COURTNEY SIMMONS Senior VP - Publicity BOB WAYNE Senior VP - Sales

GREEN LANTERN - NEW GUARDIANS VOLUME 3: LOVE AND DEATH

DC Comics, 1700 Broadway, New York, NY 10019
A Warner Bros. Entertainment Company.
Printed by RR Donnelley, Salem, VA, USA. 12/27/13. First Printing.

HC ISBN: 978-1-4012-4406-4

SUSTAINABLE FORESTRY INITIATIVE Certified Chain of Custody
At Least 20% Certified Forest Content
www.sfiprogram.org
SFI-01042
APPLIES TO TEXT STOCK ONLY

Library of Congress Cataloging-in-Publication Data

Bedard, Tony, author.
Green Lantern, New Guardians. Volume 3, Love & Death / Tony Bedard ; [illustrated by] Aaron Kuder.
pages cm
Summary: "Tying into the latest Green Lantern event masterminded by comics' hottest writer Geoff Johns, Kyle Rayner and his fellow Ring bearers must join forces to beat back "The Third Army" and survive "The Wrath of the First Lantern!" Green Lantern Kyle Rayner must master the emotional spectrum itself in order to stand a chance against the Third Army. But even then, a more dangerous threat lurks in the shadows—The First Lantern! Collects GREEN LANTERN: NEW GUARDIANS #0, 13-20"— Provided by publisher.
ISBN 978-1-4012-4406-4 (hardback)
1. Graphic novels. I. Kuder, Aaron, illustrator. II. Title. III. Title: Love & Death.
PN6728.G74B35 2014
741.5'973—dc23
2013039607

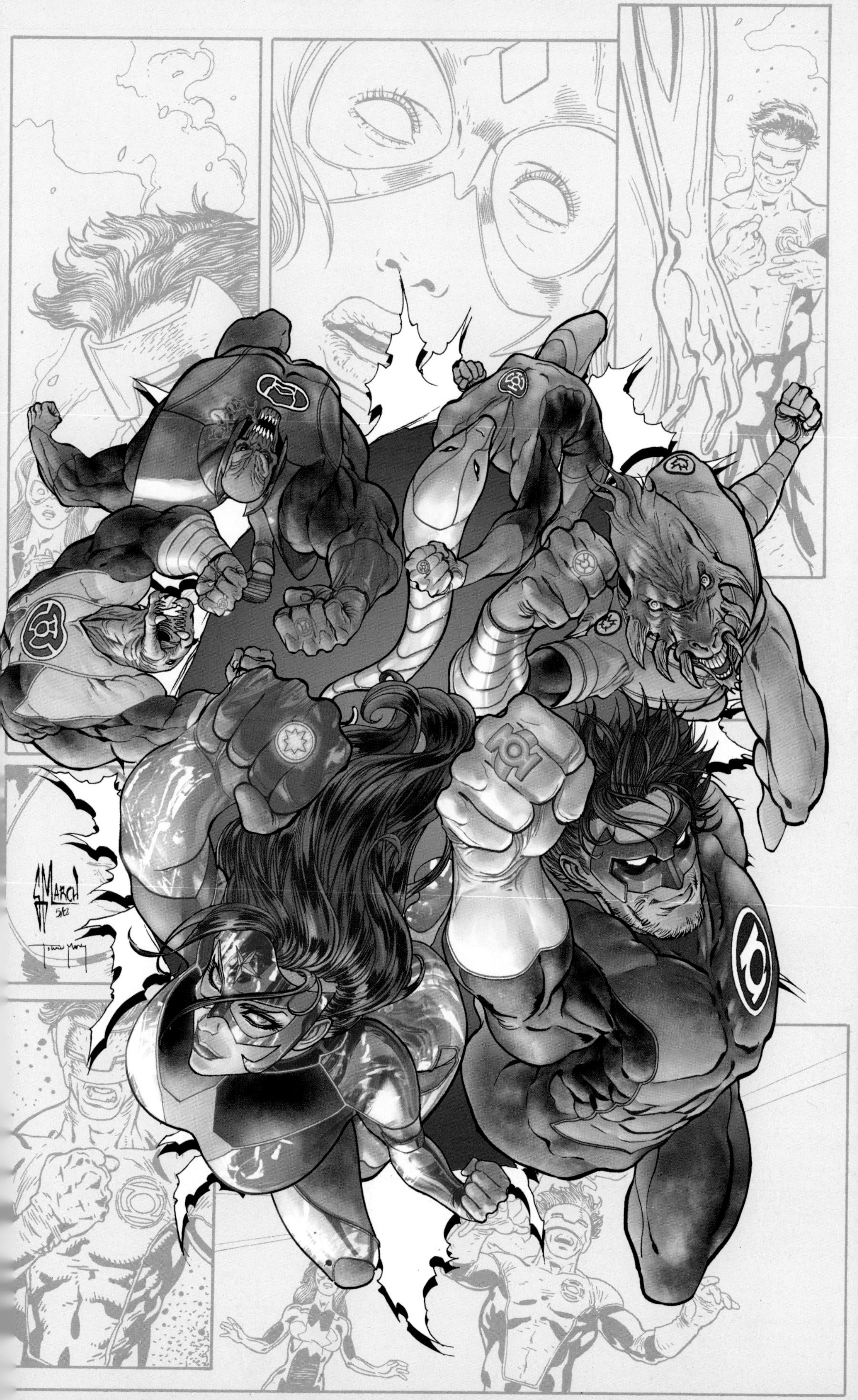

LOVE AND DEATH

TONY BEDARD writer **AARON KUDER & ANDREI BRESSAN** artists **GREG ADAMS** inker
GUILLEM MARCH cover

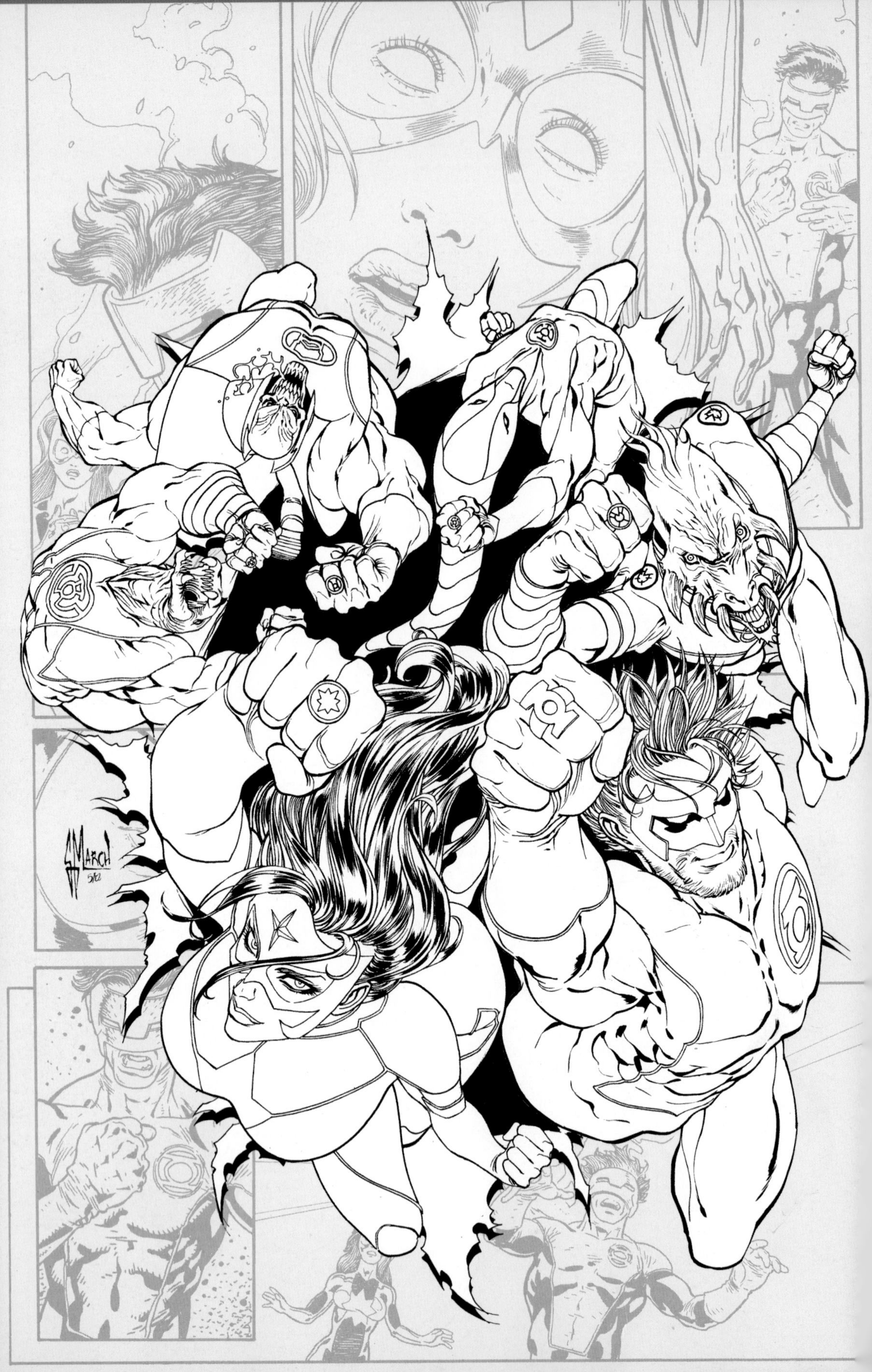

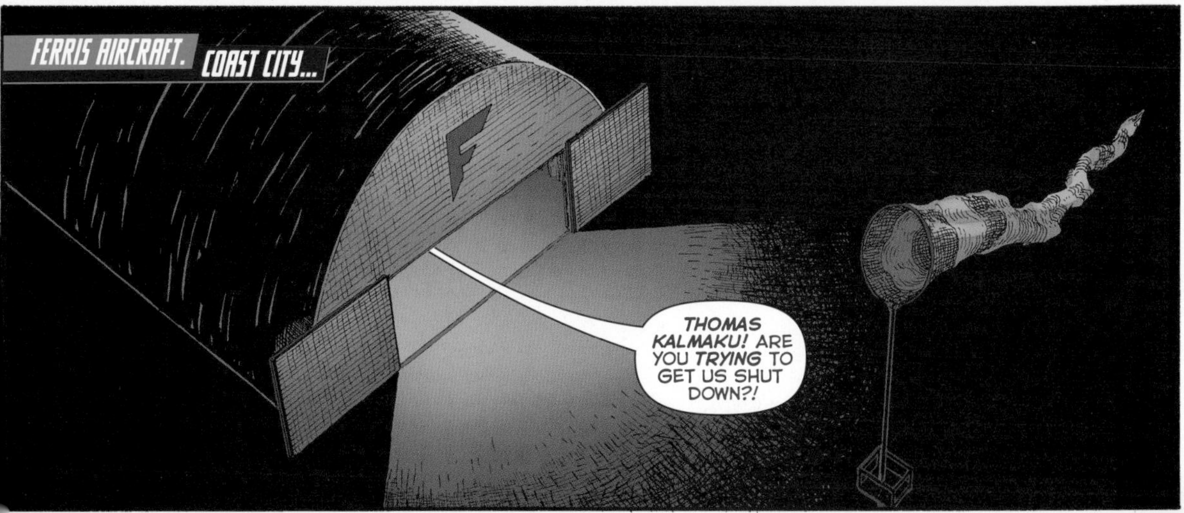
FERRIS AIRCRAFT. COAST CITY...
THOMAS KALMAKU! ARE YOU TRYING TO GET US SHUT DOWN?!

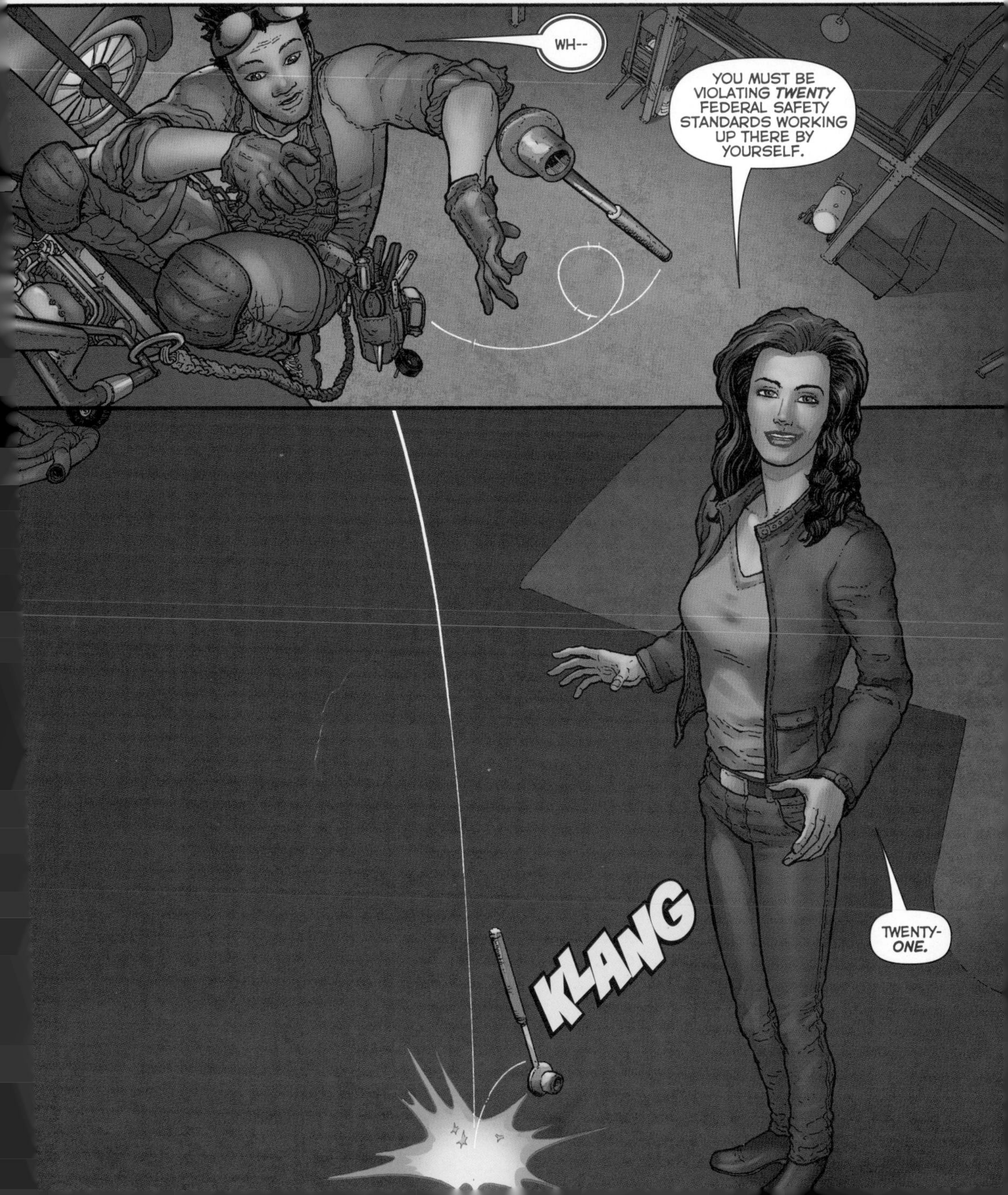
WH--
YOU MUST BE VIOLATING TWENTY FEDERAL SAFETY STANDARDS WORKING UP THERE BY YOURSELF.
KLANG
TWENTY-ONE.

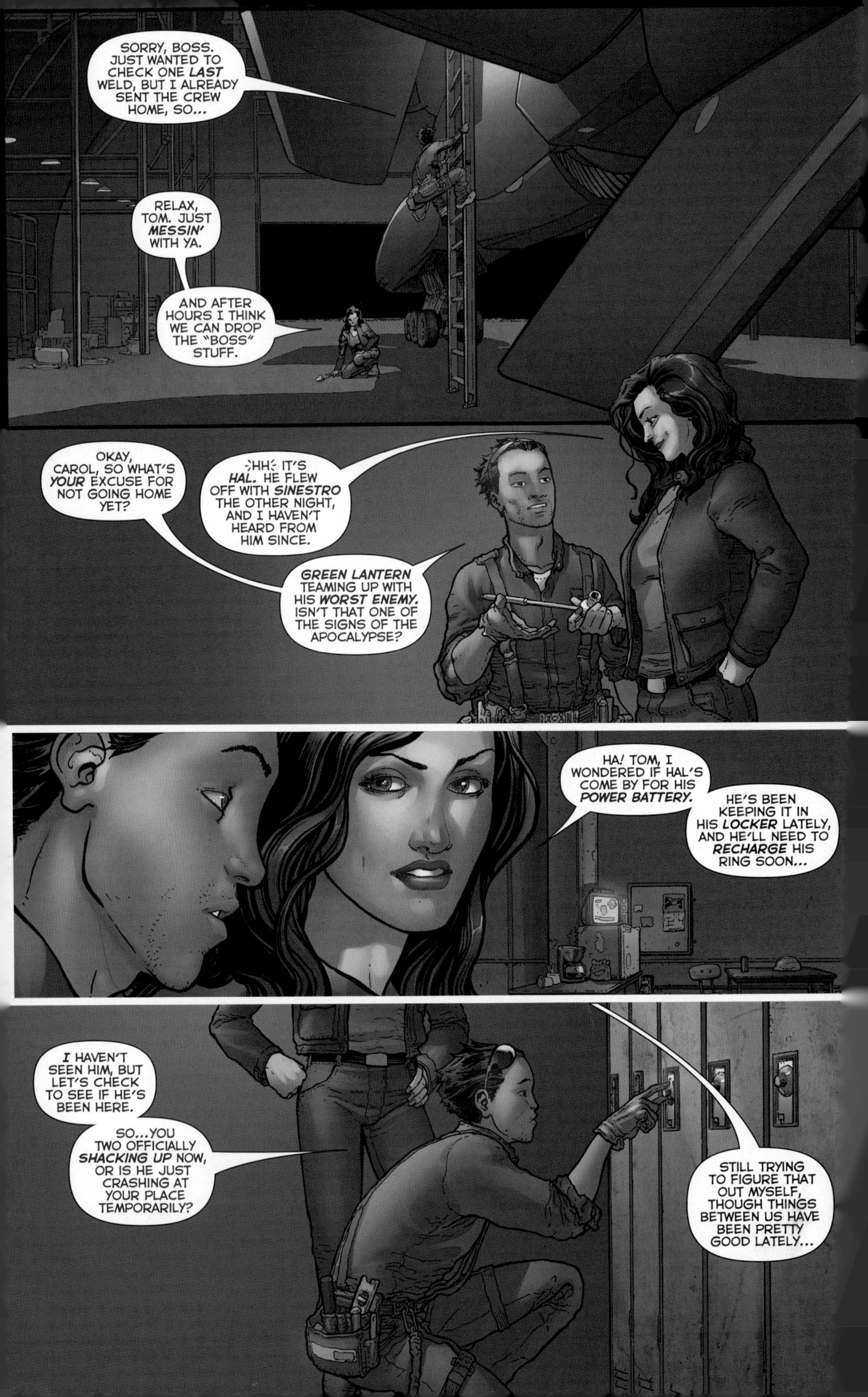
SORRY, BOSS. JUST WANTED TO CHECK ONE LAST WELD, BUT I ALREADY SENT THE CREW HOME, SO...
RELAX, TOM. JUST MESSIN' WITH YA.
AND AFTER HOURS I THINK WE CAN DROP THE "BOSS" STUFF.
OKAY, CAROL, SO WHAT'S YOUR EXCUSE FOR NOT GOING HOME YET?
HH IT'S HAL. HE FLEW OFF WITH SINESTRO THE OTHER NIGHT, AND I HAVEN'T HEARD FROM HIM SINCE.
GREEN LANTERN TEAMING UP WITH HIS WORST ENEMY. ISN'T THAT ONE OF THE SIGNS OF THE APOCALYPSE?
HA! TOM, I WONDERED IF HAL'S COME BY FOR HIS POWER BATTERY.
HE'S BEEN KEEPING IT IN HIS LOCKER LATELY, AND HE'LL NEED TO RECHARGE HIS RING SOON...
I HAVEN'T SEEN HIM, BUT LET'S CHECK TO SEE IF HE'S BEEN HERE.
SO...YOU TWO OFFICIALLY SHACKING UP NOW, OR IS HE JUST CRASHING AT YOUR PLACE TEMPORARILY?
STILL TRYING TO FIGURE THAT OUT MYSELF, THOUGH THINGS BETWEEN US HAVE BEEN PRETTY GOOD LATELY...

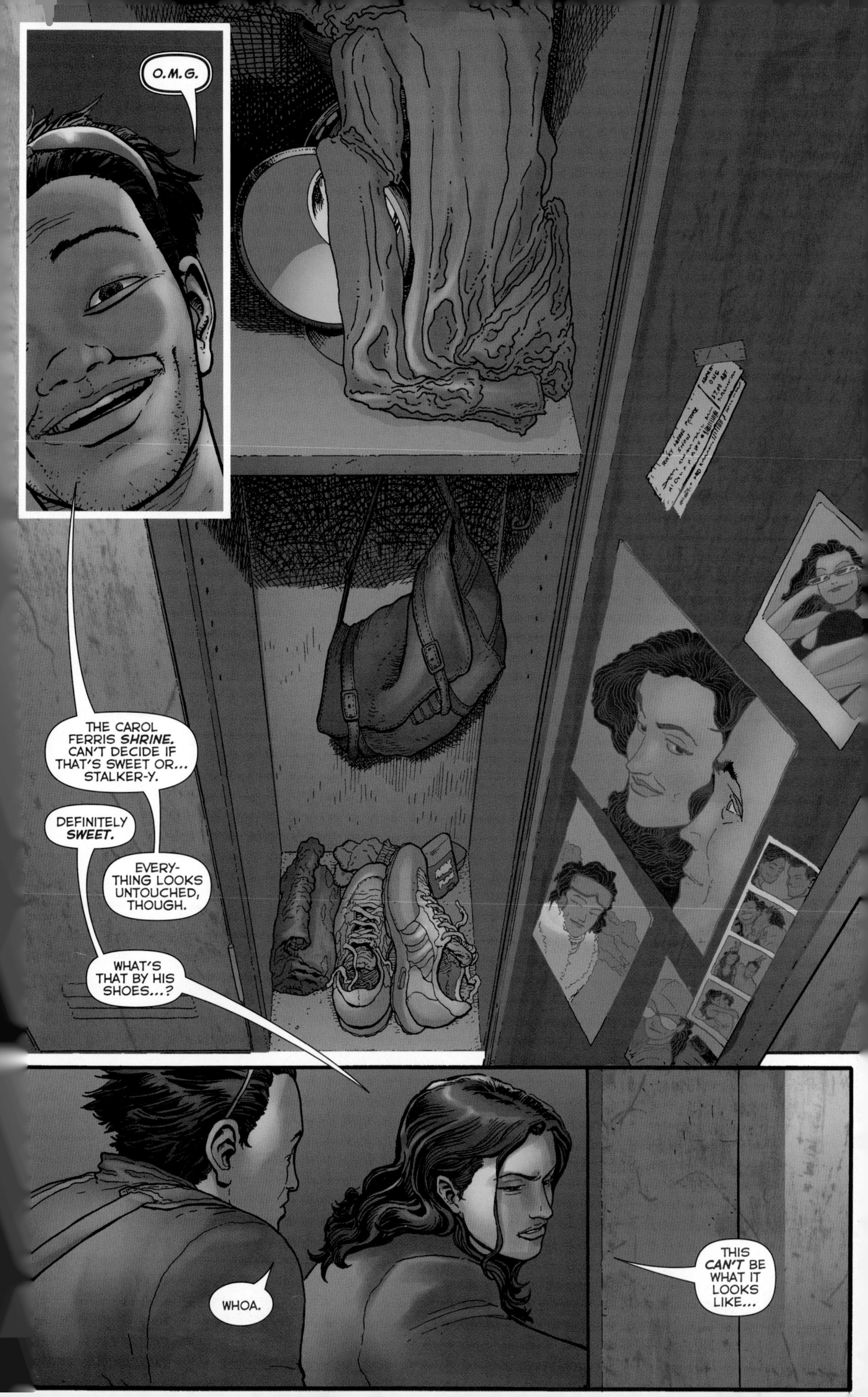
O.M.G.
THE CAROL FERRIS SHRINE. CAN'T DECIDE IF THAT'S SWEET OR... STALKER-Y.
DEFINITELY SWEET.
EVERY-THING LOOKS UNTOUCHED, THOUGH.
WHAT'S THAT BY HIS SHOES...?
WHOA.
THIS CAN'T BE WHAT IT LOOKS LIKE...

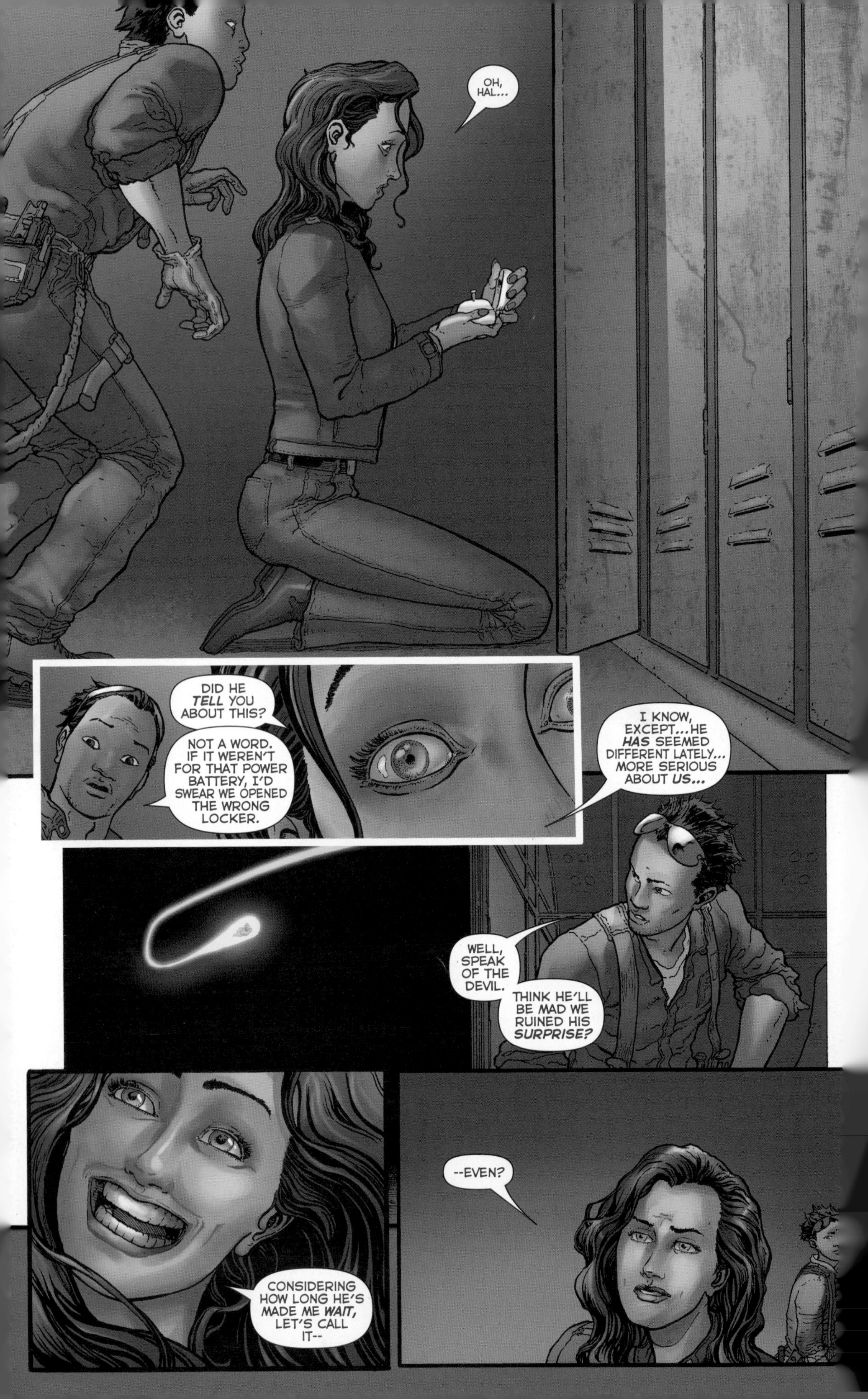
OH, HAL...
DID HE *TELL* YOU ABOUT THIS?
NOT A WORD. IF IT WEREN'T FOR THAT POWER BATTERY, I'D SWEAR WE OPENED THE WRONG LOCKER.
I KNOW, EXCEPT...HE *HAS* SEEMED DIFFERENT LATELY... MORE SERIOUS ABOUT *US*...
WELL, SPEAK OF THE DEVIL.
THINK HE'LL BE MAD WE RUINED HIS *SURPRISE?*
CONSIDERING HOW LONG HE'S MADE ME *WAIT,* LET'S CALL IT--
--EVEN?

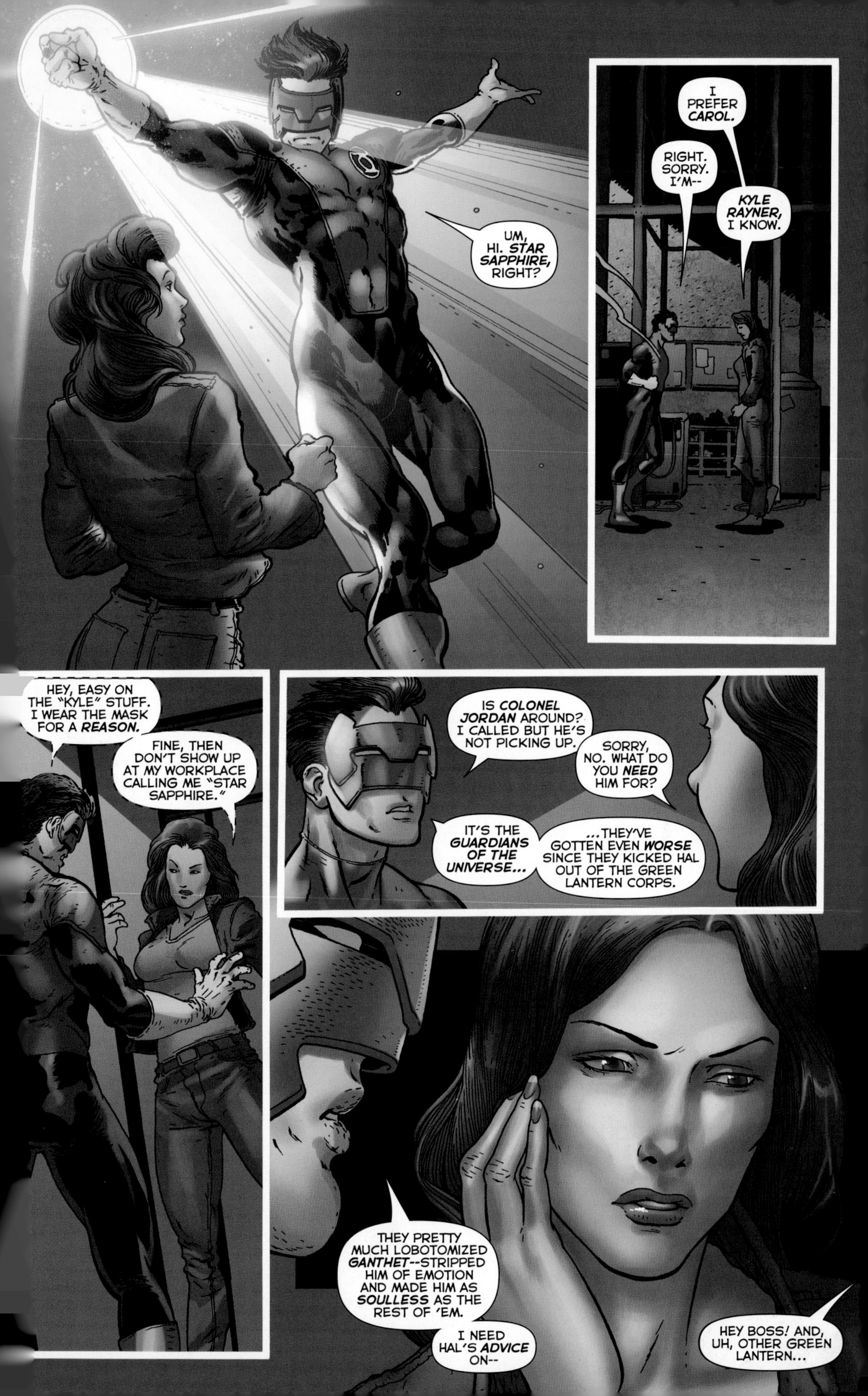
UM, HI. STAR SAPPHIRE, RIGHT?
I PREFER CAROL.
RIGHT. SORRY. I'M--
KYLE RAYNER, I KNOW.
HEY, EASY ON THE "KYLE" STUFF. I WEAR THE MASK FOR A REASON.
FINE, THEN DON'T SHOW UP AT MY WORKPLACE CALLING ME "STAR SAPPHIRE."
IS COLONEL JORDAN AROUND? I CALLED BUT HE'S NOT PICKING UP.
SORRY, NO. WHAT DO YOU NEED HIM FOR?
IT'S THE GUARDIANS OF THE UNIVERSE...
...THEY'VE GOTTEN EVEN WORSE SINCE THEY KICKED HAL OUT OF THE GREEN LANTERN CORPS.
THEY PRETTY MUCH LOBOTOMIZED GANTHET--STRIPPED HIM OF EMOTION AND MADE HIM AS SOULLESS AS THE REST OF 'EM.
I NEED HAL'S ADVICE ON--
HEY BOSS! AND, UH, OTHER GREEN LANTERN...

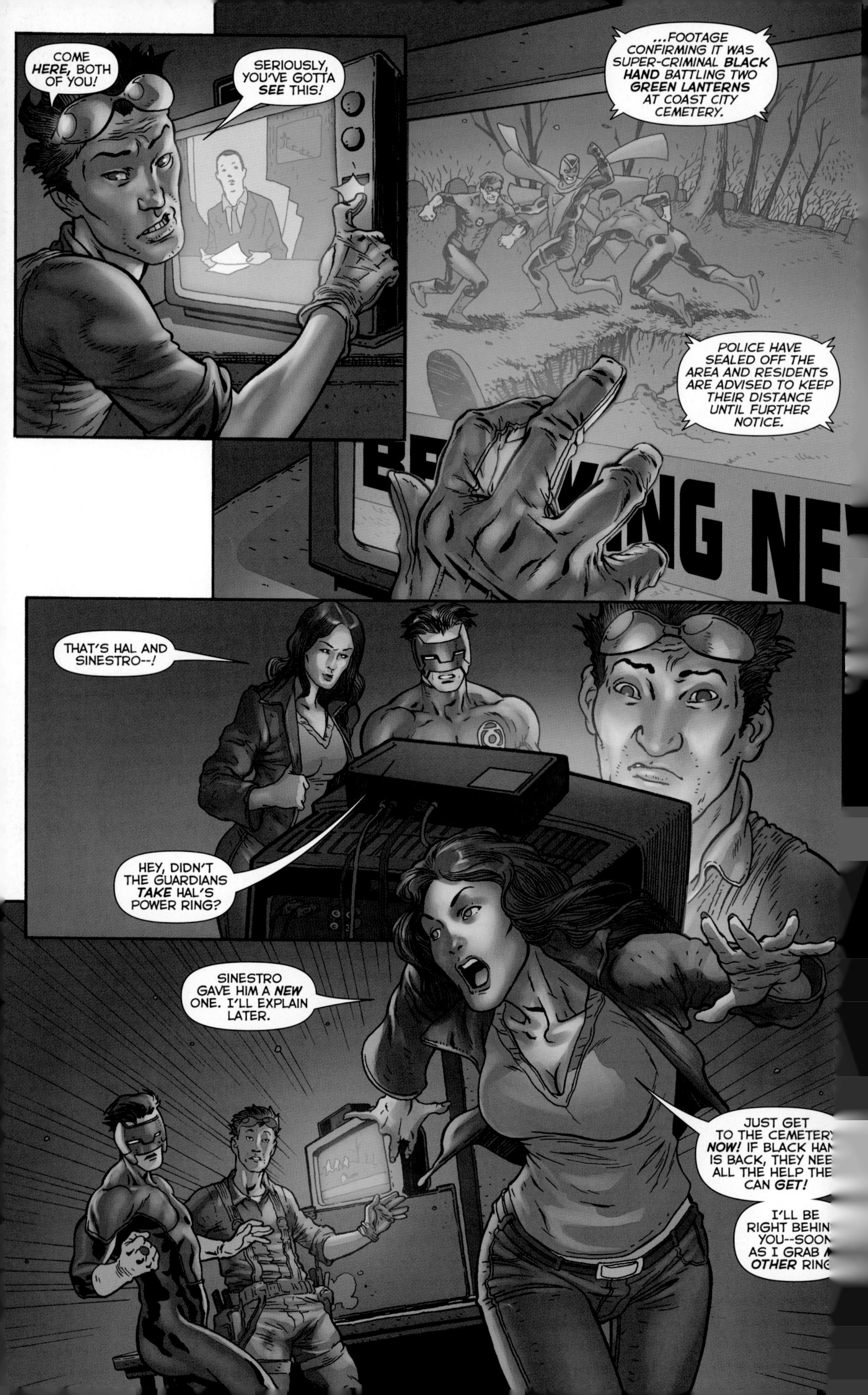
COME HERE, BOTH OF YOU!
SERIOUSLY, YOU'VE GOTTA SEE THIS!
...FOOTAGE CONFIRMING IT WAS SUPER-CRIMINAL BLACK HAND BATTLING TWO GREEN LANTERNS AT COAST CITY CEMETERY.
POLICE HAVE SEALED OFF THE AREA AND RESIDENTS ARE ADVISED TO KEEP THEIR DISTANCE UNTIL FURTHER NOTICE.
THAT'S HAL AND SINESTRO--!
HEY, DIDN'T THE GUARDIANS TAKE HAL'S POWER RING?
SINESTRO GAVE HIM A NEW ONE. I'LL EXPLAIN LATER.
JUST GET TO THE CEMETERY NOW! IF BLACK HAN IS BACK, THEY NEE ALL THE HELP THE CAN GET!
I'LL BE RIGHT BEHIN YOU--SOON AS I GRAB OTHER RING

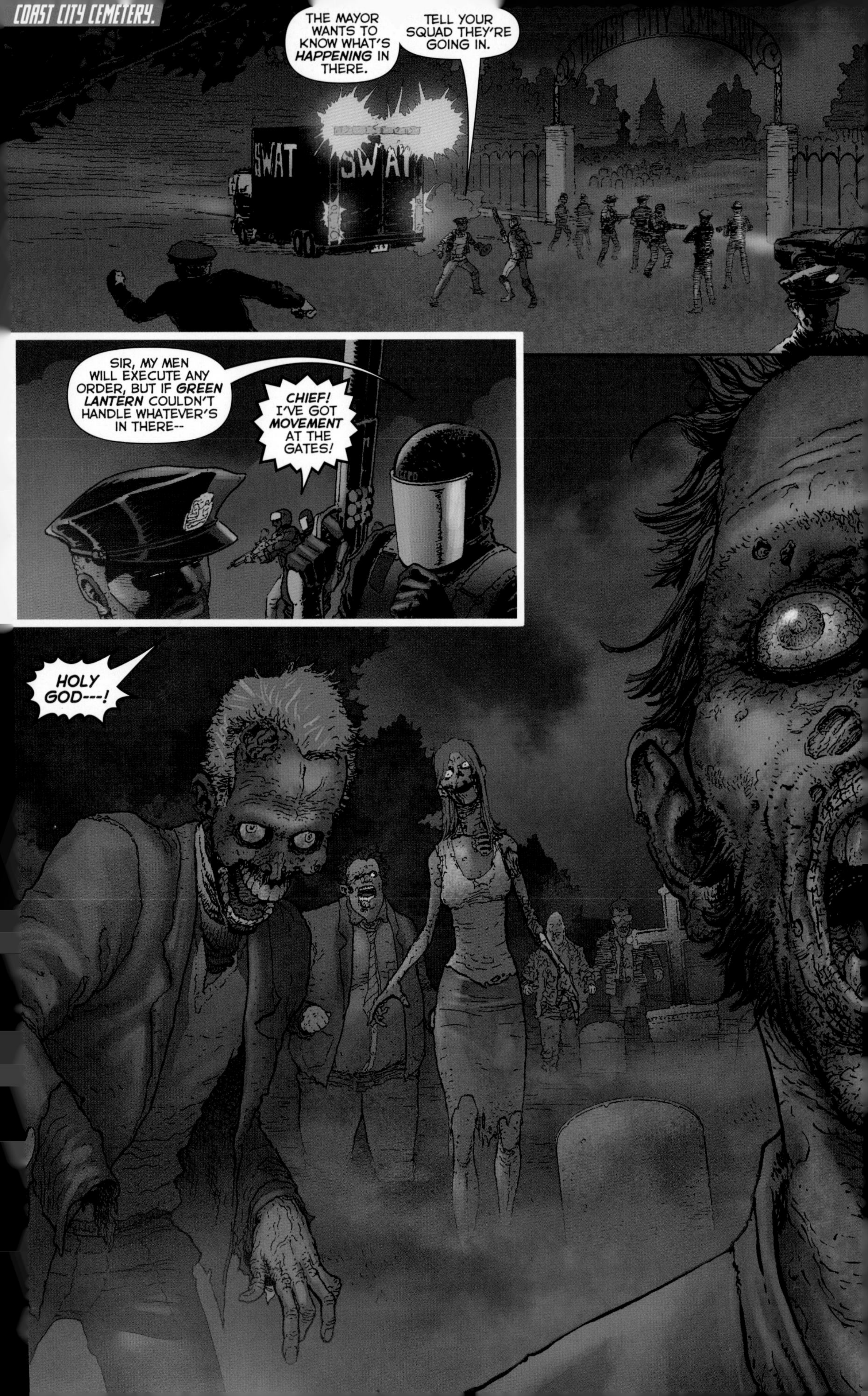
COAST CITY CEMETERY.
THE MAYOR WANTS TO KNOW WHAT'S HAPPENING IN THERE.
TELL YOUR SQUAD THEY'RE GOING IN.
SWAT
SWAT
SIR, MY MEN WILL EXECUTE ANY ORDER, BUT IF GREEN LANTERN COULDN'T HANDLE WHATEVER'S IN THERE--
CHIEF! I'VE GOT MOVEMENT AT THE GATES!
HOLY GOD---!

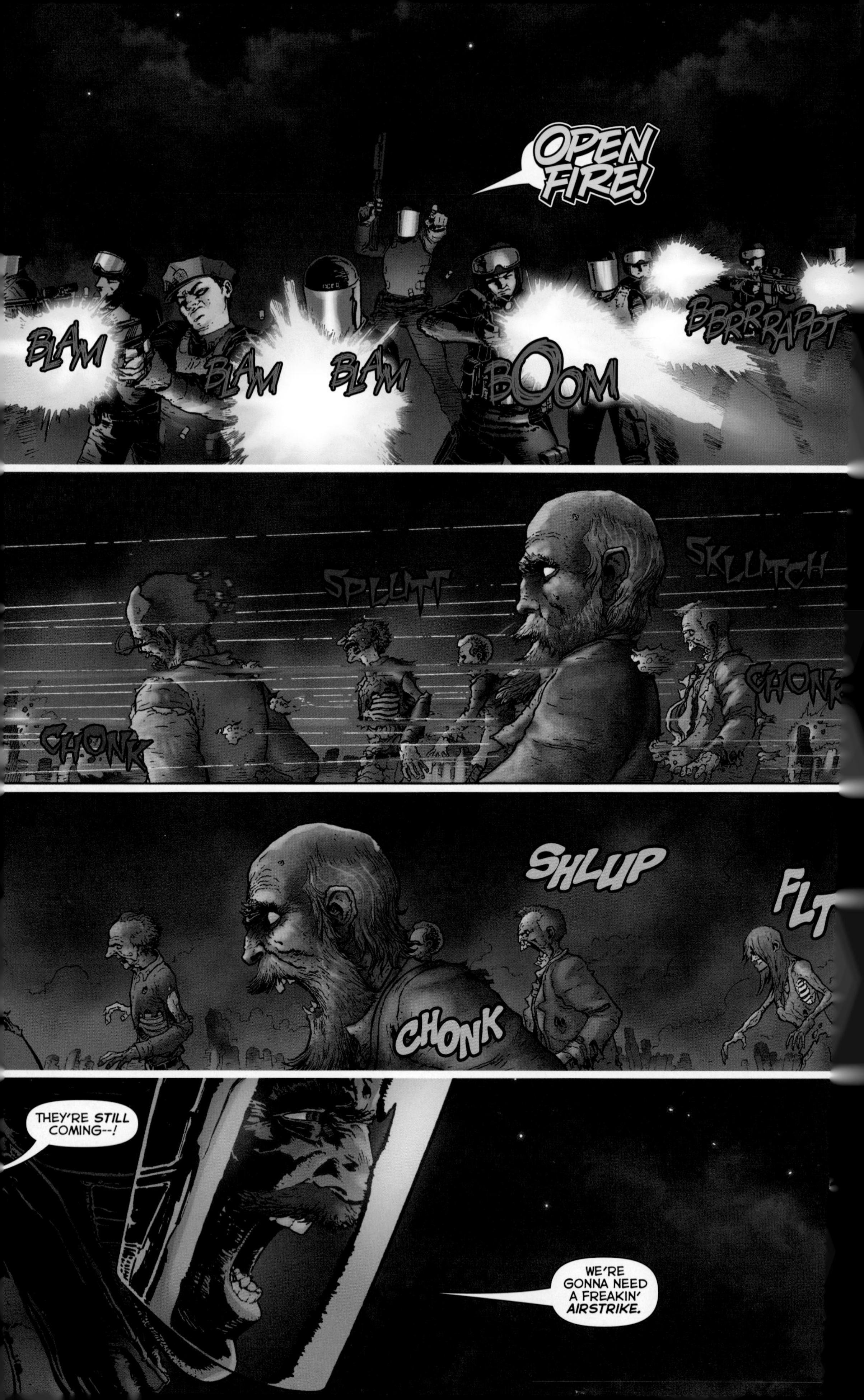
OPEN FIRE!
BLAM
BLAM
BLAM
BOOM
BBRRRRAPPT
SPLUTT
SKLUTCH
CHONK
CHONK
SHLUP
FLT
CHONK
THEY'RE STILL COMING--!
WE'RE GONNA NEED A FREAKIN' AIRSTRIKE.

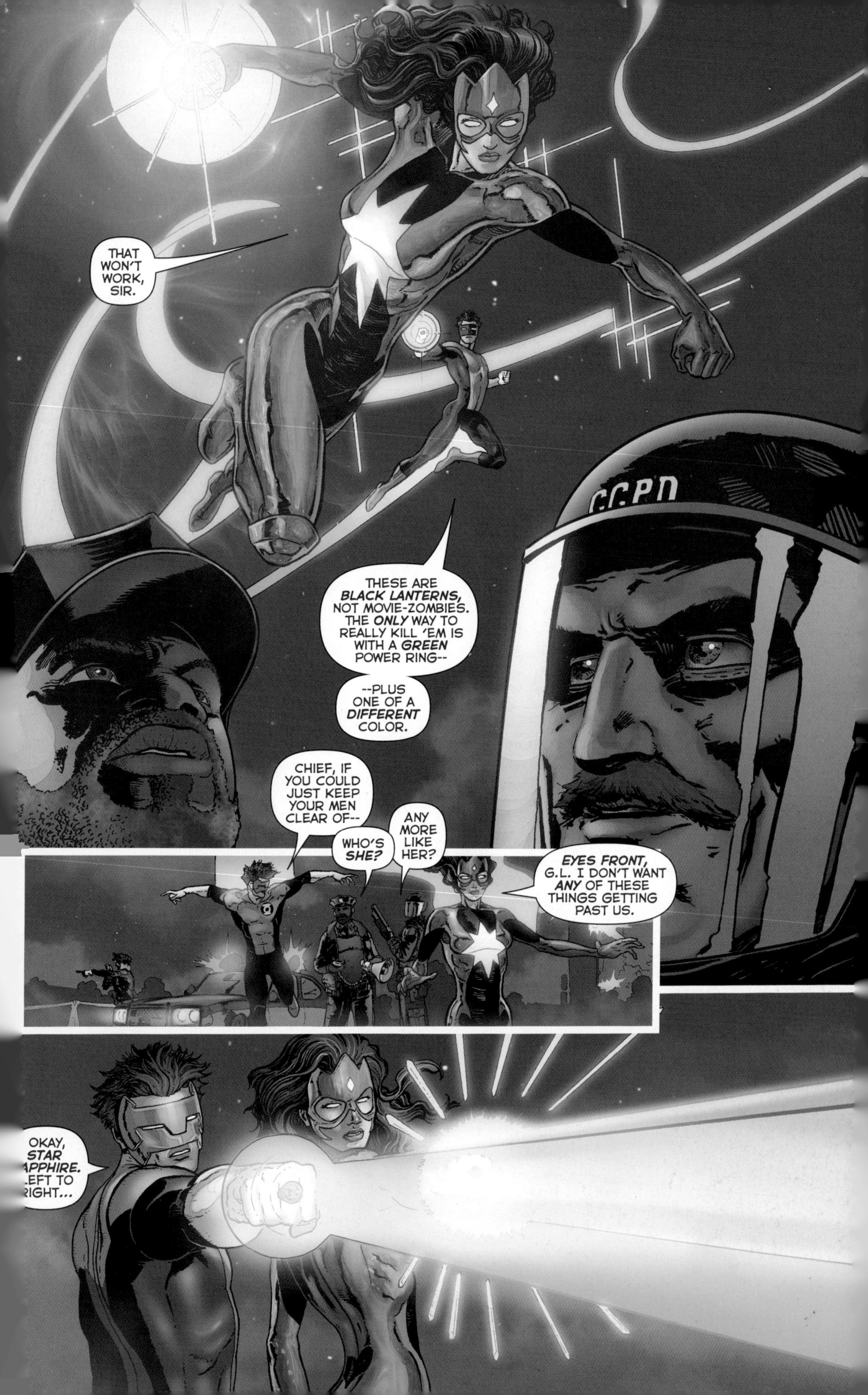
THAT WON'T WORK, SIR.
C.C.P.D
THESE ARE **BLACK LANTERNS,** NOT MOVIE-ZOMBIES. THE **ONLY** WAY TO REALLY KILL 'EM IS WITH A **GREEN** POWER RING--
--PLUS ONE OF A **DIFFERENT** COLOR.
CHIEF, IF YOU COULD JUST KEEP YOUR MEN CLEAR OF--
WHO'S **SHE?**
ANY MORE LIKE HER?
EYES FRONT, G.L. I DON'T WANT **ANY** OF THESE THINGS GETTING PAST US.
OKAY, **STAR** **APPHIRE.** **.EFT TO** **RIGHT...**

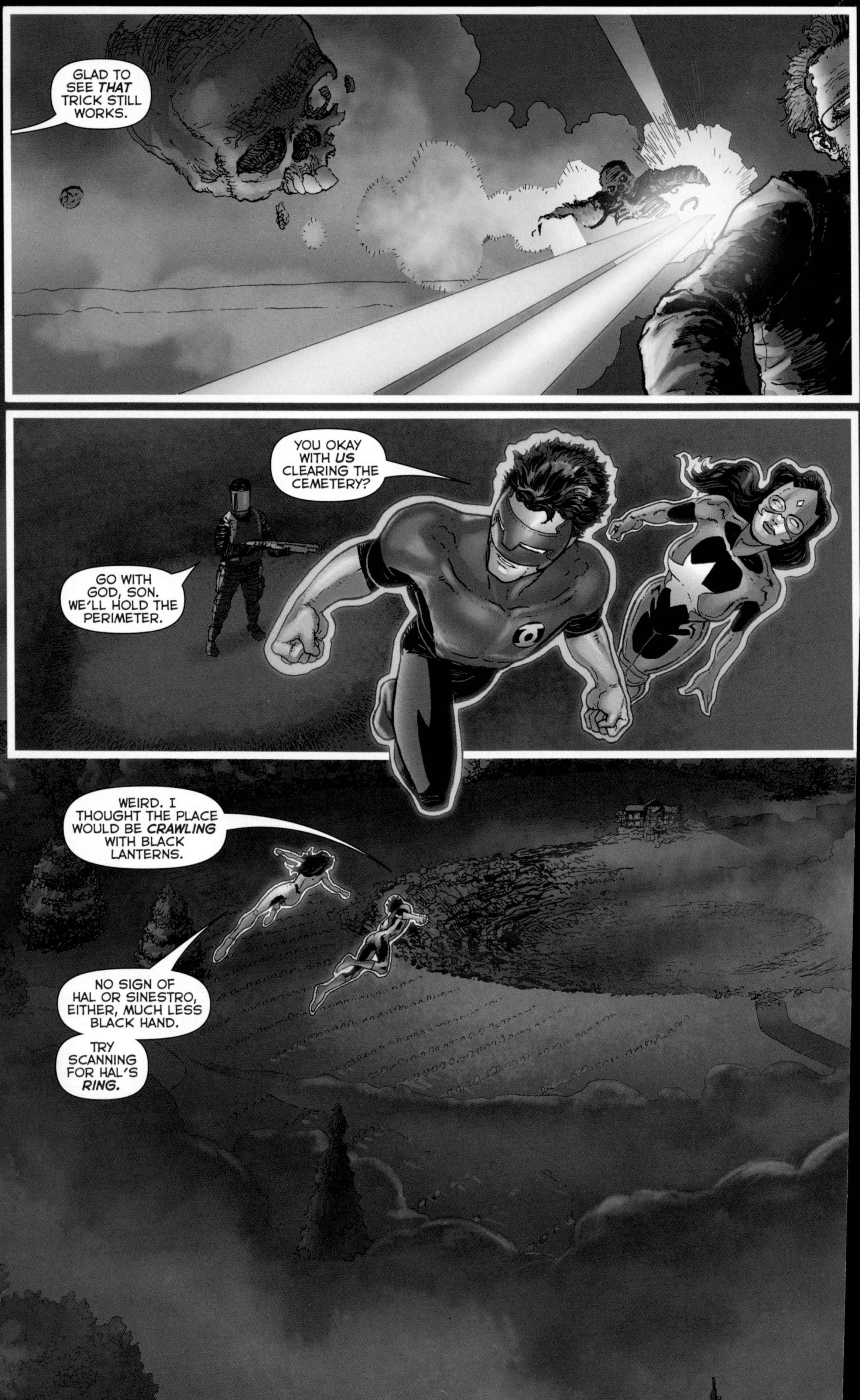
GLAD TO SEE *THAT* TRICK STILL WORKS.
YOU OKAY WITH *US* CLEARING THE CEMETERY?
GO WITH GOD, SON. WE'LL HOLD THE PERIMETER.
WEIRD. I THOUGHT THE PLACE WOULD BE *CRAWLING* WITH BLACK LANTERNS.
NO SIGN OF HAL OR SINESTRO, EITHER, MUCH LESS BLACK HAND.
TRY SCANNING FOR HAL'S *RING*.

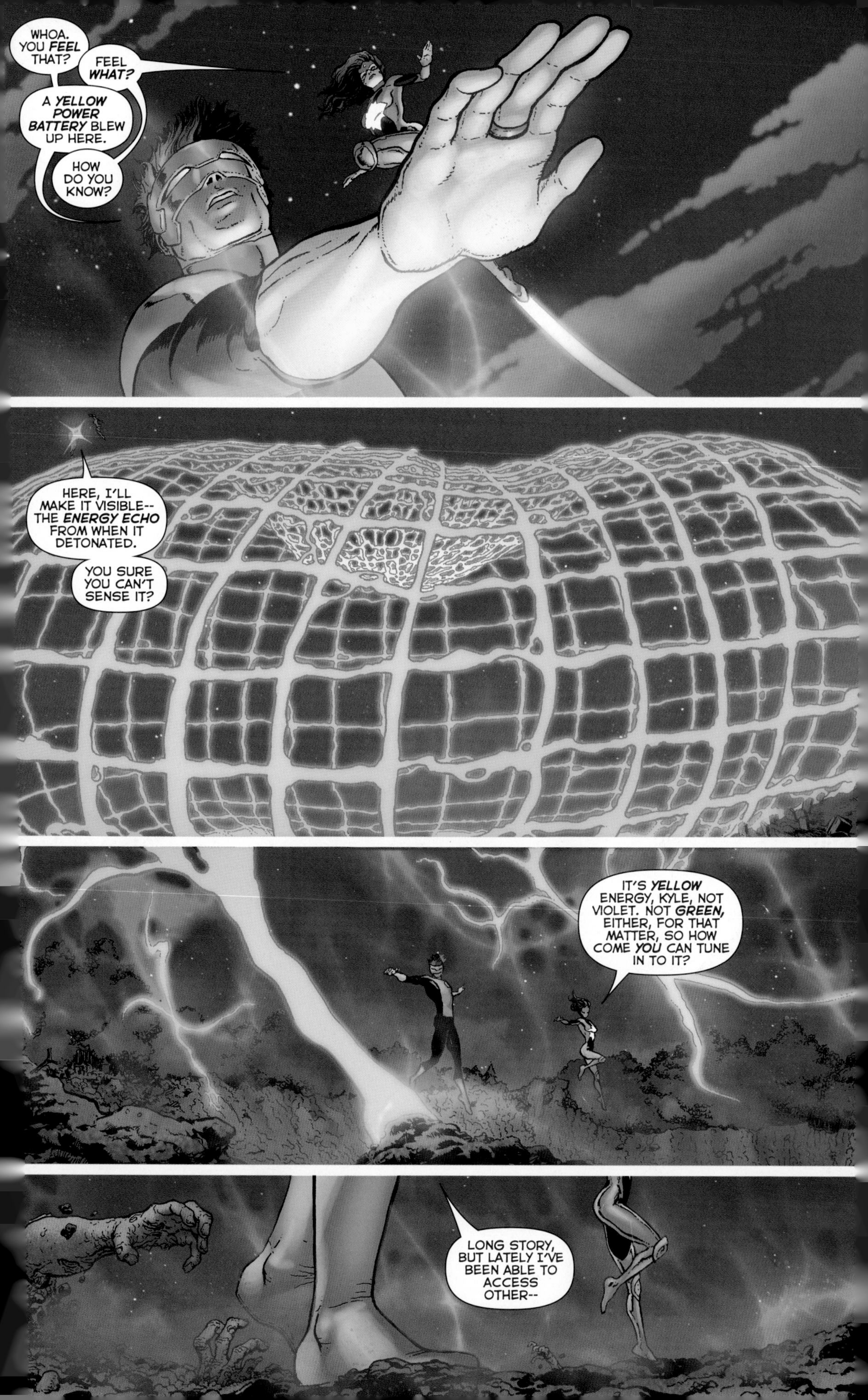
WHOA. YOU *FEEL* THAT?
FEEL *WHAT?*
A *YELLOW POWER BATTERY* BLEW UP HERE.
HOW DO YOU KNOW?
HERE, I'LL MAKE IT VISIBLE-- THE *ENERGY ECHO* FROM WHEN IT DETONATED.
YOU SURE YOU CAN'T SENSE IT?
IT'S *YELLOW* ENERGY, KYLE, NOT VIOLET. NOT *GREEN,* EITHER, FOR THAT MATTER, SO HOW COME *YOU* CAN TUNE IN TO IT?
LONG STORY, BUT LATELY I'VE BEEN ABLE TO ACCESS OTHER--

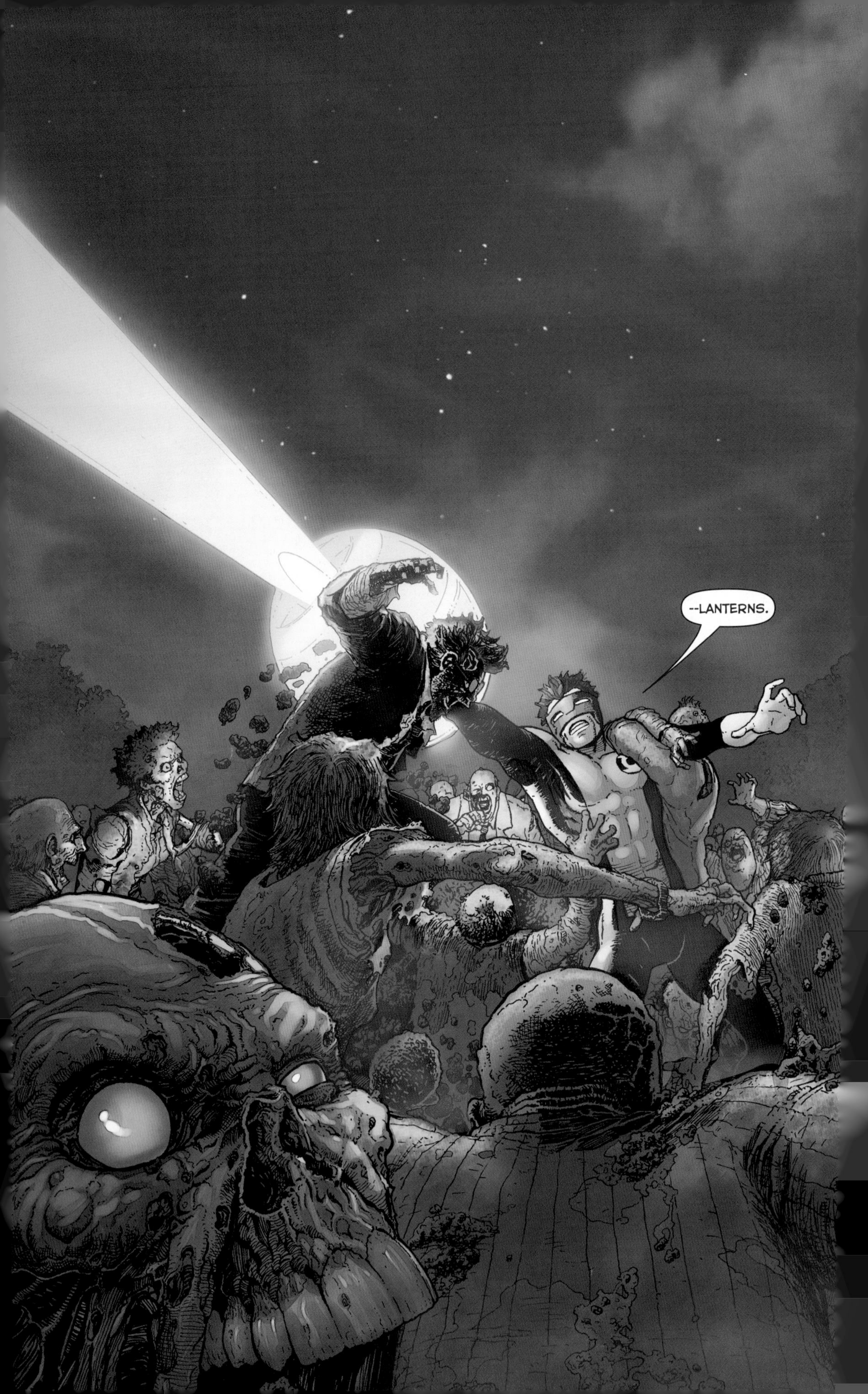
--LANTERNS.

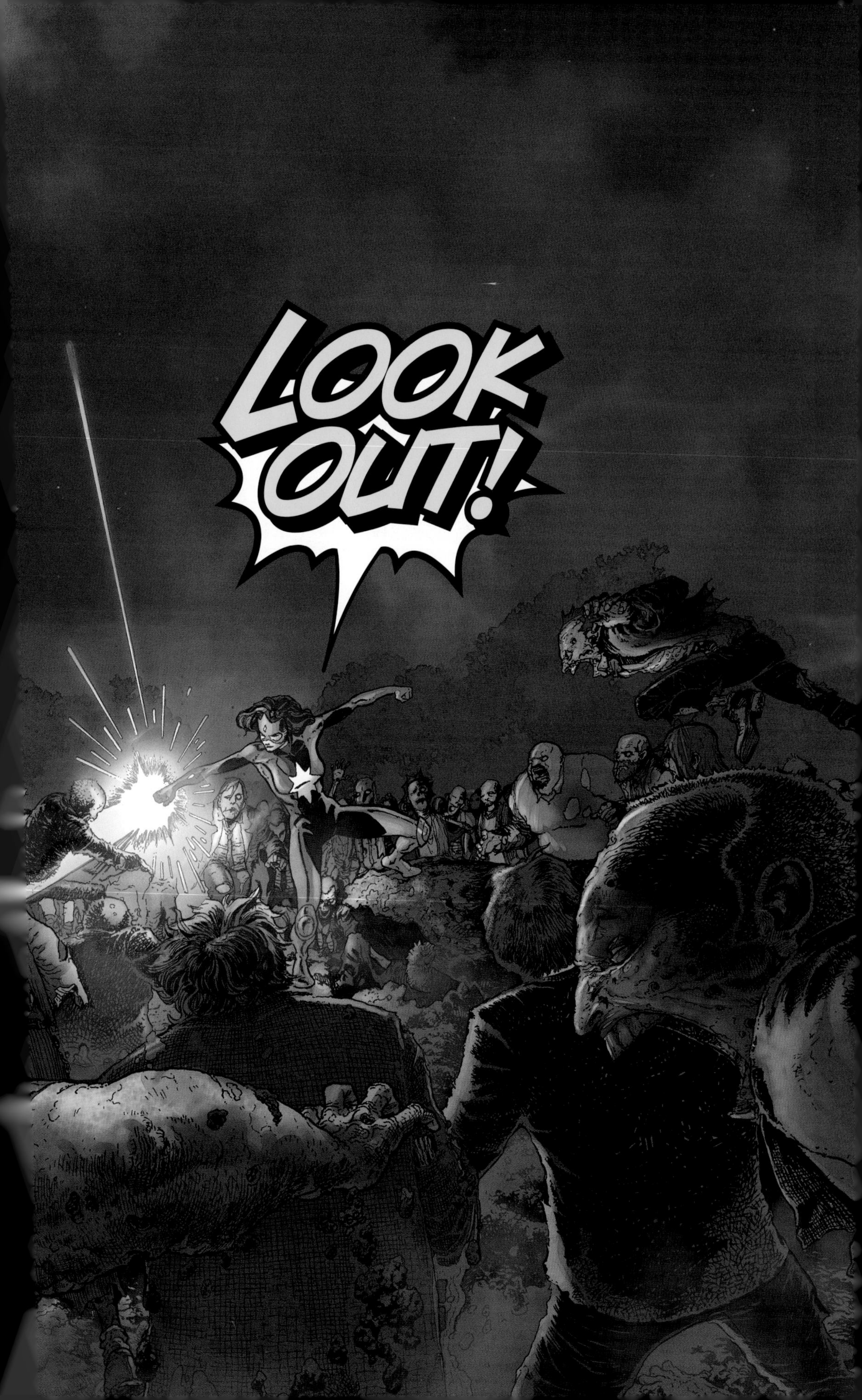
LOOK OUT!

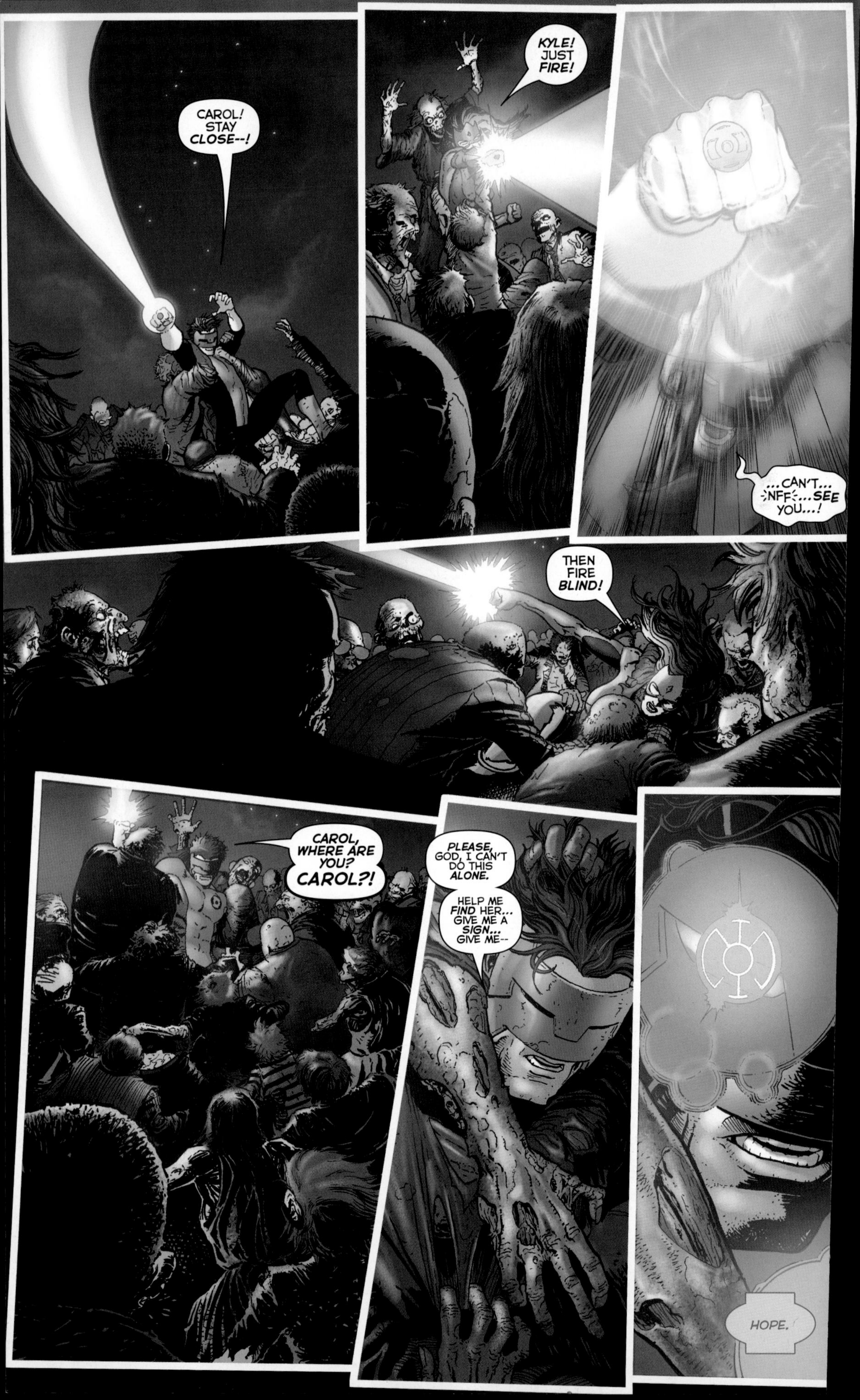
CAROL! STAY CLOSE--!
KYLE! JUST FIRE!
...CAN'T... NFF... SEE YOU...!
THEN FIRE BLIND!
CAROL, WHERE ARE YOU? CAROL?!
PLEASE, GOD, I CAN'T DO THIS ALONE.
HELP ME FIND HER... GIVE ME A SIGN... GIVE ME--
HOPE.

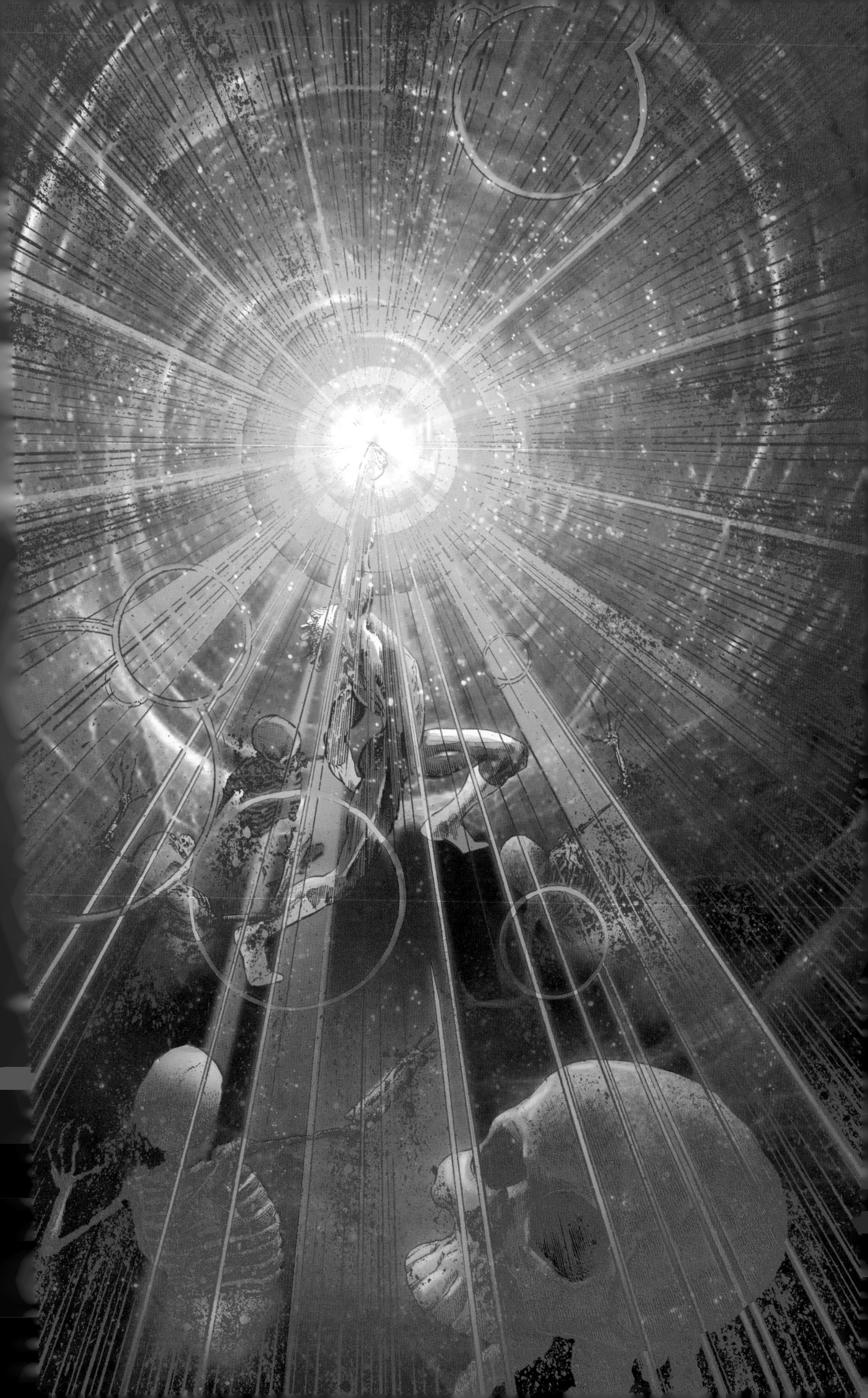

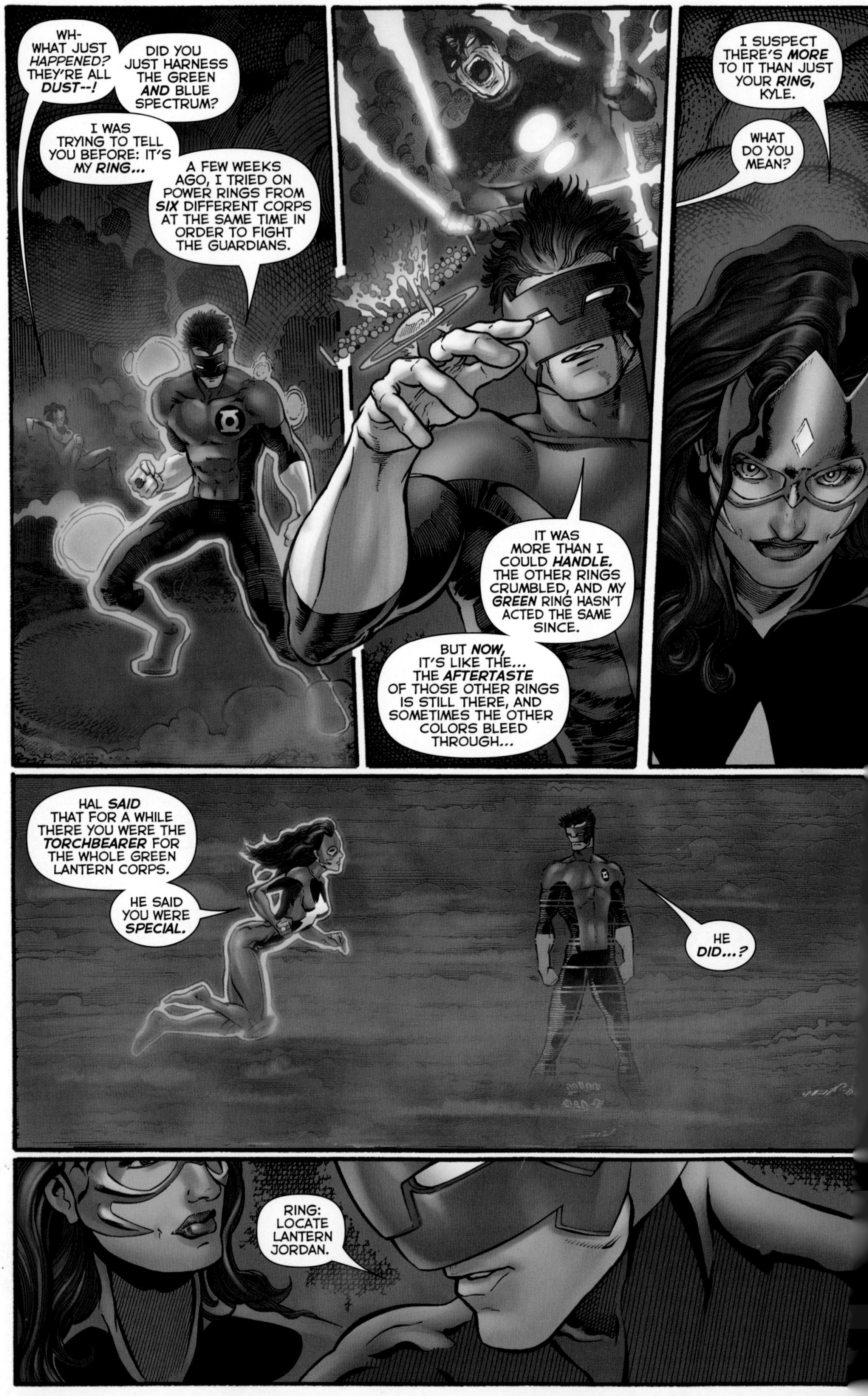
WH- WHAT JUST HAPPENED? THEY'RE ALL DUST--!
DID YOU JUST HARNESS THE GREEN AND BLUE SPECTRUM?
I WAS TRYING TO TELL YOU BEFORE: IT'S MY RING...
A FEW WEEKS AGO, I TRIED ON POWER RINGS FROM SIX DIFFERENT CORPS AT THE SAME TIME IN ORDER TO FIGHT THE GUARDIANS.
IT WAS MORE THAN I COULD HANDLE. THE OTHER RINGS CRUMBLED, AND MY GREEN RING HASN'T ACTED THE SAME SINCE.
BUT NOW, IT'S LIKE THE... THE AFTERTASTE OF THOSE OTHER RINGS IS STILL THERE, AND SOMETIMES THE OTHER COLORS BLEED THROUGH...
I SUSPECT THERE'S MORE TO IT THAN JUST YOUR RING, KYLE.
WHAT DO YOU MEAN?
HAL SAID THAT FOR A WHILE THERE YOU WERE THE TORCHBEARER FOR THE WHOLE GREEN LANTERN CORPS.
HE SAID YOU WERE SPECIAL.
HE DID...?
RING: LOCATE LANTERN JORDAN.

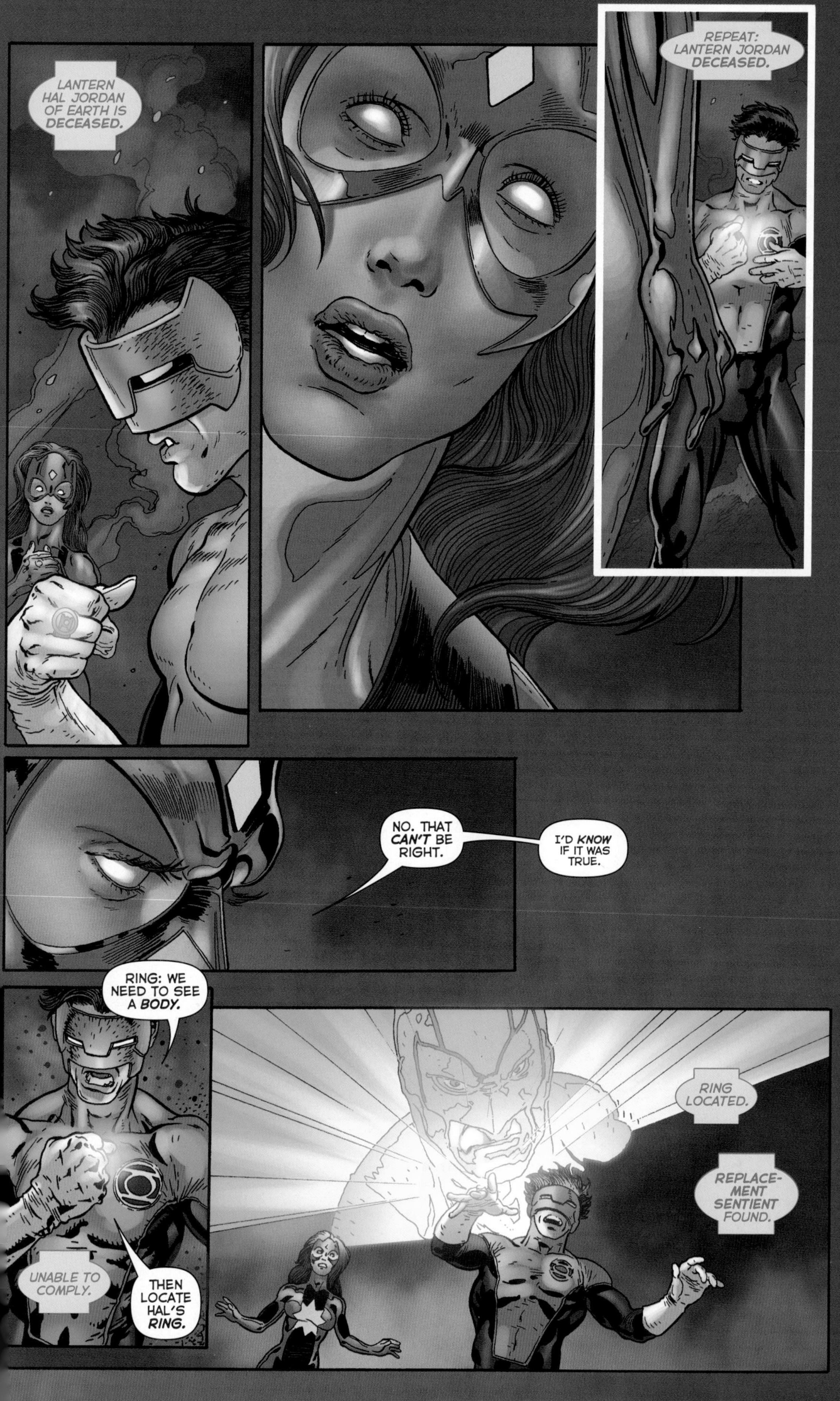
LANTERN HAL JORDAN OF EARTH IS DECEASED.
REPEAT: LANTERN JORDAN DECEASED.
NO. THAT CAN'T BE RIGHT.
I'D KNOW IF IT WAS TRUE.
RING: WE NEED TO SEE A BODY.
UNABLE TO COMPLY.
THEN LOCATE HAL'S RING.
RING LOCATED.
REPLACEMENT SENTIENT FOUND.

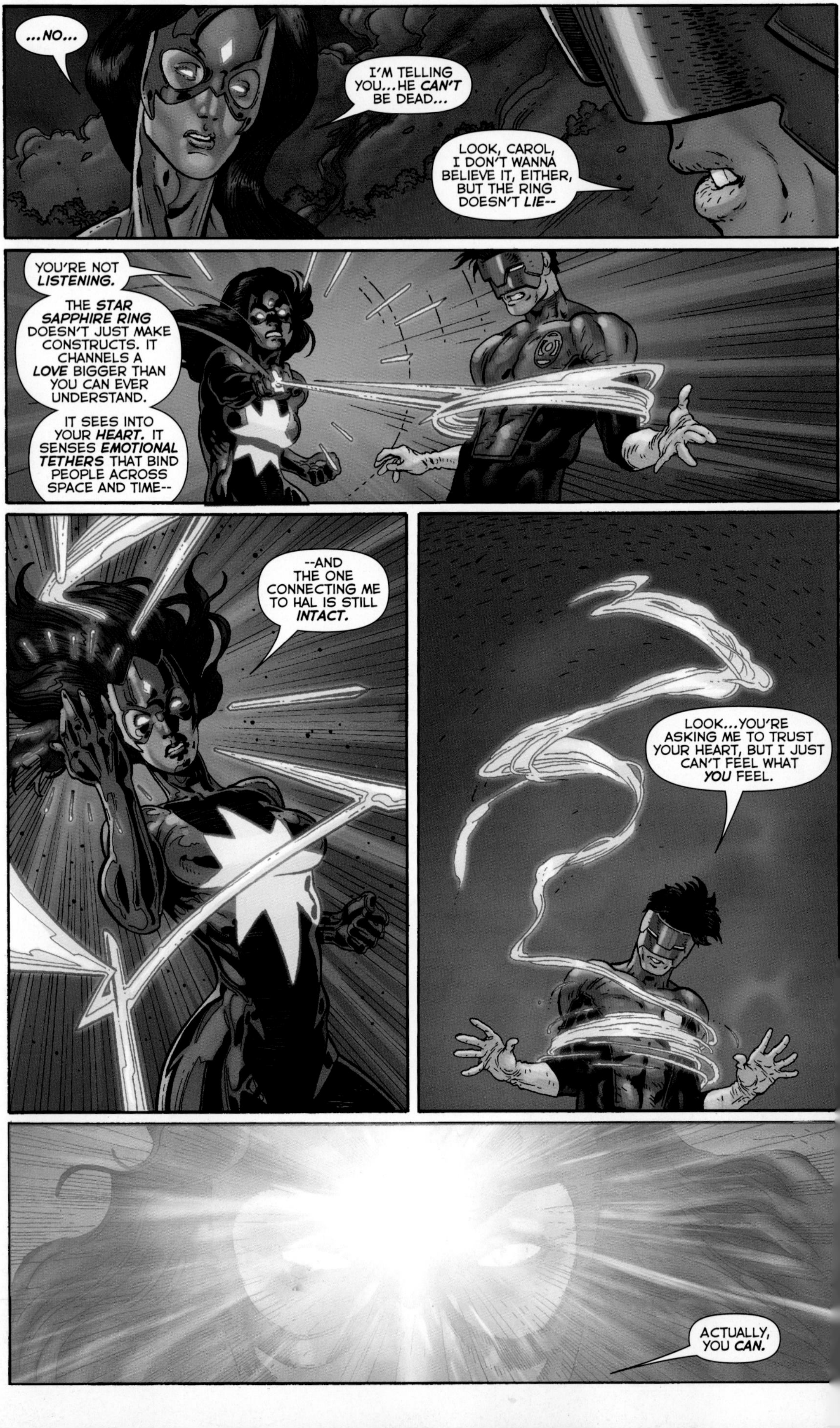
...NO...
I'M TELLING YOU...HE CAN'T BE DEAD...
LOOK, CAROL, I DON'T WANNA BELIEVE IT, EITHER, BUT THE RING DOESN'T LIE--
YOU'RE NOT LISTENING.
THE STAR SAPPHIRE RING DOESN'T JUST MAKE CONSTRUCTS. IT CHANNELS A LOVE BIGGER THAN YOU CAN EVER UNDERSTAND.
IT SEES INTO YOUR HEART. IT SENSES EMOTIONAL TETHERS THAT BIND PEOPLE ACROSS SPACE AND TIME--
--AND THE ONE CONNECTING ME TO HAL IS STILL INTACT.
LOOK...YOU'RE ASKING ME TO TRUST YOUR HEART, BUT I JUST CAN'T FEEL WHAT YOU FEEL.
ACTUALLY, YOU CAN.

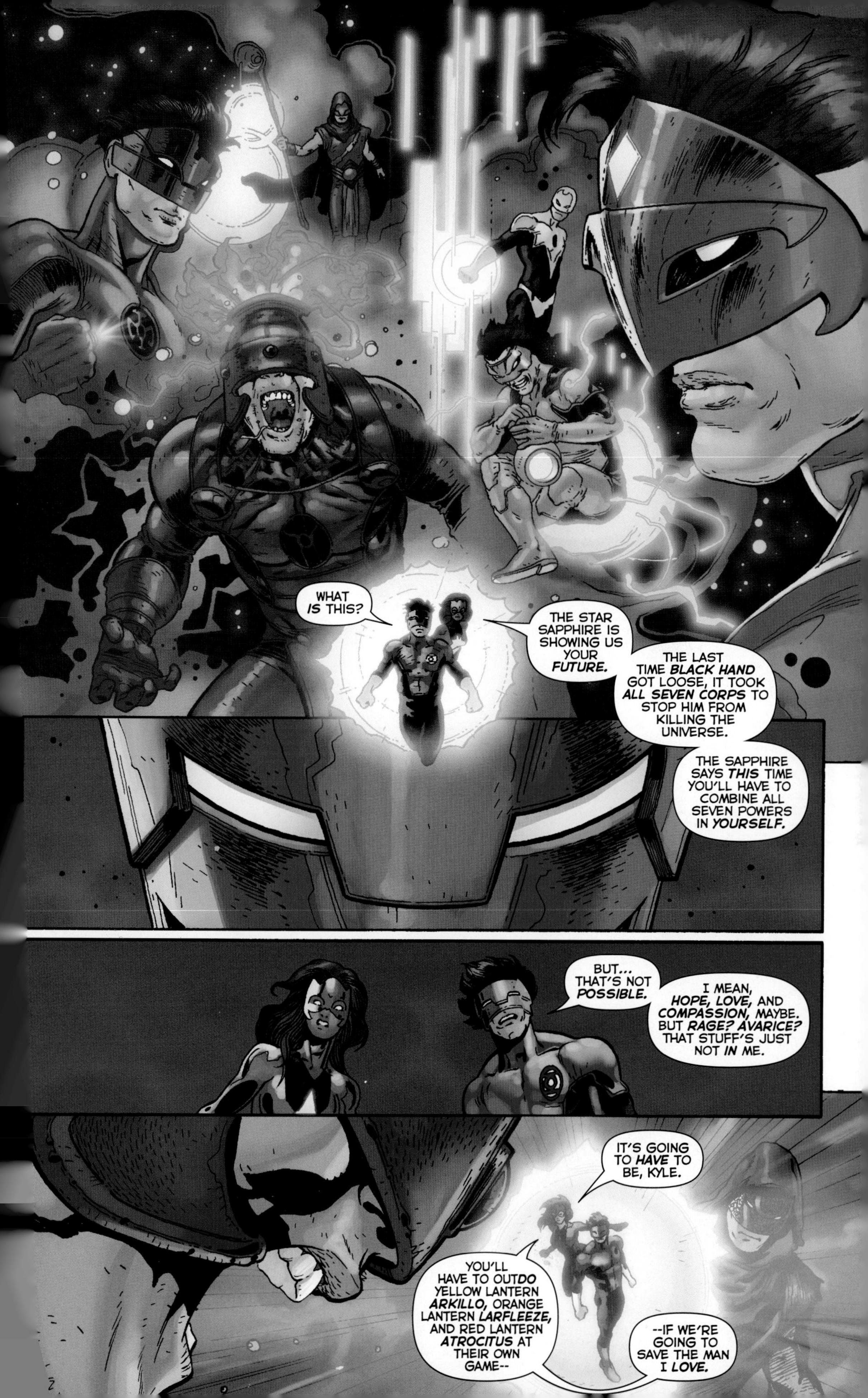
WHAT IS THIS?
THE STAR SAPPHIRE IS SHOWING US YOUR FUTURE.
THE LAST TIME BLACK HAND GOT LOOSE, IT TOOK ALL SEVEN CORPS TO STOP HIM FROM KILLING THE UNIVERSE.
THE SAPPHIRE SAYS THIS TIME YOU'LL HAVE TO COMBINE ALL SEVEN POWERS IN YOURSELF.
BUT... THAT'S NOT POSSIBLE.
I MEAN, HOPE, LOVE, AND COMPASSION, MAYBE. BUT RAGE? AVARICE? THAT STUFF'S JUST NOT IN ME.
IT'S GOING TO HAVE TO BE, KYLE.
YOU'LL HAVE TO OUTDO YELLOW LANTERN ARKILLO, ORANGE LANTERN LARFLEEZE, AND RED LANTERN ATROCITUS AT THEIR OWN GAME--
--IF WE'RE GOING TO SAVE THE MAN I LOVE.

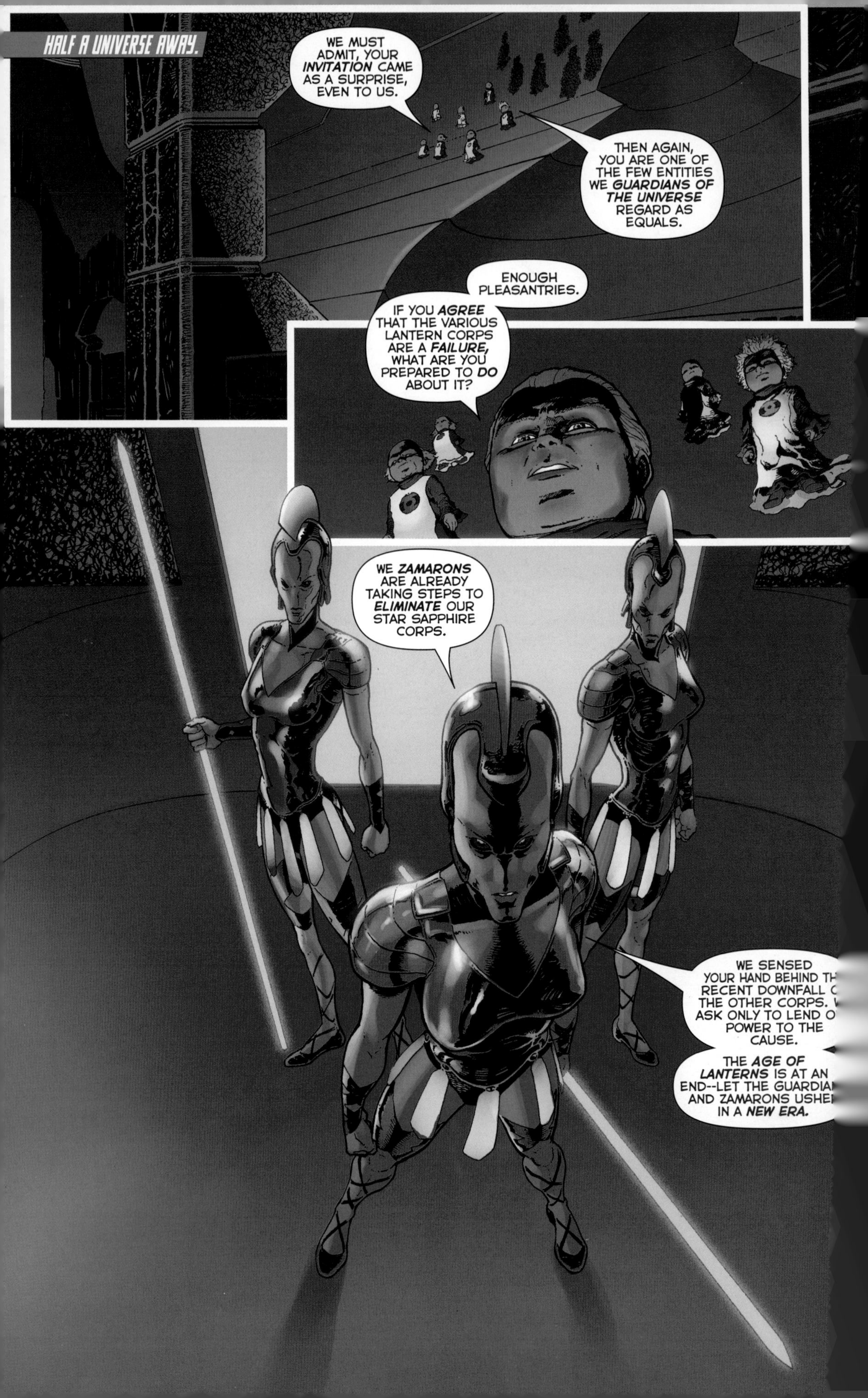
HALF A UNIVERSE AWAY.
WE MUST ADMIT, YOUR INVITATION CAME AS A SURPRISE, EVEN TO US.
THEN AGAIN, YOU ARE ONE OF THE FEW ENTITIES WE GUARDIANS OF THE UNIVERSE REGARD AS EQUALS.
ENOUGH PLEASANTRIES.
IF YOU AGREE THAT THE VARIOUS LANTERN CORPS ARE A FAILURE, WHAT ARE YOU PREPARED TO DO ABOUT IT?
WE ZAMARONS ARE ALREADY TAKING STEPS TO ELIMINATE OUR STAR SAPPHIRE CORPS.
WE SENSED YOUR HAND BEHIND TH RECENT DOWNFALL O THE OTHER CORPS. ASK ONLY TO LEND O POWER TO THE CAUSE.
THE AGE OF LANTERNS IS AT AN END--LET THE GUARDIAN AND ZAMARONS USHE IN A NEW ERA.

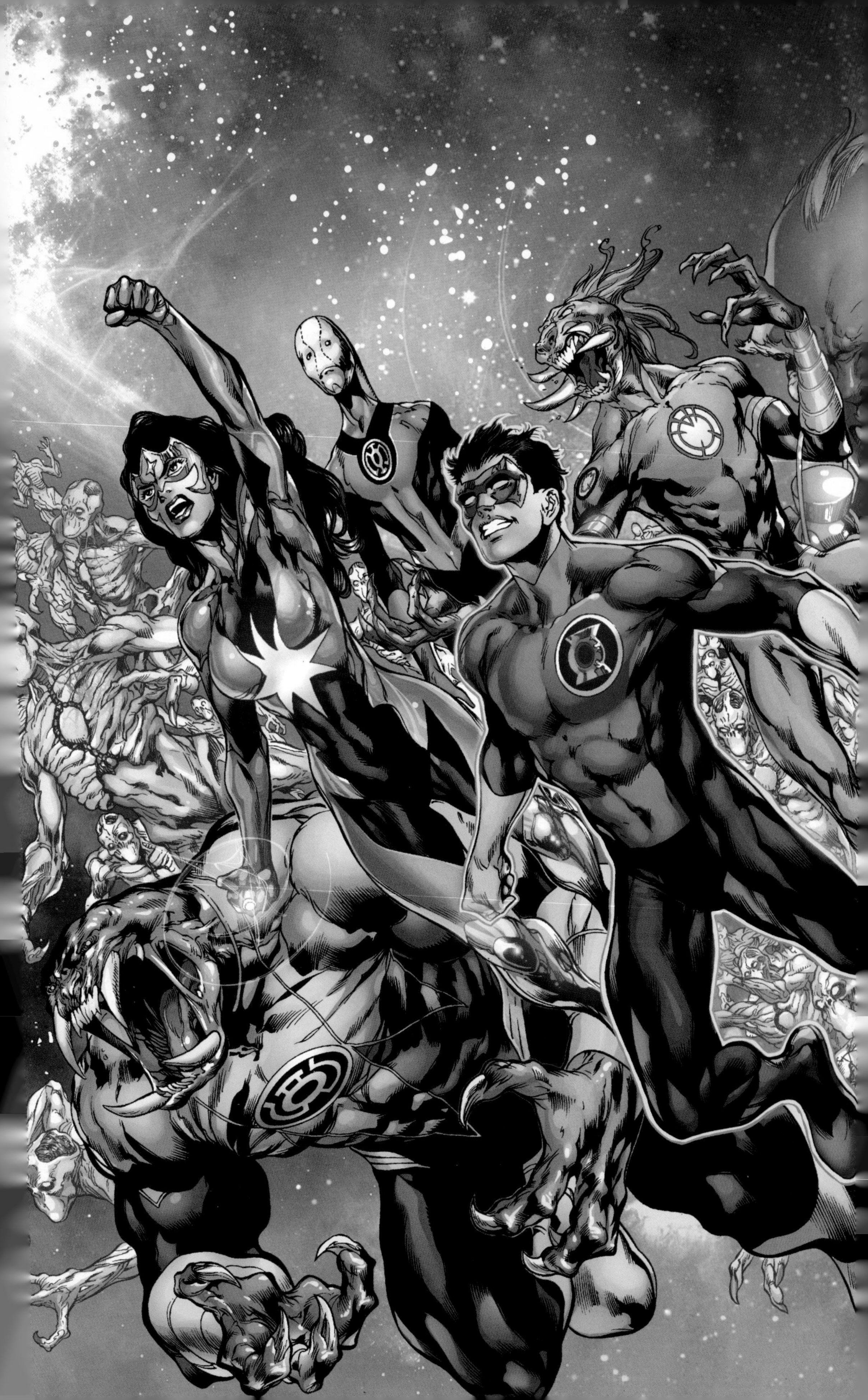

ALL THE RAGE

TONY BEDARD writer **ANDREI BRESSAN & AMILCAR PINNA** artists
IVAN REIS, OCLAIR ALBERT & ROD REIS cover

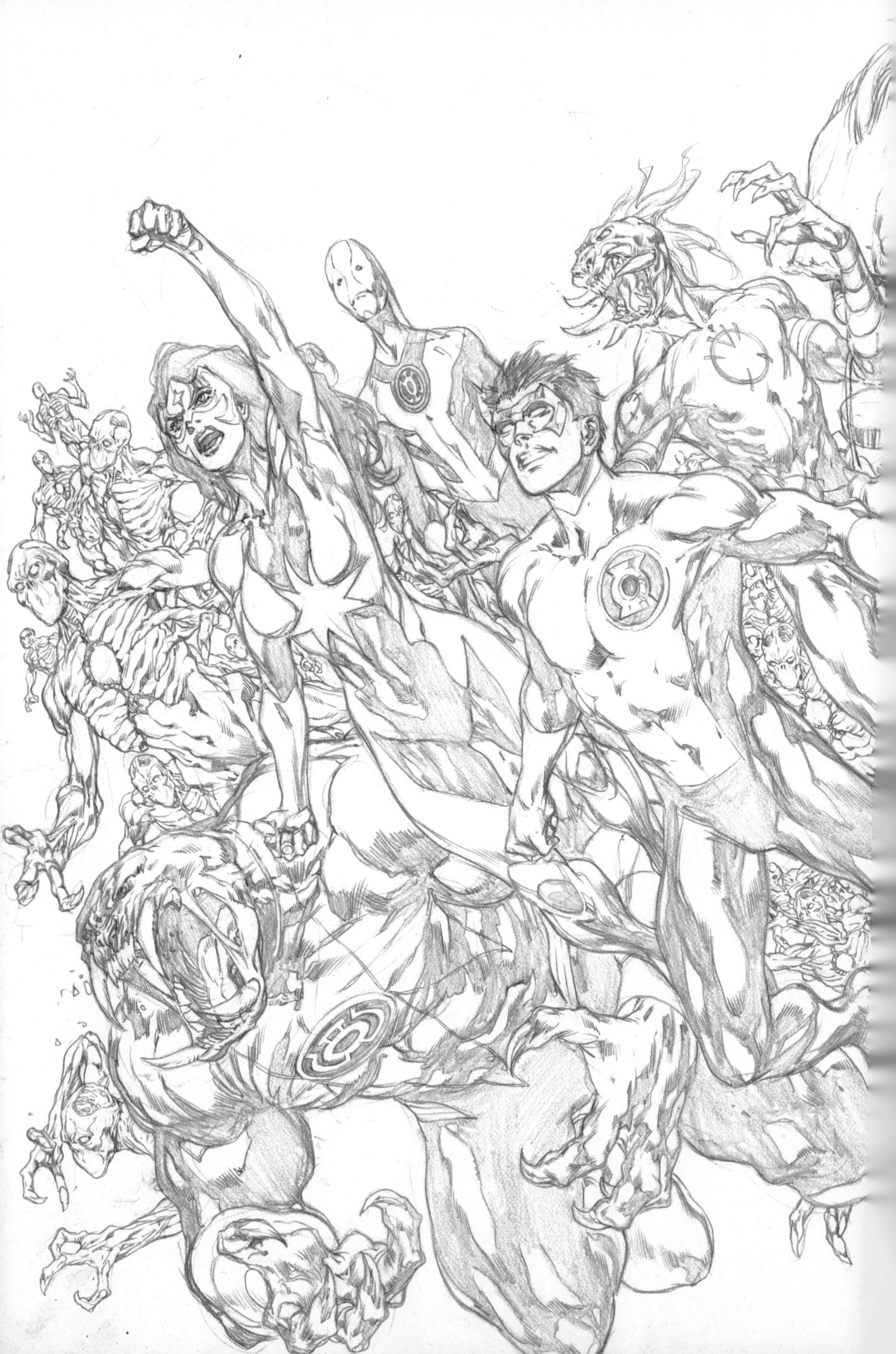

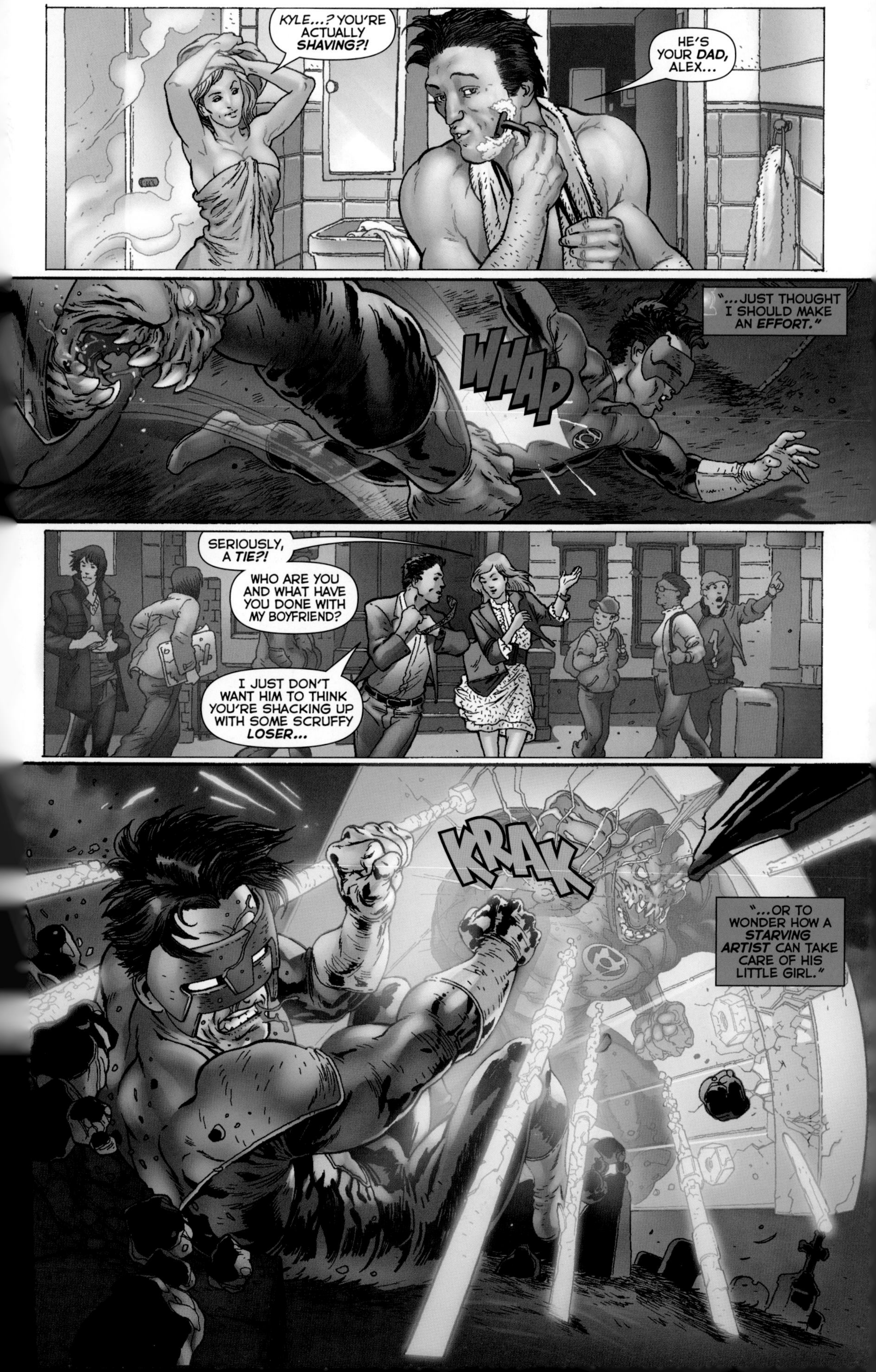

KYLE...? YOU'RE ACTUALLY SHAVING?!
HE'S YOUR DAD, ALEX...
"...JUST THOUGHT I SHOULD MAKE AN EFFORT."
WHAP
SERIOUSLY, A TIE?!
WHO ARE YOU AND WHAT HAVE YOU DONE WITH MY BOYFRIEND?
I JUST DON'T WANT HIM TO THINK YOU'RE SHACKING UP WITH SOME SCRUFFY LOSER...
KRAK
"...OR TO WONDER HOW A STARVING ARTIST CAN TAKE CARE OF HIS LITTLE GIRL."

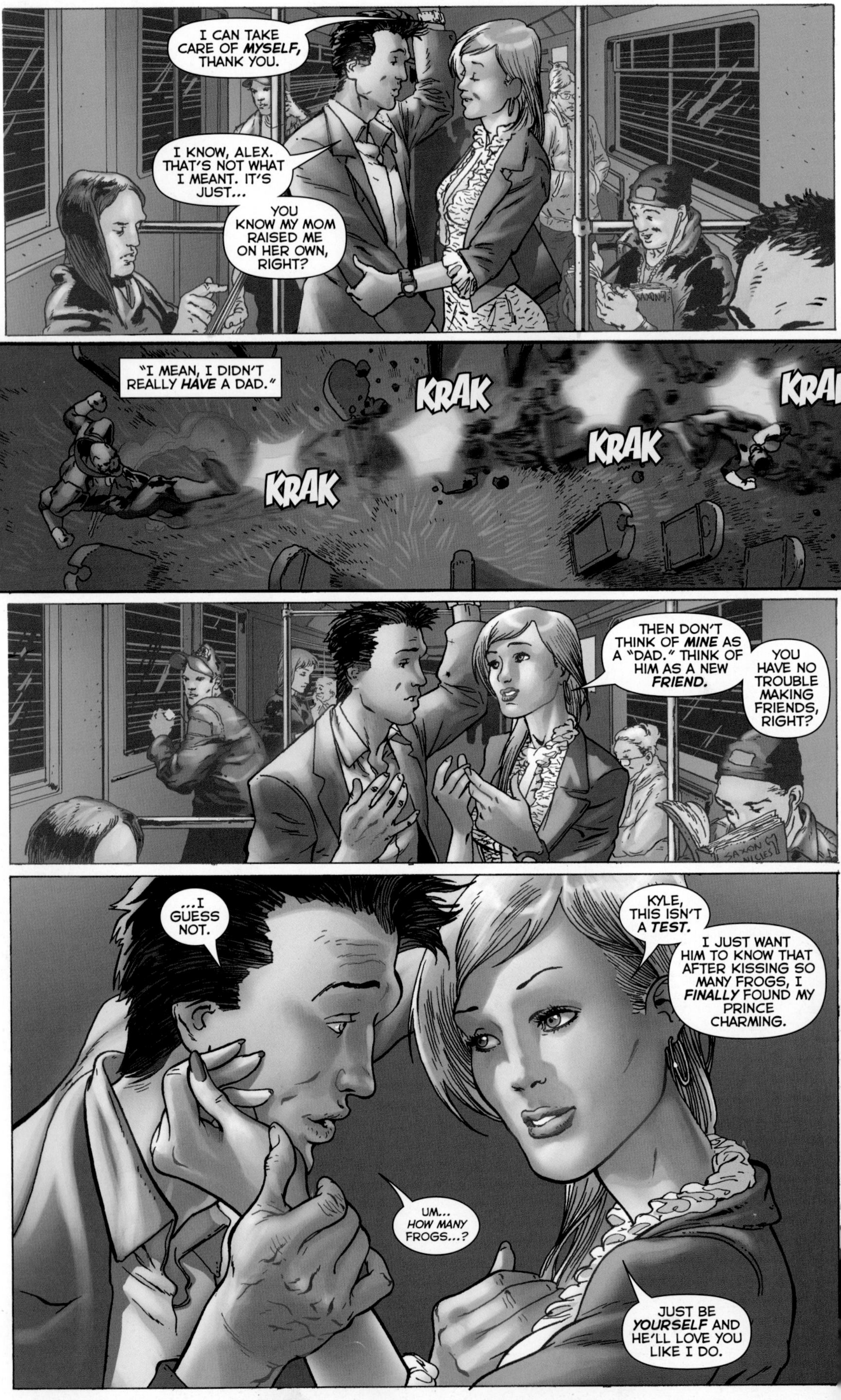
I CAN TAKE CARE OF *MYSELF,* THANK YOU.
I KNOW, ALEX. THAT'S NOT WHAT I MEANT. IT'S JUST...
YOU KNOW MY MOM RAISED ME ON HER OWN, RIGHT?
"I MEAN, I DIDN'T REALLY *HAVE* A DAD."
KRAK
KRAK
KRAK
KRAK
THEN DON'T THINK OF *MINE* AS A "DAD." THINK OF HIM AS A NEW *FRIEND.*
YOU HAVE NO TROUBLE MAKING FRIENDS, RIGHT?
...I GUESS NOT.
KYLE, THIS ISN'T A *TEST.*
I JUST WANT HIM TO KNOW THAT AFTER KISSING SO MANY FROGS, I *FINALLY* FOUND MY PRINCE CHARMING.
UM... *HOW MANY* FROGS...?
JUST BE *YOURSELF* AND HE'LL LOVE YOU LIKE I DO.

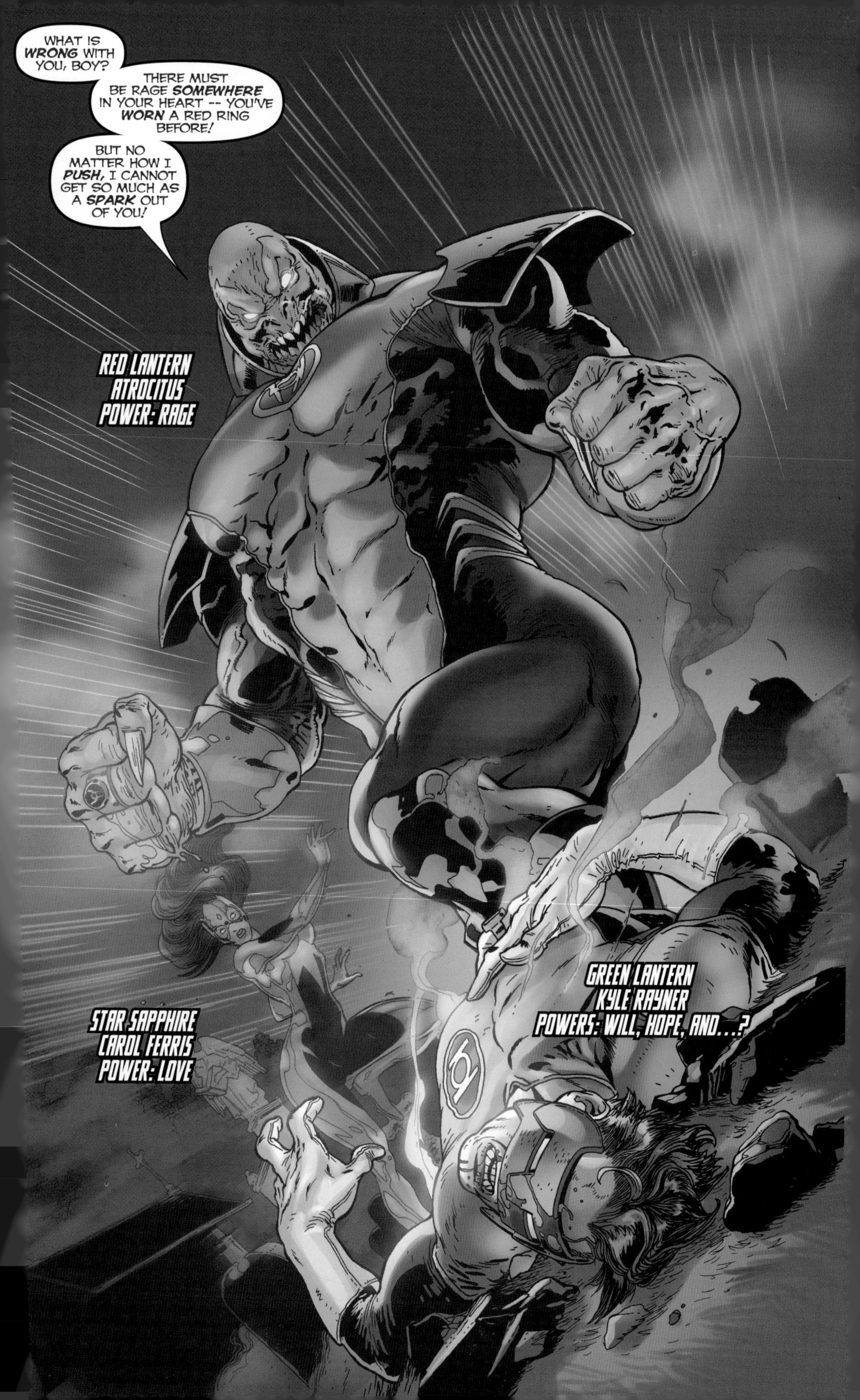
WHAT IS WRONG WITH YOU, BOY?
THERE MUST BE RAGE SOMEWHERE IN YOUR HEART -- YOU'VE WORN A RED RING BEFORE!
BUT NO MATTER HOW I PUSH, I CANNOT GET SO MUCH AS A SPARK OUT OF YOU!
RED LANTERN
ATROCITUS
POWER: RAGE
STAR SAPPHIRE
CAROL FERRIS
POWER: LOVE
GREEN LANTERN
KYLE RAYNER
POWERS: WILL, HOPE, AND...?

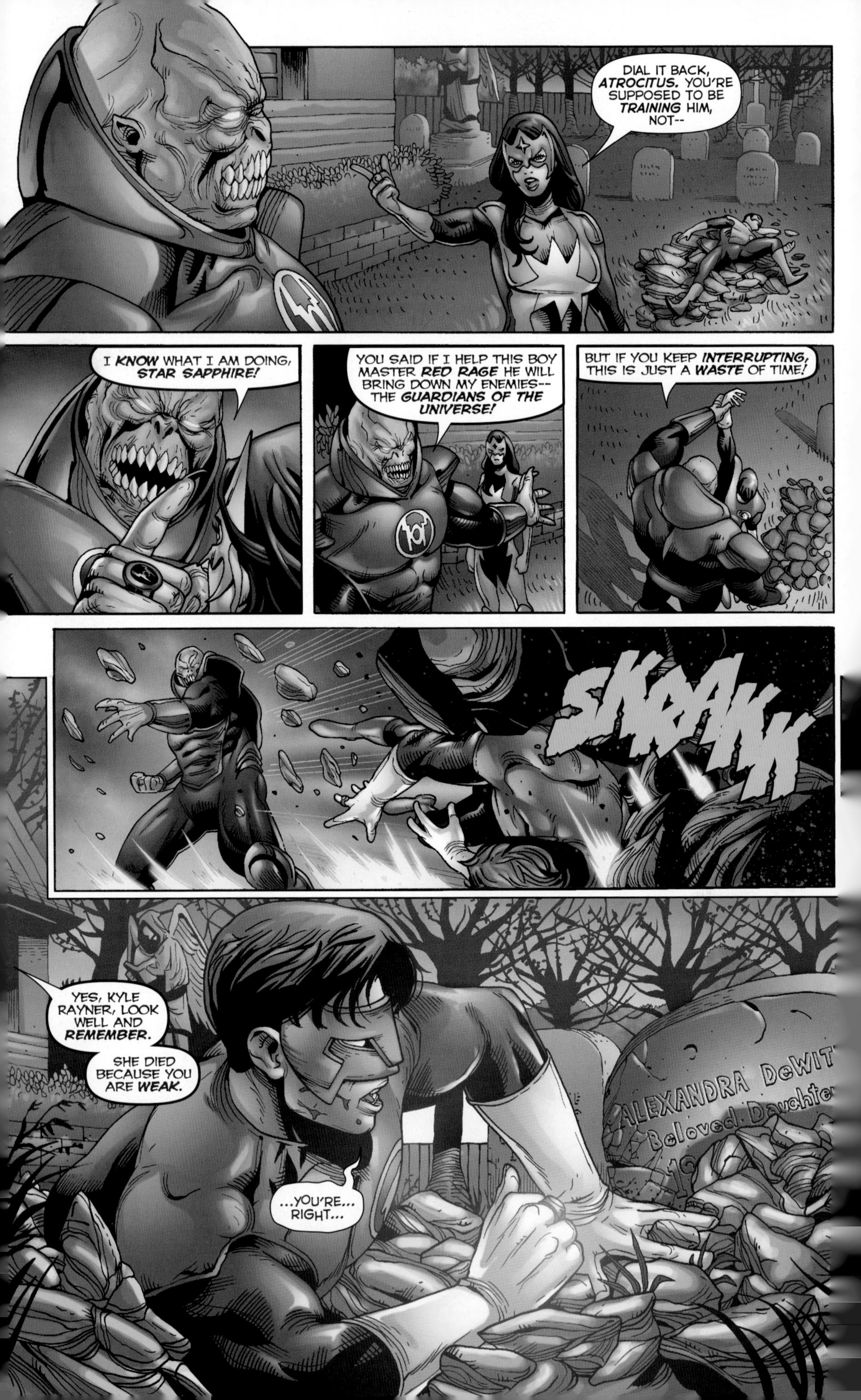
DIAL IT BACK, ATROCITUS. YOU'RE SUPPOSED TO BE TRAINING HIM, NOT--
I KNOW WHAT I AM DOING, STAR SAPPHIRE!
YOU SAID IF I HELP THIS BOY MASTER RED RAGE HE WILL BRING DOWN MY ENEMIES-- THE GUARDIANS OF THE UNIVERSE!
BUT IF YOU KEEP INTERRUPTING, THIS IS JUST A WASTE OF TIME!
SKRAKK
YES, KYLE RAYNER, LOOK WELL AND REMEMBER.
SHE DIED BECAUSE YOU ARE WEAK.
ALEXANDRA DeWIT
Beloved Daughter
...YOU'RE... RIGHT...

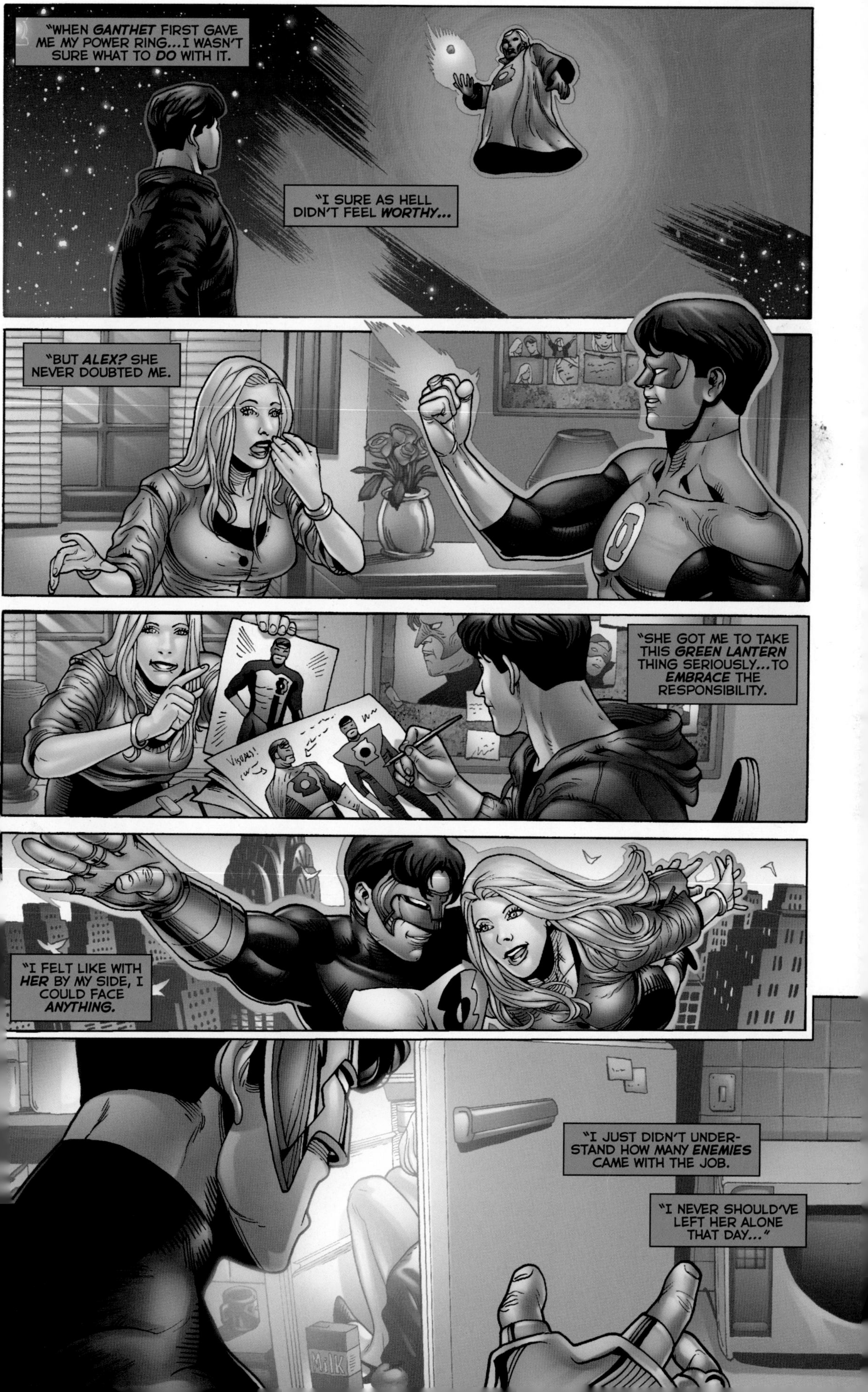
"WHEN GANTHET FIRST GAVE ME MY POWER RING... I WASN'T SURE WHAT TO DO WITH IT.
"I SURE AS HELL DIDN'T FEEL WORTHY...
"BUT ALEX? SHE NEVER DOUBTED ME.
"SHE GOT ME TO TAKE THIS GREEN LANTERN THING SERIOUSLY...TO EMBRACE THE RESPONSIBILITY.
"I FELT LIKE WITH HER BY MY SIDE, I COULD FACE ANYTHING.
"I JUST DIDN'T UNDER-STAND HOW MANY ENEMIES CAME WITH THE JOB.
"I NEVER SHOULD'VE LEFT HER ALONE THAT DAY..."
MILK

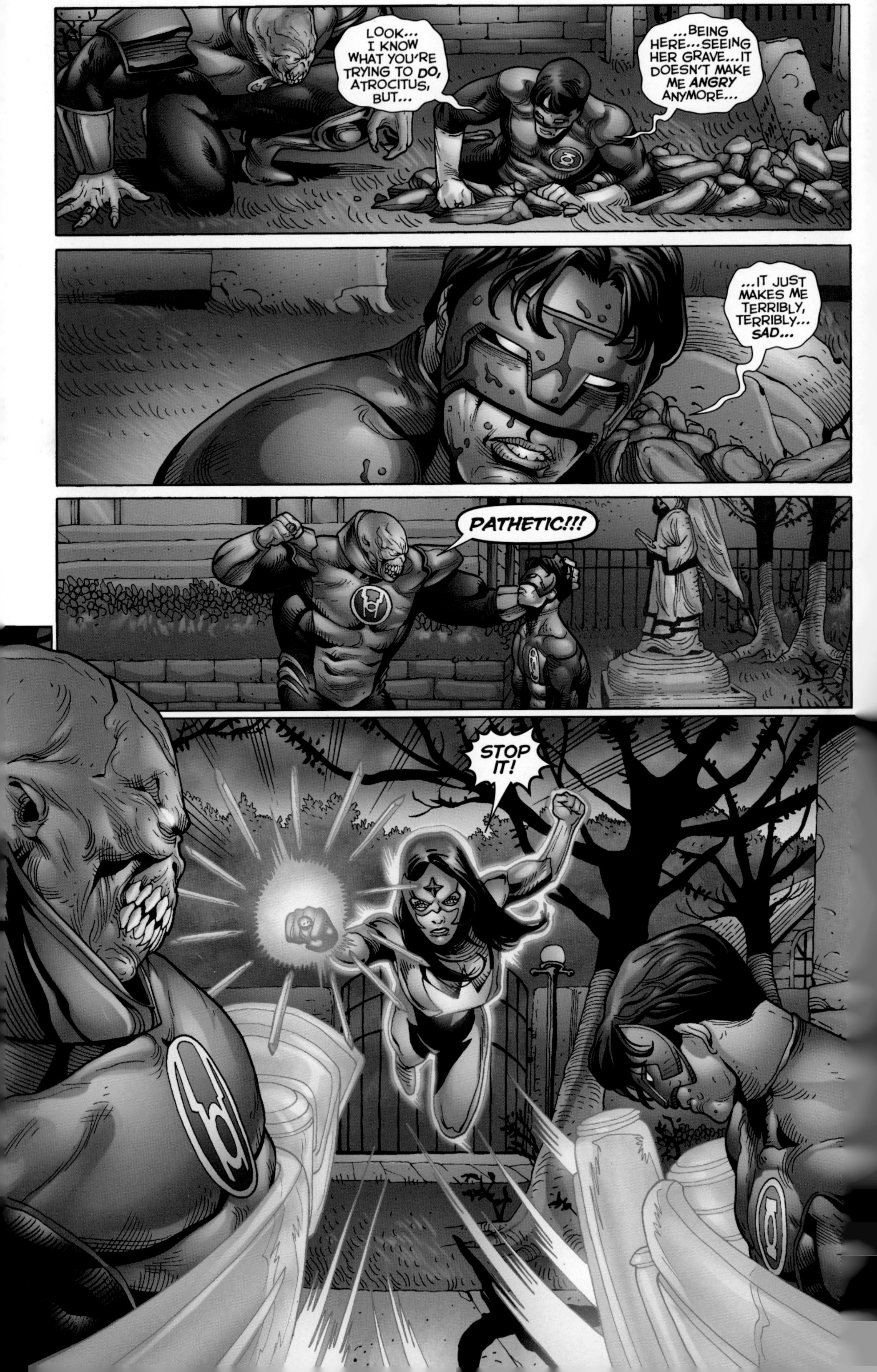
LOOK... I KNOW WHAT YOU'RE TRYING TO DO, ATROCITUS, BUT...
...BEING HERE...SEEING HER GRAVE...IT DOESN'T MAKE ME ANGRY ANYMORE...
...IT JUST MAKES ME TERRIBLY, TERRIBLY... SAD...
PATHETIC!!!
STOP IT!

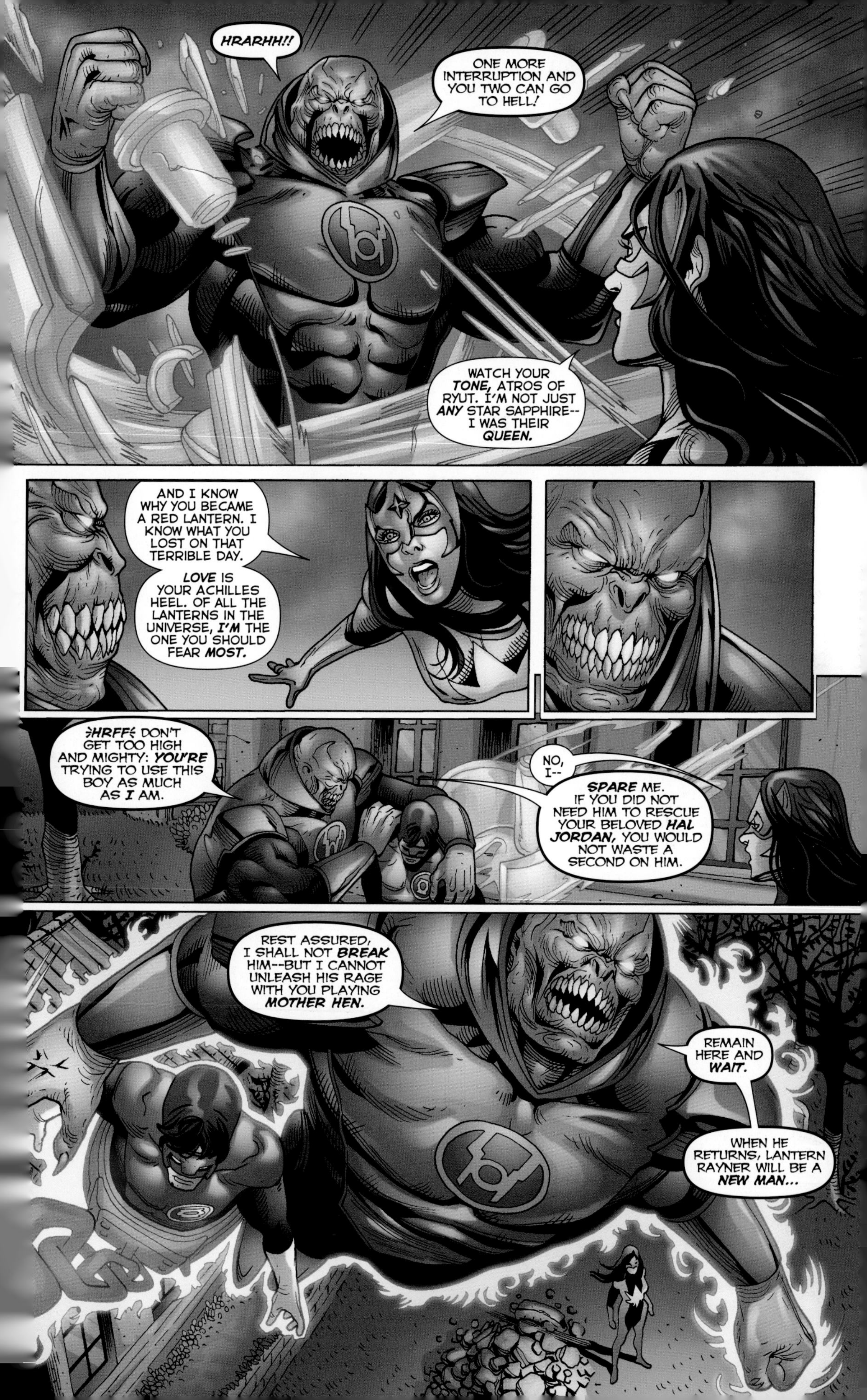
HRARHH!!
ONE MORE INTERRUPTION AND YOU TWO CAN GO TO HELL!
WATCH YOUR TONE, ATROS OF RYUT. I'M NOT JUST ANY STAR SAPPHIRE-- I WAS THEIR QUEEN.
AND I KNOW WHY YOU BECAME A RED LANTERN. I KNOW WHAT YOU LOST ON THAT TERRIBLE DAY.
LOVE IS YOUR ACHILLES HEEL. OF ALL THE LANTERNS IN THE UNIVERSE, I'M THE ONE YOU SHOULD FEAR MOST.
HRFF DON'T GET TOO HIGH AND MIGHTY: YOU'RE TRYING TO USE THIS BOY AS MUCH AS I AM.
NO, I--
SPARE ME. IF YOU DID NOT NEED HIM TO RESCUE YOUR BELOVED HAL JORDAN, YOU WOULD NOT WASTE A SECOND ON HIM.
REST ASSURED, I SHALL NOT BREAK HIM--BUT I CANNOT UNLEASH HIS RAGE WITH YOU PLAYING MOTHER HEN.
REMAIN HERE AND WAIT.
WHEN HE RETURNS, LANTERN RAYNER WILL BE A NEW MAN...

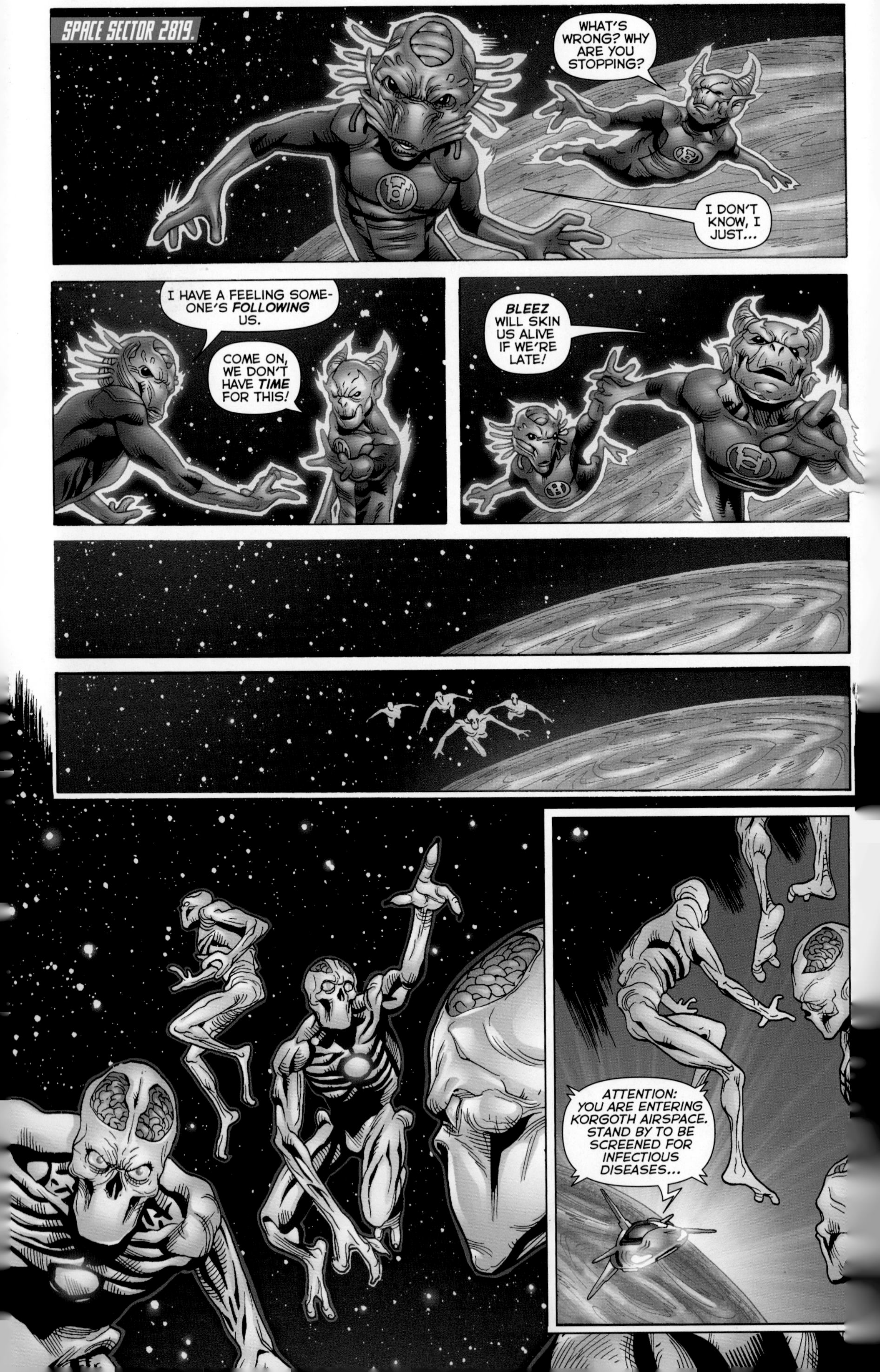
SPACE SECTOR 2819.
WHAT'S WRONG? WHY ARE YOU STOPPING?
I DON'T KNOW, I JUST...
I HAVE A FEELING SOME-ONE'S *FOLLOWING* US.
COME ON, WE DON'T HAVE *TIME* FOR THIS!
BLEEZ WILL SKIN US ALIVE IF WE'RE LATE!
ATTENTION: YOU ARE ENTERING KORGOTH AIRSPACE. STAND BY TO BE SCREENED FOR INFECTIOUS DISEASES...

PLANET EARTH.

‹YUSUF, BE **BRAVE**! GOD WILL NOT LET THIS **HAPPEN** TO US!›*

*TRANSLATED FROM ARABIC.

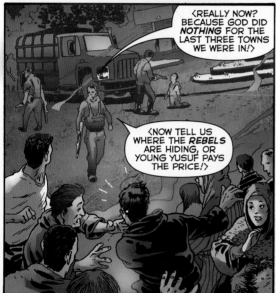

‹REALLY NOW? BECAUSE GOD DID **NOTHING** FOR THE LAST THREE TOWNS WE WERE IN!›

‹NOW TELL US WHERE THE **REBELS** ARE HIDING, OR YOUNG YUSUF PAYS THE PRICE!›

WHAT **IS** THIS, ATROCITUS? WHY BRING ME **HERE**?

TO REMIND YOU THERE'S NO SHORTAGE OF **EVIL** IN THE UNIVERSE-- EVEN ON THIS MUDBALL YOU CALL HOME.

‹WAIT! HE IS MY ONLY SON!›

‹LET **ME** TAKE HIS PLACE!›

OKAY, **LET GO** NOW. THIS HAS GONE **FAR** ENOUGH.

OH, THIS IS ONLY **BEGINNING**. SOON YOU SHALL **BURN** WITH HELPLESSNESS AND **OUTRAGE** -- JUST AS **I** DID ON THE DAY I WAS **REBORN**...

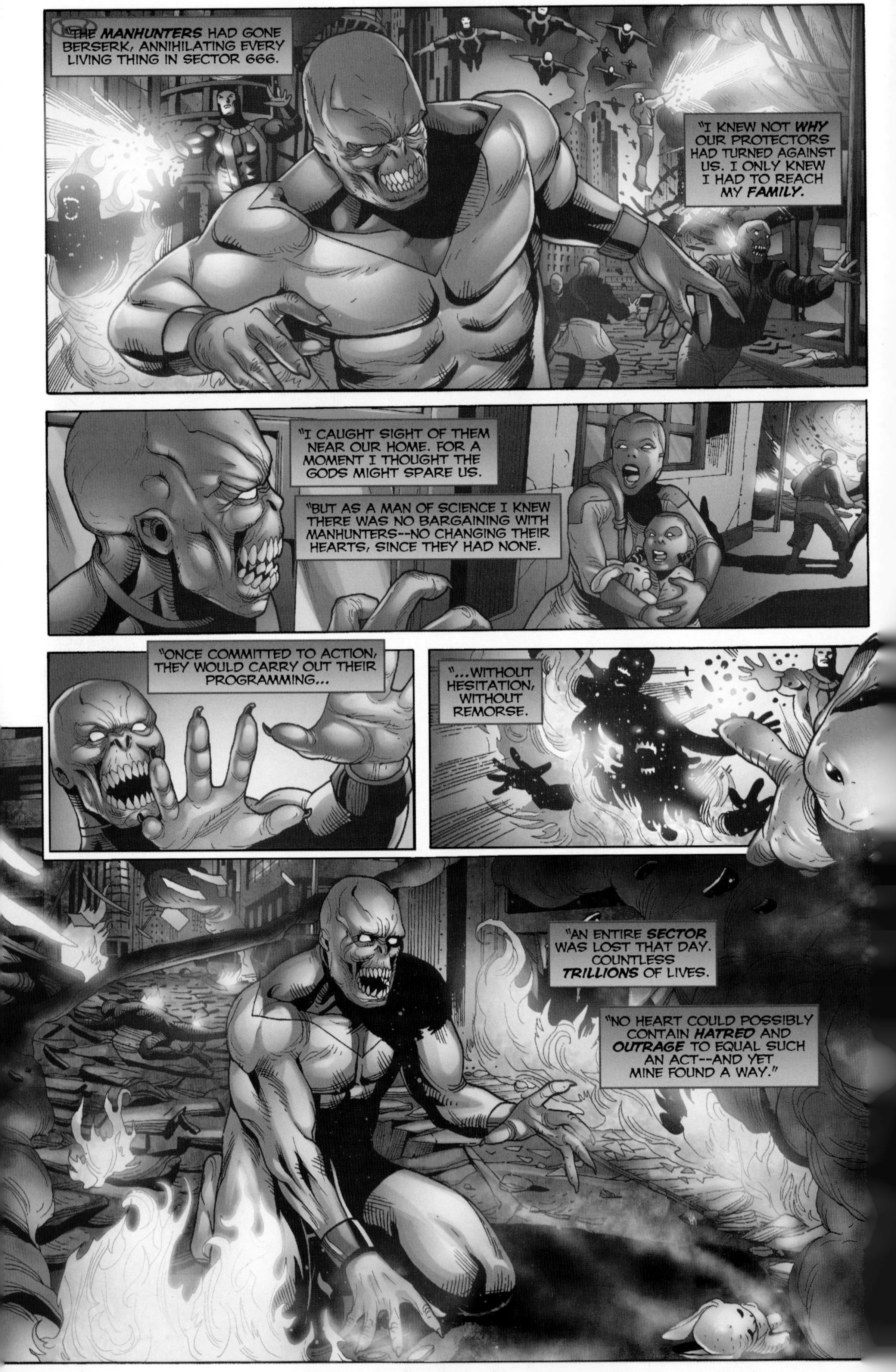
"THE MANHUNTERS HAD GONE BERSERK, ANNIHILATING EVERY LIVING THING IN SECTOR 666.
"I KNEW NOT WHY OUR PROTECTORS HAD TURNED AGAINST US. I ONLY KNEW I HAD TO REACH MY FAMILY.
"I CAUGHT SIGHT OF THEM NEAR OUR HOME. FOR A MOMENT I THOUGHT THE GODS MIGHT SPARE US.
"BUT AS A MAN OF SCIENCE I KNEW THERE WAS NO BARGAINING WITH MANHUNTERS--NO CHANGING THEIR HEARTS, SINCE THEY HAD NONE.
"ONCE COMMITTED TO ACTION, THEY WOULD CARRY OUT THEIR PROGRAMMING...
"...WITHOUT HESITATION, WITHOUT REMORSE.
"AN ENTIRE SECTOR WAS LOST THAT DAY. COUNTLESS TRILLIONS OF LIVES.
"NO HEART COULD POSSIBLY CONTAIN HATRED AND OUTRAGE TO EQUAL SUCH AN ACT--AND YET MINE FOUND A WAY."

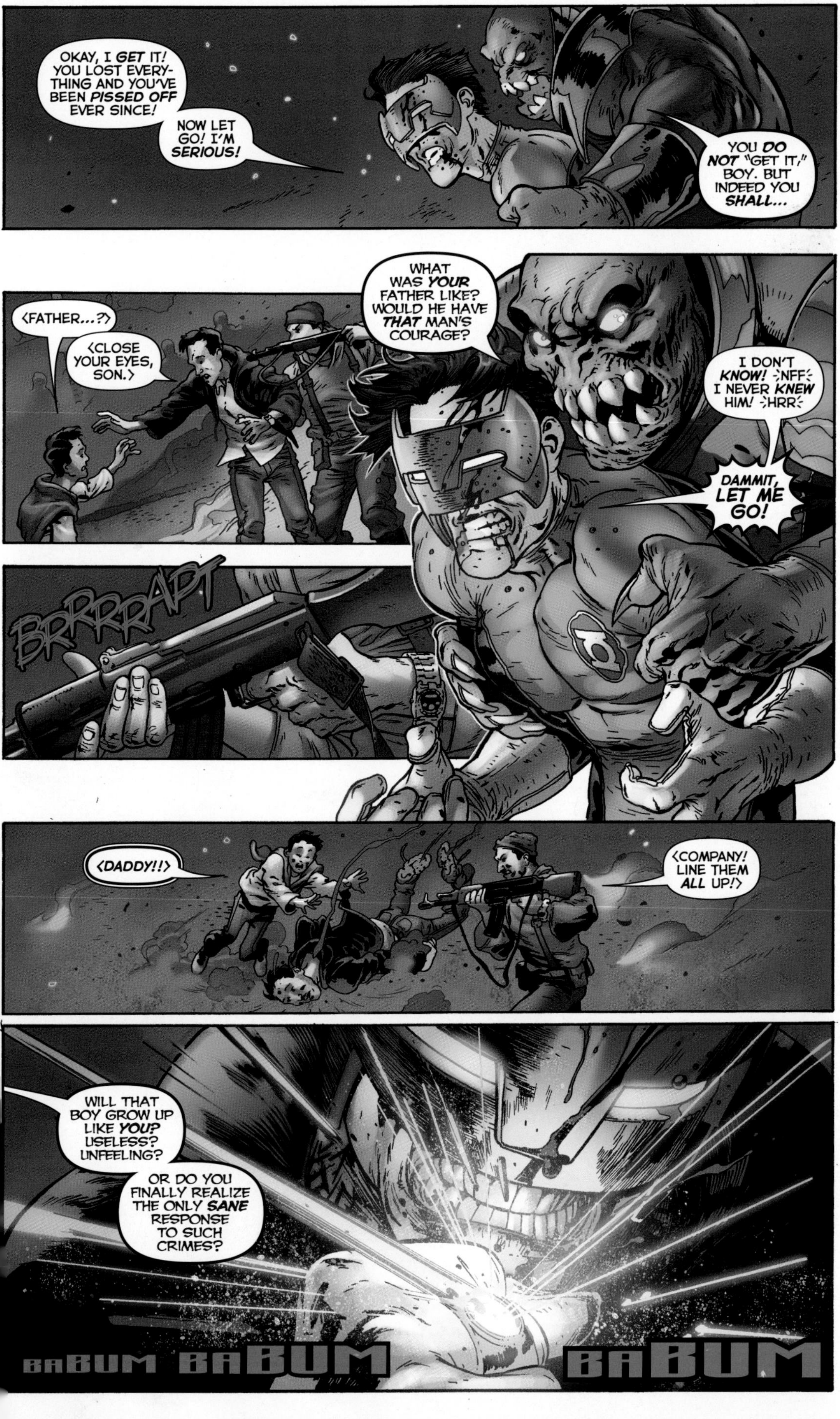
OKAY, I GET IT! YOU LOST EVERYTHING AND YOU'VE BEEN PISSED OFF EVER SINCE!
NOW LET GO! I'M SERIOUS!
YOU DO NOT "GET IT," BOY. BUT INDEED YOU SHALL...
WHAT WAS YOUR FATHER LIKE? WOULD HE HAVE THAT MAN'S COURAGE?
<FATHER...?>
<CLOSE YOUR EYES, SON.>
I DON'T KNOW! NFF I NEVER KNEW HIM! HRR
DAMMIT, LET ME GO!
BRRRRAPT
<DADDY!!>
<COMPANY! LINE THEM ALL UP!>
WILL THAT BOY GROW UP LIKE YOU? USELESS? UNFEELING?
OR DO YOU FINALLY REALIZE THE ONLY SANE RESPONSE TO SUCH CRIMES?
BABUM BABUM BABUM

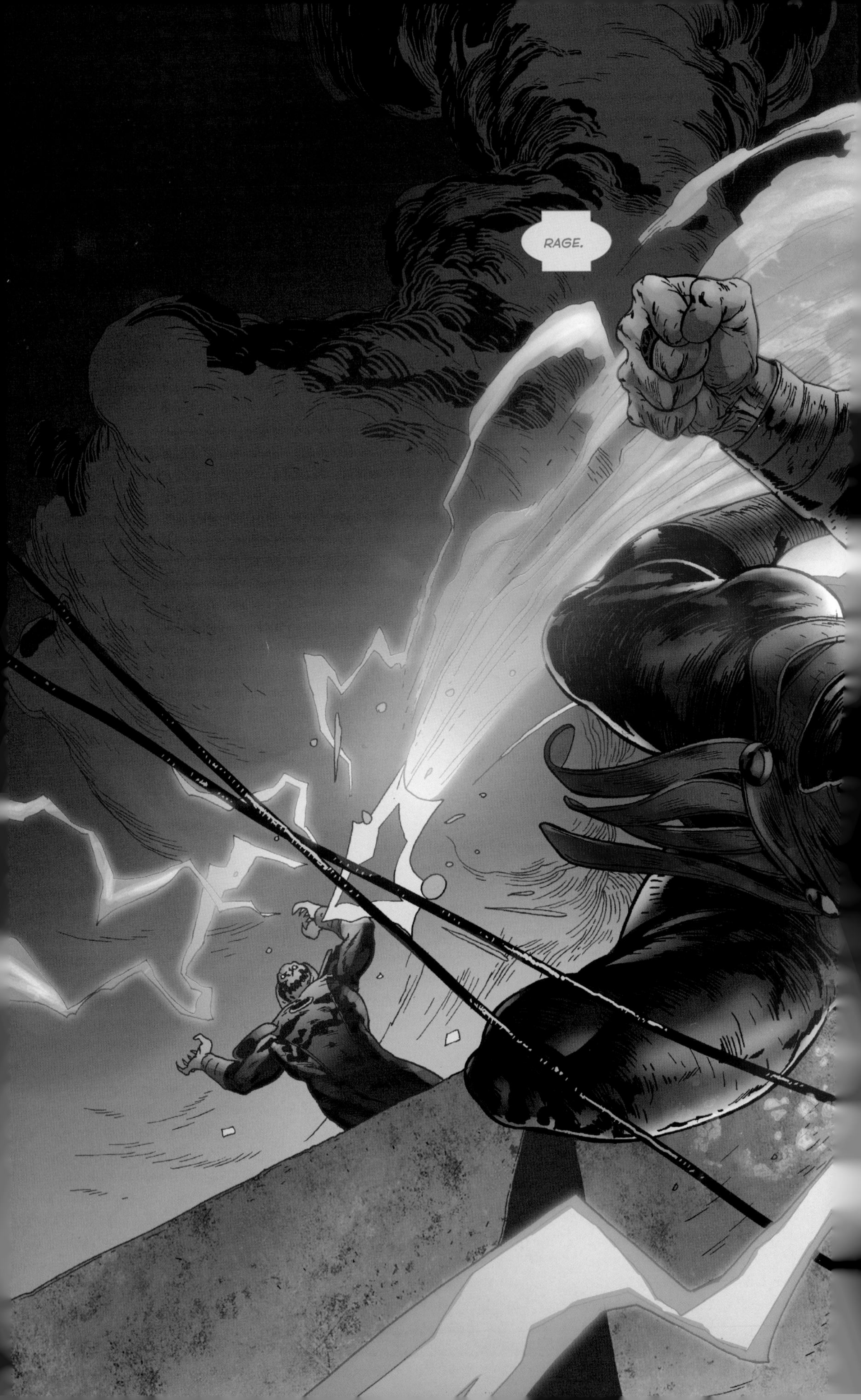
RAGE.

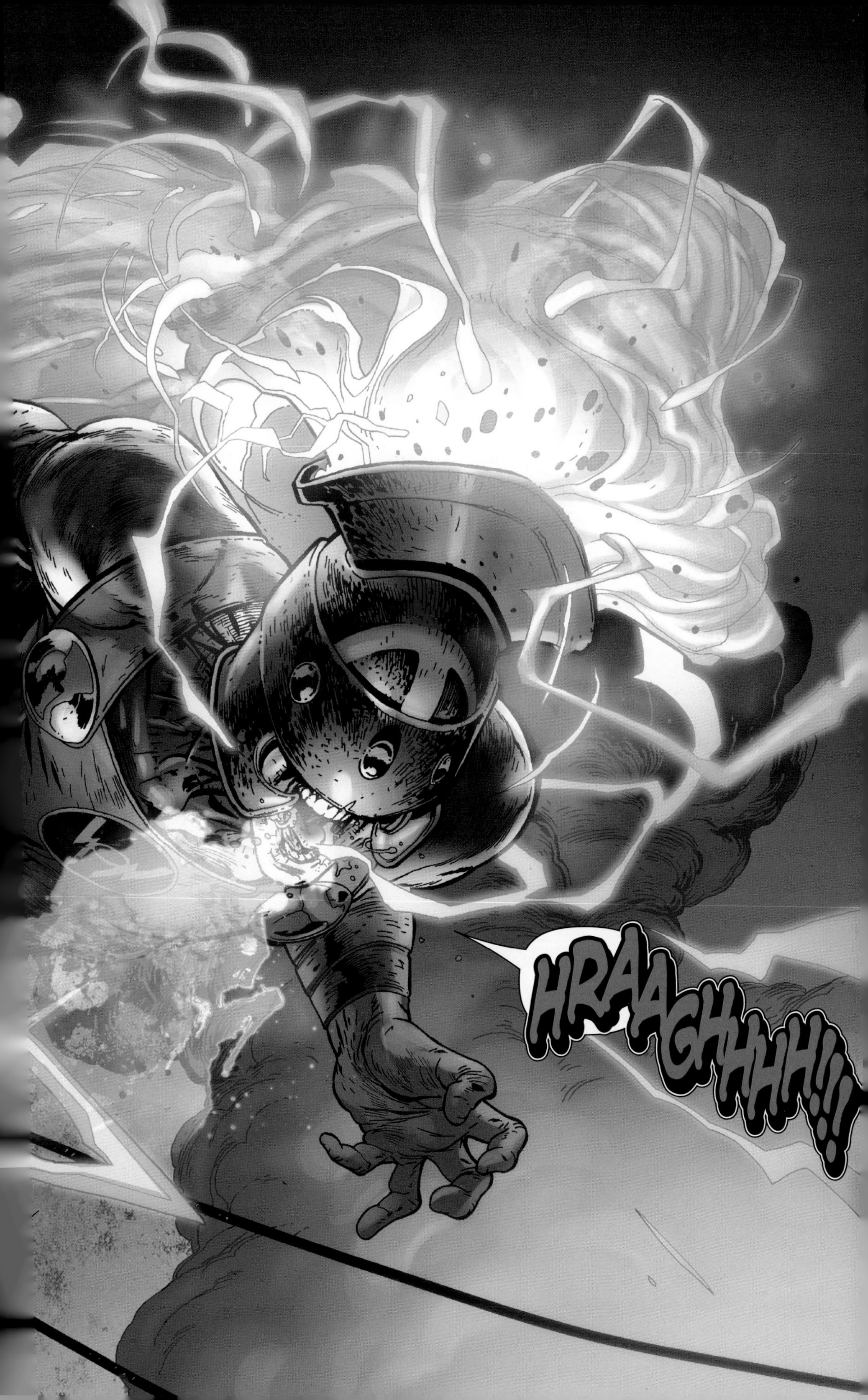
HRAAGHHHH!!!

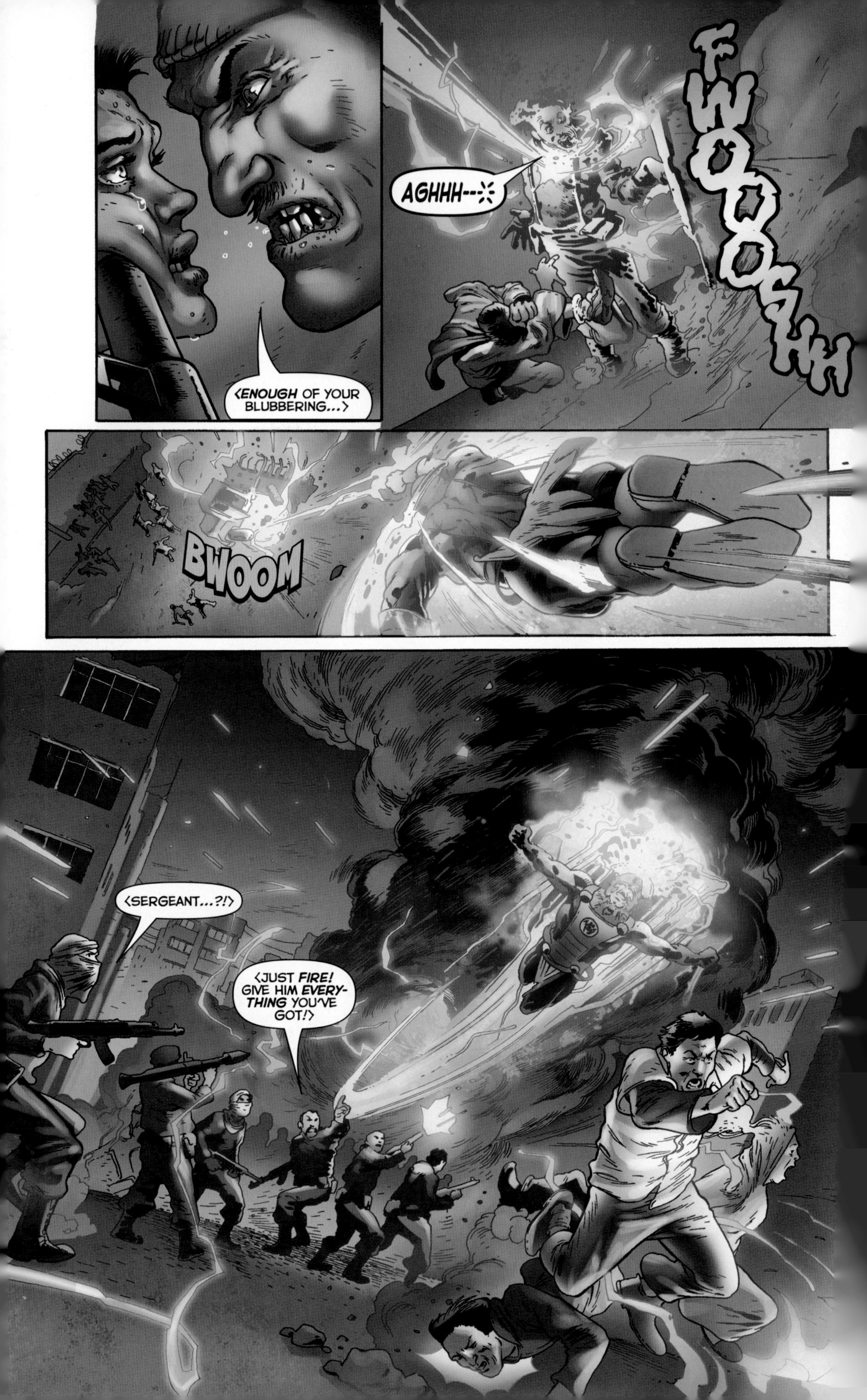

‹ENOUGH OF YOUR BLUBBERING...›
AGHHH--⁂
FWOOOSHH
BWOOM
‹SERGEANT...?!›
‹JUST FIRE! GIVE HIM EVERYTHING YOU'VE GOT!›

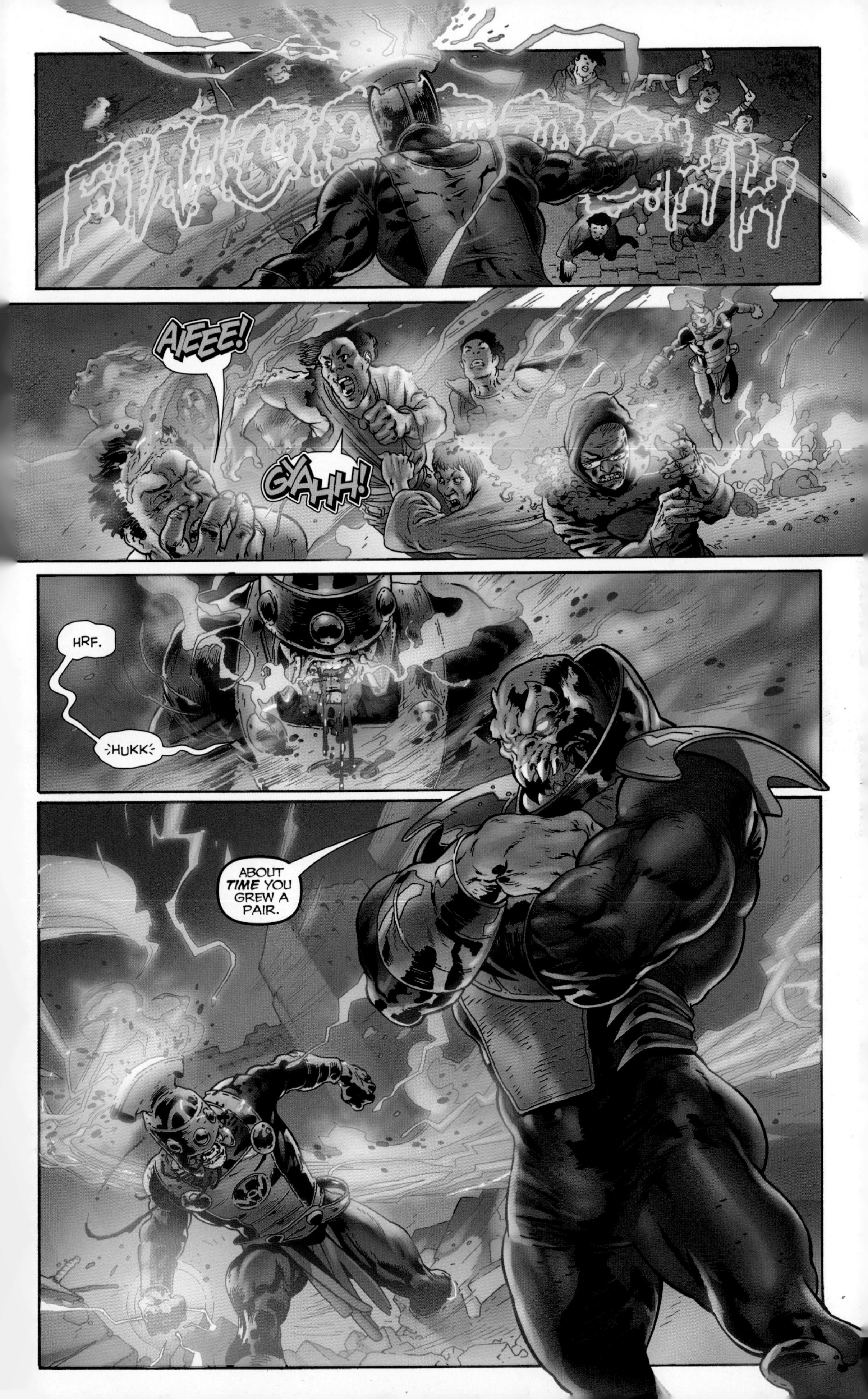
AIEEE!
GYAHH!
HRF.
HUKK
ABOUT TIME YOU GREW A PAIR.

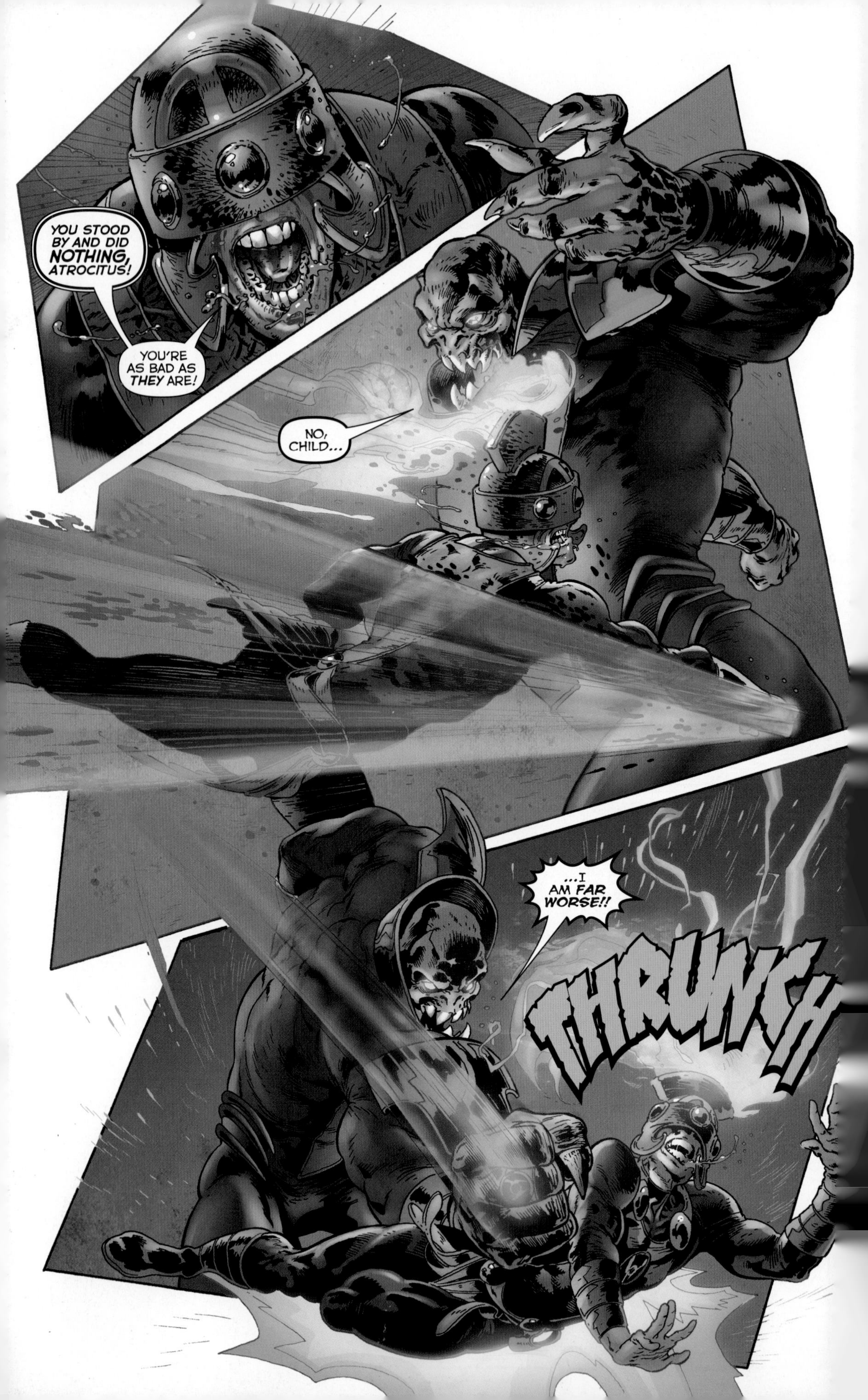
YOU STOOD BY AND DID NOTHING, ATROCITUS!
YOU'RE AS BAD AS THEY ARE!
NO, CHILD...
...I AM FAR WORSE!!
THRUNCH

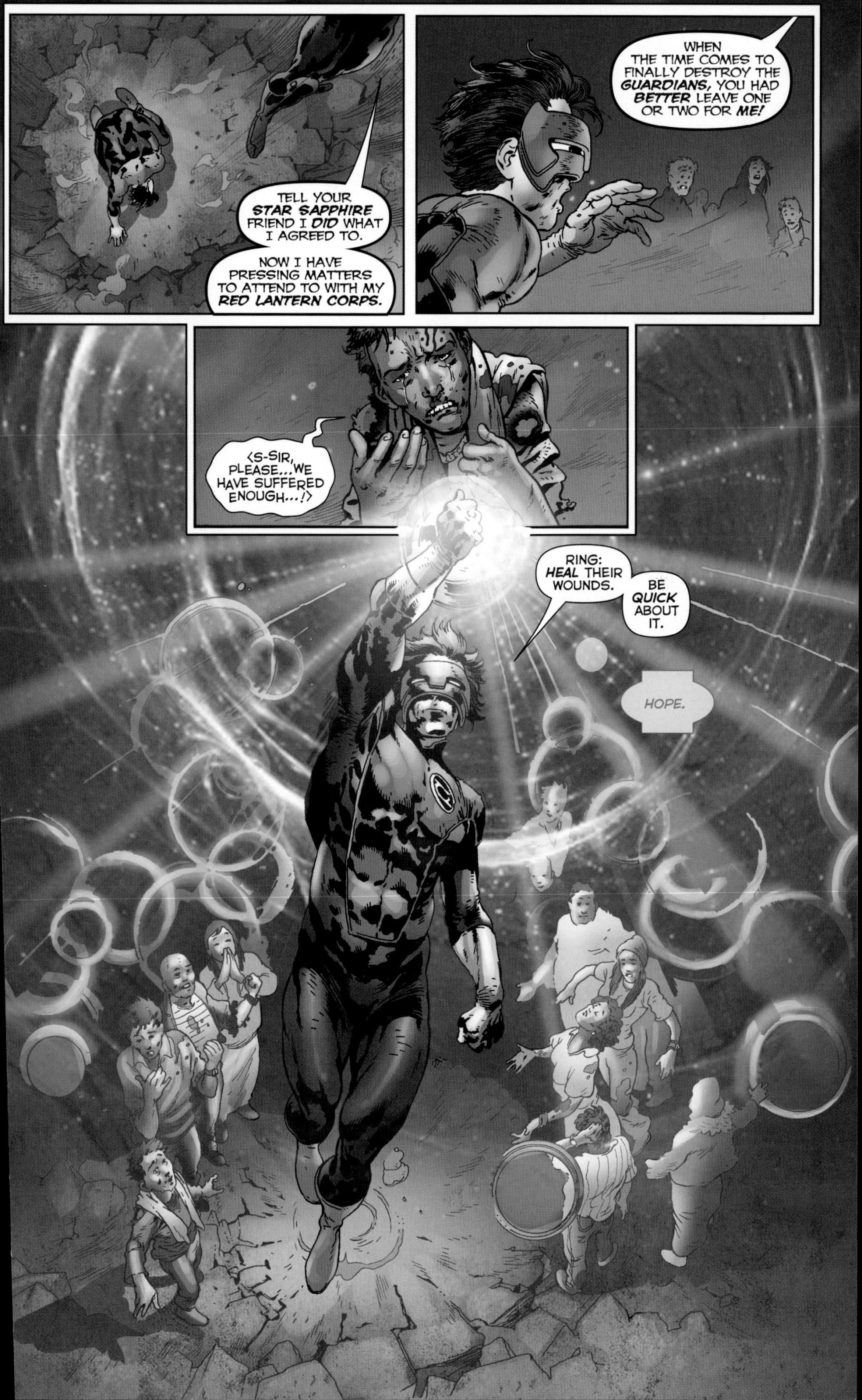

TELL YOUR STAR SAPPHIRE FRIEND I DID WHAT I AGREED TO.
NOW I HAVE PRESSING MATTERS TO ATTEND TO WITH MY RED LANTERN CORPS.
WHEN THE TIME COMES TO FINALLY DESTROY THE GUARDIANS, YOU HAD BETTER LEAVE ONE OR TWO FOR ME!
<S-SIR, PLEASE... WE HAVE SUFFERED ENOUGH...!>
RING: HEAL THEIR WOUNDS.
BE QUICK ABOUT IT.
HOPE.

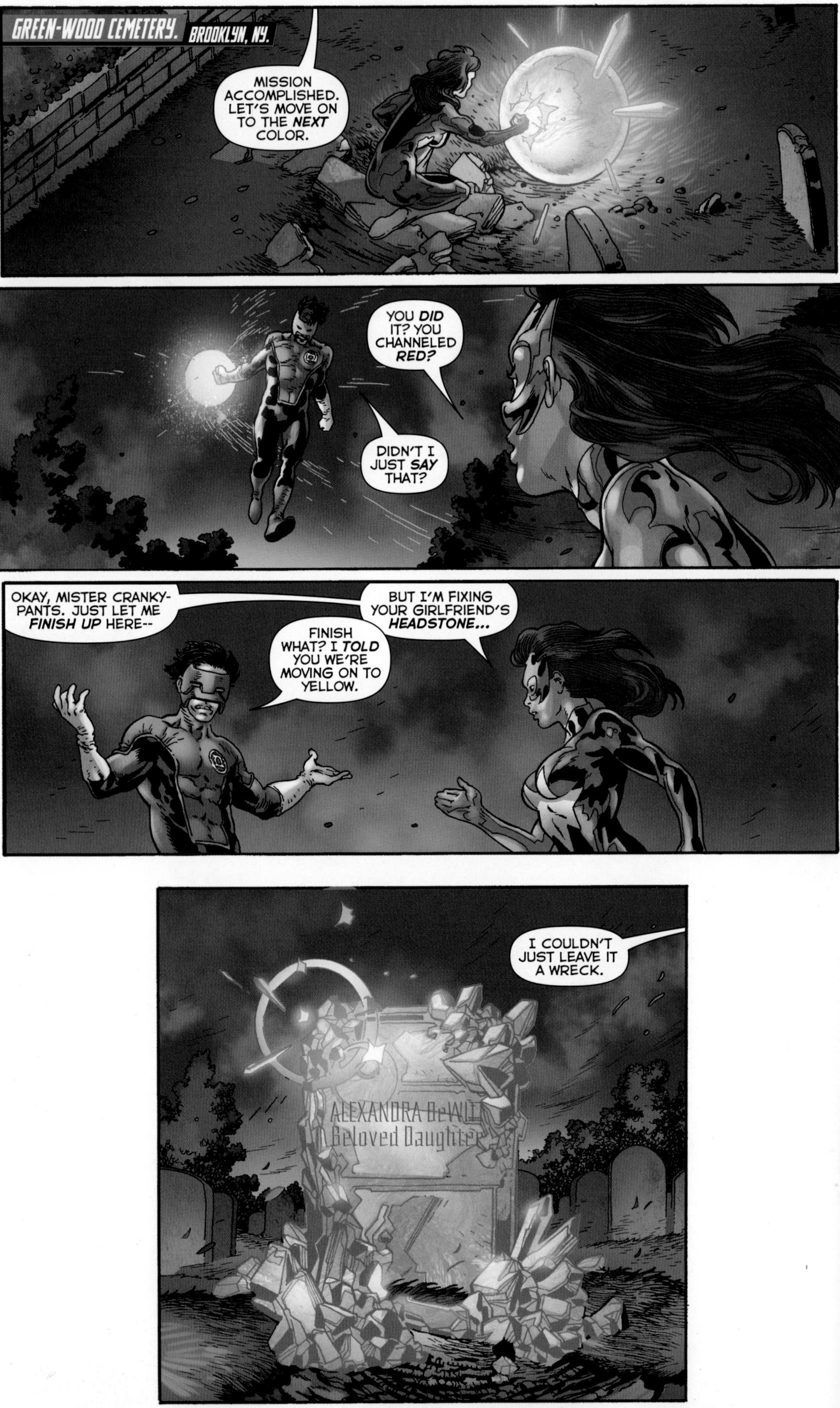
GREEN-WOOD CEMETERY. BROOKLYN, NY.
MISSION ACCOMPLISHED. LET'S MOVE ON TO THE NEXT COLOR.
YOU DID IT? YOU CHANNELED RED?
DIDN'T I JUST SAY THAT?
OKAY, MISTER CRANKY-PANTS. JUST LET ME FINISH UP HERE--
FINISH WHAT? I TOLD YOU WE'RE MOVING ON TO YELLOW.
BUT I'M FIXING YOUR GIRLFRIEND'S HEADSTONE...
I COULDN'T JUST LEAVE IT A WRECK.
ALEXANDRA DeWIT
Beloved Daughter

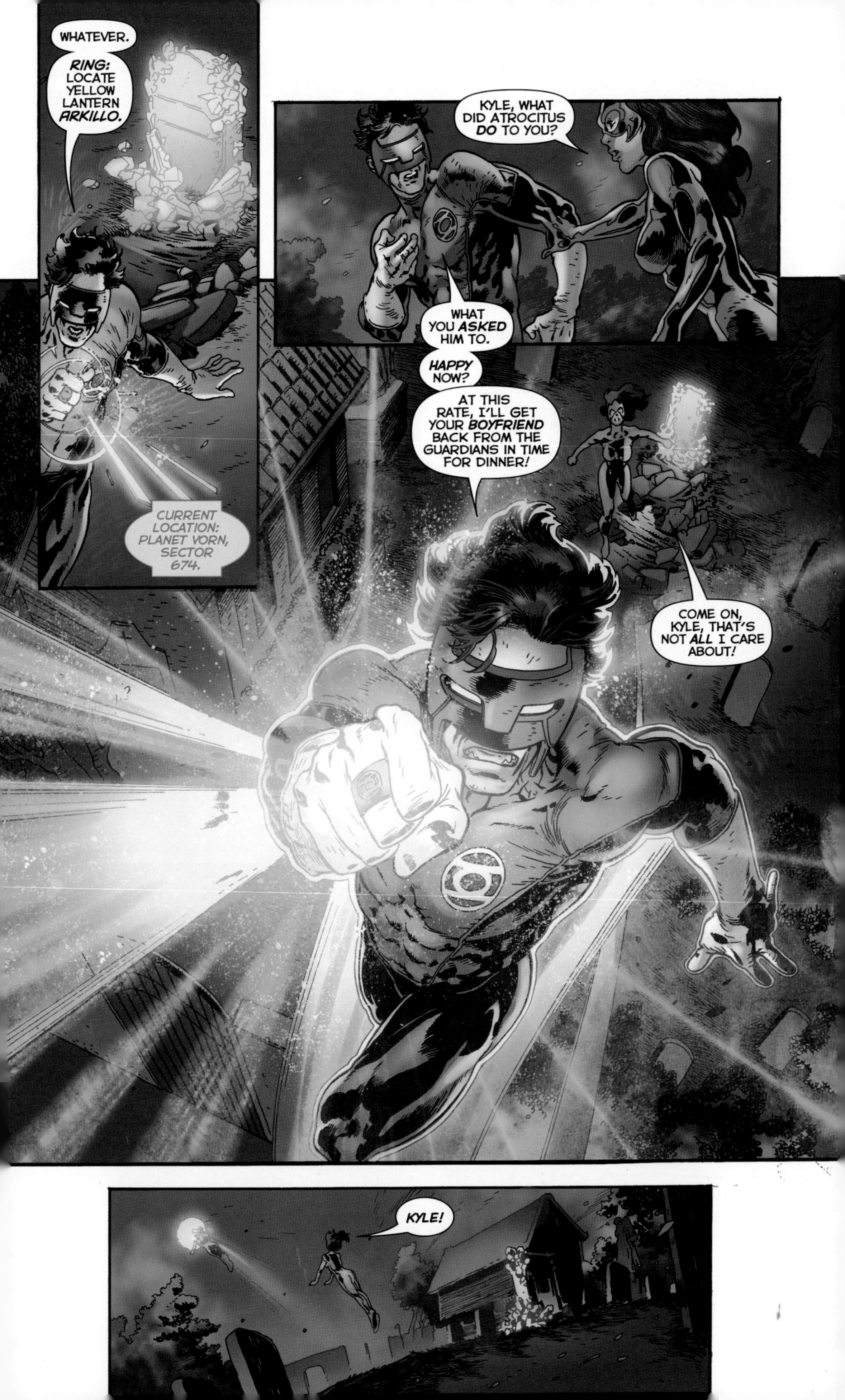
WHATEVER.
RING: LOCATE YELLOW LANTERN ARKILLO.
CURRENT LOCATION: PLANET VORN, SECTOR 674.
KYLE, WHAT DID ATROCITUS DO TO YOU?
WHAT YOU ASKED HIM TO.
HAPPY NOW?
AT THIS RATE, I'LL GET YOUR BOYFRIEND BACK FROM THE GUARDIANS IN TIME FOR DINNER!
COME ON, KYLE, THAT'S NOT ALL I CARE ABOUT!
KYLE!

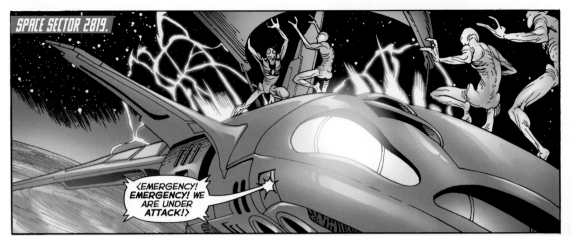

SPACE SECTOR 2819.

<EMERGENCY! EMERGENCY! WE ARE UNDER ATTACK!>

<HULL *BREACHED!* SHIP VENTING *ATMO-SPHERE...*>

<NO! STOP!>

<GET OFF ME!>

<GET OMMPH!>

ANALYSIS:
RAPID INFECTION/
CELLULAR CONVERSION.
EXPONENTIAL
INFECTION RATE.
PROGNOSIS:
DISEASE VECTOR
UNSTOPPABLE.
FORECAST:
UNIVERSAL PANDEMI

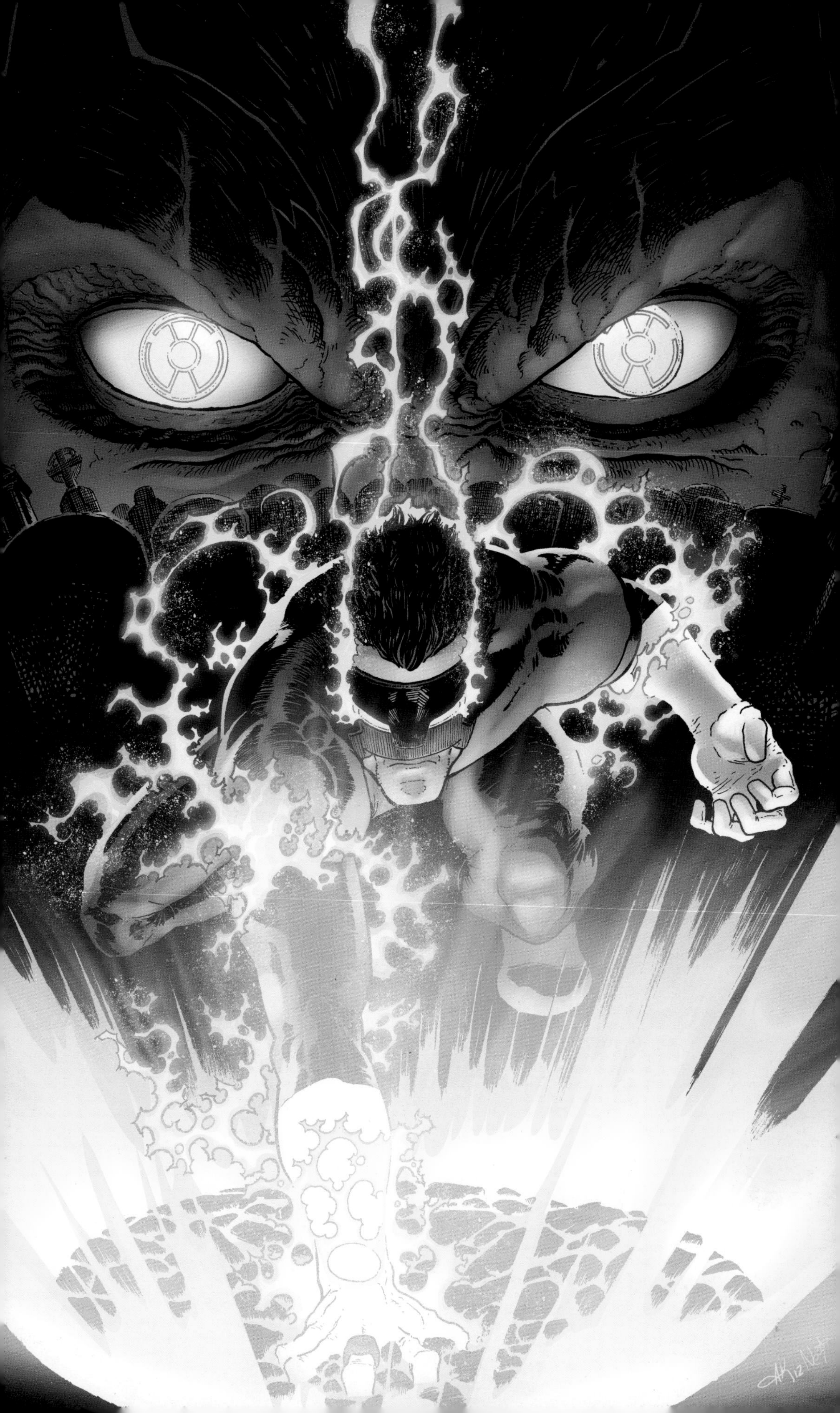

FEAR FACTOR

TONY BEDARD writer ANDREI BRESSAN & AMILCAR PINNA artists
AARON KUDER & NEI RUFFINO cover

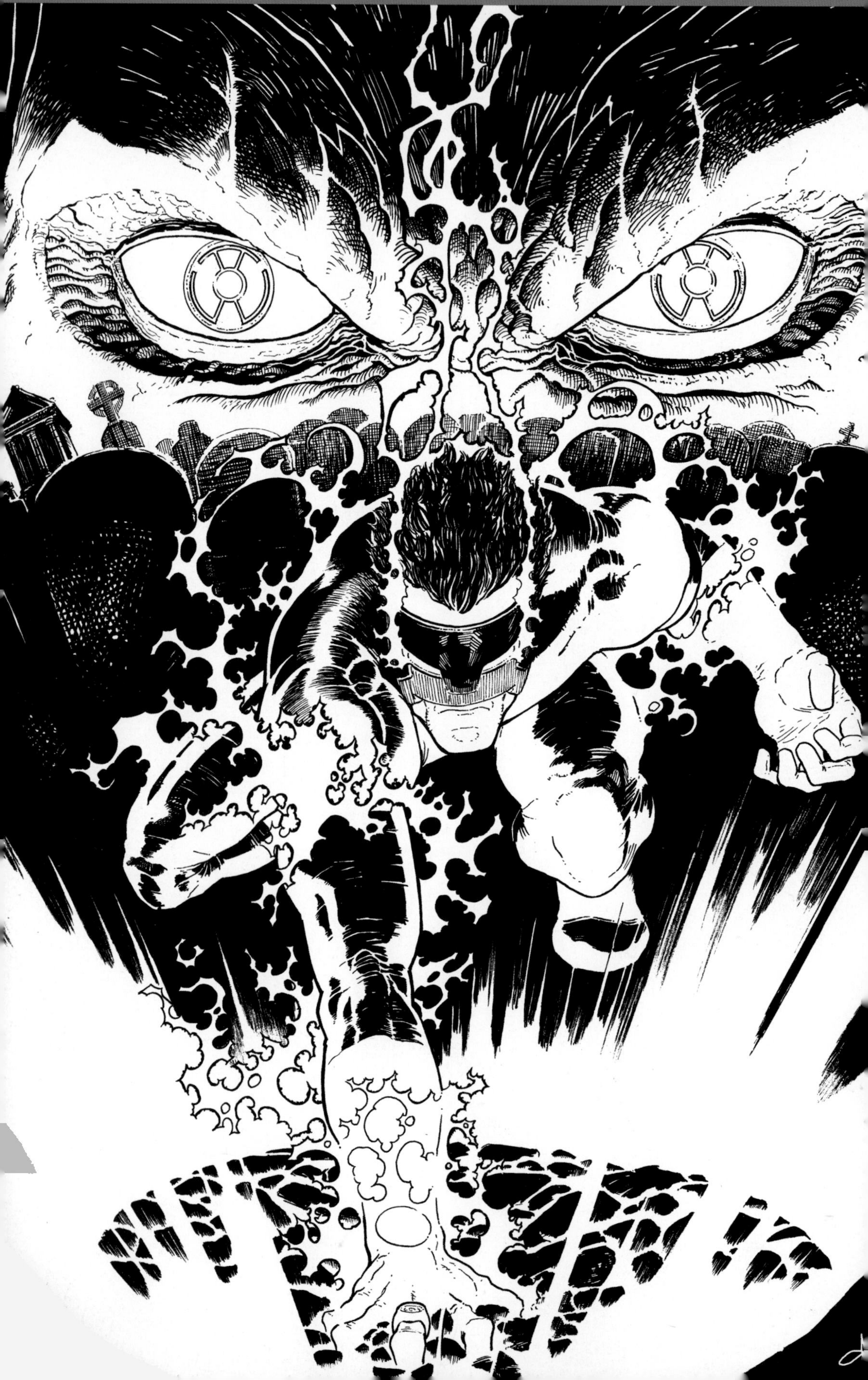

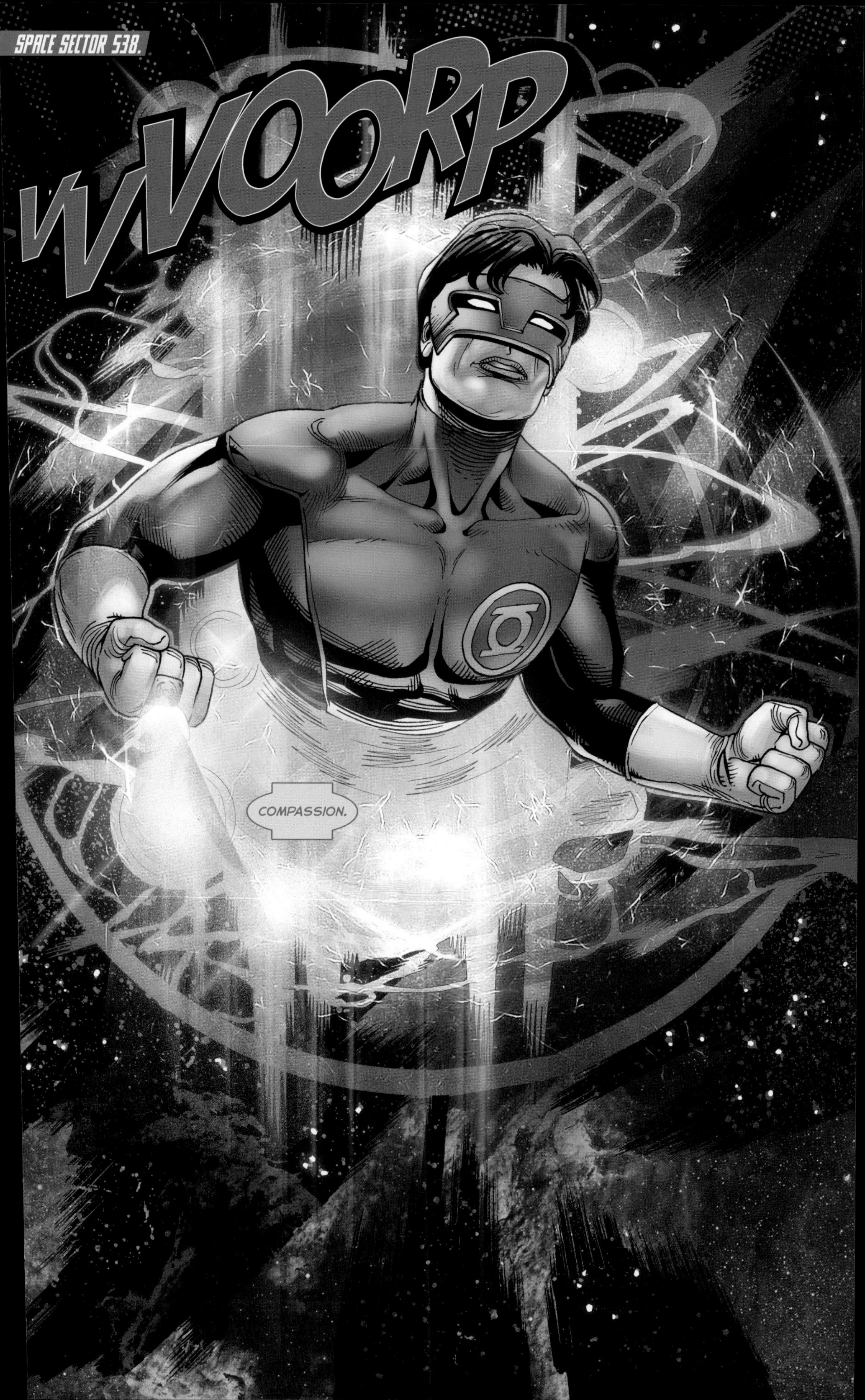
SPACE SECTOR 538.
WVOORP
COMPASSION.

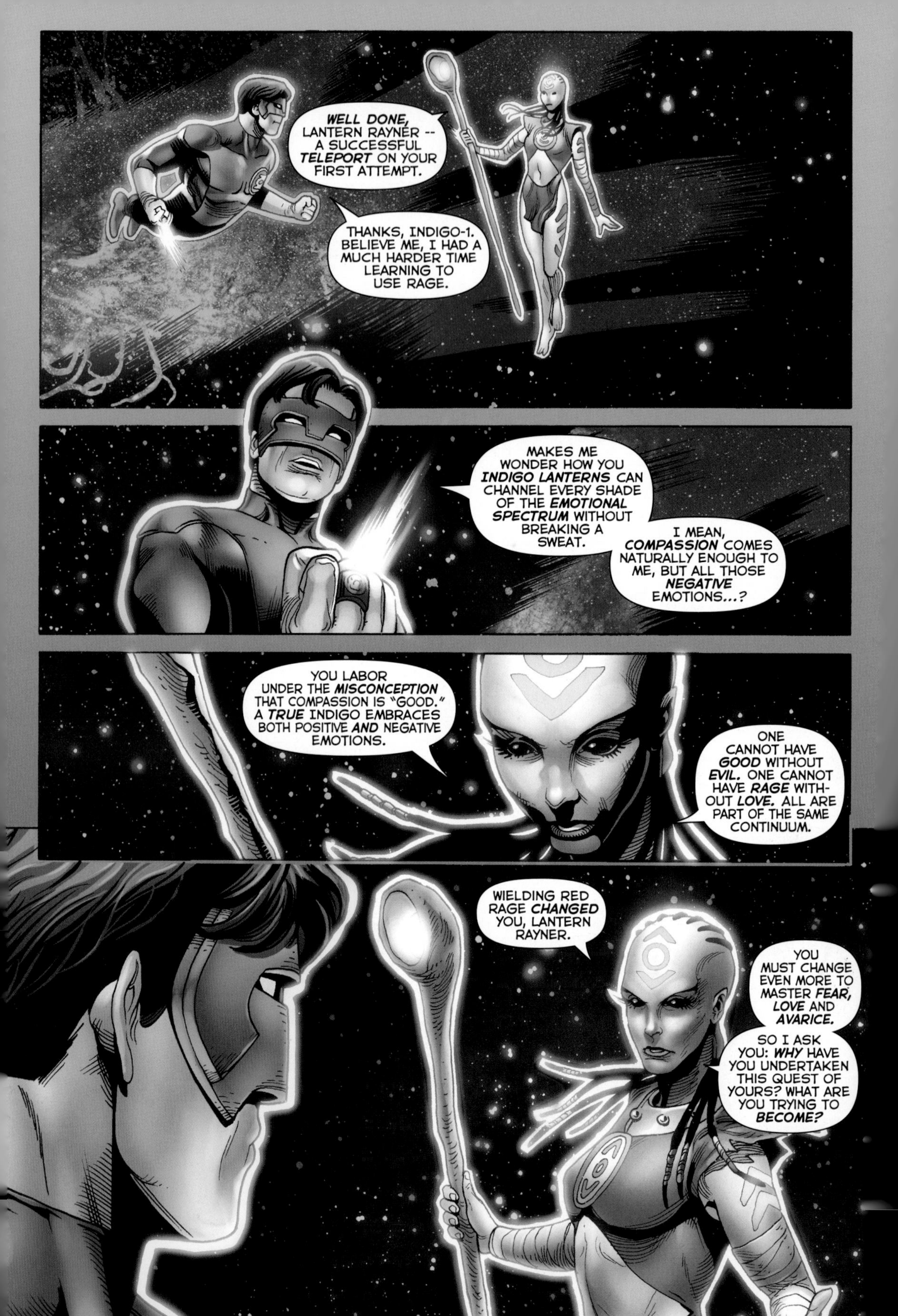
WELL DONE, LANTERN RAYNER -- A SUCCESSFUL TELEPORT ON YOUR FIRST ATTEMPT.
THANKS, INDIGO-1. BELIEVE ME, I HAD A MUCH HARDER TIME LEARNING TO USE RAGE.
MAKES ME WONDER HOW YOU INDIGO LANTERNS CAN CHANNEL EVERY SHADE OF THE EMOTIONAL SPECTRUM WITHOUT BREAKING A SWEAT.
I MEAN, COMPASSION COMES NATURALLY ENOUGH TO ME, BUT ALL THOSE NEGATIVE EMOTIONS...?
YOU LABOR UNDER THE MISCONCEPTION THAT COMPASSION IS "GOOD." A TRUE INDIGO EMBRACES BOTH POSITIVE AND NEGATIVE EMOTIONS.
ONE CANNOT HAVE GOOD WITHOUT EVIL. ONE CANNOT HAVE RAGE WITHOUT LOVE. ALL ARE PART OF THE SAME CONTINUUM.
WIELDING RED RAGE CHANGED YOU, LANTERN RAYNER.
YOU MUST CHANGE EVEN MORE TO MASTER FEAR, LOVE AND AVARICE.
SO I ASK YOU: WHY HAVE YOU UNDERTAKEN THIS QUEST OF YOURS? WHAT ARE YOU TRYING TO BECOME?

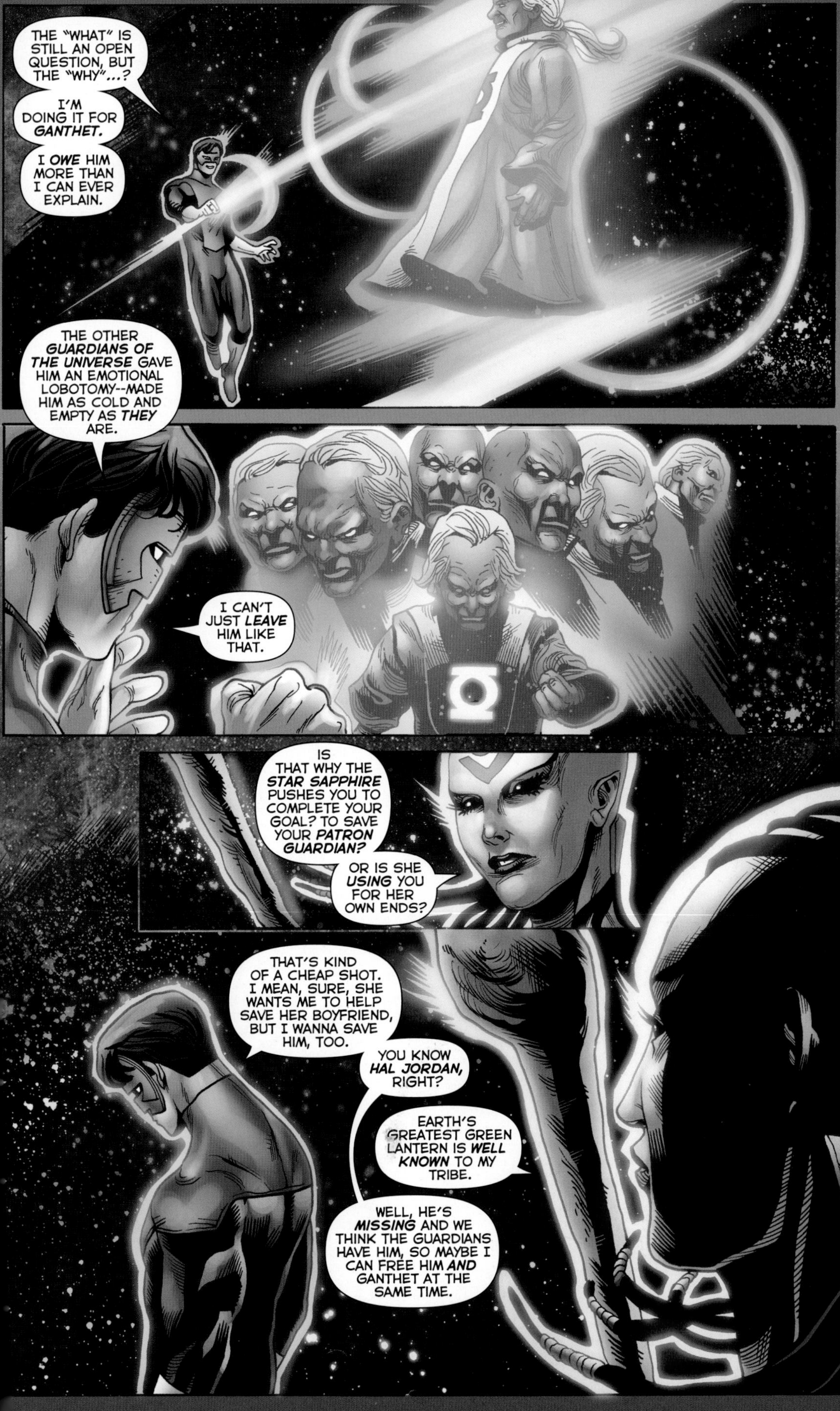
THE "WHAT" IS STILL AN OPEN QUESTION, BUT THE "WHY"...?
I'M DOING IT FOR GANTHET.
I OWE HIM MORE THAN I CAN EVER EXPLAIN.
THE OTHER GUARDIANS OF THE UNIVERSE GAVE HIM AN EMOTIONAL LOBOTOMY--MADE HIM AS COLD AND EMPTY AS THEY ARE.
I CAN'T JUST LEAVE HIM LIKE THAT.
IS THAT WHY THE STAR SAPPHIRE PUSHES YOU TO COMPLETE YOUR GOAL? TO SAVE YOUR PATRON GUARDIAN?
OR IS SHE USING YOU FOR HER OWN ENDS?
THAT'S KIND OF A CHEAP SHOT. I MEAN, SURE, SHE WANTS ME TO HELP SAVE HER BOYFRIEND, BUT I WANNA SAVE HIM, TOO.
YOU KNOW HAL JORDAN, RIGHT?
EARTH'S GREATEST GREEN LANTERN IS WELL KNOWN TO MY TRIBE.
WELL, HE'S MISSING AND WE THINK THE GUARDIANS HAVE HIM, SO MAYBE I CAN FREE HIM AND GANTHET AT THE SAME TIME.

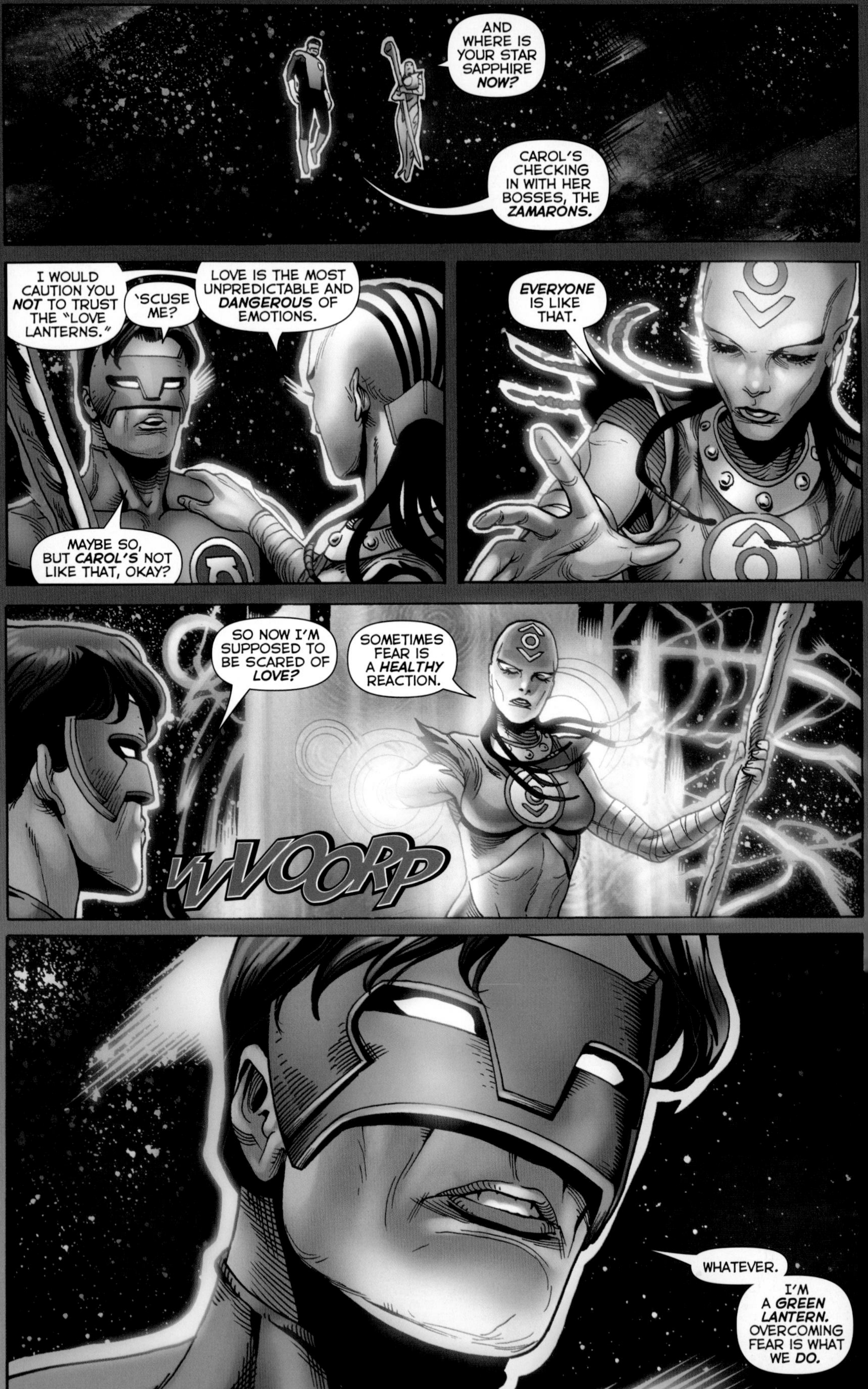
AND WHERE IS YOUR STAR SAPPHIRE NOW?
CAROL'S CHECKING IN WITH HER BOSSES, THE ZAMARONS.
I WOULD CAUTION YOU NOT TO TRUST THE "LOVE LANTERNS."
'SCUSE ME?
LOVE IS THE MOST UNPREDICTABLE AND DANGEROUS OF EMOTIONS.
MAYBE SO, BUT CAROL'S NOT LIKE THAT, OKAY?
EVERYONE IS LIKE THAT.
SO NOW I'M SUPPOSED TO BE SCARED OF LOVE?
SOMETIMES FEAR IS A HEALTHY REACTION.
VVVOORP
WHATEVER.
I'M A GREEN LANTERN. OVERCOMING FEAR IS WHAT WE DO.

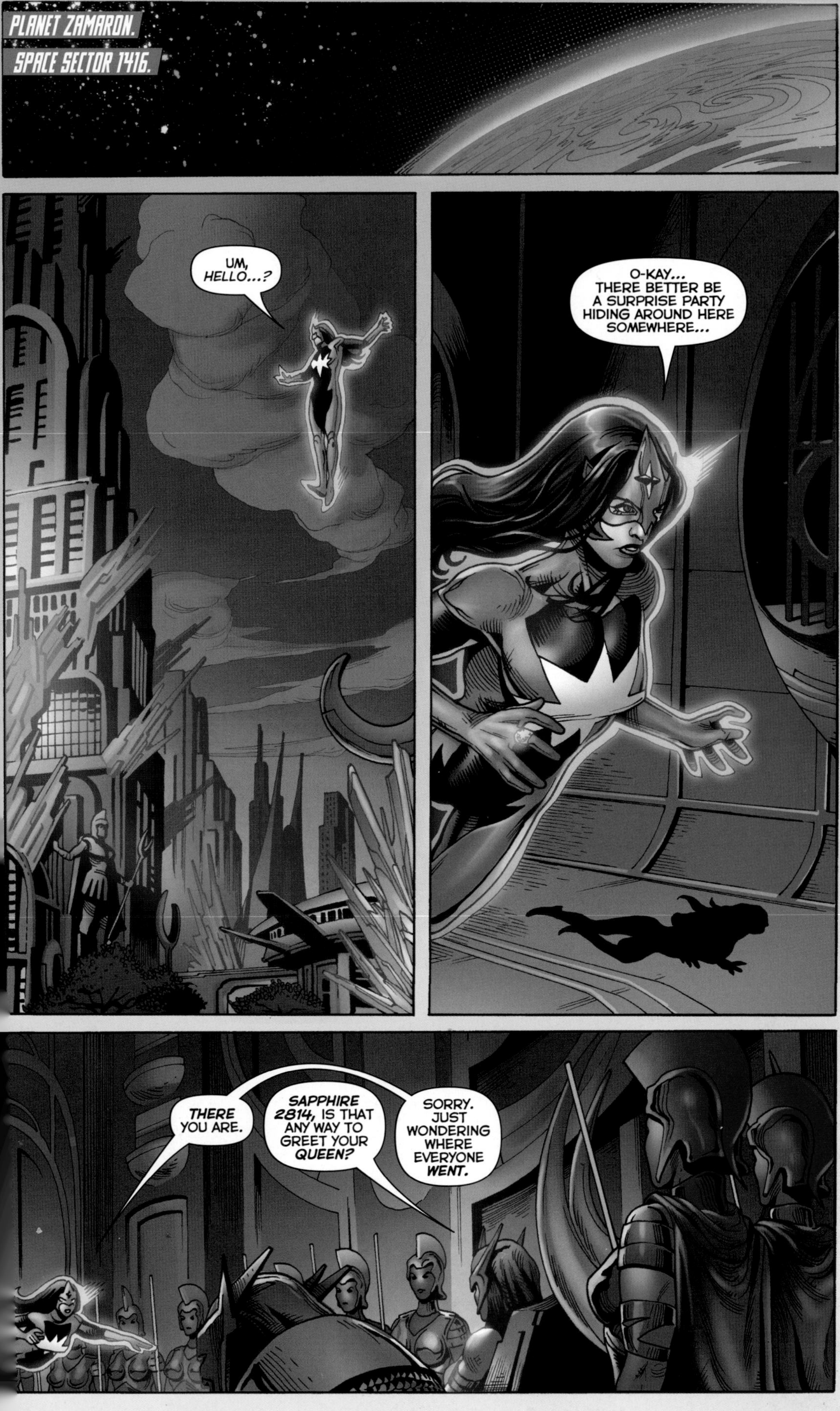
PLANET ZAMARON.
SPACE SECTOR 1416.
UM, HELLO...?
O-KAY... THERE BETTER BE A SURPRISE PARTY HIDING AROUND HERE SOMEWHERE...
THERE YOU ARE.
SAPPHIRE 2814, IS THAT ANY WAY TO GREET YOUR QUEEN?
SORRY. JUST WONDERING WHERE EVERYONE WENT.

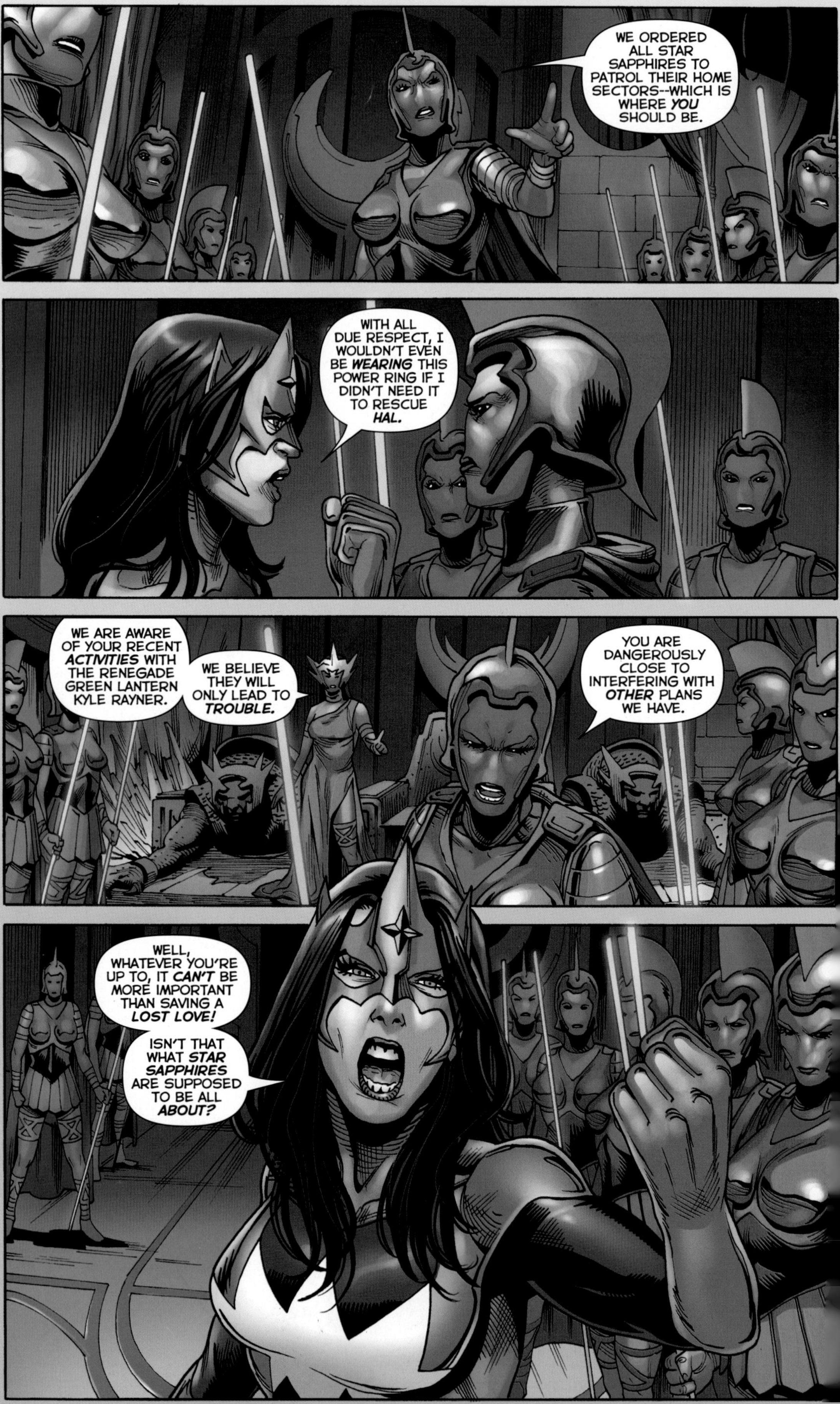
WE ORDERED ALL STAR SAPPHIRES TO PATROL THEIR HOME SECTORS--WHICH IS WHERE YOU SHOULD BE.
WITH ALL DUE RESPECT, I WOULDN'T EVEN BE WEARING THIS POWER RING IF I DIDN'T NEED IT TO RESCUE HAL.
WE ARE AWARE OF YOUR RECENT ACTIVITIES WITH THE RENEGADE GREEN LANTERN KYLE RAYNER.
WE BELIEVE THEY WILL ONLY LEAD TO TROUBLE.
YOU ARE DANGEROUSLY CLOSE TO INTERFERING WITH OTHER PLANS WE HAVE.
WELL, WHATEVER YOU'RE UP TO, IT CAN'T BE MORE IMPORTANT THAN SAVING A LOST LOVE!
ISN'T THAT WHAT STAR SAPPHIRES ARE SUPPOSED TO BE ALL ABOUT?

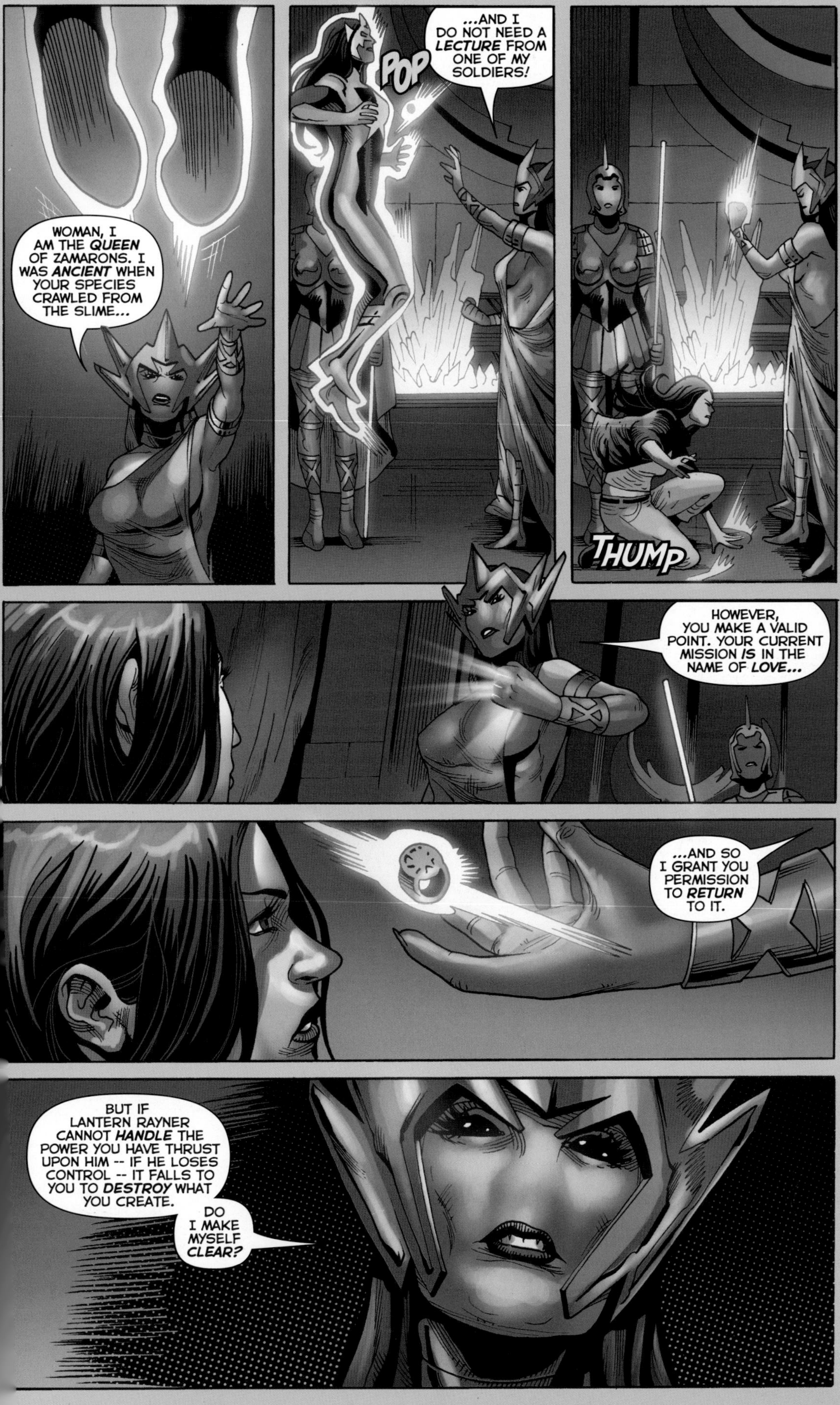
WOMAN, I AM THE QUEEN OF ZAMARONS. I WAS ANCIENT WHEN YOUR SPECIES CRAWLED FROM THE SLIME...
POP
...AND I DO NOT NEED A LECTURE FROM ONE OF MY SOLDIERS!
THUMP
HOWEVER, YOU MAKE A VALID POINT. YOUR CURRENT MISSION IS IN THE NAME OF LOVE...
...AND SO I GRANT YOU PERMISSION TO RETURN TO IT.
BUT IF LANTERN RAYNER CANNOT HANDLE THE POWER YOU HAVE THRUST UPON HIM -- IF HE LOSES CONTROL -- IT FALLS TO YOU TO DESTROY WHAT YOU CREATE.
DO I MAKE MYSELF CLEAR?

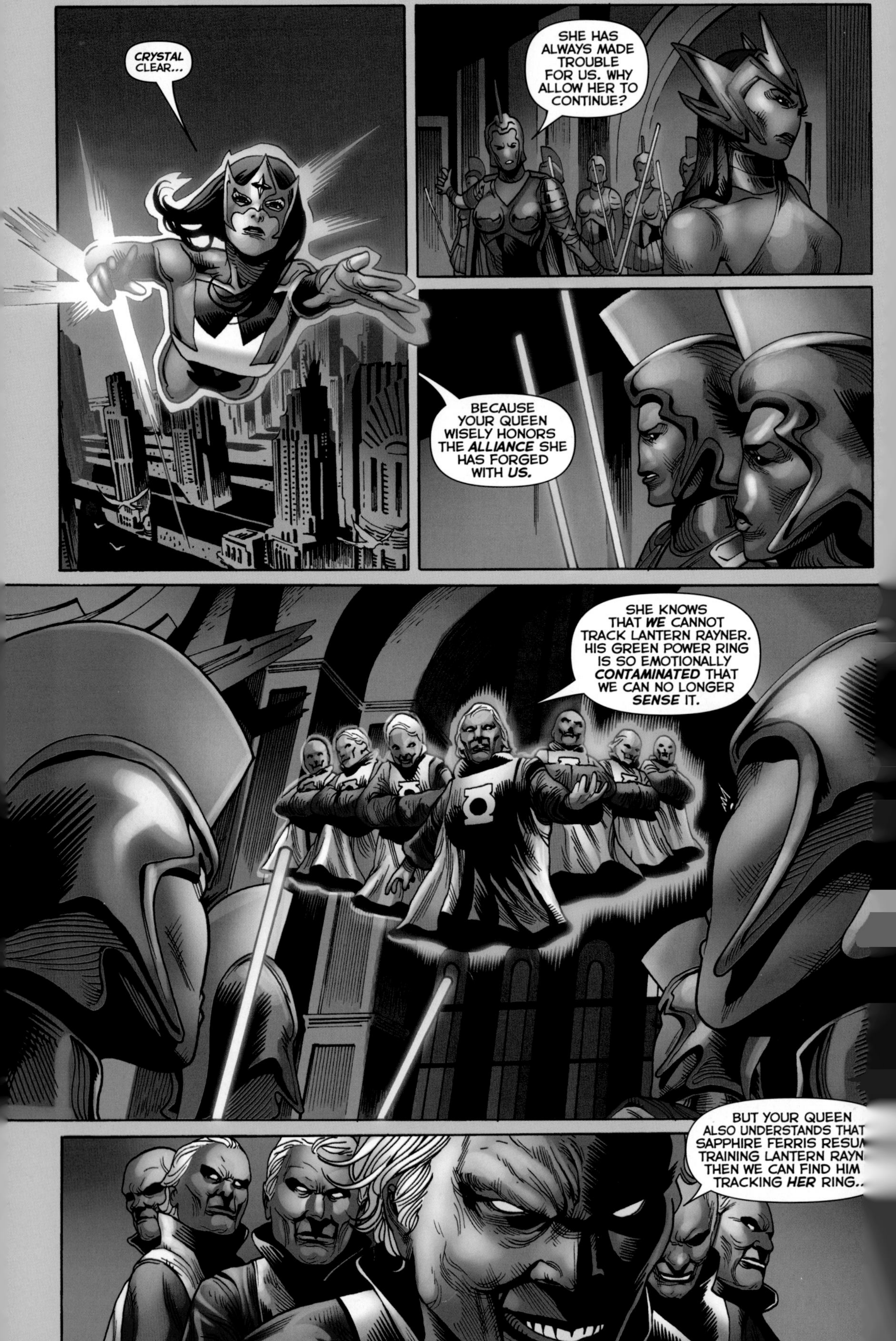
CRYSTAL CLEAR...
SHE HAS ALWAYS MADE TROUBLE FOR US. WHY ALLOW HER TO CONTINUE?
BECAUSE YOUR QUEEN WISELY HONORS THE ALLIANCE SHE HAS FORGED WITH US.
SHE KNOWS THAT WE CANNOT TRACK LANTERN RAYNER. HIS GREEN POWER RING IS SO EMOTIONALLY CONTAMINATED THAT WE CAN NO LONGER SENSE IT.
BUT YOUR QUEEN ALSO UNDERSTANDS THAT SAPPHIRE FERRIS RESUM TRAINING LANTERN RAYN THEN WE CAN FIND HIM TRACKING HER RING..

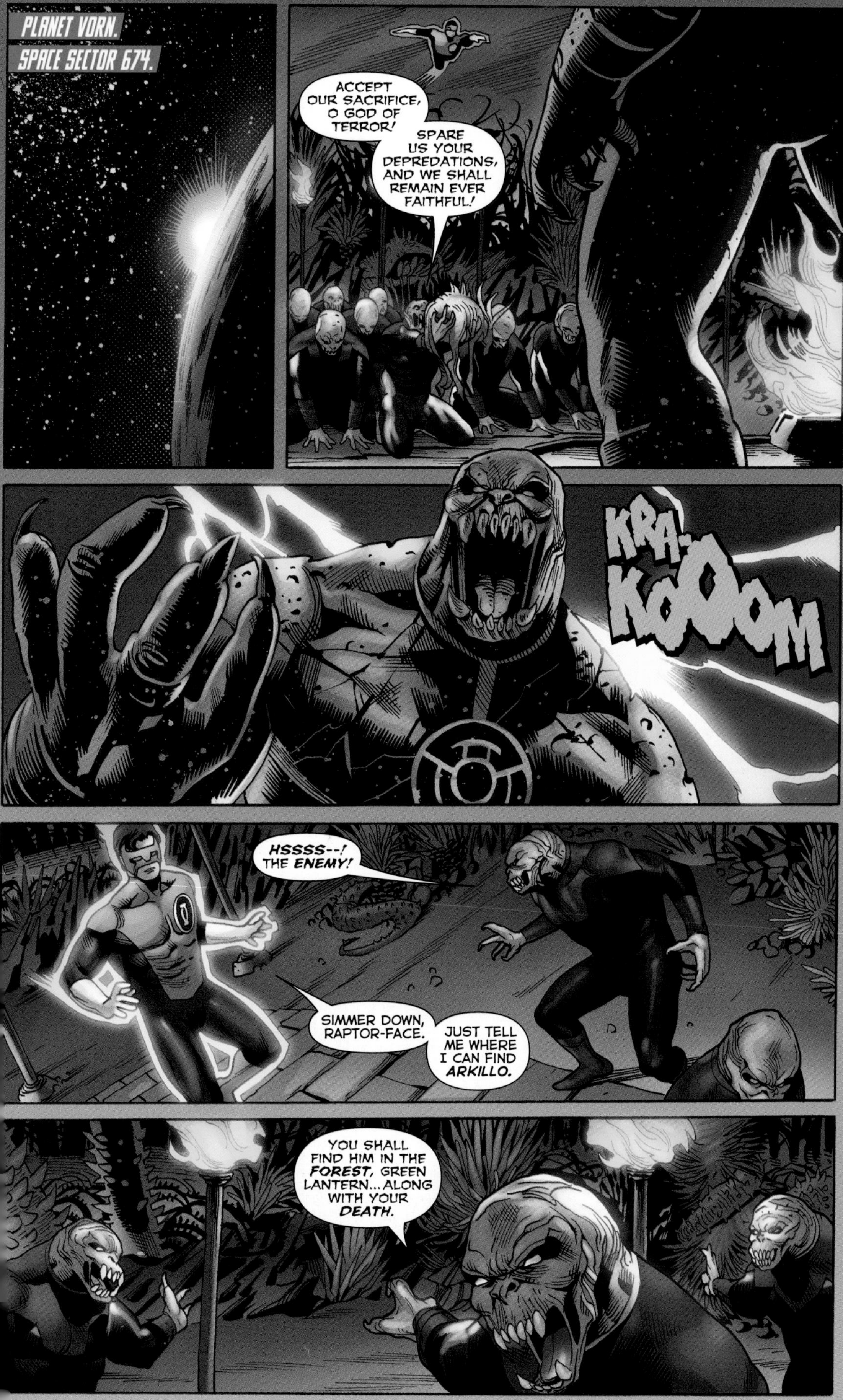
PLANET VORN.
SPACE SECTOR 674.
ACCEPT OUR SACRIFICE, O GOD OF TERROR!
SPARE US YOUR DEPREDATIONS, AND WE SHALL REMAIN EVER FAITHFUL!
KRA-KOOOM
HSSSS--! THE ENEMY!
SIMMER DOWN, RAPTOR-FACE.
JUST TELL ME WHERE I CAN FIND ARKILLO.
YOU SHALL FIND HIM IN THE FOREST, GREEN LANTERN...ALONG WITH YOUR DEATH.

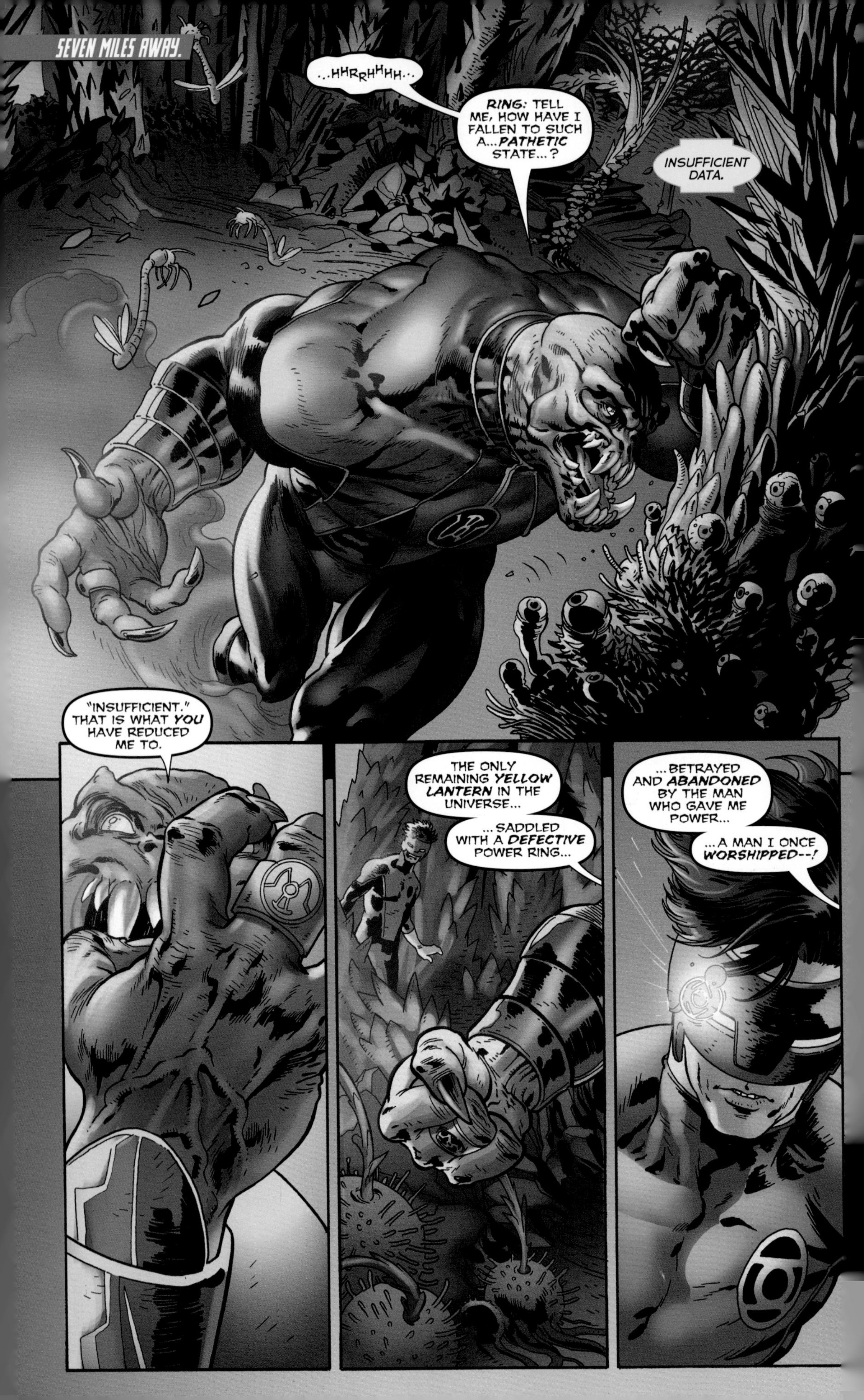
SEVEN MILES AWAY.
...HHRRHHHH...
RING: TELL ME, HOW HAVE I FALLEN TO SUCH A...PATHETIC STATE...?
INSUFFICIENT DATA.
"INSUFFICIENT." THAT IS WHAT YOU HAVE REDUCED ME TO.
THE ONLY REMAINING YELLOW LANTERN IN THE UNIVERSE...
...SADDLED WITH A DEFECTIVE POWER RING...
...BETRAYED AND ABANDONED BY THE MAN WHO GAVE ME POWER...
...A MAN I ONCE WORSHIPPED--!

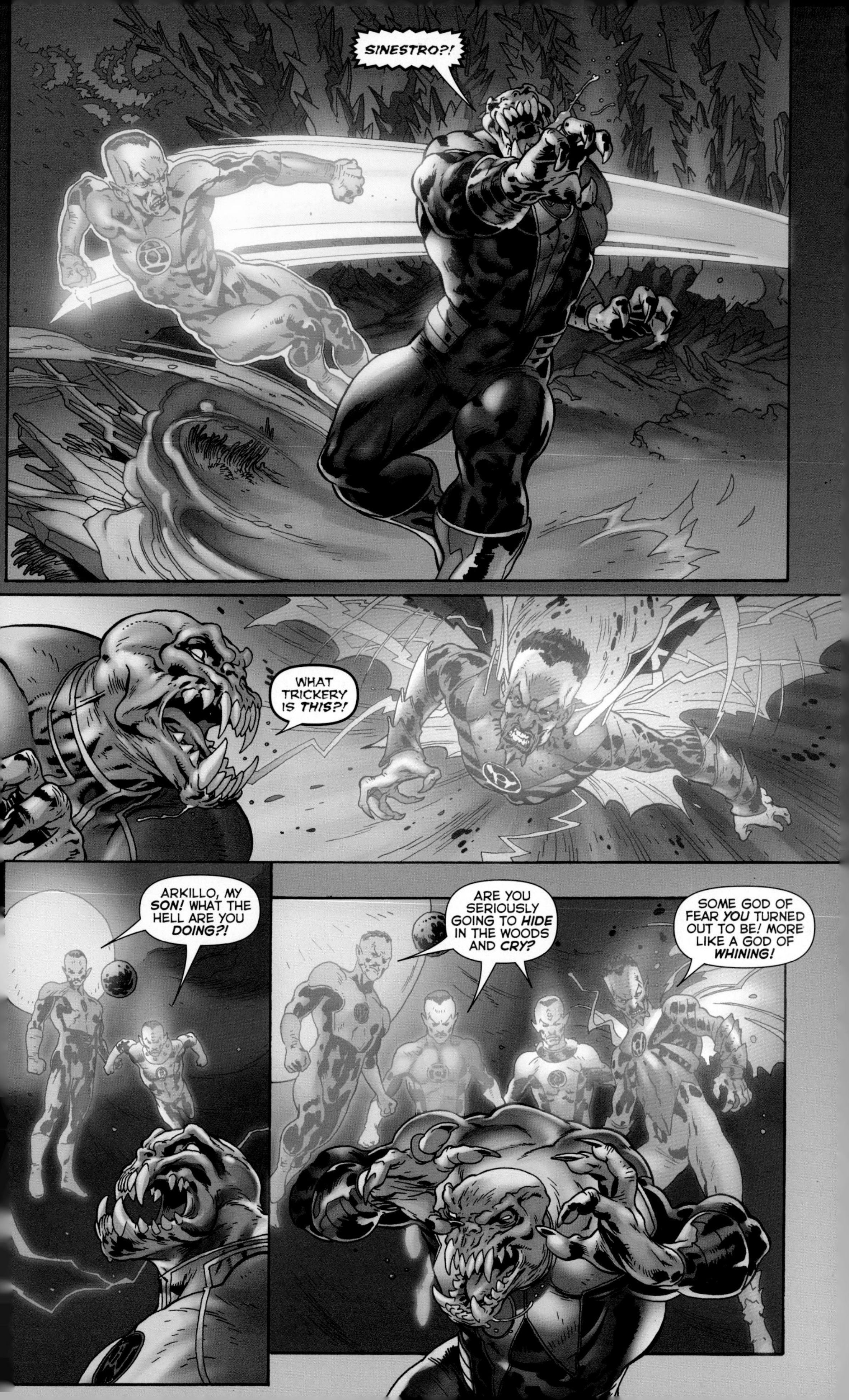
SINESTRO?!
WHAT TRICKERY IS THIS?!
ARKILLO, MY SON! WHAT THE HELL ARE YOU DOING?!
ARE YOU SERIOUSLY GOING TO HIDE IN THE WOODS AND CRY?
SOME GOD OF FEAR YOU TURNED OUT TO BE! MORE LIKE A GOD OF WHINING!

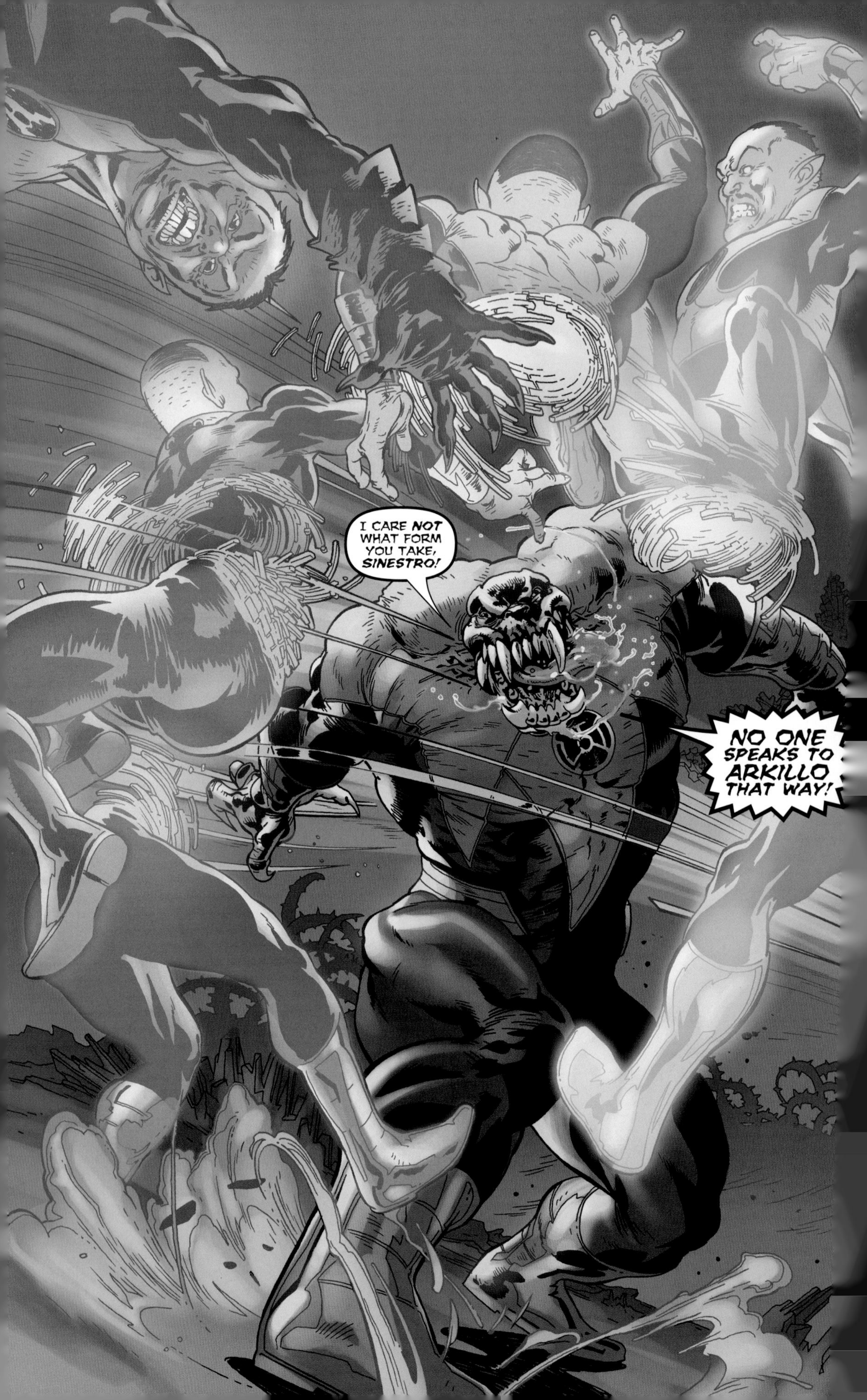
I CARE NOT WHAT FORM YOU TAKE, SINESTRO!
NO ONE SPEAKS TO ARKILLO THAT WAY!

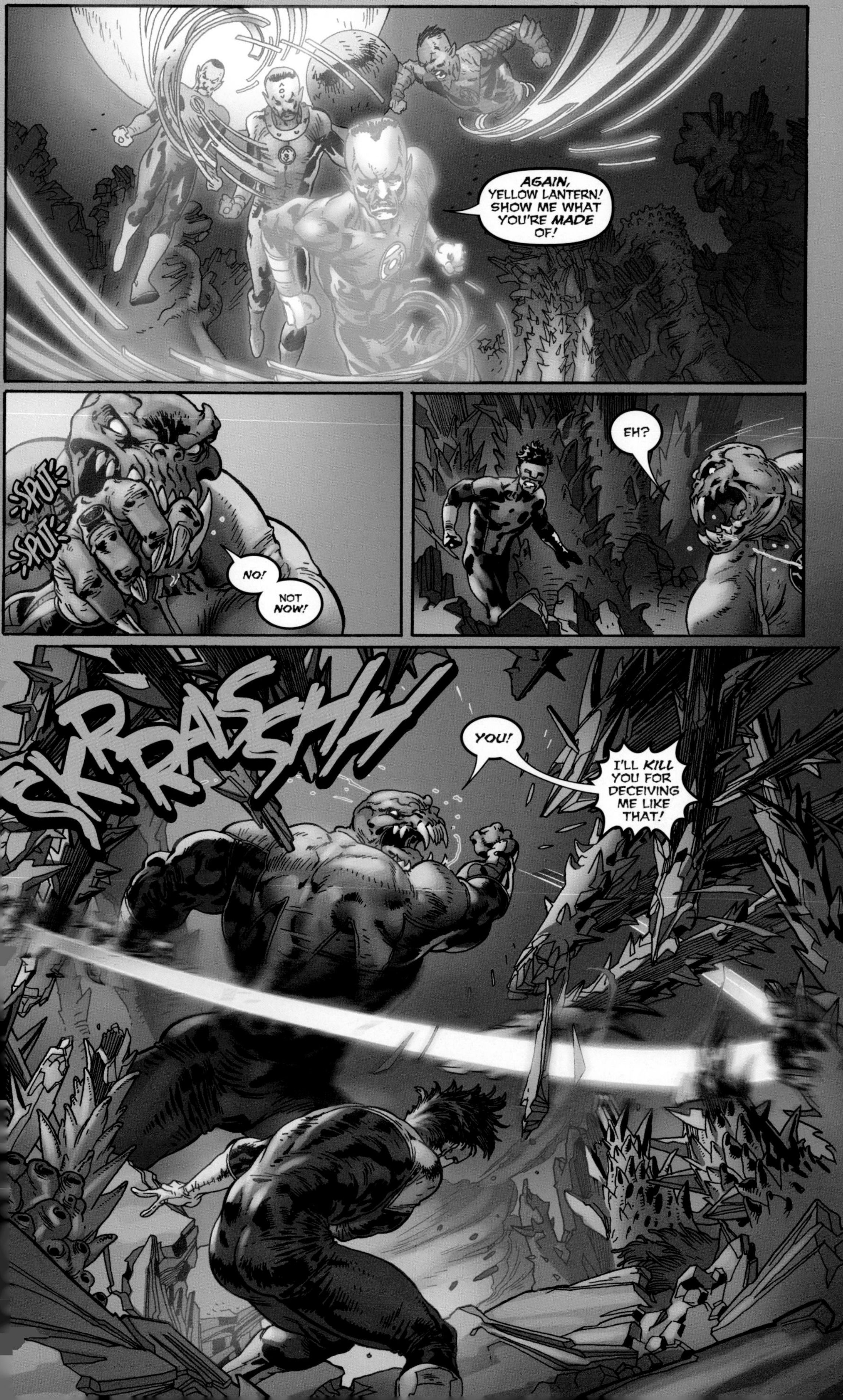
AGAIN, YELLOW LANTERN! SHOW ME WHAT YOU'RE MADE OF!
SPUT
SPUT
NO!
NOT NOW!
EH?
SKRASHH
YOU!
I'LL KILL YOU FOR DECEIVING ME LIKE THAT!

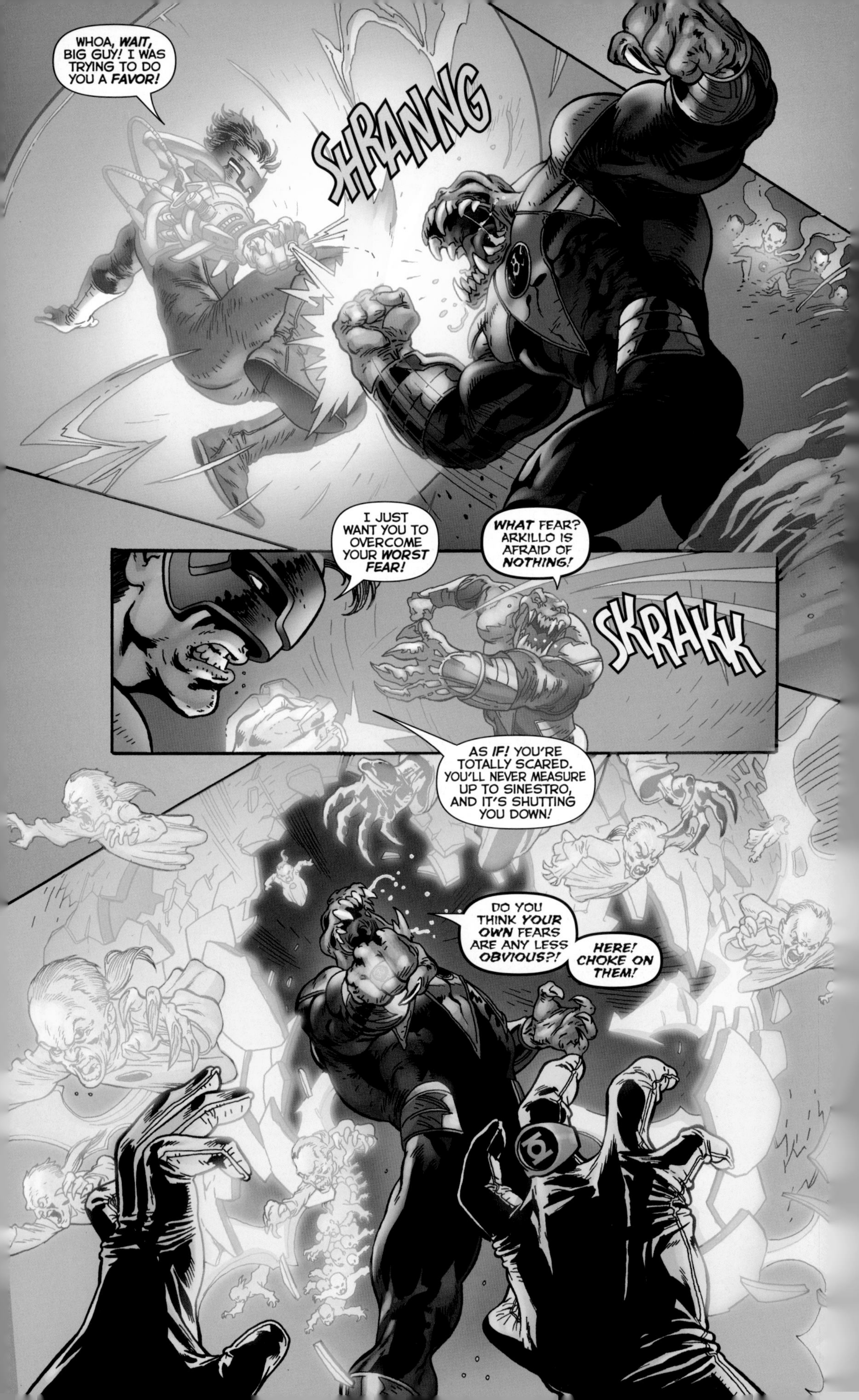
WHOA, WAIT, BIG GUY! I WAS TRYING TO DO YOU A FAVOR!
SHRANNG
I JUST WANT YOU TO OVERCOME YOUR WORST FEAR!
WHAT FEAR? ARKILLO IS AFRAID OF NOTHING!
SKRAKK
AS IF! YOU'RE TOTALLY SCARED. YOU'LL NEVER MEASURE UP TO SINESTRO, AND IT'S SHUTTING YOU DOWN!
DO YOU THINK YOUR OWN FEARS ARE ANY LESS OBVIOUS?!
HERE! CHOKE ON THEM!

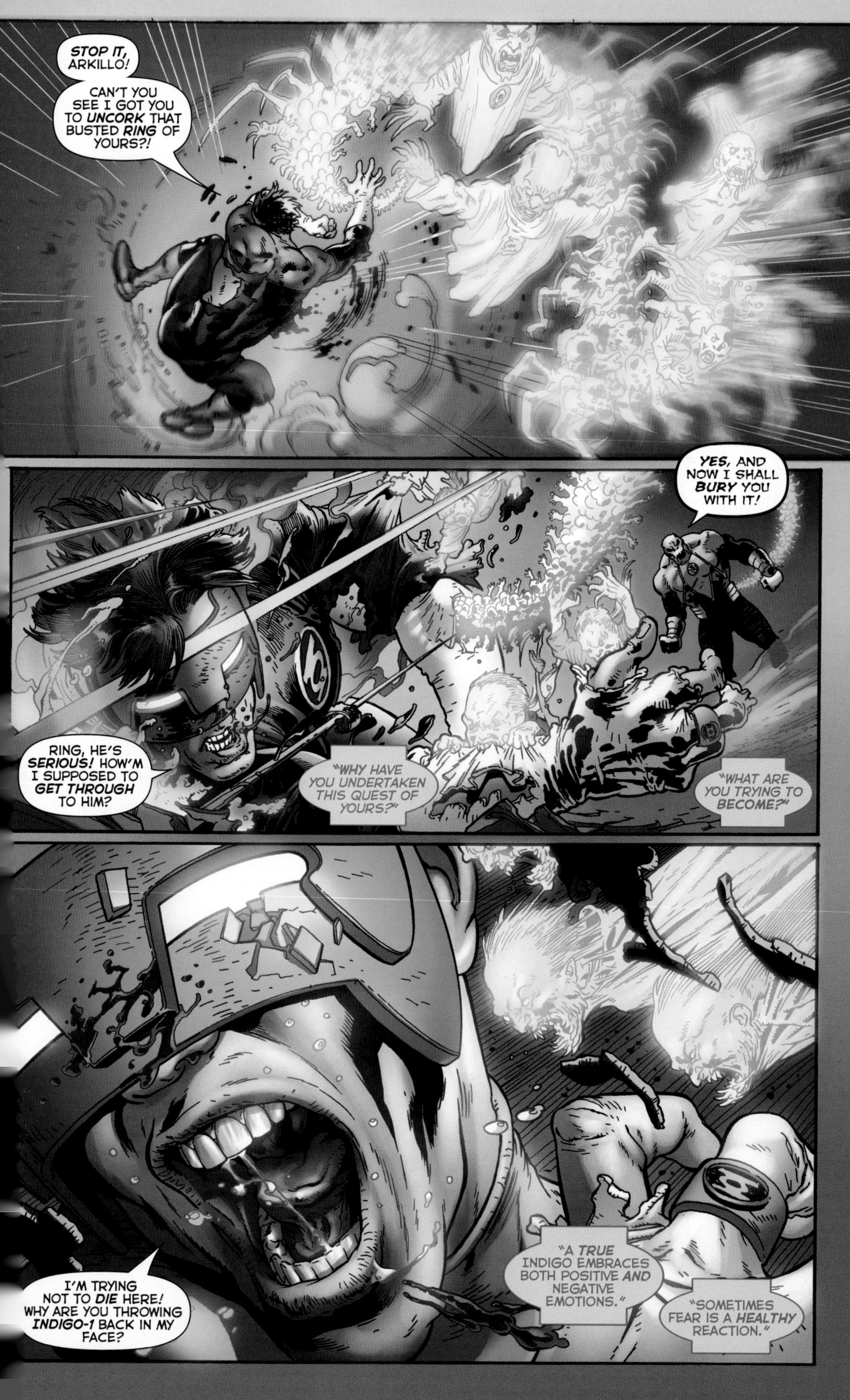
STOP IT, ARKILLO!
CAN'T YOU SEE I GOT YOU TO UNCORK THAT BUSTED RING OF YOURS?!
YES, AND NOW I SHALL BURY YOU WITH IT!
RING, HE'S SERIOUS! HOW'M I SUPPOSED TO GET THROUGH TO HIM?
"WHY HAVE YOU UNDERTAKEN THIS QUEST OF YOURS?"
"WHAT ARE YOU TRYING TO BECOME?"
I'M TRYING NOT TO DIE HERE! WHY ARE YOU THROWING INDIGO-1 BACK IN MY FACE?
"A TRUE INDIGO EMBRACES BOTH POSITIVE AND NEGATIVE EMOTIONS."
"SOMETIMES FEAR IS A HEALTHY REACTION."

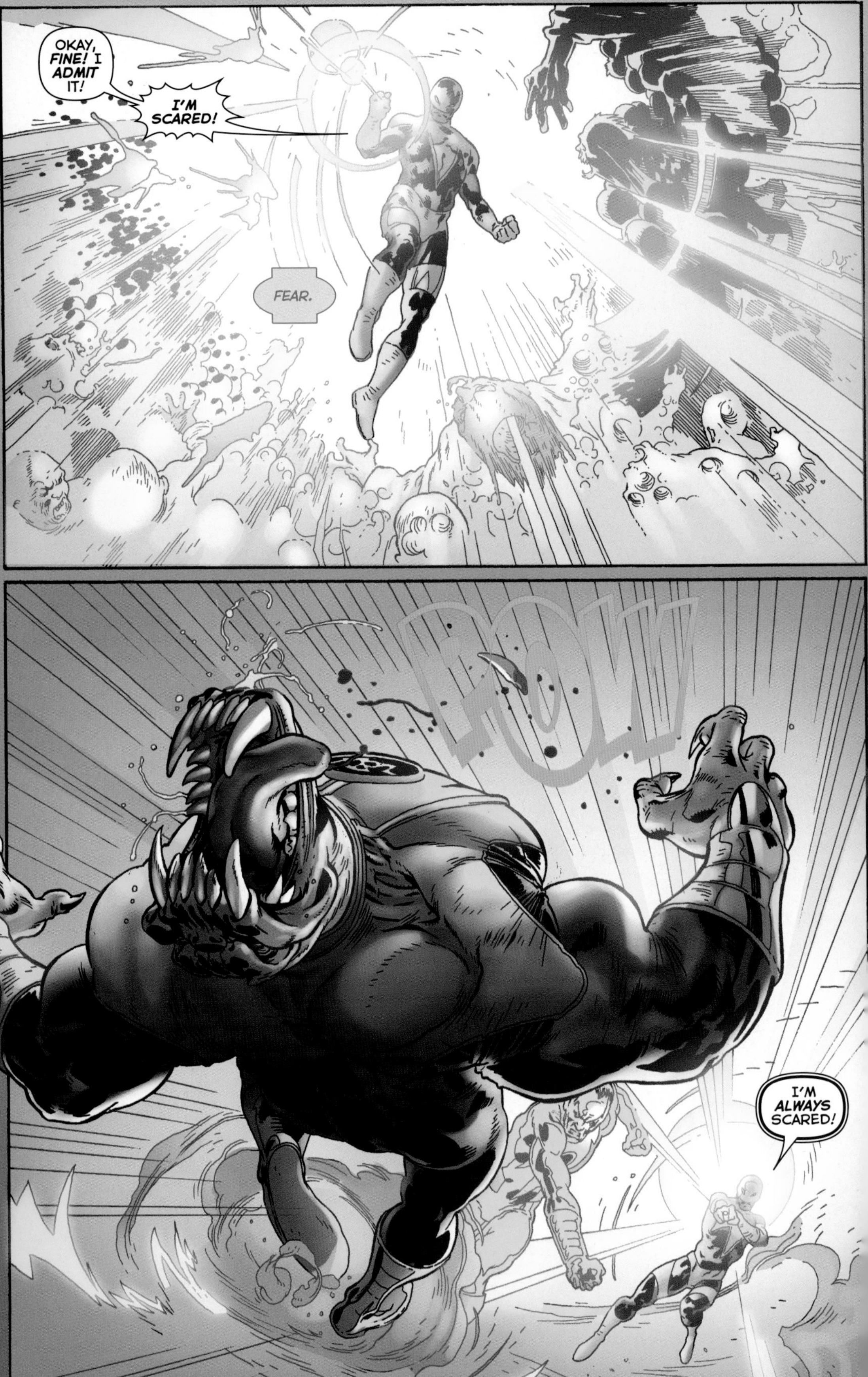
OKAY, FINE! I ADMIT IT!
I'M SCARED!
FEAR.
POW
I'M ALWAYS SCARED!

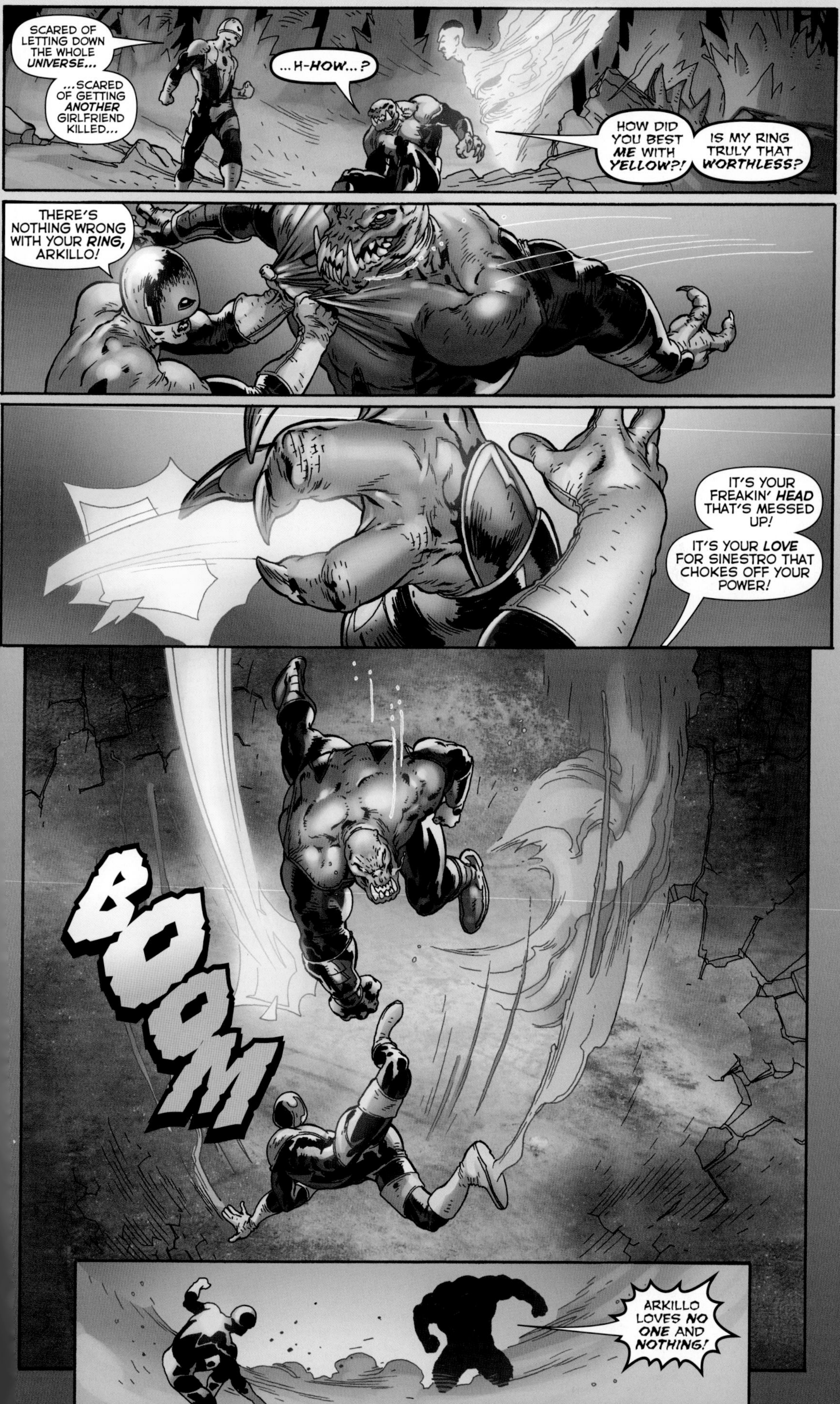

SCARED OF LETTING DOWN THE WHOLE UNIVERSE...
...SCARED OF GETTING ANOTHER GIRLFRIEND KILLED...
...H-HOW...?
HOW DID YOU BEST ME WITH YELLOW?!
IS MY RING TRULY THAT WORTHLESS?
THERE'S NOTHING WRONG WITH YOUR RING, ARKILLO!
IT'S YOUR FREAKIN' HEAD THAT'S MESSED UP!
IT'S YOUR LOVE FOR SINESTRO THAT CHOKES OFF YOUR POWER!
BOOM
ARKILLO LOVES NO ONE AND NOTHING!

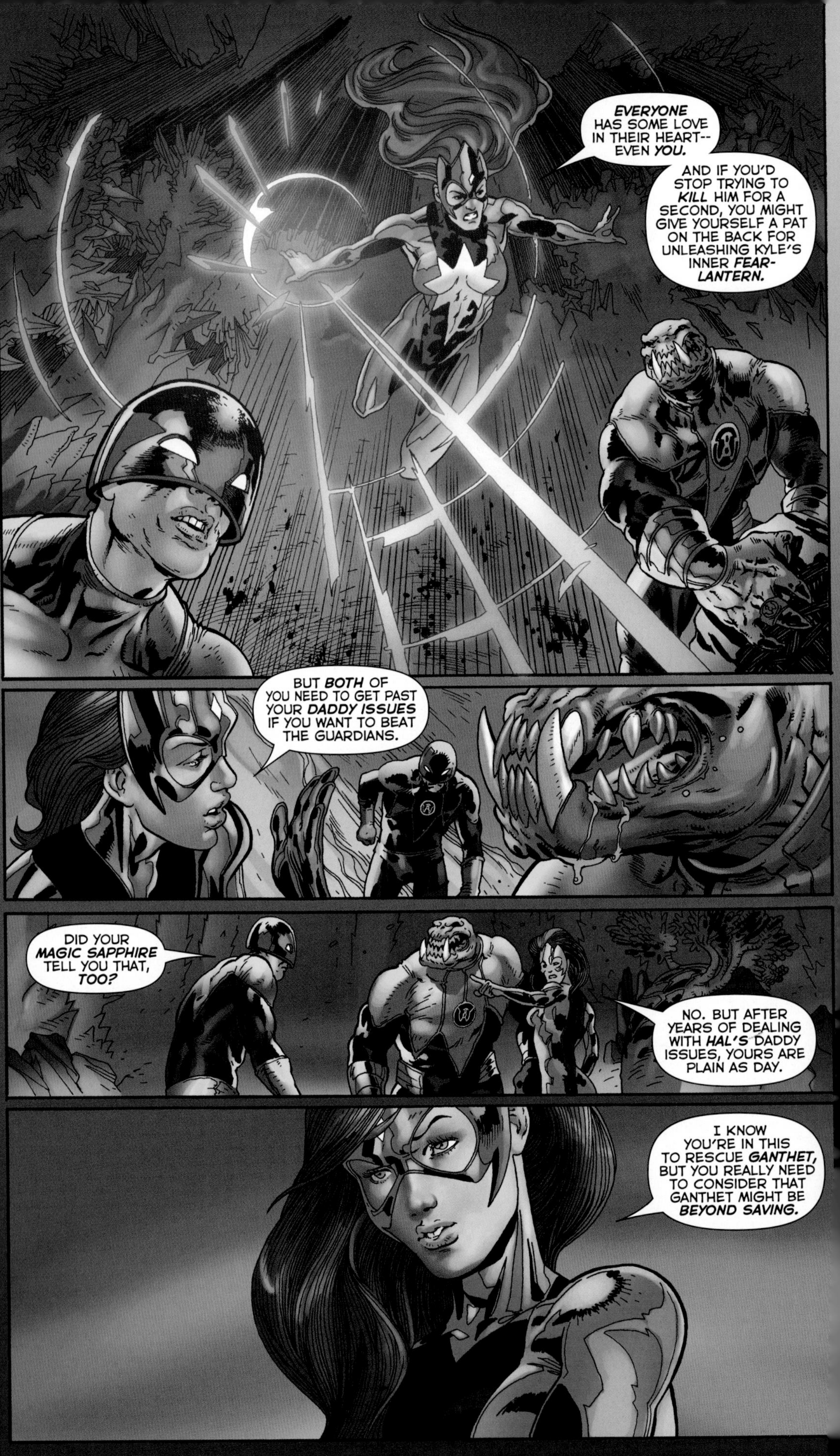
EVERYONE HAS SOME LOVE IN THEIR HEART-- EVEN YOU.
AND IF YOU'D STOP TRYING TO KILL HIM FOR A SECOND, YOU MIGHT GIVE YOURSELF A PAT ON THE BACK FOR UNLEASHING KYLE'S INNER FEAR-LANTERN.
BUT BOTH OF YOU NEED TO GET PAST YOUR DADDY ISSUES IF YOU WANT TO BEAT THE GUARDIANS.
DID YOUR MAGIC SAPPHIRE TELL YOU THAT, TOO?
NO. BUT AFTER YEARS OF DEALING WITH HAL'S DADDY ISSUES, YOURS ARE PLAIN AS DAY.
I KNOW YOU'RE IN THIS TO RESCUE GANTHET, BUT YOU REALLY NEED TO CONSIDER THAT GANTHET MIGHT BE BEYOND SAVING.

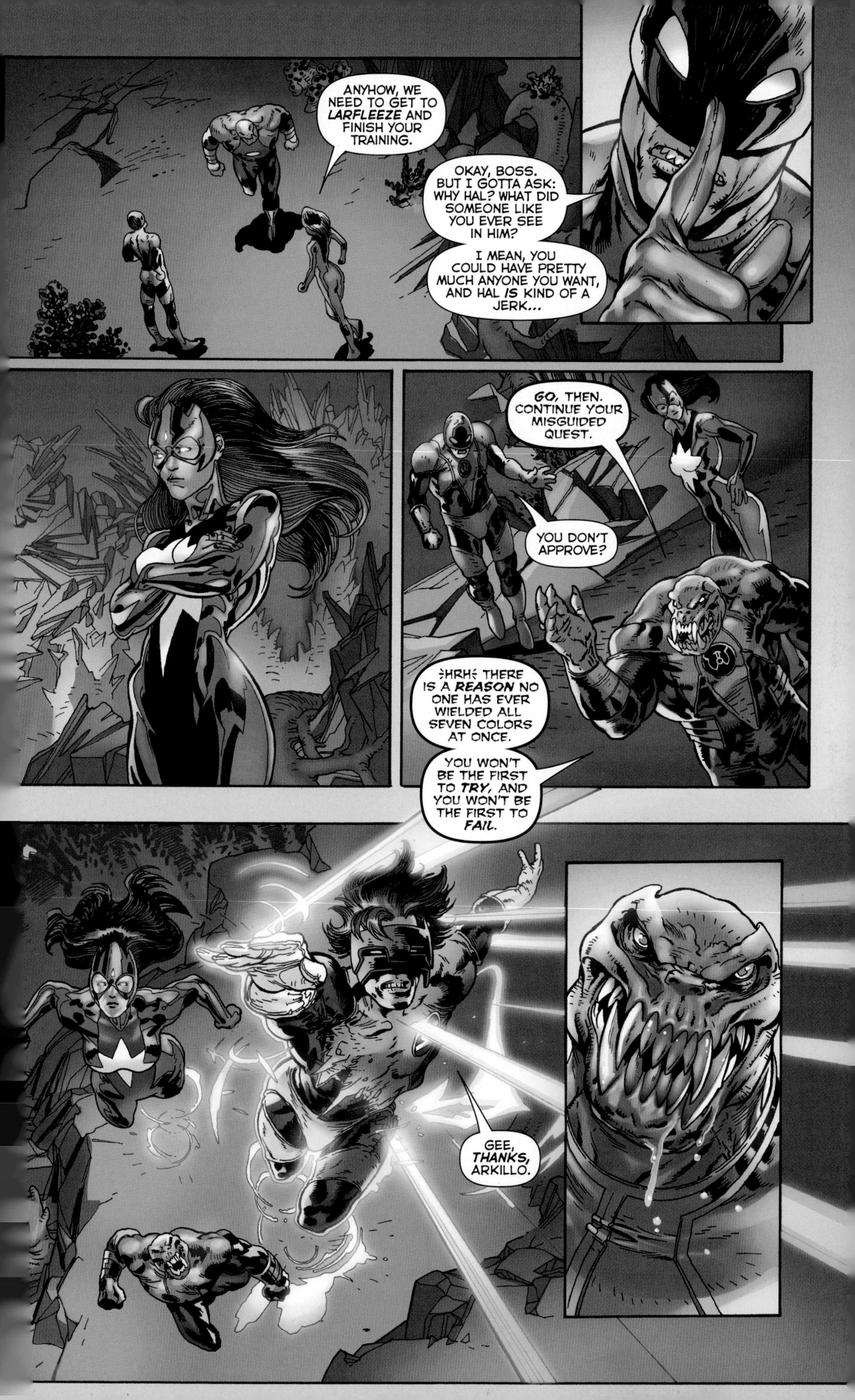

ANYHOW, WE NEED TO GET TO *LARFLEEZE* AND FINISH YOUR TRAINING.
OKAY, BOSS. BUT I GOTTA ASK: WHY HAL? WHAT DID SOMEONE LIKE YOU EVER SEE IN HIM?
I MEAN, YOU COULD HAVE PRETTY MUCH ANYONE YOU WANT, AND HAL *IS* KIND OF A JERK...
GO, THEN. CONTINUE YOUR MISGUIDED QUEST.
YOU DON'T APPROVE?
HRH THERE IS A *REASON* NO ONE HAS EVER WIELDED ALL SEVEN COLORS AT ONCE.
YOU WON'T BE THE FIRST TO *TRY,* AND YOU WON'T BE THE FIRST TO *FAIL.*
GEE, *THANKS,* ARKILLO.

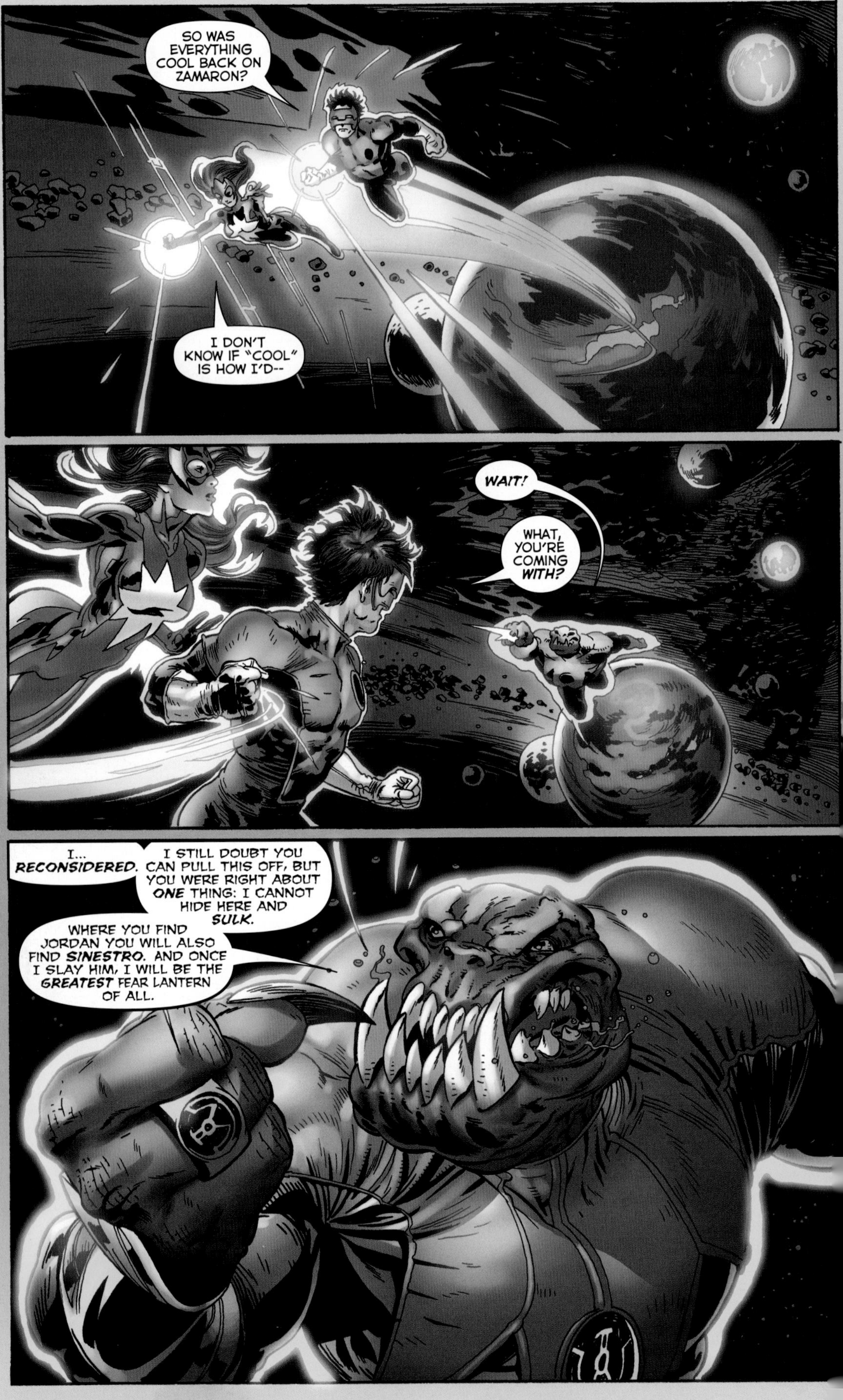
SO WAS EVERYTHING COOL BACK ON ZAMARON?
I DON'T KNOW IF "COOL" IS HOW I'D--
WAIT!
WHAT, YOU'RE COMING WITH?
I... RECONSIDERED.
I STILL DOUBT YOU CAN PULL THIS OFF, BUT YOU WERE RIGHT ABOUT ONE THING: I CANNOT HIDE HERE AND SULK.
WHERE YOU FIND JORDAN YOU WILL ALSO FIND SINESTRO. AND ONCE I SLAY HIM, I WILL BE THE GREATEST FEAR LANTERN OF ALL.

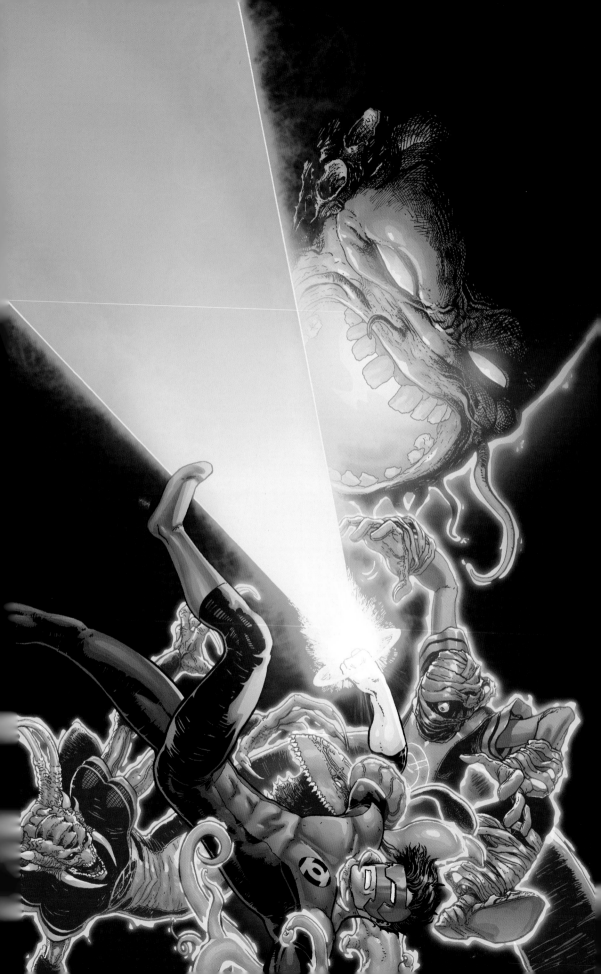

THE NEED FOR GREED

TONY BEDARD writer **AARON KUDER** artist

AARON KUDER & HI-FI cover

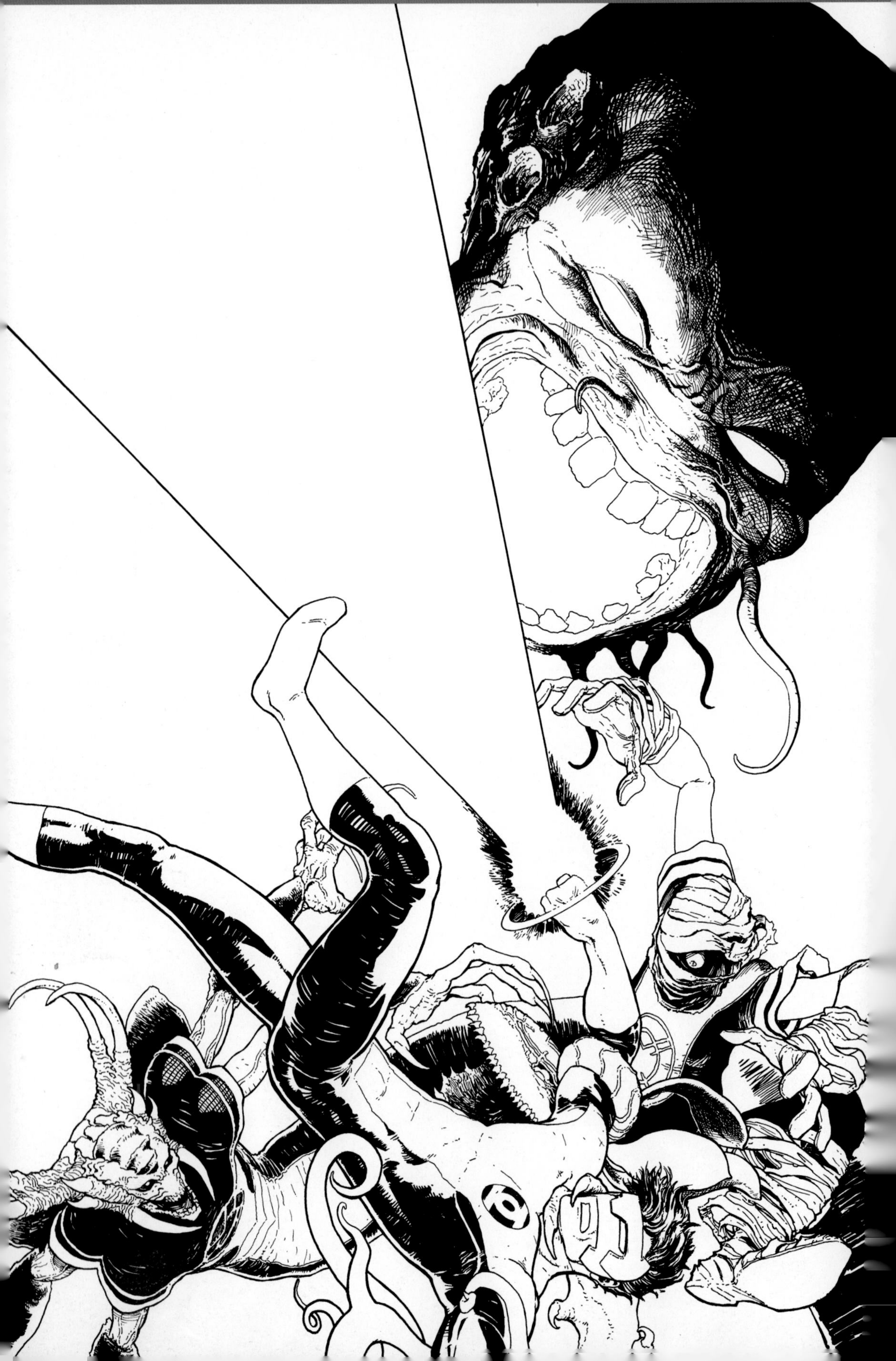

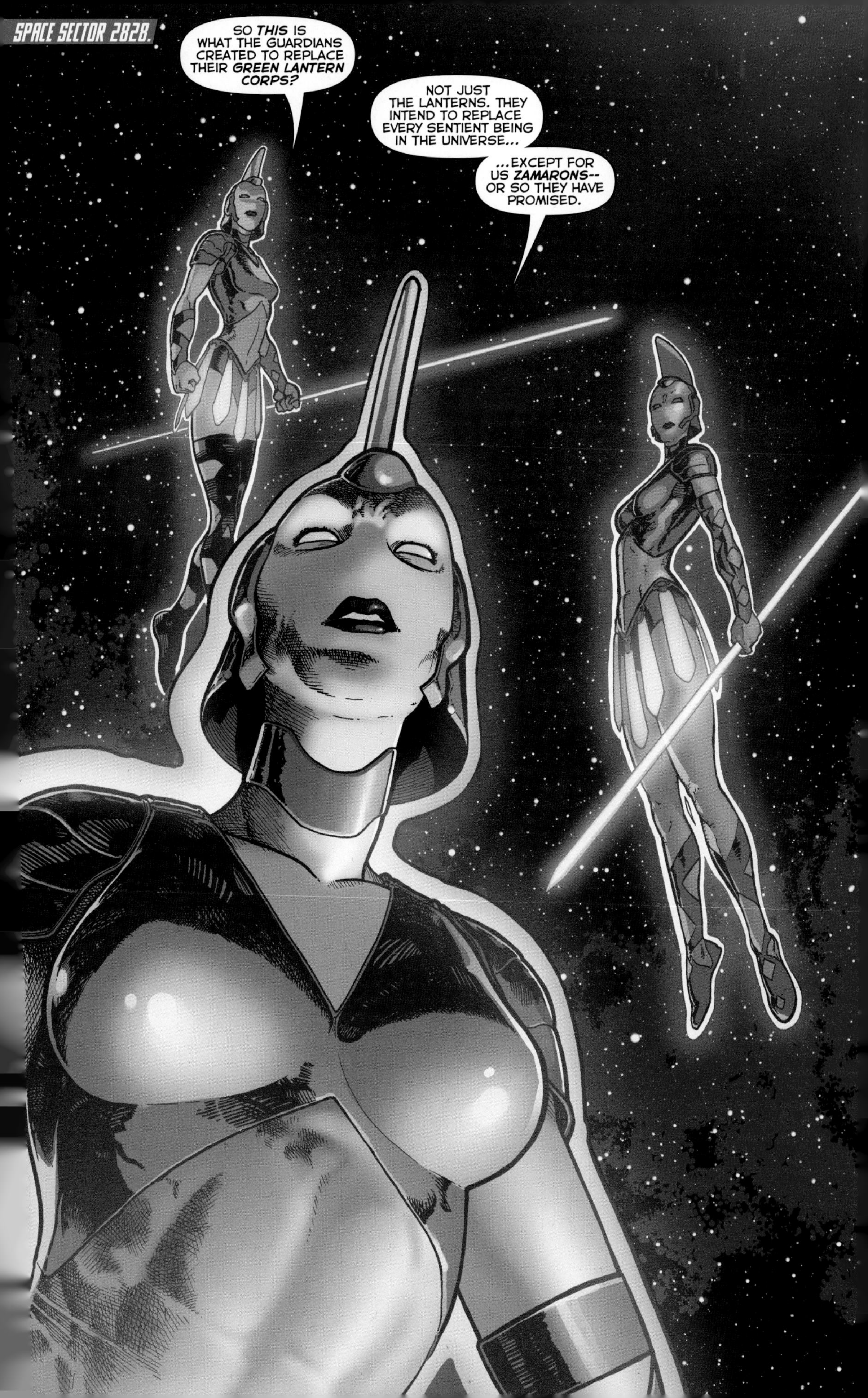
SPACE SECTOR 2828.
SO THIS IS WHAT THE GUARDIANS CREATED TO REPLACE THEIR GREEN LANTERN CORPS?
NOT JUST THE LANTERNS. THEY INTEND TO REPLACE EVERY SENTIENT BEING IN THE UNIVERSE...
...EXCEPT FOR US ZAMARONS-- OR SO THEY HAVE PROMISED.

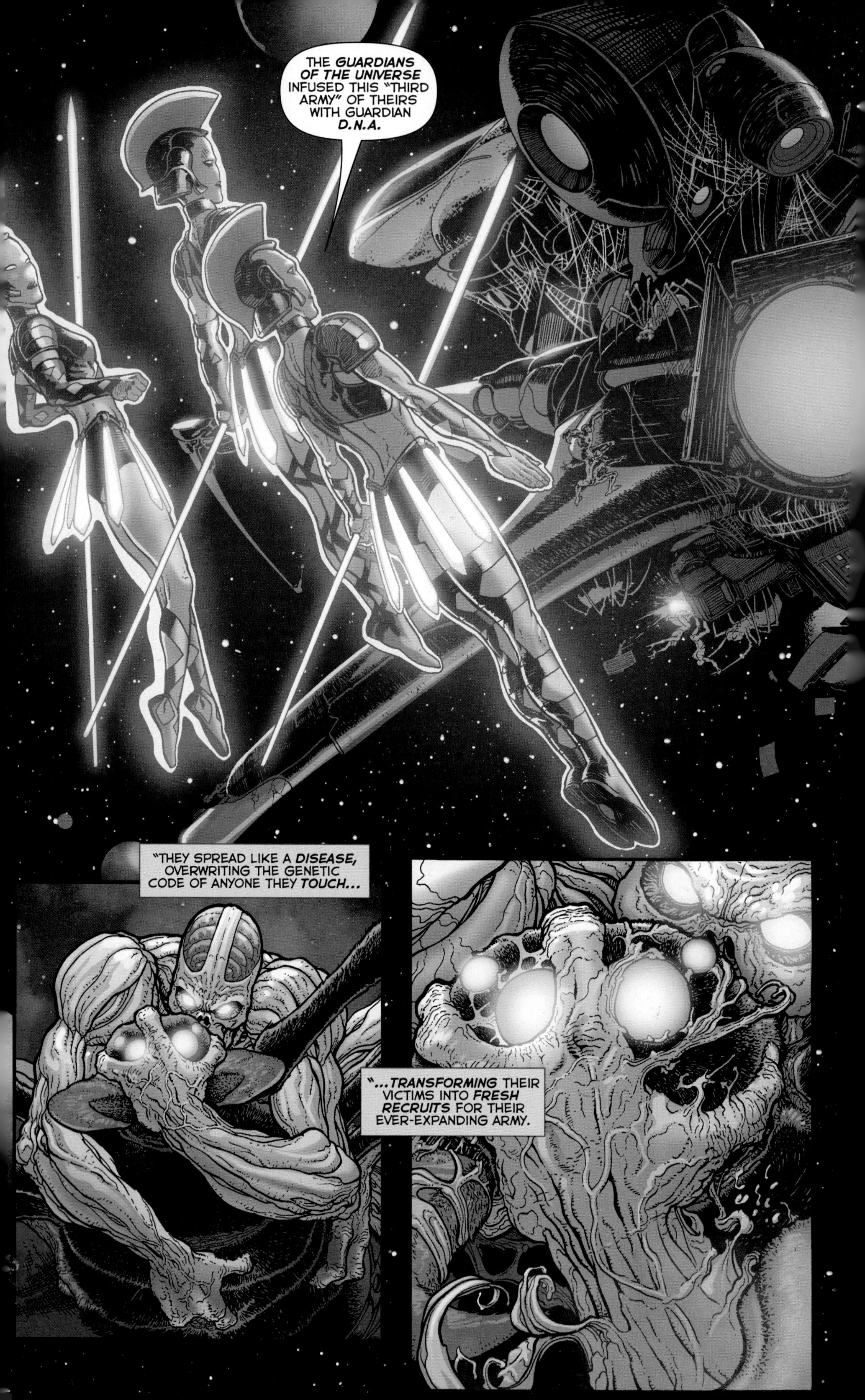
THE GUARDIANS OF THE UNIVERSE INFUSED THIS "THIRD ARMY" OF THEIRS WITH GUARDIAN D.N.A.
"THEY SPREAD LIKE A DISEASE, OVERWRITING THE GENETIC CODE OF ANYONE THEY TOUCH...
"...TRANSFORMING THEIR VICTIMS INTO FRESH RECRUITS FOR THEIR EVER-EXPANDING ARMY.

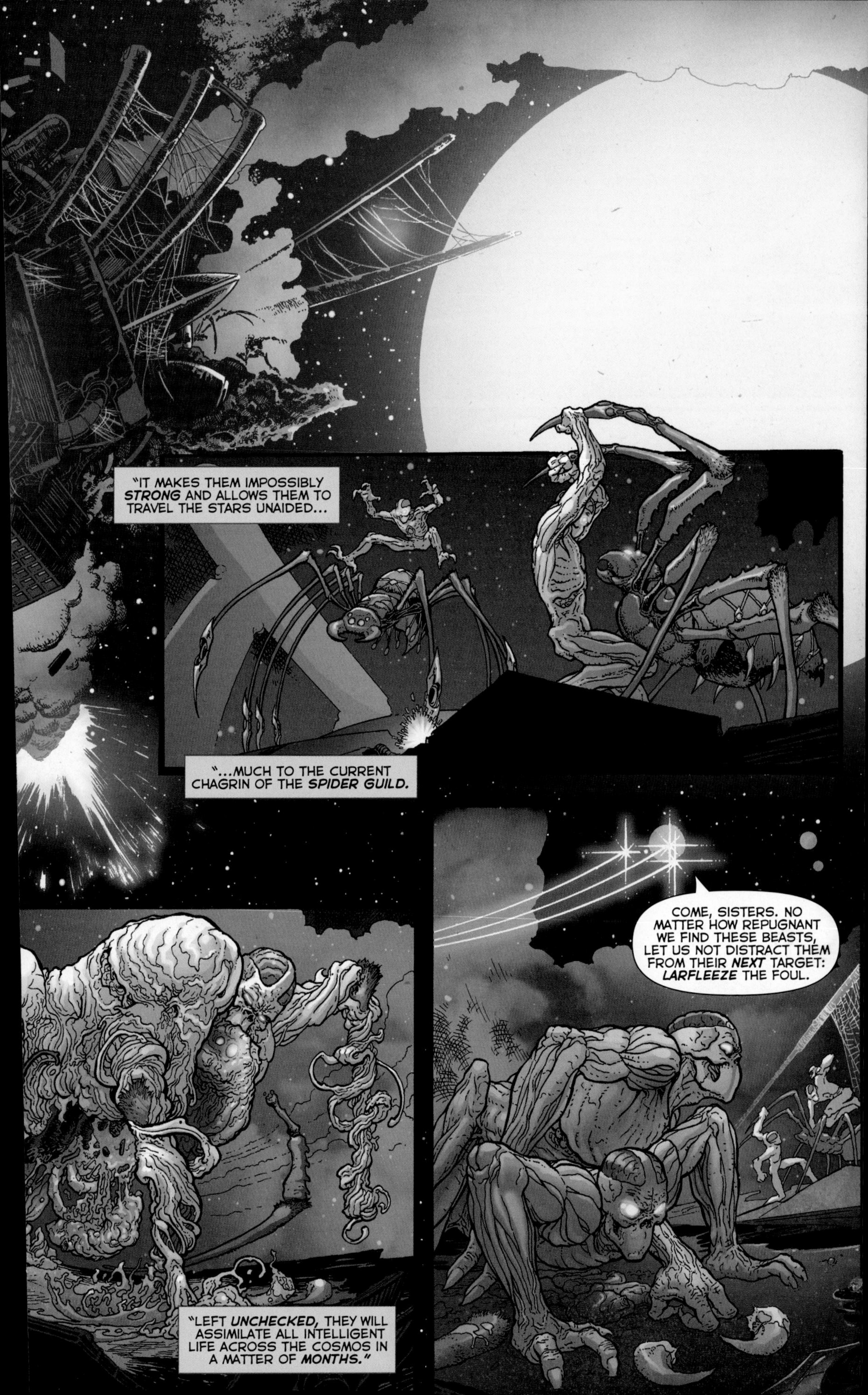
"IT MAKES THEM IMPOSSIBLY STRONG AND ALLOWS THEM TO TRAVEL THE STARS UNAIDED...
"...MUCH TO THE CURRENT CHAGRIN OF THE SPIDER GUILD.
COME, SISTERS. NO MATTER HOW REPUGNANT WE FIND THESE BEASTS, LET US NOT DISTRACT THEM FROM THEIR NEXT TARGET: LARFLEEZE THE FOUL.
"LEFT UNCHECKED, THEY WILL ASSIMILATE ALL INTELLIGENT LIFE ACROSS THE COSMOS IN A MATTER OF MONTHS."

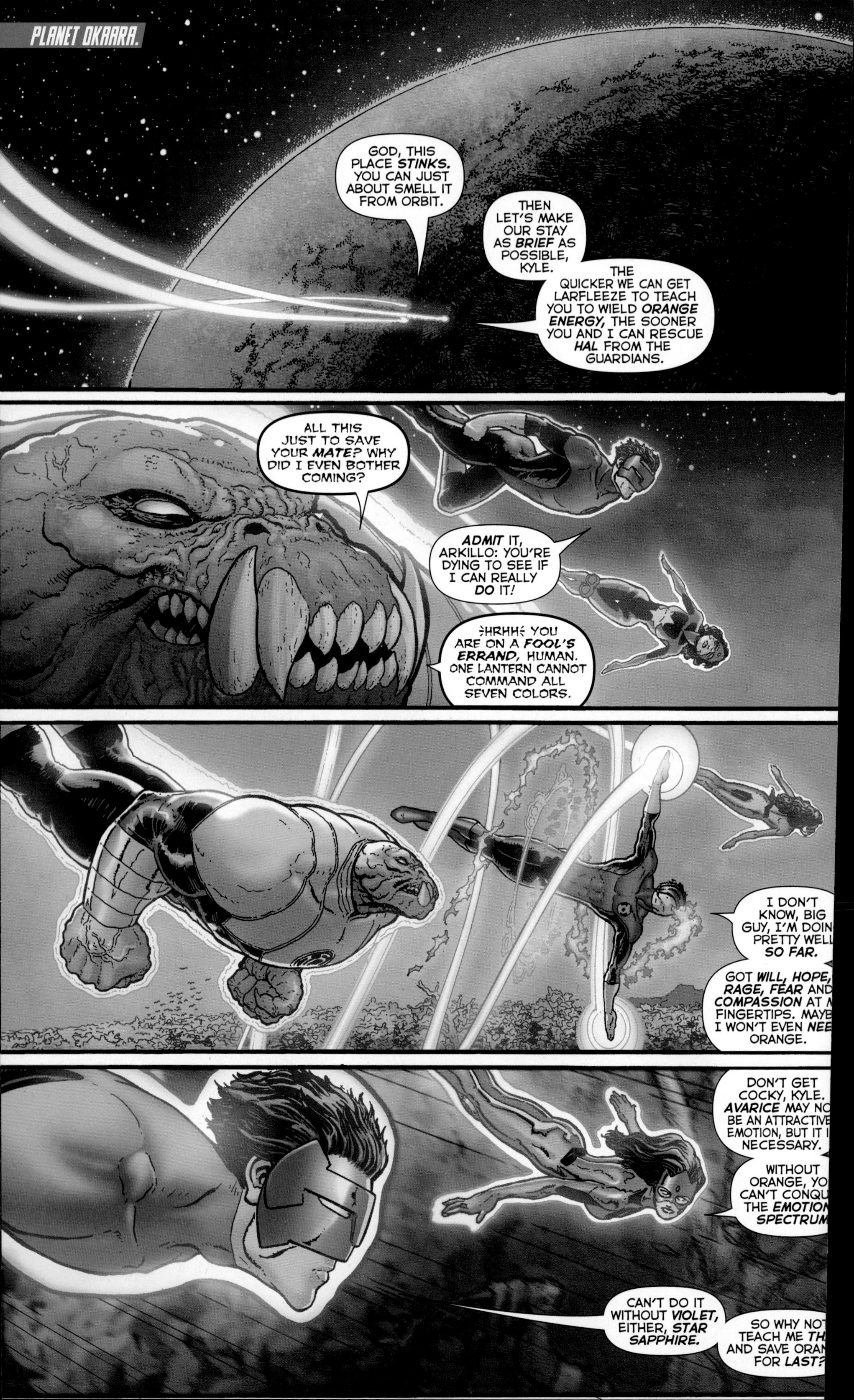
PLANET OKAARA.
GOD, THIS PLACE STINKS. YOU CAN JUST ABOUT SMELL IT FROM ORBIT.
THEN LET'S MAKE OUR STAY AS BRIEF AS POSSIBLE, KYLE.
THE QUICKER WE CAN GET LARFLEEZE TO TEACH YOU TO WIELD ORANGE ENERGY, THE SOONER YOU AND I CAN RESCUE HAL FROM THE GUARDIANS.
ALL THIS JUST TO SAVE YOUR MATE? WHY DID I EVEN BOTHER COMING?
ADMIT IT, ARKILLO: YOU'RE DYING TO SEE IF I CAN REALLY DO IT!
HRHH YOU ARE ON A FOOL'S ERRAND, HUMAN. ONE LANTERN CANNOT COMMAND ALL SEVEN COLORS.
I DON'T KNOW, BIG GUY, I'M DOIN PRETTY WELL SO FAR.
GOT WILL, HOPE, RAGE, FEAR AND COMPASSION AT M FINGERTIPS. MAYB I WON'T EVEN NEE ORANGE.
DON'T GET COCKY, KYLE. AVARICE MAY NO BE AN ATTRACTIVE EMOTION, BUT IT I NECESSARY.
WITHOUT ORANGE, YO CAN'T CONQU THE EMOTION SPECTRUM
CAN'T DO IT WITHOUT VIOLET, EITHER, STAR SAPPHIRE.
SO WHY NOT TEACH ME TH AND SAVE ORAN FOR LAST?

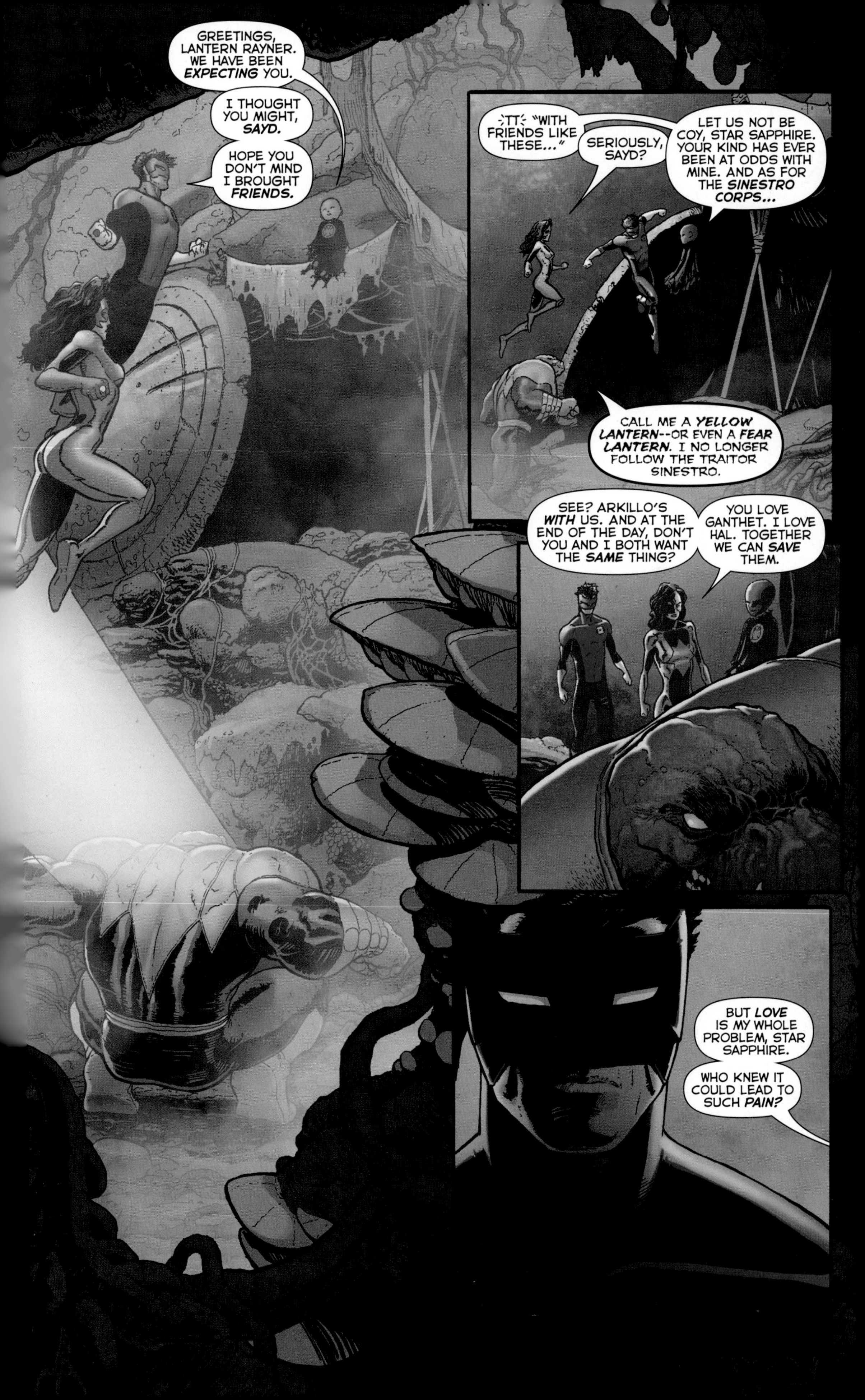
GREETINGS, LANTERN RAYNER. WE HAVE BEEN EXPECTING YOU.
I THOUGHT YOU MIGHT, SAYD.
HOPE YOU DON'T MIND I BROUGHT FRIENDS.
TT "WITH FRIENDS LIKE THESE..."
SERIOUSLY, SAYD?
LET US NOT BE COY, STAR SAPPHIRE. YOUR KIND HAS EVER BEEN AT ODDS WITH MINE. AND AS FOR THE SINESTRO CORPS...
CALL ME A YELLOW LANTERN--OR EVEN A FEAR LANTERN. I NO LONGER FOLLOW THE TRAITOR SINESTRO.
SEE? ARKILLO'S WITH US. AND AT THE END OF THE DAY, DON'T YOU AND I BOTH WANT THE SAME THING?
YOU LOVE GANTHET. I LOVE HAL. TOGETHER WE CAN SAVE THEM.
BUT LOVE IS MY WHOLE PROBLEM, STAR SAPPHIRE.
WHO KNEW IT COULD LEAD TO SUCH PAIN?

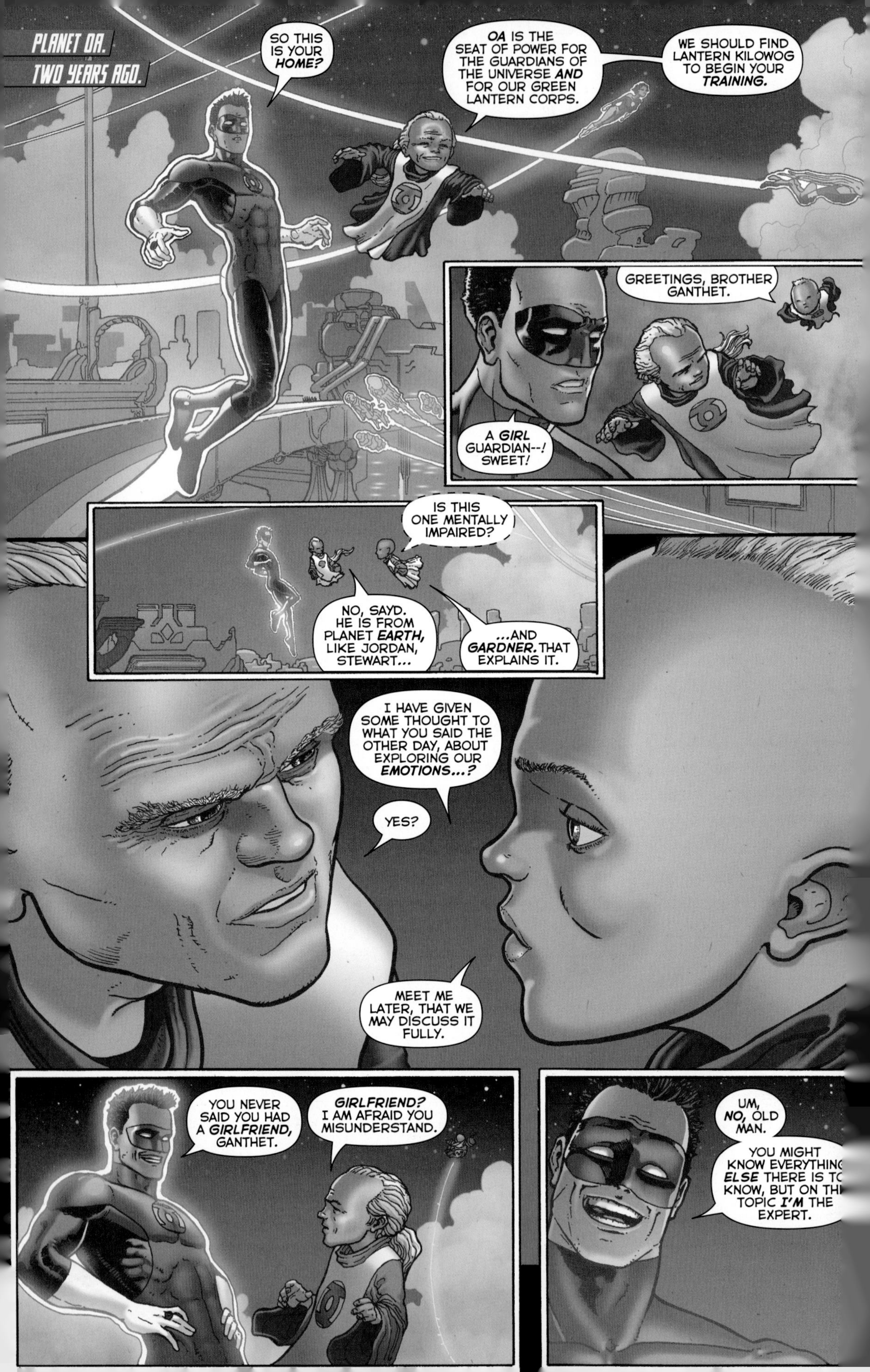
PLANET OA. TWO YEARS AGO.
SO THIS IS YOUR HOME?
OA IS THE SEAT OF POWER FOR THE GUARDIANS OF THE UNIVERSE AND FOR OUR GREEN LANTERN CORPS.
WE SHOULD FIND LANTERN KILOWOG TO BEGIN YOUR TRAINING.
GREETINGS, BROTHER GANTHET.
A GIRL GUARDIAN--! SWEET!
IS THIS ONE MENTALLY IMPAIRED?
NO, SAYD. HE IS FROM PLANET EARTH, LIKE JORDAN, STEWART...
...AND GARDNER. THAT EXPLAINS IT.
I HAVE GIVEN SOME THOUGHT TO WHAT YOU SAID THE OTHER DAY, ABOUT EXPLORING OUR EMOTIONS...?
YES?
MEET ME LATER, THAT WE MAY DISCUSS IT FULLY.
YOU NEVER SAID YOU HAD A GIRLFRIEND, GANTHET.
GIRLFRIEND? I AM AFRAID YOU MISUNDERSTAND.
UM, NO, OLD MAN.
YOU MIGHT KNOW EVERYTHING ELSE THERE IS TO KNOW, BUT ON THI TOPIC I'M THE EXPERT.

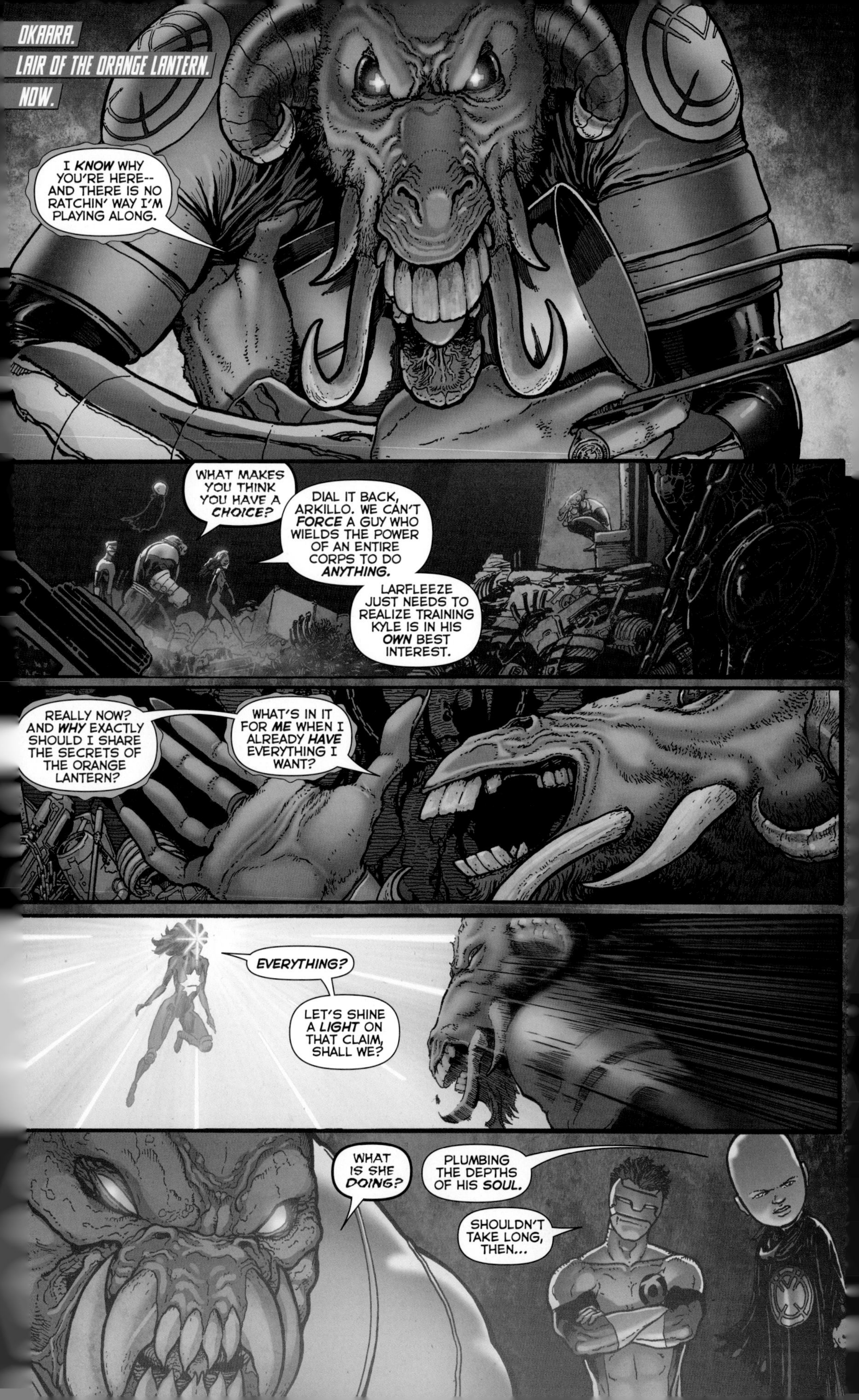
OKAARA.
LAIR OF THE ORANGE LANTERN.
NOW.
I KNOW WHY YOU'RE HERE-- AND THERE IS NO RATCHIN' WAY I'M PLAYING ALONG.
WHAT MAKES YOU THINK YOU HAVE A CHOICE?
DIAL IT BACK, ARKILLO. WE CAN'T FORCE A GUY WHO WIELDS THE POWER OF AN ENTIRE CORPS TO DO ANYTHING.
LARFLEEZE JUST NEEDS TO REALIZE TRAINING KYLE IS IN HIS OWN BEST INTEREST.
REALLY NOW? AND WHY EXACTLY SHOULD I SHARE THE SECRETS OF THE ORANGE LANTERN?
WHAT'S IN IT FOR ME WHEN I ALREADY HAVE EVERYTHING I WANT?
EVERYTHING?
LET'S SHINE A LIGHT ON THAT CLAIM, SHALL WE?
WHAT IS SHE DOING?
PLUMBING THE DEPTHS OF HIS SOUL.
SHOULDN'T TAKE LONG, THEN...

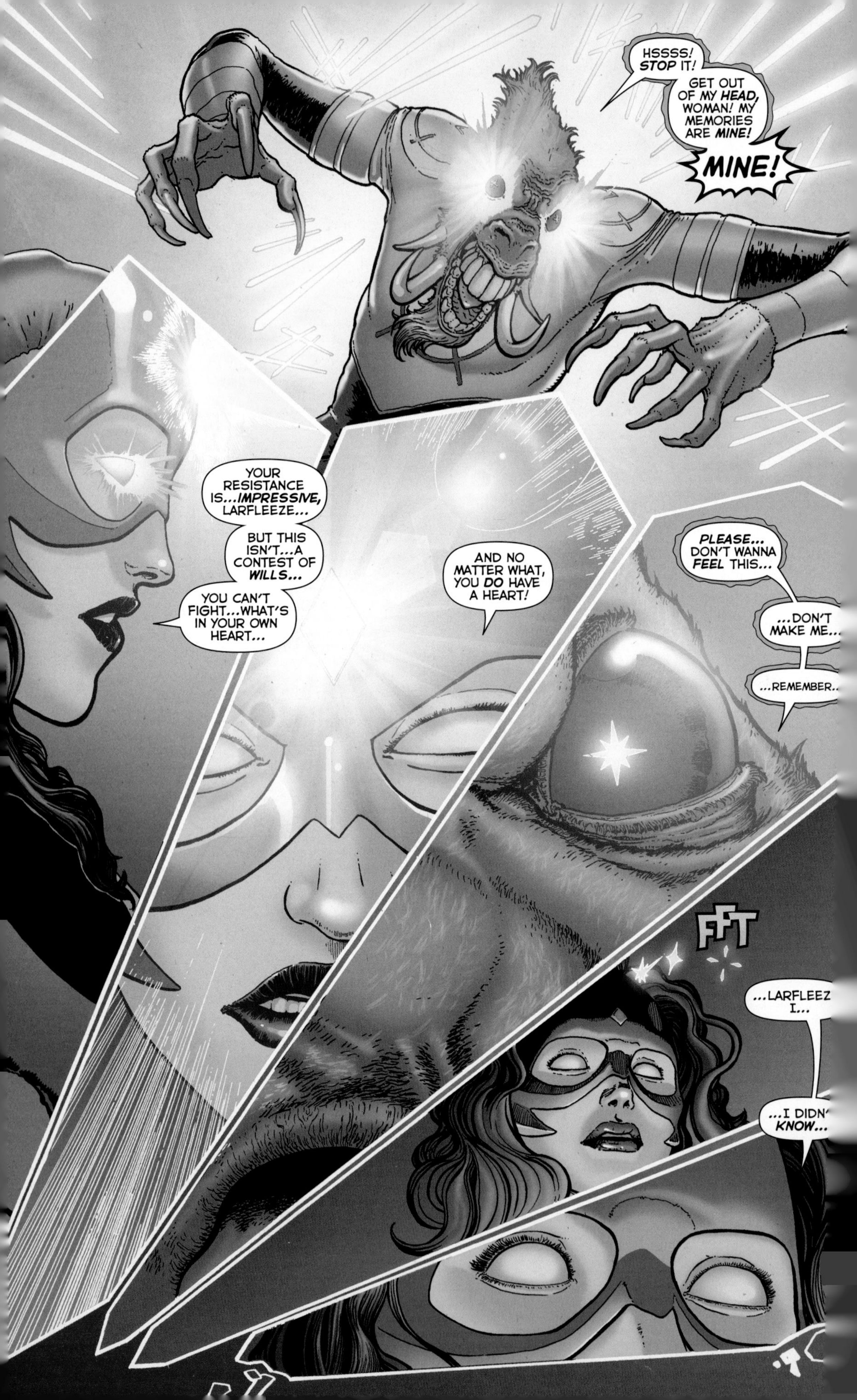
HSSSS! STOP IT!
GET OUT OF MY HEAD, WOMAN! MY MEMORIES ARE MINE!
MINE!
YOUR RESISTANCE IS...IMPRESSIVE, LARFLEEZE...
BUT THIS ISN'T...A CONTEST OF WILLS...
YOU CAN'T FIGHT...WHAT'S IN YOUR OWN HEART...
AND NO MATTER WHAT, YOU DO HAVE A HEART!
PLEASE... DON'T WANNA FEEL THIS...
...DON'T MAKE ME...
...REMEMBER...
FFT
...LARFLEEZ I...
...I DIDN' KNOW...

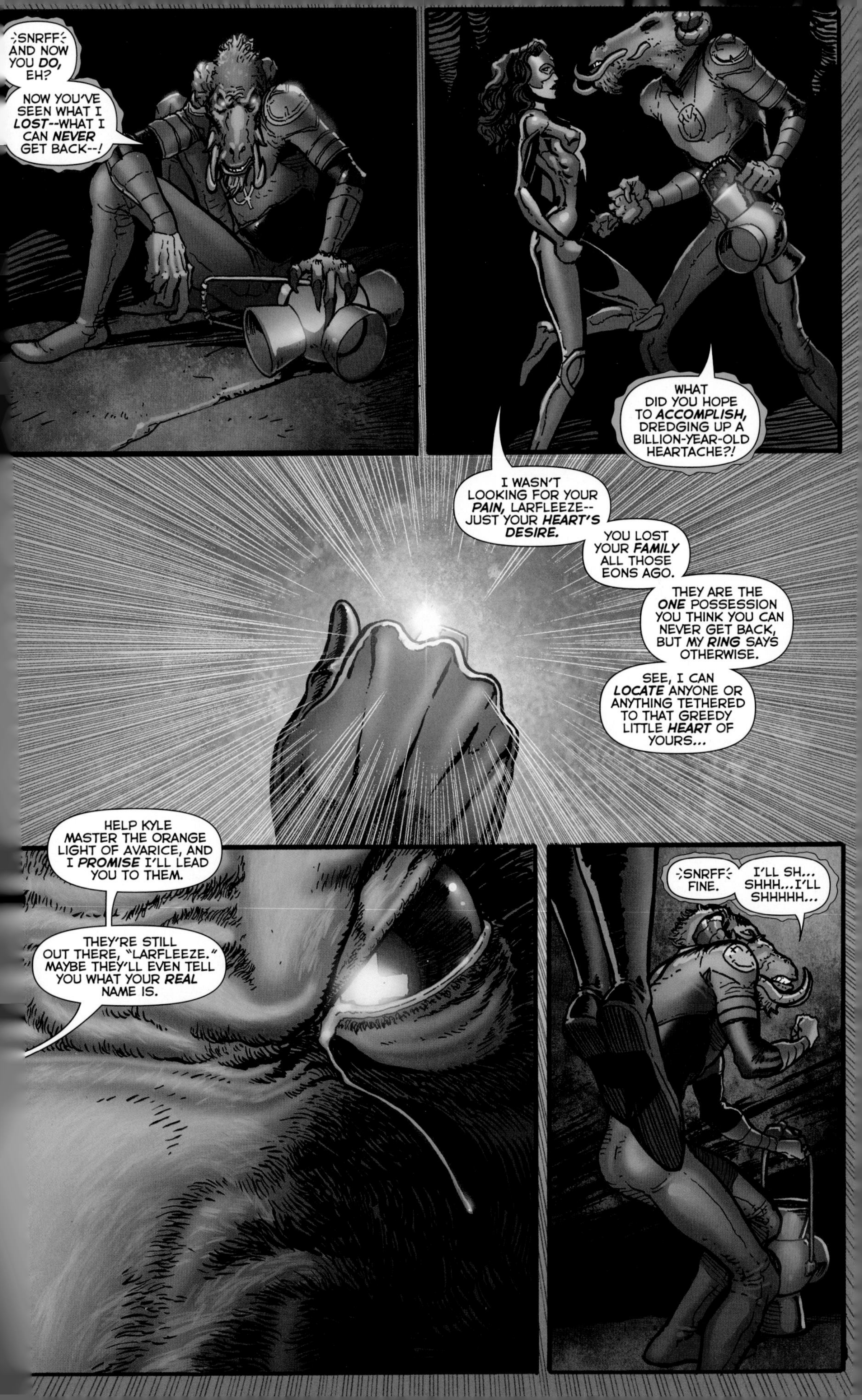
-SNRFF- AND NOW YOU DO, EH?
NOW YOU'VE SEEN WHAT I LOST--WHAT I CAN NEVER GET BACK--!
WHAT DID YOU HOPE TO ACCOMPLISH, DREDGING UP A BILLION-YEAR-OLD HEARTACHE?!
I WASN'T LOOKING FOR YOUR PAIN, LARFLEEZE-- JUST YOUR HEART'S DESIRE.
YOU LOST YOUR FAMILY ALL THOSE EONS AGO.
THEY ARE THE ONE POSSESSION YOU THINK YOU CAN NEVER GET BACK, BUT MY RING SAYS OTHERWISE.
SEE, I CAN LOCATE ANYONE OR ANYTHING TETHERED TO THAT GREEDY LITTLE HEART OF YOURS...
HELP KYLE MASTER THE ORANGE LIGHT OF AVARICE, AND I PROMISE I'LL LEAD YOU TO THEM.
THEY'RE STILL OUT THERE, "LARFLEEZE." MAYBE THEY'LL EVEN TELL YOU WHAT YOUR REAL NAME IS.
-SNRFF- FINE.
I'LL SH... SHHH...I'LL SHHHHH...

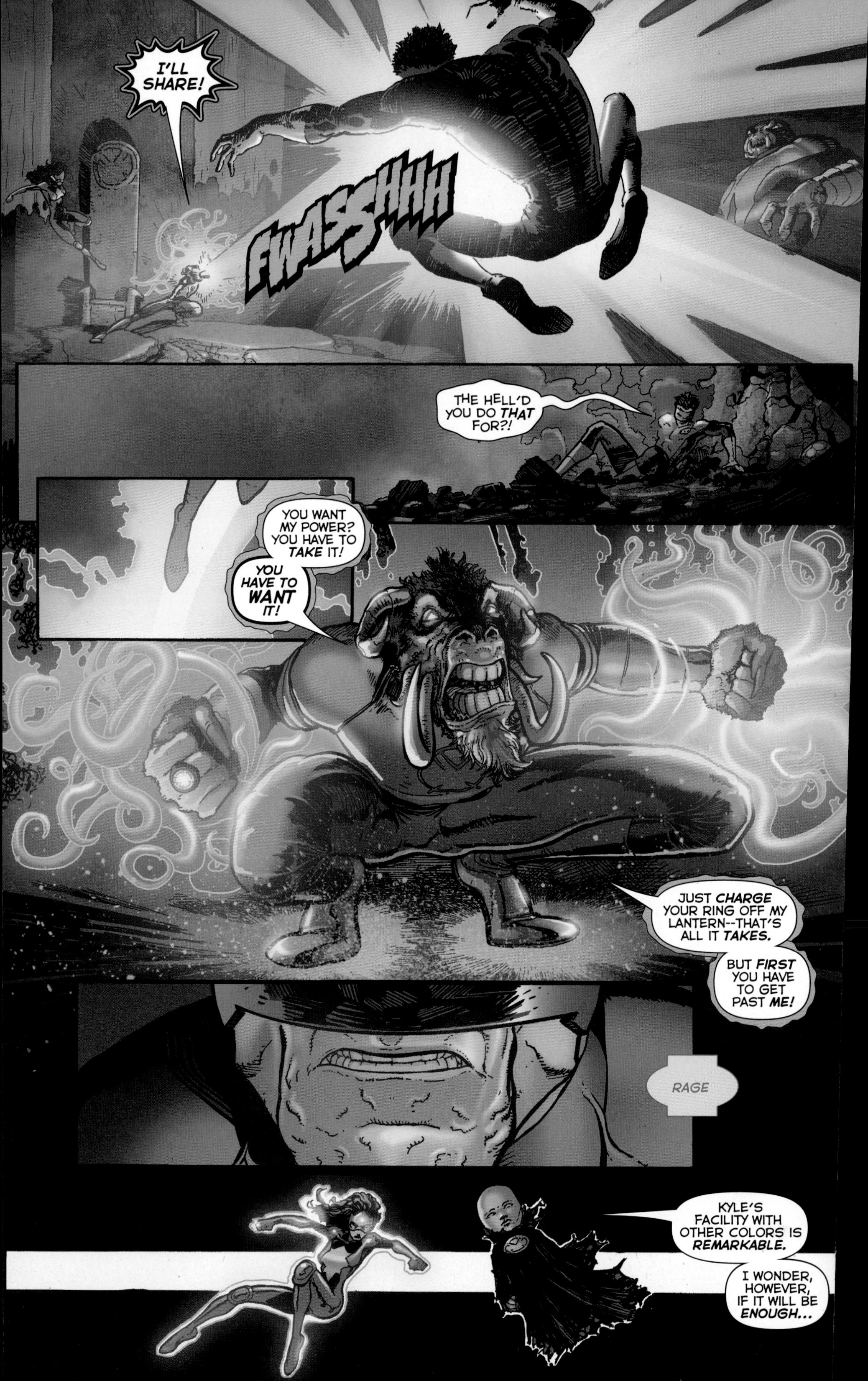
I'LL SHARE!
FWASSHHH
THE HELL'D YOU DO *THAT* FOR?!
YOU WANT MY POWER? YOU HAVE TO *TAKE* IT!
YOU HAVE TO WANT IT!
JUST *CHARGE* YOUR RING OFF MY LANTERN--THAT'S ALL IT *TAKES.*
BUT *FIRST* YOU HAVE TO GET PAST *ME!*
RAGE
KYLE'S FACILITY WITH OTHER COLORS IS *REMARKABLE.*
I WONDER, HOWEVER, IF IT WILL BE *ENOUGH...*

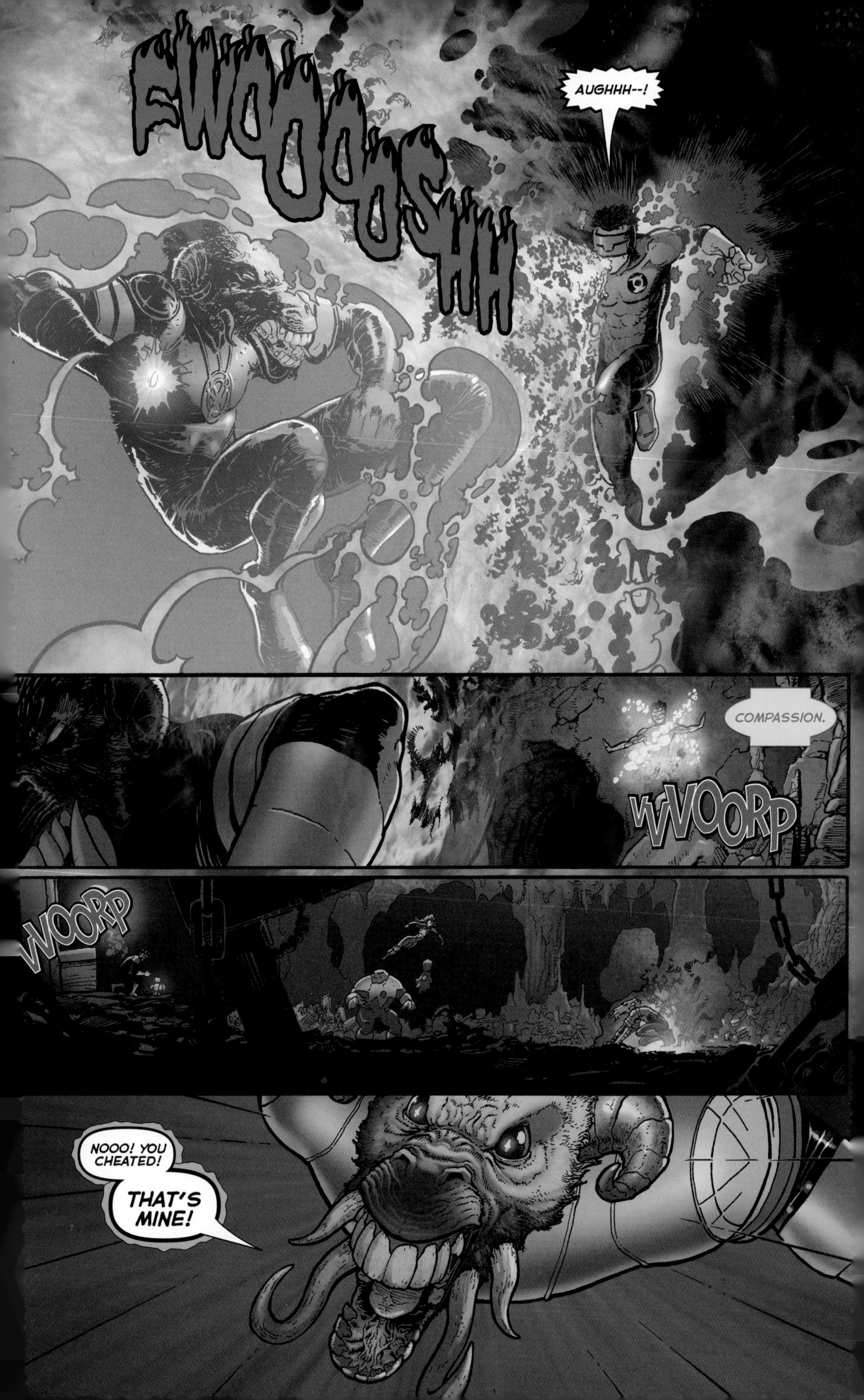
FWOOOOSHH
AUGHHH--!
COMPASSION.
VVVOORP
WOORP
NOOO! YOU CHEATED!
THAT'S MINE!

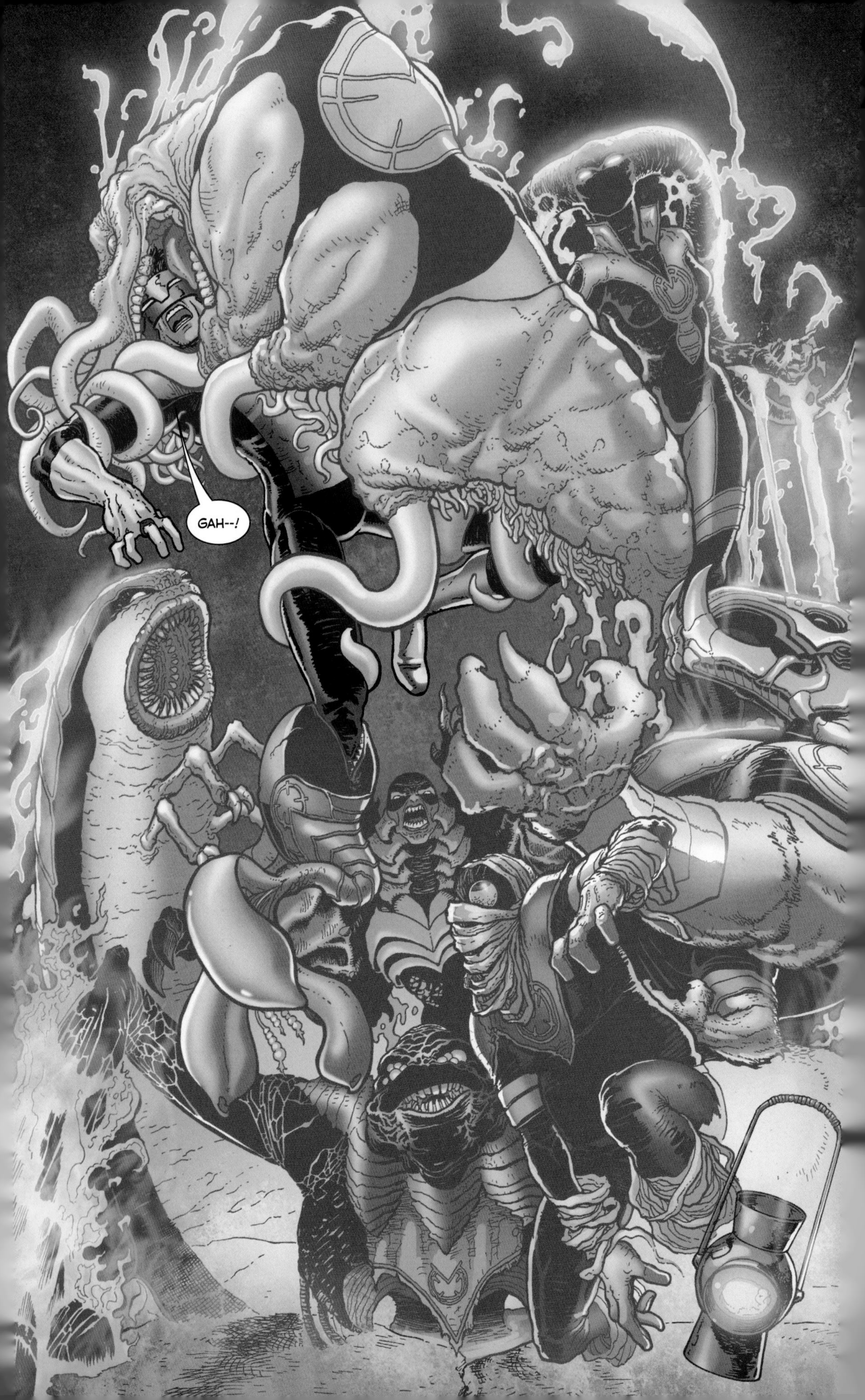
GAH--!

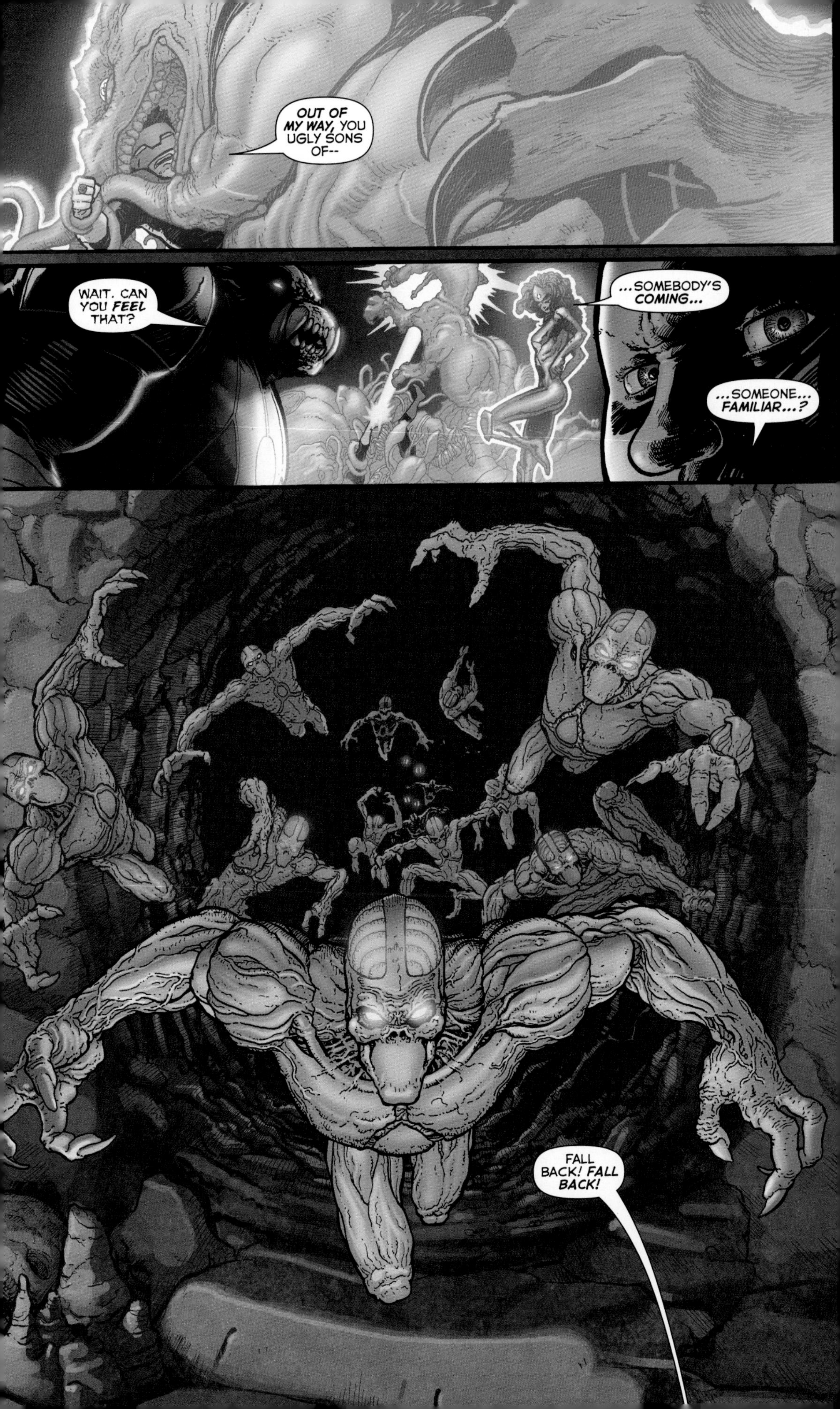
OUT OF MY WAY, YOU UGLY SONS OF--
WAIT. CAN YOU FEEL THAT?
...SOMEBODY'S COMING...
...SOMEONE... FAMILIAR...?
FALL BACK! FALL BACK!

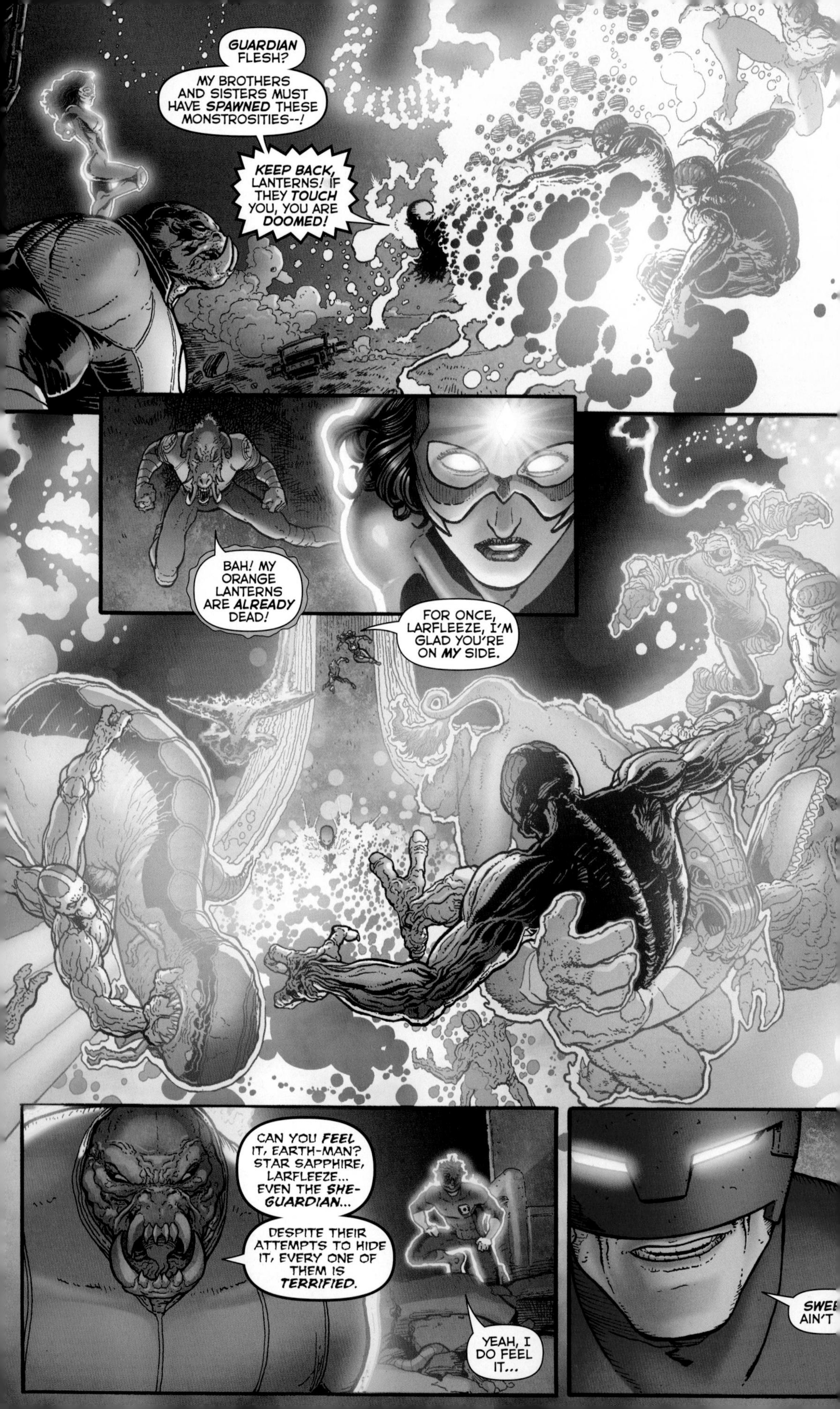
GUARDIAN FLESH?
MY BROTHERS AND SISTERS MUST HAVE SPAWNED THESE MONSTROSITIES--!
KEEP BACK, LANTERNS! IF THEY TOUCH YOU, YOU ARE DOOMED!
BAH! MY ORANGE LANTERNS ARE ALREADY DEAD!
FOR ONCE, LARFLEEZE, I'M GLAD YOU'RE ON MY SIDE.
CAN YOU FEEL IT, EARTH-MAN? STAR SAPPHIRE, LARFLEEZE... EVEN THE SHE-GUARDIAN...
DESPITE THEIR ATTEMPTS TO HIDE IT, EVERY ONE OF THEM IS TERRIFIED.
YEAH, I DO FEEL IT...

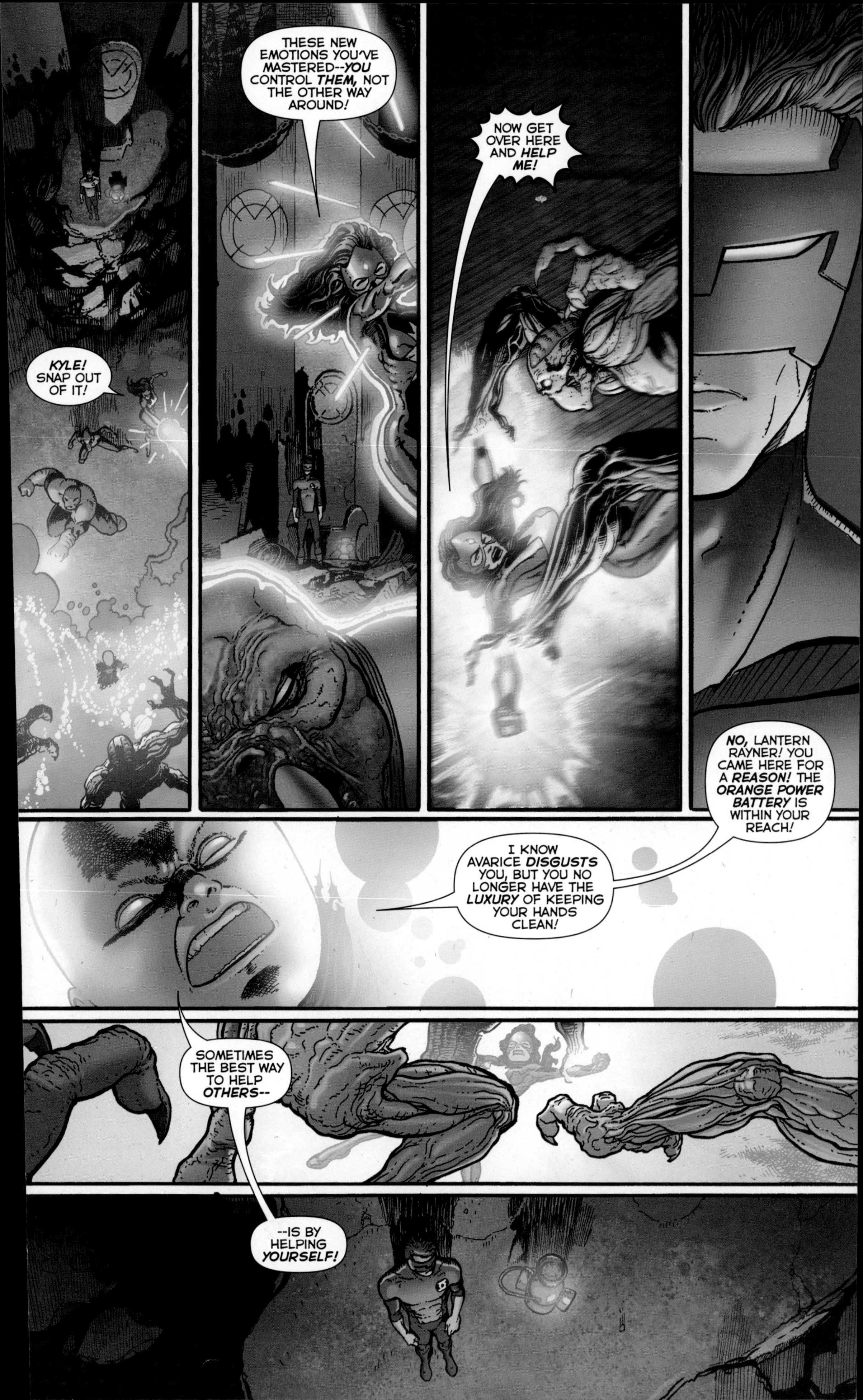
KYLE! SNAP OUT OF IT!
THESE NEW EMOTIONS YOU'VE MASTERED--YOU CONTROL THEM, NOT THE OTHER WAY AROUND!
NOW GET OVER HERE AND HELP ME!
NO, LANTERN RAYNER! YOU CAME HERE FOR A REASON! THE ORANGE POWER BATTERY IS WITHIN YOUR REACH!
I KNOW AVARICE DISGUSTS YOU, BUT YOU NO LONGER HAVE THE LUXURY OF KEEPING YOUR HANDS CLEAN!
SOMETIMES THE BEST WAY TO HELP OTHERS--
--IS BY HELPING YOURSELF!

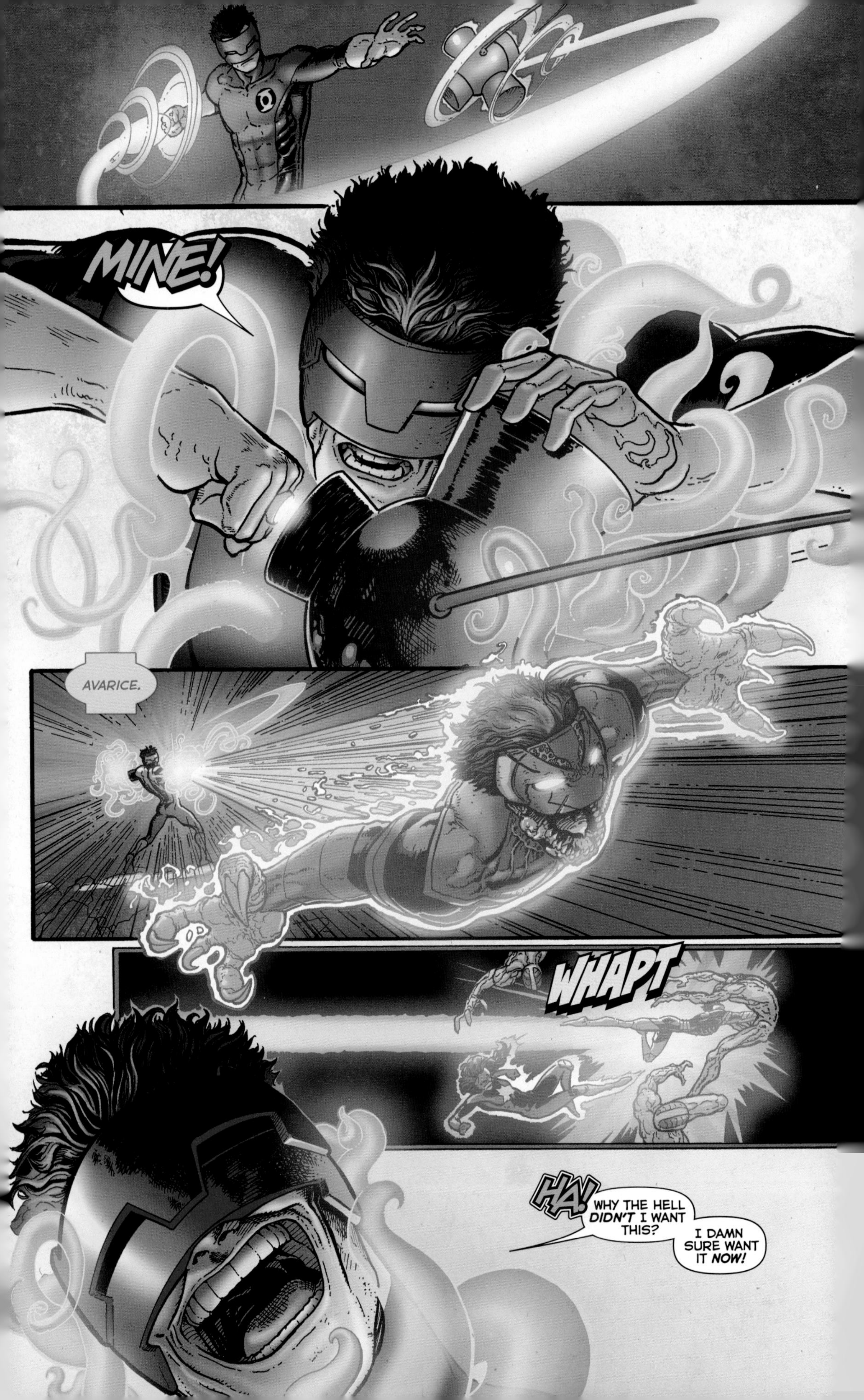
MINE!
AVARICE.
WHAPT
HA!
WHY THE HELL DIDN'T I WANT THIS?
I DAMN SURE WANT IT NOW!

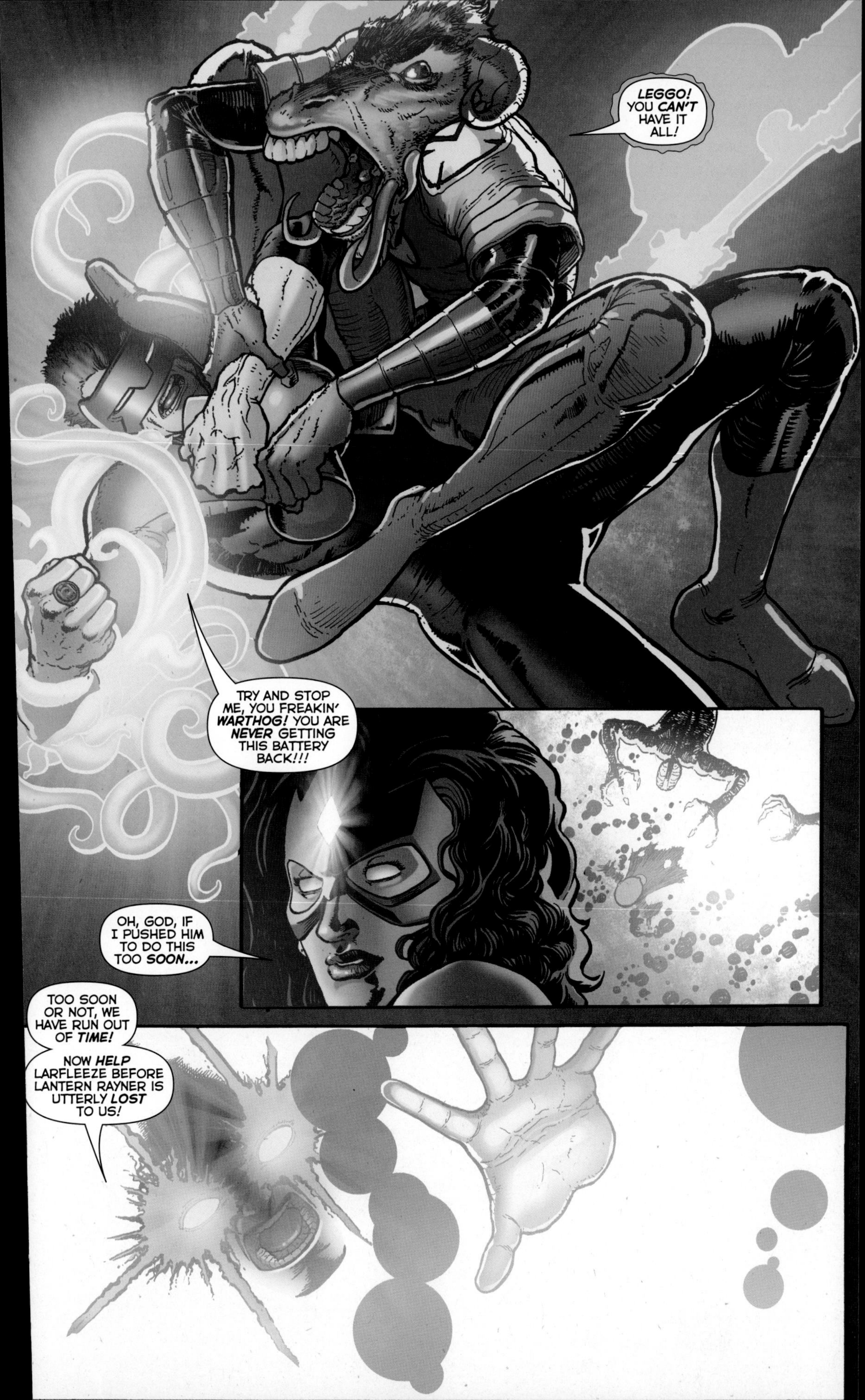

LEGGO! YOU CAN'T HAVE IT ALL!
TRY AND STOP ME, YOU FREAKIN' WARTHOG! YOU ARE NEVER GETTING THIS BATTERY BACK!!!
OH, GOD, IF I PUSHED HIM TO DO THIS TOO SOON...
TOO SOON OR NOT, WE HAVE RUN OUT OF TIME!
NOW HELP LARFLEEZE BEFORE LANTERN RAYNER IS UTTERLY LOST TO US!

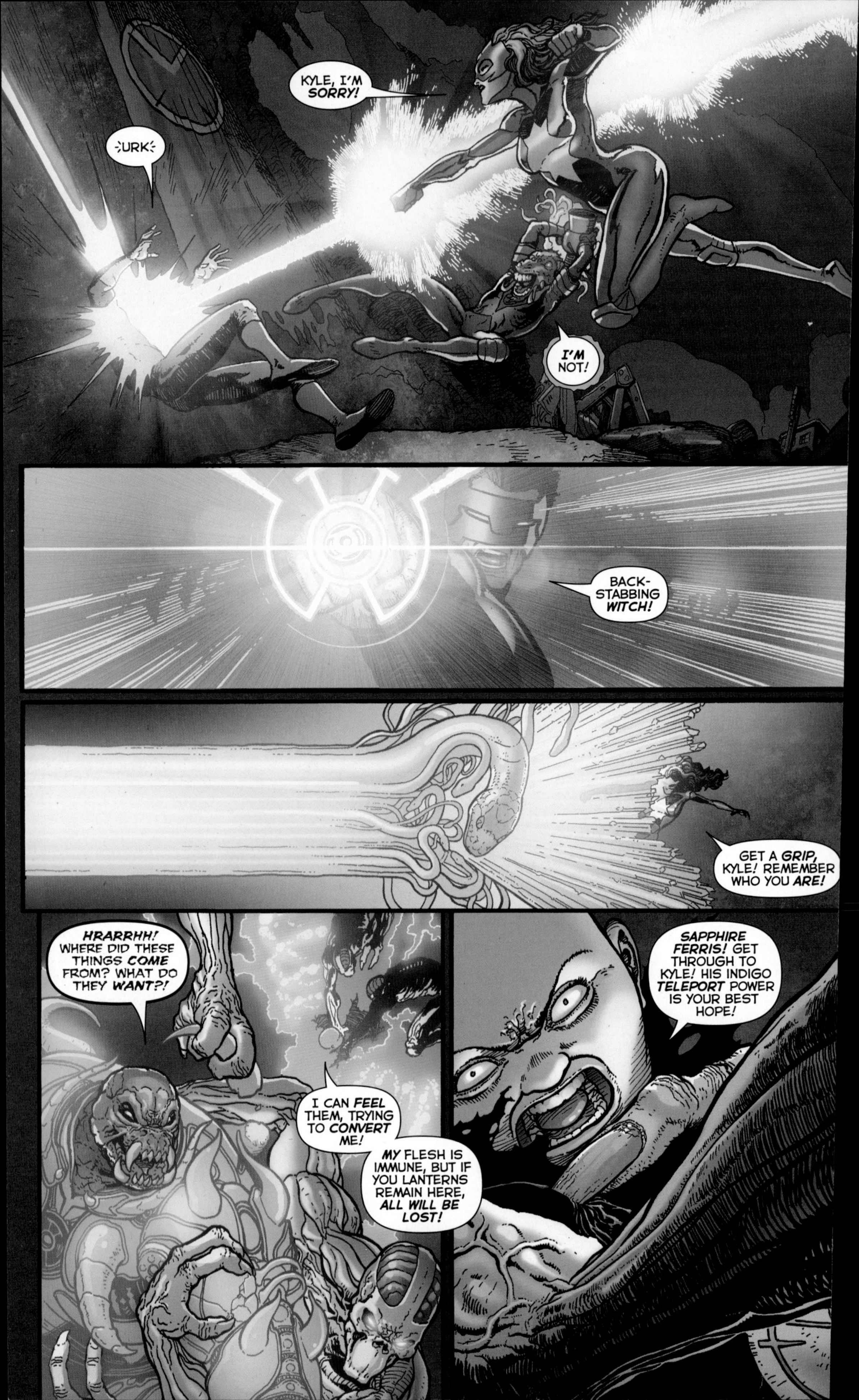
KYLE, I'M SORRY!
URK
I'M NOT!
BACK-STABBING WITCH!
GET A GRIP, KYLE! REMEMBER WHO YOU ARE!
HRARRHH! WHERE DID THESE THINGS COME FROM? WHAT DO THEY WANT?!
I CAN FEEL THEM, TRYING TO CONVERT ME!
MY FLESH IS IMMUNE, BUT IF YOU LANTERNS REMAIN HERE, ALL WILL BE LOST!
SAPPHIRE FERRIS! GET THROUGH TO KYLE! HIS INDIGO TELEPORT POWER IS YOUR BEST HOPE!

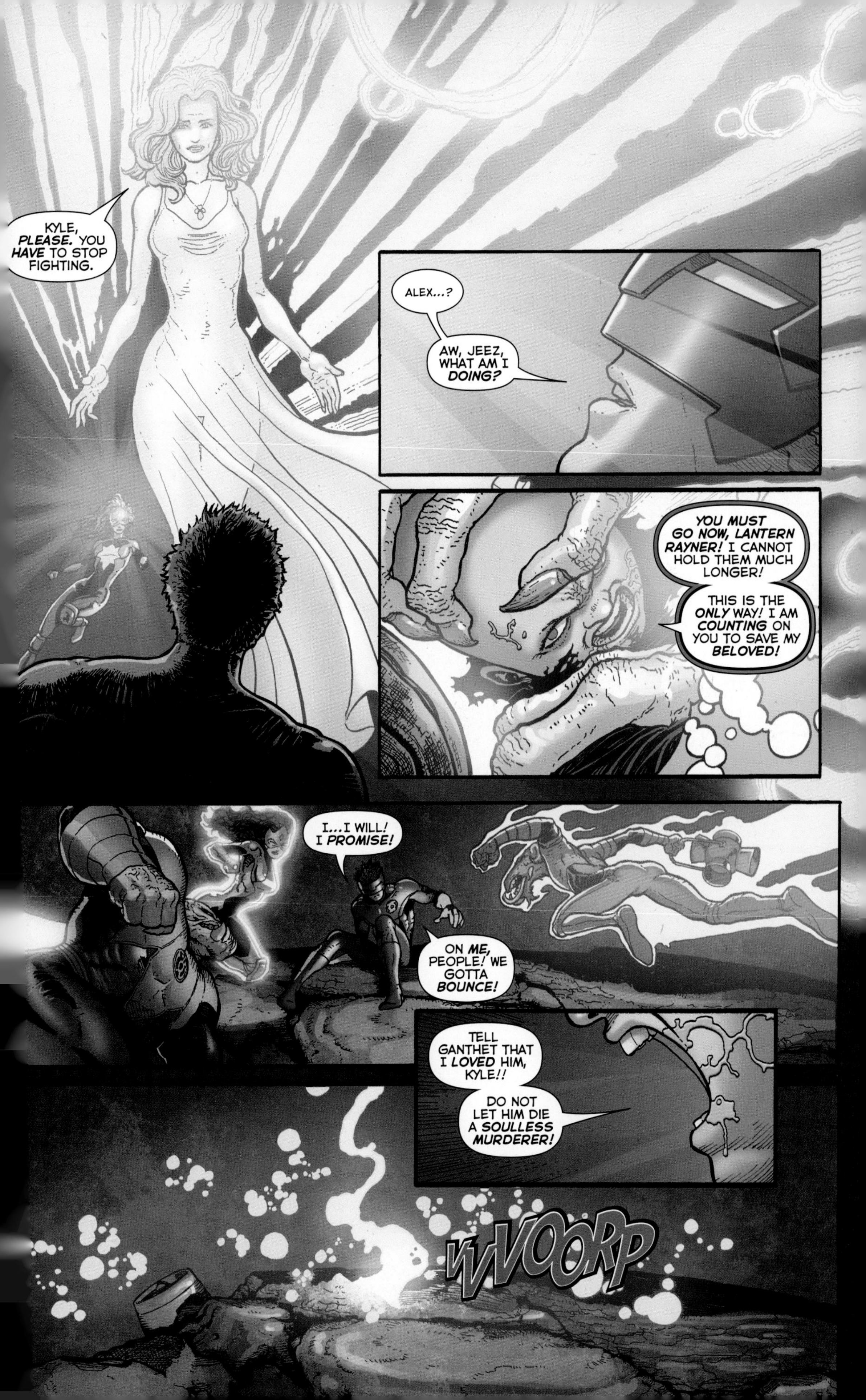
KYLE, PLEASE. YOU HAVE TO STOP FIGHTING.
ALEX...?
AW, JEEZ, WHAT AM I DOING?
YOU MUST GO NOW, LANTERN RAYNER! I CANNOT HOLD THEM MUCH LONGER!
THIS IS THE ONLY WAY! I AM COUNTING ON YOU TO SAVE MY BELOVED!
I...I WILL! I PROMISE!
ON ME, PEOPLE! WE GOTTA BOUNCE!
TELL GANTHET THAT I LOVED HIM, KYLE!!
DO NOT LET HIM DIE A SOULLESS MURDERER!
VVVOORP

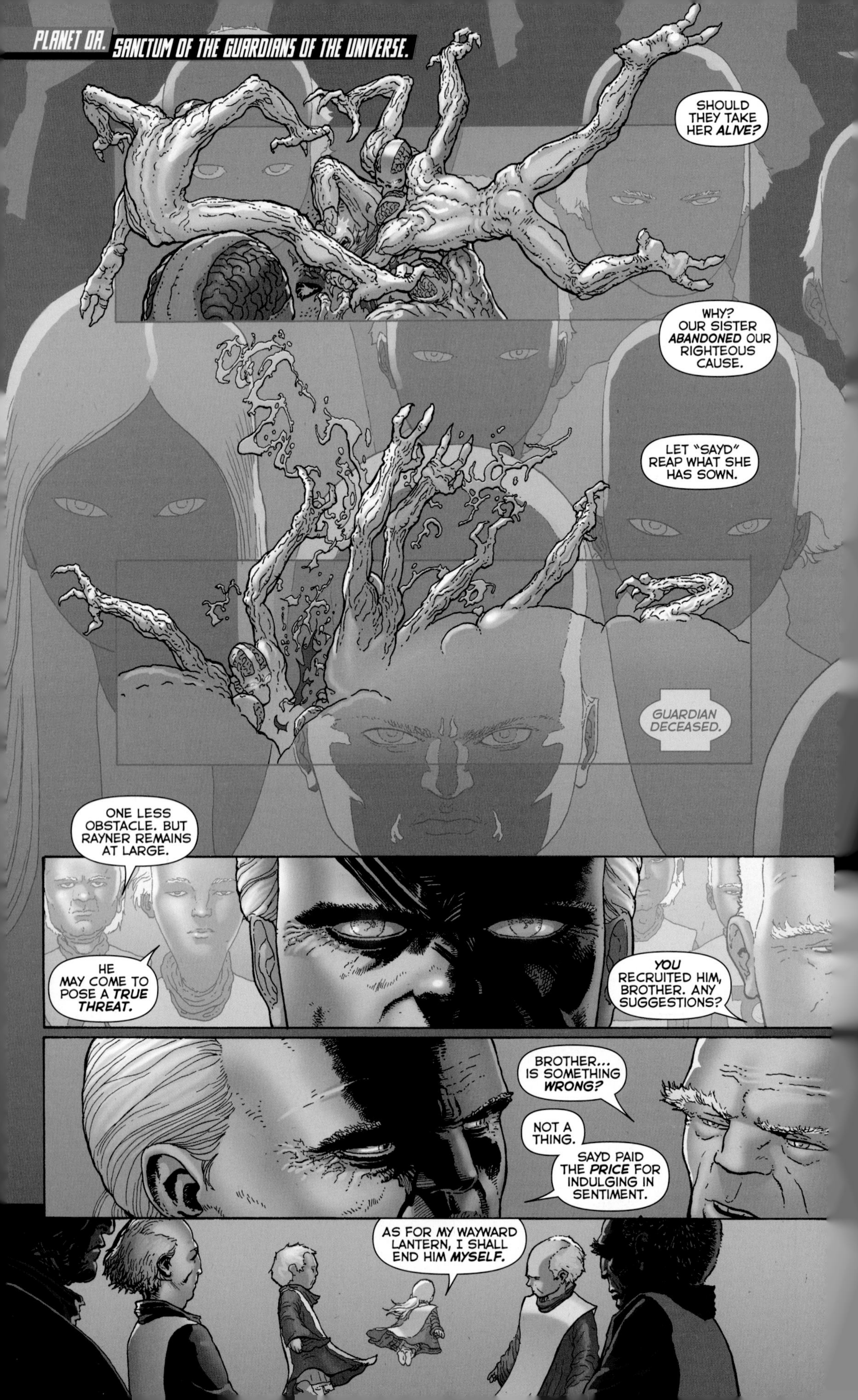
PLANET OA. SANCTUM OF THE GUARDIANS OF THE UNIVERSE.
SHOULD THEY TAKE HER ALIVE?
WHY? OUR SISTER ABANDONED OUR RIGHTEOUS CAUSE.
LET "SAYD" REAP WHAT SHE HAS SOWN.
GUARDIAN DECEASED.
ONE LESS OBSTACLE. BUT RAYNER REMAINS AT LARGE.
HE MAY COME TO POSE A TRUE THREAT.
YOU RECRUITED HIM, BROTHER. ANY SUGGESTIONS?
BROTHER... IS SOMETHING WRONG?
NOT A THING.
SAYD PAID THE PRICE FOR INDULGING IN SENTIMENT.
AS FOR MY WAYWARD LANTERN, I SHALL END HIM MYSELF.

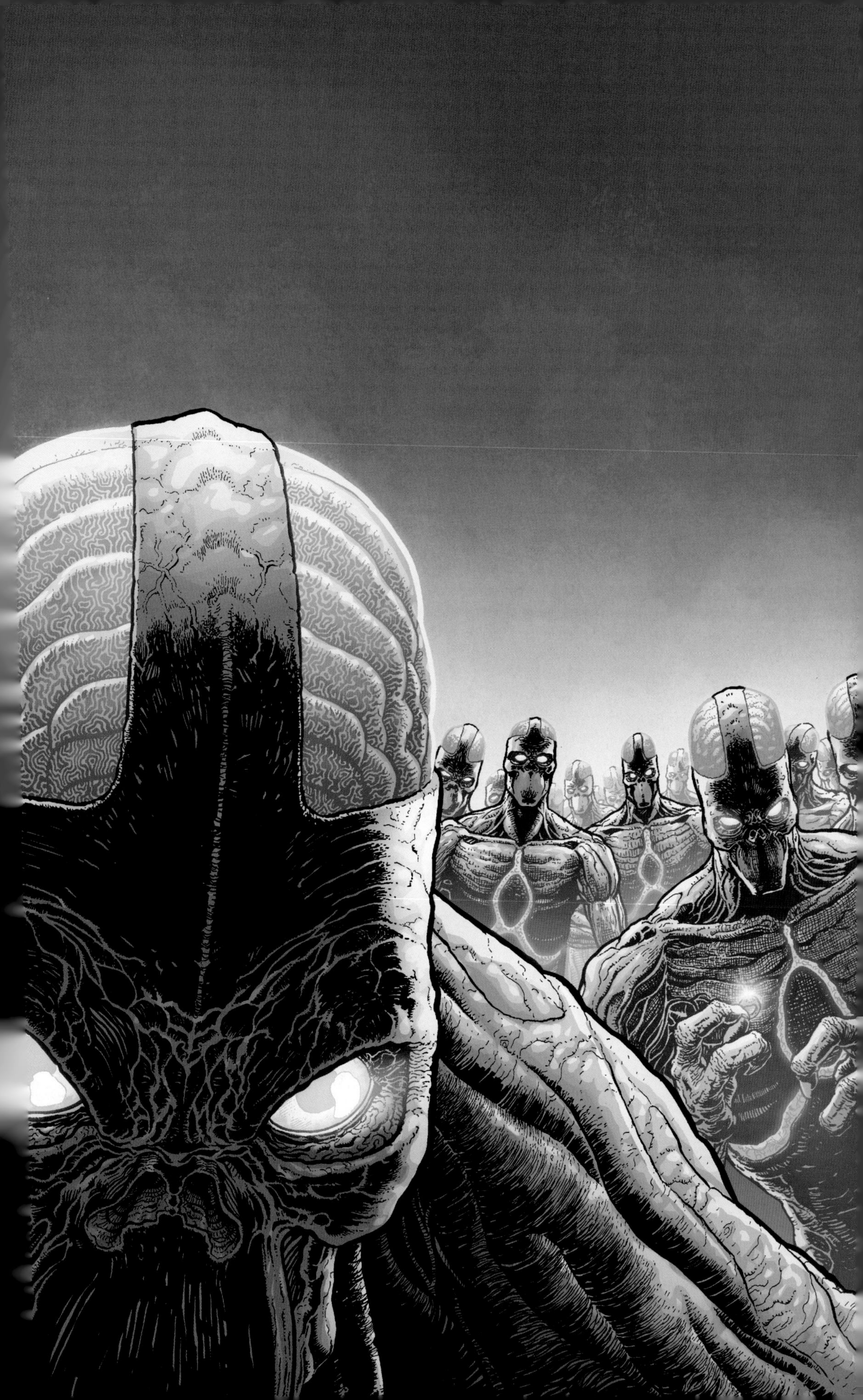

LET LOVE RULE

TONY BEDARD writer AARON KUDER artist
AARON KUDER & HI-FI cover

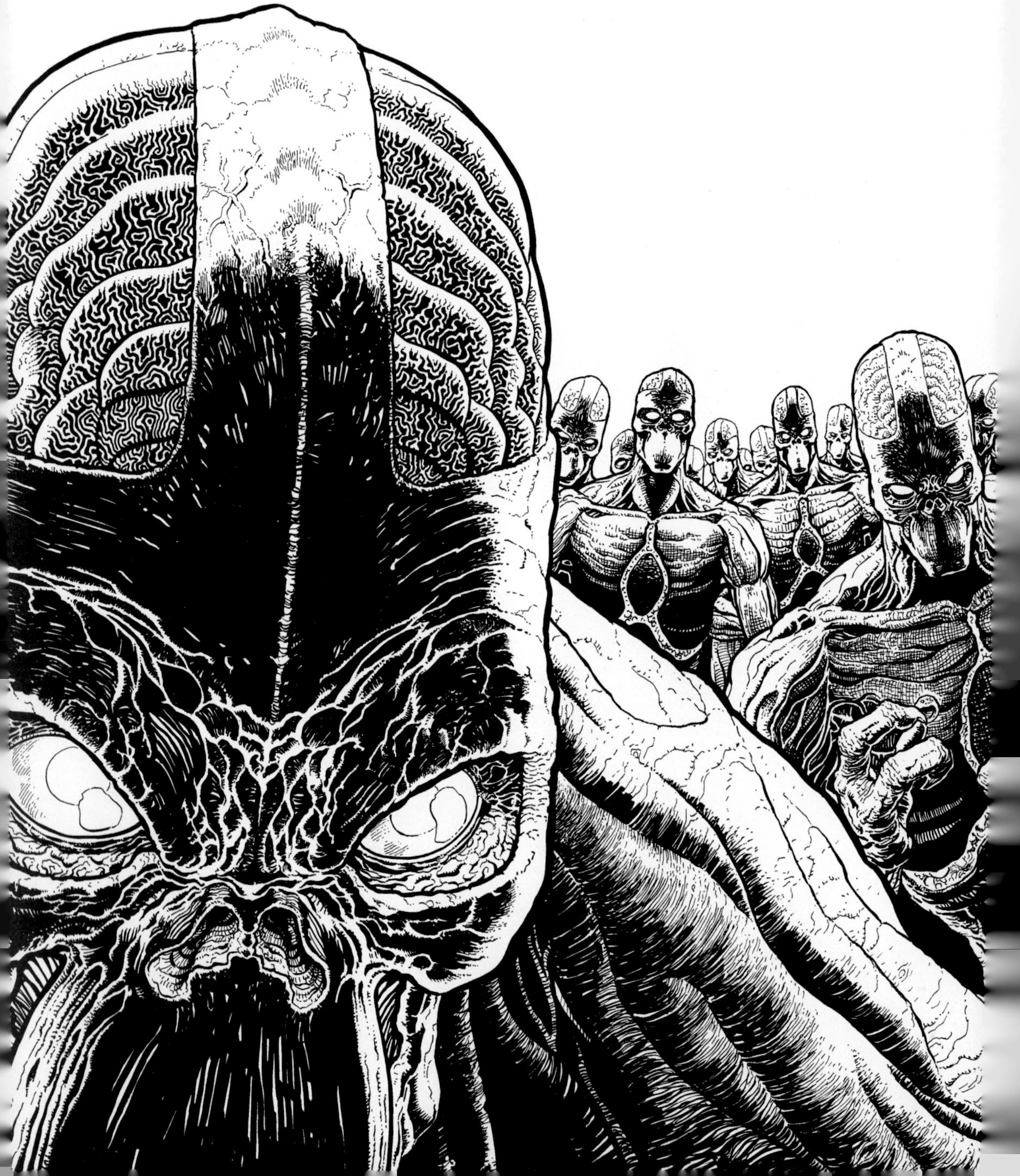

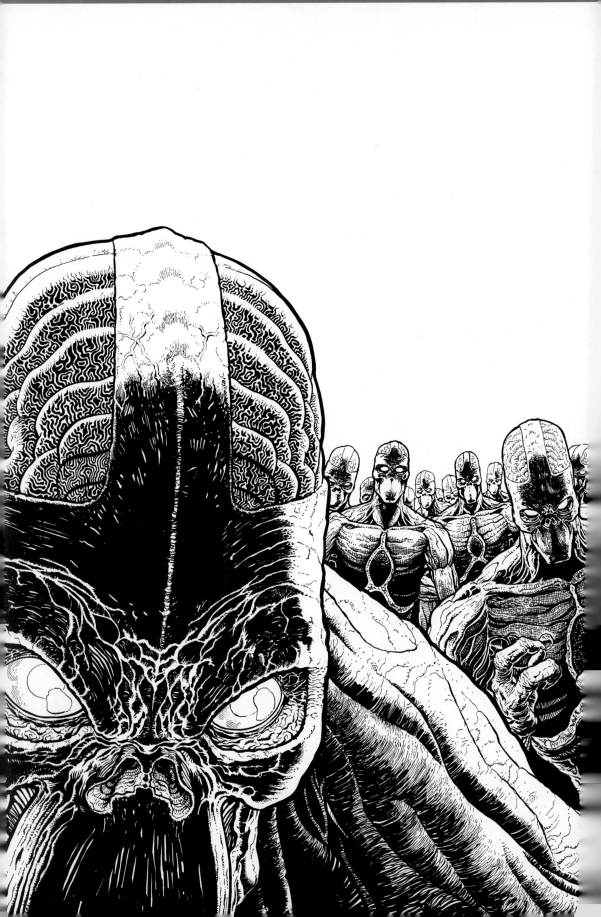

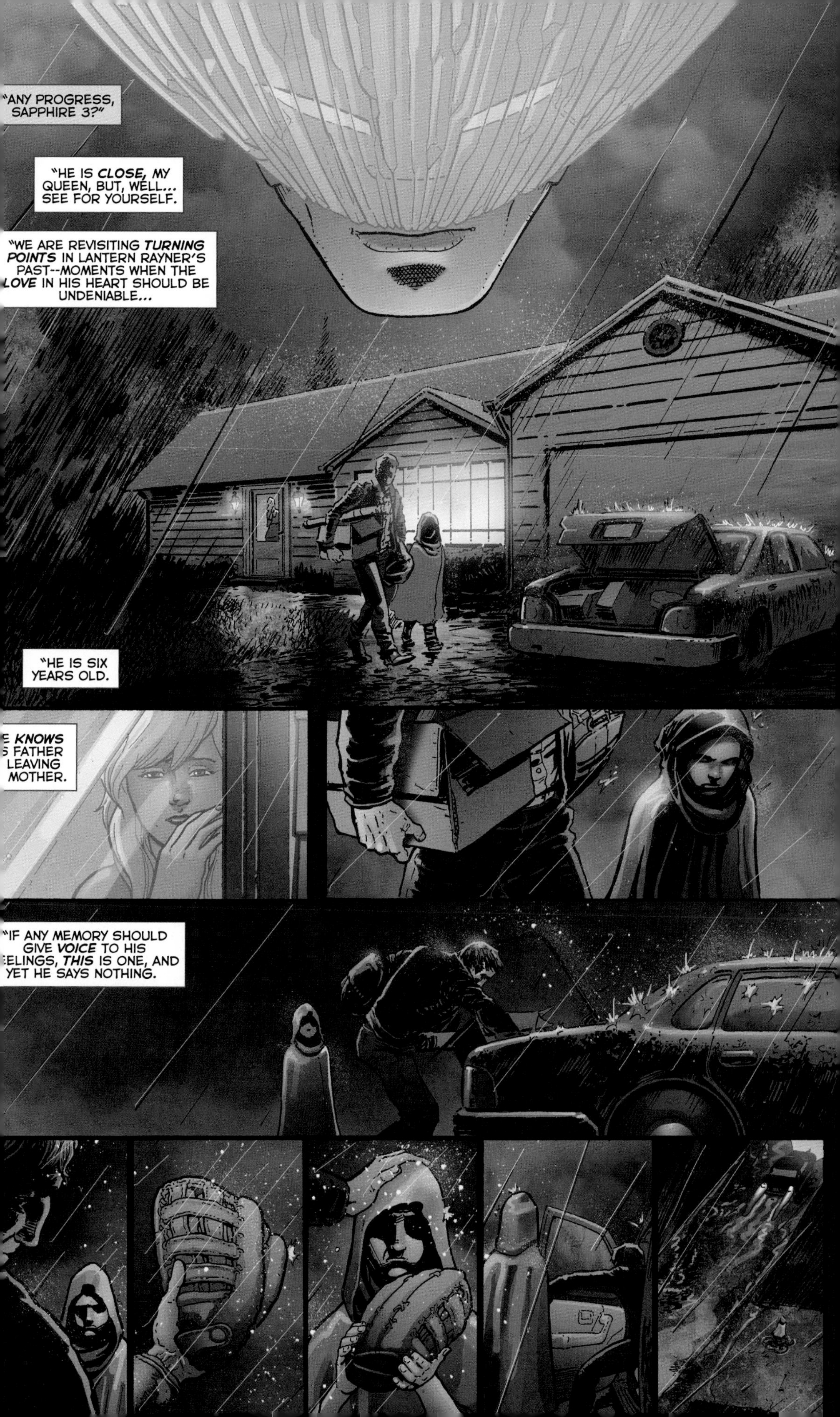
"ANY PROGRESS, SAPPHIRE 3?"
"HE IS CLOSE, MY QUEEN, BUT, WELL... SEE FOR YOURSELF.
"WE ARE REVISITING TURNING POINTS IN LANTERN RAYNER'S PAST--MOMENTS WHEN THE LOVE IN HIS HEART SHOULD BE UNDENIABLE...
"HE IS SIX YEARS OLD.
E KNOWS S FATHER LEAVING MOTHER.
"IF ANY MEMORY SHOULD GIVE VOICE TO HIS EELINGS, THIS IS ONE, AND YET HE SAYS NOTHING.

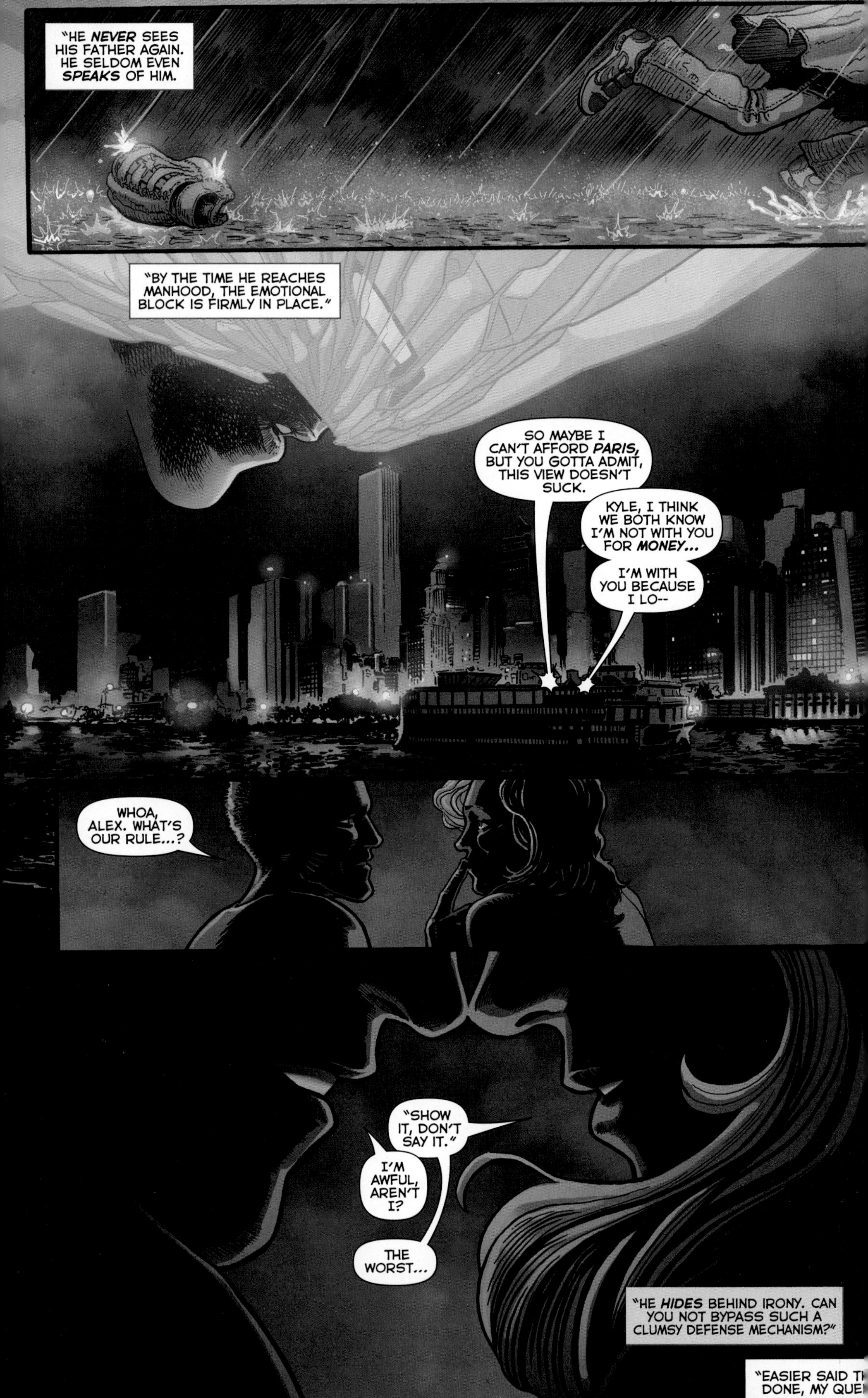
"HE NEVER SEES HIS FATHER AGAIN. HE SELDOM EVEN SPEAKS OF HIM.
"BY THE TIME HE REACHES MANHOOD, THE EMOTIONAL BLOCK IS FIRMLY IN PLACE."
SO MAYBE I CAN'T AFFORD PARIS, BUT YOU GOTTA ADMIT, THIS VIEW DOESN'T SUCK.
KYLE, I THINK WE BOTH KNOW I'M NOT WITH YOU FOR MONEY...
I'M WITH YOU BECAUSE I LO--
WHOA, ALEX. WHAT'S OUR RULE...?
"SHOW IT, DON'T SAY IT."
I'M AWFUL, AREN'T I?
THE WORST...
"HE HIDES BEHIND IRONY. CAN YOU NOT BYPASS SUCH A CLUMSY DEFENSE MECHANISM?"

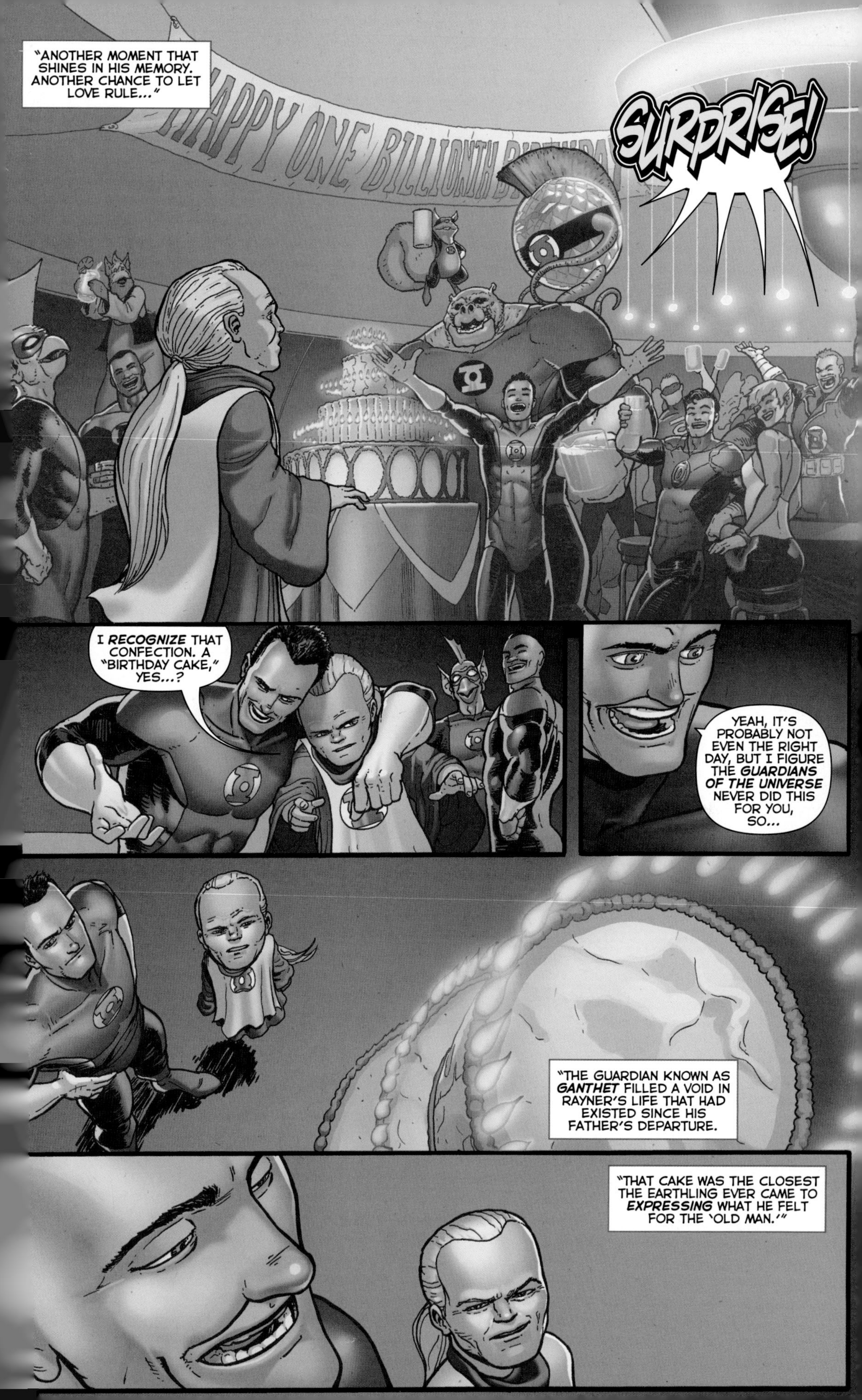
"ANOTHER MOMENT THAT SHINES IN HIS MEMORY. ANOTHER CHANCE TO LET LOVE RULE..."
SURPRISE!
I *RECOGNIZE* THAT CONFECTION. A "BIRTHDAY CAKE," YES...?
YEAH, IT'S PROBABLY NOT EVEN THE RIGHT DAY, BUT I FIGURE THE *GUARDIANS OF THE UNIVERSE* NEVER DID THIS FOR YOU, SO...
"THE GUARDIAN KNOWN AS *GANTHET* FILLED A VOID IN RAYNER'S LIFE THAT HAD EXISTED SINCE HIS FATHER'S DEPARTURE.
"THAT CAKE WAS THE CLOSEST THE EARTHLING EVER CAME TO *EXPRESSING* WHAT HE FELT FOR THE 'OLD MAN.'"

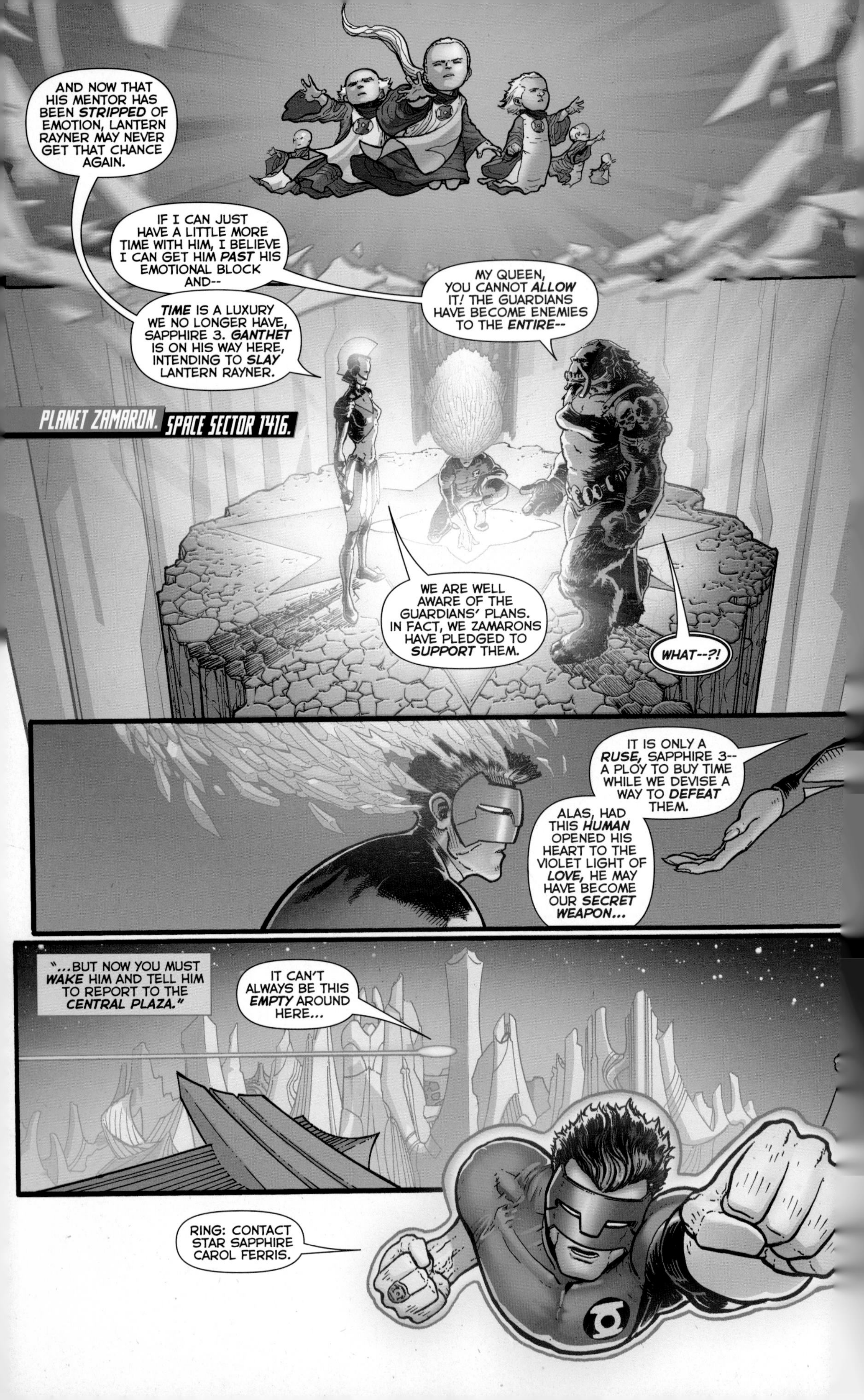
AND NOW THAT HIS MENTOR HAS BEEN STRIPPED OF EMOTION, LANTERN RAYNER MAY NEVER GET THAT CHANCE AGAIN.
IF I CAN JUST HAVE A LITTLE MORE TIME WITH HIM, I BELIEVE I CAN GET HIM PAST HIS EMOTIONAL BLOCK AND--
PLANET ZAMARON.
SPACE SECTOR 1416.
TIME IS A LUXURY WE NO LONGER HAVE, SAPPHIRE 3. GANTHET IS ON HIS WAY HERE, INTENDING TO SLAY LANTERN RAYNER.
MY QUEEN, YOU CANNOT ALLOW IT! THE GUARDIANS HAVE BECOME ENEMIES TO THE ENTIRE--
WE ARE WELL AWARE OF THE GUARDIANS' PLANS. IN FACT, WE ZAMARONS HAVE PLEDGED TO SUPPORT THEM.
WHAT--?!
IT IS ONLY A RUSE, SAPPHIRE 3-- A PLOY TO BUY TIME WHILE WE DEVISE A WAY TO DEFEAT THEM.
ALAS, HAD THIS HUMAN OPENED HIS HEART TO THE VIOLET LIGHT OF LOVE, HE MAY HAVE BECOME OUR SECRET WEAPON...
"...BUT NOW YOU MUST WAKE HIM AND TELL HIM TO REPORT TO THE CENTRAL PLAZA."
IT CAN'T ALWAYS BE THIS EMPTY AROUND HERE...
RING: CONTACT STAR SAPPHIRE CAROL FERRIS.

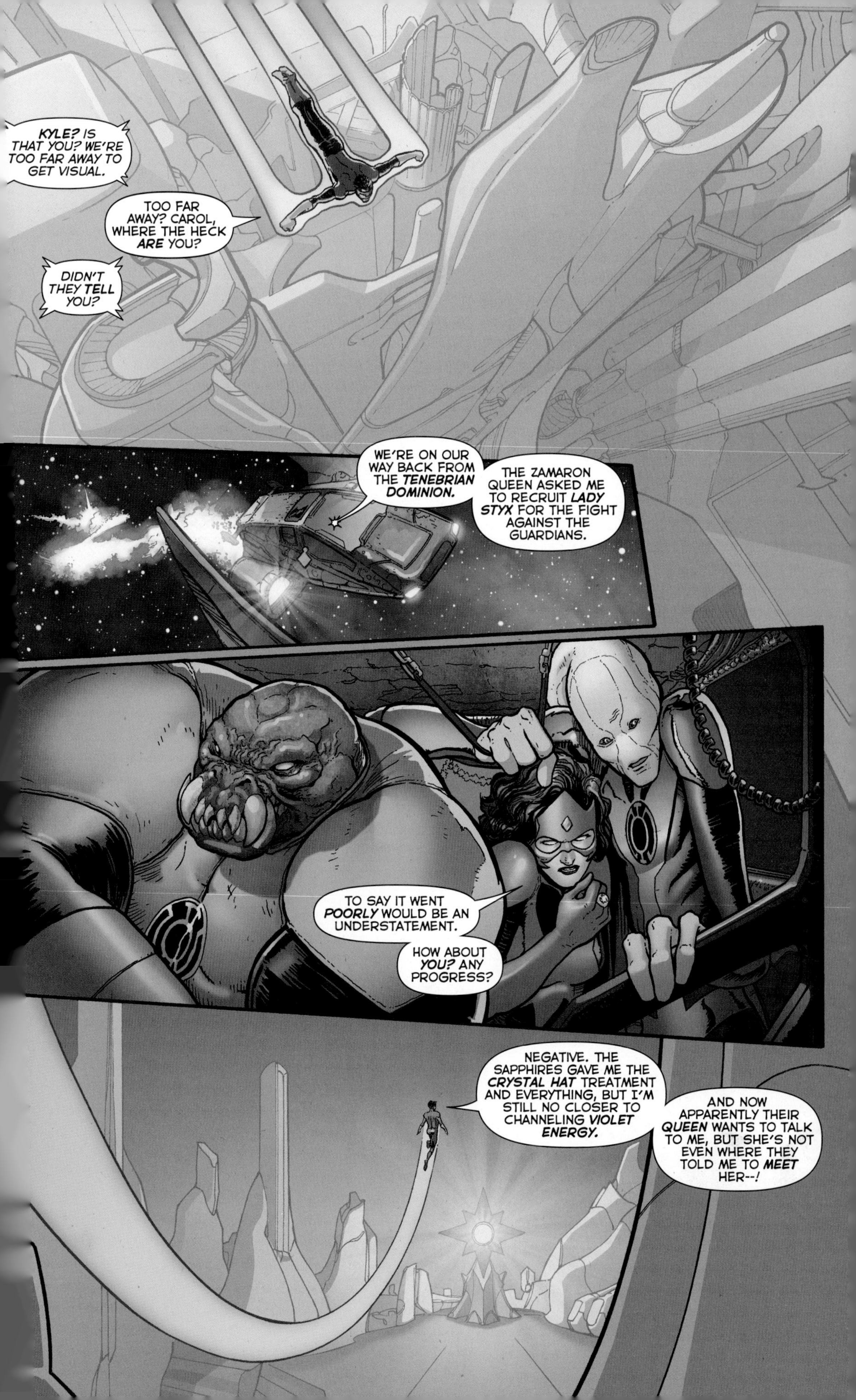
KYLE? IS THAT YOU? WE'RE TOO FAR AWAY TO GET VISUAL.
TOO FAR AWAY? CAROL, WHERE THE HECK ARE YOU?
DIDN'T THEY TELL YOU?
WE'RE ON OUR WAY BACK FROM THE TENEBRIAN DOMINION.
THE ZAMARON QUEEN ASKED ME TO RECRUIT LADY STYX FOR THE FIGHT AGAINST THE GUARDIANS.
TO SAY IT WENT POORLY WOULD BE AN UNDERSTATEMENT.
HOW ABOUT YOU? ANY PROGRESS?
NEGATIVE. THE SAPPHIRES GAVE ME THE CRYSTAL HAT TREATMENT AND EVERYTHING, BUT I'M STILL NO CLOSER TO CHANNELING VIOLET ENERGY.
AND NOW APPARENTLY THEIR QUEEN WANTS TO TALK TO ME, BUT SHE'S NOT EVEN WHERE THEY TOLD ME TO MEET HER--!

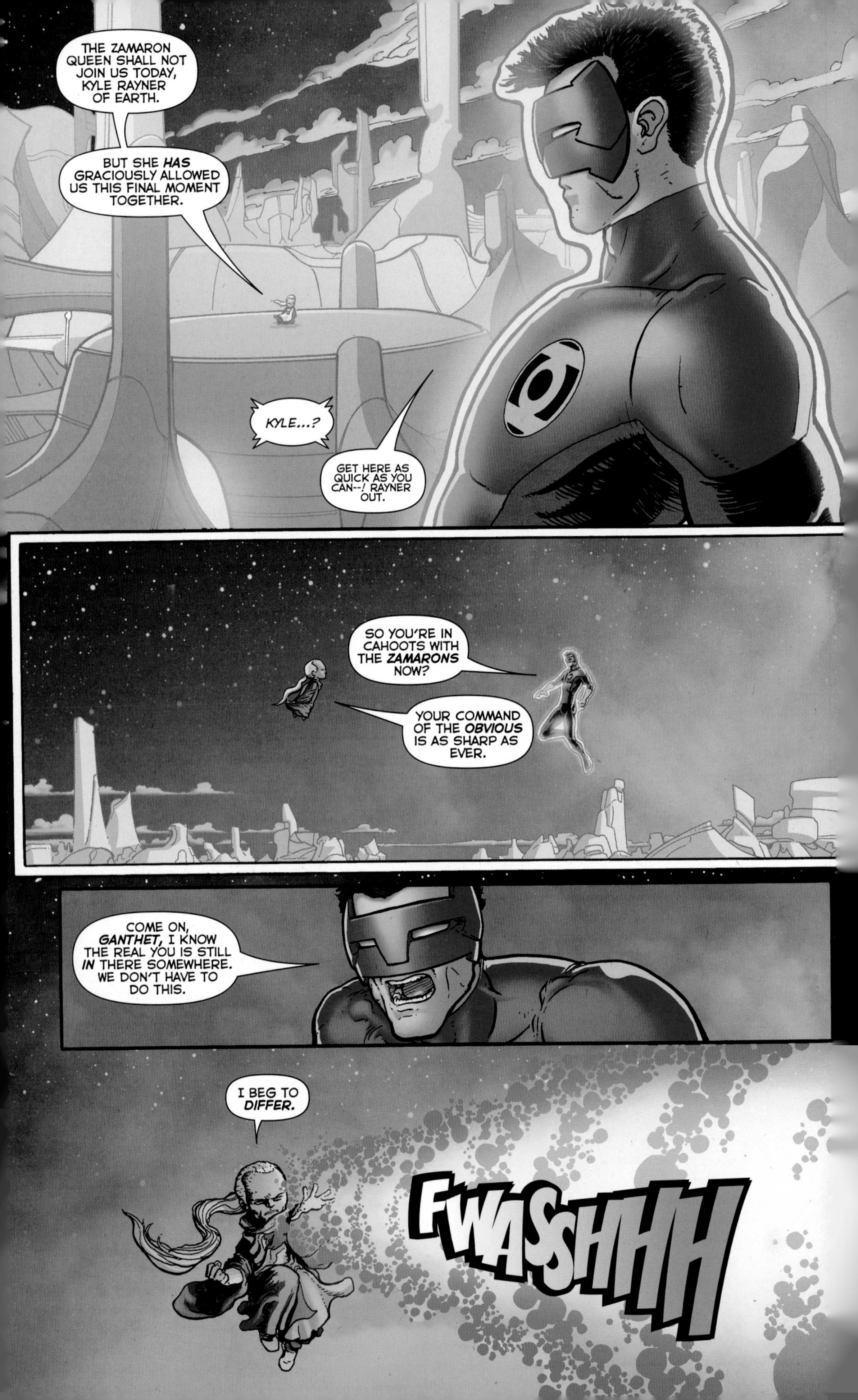
THE ZAMARON QUEEN SHALL NOT JOIN US TODAY, KYLE RAYNER OF EARTH.
BUT SHE HAS GRACIOUSLY ALLOWED US THIS FINAL MOMENT TOGETHER.
KYLE...?
GET HERE AS QUICK AS YOU CAN--! RAYNER OUT.
SO YOU'RE IN CAHOOTS WITH THE ZAMARONS NOW?
YOUR COMMAND OF THE OBVIOUS IS AS SHARP AS EVER.
COME ON, GANTHET, I KNOW THE REAL YOU IS STILL IN THERE SOMEWHERE. WE DON'T HAVE TO DO THIS.
I BEG TO DIFFER.
FWASHHH

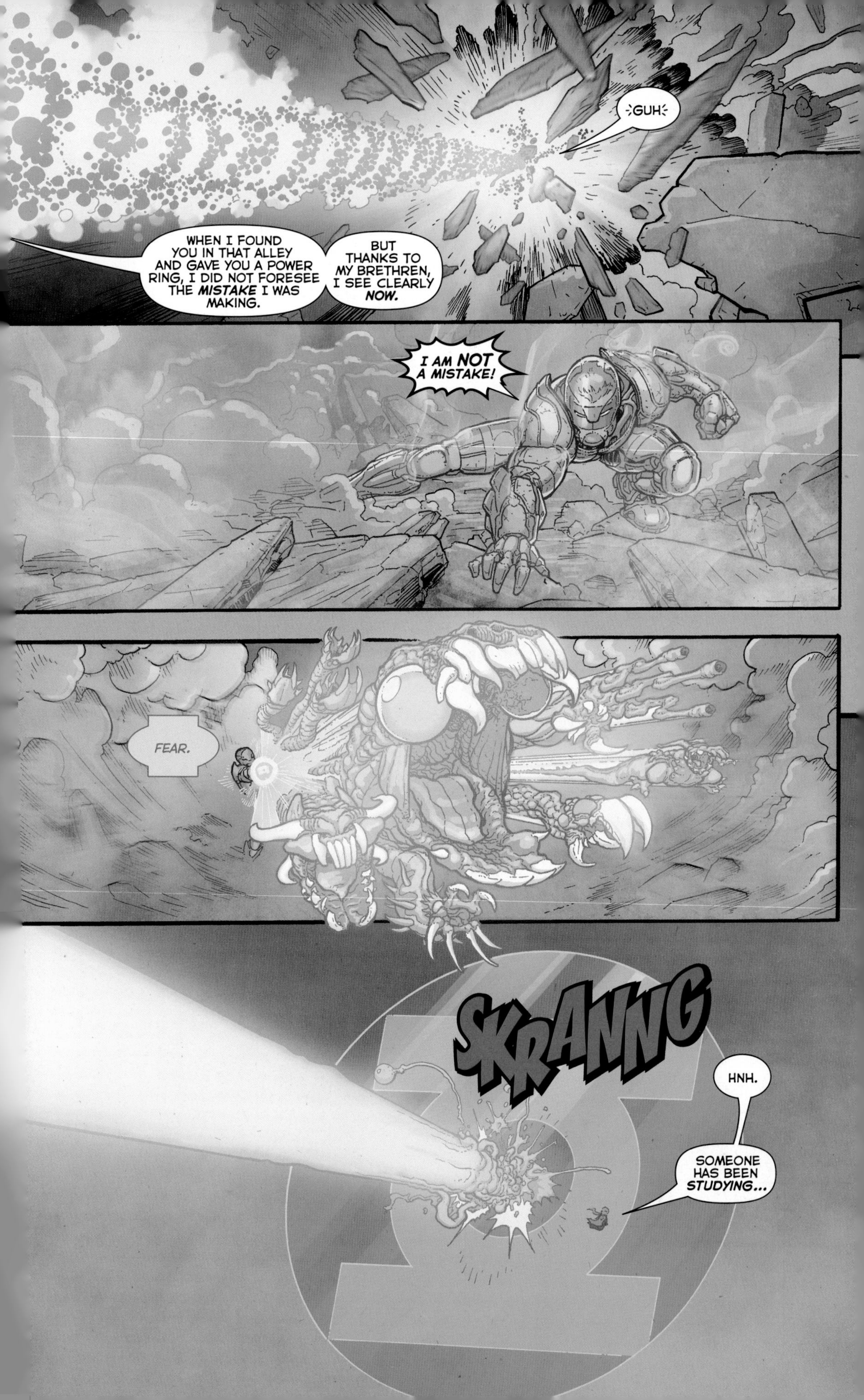
GUH
WHEN I FOUND YOU IN THAT ALLEY AND GAVE YOU A POWER RING, I DID NOT FORESEE THE MISTAKE I WAS MAKING.
BUT THANKS TO MY BRETHREN, I SEE CLEARLY NOW.
I AM NOT A MISTAKE!
FEAR.
SKRANNG
HNH.
SOMEONE HAS BEEN STUDYING...

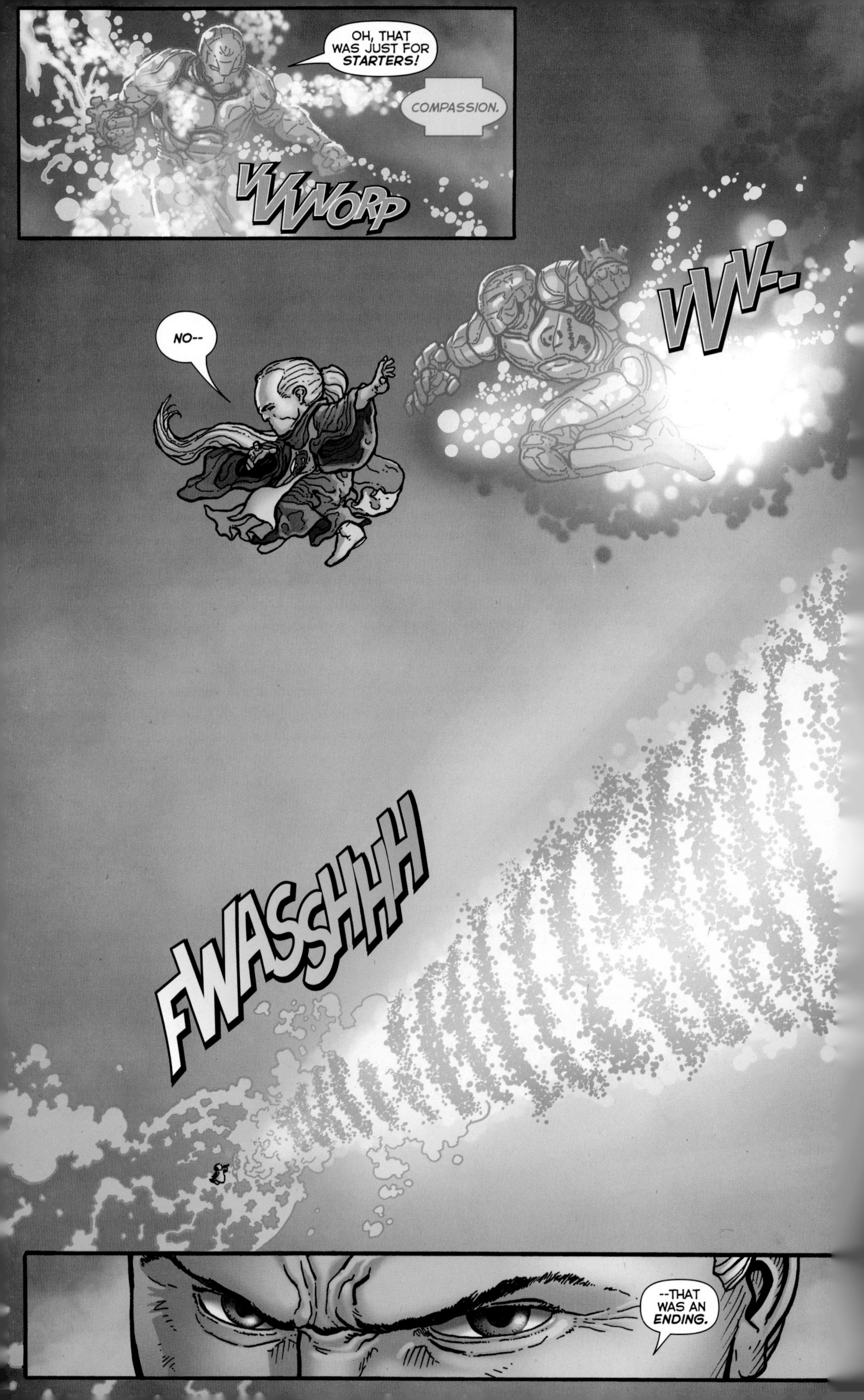

OH, THAT WAS JUST FOR STARTERS!
COMPASSION.
VVVWORP
NO--
VVV--
FWASSHHH
--THAT WAS AN ENDING.

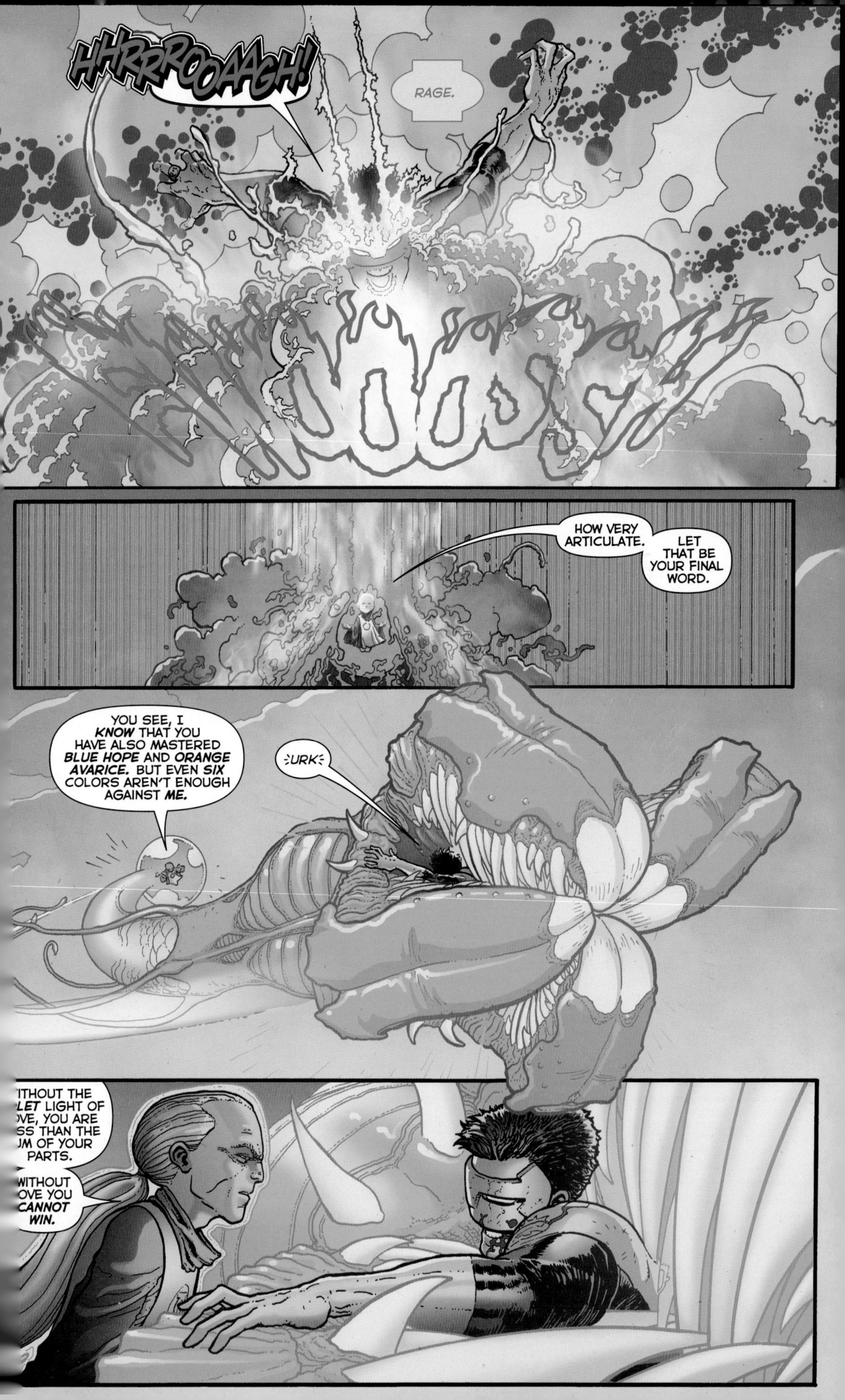
HHRRROOAAAGH!
RAGE.
WOOSH
HOW VERY ARTICULATE.
LET THAT BE YOUR FINAL WORD.
YOU SEE, I KNOW THAT YOU HAVE ALSO MASTERED BLUE HOPE AND ORANGE AVARICE. BUT EVEN SIX COLORS AREN'T ENOUGH AGAINST ME.
URK
ITHOUT THE OLET LIGHT OF OVE, YOU ARE SS THAN THE UM OF YOUR PARTS.
WITHOUT OVE YOU CANNOT WIN.

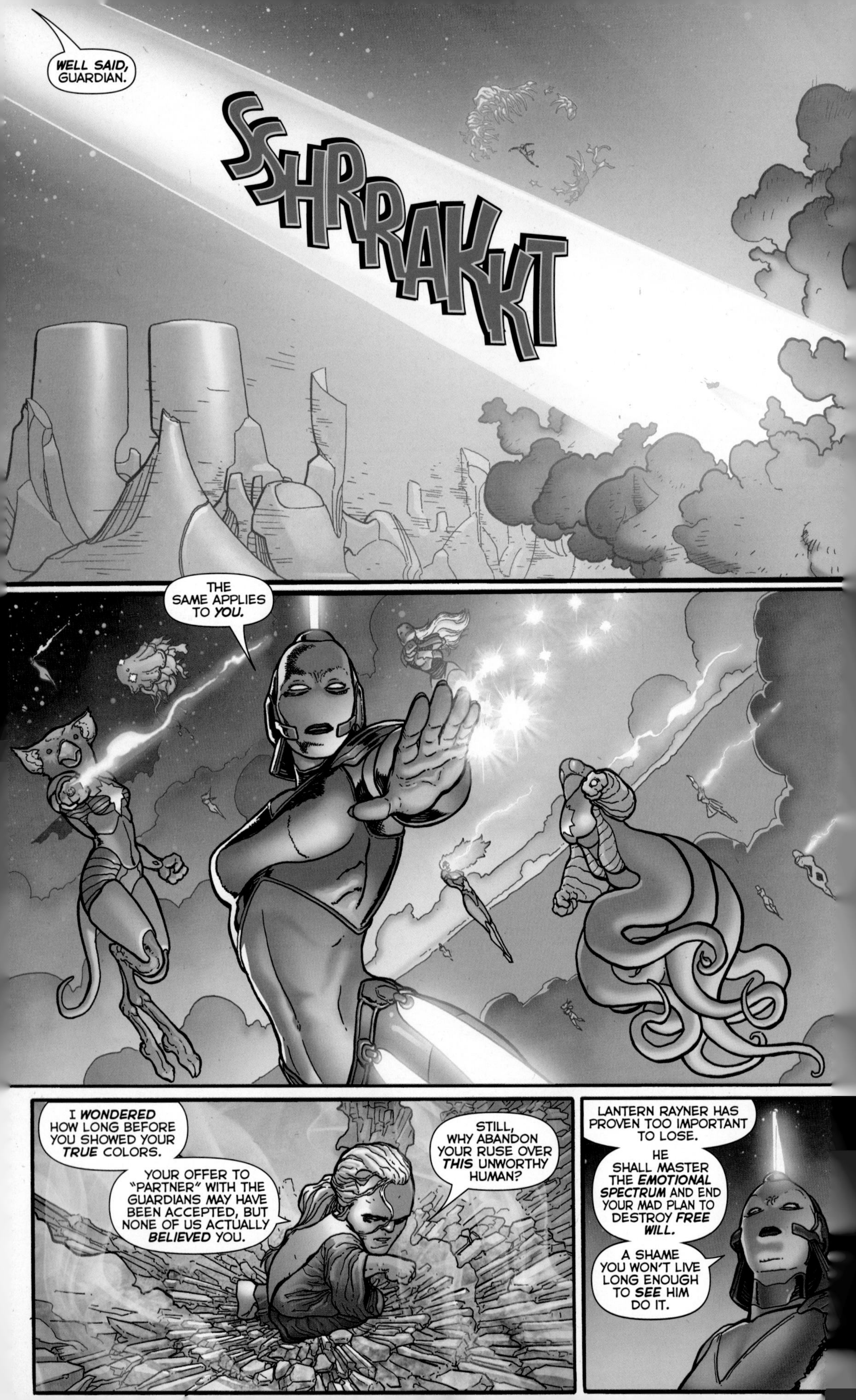
WELL SAID, GUARDIAN.
SSHRRAKKT
THE SAME APPLIES TO YOU.
I WONDERED HOW LONG BEFORE YOU SHOWED YOUR TRUE COLORS.
YOUR OFFER TO "PARTNER" WITH THE GUARDIANS MAY HAVE BEEN ACCEPTED, BUT NONE OF US ACTUALLY BELIEVED YOU.
STILL, WHY ABANDON YOUR RUSE OVER THIS UNWORTHY HUMAN?
LANTERN RAYNER HAS PROVEN TOO IMPORTANT TO LOSE.
HE SHALL MASTER THE EMOTIONAL SPECTRUM AND END YOUR MAD PLAN TO DESTROY FREE WILL.
A SHAME YOU WON'T LIVE LONG ENOUGH TO SEE HIM DO IT.

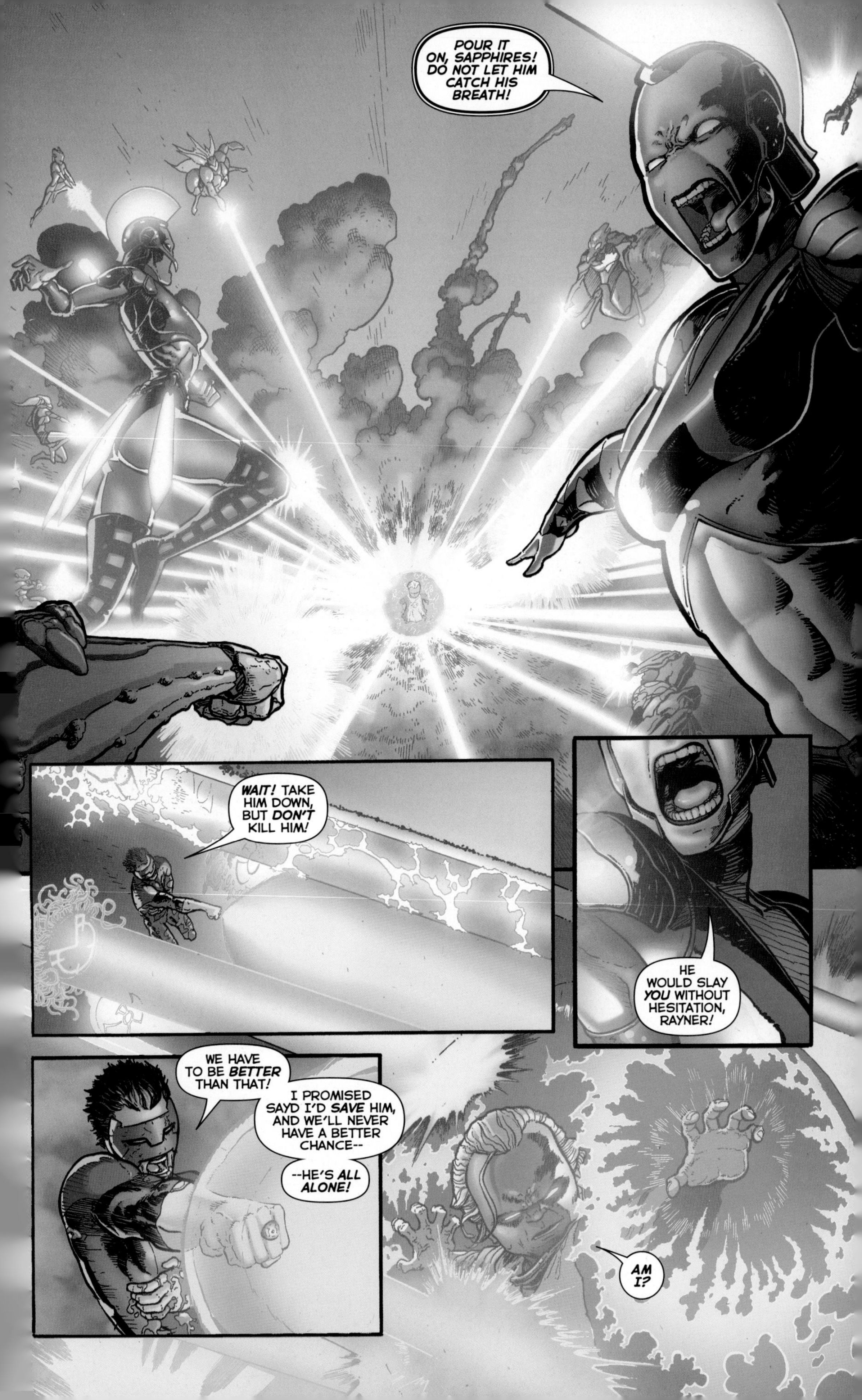
POUR IT ON, SAPPHIRES! DO NOT LET HIM CATCH HIS BREATH!
WAIT! TAKE HIM DOWN, BUT DON'T KILL HIM!
HE WOULD SLAY YOU WITHOUT HESITATION, RAYNER!
WE HAVE TO BE BETTER THAN THAT!
I PROMISED SAYD I'D SAVE HIM, AND WE'LL NEVER HAVE A BETTER CHANCE--
--HE'S ALL ALONE!
AM I?

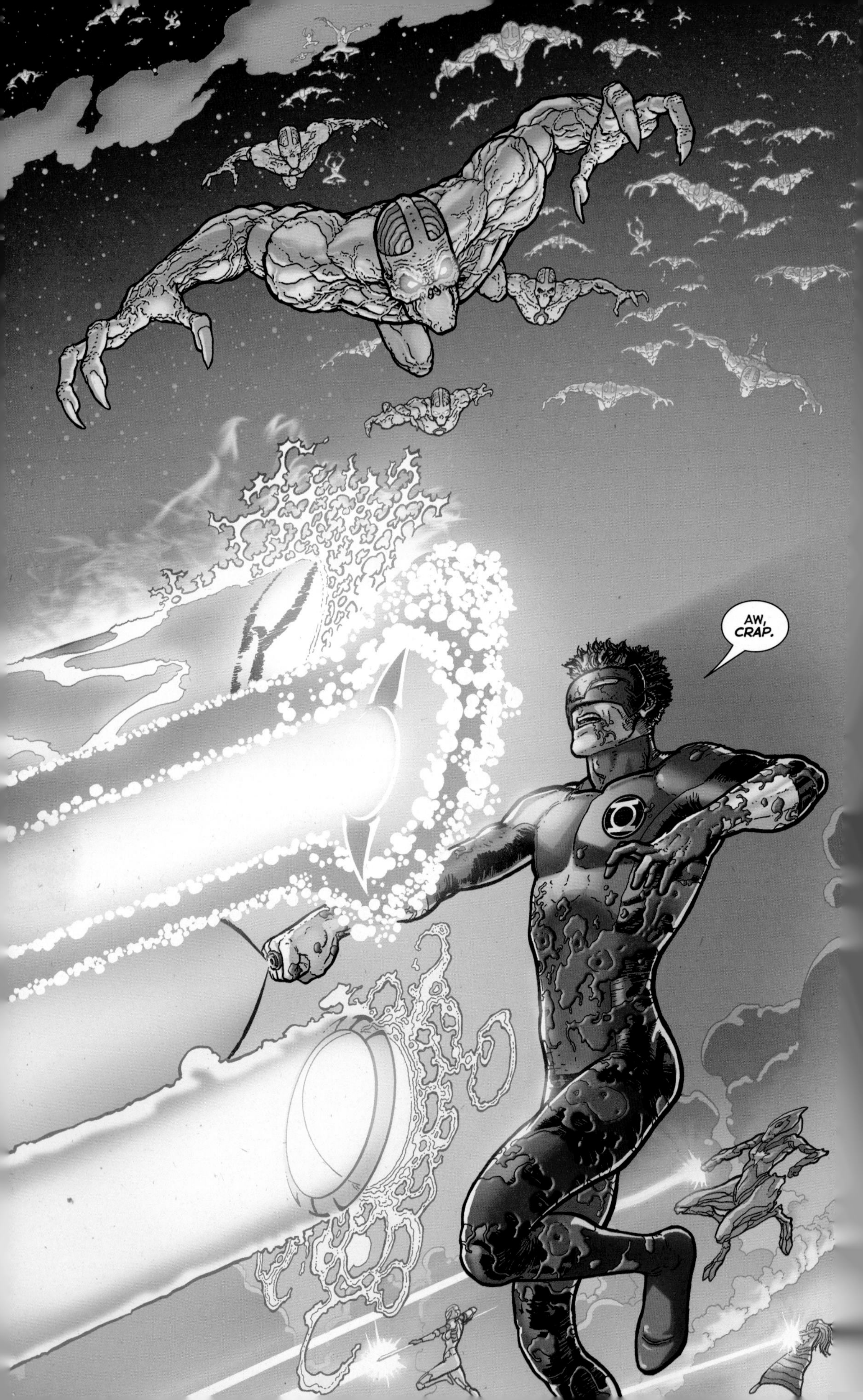
AW, CRAP.

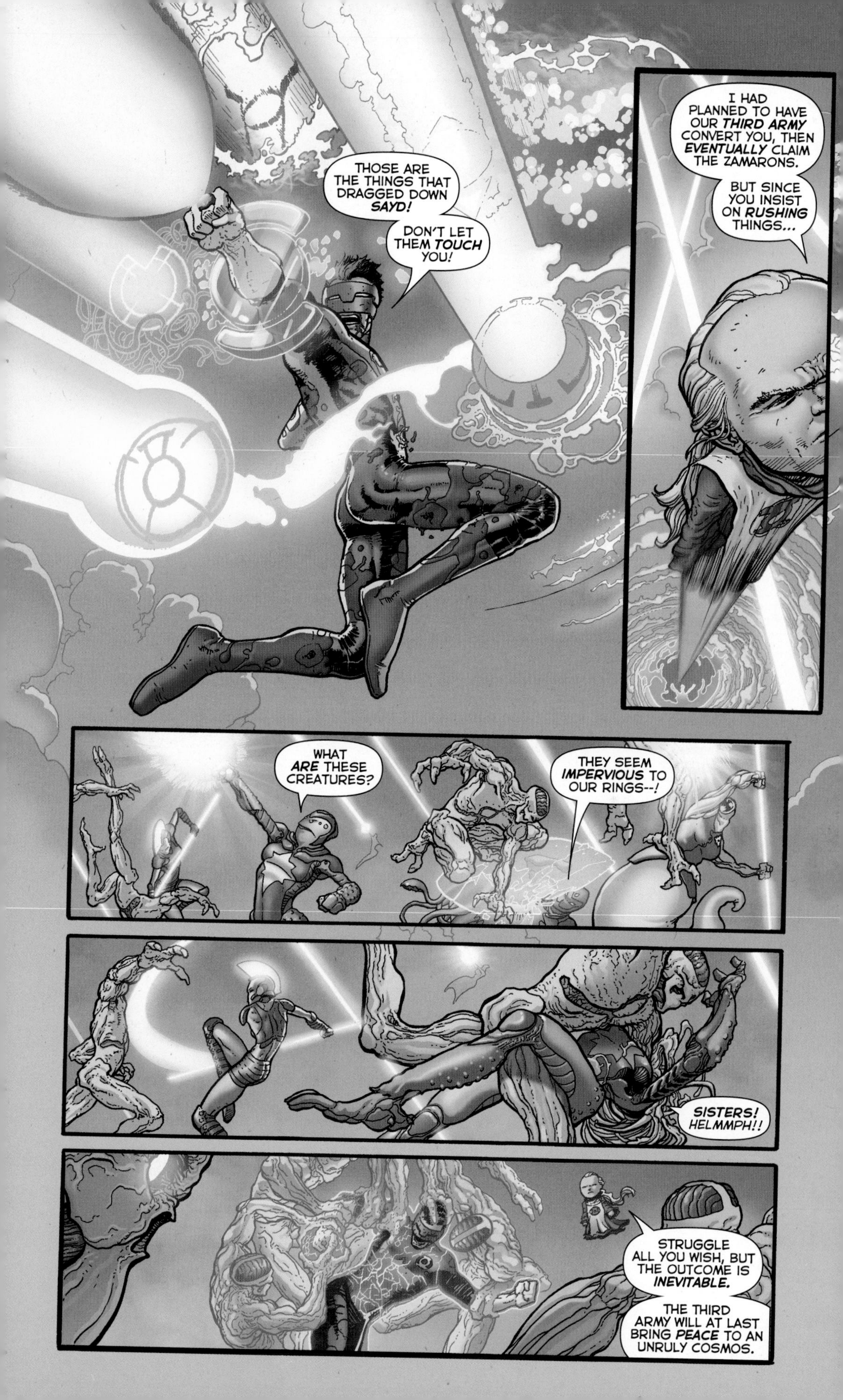
THOSE ARE THE THINGS THAT DRAGGED DOWN SAYD!
DON'T LET THEM TOUCH YOU!
I HAD PLANNED TO HAVE OUR THIRD ARMY CONVERT YOU, THEN EVENTUALLY CLAIM THE ZAMARONS.
BUT SINCE YOU INSIST ON RUSHING THINGS...
WHAT ARE THESE CREATURES?
THEY SEEM IMPERVIOUS TO OUR RINGS--!
SISTERS! HELMMPH!!
STRUGGLE ALL YOU WISH, BUT THE OUTCOME IS INEVITABLE.
THE THIRD ARMY WILL AT LAST BRING PEACE TO AN UNRULY COSMOS.

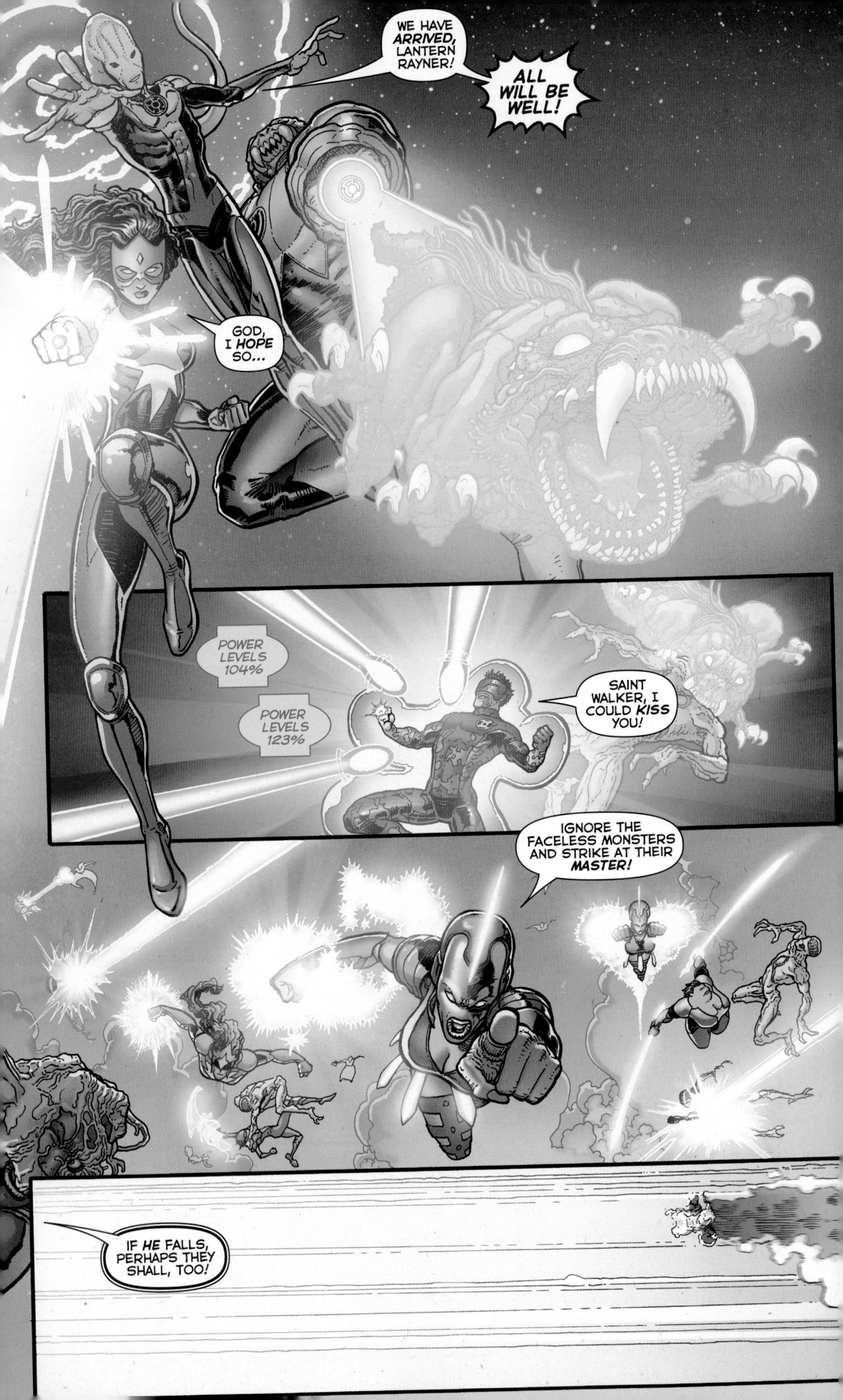
WE HAVE ARRIVED, LANTERN RAYNER!
ALL WILL BE WELL!
GOD, I HOPE SO...
POWER LEVELS 104%
POWER LEVELS 123%
SAINT WALKER, I COULD KISS YOU!
IGNORE THE FACELESS MONSTERS AND STRIKE AT THEIR MASTER!
IF HE FALLS, PERHAPS THEY SHALL, TOO!

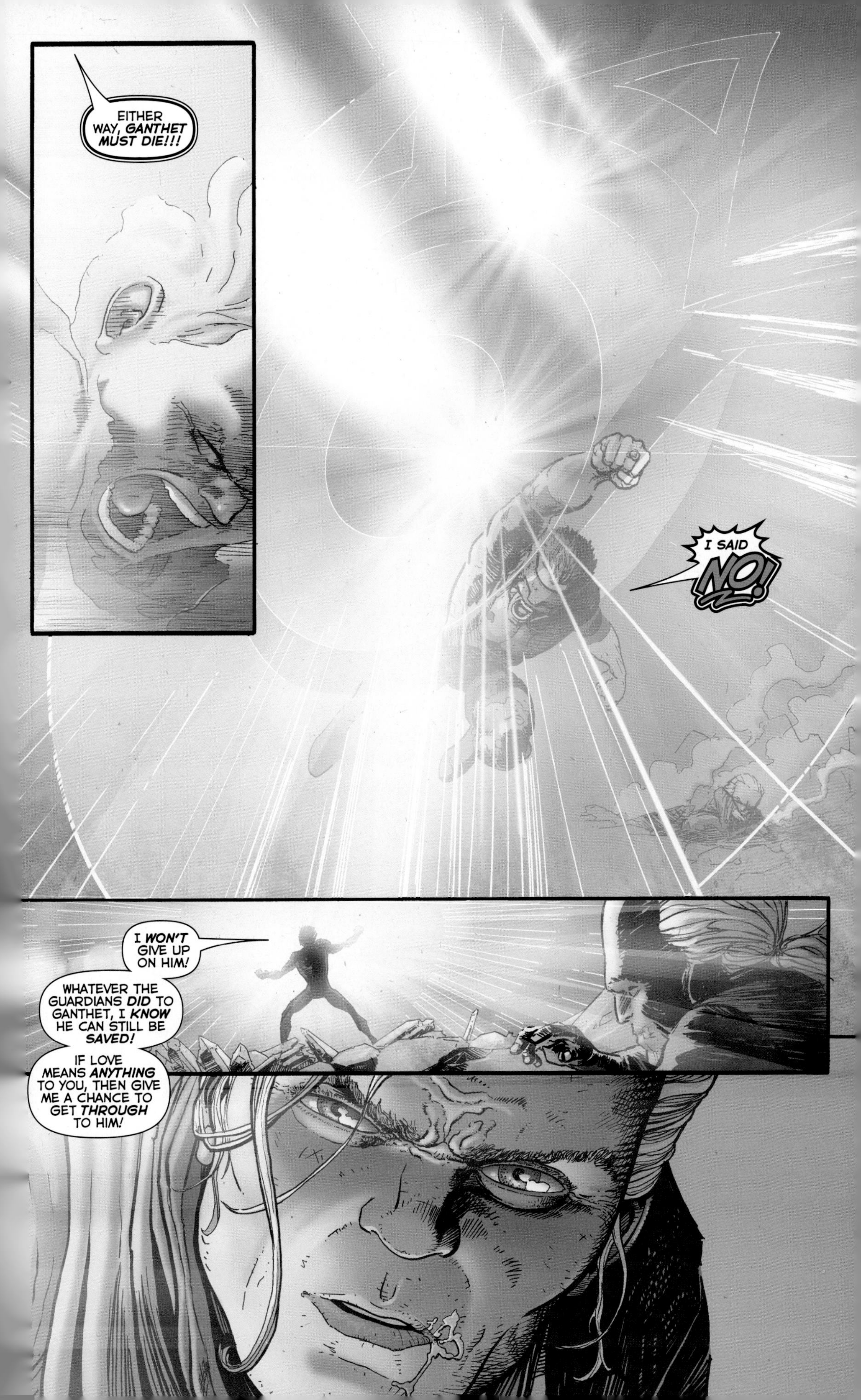
EITHER WAY, GANTHET MUST DIE!!!
I SAID NO!
I WON'T GIVE UP ON HIM!
WHATEVER THE GUARDIANS DID TO GANTHET, I KNOW HE CAN STILL BE SAVED!
IF LOVE MEANS ANYTHING TO YOU, THEN GIVE ME A CHANCE TO GET THROUGH TO HIM!

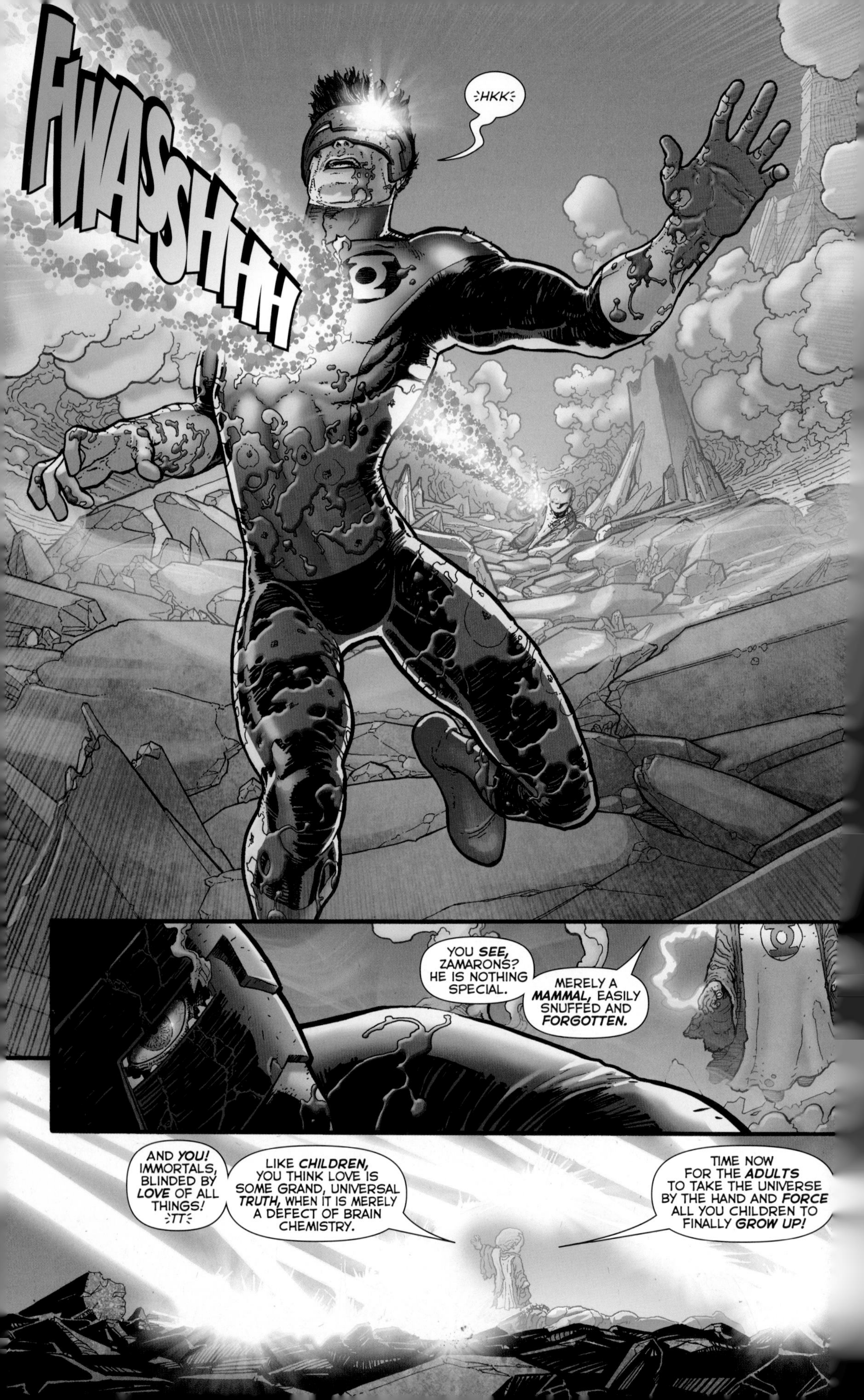
FWASHHH
HKK
YOU SEE, ZAMARONS? HE IS NOTHING SPECIAL.
MERELY A MAMMAL, EASILY SNUFFED AND FORGOTTEN.
AND YOU! IMMORTALS, BLINDED BY LOVE OF ALL THINGS! TT
LIKE CHILDREN, YOU THINK LOVE IS SOME GRAND, UNIVERSAL TRUTH, WHEN IT IS MERELY A DEFECT OF BRAIN CHEMISTRY.
TIME NOW FOR THE ADULTS TO TAKE THE UNIVERSE BY THE HAND AND FORCE ALL YOU CHILDREN TO FINALLY GROW UP!

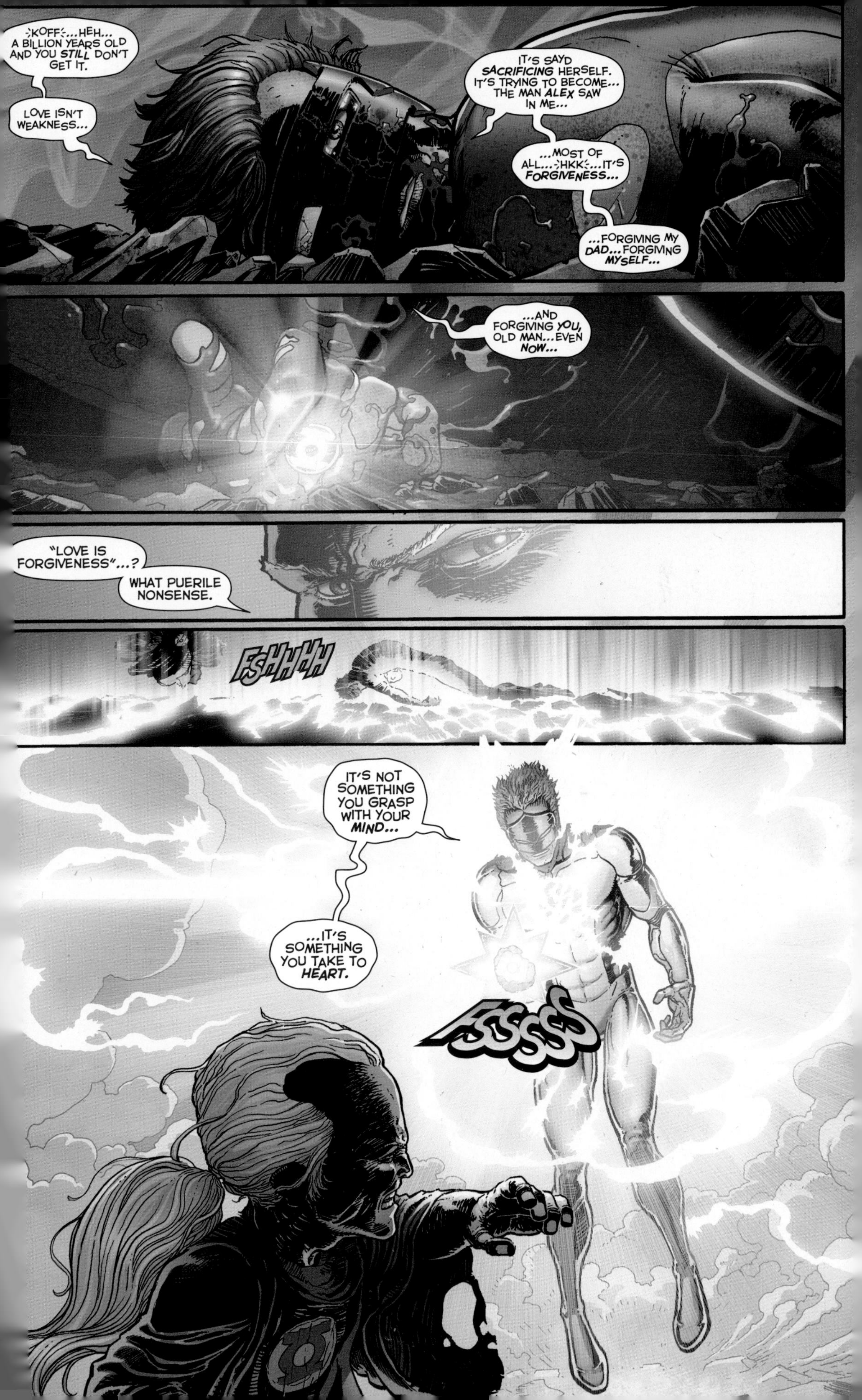

¦KOFF¦...HEH... A BILLION YEARS OLD AND YOU STILL DON'T GET IT.
LOVE ISN'T WEAKNESS...
IT'S SAYD SACRIFICING HERSELF. IT'S TRYING TO BECOME... THE MAN ALEX SAW IN ME...
...MOST OF ALL...¦HKK¦...IT'S FORGIVENESS...
...FORGIVING MY DAD...FORGIVING MYSELF...
...AND FORGIVING YOU, OLD MAN...EVEN NOW...
"LOVE IS FORGIVENESS"...?
WHAT PUERILE NONSENSE.
FSHHHH
IT'S NOT SOMETHING YOU GRASP WITH YOUR MIND...
...IT'S SOMETHING YOU TAKE TO HEART.
FSSSSS

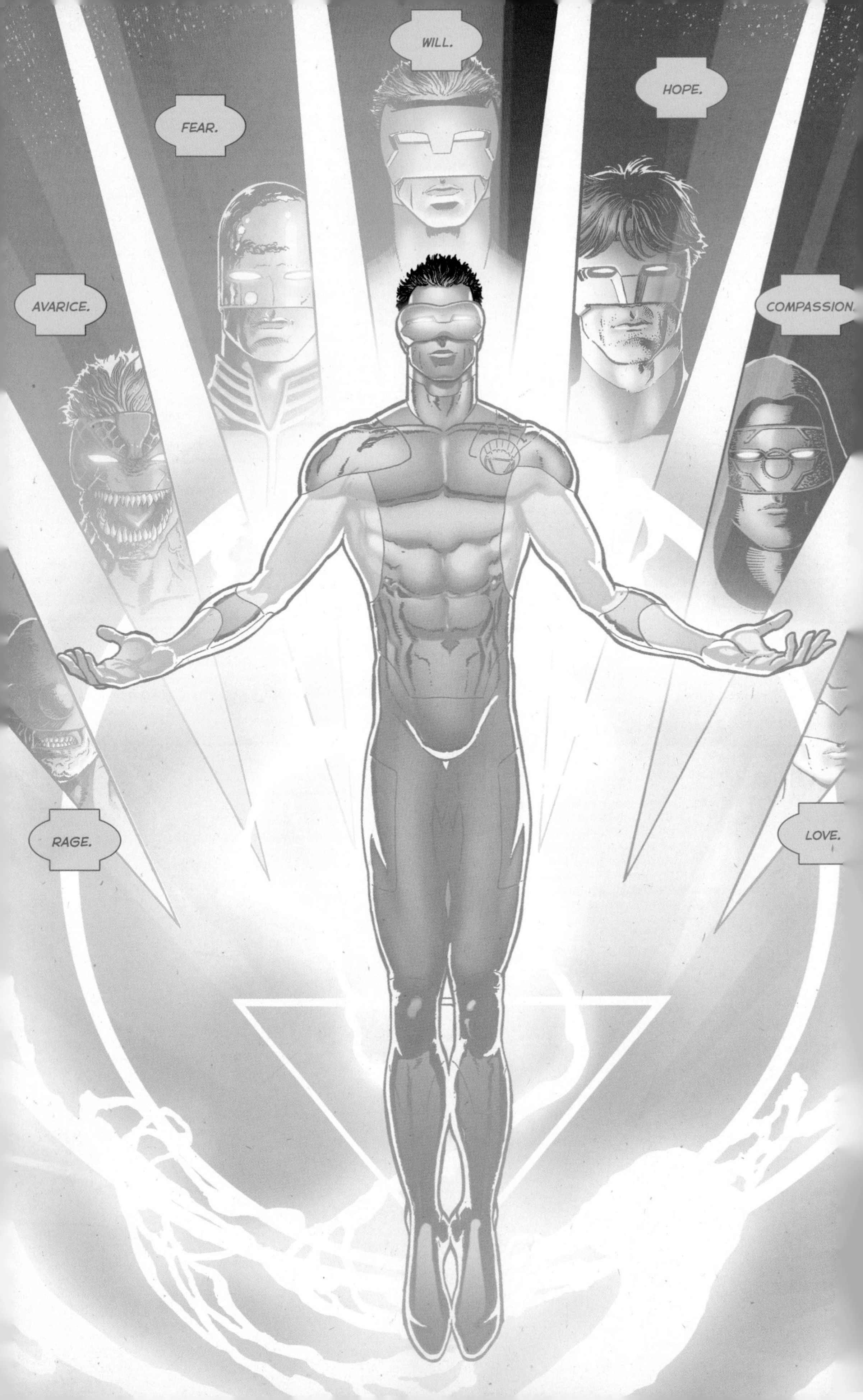
WILL.
HOPE.
FEAR.
AVARICE.
COMPASSION.
RAGE.
LOVE.

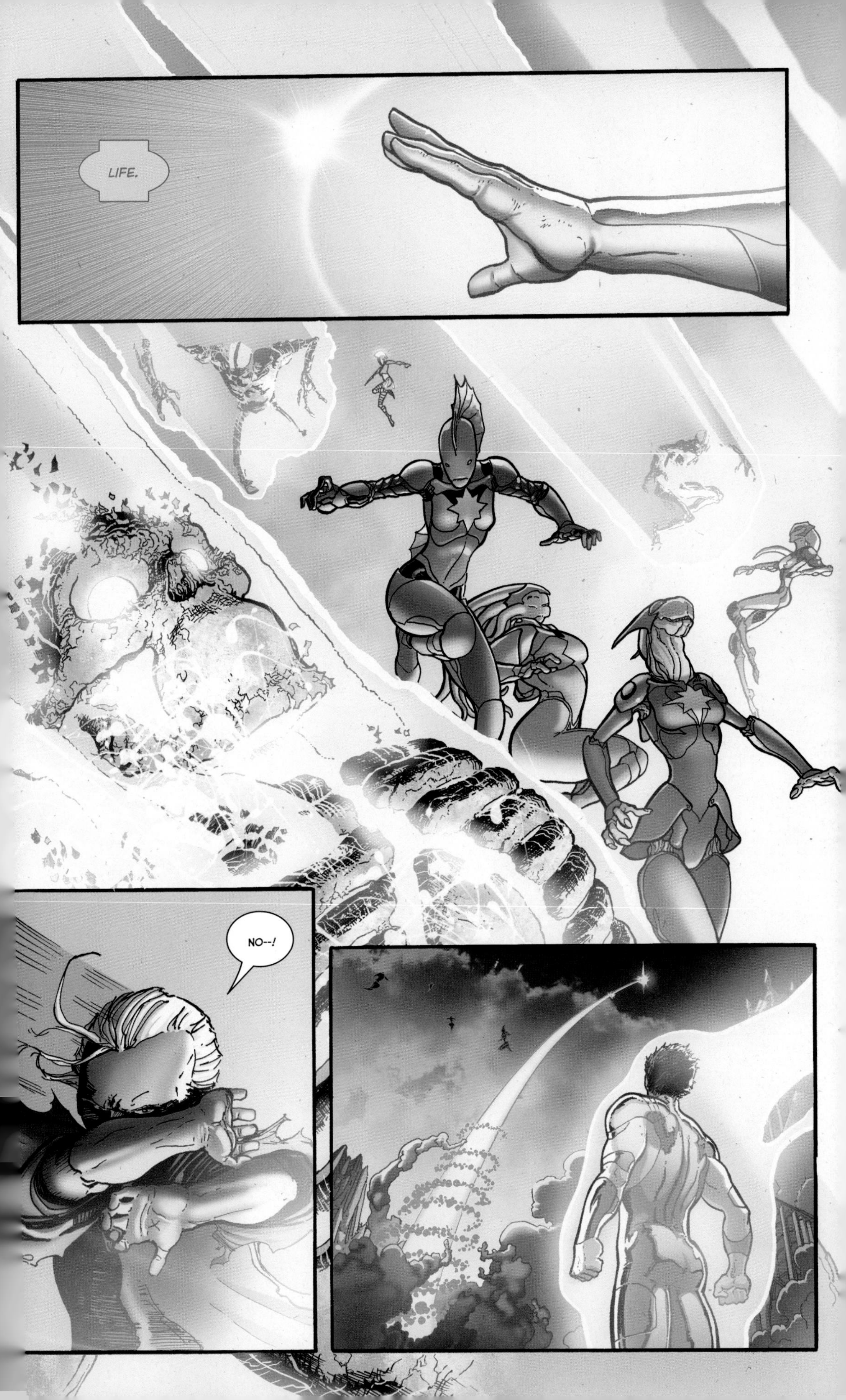
LIFE.
NO--!

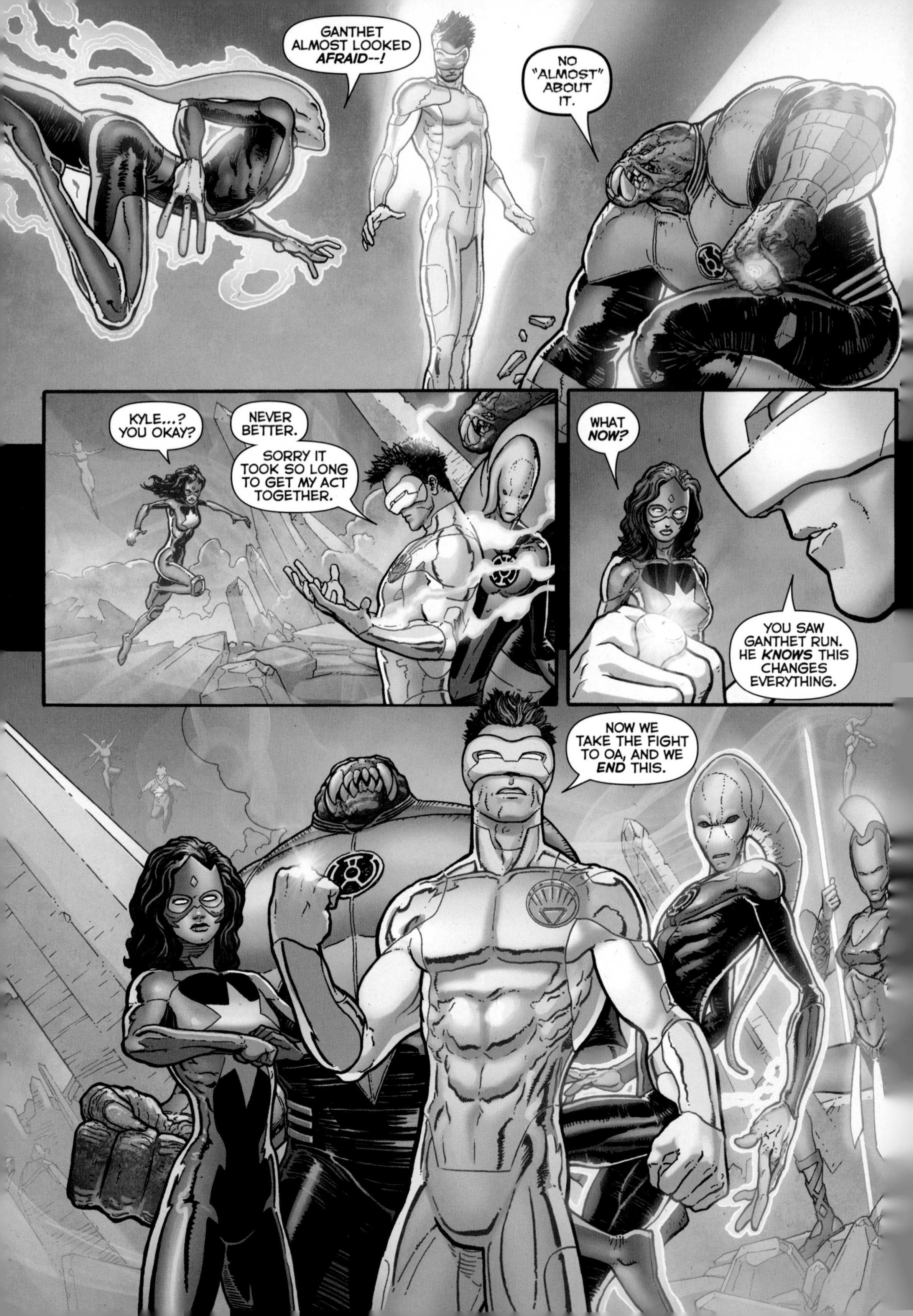
GANTHET ALMOST LOOKED AFRAID--!
NO "ALMOST" ABOUT IT.
KYLE...? YOU OKAY?
NEVER BETTER.
SORRY IT TOOK SO LONG TO GET MY ACT TOGETHER.
WHAT NOW?
YOU SAW GANTHET RUN. HE KNOWS THIS CHANGES EVERYTHING.
NOW WE TAKE THE FIGHT TO OA, AND WE END THIS.

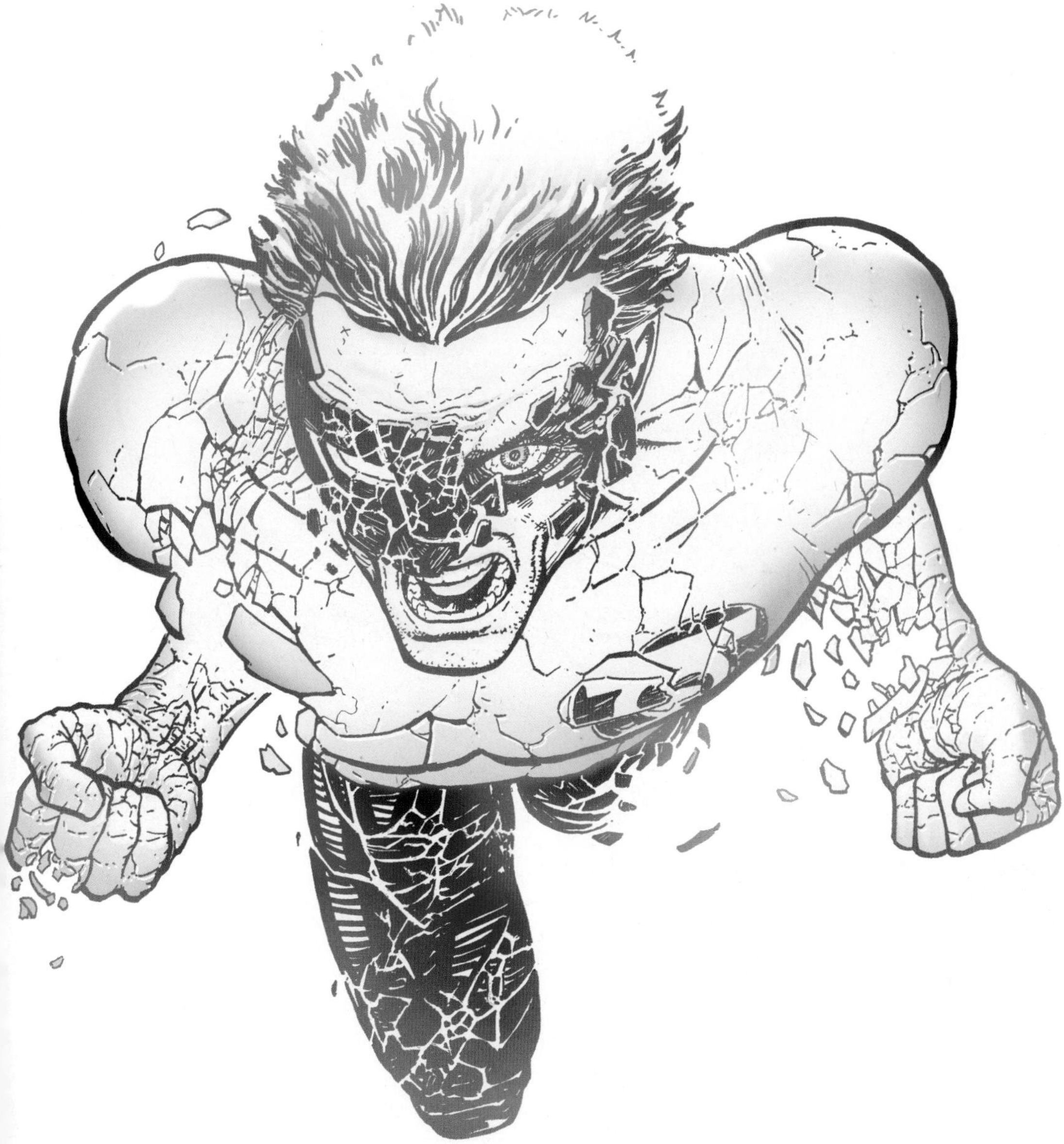

2 REUNIONS AND A FUNERAL

TONY BEDARD writer **AARON KUDER** artist
AARON KUDER & WIL QUINTANA cover

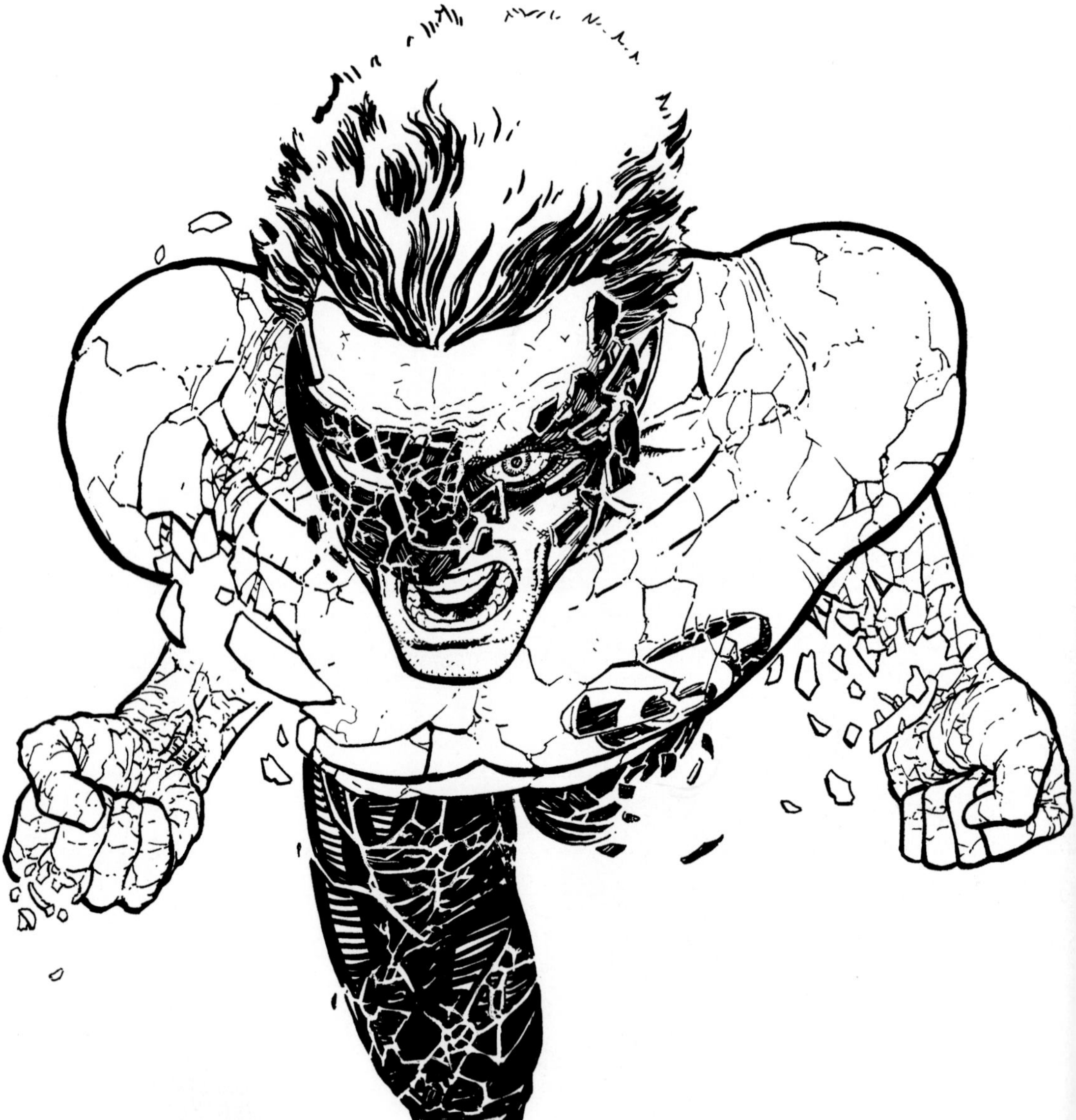

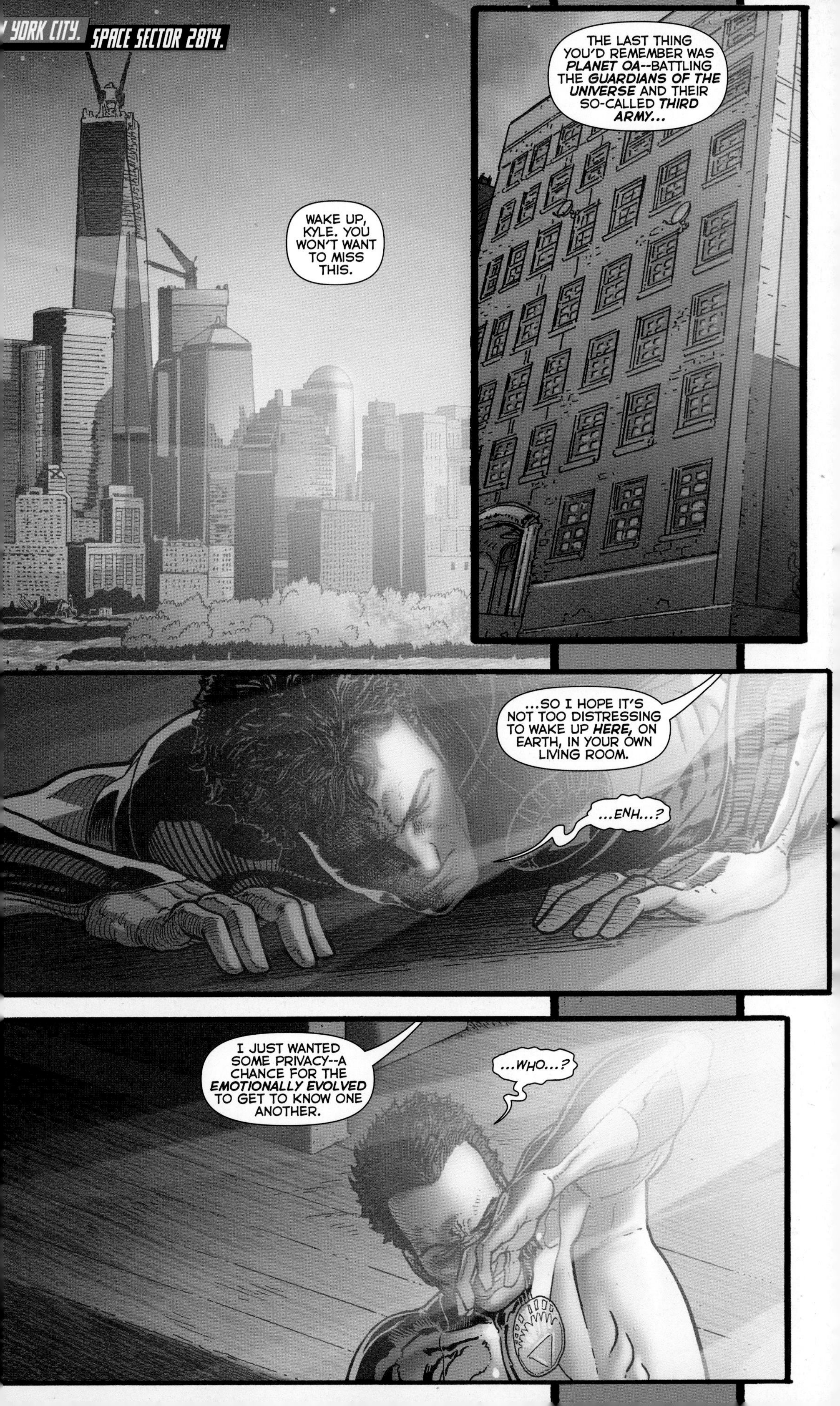
YORK CITY.
SPACE SECTOR 2814.
WAKE UP, KYLE. YOU WON'T WANT TO MISS THIS.
THE LAST THING YOU'D REMEMBER WAS PLANET OA--BATTLING THE GUARDIANS OF THE UNIVERSE AND THEIR SO-CALLED THIRD ARMY...
...SO I HOPE IT'S NOT TOO DISTRESSING TO WAKE UP HERE, ON EARTH, IN YOUR OWN LIVING ROOM.
...ENH...?
I JUST WANTED SOME PRIVACY--A CHANCE FOR THE EMOTIONALLY EVOLVED TO GET TO KNOW ONE ANOTHER.
...WHO...?

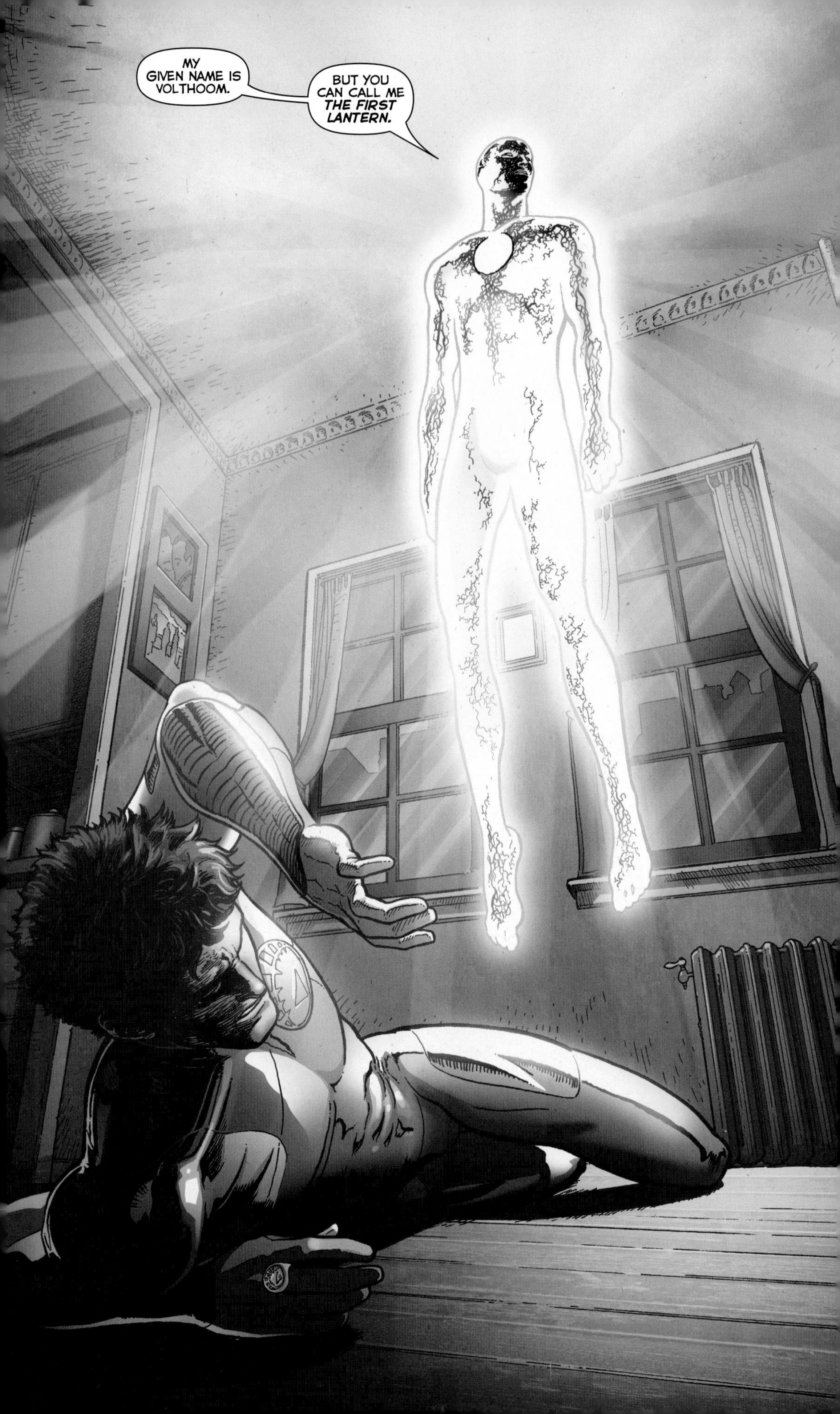
MY GIVEN NAME IS VOLTHOOM.
BUT YOU CAN CALL ME THE FIRST LANTERN.

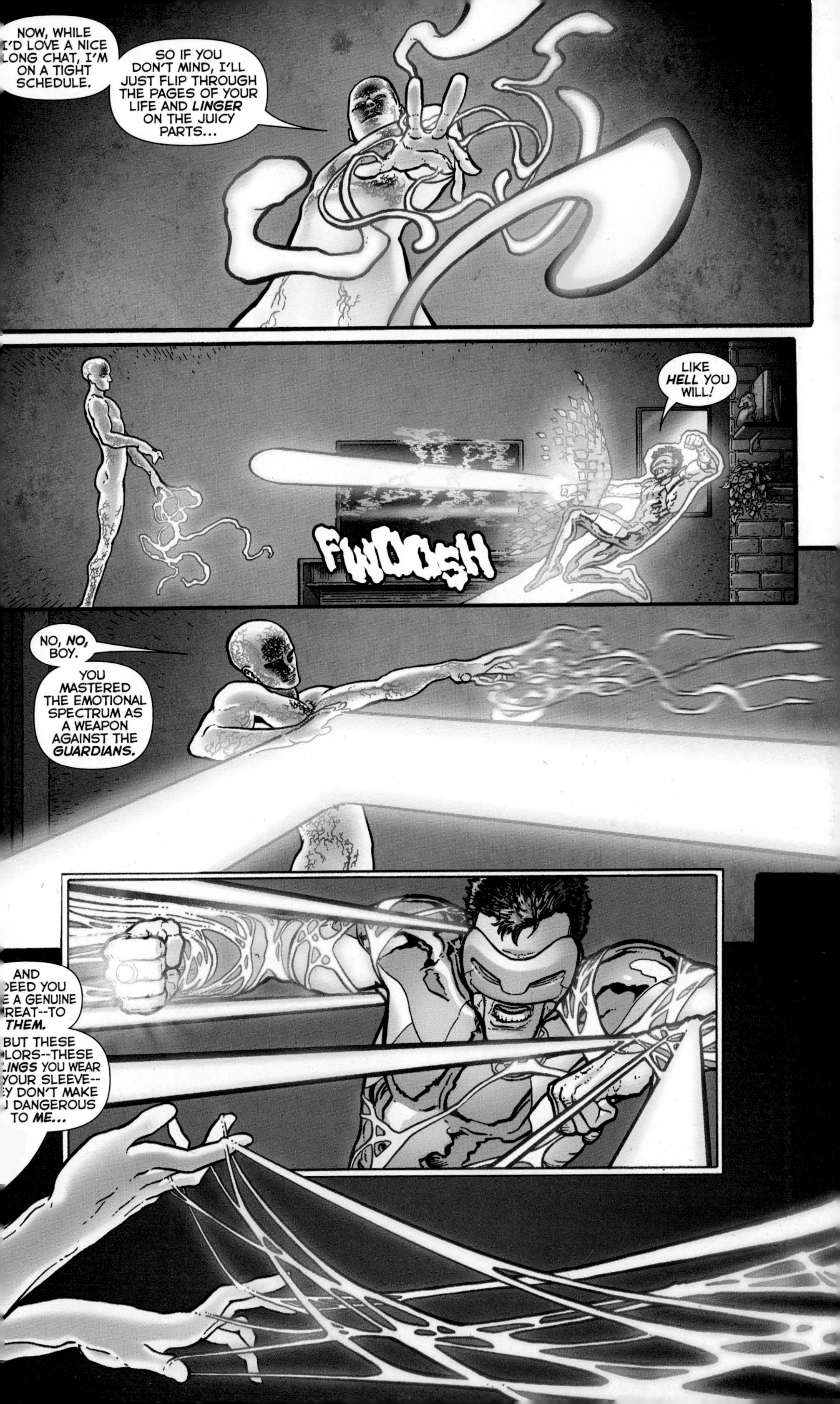

NOW, WHILE I'D LOVE A NICE LONG CHAT, I'M ON A TIGHT SCHEDULE.
SO IF YOU DON'T MIND, I'LL JUST FLIP THROUGH THE PAGES OF YOUR LIFE AND *LINGER* ON THE JUICY PARTS...
LIKE *HELL* YOU WILL!
FWOOSH
NO, *NO,* BOY.
YOU MASTERED THE EMOTIONAL SPECTRUM AS A WEAPON AGAINST THE *GUARDIANS.*
AND DEED YOU E A GENUINE REAT--TO *THEM.*
BUT THESE LORS--THESE *LINGS* YOU WEAR YOUR SLEEVE-- Y DON'T MAKE DANGEROUS TO *ME...*

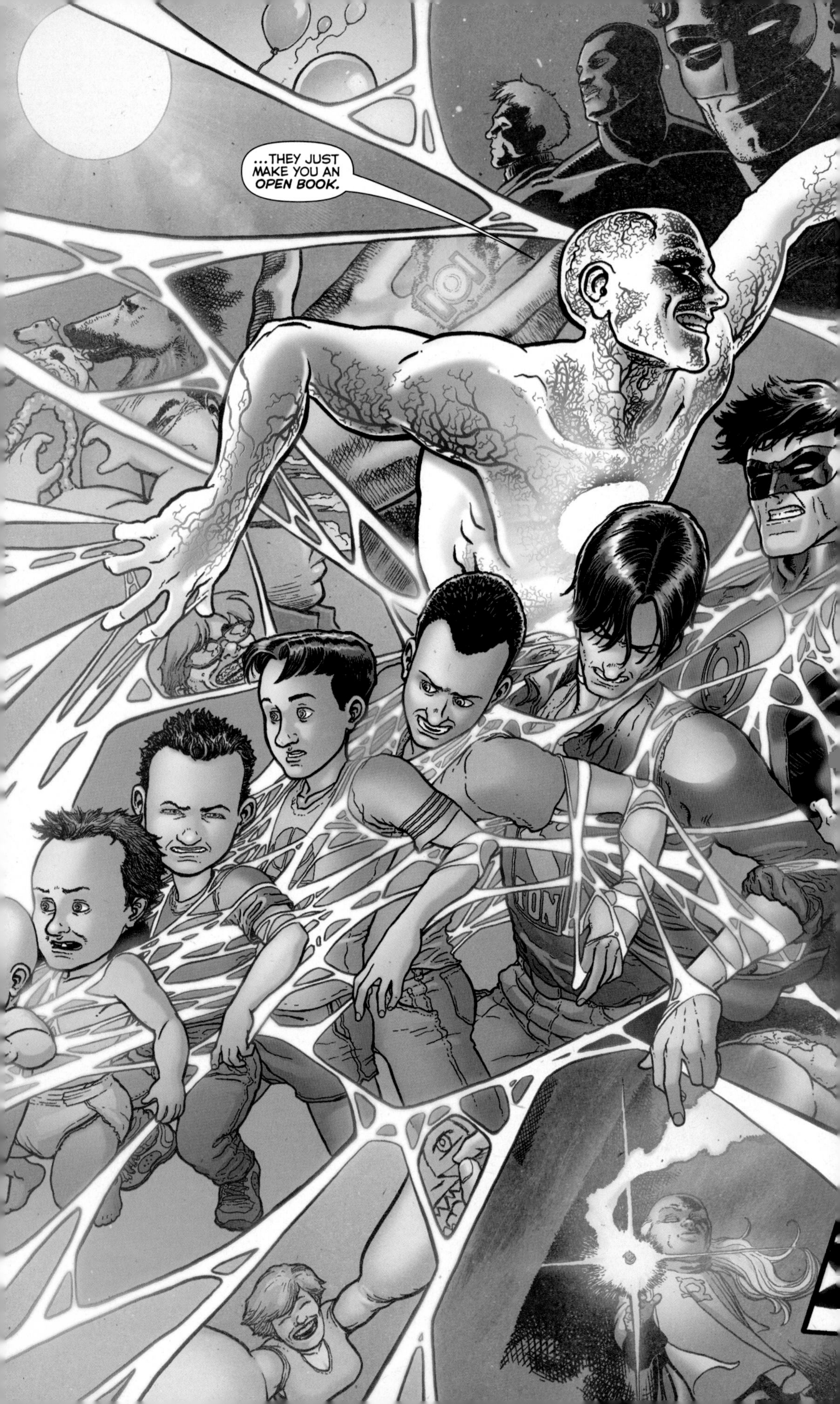
...THEY JUST MAKE YOU AN OPEN BOOK.

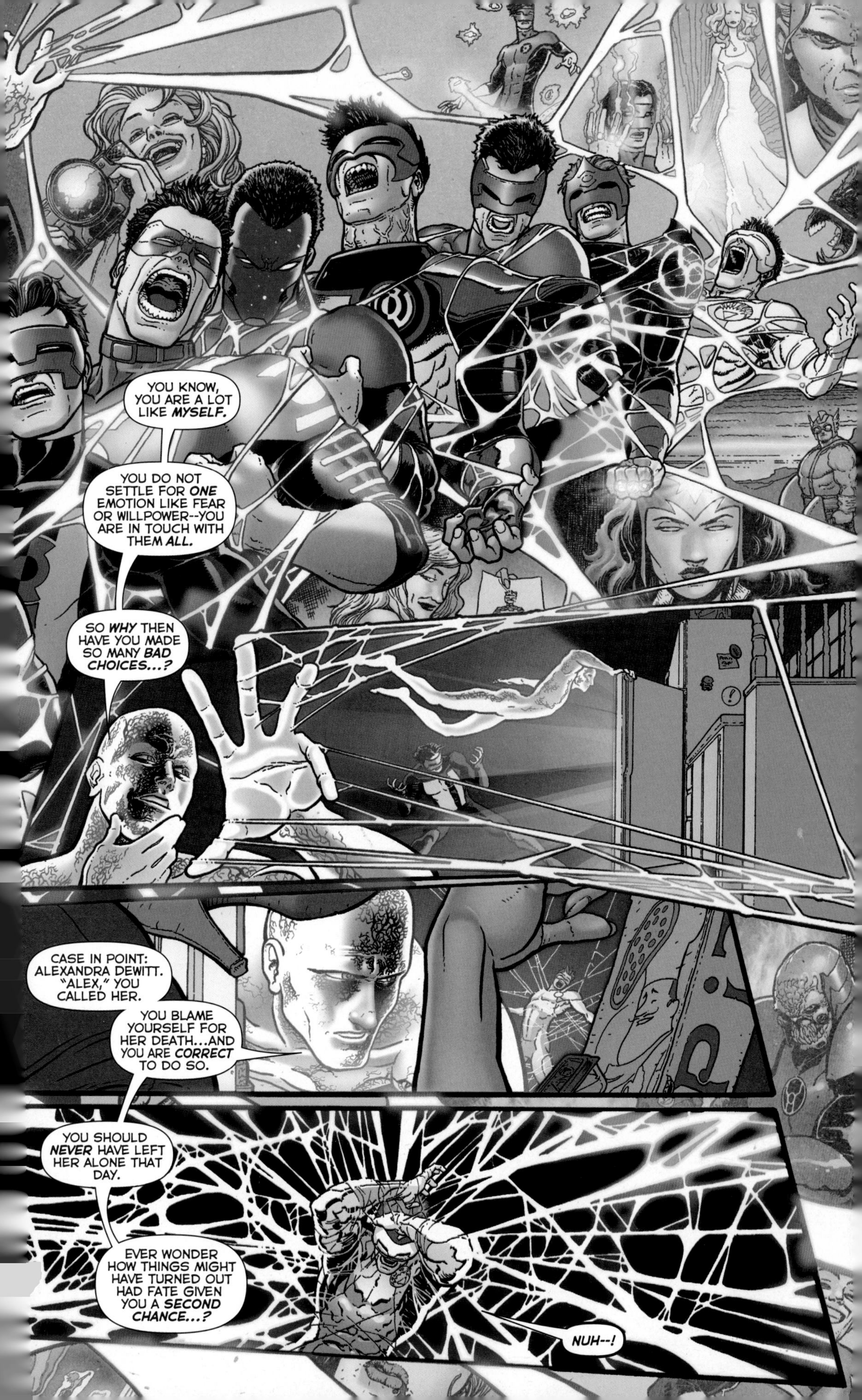
YOU KNOW, YOU ARE A LOT LIKE *MYSELF.*
YOU DO NOT SETTLE FOR *ONE* EMOTION LIKE FEAR OR WILLPOWER--YOU ARE IN TOUCH WITH THEM *ALL.*
SO *WHY* THEN HAVE YOU MADE SO MANY *BAD CHOICES...?*
CASE IN POINT: ALEXANDRA DEWITT. "ALEX," YOU CALLED HER.
YOU BLAME YOURSELF FOR HER DEATH...AND YOU ARE *CORRECT* TO DO SO.
YOU SHOULD *NEVER* HAVE LEFT HER ALONE THAT DAY.
EVER WONDER HOW THINGS MIGHT HAVE TURNED OUT HAD FATE GIVEN YOU A *SECOND CHANCE...?*
NUH--!

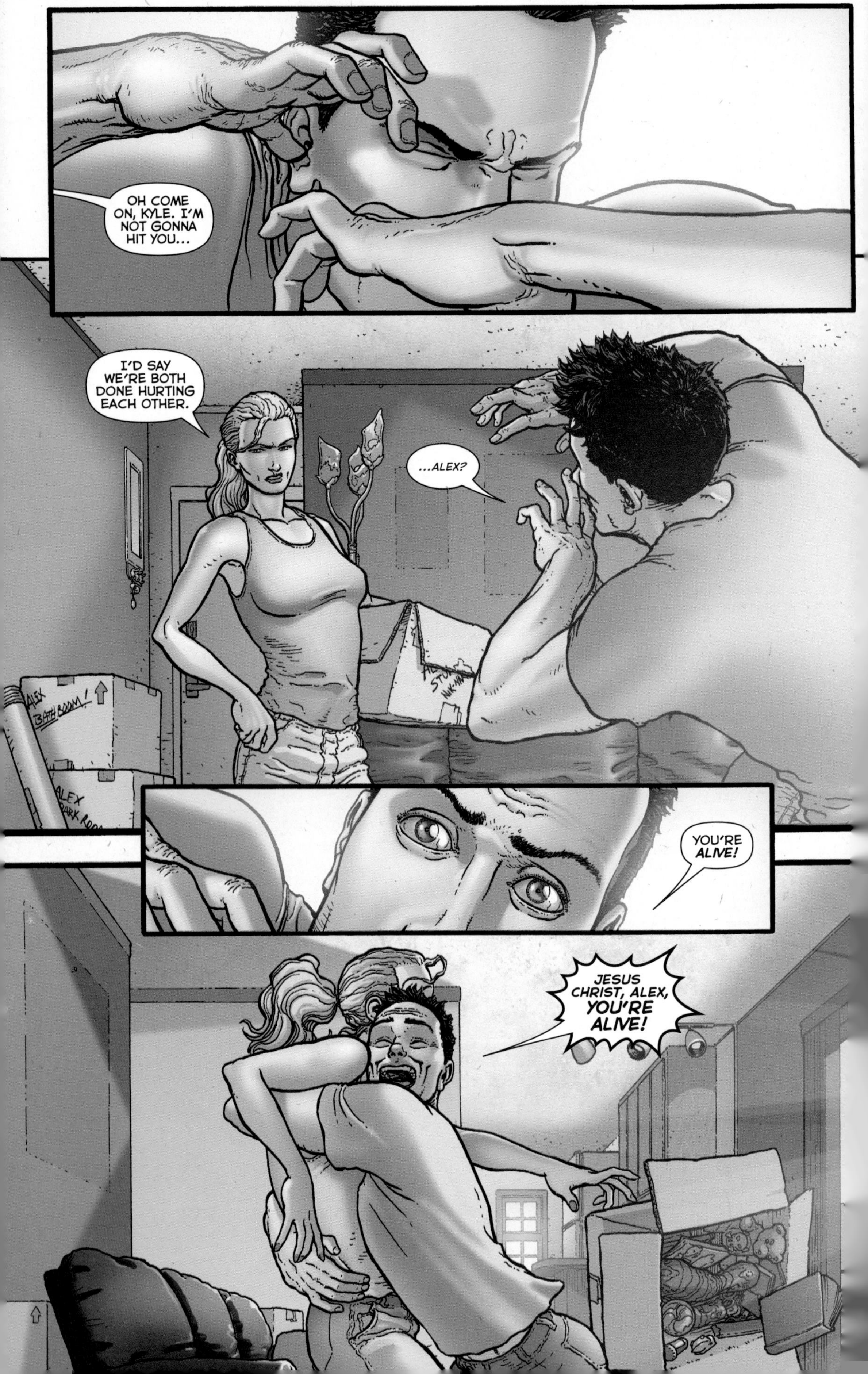
OH COME ON, KYLE. I'M NOT GONNA HIT YOU...
I'D SAY WE'RE BOTH DONE HURTING EACH OTHER.
...ALEX?
ALEX BATHROOM!
YOU'RE ALIVE!
JESUS CHRIST, ALEX, YOU'RE ALIVE!

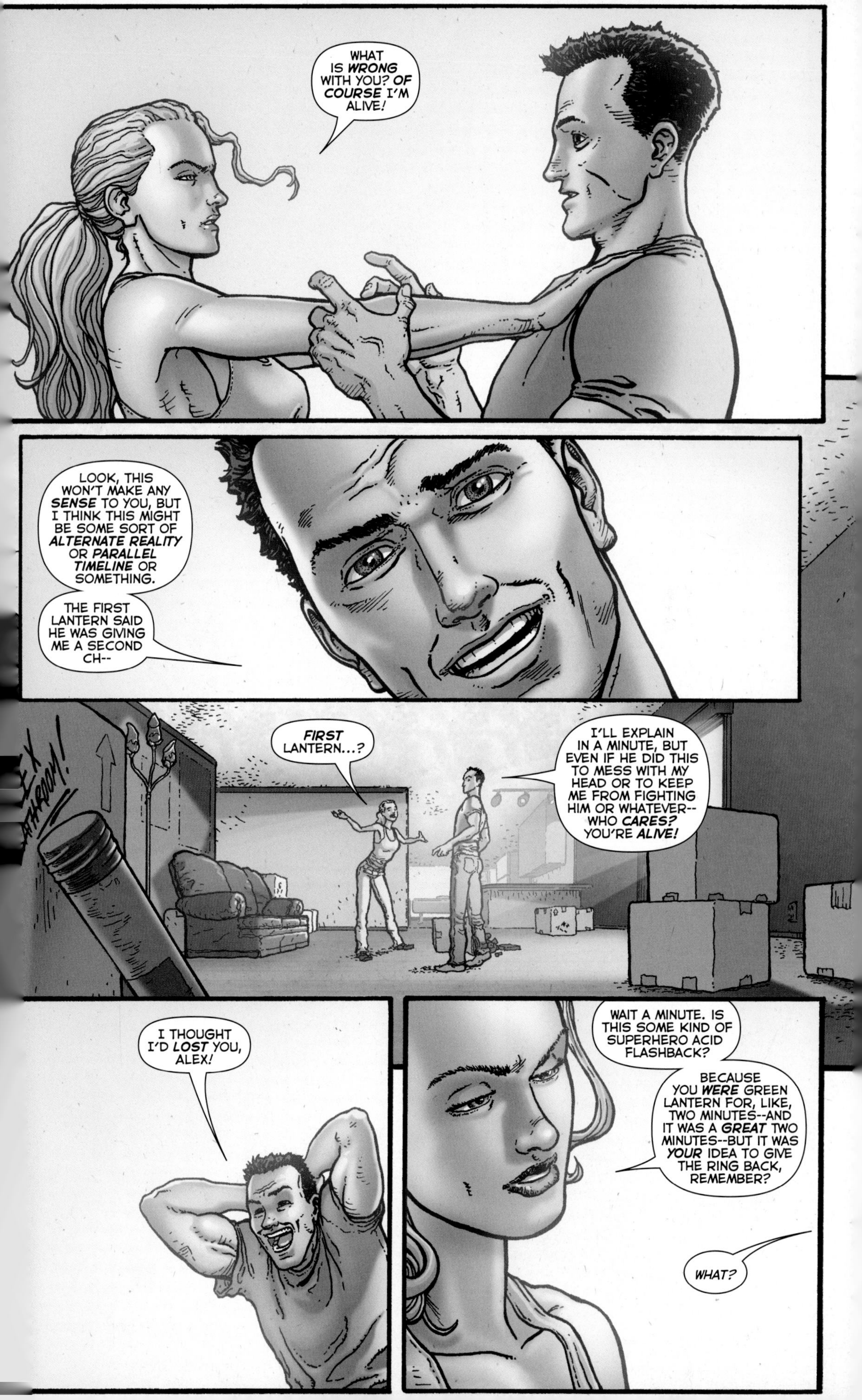

WHAT IS WRONG WITH YOU? OF COURSE I'M ALIVE!
LOOK, THIS WON'T MAKE ANY SENSE TO YOU, BUT I THINK THIS MIGHT BE SOME SORT OF ALTERNATE REALITY OR PARALLEL TIMELINE OR SOMETHING.
THE FIRST LANTERN SAID HE WAS GIVING ME A SECOND CH--
FIRST LANTERN...?
I'LL EXPLAIN IN A MINUTE, BUT EVEN IF HE DID THIS TO MESS WITH MY HEAD OR TO KEEP ME FROM FIGHTING HIM OR WHATEVER-- WHO CARES? YOU'RE ALIVE!
I THOUGHT I'D LOST YOU, ALEX!
WAIT A MINUTE. IS THIS SOME KIND OF SUPERHERO ACID FLASHBACK?
BECAUSE YOU WERE GREEN LANTERN FOR, LIKE, TWO MINUTES--AND IT WAS A GREAT TWO MINUTES--BUT IT WAS YOUR IDEA TO GIVE THE RING BACK, REMEMBER?
WHAT?

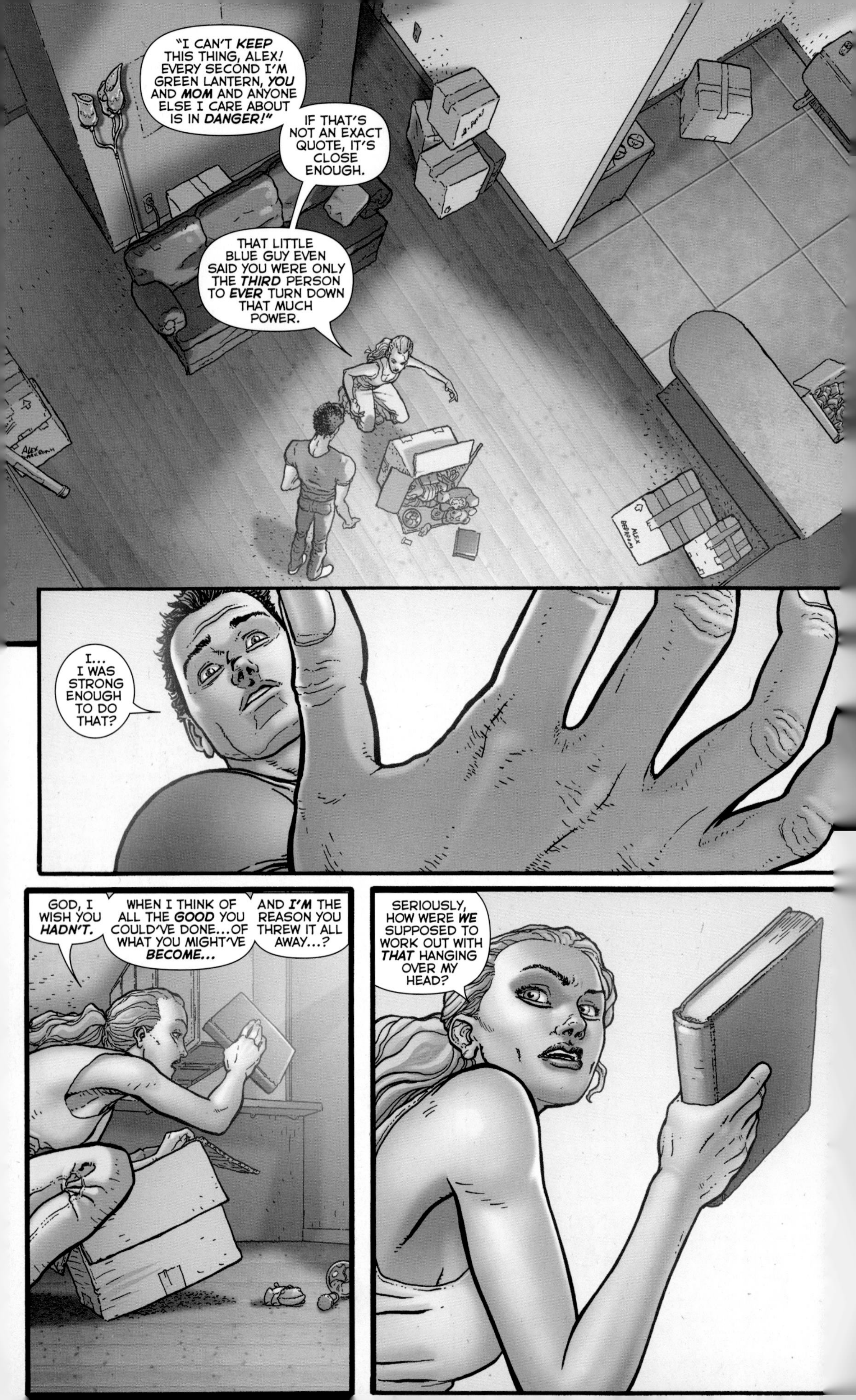
"I CAN'T KEEP THIS THING, ALEX! EVERY SECOND I'M GREEN LANTERN, YOU AND MOM AND ANYONE ELSE I CARE ABOUT IS IN DANGER!"
IF THAT'S NOT AN EXACT QUOTE, IT'S CLOSE ENOUGH.
THAT LITTLE BLUE GUY EVEN SAID YOU WERE ONLY THE THIRD PERSON TO EVER TURN DOWN THAT MUCH POWER.
I... I WAS STRONG ENOUGH TO DO THAT?
GOD, I WISH YOU HADN'T.
WHEN I THINK OF ALL THE GOOD YOU COULD'VE DONE...OF WHAT YOU MIGHT'VE BECOME...
AND I'M THE REASON YOU THREW IT ALL AWAY...?
SERIOUSLY, HOW WERE WE SUPPOSED TO WORK OUT WITH THAT HANGING OVER MY HEAD?

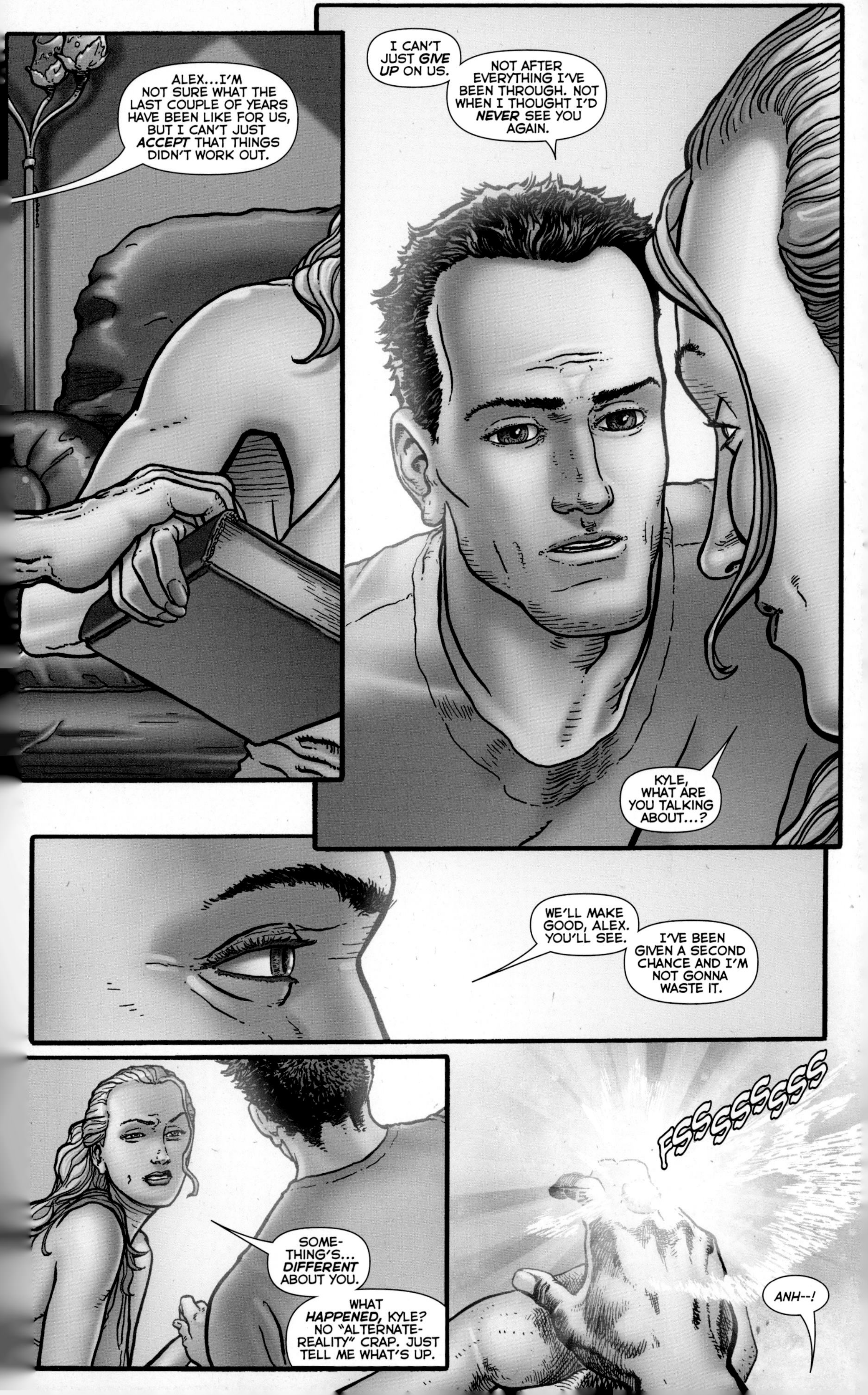
ALEX...I'M NOT SURE WHAT THE LAST COUPLE OF YEARS HAVE BEEN LIKE FOR US, BUT I CAN'T JUST ACCEPT THAT THINGS DIDN'T WORK OUT.
I CAN'T JUST GIVE UP ON US.
NOT AFTER EVERYTHING I'VE BEEN THROUGH. NOT WHEN I THOUGHT I'D NEVER SEE YOU AGAIN.
KYLE, WHAT ARE YOU TALKING ABOUT...?
WE'LL MAKE GOOD, ALEX. YOU'LL SEE.
I'VE BEEN GIVEN A SECOND CHANCE AND I'M NOT GONNA WASTE IT.
SOME-THING'S... DIFFERENT ABOUT YOU.
WHAT HAPPENED, KYLE? NO "ALTERNATE-REALITY" CRAP. JUST TELL ME WHAT'S UP.
FSSSSSSSS
ANH--!

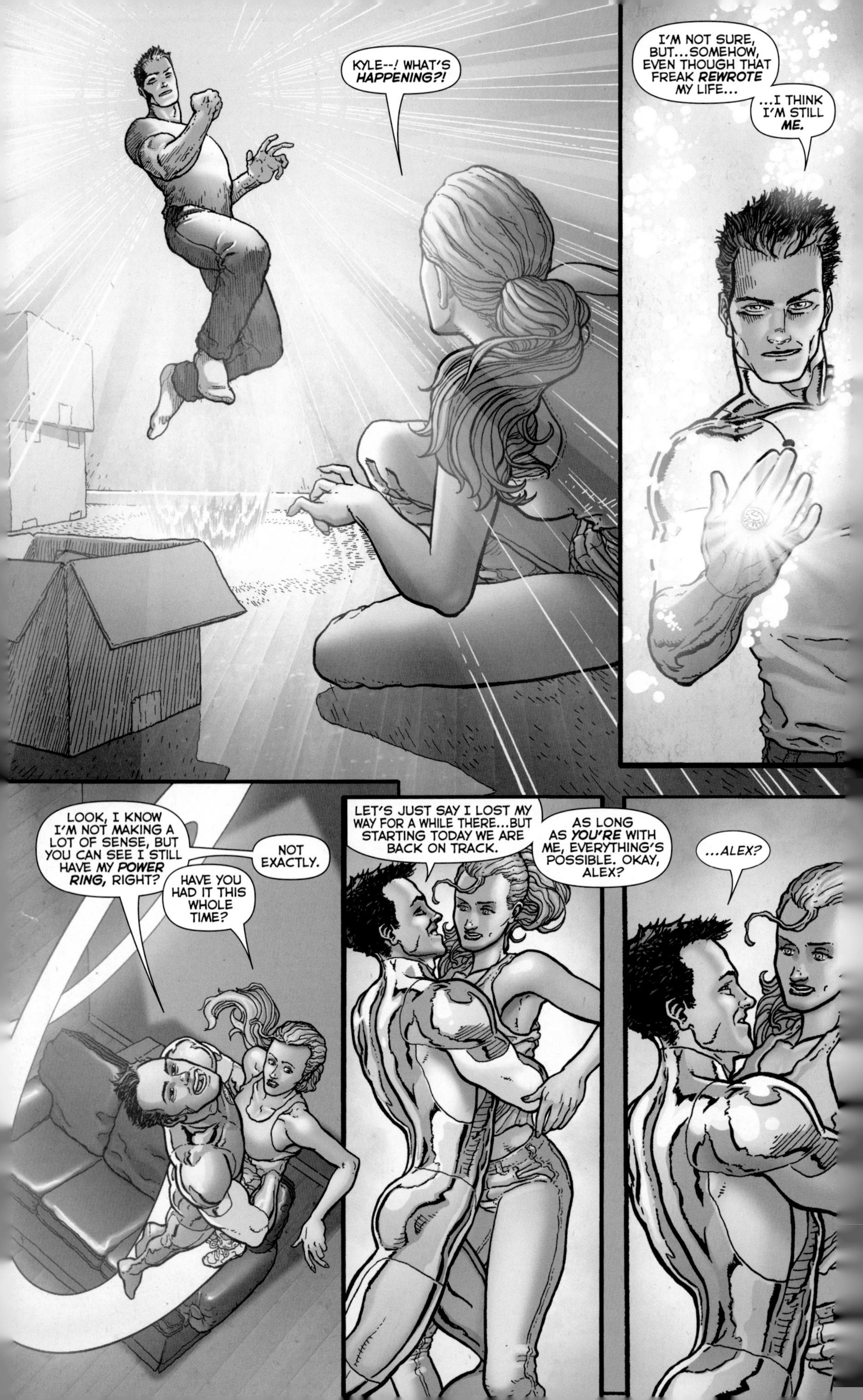
KYLE--! WHAT'S *HAPPENING?!*
I'M NOT SURE, BUT...SOMEHOW, EVEN THOUGH THAT FREAK *REWROTE* MY LIFE...
...I THINK I'M STILL *ME.*
LOOK, I KNOW I'M NOT MAKING A LOT OF SENSE, BUT YOU CAN SEE I STILL HAVE MY *POWER RING,* RIGHT?
NOT EXACTLY.
HAVE YOU HAD IT THIS WHOLE TIME?
LET'S JUST SAY I LOST MY WAY FOR A WHILE THERE...BUT STARTING TODAY WE ARE BACK ON TRACK.
AS LONG AS *YOU'RE* WITH ME, EVERYTHING'S POSSIBLE. OKAY, ALEX?
...ALEX?

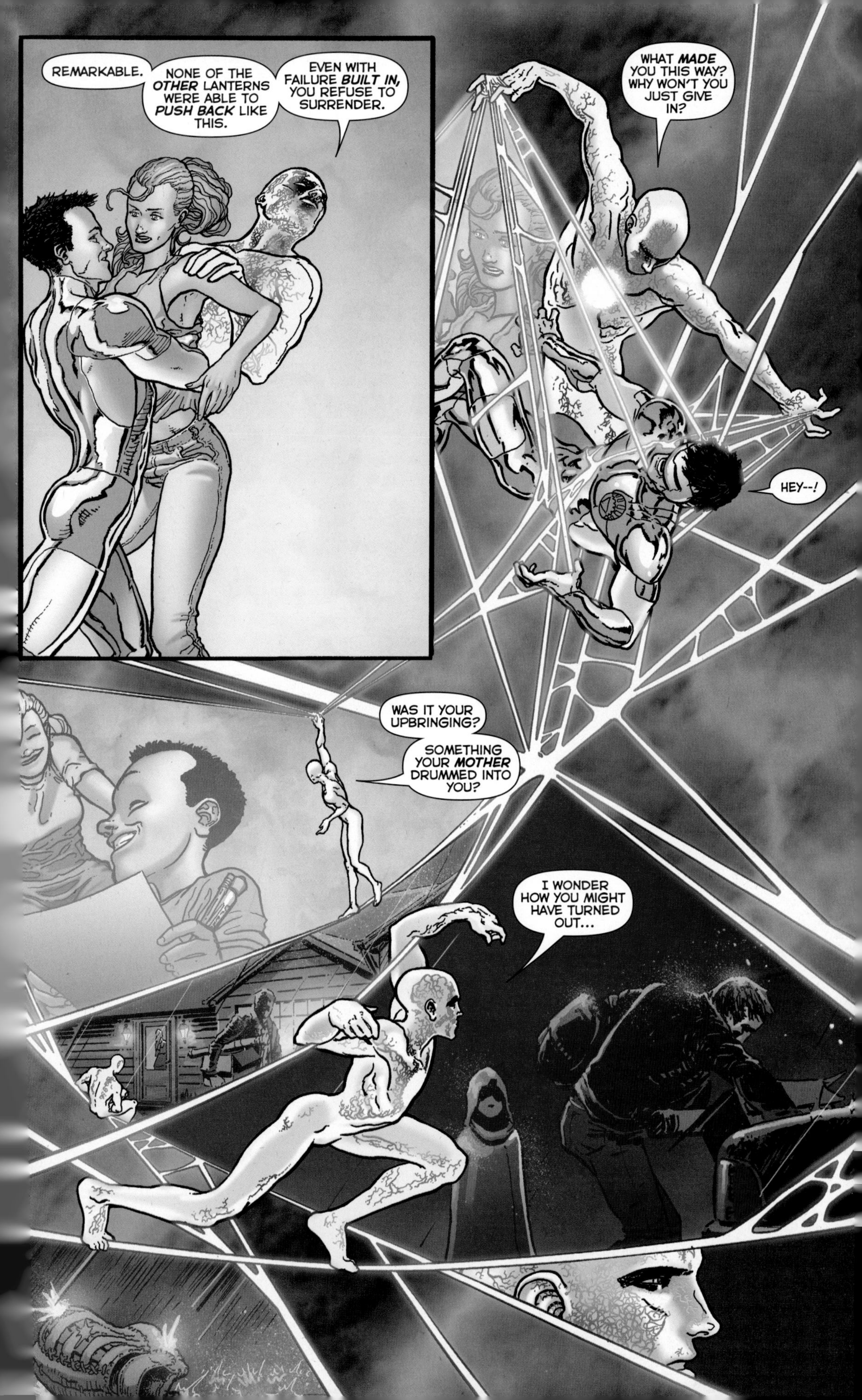
REMARKABLE.
NONE OF THE *OTHER* LANTERNS WERE ABLE TO *PUSH BACK* LIKE THIS.
EVEN WITH FAILURE *BUILT IN,* YOU REFUSE TO SURRENDER.
WHAT *MADE* YOU THIS WAY? WHY WON'T YOU JUST GIVE IN?
HEY--!
WAS IT YOUR UPBRINGING?
SOMETHING YOUR *MOTHER* DRUMMED INTO YOU?
I WONDER HOW YOU MIGHT HAVE TURNED OUT...

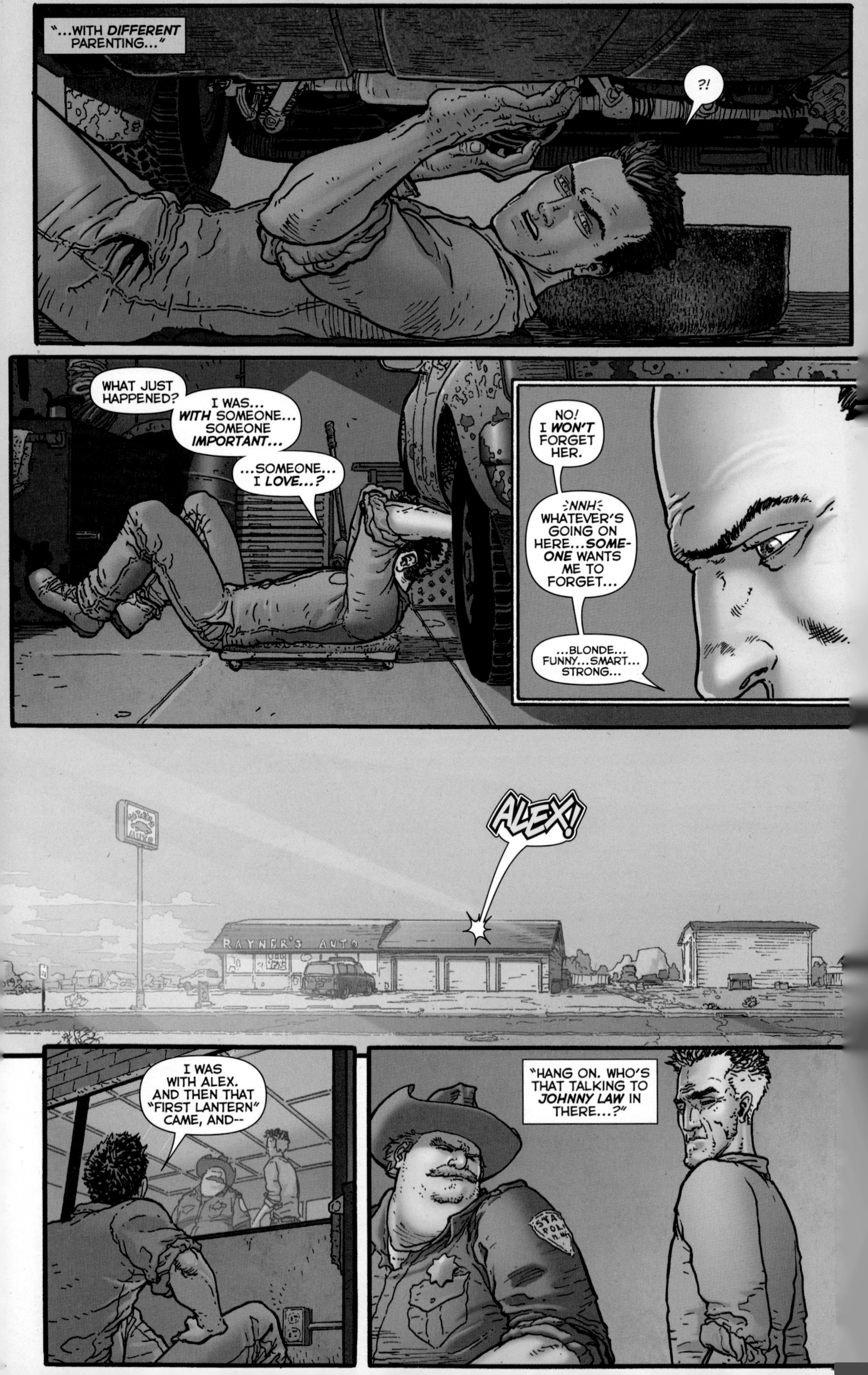
"...WITH DIFFERENT PARENTING..."
?!
WHAT JUST HAPPENED?
I WAS... WITH SOMEONE... SOMEONE IMPORTANT...
...SOMEONE... I LOVE...?
NO! I WON'T FORGET HER.
NNH WHATEVER'S GOING ON HERE...SOMEONE WANTS ME TO FORGET...
...BLONDE... FUNNY...SMART... STRONG...
ALEX!
RAYNER'S AUTO
I WAS WITH ALEX. AND THEN THAT "FIRST LANTERN" CAME, AND--
"HANG ON. WHO'S THAT TALKING TO JOHNNY LAW IN THERE...?"

HOLY CRAP, THAT'S MY *DAD*--!

HEY! SINCE WHEN DOES THE STORE PAY THE CUSTOMER?

GET BACK TO *WORK*, KYLE.

HANKS FOR RENT, CHIEF. HAVE A NICE DAY.

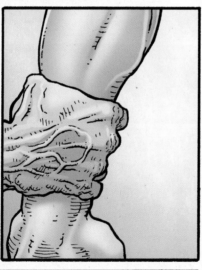

KYLE, WHAT'RE YOU *THINKING*--?!

WHAT, I'M JUST SUPPOSED TO LOOK THE OTHER WAY WHILE SHERIFF LARD-BUTT *SHAKES YOU DOWN?*

YES!

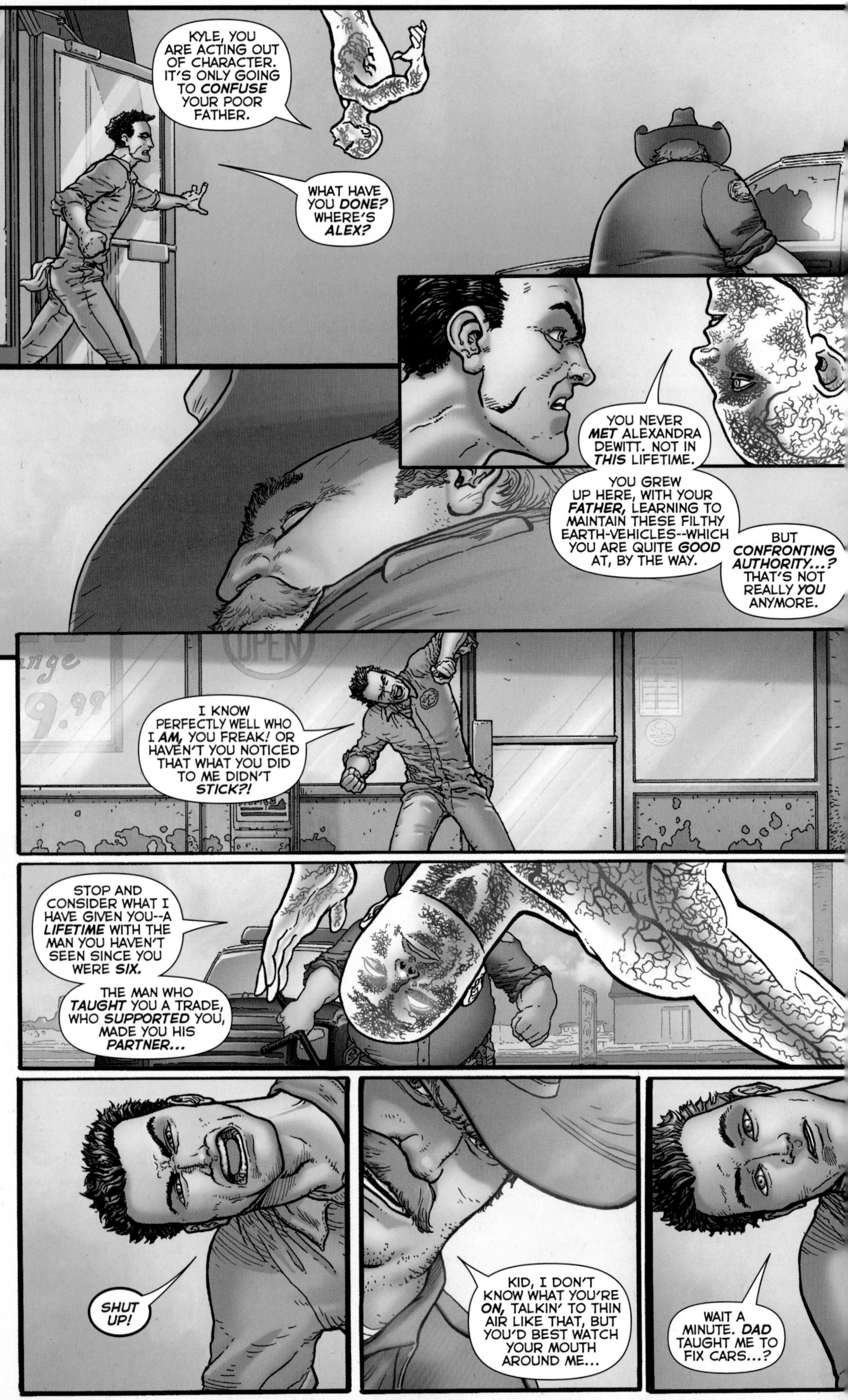
KYLE, YOU ARE ACTING OUT OF CHARACTER. IT'S ONLY GOING TO CONFUSE YOUR POOR FATHER.
WHAT HAVE YOU DONE? WHERE'S ALEX?
YOU NEVER MET ALEXANDRA DEWITT. NOT IN THIS LIFETIME.
YOU GREW UP HERE, WITH YOUR FATHER, LEARNING TO MAINTAIN THESE FILTHY EARTH-VEHICLES--WHICH YOU ARE QUITE GOOD AT, BY THE WAY.
BUT CONFRONTING AUTHORITY...? THAT'S NOT REALLY YOU ANYMORE.
OPEN
I KNOW PERFECTLY WELL WHO I AM, YOU FREAK! OR HAVEN'T YOU NOTICED THAT WHAT YOU DID TO ME DIDN'T STICK?!
STOP AND CONSIDER WHAT I HAVE GIVEN YOU--A LIFETIME WITH THE MAN YOU HAVEN'T SEEN SINCE YOU WERE SIX.
THE MAN WHO TAUGHT YOU A TRADE, WHO SUPPORTED YOU, MADE YOU HIS PARTNER...
SHUT UP!
KID, I DON'T KNOW WHAT YOU'RE ON, TALKIN' TO THIN AIR LIKE THAT, BUT YOU'D BEST WATCH YOUR MOUTH AROUND ME...
WAIT A MINUTE. DAD TAUGHT ME TO FIX CARS...?

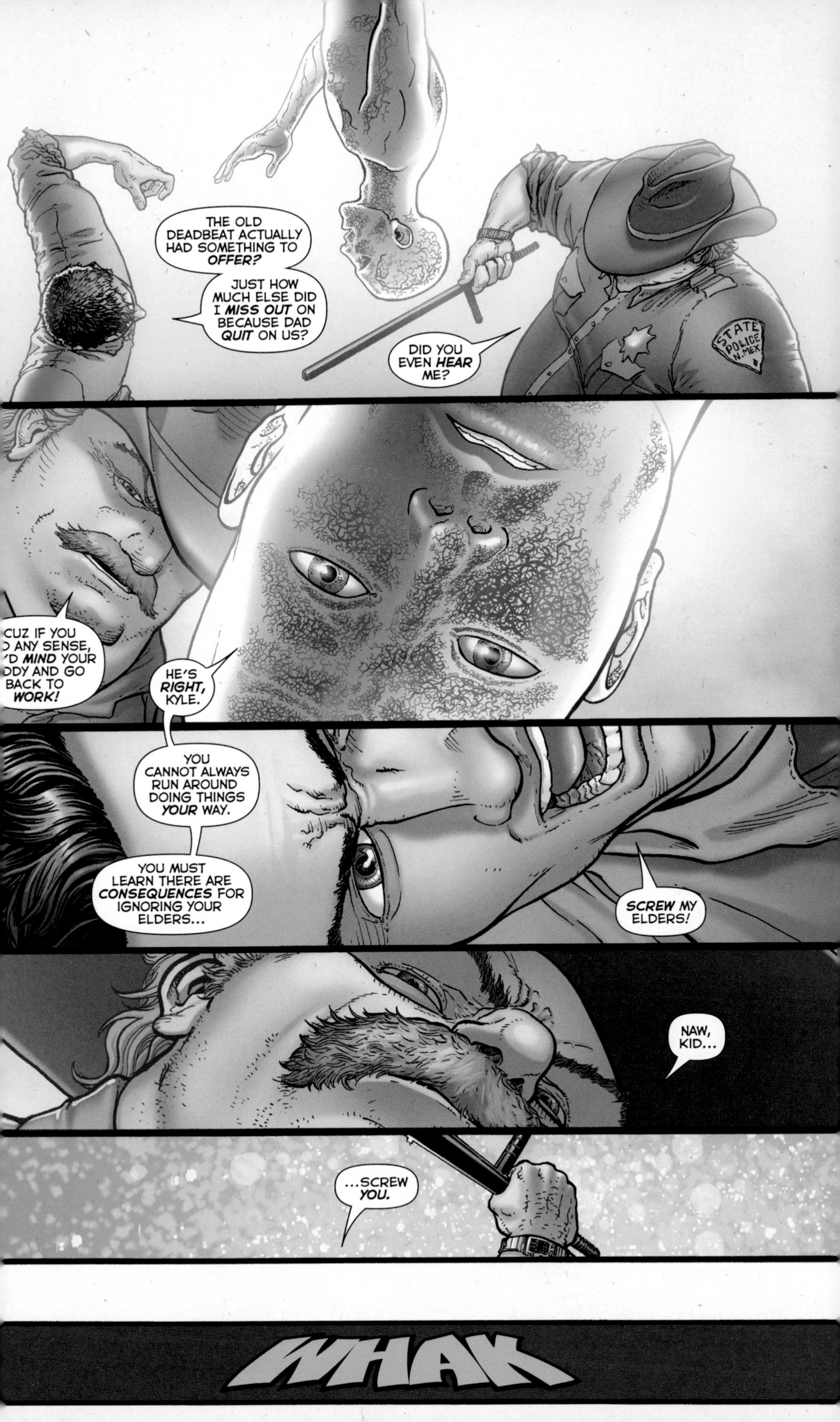
THE OLD DEADBEAT ACTUALLY HAD SOMETHING TO *OFFER?*
JUST HOW MUCH ELSE DID I *MISS OUT* ON BECAUSE DAD *QUIT* ON US?
DID YOU EVEN *HEAR* ME?
CUZ IF YOU D ANY SENSE, 'D *MIND* YOUR DDY AND GO BACK TO *WORK!*
HE'S *RIGHT,* KYLE.
YOU CANNOT ALWAYS RUN AROUND DOING THINGS *YOUR* WAY.
YOU MUST LEARN THERE ARE *CONSEQUENCES* FOR IGNORING YOUR ELDERS...
SCREW MY ELDERS!
NAW, KID...
...SCREW *YOU.*
WHAK

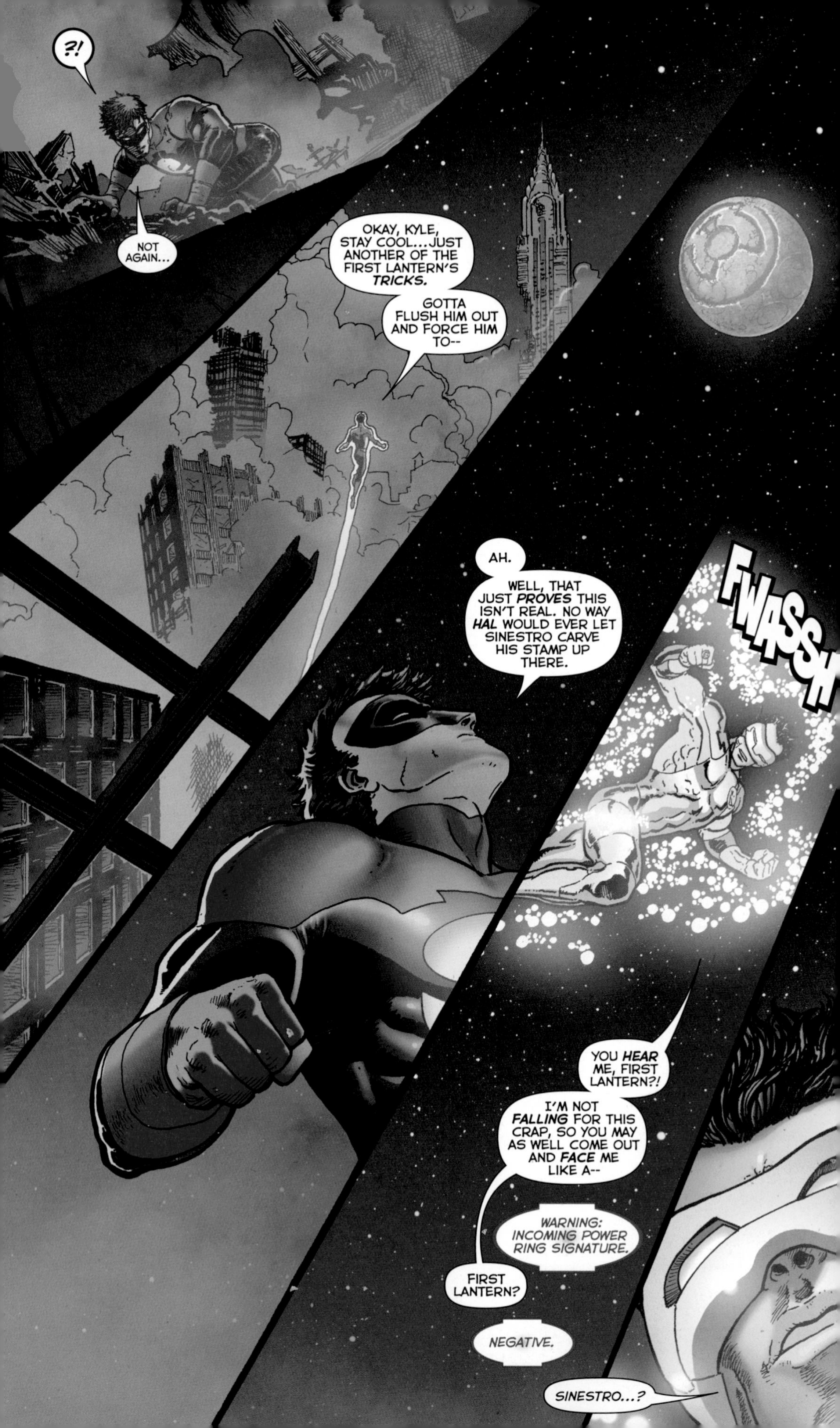
?!
NOT AGAIN...
OKAY, KYLE, STAY COOL...JUST ANOTHER OF THE FIRST LANTERN'S *TRICKS.*
GOTTA FLUSH HIM OUT AND FORCE HIM TO--
AH.
WELL, THAT JUST *PROVES* THIS ISN'T REAL. NO WAY *HAL* WOULD EVER LET SINESTRO CARVE HIS STAMP UP THERE.
FWASSH
YOU *HEAR* ME, FIRST LANTERN?!
I'M NOT *FALLING* FOR THIS CRAP, SO YOU MAY AS WELL COME OUT AND *FACE* ME LIKE A--
WARNING: INCOMING POWER RING SIGNATURE.
FIRST LANTERN?
NEGATIVE.
SINESTRO...?

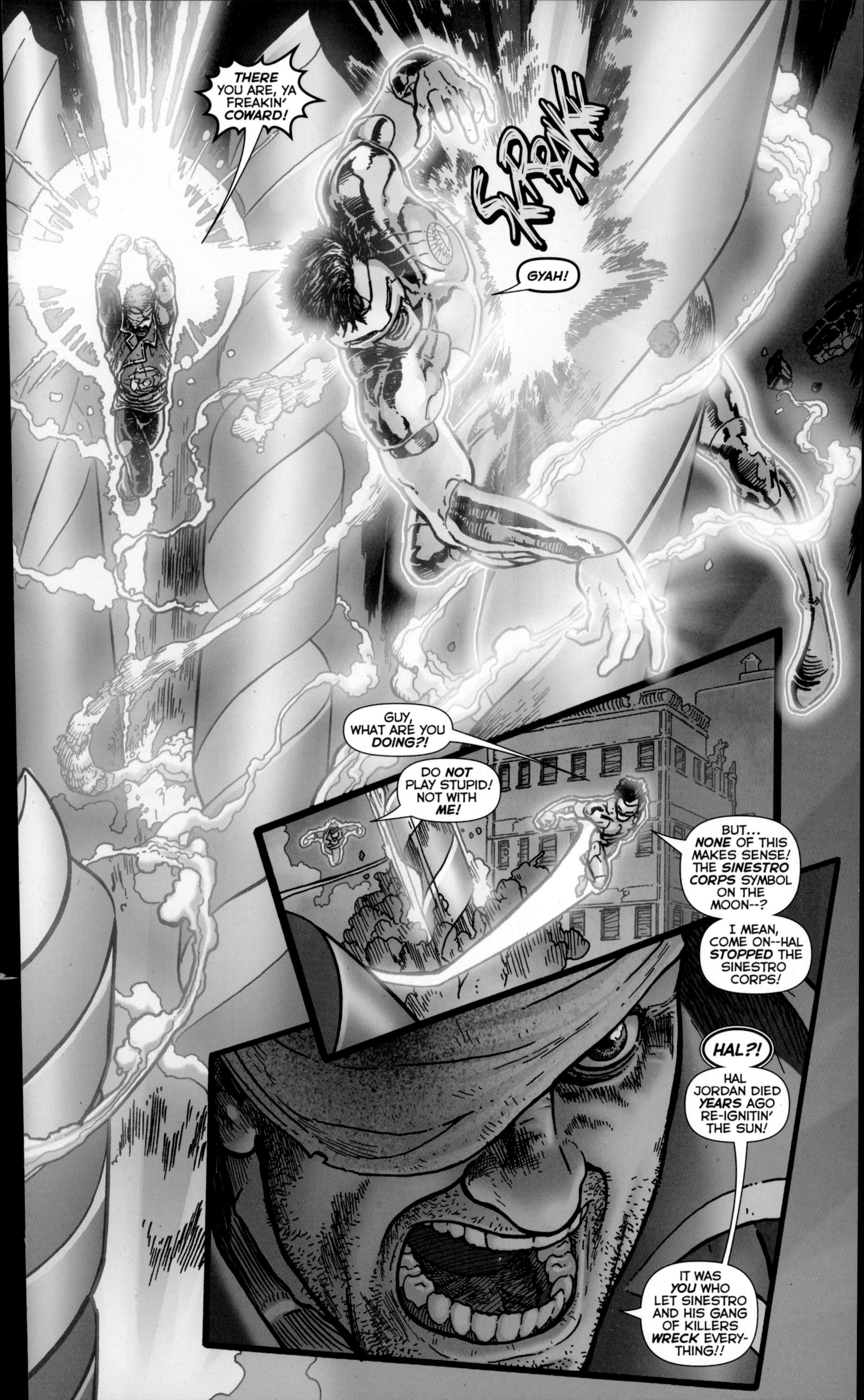

THERE YOU ARE, YA FREAKIN' COWARD!
SPRAKK
GYAH!
GUY, WHAT ARE YOU DOING?!
DO NOT PLAY STUPID! NOT WITH ME!
BUT... NONE OF THIS MAKES SENSE! THE SINESTRO CORPS SYMBOL ON THE MOON--?
I MEAN, COME ON--HAL STOPPED THE SINESTRO CORPS!
HAL?!
HAL JORDAN DIED YEARS AGO RE-IGNITIN' THE SUN!
IT WAS YOU WHO LET SINESTRO AND HIS GANG OF KILLERS WRECK EVERY-THING!!

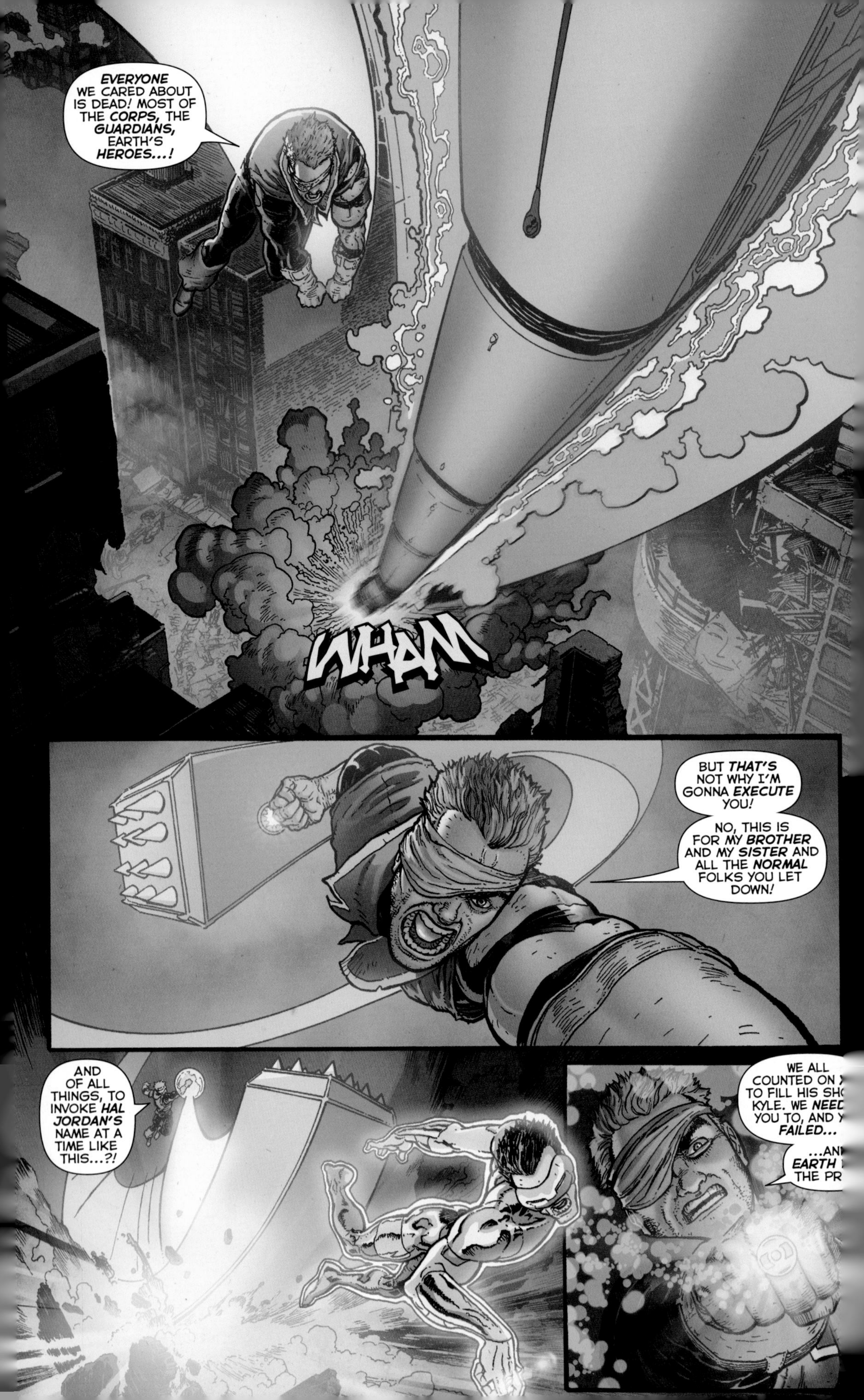
EVERYONE WE CARED ABOUT IS DEAD! MOST OF THE CORPS, THE GUARDIANS, EARTH'S HEROES...!
WHAM
BUT THAT'S NOT WHY I'M GONNA EXECUTE YOU!
NO, THIS IS FOR MY BROTHER AND MY SISTER AND ALL THE NORMAL FOLKS YOU LET DOWN!
AND OF ALL THINGS, TO INVOKE HAL JORDAN'S NAME AT A TIME LIKE THIS...?!
WE ALL COUNTED ON TO FILL HIS SHO KYLE. WE NEED YOU TO, AND FAILED...
...AN EARTH THE PR

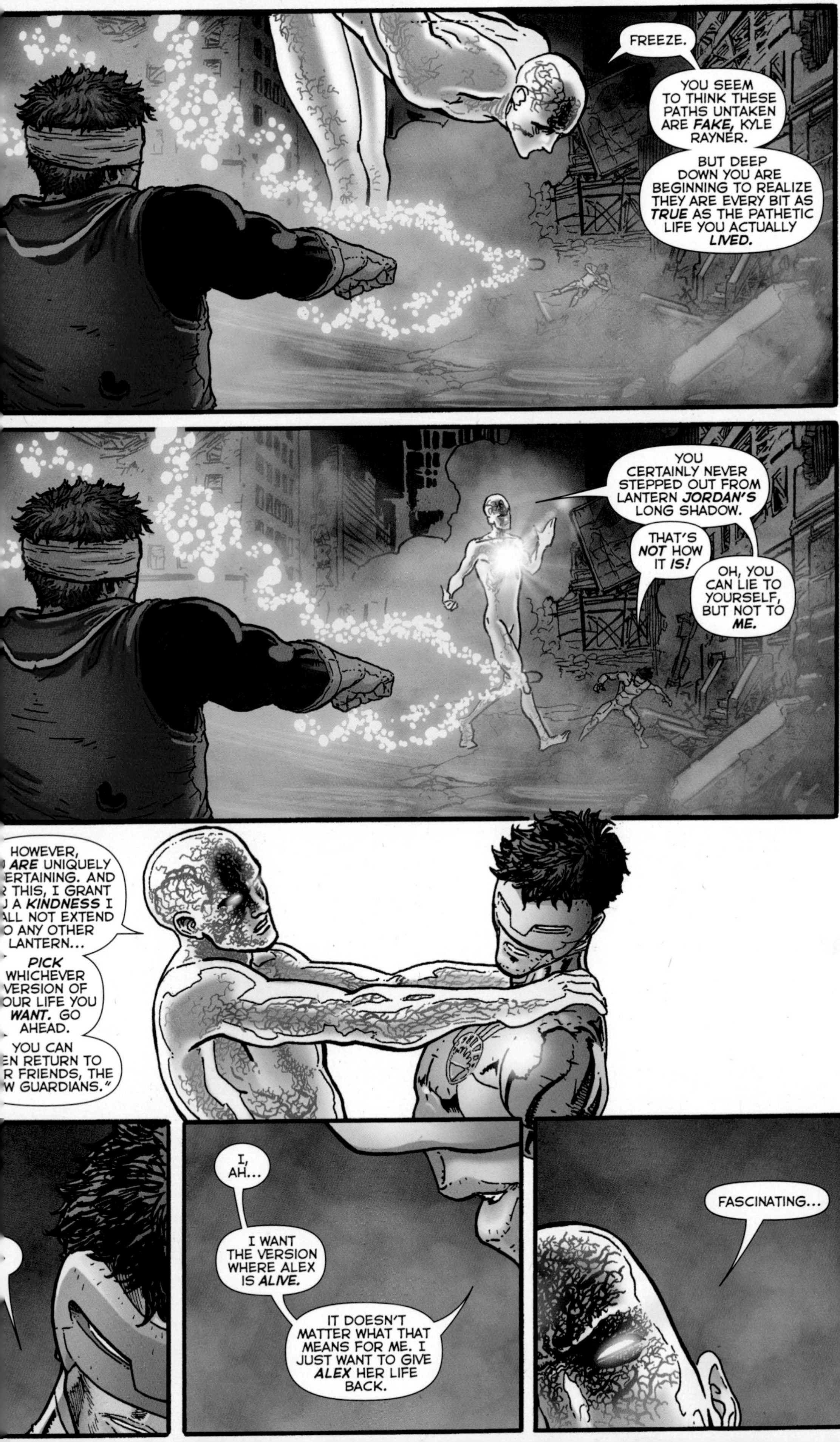
FREEZE.
YOU SEEM TO THINK THESE PATHS UNTAKEN ARE FAKE, KYLE RAYNER.
BUT DEEP DOWN YOU ARE BEGINNING TO REALIZE THEY ARE EVERY BIT AS TRUE AS THE PATHETIC LIFE YOU ACTUALLY LIVED.
YOU CERTAINLY NEVER STEPPED OUT FROM LANTERN JORDAN'S LONG SHADOW.
THAT'S NOT HOW IT IS!
OH, YOU CAN LIE TO YOURSELF, BUT NOT TO ME.
HOWEVER, ARE UNIQUELY ERTAINING. AND R THIS, I GRANT A KINDNESS I ALL NOT EXTEND O ANY OTHER LANTERN...
PICK WHICHEVER VERSION OF OUR LIFE YOU WANT. GO AHEAD.
YOU CAN EN RETURN TO R FRIENDS, THE W GUARDIANS."
I, AH...
I WANT THE VERSION WHERE ALEX IS ALIVE.
IT DOESN'T MATTER WHAT THAT MEANS FOR ME. I JUST WANT TO GIVE ALEX HER LIFE BACK.
FASCINATING...

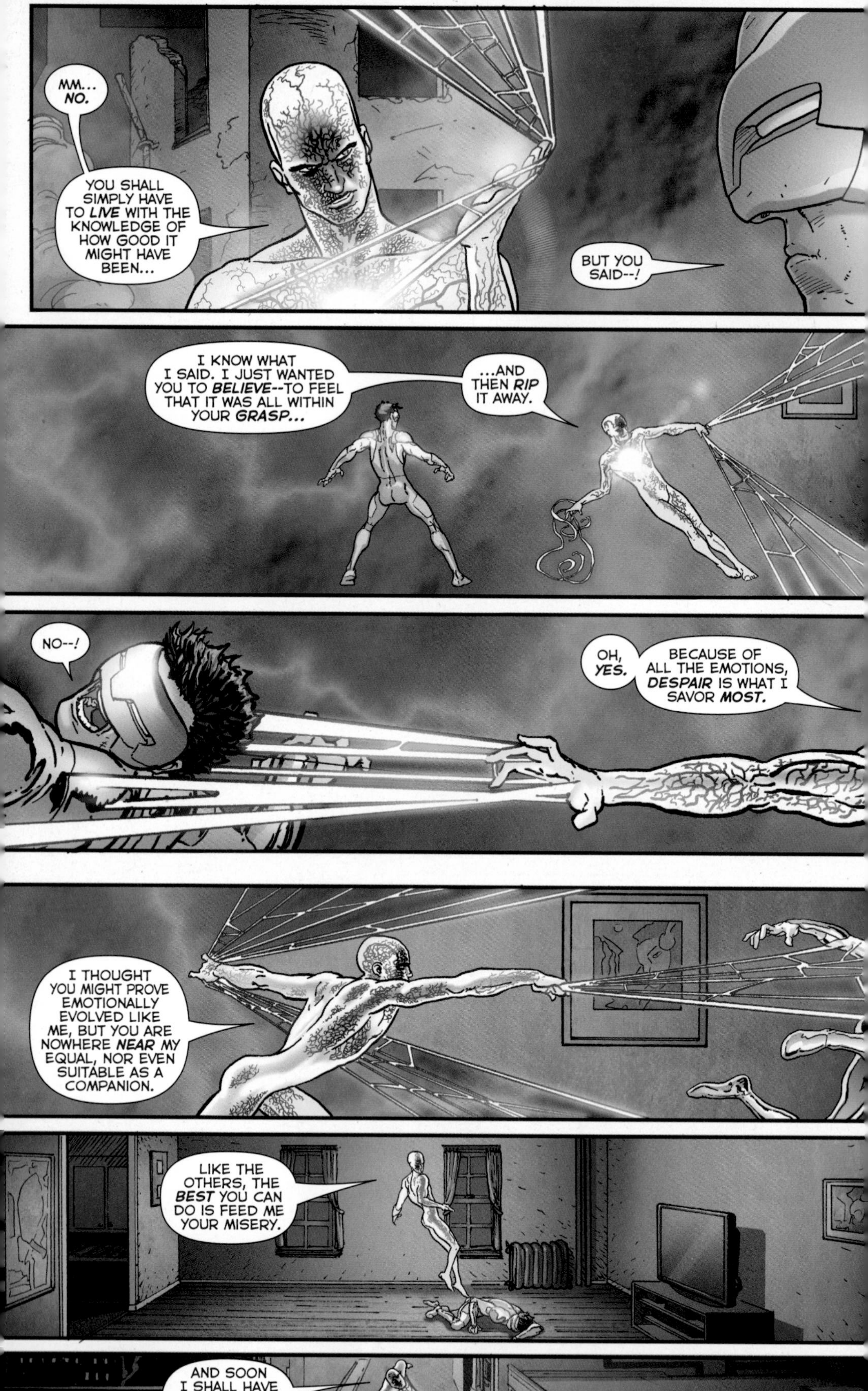
MM... NO.
YOU SHALL SIMPLY HAVE TO LIVE WITH THE KNOWLEDGE OF HOW GOOD IT MIGHT HAVE BEEN...
BUT YOU SAID--!
I KNOW WHAT I SAID. I JUST WANTED YOU TO BELIEVE--TO FEEL THAT IT WAS ALL WITHIN YOUR GRASP...
...AND THEN RIP IT AWAY.
NO--!
OH, YES.
BECAUSE OF ALL THE EMOTIONS, DESPAIR IS WHAT I SAVOR MOST.
I THOUGHT YOU MIGHT PROVE EMOTIONALLY EVOLVED LIKE ME, BUT YOU ARE NOWHERE NEAR MY EQUAL, NOR EVEN SUITABLE AS A COMPANION.
LIKE THE OTHERS, THE BEST YOU CAN DO IS FEED ME YOUR MISERY.
AND SOON I SHALL HAVE ENOUGH POWER TO MAKE ALL OF REALITY MY OWN...

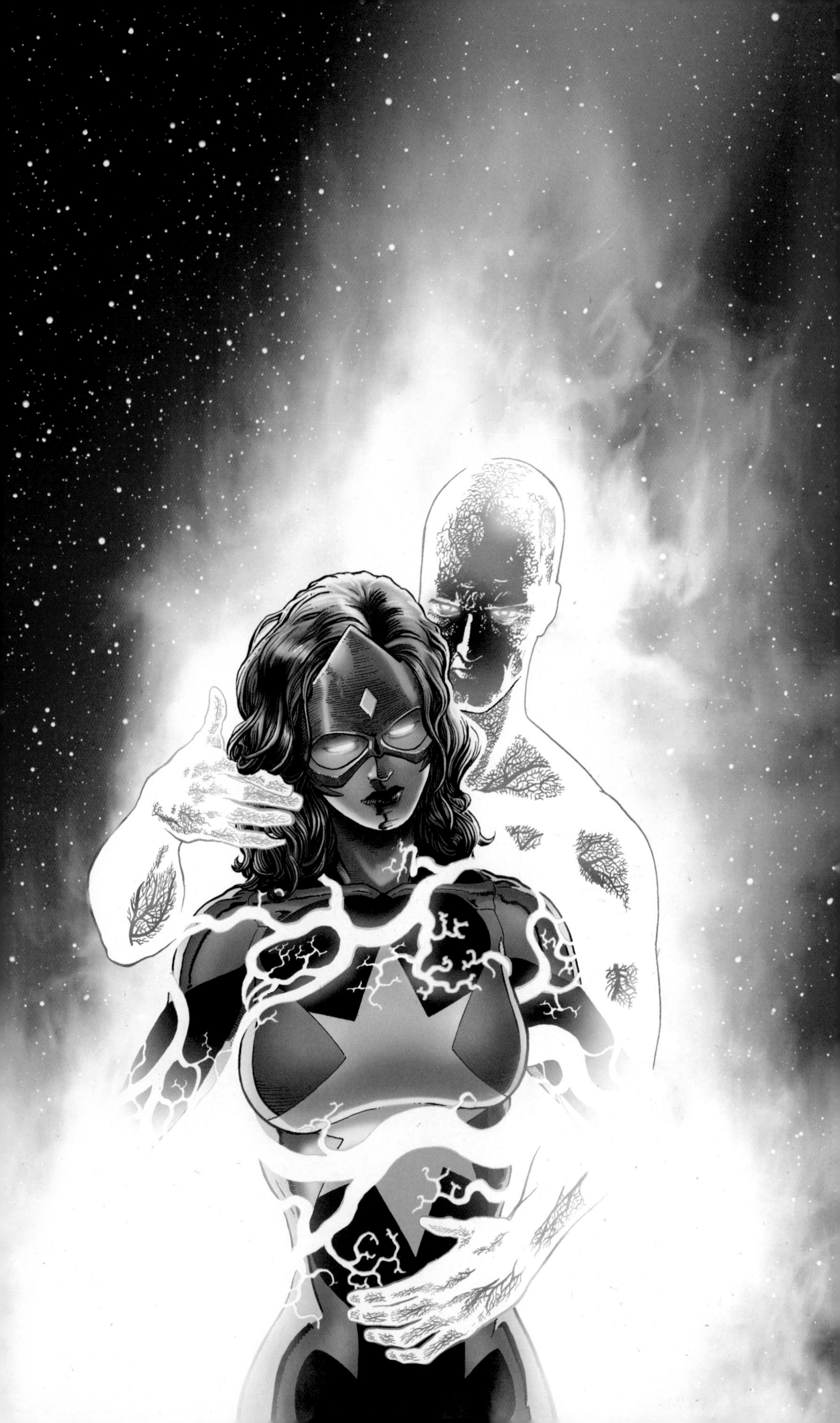

PATHS UNTAKEN

TONY BEDARD writer **HENDRY PRASETYO, JIM CALAFIORE & JAVIER PULIDO** artists
AARON KUDER & WIL QUINTANA cover

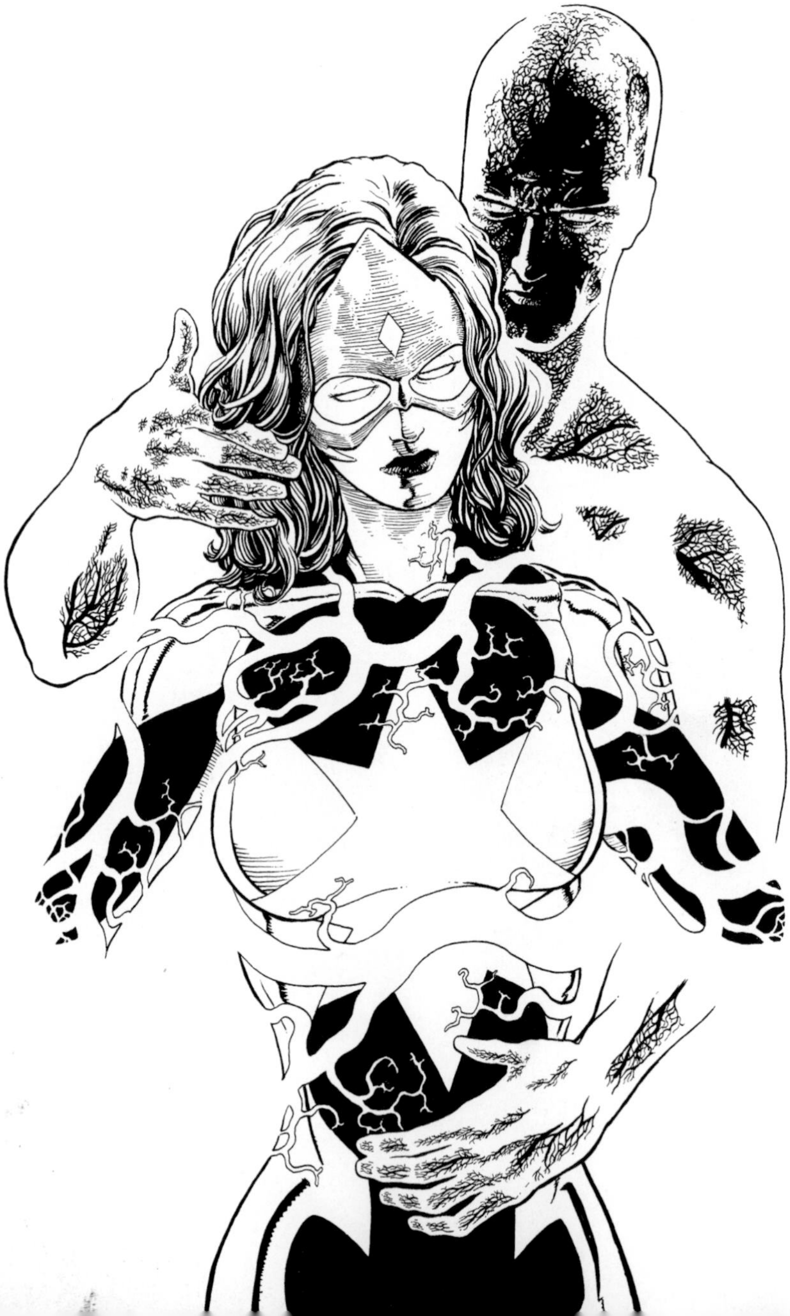

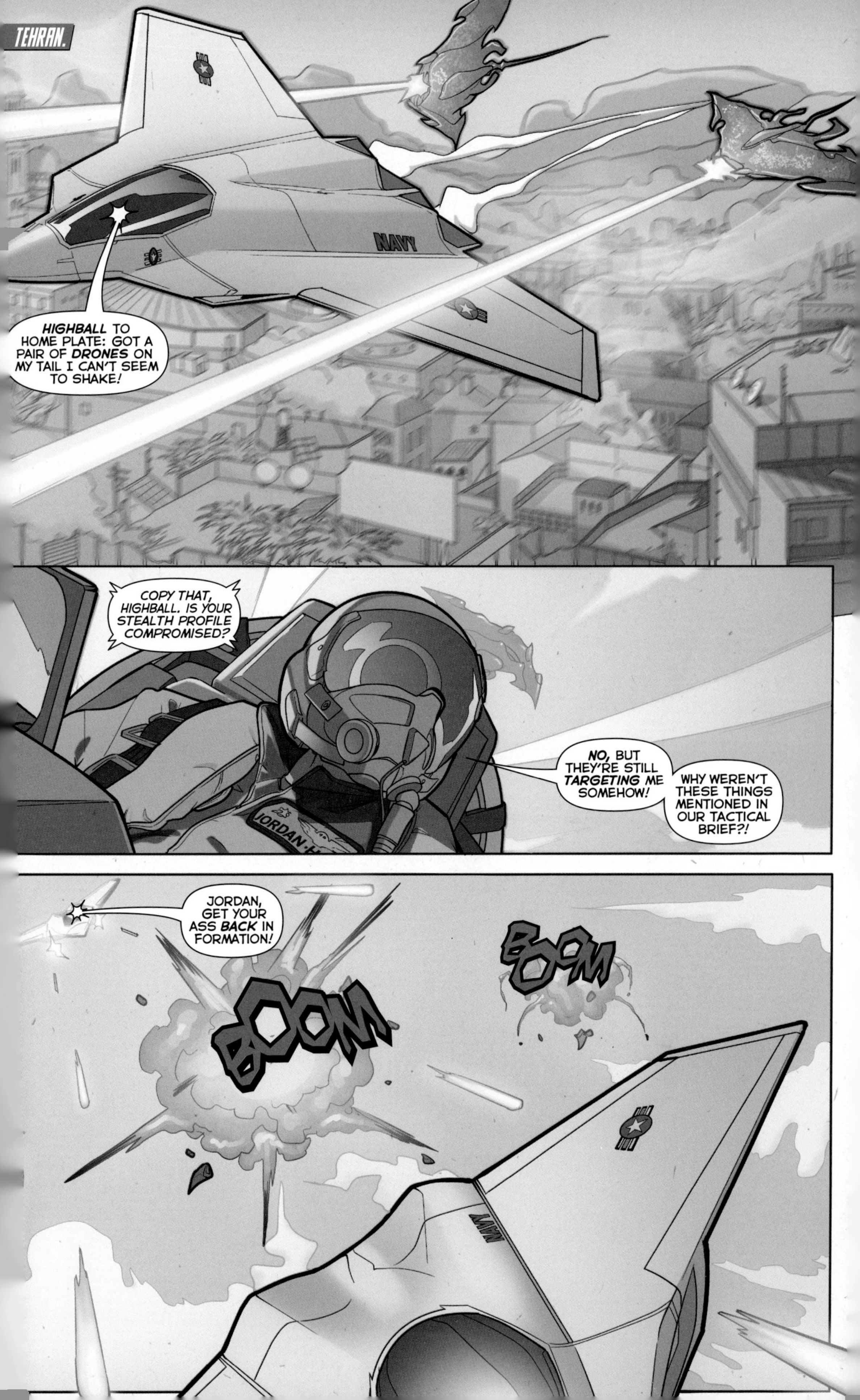
TEHRAN.
HIGHBALL TO HOME PLATE: GOT A PAIR OF DRONES ON MY TAIL I CAN'T SEEM TO SHAKE!
NAVY
COPY THAT, HIGHBALL. IS YOUR STEALTH PROFILE COMPROMISED?
NO, BUT THEY'RE STILL TARGETING ME SOMEHOW!
WHY WEREN'T THESE THINGS MENTIONED IN OUR TACTICAL BRIEF?!
JORDAN, GET YOUR ASS BACK IN FORMATION!
BOOM
BOOM
NAVY

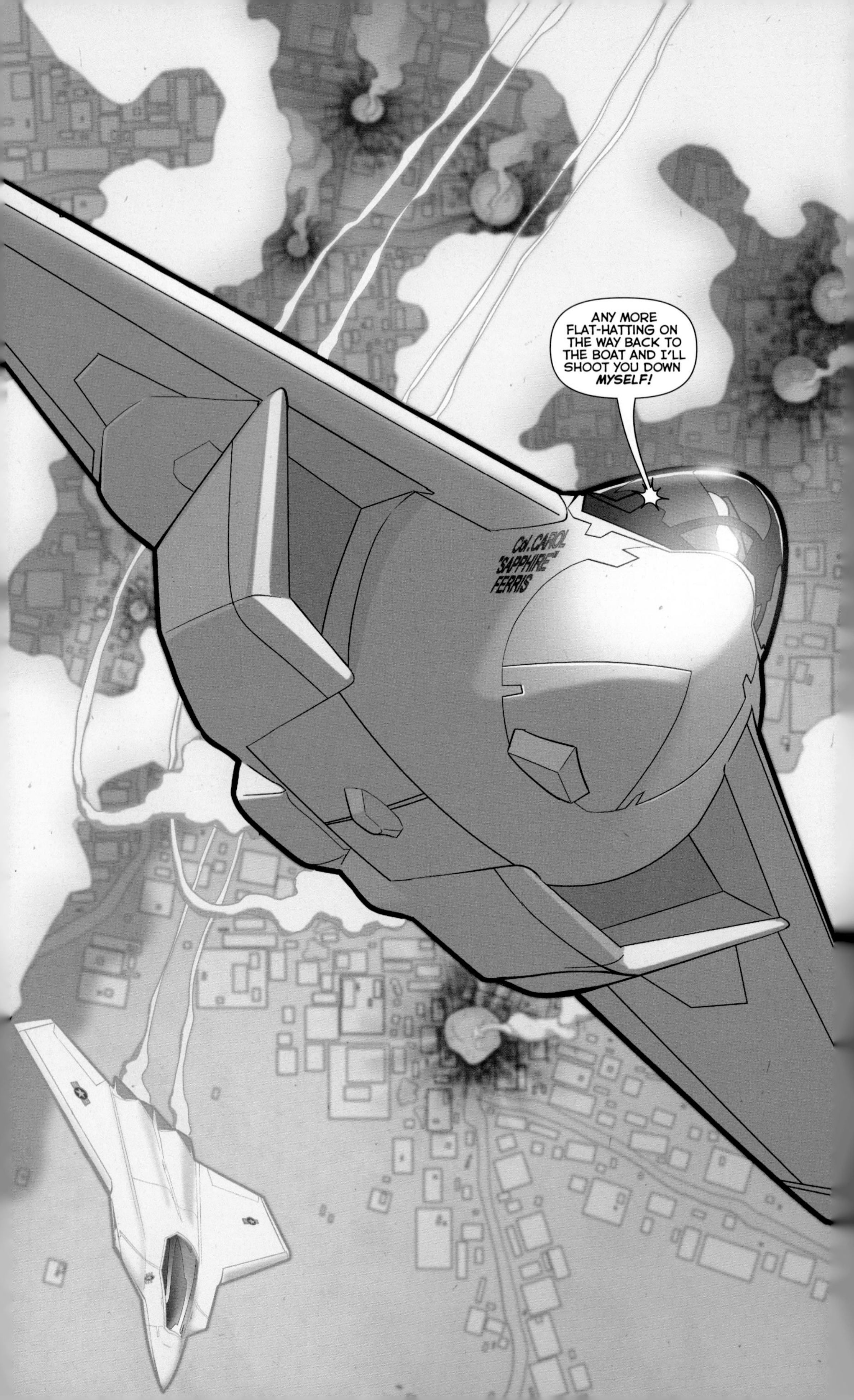
ANY MORE FLAT-HATTING ON THE WAY BACK TO THE BOAT AND I'LL SHOOT YOU DOWN MYSELF!
Col. CAROL "SAPPHIRE" FERRIS

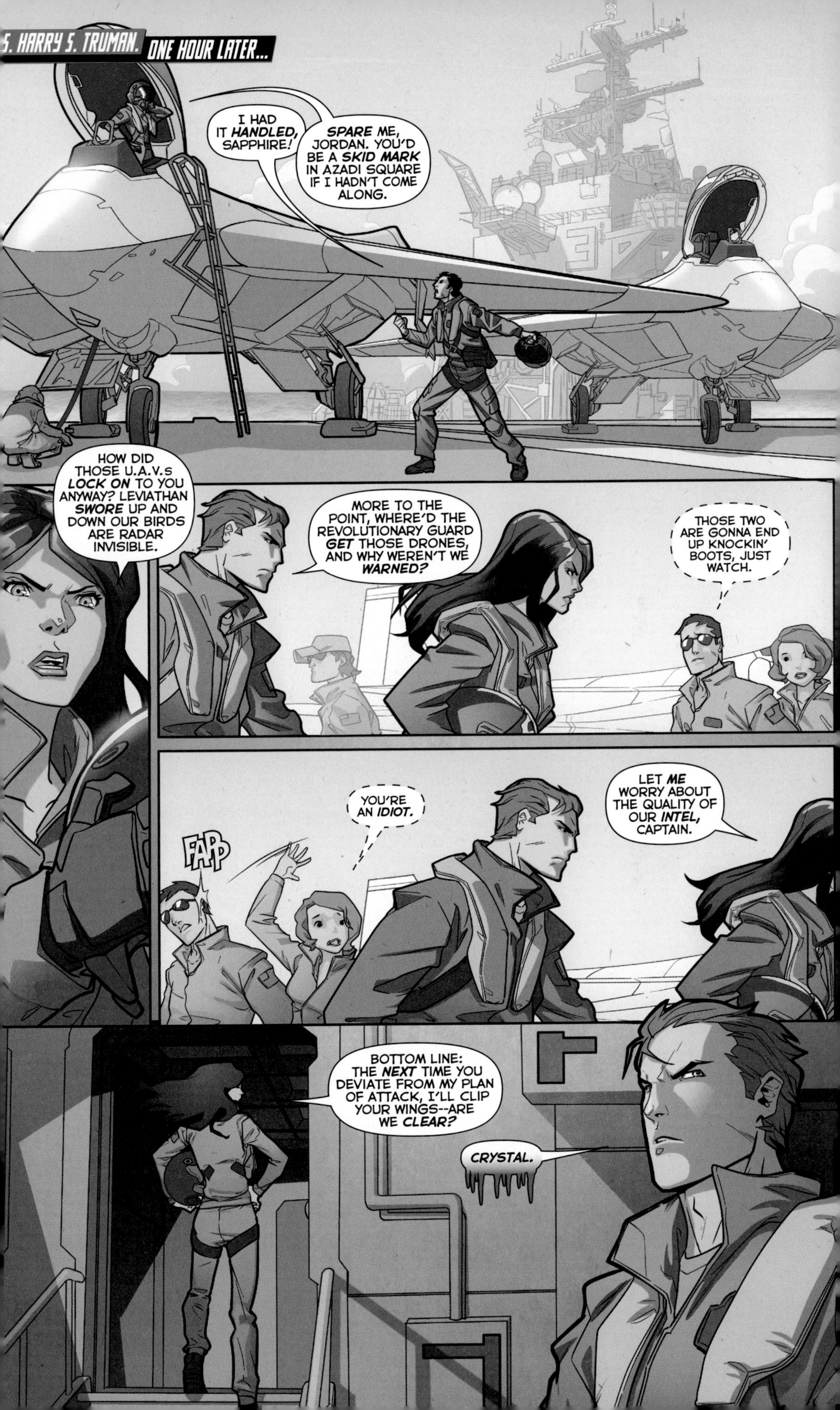

S. HARRY S. TRUMAN. ONE HOUR LATER...
I HAD IT HANDLED, SAPPHIRE!
SPARE ME, JORDAN. YOU'D BE A SKID MARK IN AZADI SQUARE IF I HADN'T COME ALONG.
HOW DID THOSE U.A.V.s LOCK ON TO YOU ANYWAY? LEVIATHAN SWORE UP AND DOWN OUR BIRDS ARE RADAR INVISIBLE.
MORE TO THE POINT, WHERE'D THE REVOLUTIONARY GUARD GET THOSE DRONES, AND WHY WEREN'T WE WARNED?
THOSE TWO ARE GONNA END UP KNOCKIN' BOOTS, JUST WATCH.
FAPP
YOU'RE AN IDIOT.
LET ME WORRY ABOUT THE QUALITY OF OUR INTEL, CAPTAIN.
BOTTOM LINE: THE NEXT TIME YOU DEVIATE FROM MY PLAN OF ATTACK, I'LL CLIP YOUR WINGS--ARE WE CLEAR?
CRYSTAL.

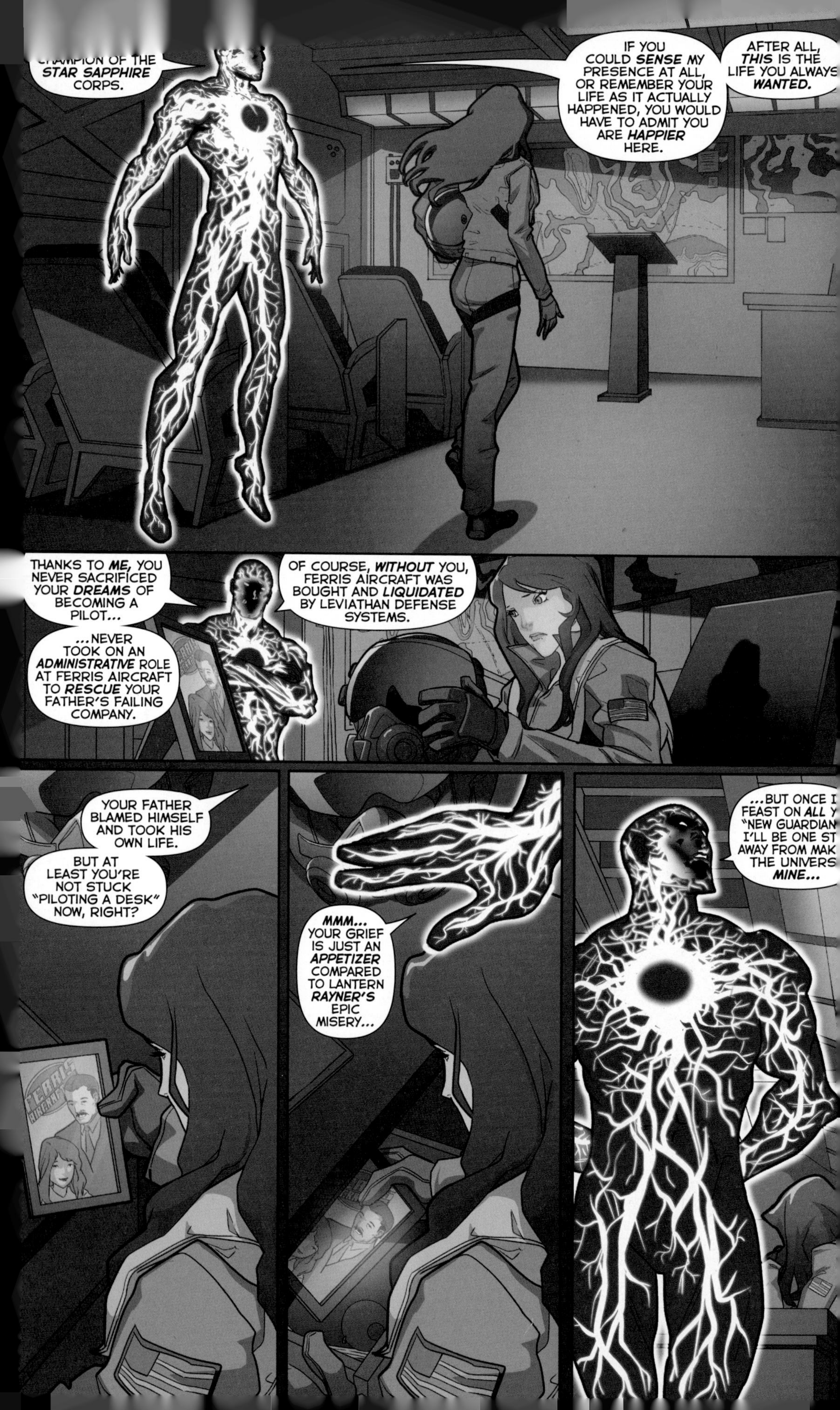
CHAMPION OF THE STAR SAPPHIRE CORPS.
IF YOU COULD SENSE MY PRESENCE AT ALL, OR REMEMBER YOUR LIFE AS IT ACTUALLY HAPPENED, YOU WOULD HAVE TO ADMIT YOU ARE HAPPIER HERE.
AFTER ALL, THIS IS THE LIFE YOU ALWAYS WANTED.
THANKS TO ME, YOU NEVER SACRIFICED YOUR DREAMS OF BECOMING A PILOT...
...NEVER TOOK ON AN ADMINISTRATIVE ROLE AT FERRIS AIRCRAFT TO RESCUE YOUR FATHER'S FAILING COMPANY.
OF COURSE, WITHOUT YOU, FERRIS AIRCRAFT WAS BOUGHT AND LIQUIDATED BY LEVIATHAN DEFENSE SYSTEMS.
YOUR FATHER BLAMED HIMSELF AND TOOK HIS OWN LIFE.
BUT AT LEAST YOU'RE NOT STUCK "PILOTING A DESK" NOW, RIGHT?
MMM... YOUR GRIEF IS JUST AN APPETIZER COMPARED TO LANTERN RAYNER'S EPIC MISERY...
...BUT ONCE I FEAST ON ALL Y "NEW GUARDIAN I'LL BE ONE ST AWAY FROM MAK THE UNIVERS MINE...

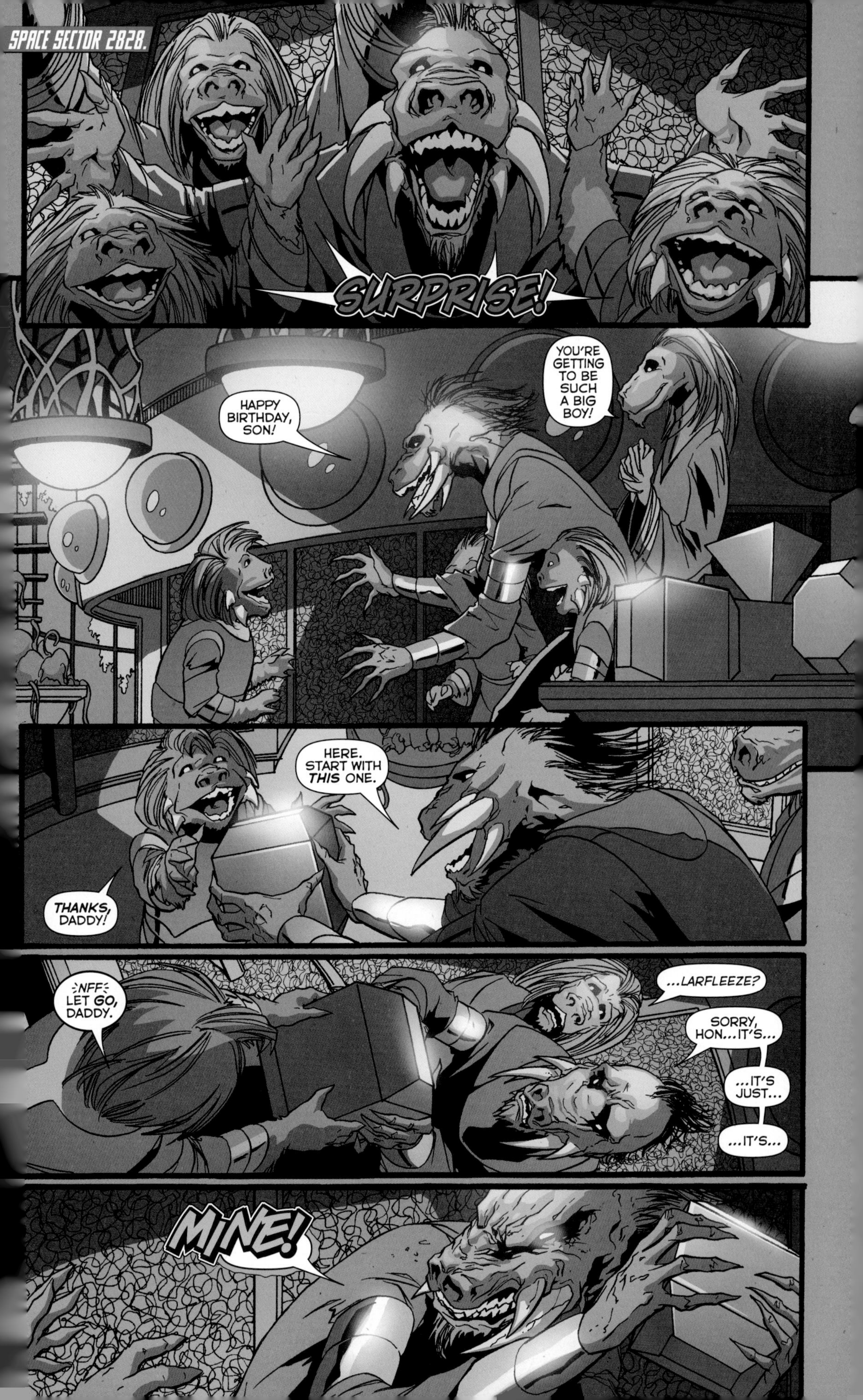
SPACE SECTOR 2828.
SURPRISE!
HAPPY BIRTHDAY, SON!
YOU'RE GETTING TO BE SUCH A BIG BOY!
HERE. START WITH *THIS* ONE.
THANKS, DADDY!
NFF LET *GO,* DADDY.
...LARFLEEZE?
SORRY, HON...IT'S...
...IT'S JUST...
...IT'S...
MINE!

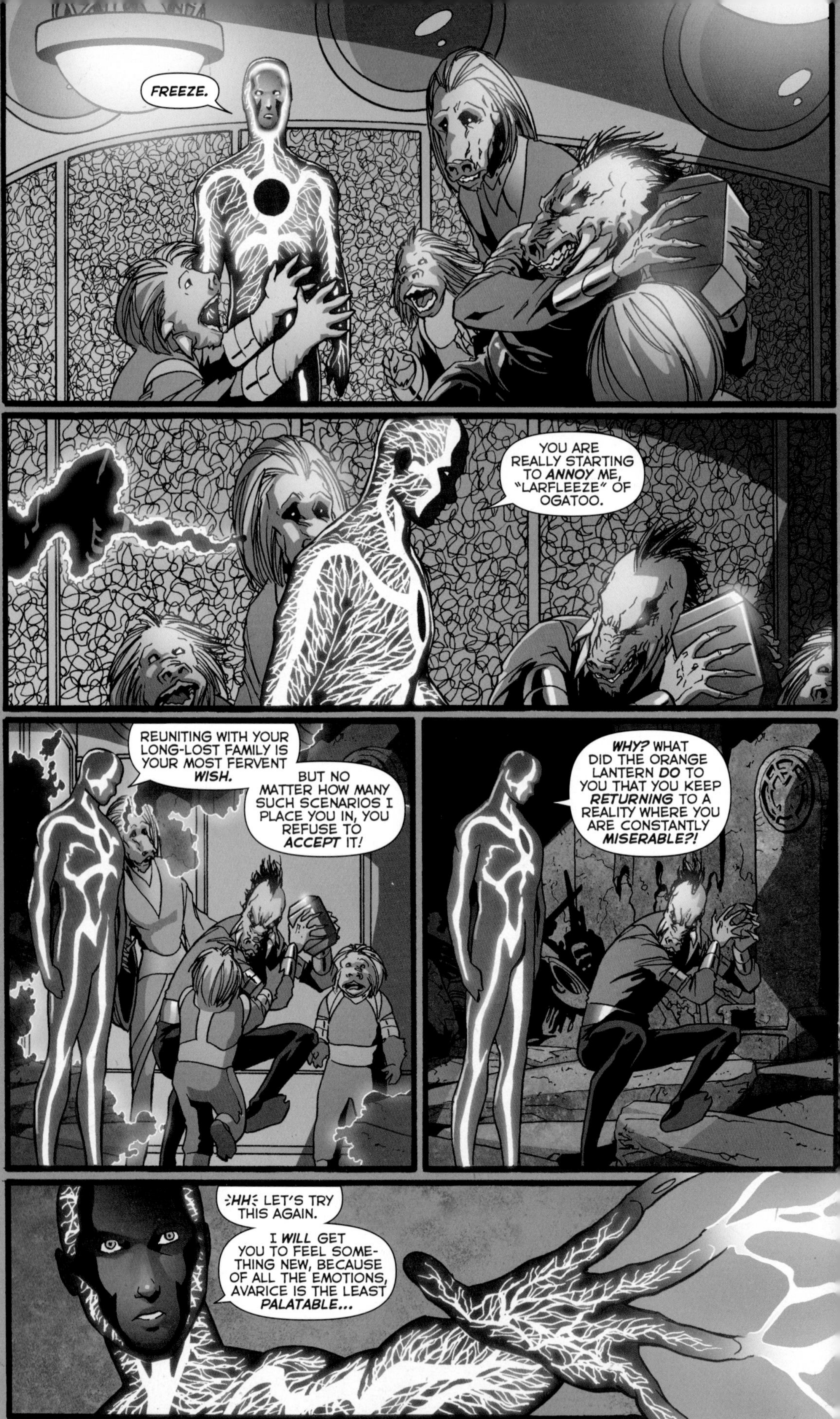
FREEZE.
YOU ARE REALLY STARTING TO ANNOY ME, "LARFLEEZE" OF OGATOO.
REUNITING WITH YOUR LONG-LOST FAMILY IS YOUR MOST FERVENT WISH.
BUT NO MATTER HOW MANY SUCH SCENARIOS I PLACE YOU IN, YOU REFUSE TO ACCEPT IT!
WHY? WHAT DID THE ORANGE LANTERN DO TO YOU THAT YOU KEEP RETURNING TO A REALITY WHERE YOU ARE CONSTANTLY MISERABLE?!
HH LET'S TRY THIS AGAIN.
I WILL GET YOU TO FEEL SOMETHING NEW, BECAUSE OF ALL THE EMOTIONS, AVARICE IS THE LEAST PALATABLE...

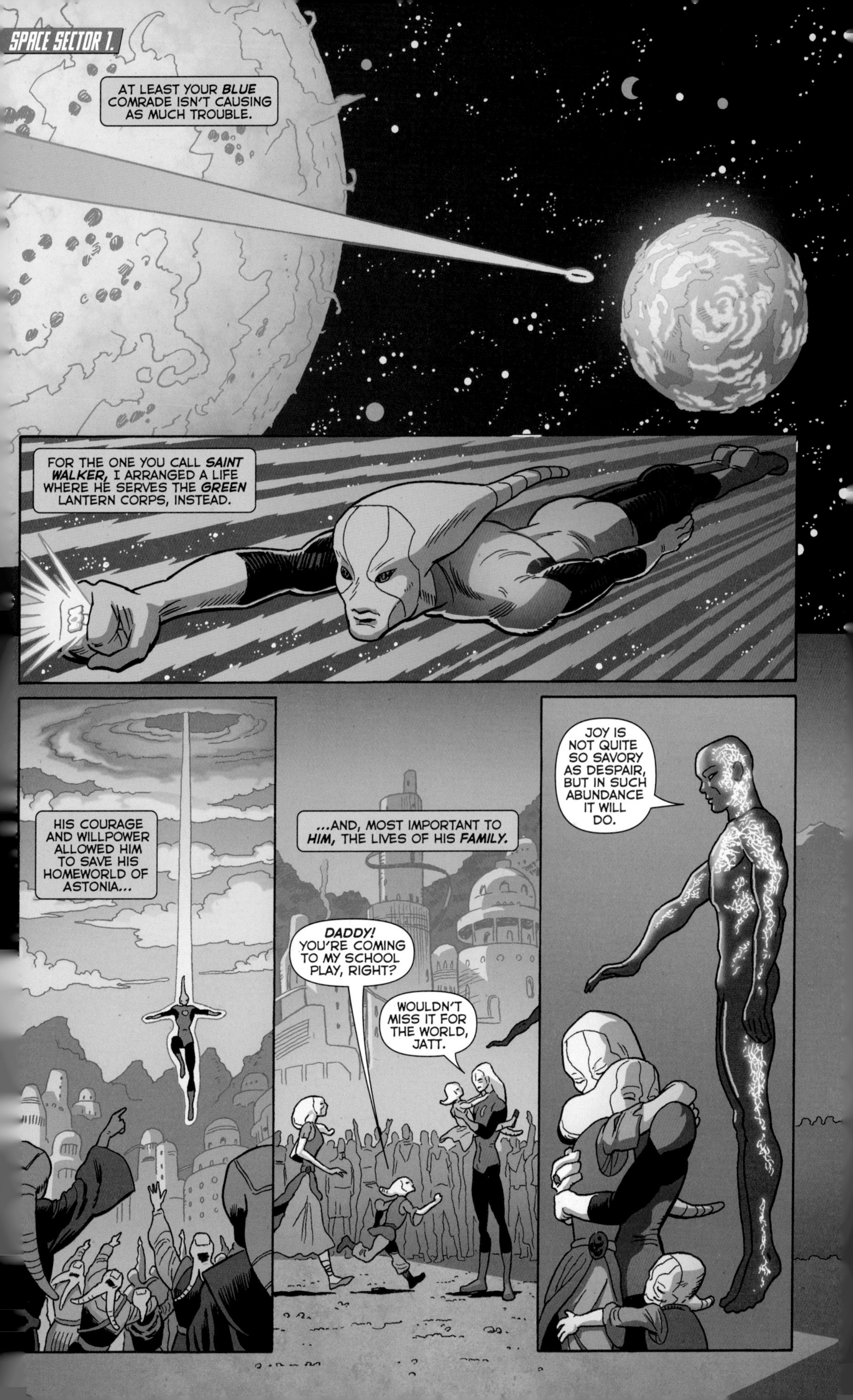
SPACE SECTOR 1.
AT LEAST YOUR BLUE COMRADE ISN'T CAUSING AS MUCH TROUBLE.
FOR THE ONE YOU CALL SAINT WALKER, I ARRANGED A LIFE WHERE HE SERVES THE GREEN LANTERN CORPS, INSTEAD.
HIS COURAGE AND WILLPOWER ALLOWED HIM TO SAVE HIS HOMEWORLD OF ASTONIA...
...AND, MOST IMPORTANT TO HIM, THE LIVES OF HIS FAMILY.
DADDY! YOU'RE COMING TO MY SCHOOL PLAY, RIGHT?
WOULDN'T MISS IT FOR THE WORLD, JATT.
JOY IS NOT QUITE SO SAVORY AS DESPAIR, BUT IN SUCH ABUNDANCE IT WILL DO.

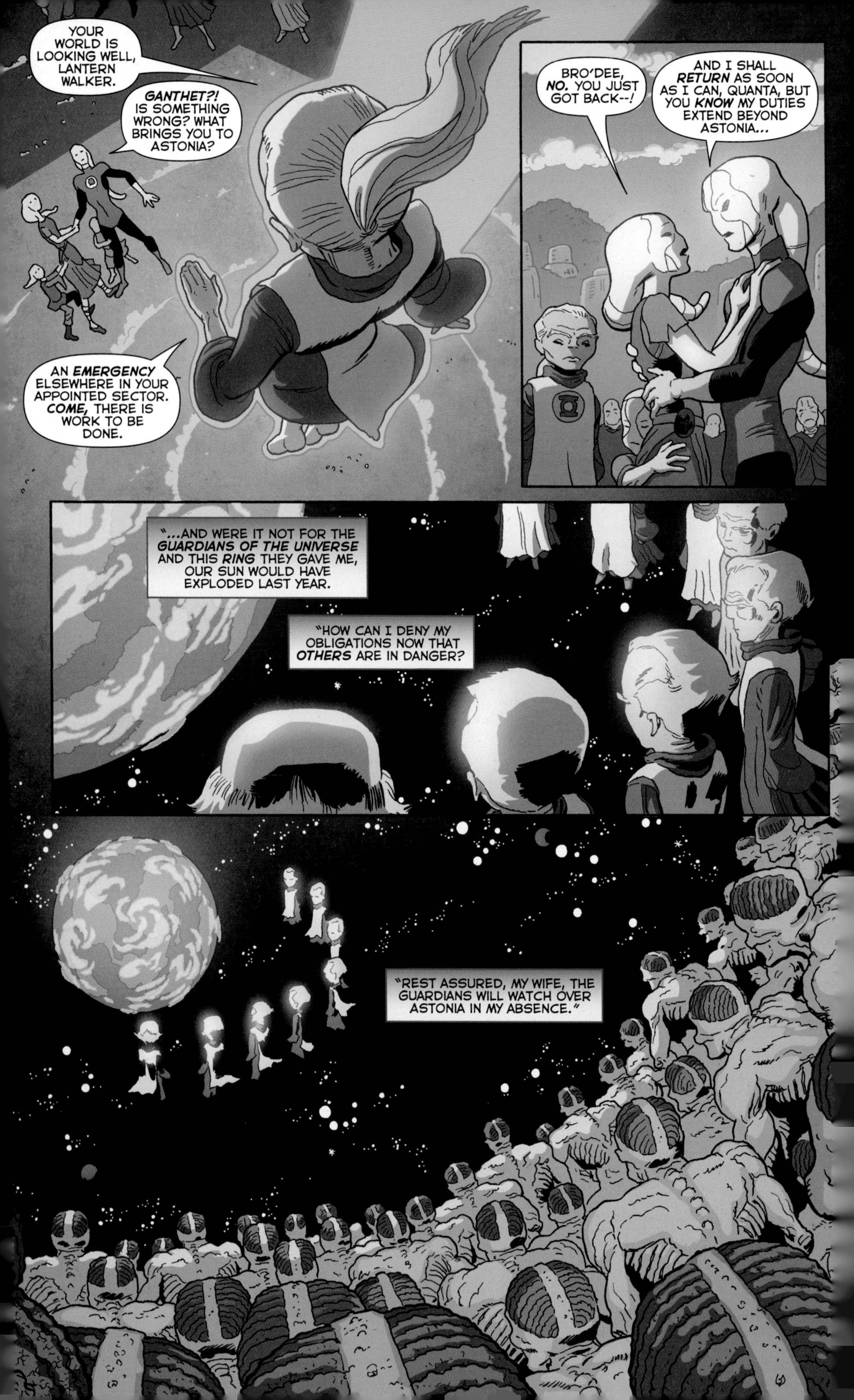
YOUR WORLD IS LOOKING WELL, LANTERN WALKER.
GANTHET?! IS SOMETHING WRONG? WHAT BRINGS YOU TO ASTONIA?
AN EMERGENCY ELSEWHERE IN YOUR APPOINTED SECTOR. COME, THERE IS WORK TO BE DONE.
BRO'DEE, NO. YOU JUST GOT BACK--!
AND I SHALL RETURN AS SOON AS I CAN, QUANTA, BUT YOU KNOW MY DUTIES EXTEND BEYOND ASTONIA...
"...AND WERE IT NOT FOR THE GUARDIANS OF THE UNIVERSE AND THIS RING THEY GAVE ME, OUR SUN WOULD HAVE EXPLODED LAST YEAR.
"HOW CAN I DENY MY OBLIGATIONS NOW THAT OTHERS ARE IN DANGER?
"REST ASSURED, MY WIFE, THE GUARDIANS WILL WATCH OVER ASTONIA IN MY ABSENCE."

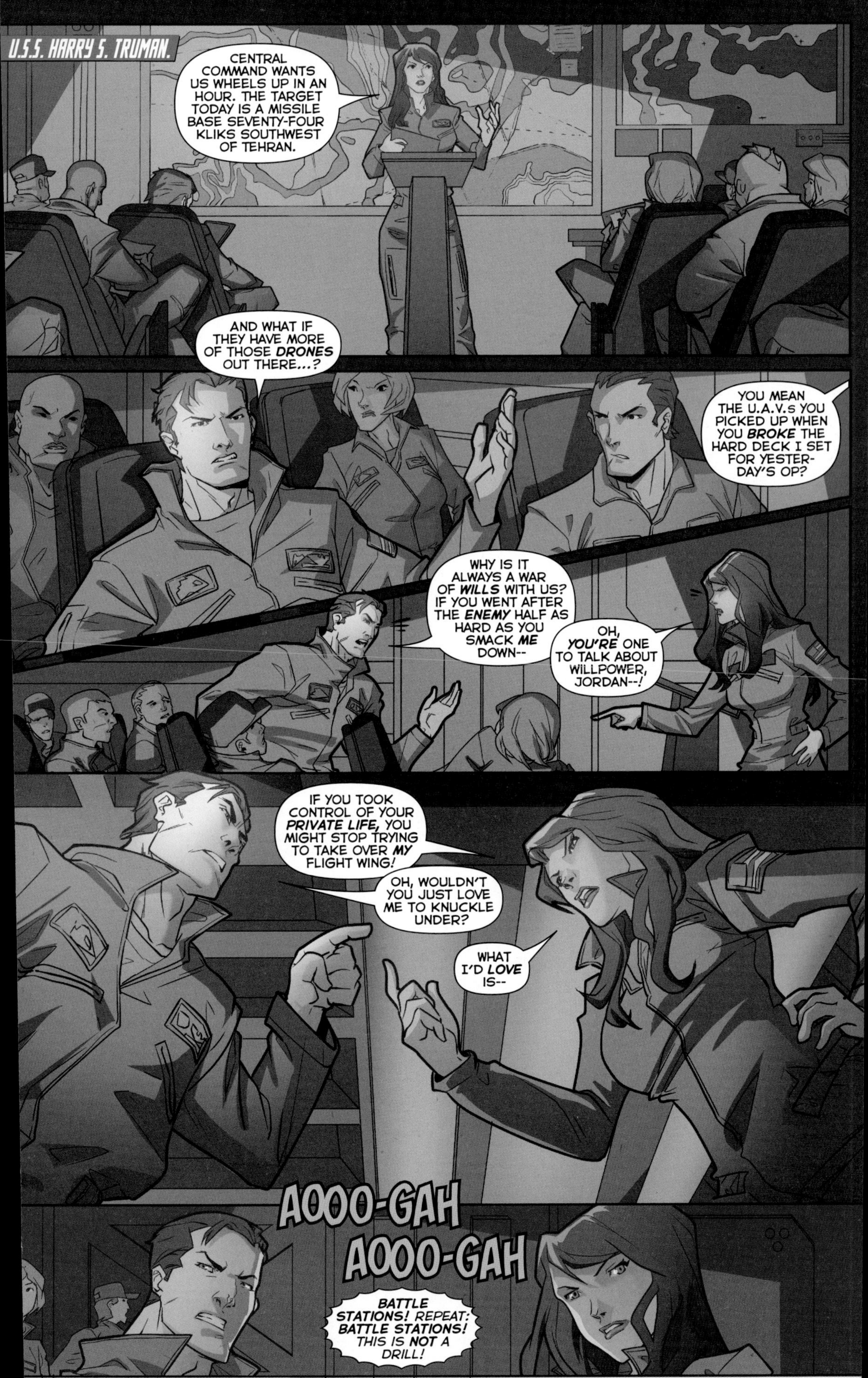
U.S.S. HARRY S. TRUMAN.
CENTRAL COMMAND WANTS US WHEELS UP IN AN HOUR. THE TARGET TODAY IS A MISSILE BASE SEVENTY-FOUR KLIKS SOUTHWEST OF TEHRAN.
AND WHAT IF THEY HAVE MORE OF THOSE DRONES OUT THERE...?
YOU MEAN THE U.A.V.s YOU PICKED UP WHEN YOU BROKE THE HARD DECK I SET FOR YESTERDAY'S OP?
WHY IS IT ALWAYS A WAR OF WILLS WITH US? IF YOU WENT AFTER THE ENEMY HALF AS HARD AS YOU SMACK ME DOWN--
OH, YOU'RE ONE TO TALK ABOUT WILLPOWER, JORDAN--!
IF YOU TOOK CONTROL OF YOUR PRIVATE LIFE, YOU MIGHT STOP TRYING TO TAKE OVER MY FLIGHT WING!
OH, WOULDN'T YOU JUST LOVE ME TO KNUCKLE UNDER?
WHAT I'D LOVE IS--
AOOO-GAH
AOOO-GAH
BATTLE STATIONS! REPEAT: BATTLE STATIONS! THIS IS NOT A DRILL!

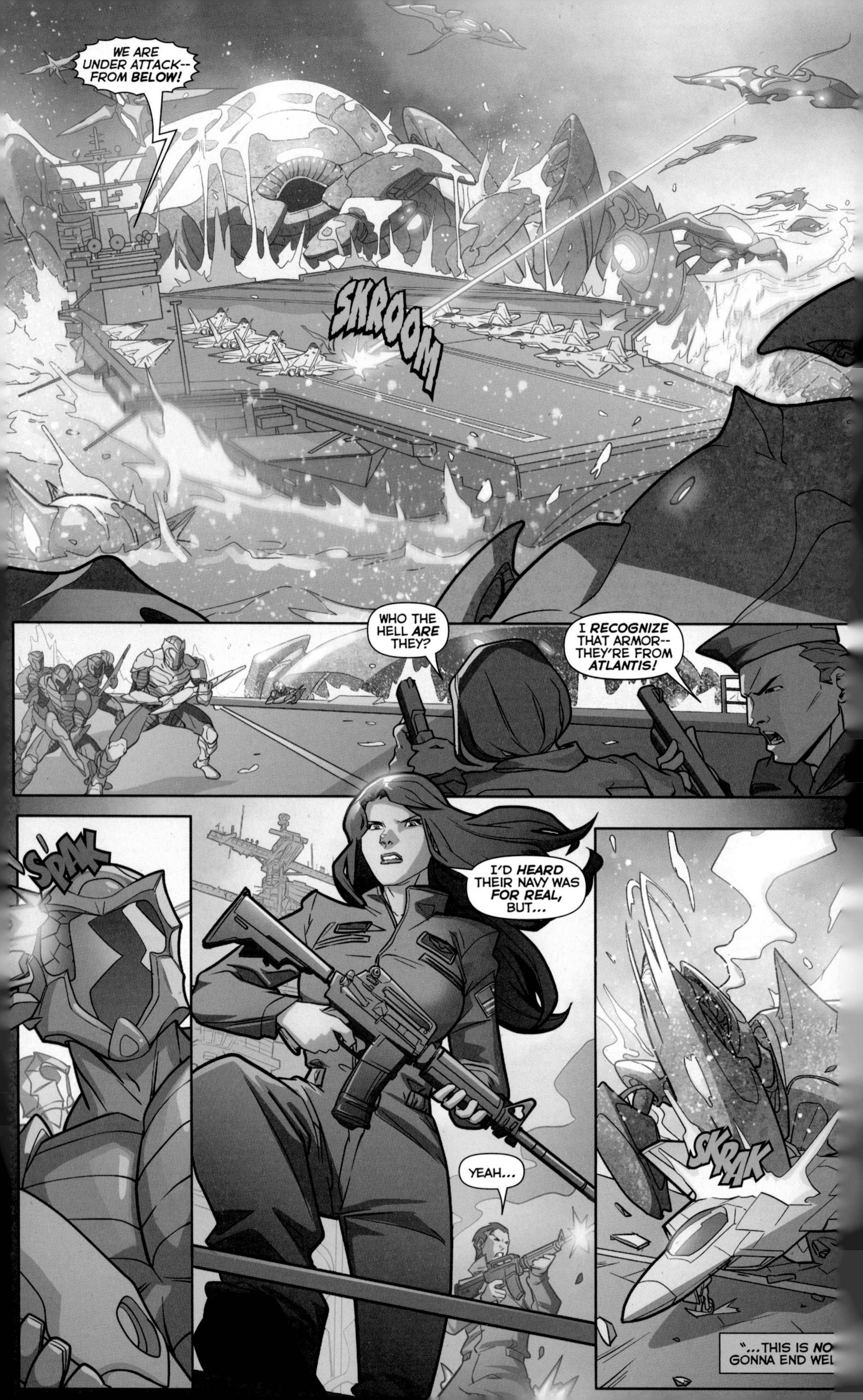
WE ARE UNDER ATTACK-- FROM BELOW!
SKROOM
WHO THE HELL ARE THEY?
I RECOGNIZE THAT ARMOR-- THEY'RE FROM ATLANTIS!
SPAK
I'D HEARD THEIR NAVY WAS FOR REAL, BUT...
YEAH...
SKRAK
"...THIS IS NO
GONNA END WEL

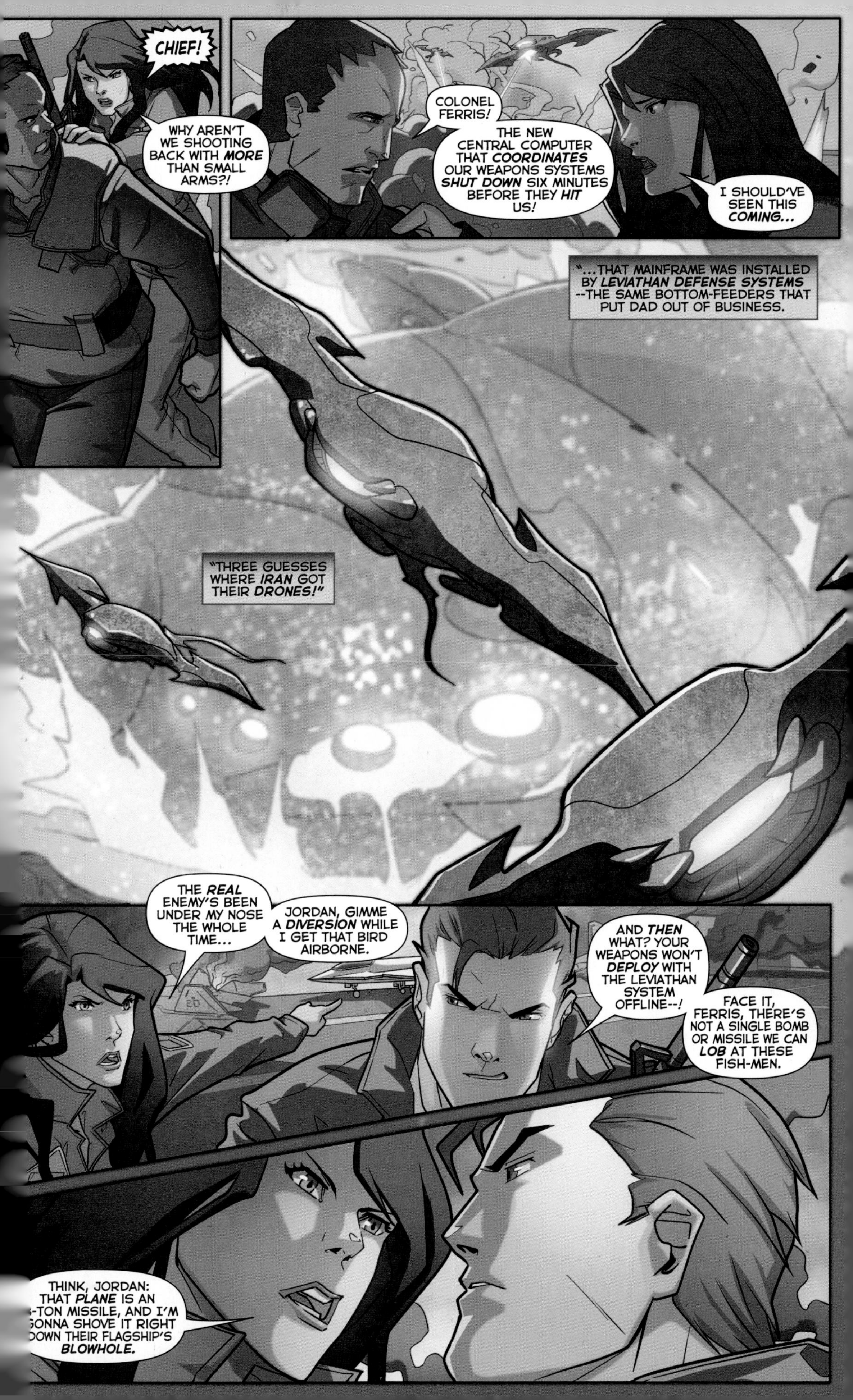

CHIEF!
WHY AREN'T WE SHOOTING BACK WITH MORE THAN SMALL ARMS?!
COLONEL FERRIS!
THE NEW CENTRAL COMPUTER THAT COORDINATES OUR WEAPONS SYSTEMS SHUT DOWN SIX MINUTES BEFORE THEY HIT US!
I SHOULD'VE SEEN THIS COMING...
"...THAT MAINFRAME WAS INSTALLED BY LEVIATHAN DEFENSE SYSTEMS --THE SAME BOTTOM-FEEDERS THAT PUT DAD OUT OF BUSINESS.
"THREE GUESSES WHERE IRAN GOT THEIR DRONES!"
THE REAL ENEMY'S BEEN UNDER MY NOSE THE WHOLE TIME...
JORDAN, GIMME A DIVERSION WHILE I GET THAT BIRD AIRBORNE.
AND THEN WHAT? YOUR WEAPONS WON'T DEPLOY WITH THE LEVIATHAN SYSTEM OFFLINE--!
FACE IT, FERRIS, THERE'S NOT A SINGLE BOMB OR MISSILE WE CAN LOB AT THESE FISH-MEN.
THINK, JORDAN: THAT PLANE IS AN -TON MISSILE, AND I'M GONNA SHOVE IT RIGHT DOWN THEIR FLAGSHIP'S BLOWHOLE.

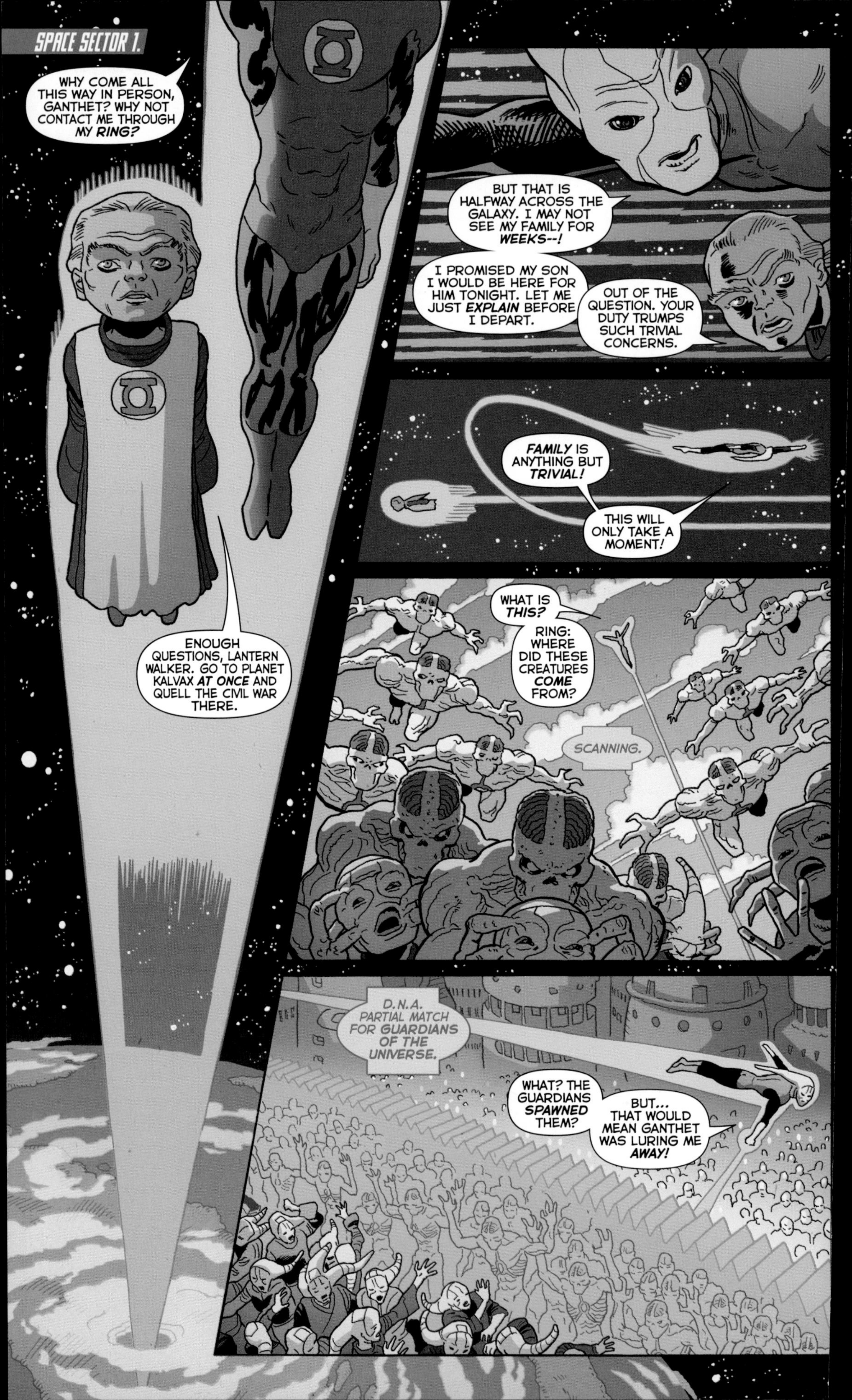
SPACE SECTOR 1.
WHY COME ALL THIS WAY IN PERSON, GANTHET? WHY NOT CONTACT ME THROUGH MY RING?
ENOUGH QUESTIONS, LANTERN WALKER. GO TO PLANET KALVAX AT ONCE AND QUELL THE CIVIL WAR THERE.
BUT THAT IS HALFWAY ACROSS THE GALAXY. I MAY NOT SEE MY FAMILY FOR WEEKS--!
I PROMISED MY SON I WOULD BE HERE FOR HIM TONIGHT. LET ME JUST EXPLAIN BEFORE I DEPART.
OUT OF THE QUESTION. YOUR DUTY TRUMPS SUCH TRIVIAL CONCERNS.
FAMILY IS ANYTHING BUT TRIVIAL!
THIS WILL ONLY TAKE A MOMENT!
WHAT IS THIS?
RING: WHERE DID THESE CREATURES COME FROM?
SCANNING.
D.N.A. PARTIAL MATCH FOR GUARDIANS OF THE UNIVERSE.
WHAT? THE GUARDIANS SPAWNED THEM?
BUT... THAT WOULD MEAN GANTHET WAS LURING ME AWAY!

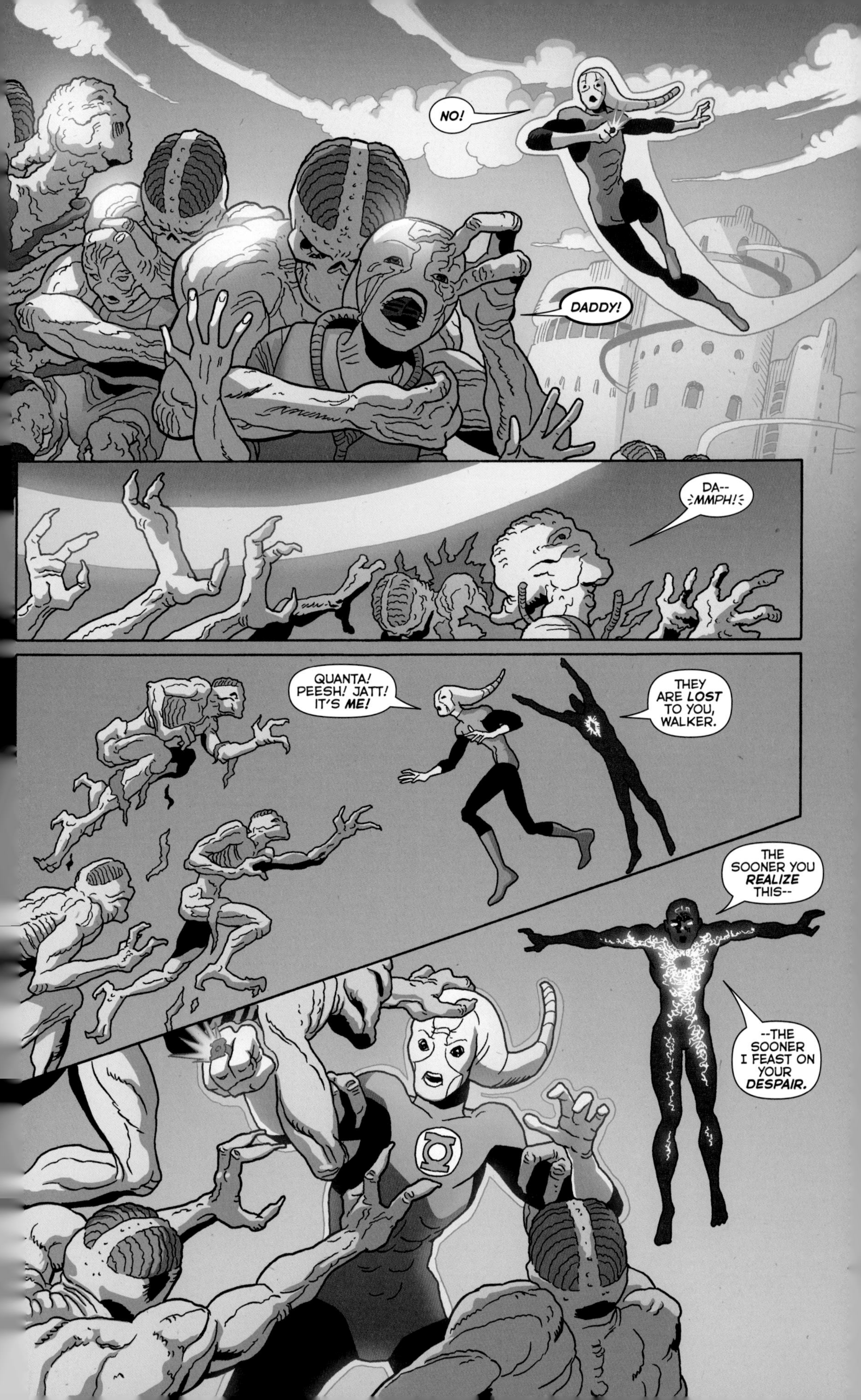

NO!
DADDY!
DA-- MMPH!
QUANTA! PEESH! JATT! IT'S ME!
THEY ARE LOST TO YOU, WALKER.
THE SOONER YOU REALIZE THIS--
--THE SOONER I FEAST ON YOUR DESPAIR.

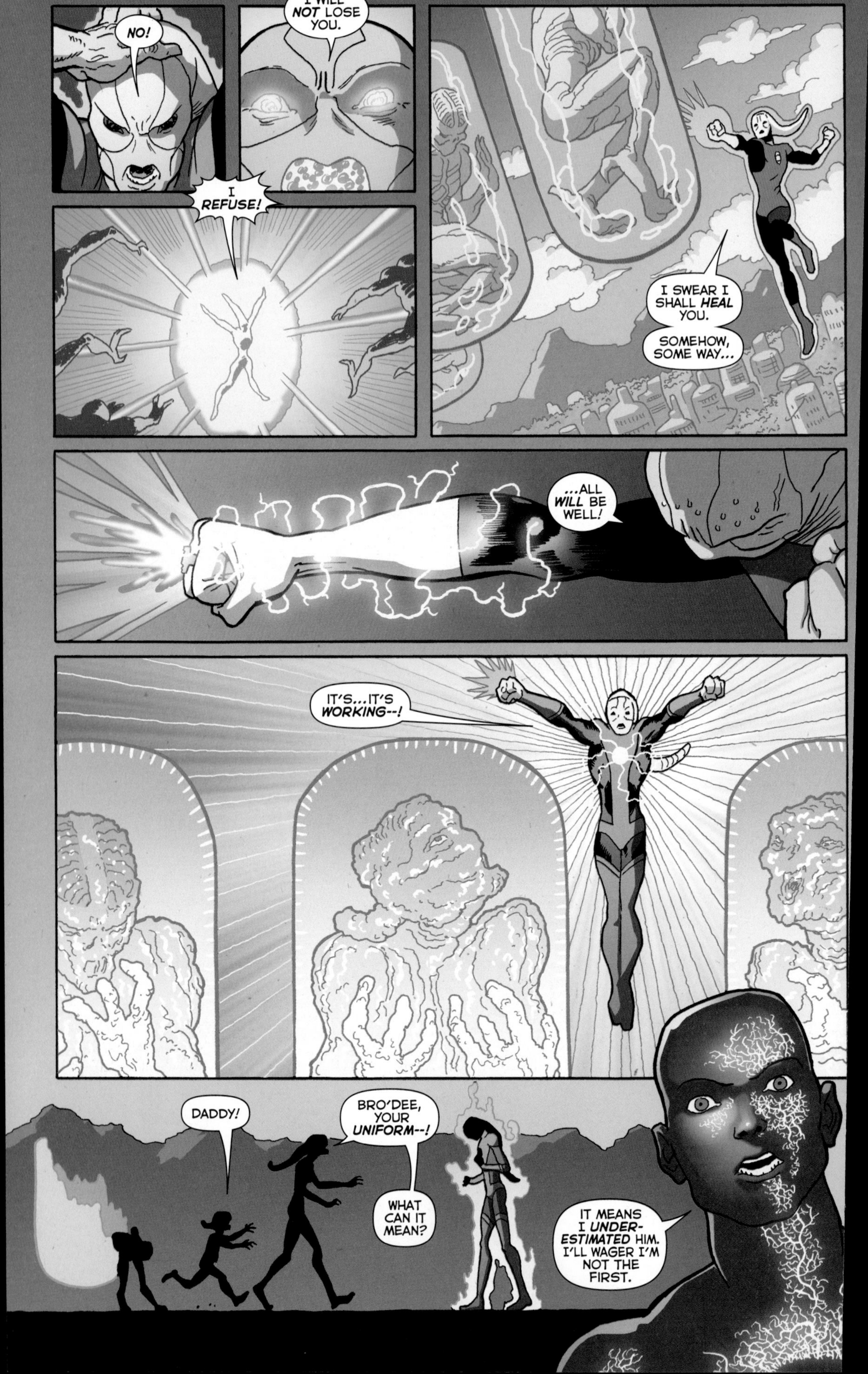
NO!
I WILL NOT LOSE YOU.
I REFUSE!
I SWEAR I SHALL HEAL YOU.
SOMEHOW, SOME WAY...
...ALL WILL BE WELL!
IT'S...IT'S WORKING--!
DADDY!
BRO'DEE, YOUR UNIFORM--!
WHAT CAN IT MEAN?
IT MEANS I UNDER-ESTIMATED HIM. I'LL WAGER I'M NOT THE FIRST.

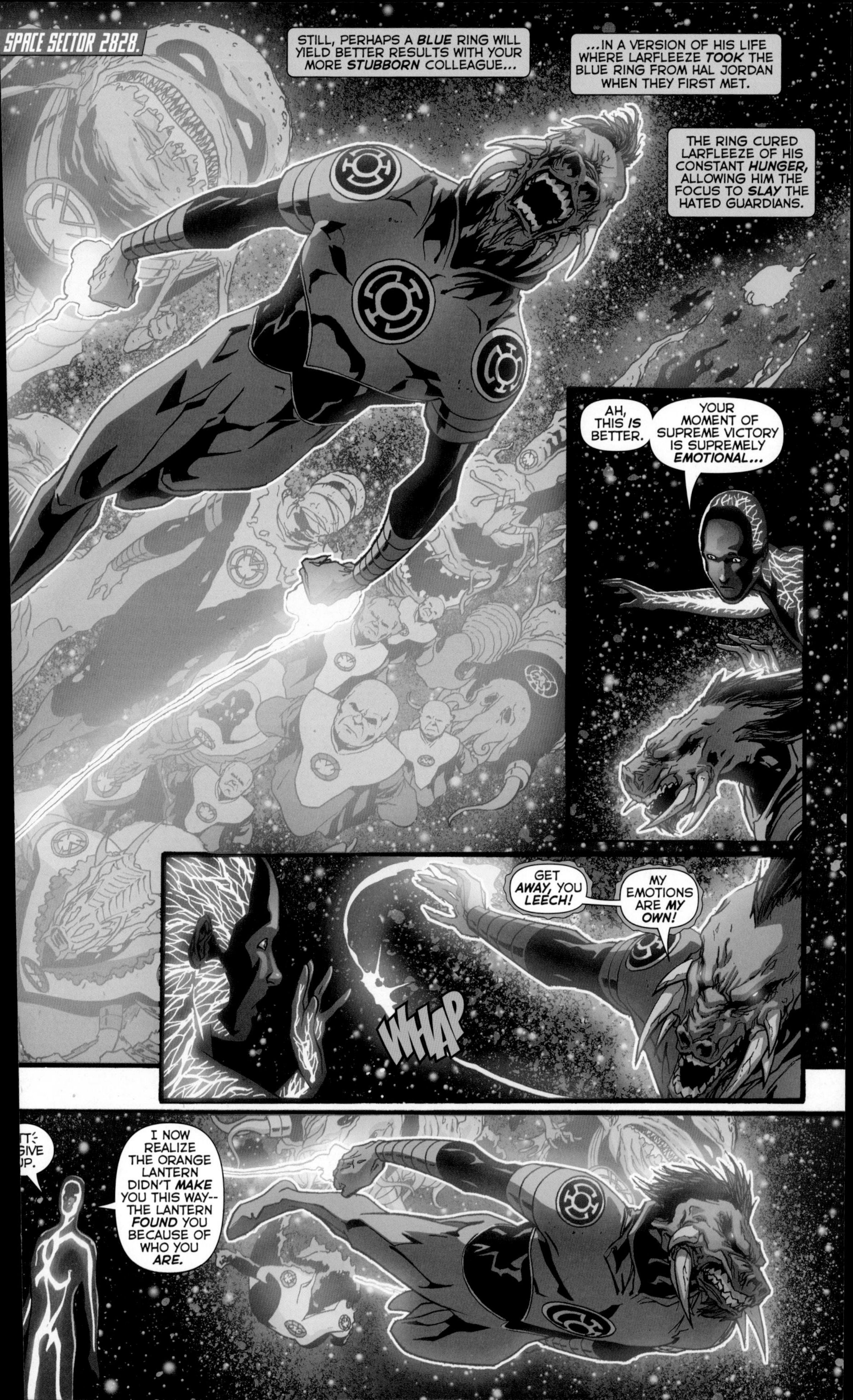
SPACE SECTOR 2828.
STILL, PERHAPS A BLUE RING WILL YIELD BETTER RESULTS WITH YOUR MORE STUBBORN COLLEAGUE...
...IN A VERSION OF HIS LIFE WHERE LARFLEEZE TOOK THE BLUE RING FROM HAL JORDAN WHEN THEY FIRST MET.
THE RING CURED LARFLEEZE OF HIS CONSTANT HUNGER, ALLOWING HIM THE FOCUS TO SLAY THE HATED GUARDIANS.
AH, THIS IS BETTER.
YOUR MOMENT OF SUPREME VICTORY IS SUPREMELY EMOTIONAL...
GET AWAY, YOU LEECH!
MY EMOTIONS ARE MY OWN!
WHAP
GIVE UP.
I NOW REALIZE THE ORANGE LANTERN DIDN'T MAKE YOU THIS WAY-- THE LANTERN FOUND YOU BECAUSE OF WHO YOU ARE.

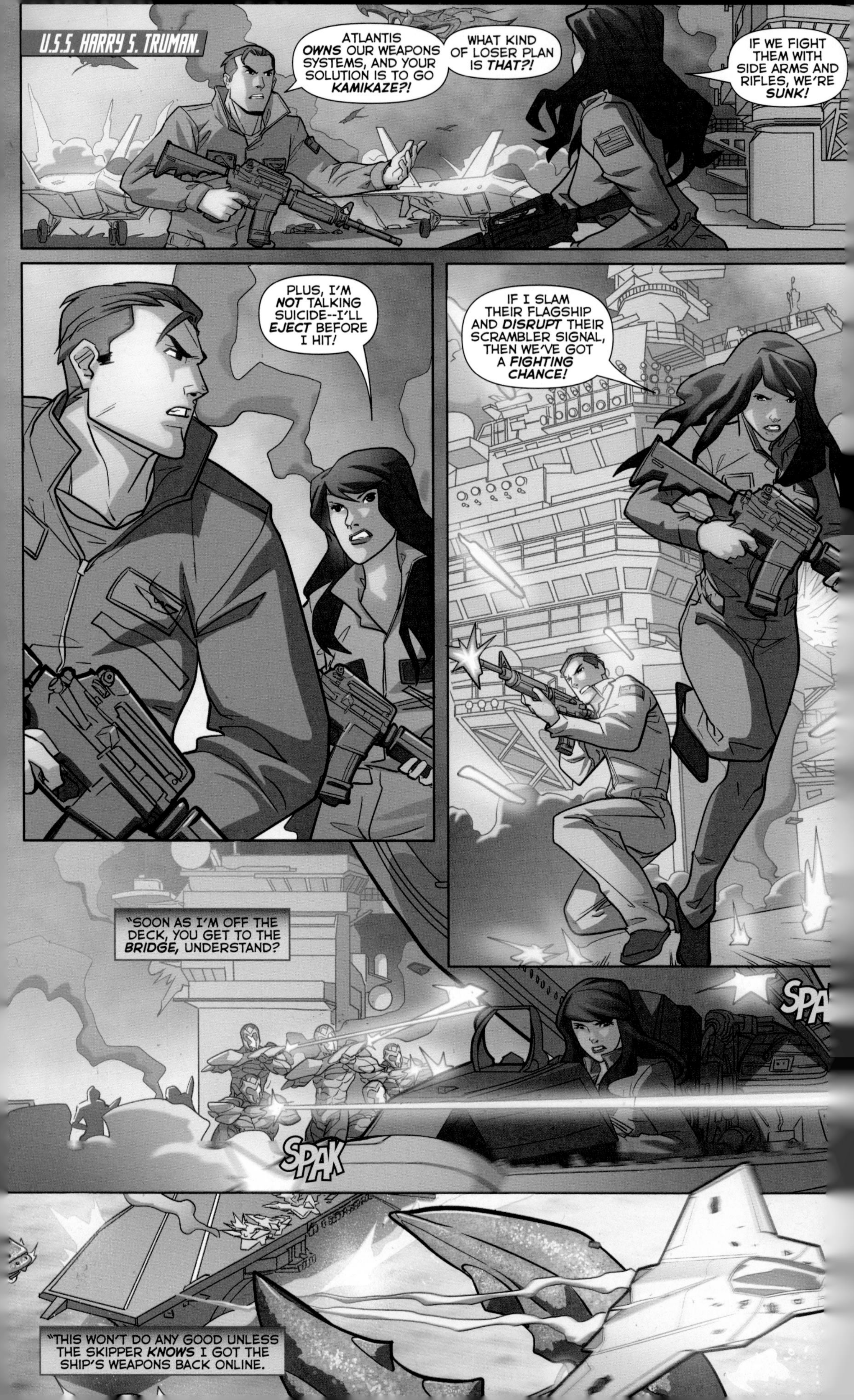
U.S.S. HARRY S. TRUMAN.
ATLANTIS OWNS OUR WEAPONS SYSTEMS, AND YOUR SOLUTION IS TO GO KAMIKAZE?!
WHAT KIND OF LOSER PLAN IS THAT?!
IF WE FIGHT THEM WITH SIDE ARMS AND RIFLES, WE'RE SUNK!
PLUS, I'M NOT TALKING SUICIDE--I'LL EJECT BEFORE I HIT!
IF I SLAM THEIR FLAGSHIP AND DISRUPT THEIR SCRAMBLER SIGNAL, THEN WE'VE GOT A FIGHTING CHANCE!
"SOON AS I'M OFF THE DECK, YOU GET TO THE BRIDGE, UNDERSTAND?
SPAK
"THIS WON'T DO ANY GOOD UNLESS THE SKIPPER KNOWS I GOT THE SHIP'S WEAPONS BACK ONLINE.

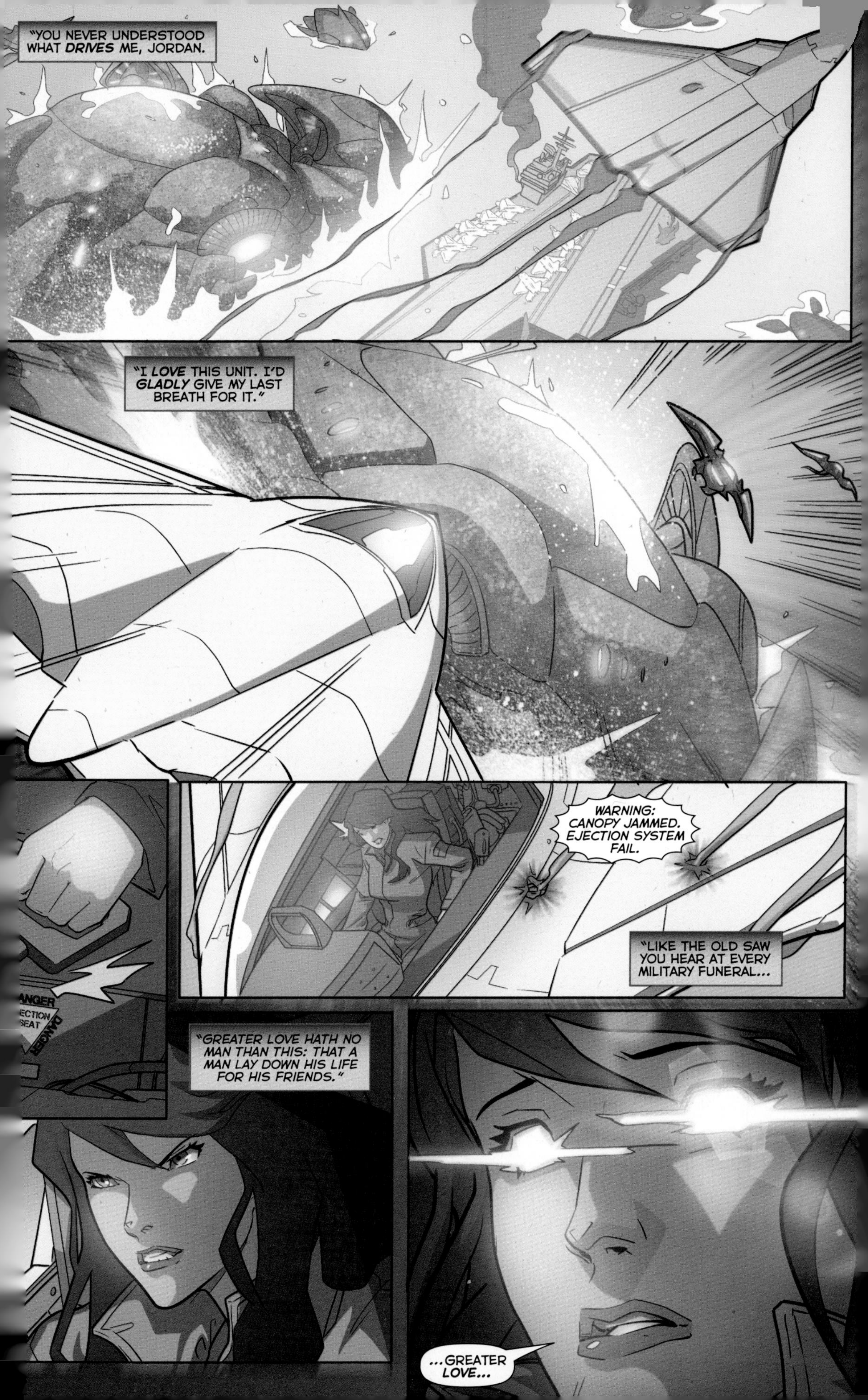
"YOU NEVER UNDERSTOOD WHAT DRIVES ME, JORDAN.
"I LOVE THIS UNIT. I'D GLADLY GIVE MY LAST BREATH FOR IT."
WARNING: CANOPY JAMMED. EJECTION SYSTEM FAIL.
"LIKE THE OLD SAW YOU HEAR AT EVERY MILITARY FUNERAL...
"GREATER LOVE HATH NO MAN THAN THIS: THAT A MAN LAY DOWN HIS LIFE FOR HIS FRIENDS."
...GREATER LOVE...

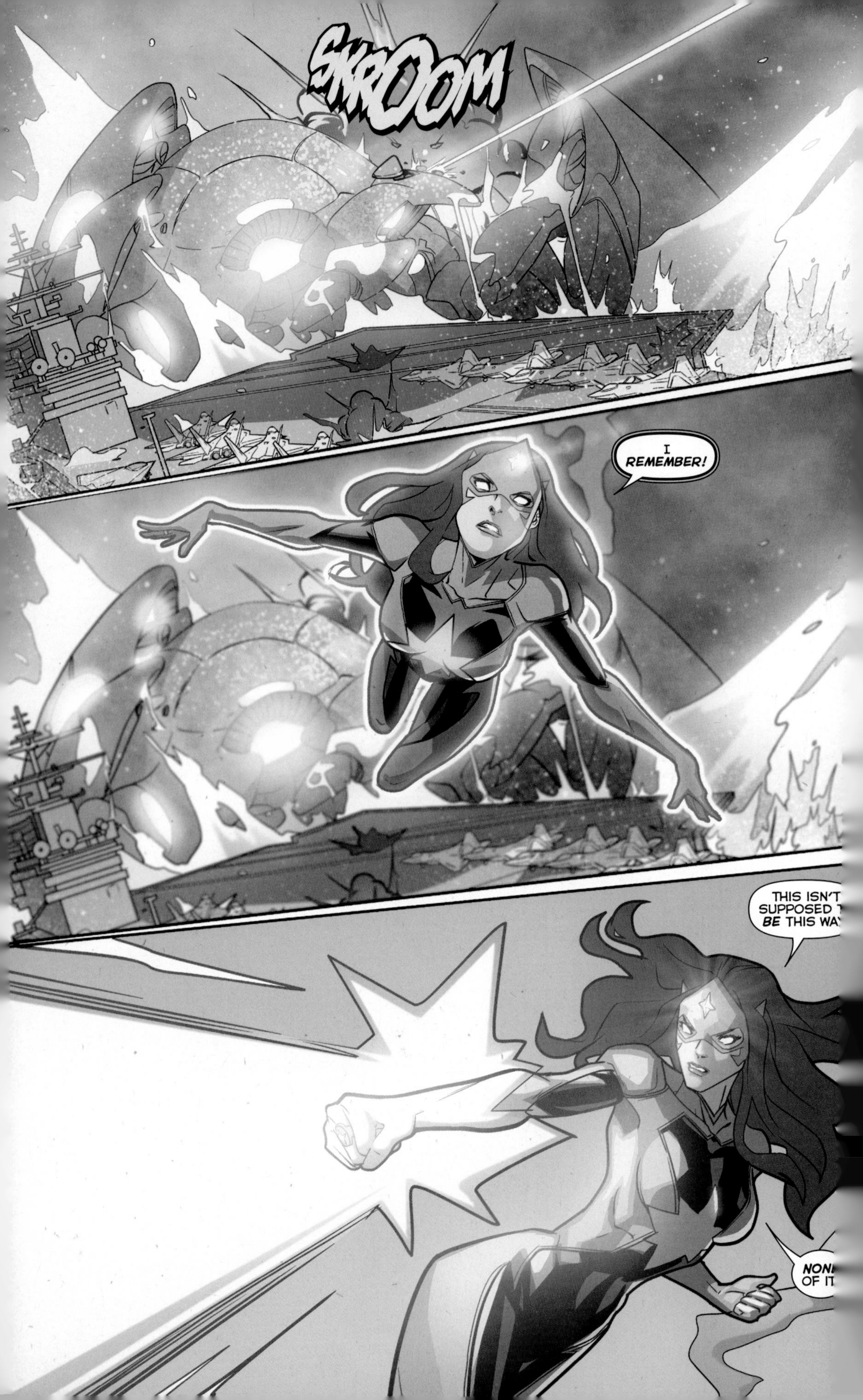
SKROOM
I REMEMBER!
THIS ISN'T SUPPOSED T BE THIS WAY
NON OF IT

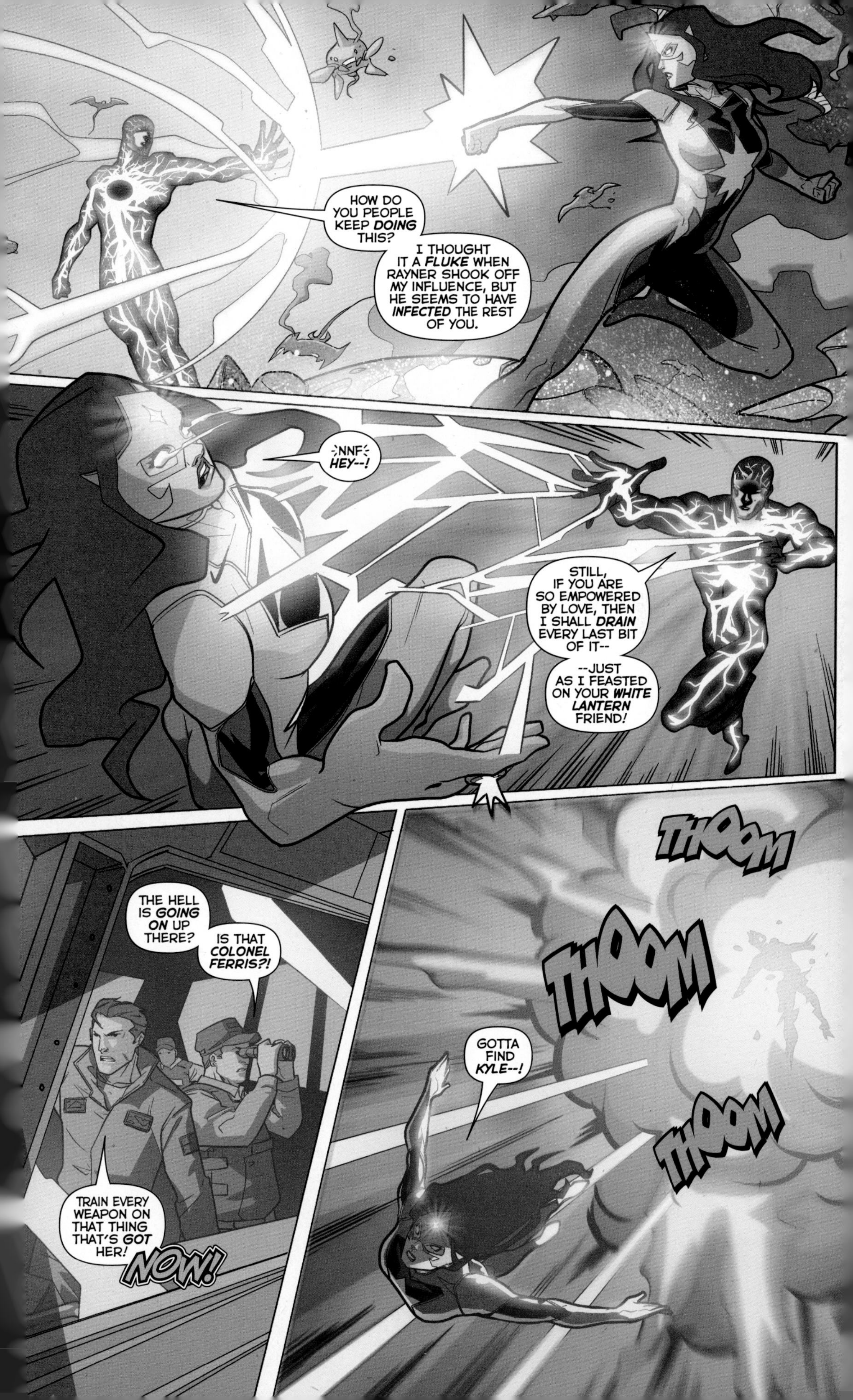
HOW DO YOU PEOPLE KEEP DOING THIS?
I THOUGHT IT A FLUKE WHEN RAYNER SHOOK OFF MY INFLUENCE, BUT HE SEEMS TO HAVE INFECTED THE REST OF YOU.
-NNF- HEY--!
STILL, IF YOU ARE SO EMPOWERED BY LOVE, THEN I SHALL DRAIN EVERY LAST BIT OF IT--
--JUST AS I FEASTED ON YOUR WHITE LANTERN FRIEND!
THE HELL IS GOING ON UP THERE?
IS THAT COLONEL FERRIS?!
TRAIN EVERY WEAPON ON THAT THING THAT'S GOT HER!
NOW!
THOOM
THOOM
THOOM
GOTTA FIND KYLE--!

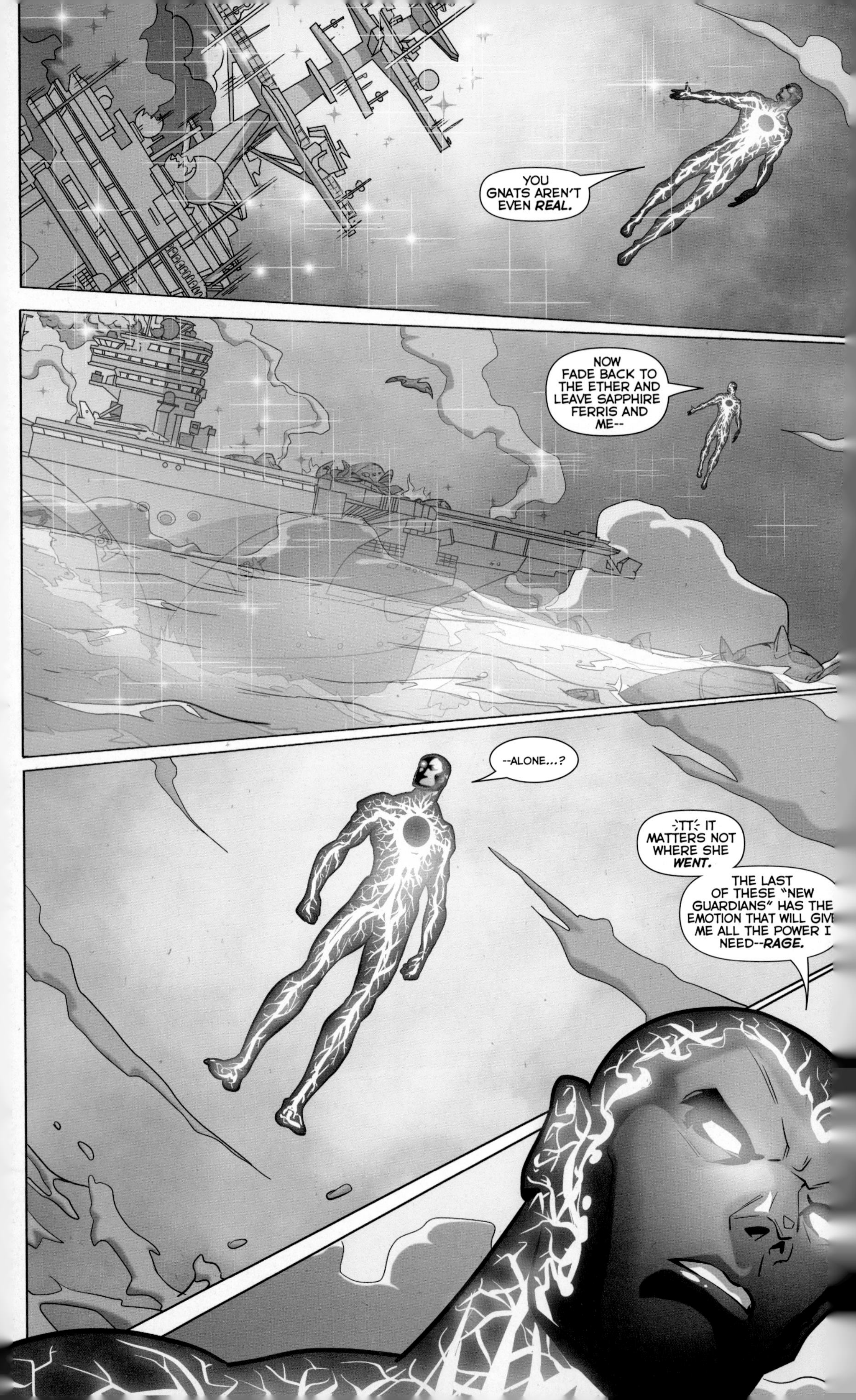
YOU GNATS AREN'T EVEN REAL.
NOW FADE BACK TO THE ETHER AND LEAVE SAPPHIRE FERRIS AND ME--
--ALONE...?
TT IT MATTERS NOT WHERE SHE WENT.
THE LAST OF THESE "NEW GUARDIANS" HAS THE EMOTION THAT WILL GIVE ME ALL THE POWER I NEED--RAGE.

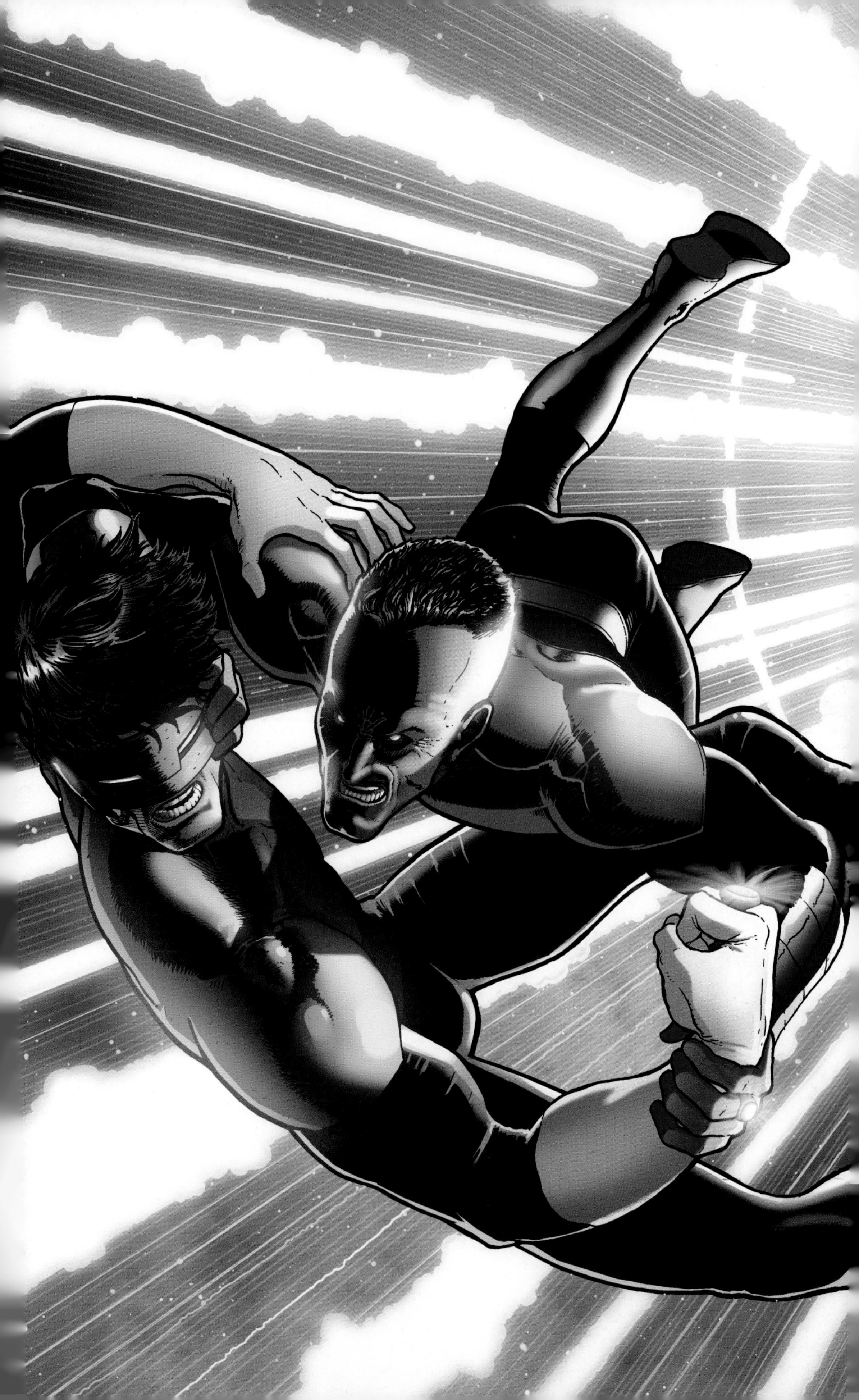

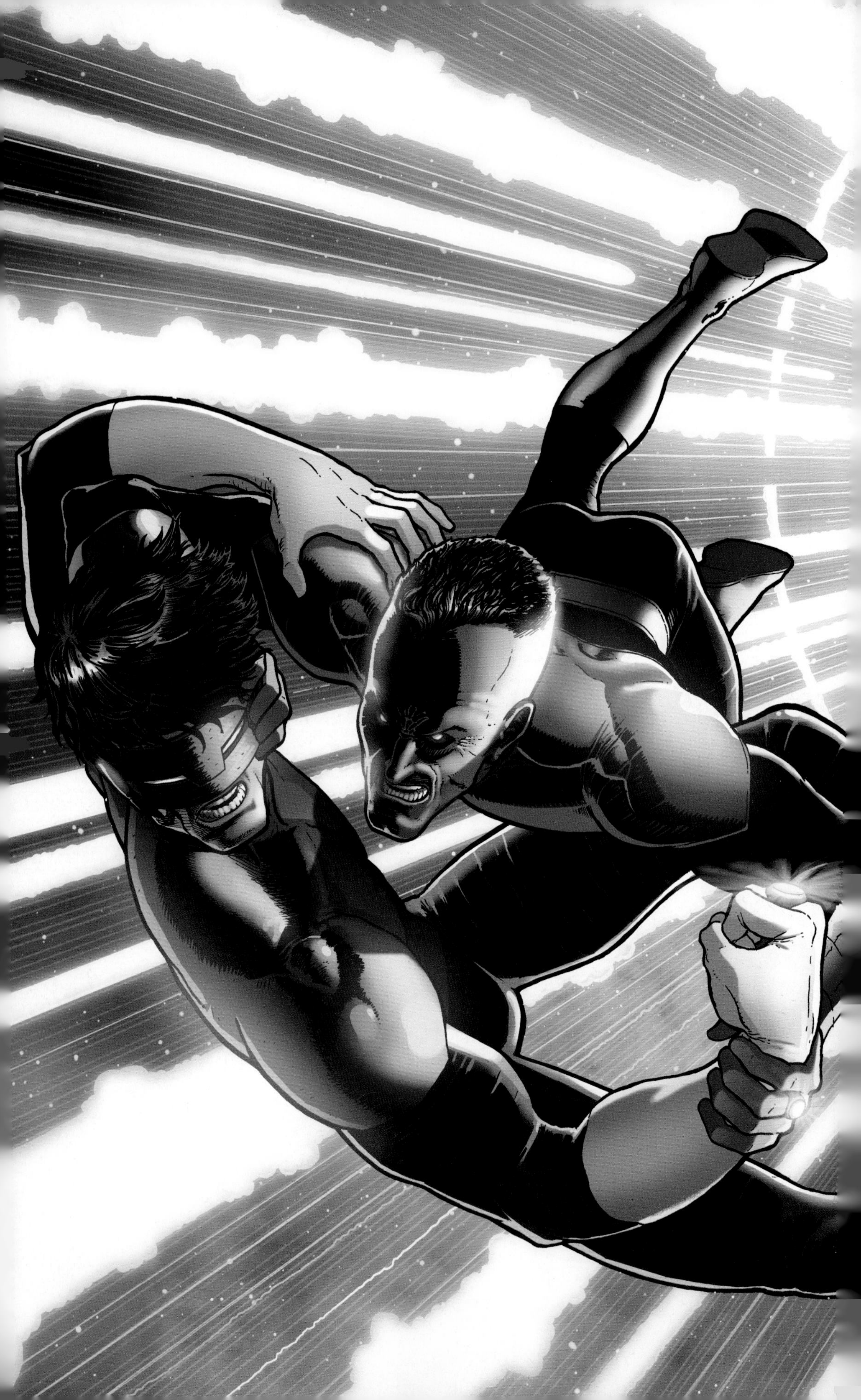

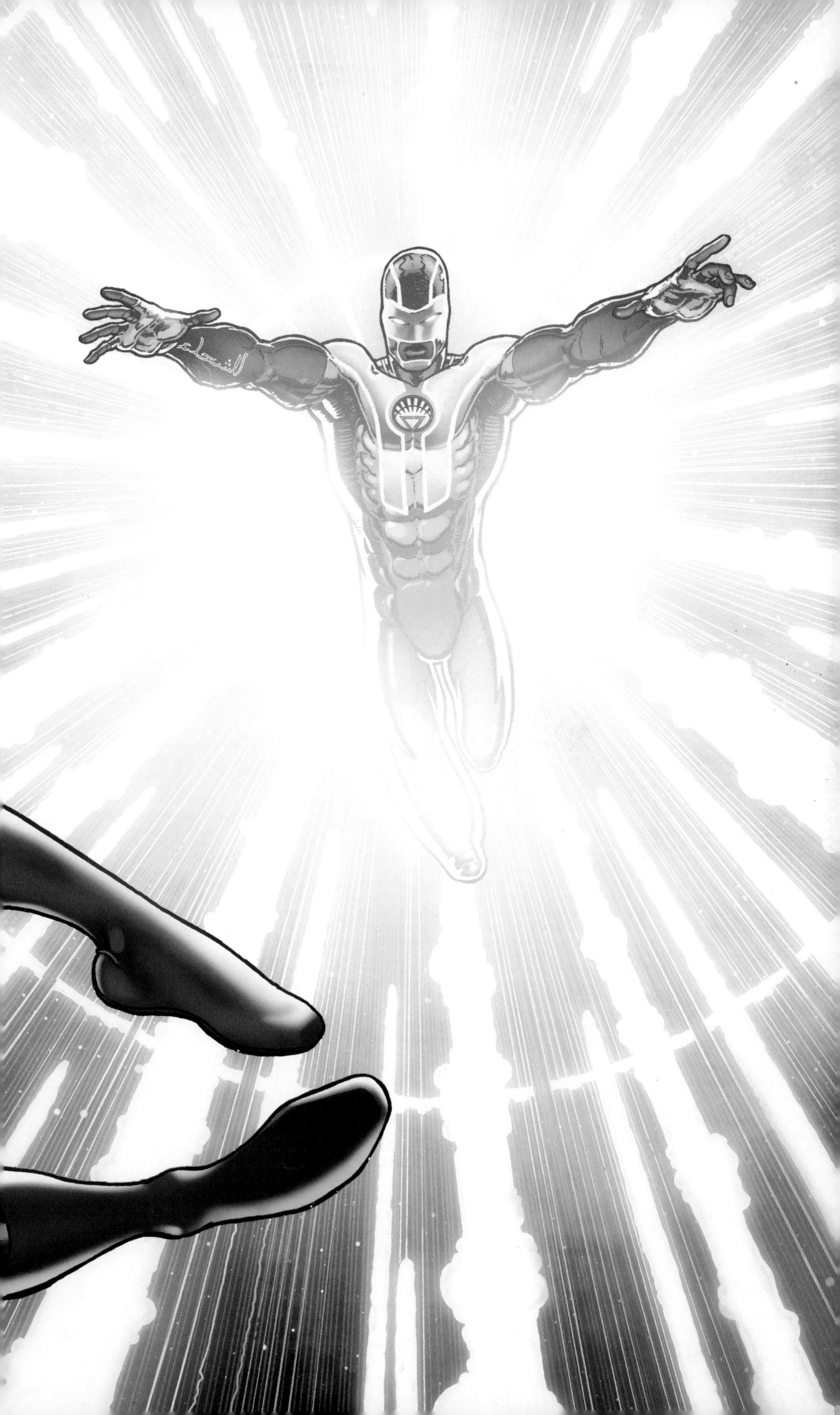

SHADOW OF DEATH

TONY BEDARD writer **ANDRES GUINALDO** penciller **RAUL FERNANDEZ** inker
AARON KUDER & WIL QUINTANA cover

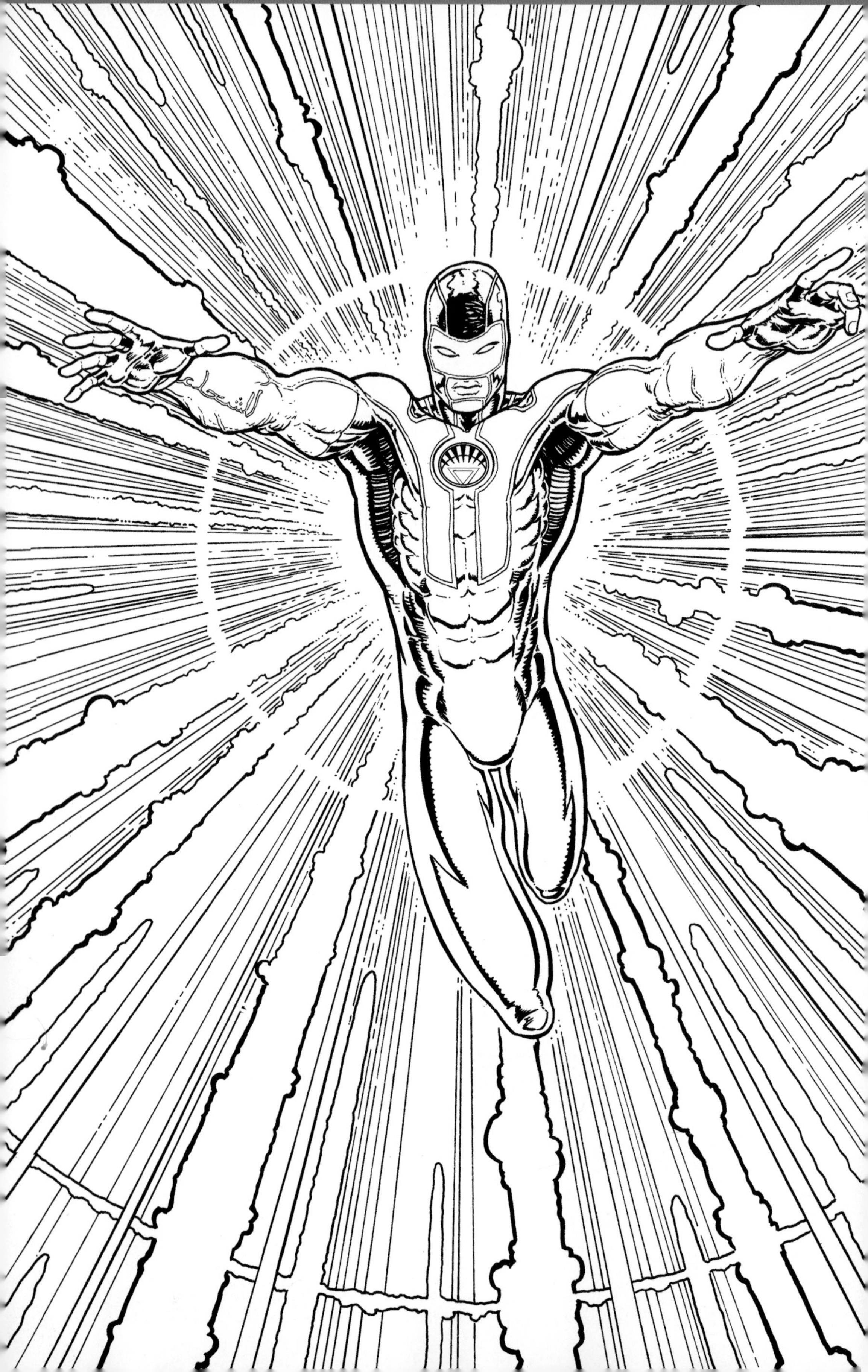

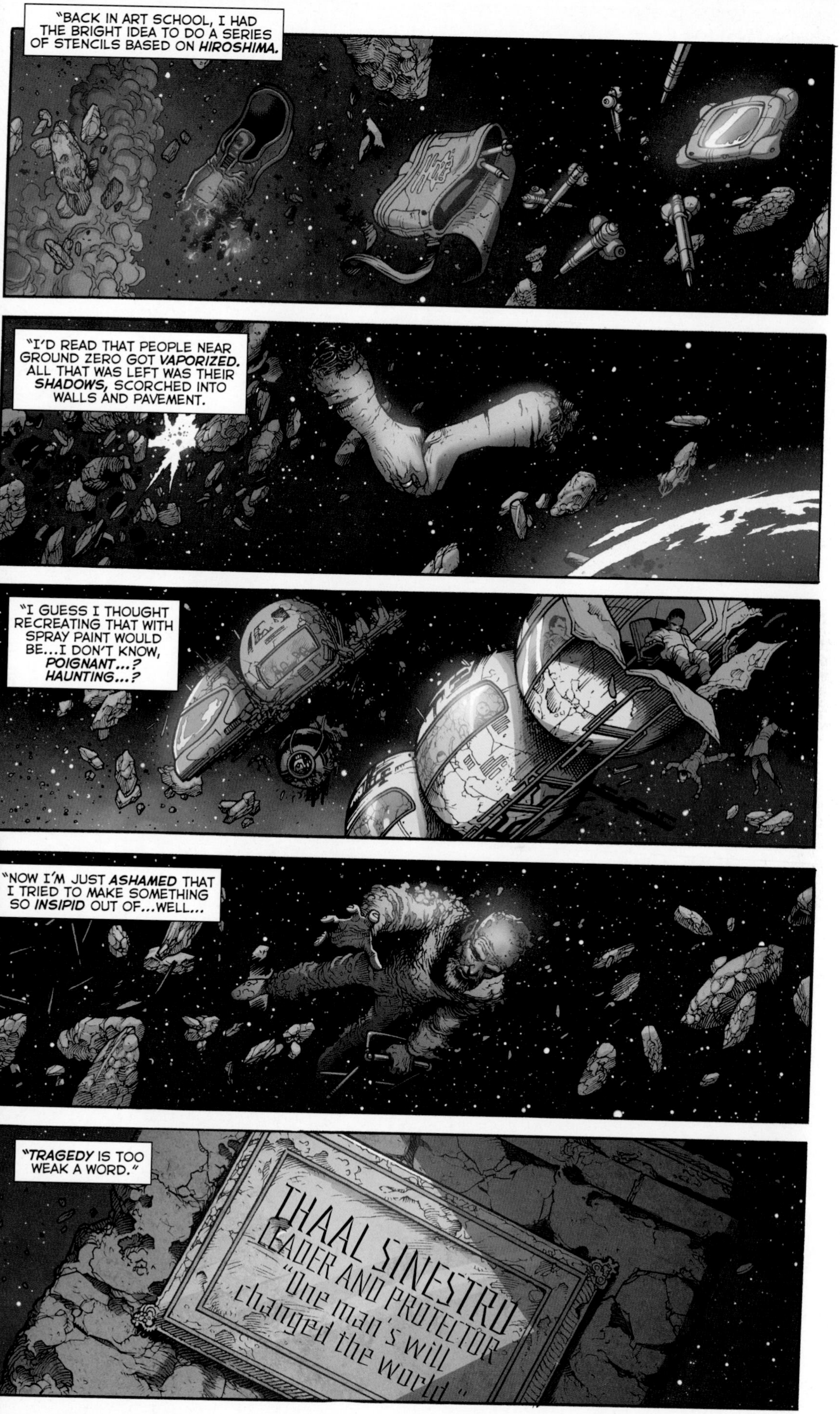
"BACK IN ART SCHOOL, I HAD THE BRIGHT IDEA TO DO A SERIES OF STENCILS BASED ON HIROSHIMA.
"I'D READ THAT PEOPLE NEAR GROUND ZERO GOT VAPORIZED. ALL THAT WAS LEFT WAS THEIR SHADOWS, SCORCHED INTO WALLS AND PAVEMENT.
"I GUESS I THOUGHT RECREATING THAT WITH SPRAY PAINT WOULD BE...I DON'T KNOW, POIGNANT...? HAUNTING...?
"NOW I'M JUST ASHAMED THAT I TRIED TO MAKE SOMETHING SO INSIPID OUT OF...WELL...
"TRAGEDY IS TOO WEAK A WORD."
THAAL SINESTRO
LEADER AND PROTECTOR
"One man's will changed the world."

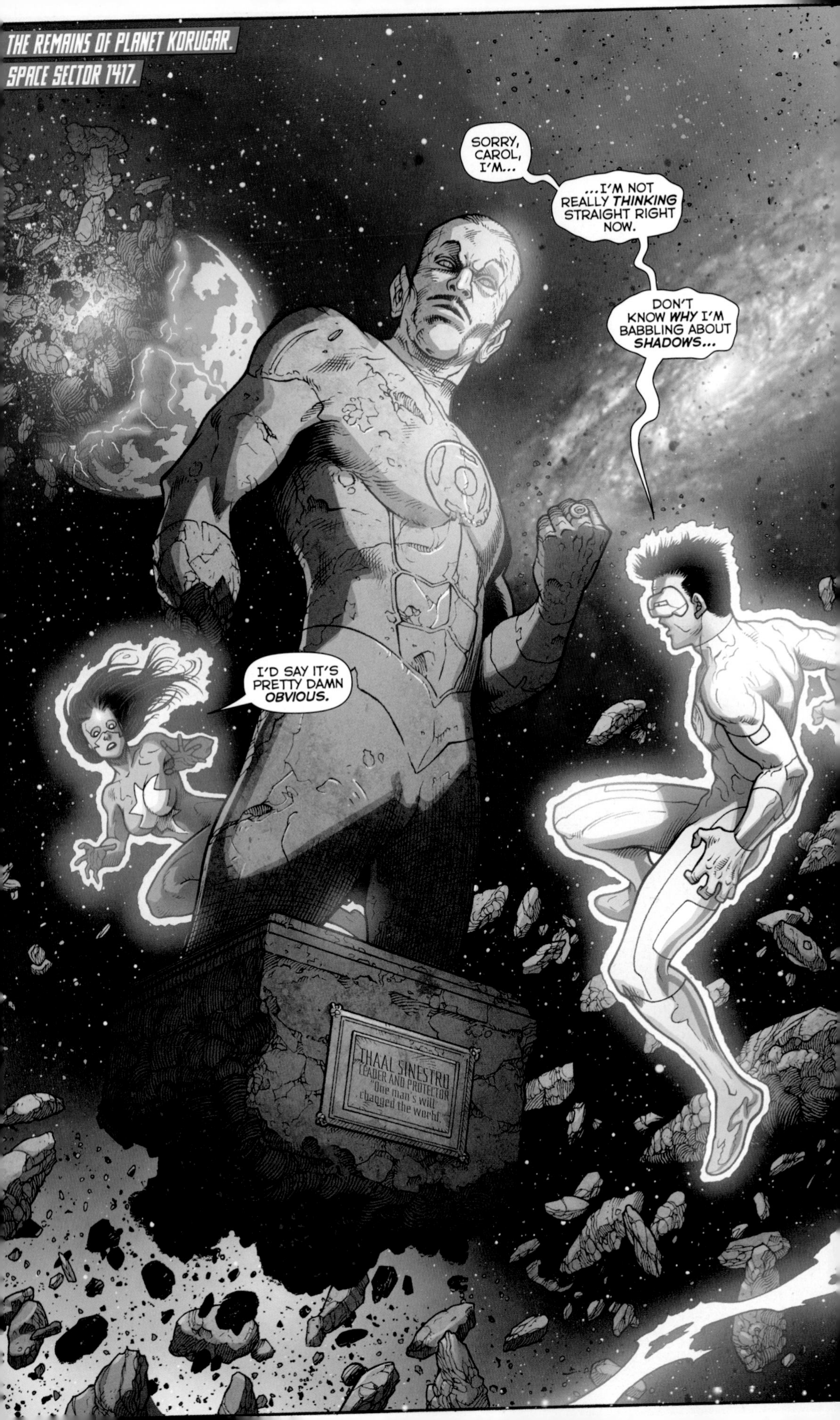
THE REMAINS OF PLANET KORUGAR.
SPACE SECTOR 1417.
SORRY, CAROL, I'M...
...I'M NOT REALLY THINKING STRAIGHT RIGHT NOW.
DON'T KNOW WHY I'M BABBLING ABOUT SHADOWS...
I'D SAY IT'S PRETTY DAMN OBVIOUS.
THAAL SINESTRO
LEADER AND PROTECTOR
"One man's will changed the world."

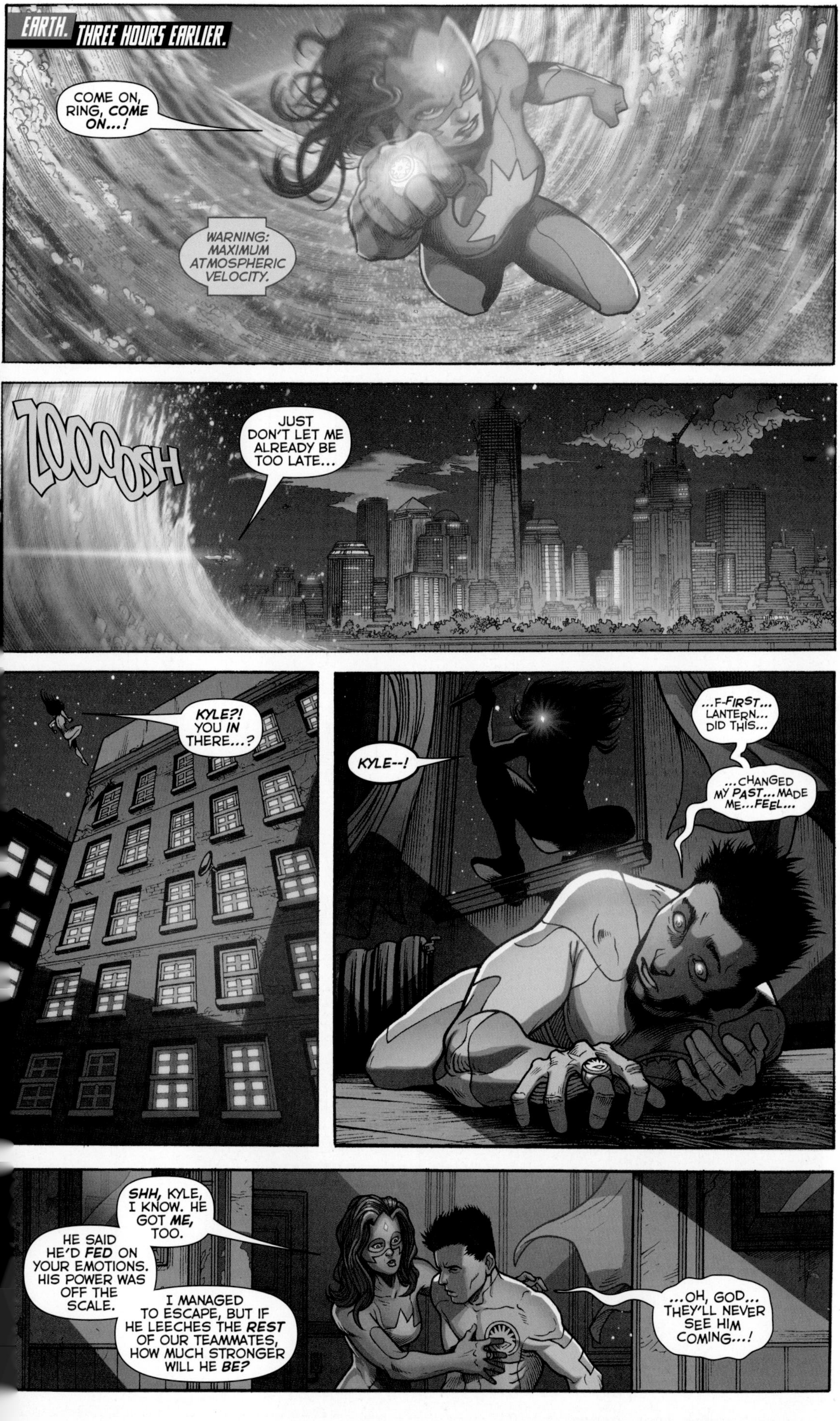
EARTH. THREE HOURS EARLIER.
COME ON, RING, COME ON...!
WARNING: MAXIMUM ATMOSPHERIC VELOCITY.
ZOOOOSH
JUST DON'T LET ME ALREADY BE TOO LATE...
KYLE?! YOU IN THERE...?
KYLE--!
...F-FIRST... LANTERN... DID THIS...
...CHANGED MY PAST...MADE ME...FEEL...
SHH, KYLE, I KNOW. HE GOT ME, TOO.
HE SAID HE'D FED ON YOUR EMOTIONS. HIS POWER WAS OFF THE SCALE.
I MANAGED TO ESCAPE, BUT IF HE LEECHES THE REST OF OUR TEAMMATES, HOW MUCH STRONGER WILL HE BE?
...OH, GOD... THEY'LL NEVER SEE HIM COMING...!

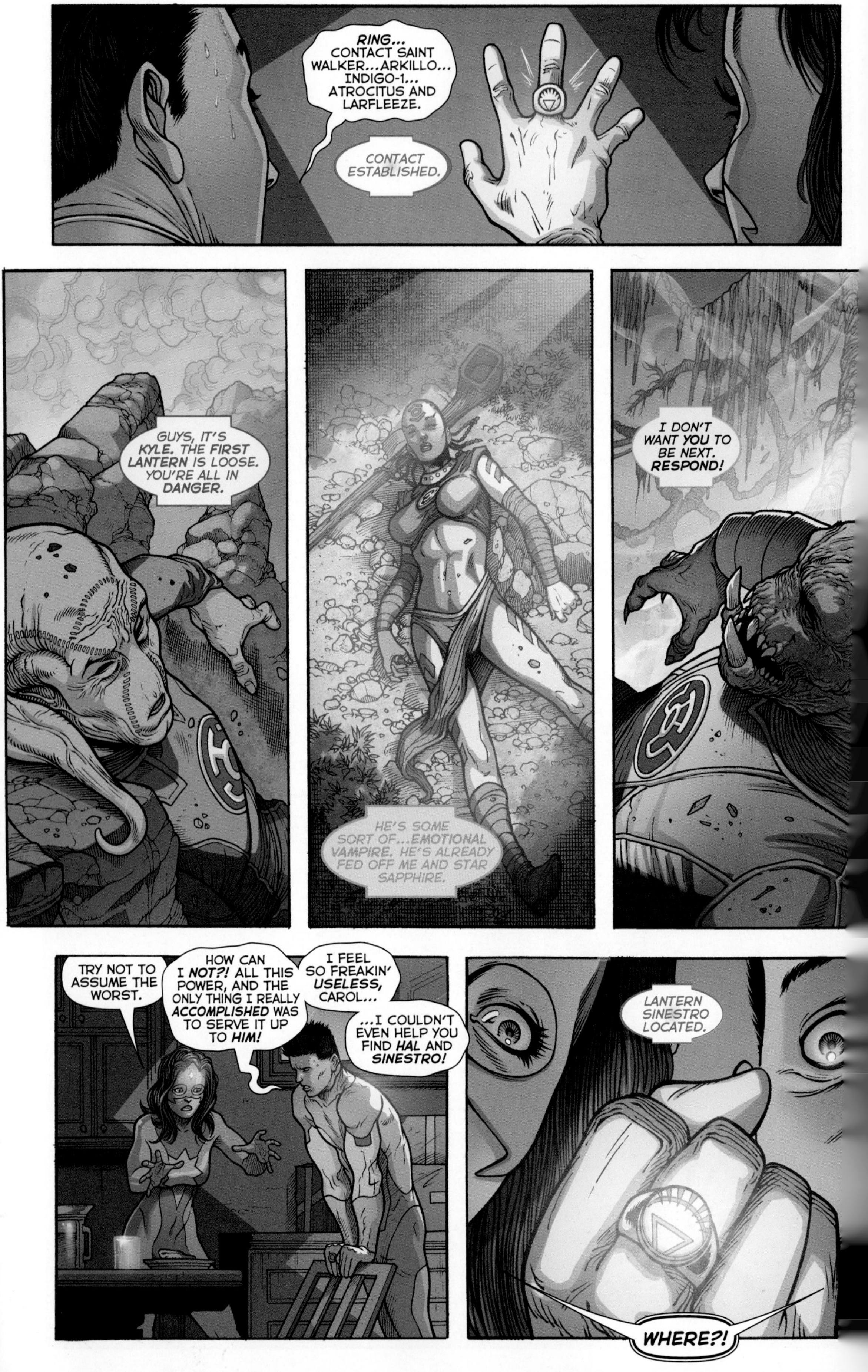
RING... CONTACT SAINT WALKER...ARKILLO... INDIGO-1... ATROCITUS AND LARFLEEZE.
CONTACT ESTABLISHED.
GUYS, IT'S KYLE. THE FIRST LANTERN IS LOOSE. YOU'RE ALL IN DANGER.
HE'S SOME SORT OF...EMOTIONAL VAMPIRE. HE'S ALREADY FED OFF ME AND STAR SAPPHIRE.
I DON'T WANT YOU TO BE NEXT. RESPOND!
TRY NOT TO ASSUME THE WORST.
HOW CAN I NOT?! ALL THIS POWER, AND THE ONLY THING I REALLY ACCOMPLISHED WAS TO SERVE IT UP TO HIM!
I FEEL SO FREAKIN' USELESS, CAROL...
...I COULDN'T EVEN HELP YOU FIND HAL AND SINESTRO!
LANTERN SINESTRO LOCATED.
WHERE?!

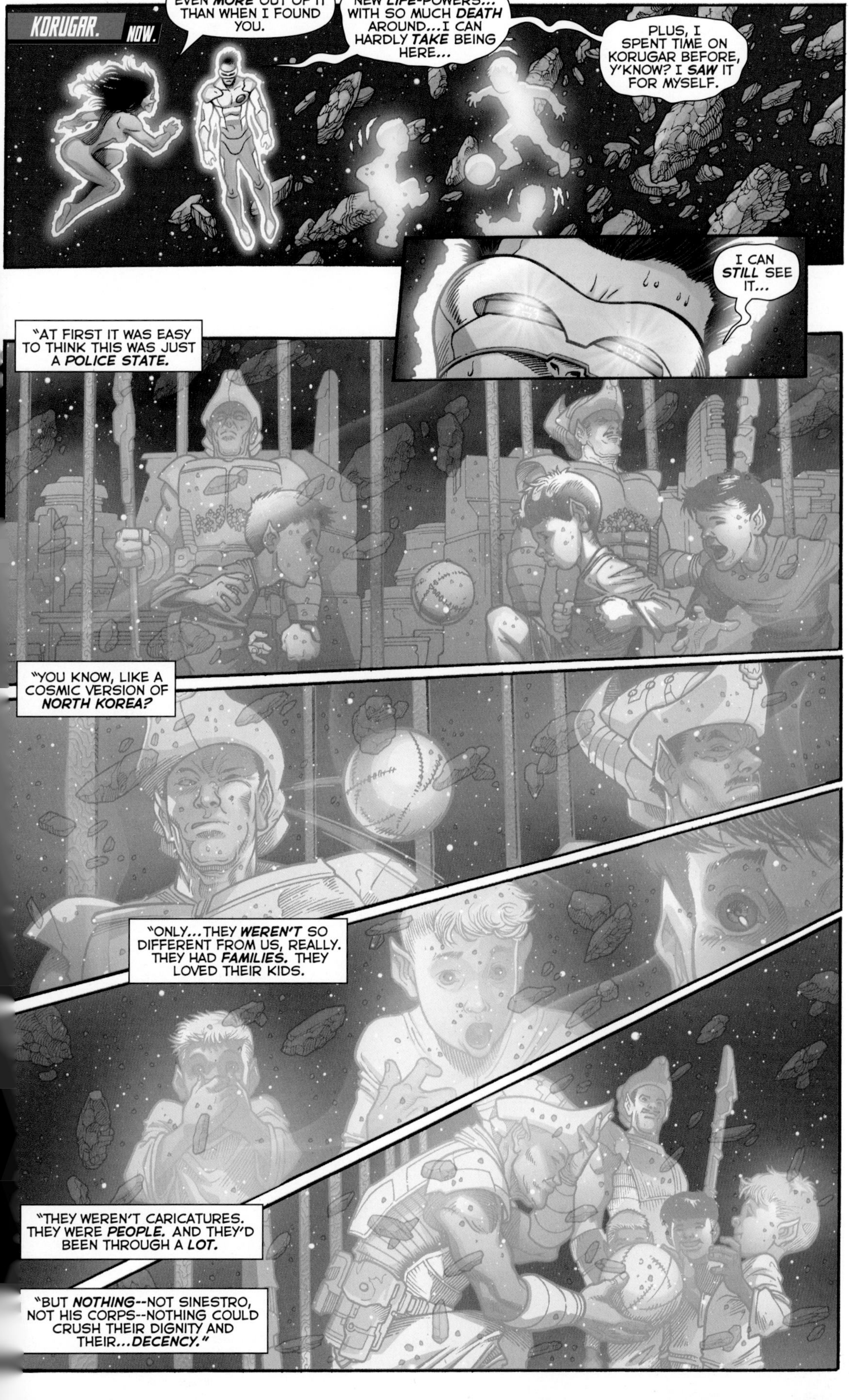

KORUGAR.
NOW.
KYLE, YOU SEEM EVEN MORE OUT OF IT THAN WHEN I FOUND YOU.
...IT'S THESE NEW LIFE-POWERS... WITH SO MUCH DEATH AROUND...I CAN HARDLY TAKE BEING HERE...
PLUS, I SPENT TIME ON KORUGAR BEFORE, Y'KNOW? I SAW IT FOR MYSELF.
I CAN STILL SEE IT...
"AT FIRST IT WAS EASY TO THINK THIS WAS JUST A POLICE STATE.
"YOU KNOW, LIKE A COSMIC VERSION OF NORTH KOREA?
"ONLY...THEY WEREN'T SO DIFFERENT FROM US, REALLY. THEY HAD FAMILIES. THEY LOVED THEIR KIDS.
"THEY WEREN'T CARICATURES. THEY WERE PEOPLE. AND THEY'D BEEN THROUGH A LOT.
"BUT NOTHING--NOT SINESTRO, NOT HIS CORPS--NOTHING COULD CRUSH THEIR DIGNITY AND THEIR...DECENCY."

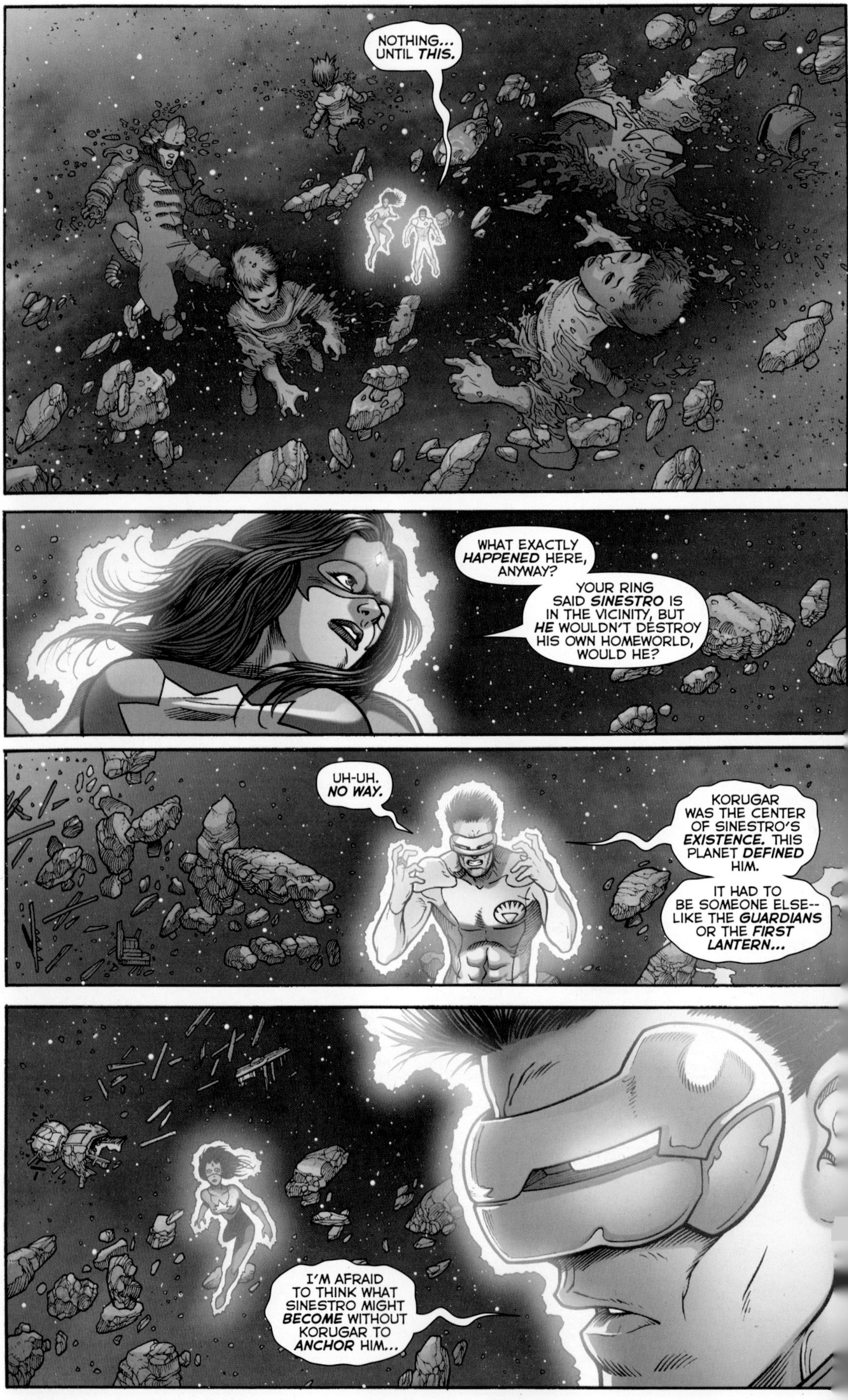
NOTHING... UNTIL THIS.
WHAT EXACTLY HAPPENED HERE, ANYWAY?
YOUR RING SAID SINESTRO IS IN THE VICINITY, BUT HE WOULDN'T DESTROY HIS OWN HOMEWORLD, WOULD HE?
UH-UH. NO WAY.
KORUGAR WAS THE CENTER OF SINESTRO'S EXISTENCE. THIS PLANET DEFINED HIM.
IT HAD TO BE SOMEONE ELSE--LIKE THE GUARDIANS OR THE FIRST LANTERN...
I'M AFRAID TO THINK WHAT SINESTRO MIGHT BECOME WITHOUT KORUGAR TO ANCHOR HIM...

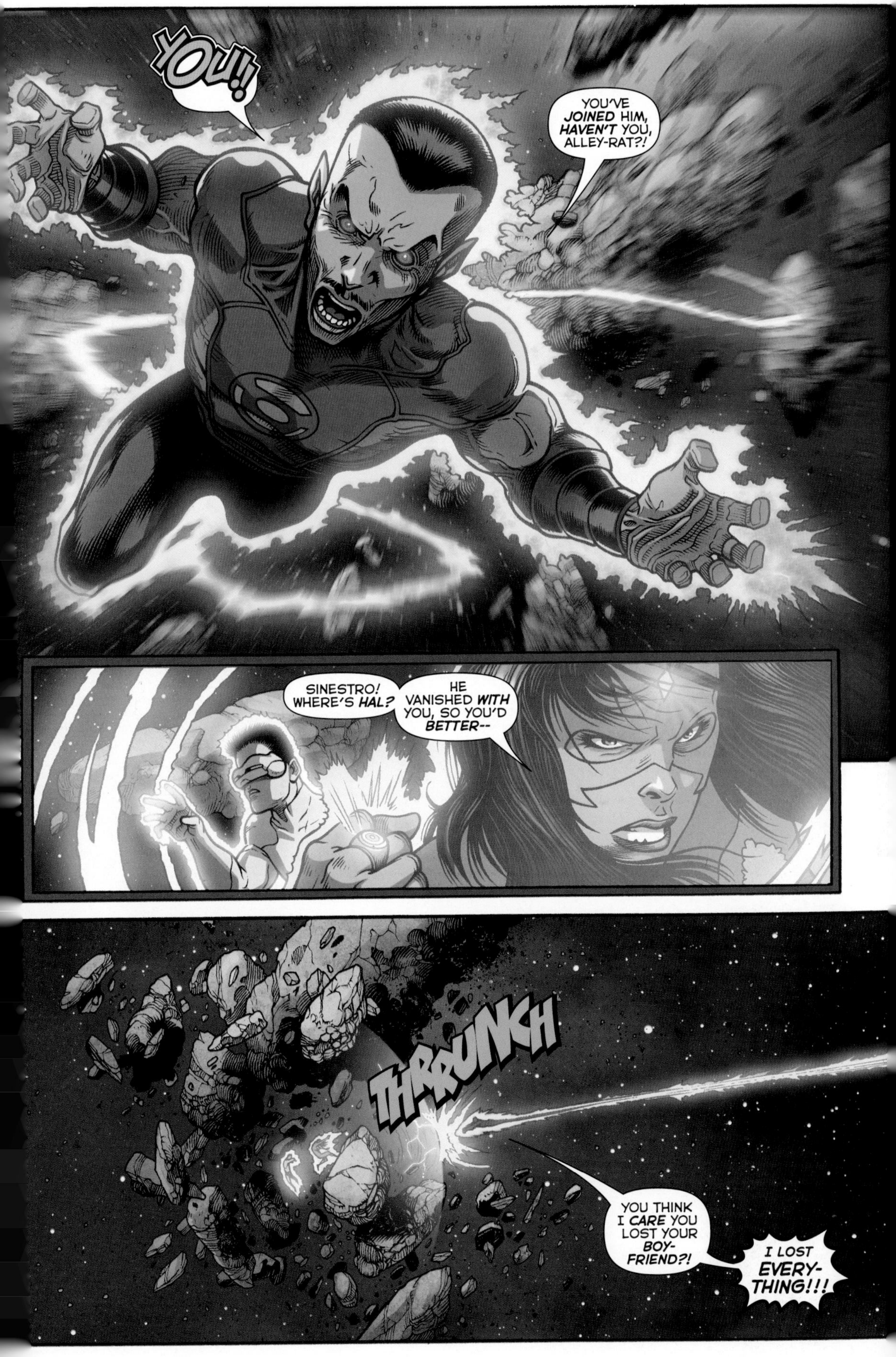
YOU!!
YOU'VE JOINED HIM, HAVEN'T YOU, ALLEY-RAT?!
SINESTRO! WHERE'S HAL?
HE VANISHED WITH YOU, SO YOU'D BETTER--
THRRUNCH
YOU THINK I CARE YOU LOST YOUR BOY-FRIEND?!
I LOST EVERY-THING!!!

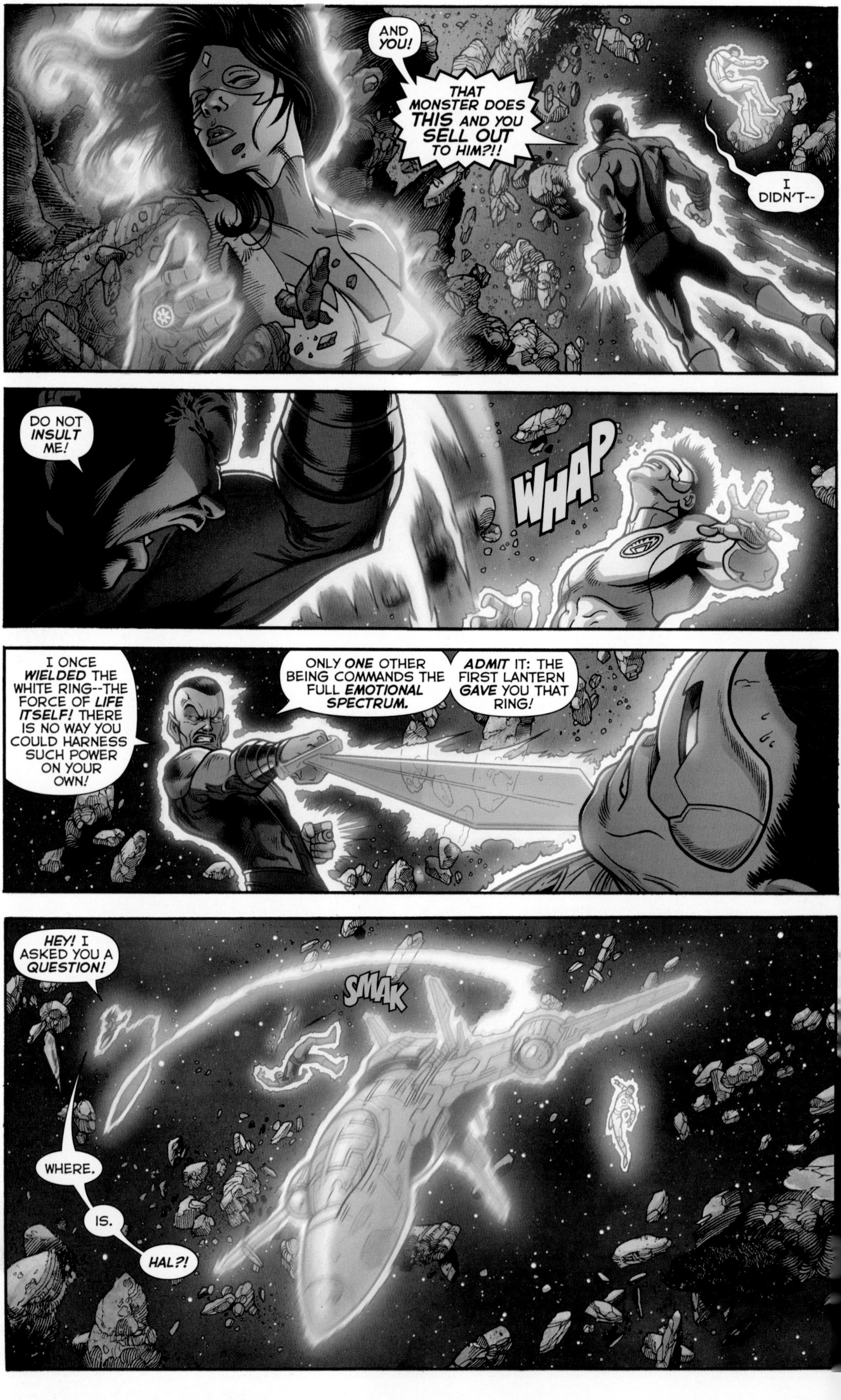
AND YOU!
THAT MONSTER DOES THIS AND YOU SELL OUT TO HIM?!!
I DIDN'T--
DO NOT INSULT ME!
WHAP
I ONCE WIELDED THE WHITE RING--THE FORCE OF LIFE ITSELF! THERE IS NO WAY YOU COULD HARNESS SUCH POWER ON YOUR OWN!
ONLY ONE OTHER BEING COMMANDS THE FULL EMOTIONAL SPECTRUM.
ADMIT IT: THE FIRST LANTERN GAVE YOU THAT RING!
HEY! I ASKED YOU A QUESTION!
SMAK
WHERE.
IS.
HAL?!

ENOUGH OF YOUR *WHINING!*

JORDAN IS *DEAD!* AND THIS TIME HE'S *NOT* COMING BACK!

YOU...

YOU'RE *LYING!* I'LL...

I'LL RIP THE *TRUTH* OUT OF YOU!

NO.

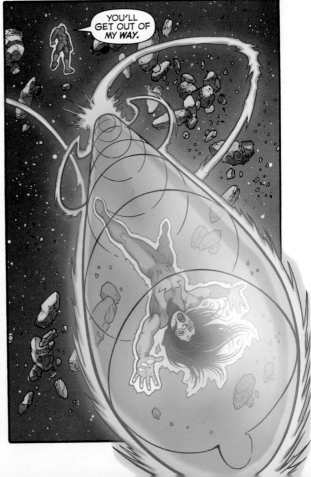

YOU'LL GET OUT OF *MY WAY.*

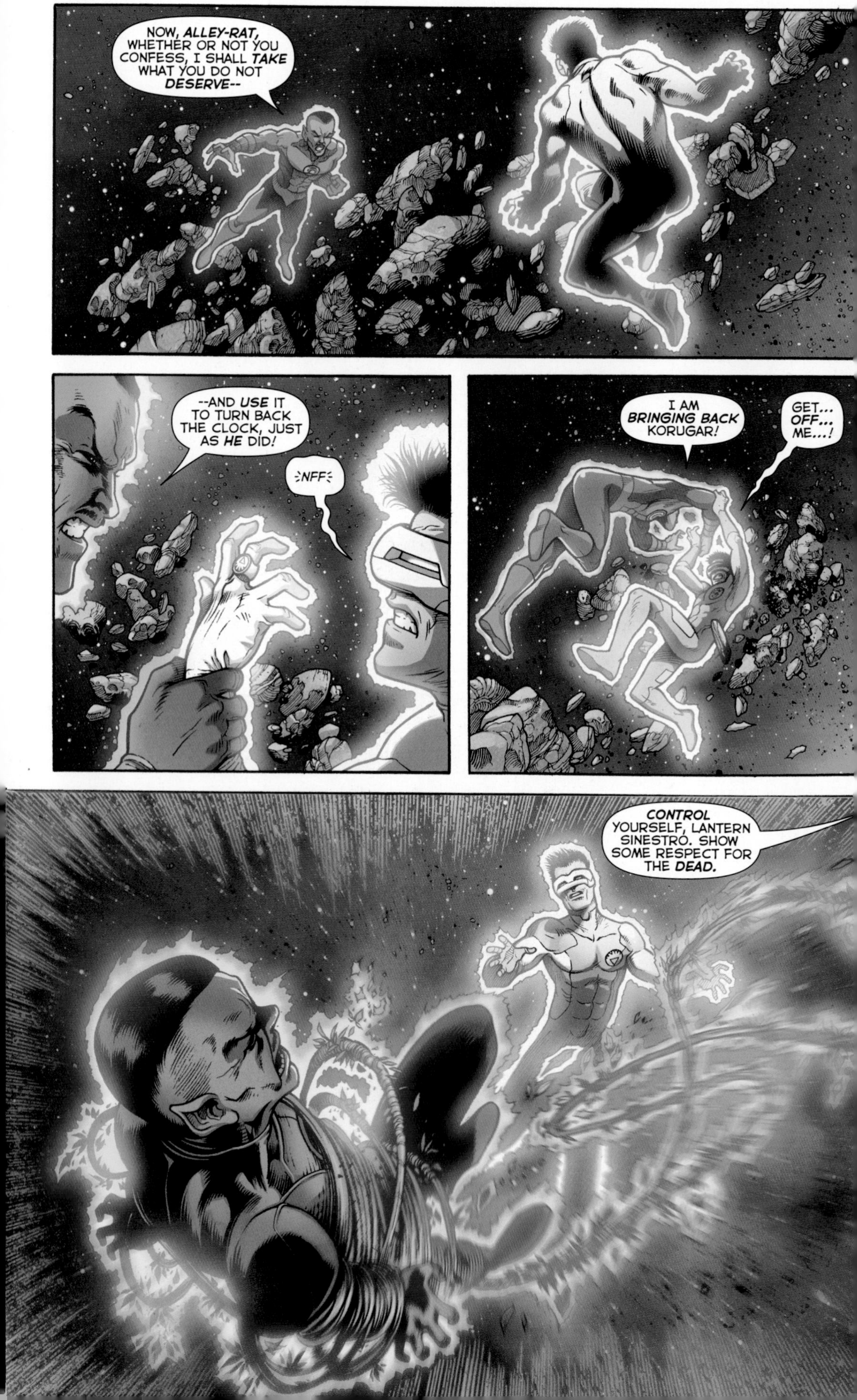
NOW, ALLEY-RAT, WHETHER OR NOT YOU CONFESS, I SHALL TAKE WHAT YOU DO NOT DESERVE--
--AND USE IT TO TURN BACK THE CLOCK, JUST AS HE DID!
NFF
I AM BRINGING BACK KORUGAR!
GET... OFF... ME...!
CONTROL YOURSELF, LANTERN SINESTRO. SHOW SOME RESPECT FOR THE DEAD.

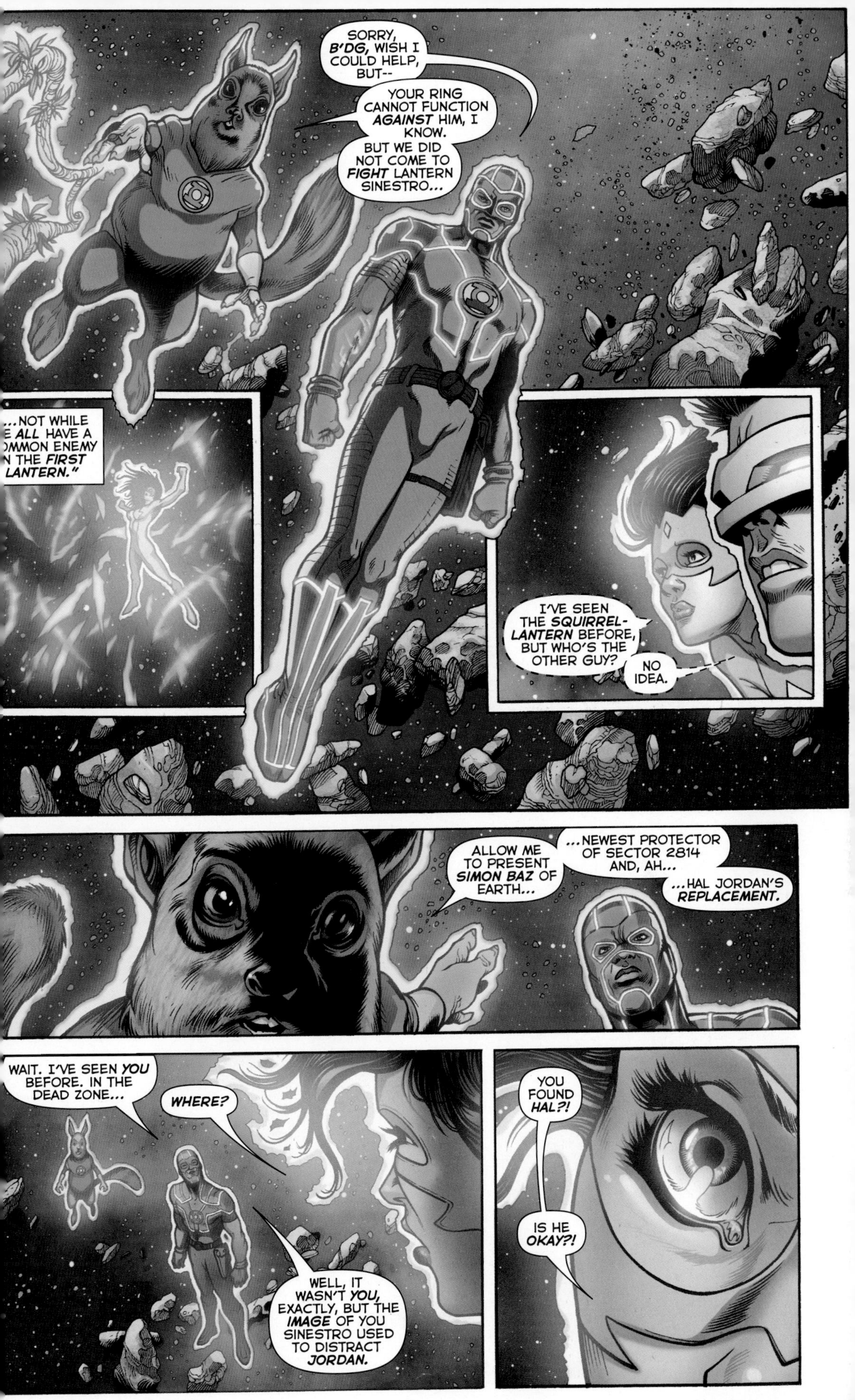
SORRY, B'DG, WISH I COULD HELP, BUT--
YOUR RING CANNOT FUNCTION AGAINST HIM, I KNOW.
BUT WE DID NOT COME TO FIGHT LANTERN SINESTRO...
...NOT WHILE
E ALL HAVE A
OMMON ENEMY
N THE FIRST
LANTERN."
I'VE SEEN THE SQUIRREL-LANTERN BEFORE, BUT WHO'S THE OTHER GUY?
NO IDEA.
ALLOW ME TO PRESENT SIMON BAZ OF EARTH...
...NEWEST PROTECTOR OF SECTOR 2814 AND, AH...
...HAL JORDAN'S REPLACEMENT.
WAIT. I'VE SEEN YOU BEFORE. IN THE DEAD ZONE...
WHERE?
WELL, IT WASN'T YOU, EXACTLY, BUT THE IMAGE OF YOU SINESTRO USED TO DISTRACT JORDAN.
YOU FOUND HAL?!
IS HE OKAY?!

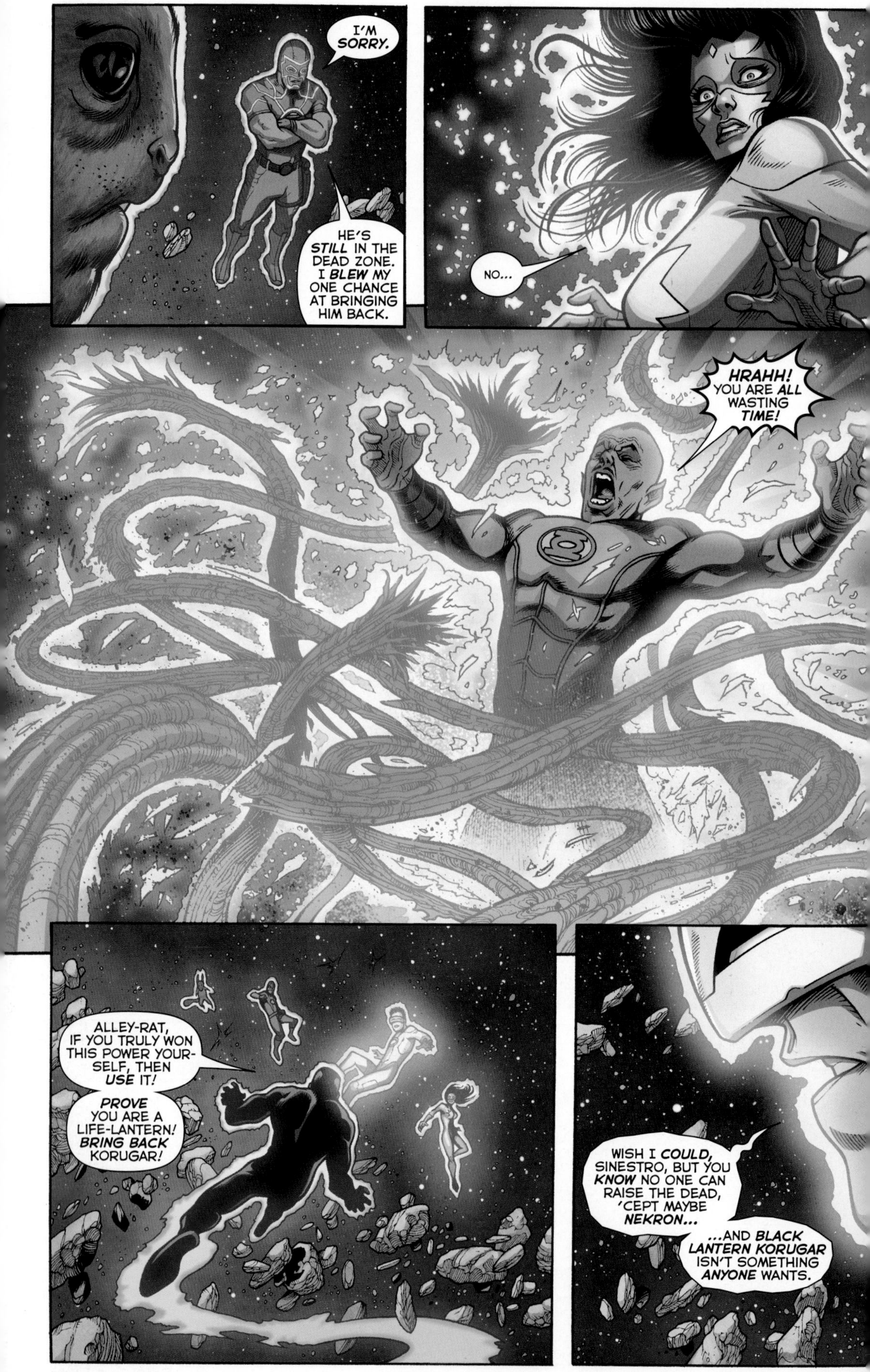
I'M SORRY.
HE'S STILL IN THE DEAD ZONE. I BLEW MY ONE CHANCE AT BRINGING HIM BACK.
NO...
HRAHH! YOU ARE ALL WASTING TIME!
ALLEY-RAT, IF YOU TRULY WON THIS POWER YOURSELF, THEN USE IT!
PROVE YOU ARE A LIFE-LANTERN! BRING BACK KORUGAR!
WISH I COULD, SINESTRO, BUT YOU KNOW NO ONE CAN RAISE THE DEAD, 'CEPT MAYBE NEKRON...
...AND BLACK LANTERN KORUGAR ISN'T SOMETHING ANYONE WANTS.

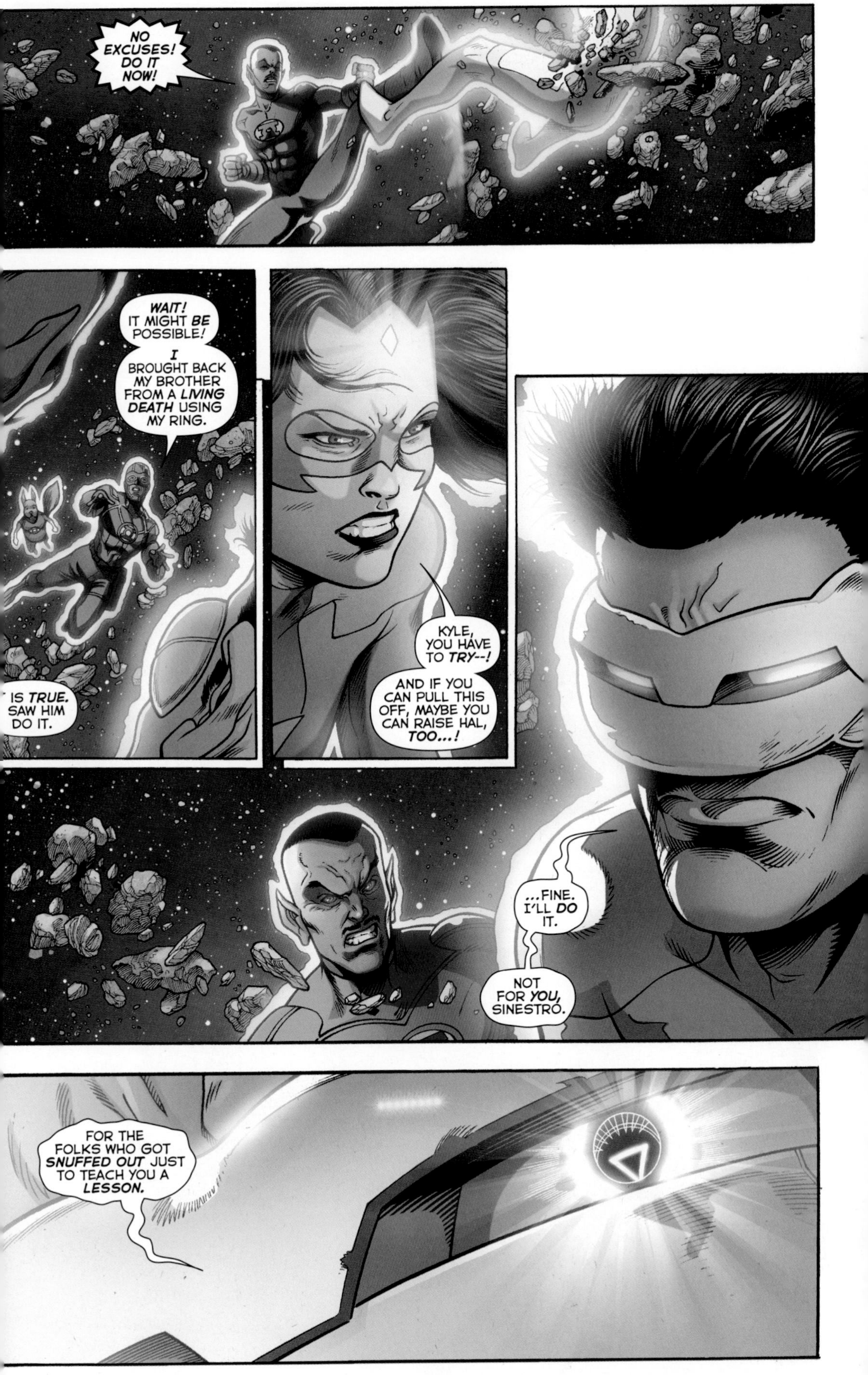
NO EXCUSES! DO IT NOW!
WAIT! IT MIGHT BE POSSIBLE!
I BROUGHT BACK MY BROTHER FROM A LIVING DEATH USING MY RING.
IS TRUE. SAW HIM DO IT.
KYLE, YOU HAVE TO TRY--!
AND IF YOU CAN PULL THIS OFF, MAYBE YOU CAN RAISE HAL, TOO...!
...FINE. I'LL DO IT.
NOT FOR YOU, SINESTRO.
FOR THE FOLKS WHO GOT SNUFFED OUT JUST TO TEACH YOU A LESSON.

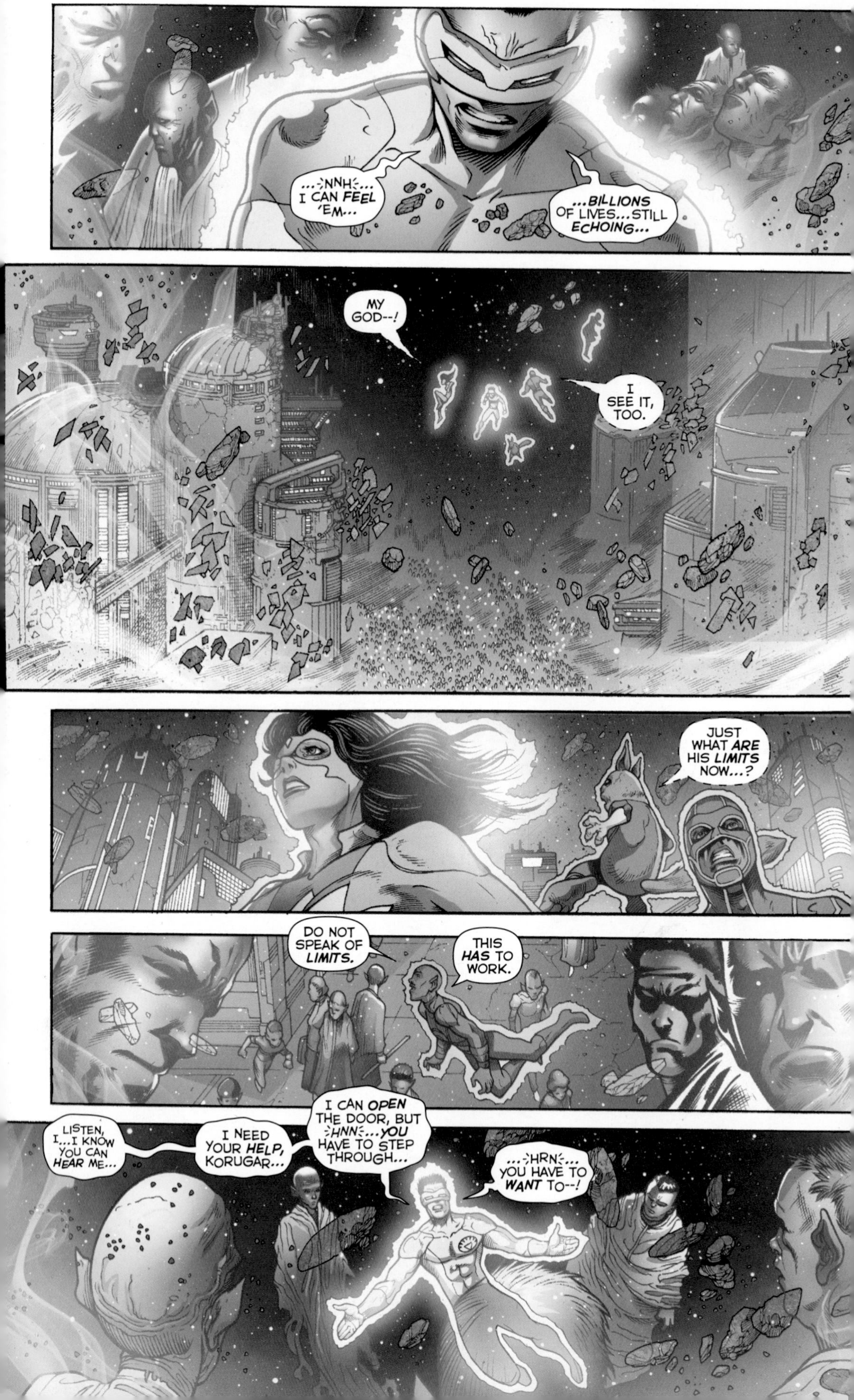
...NNH... I CAN FEEL 'EM...
...BILLIONS OF LIVES...STILL ECHOING...
MY GOD--!
I SEE IT, TOO.
JUST WHAT ARE HIS LIMITS NOW...?
DO NOT SPEAK OF LIMITS.
THIS HAS TO WORK.
LISTEN, I...I KNOW YOU CAN HEAR ME...
I NEED YOUR HELP, KORUGAR...
I CAN OPEN THE DOOR, BUT HNN...YOU HAVE TO STEP THROUGH...
...HRN... YOU HAVE TO WANT TO--!

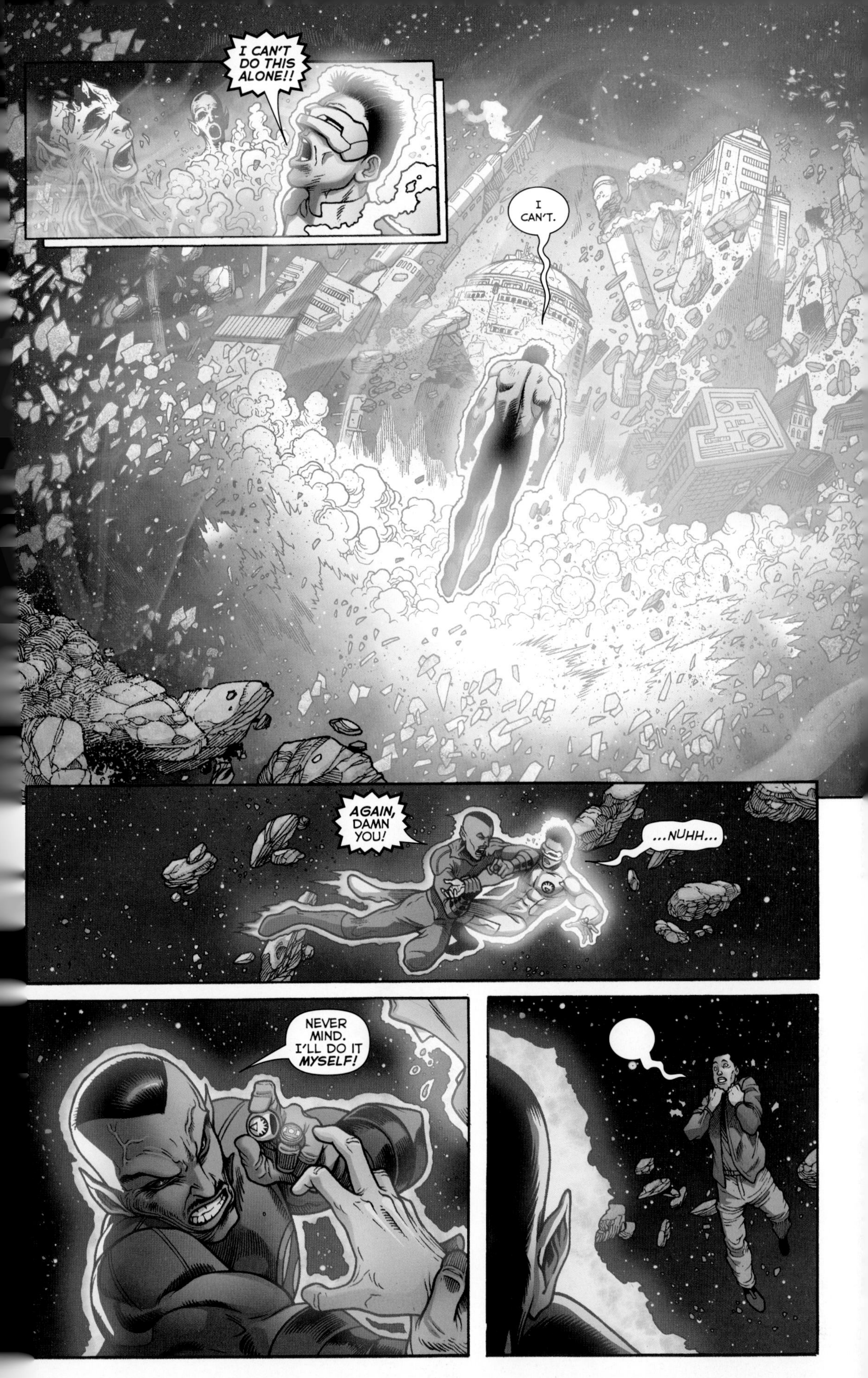
I CAN'T DO THIS ALONE!!
I CAN'T.
AGAIN, DAMN YOU!
...NUHH...
NEVER MIND. I'LL DO IT MYSELF!

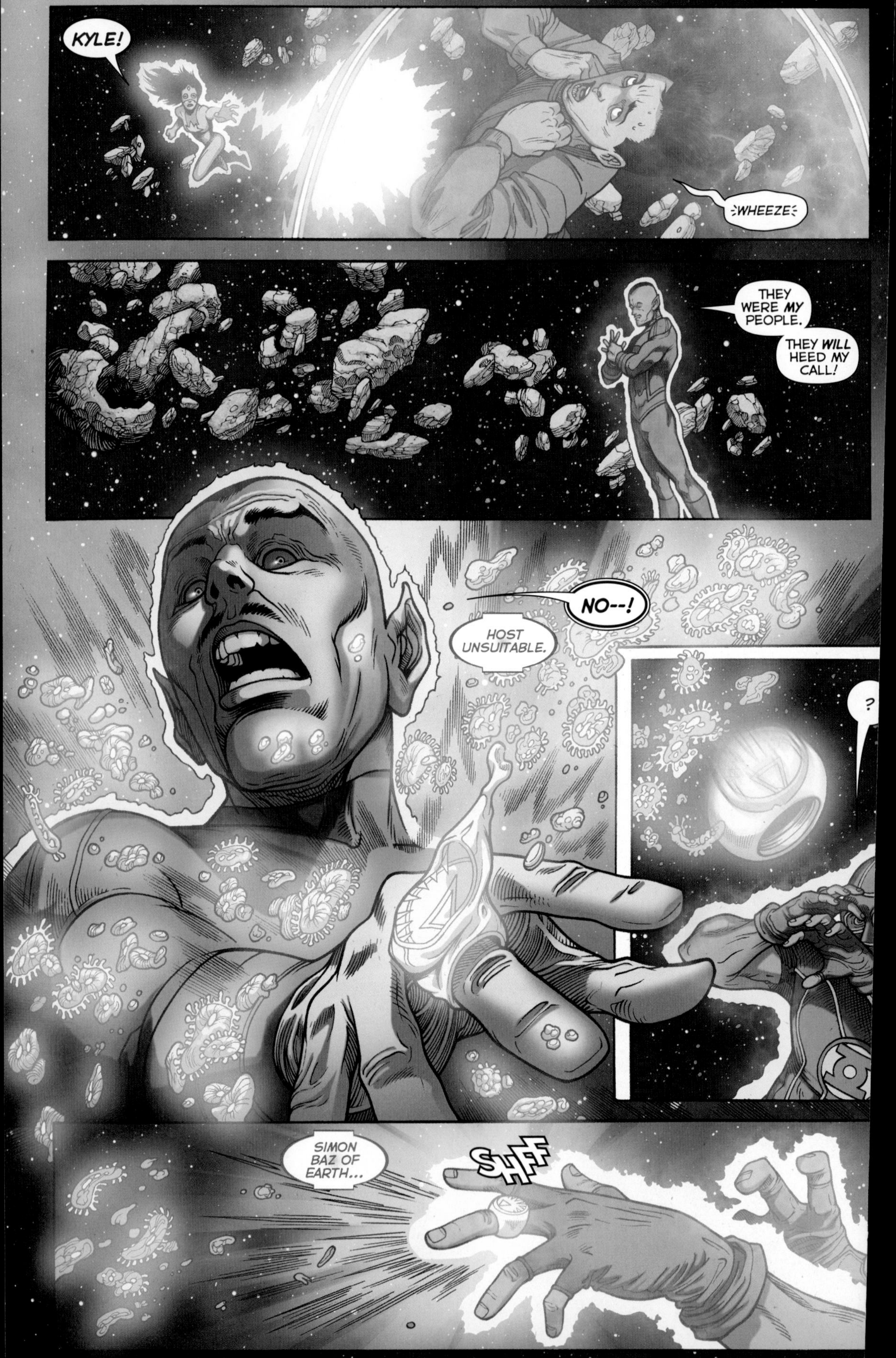
KYLE!
WHEEZE
THEY WERE MY PEOPLE.
THEY WILL HEED MY CALL!
NO--!
HOST UNSUITABLE.
?
SIMON BAZ OF EARTH...
SHFF

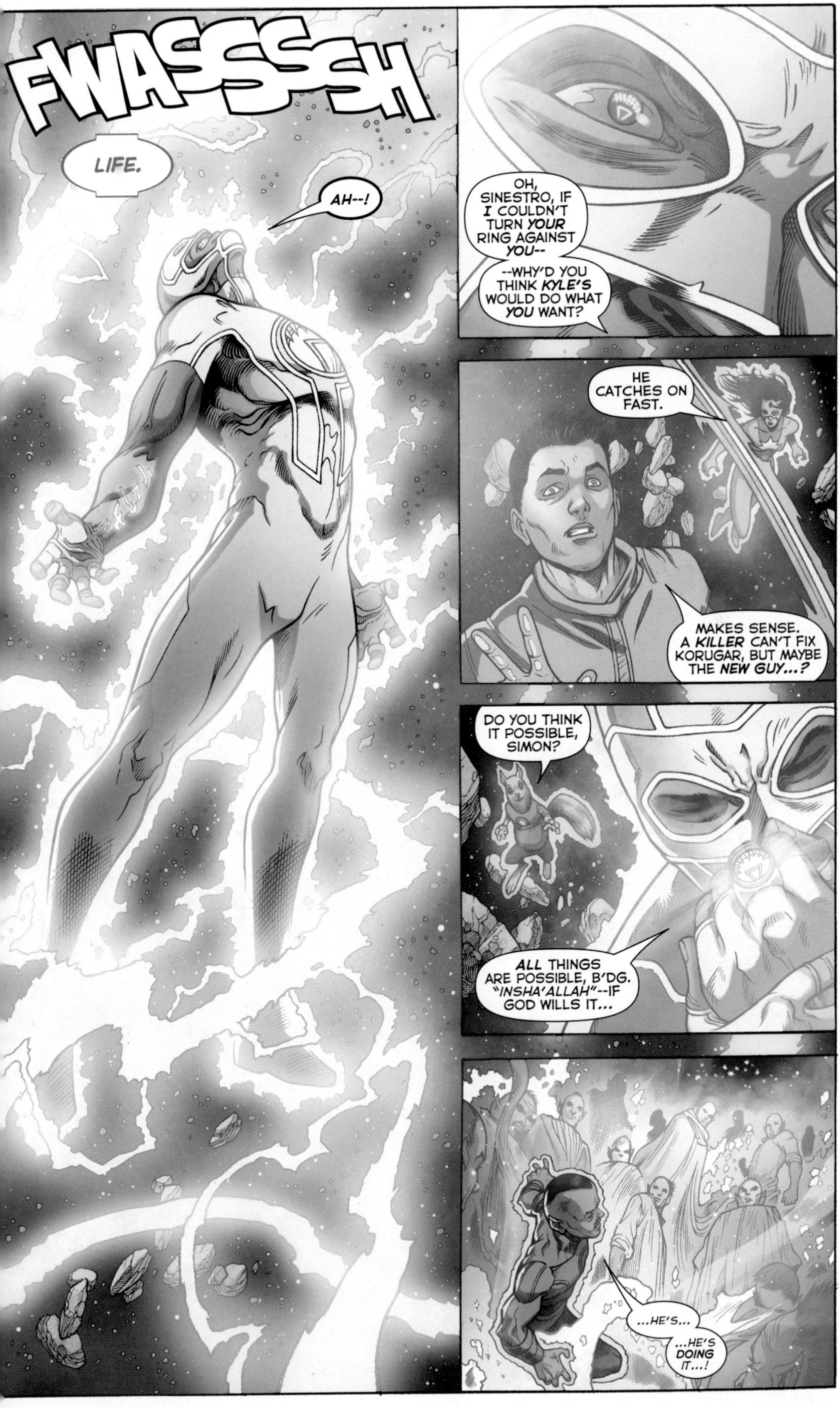
FWASSSSH
LIFE.
AH--!
OH, SINESTRO, IF I COULDN'T TURN YOUR RING AGAINST YOU--
--WHY'D YOU THINK KYLE'S WOULD DO WHAT YOU WANT?
HE CATCHES ON FAST.
MAKES SENSE. A KILLER CAN'T FIX KORUGAR, BUT MAYBE THE NEW GUY...?
DO YOU THINK IT POSSIBLE, SIMON?
ALL THINGS ARE POSSIBLE, B'DG. "INSHA'ALLAH"--IF GOD WILLS IT...
...HE'S...
...HE'S DOING IT...!

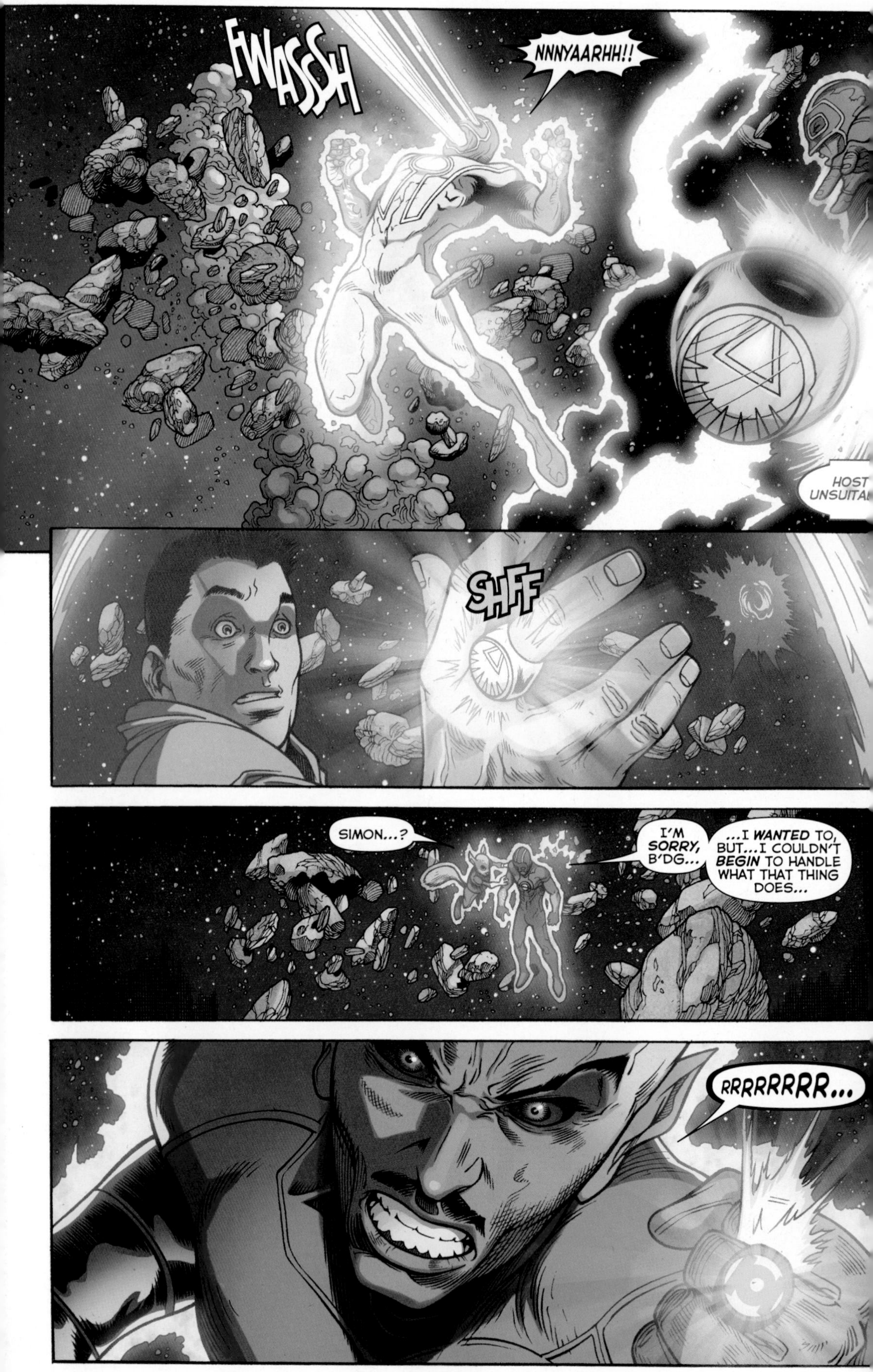
FWASSSH
NNNYAARHH!!
HOST UNSUITA
SHFF
SIMON...?
I'M SORRY, B'DG...
...I WANTED TO, BUT...I COULDN'T BEGIN TO HANDLE WHAT THAT THING DOES...
RRRRRRRR...

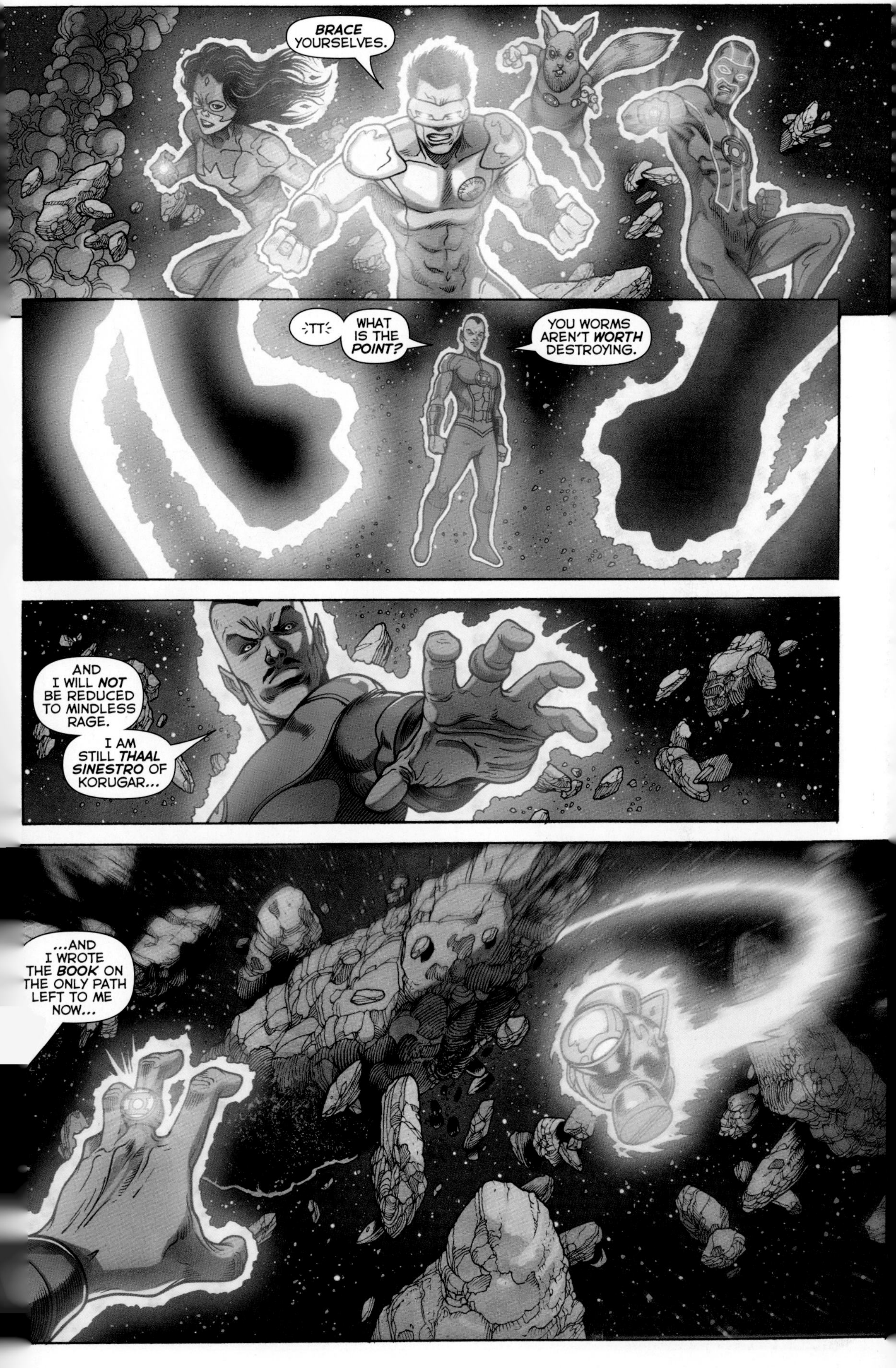
BRACE YOURSELVES.
TT
WHAT IS THE POINT?
YOU WORMS AREN'T WORTH DESTROYING.
AND I WILL NOT BE REDUCED TO MINDLESS RAGE.
I AM STILL THAAL SINESTRO OF KORUGAR...
...AND I WROTE THE BOOK ON THE ONLY PATH LEFT TO ME NOW...

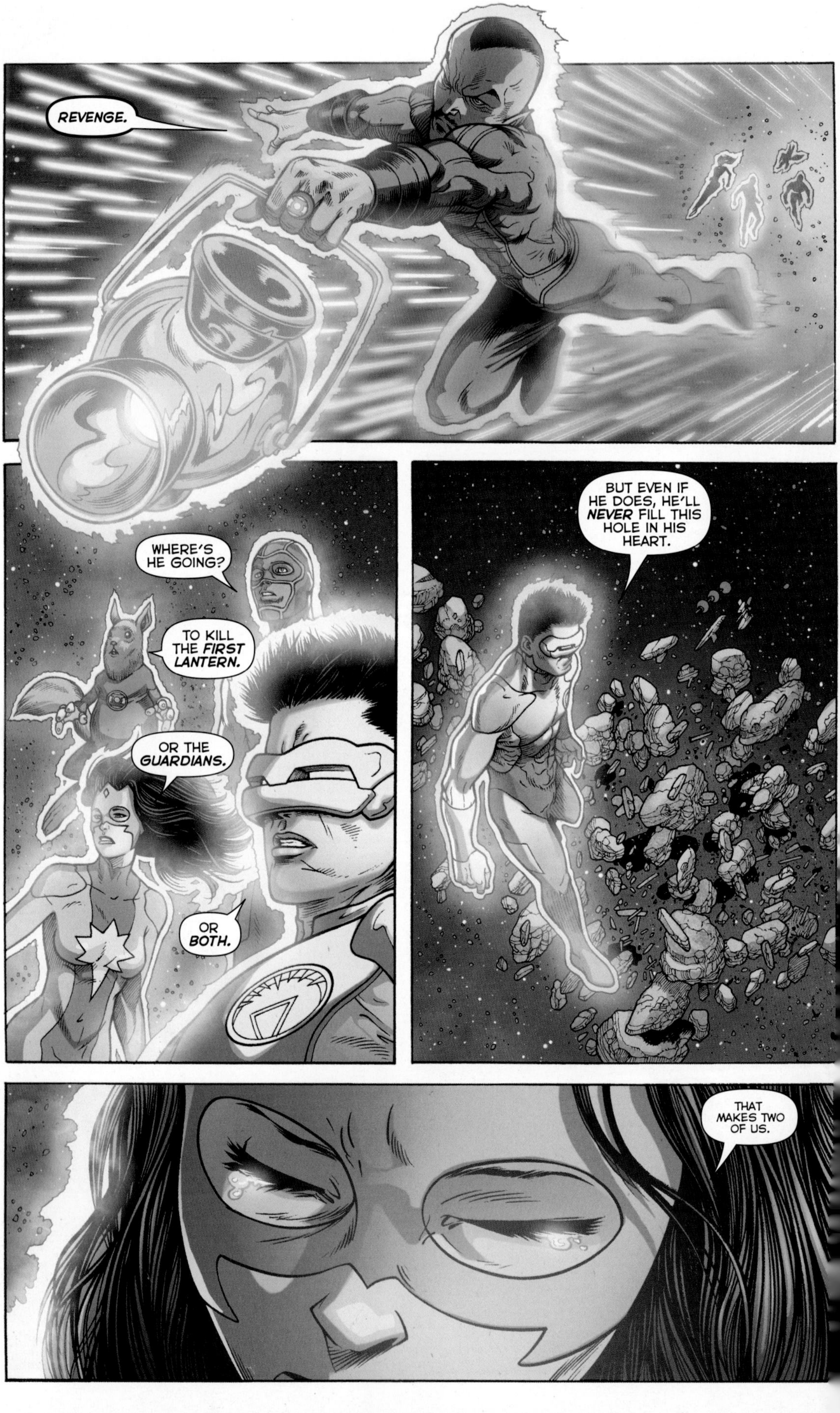
REVENGE.
WHERE'S HE GOING?
TO KILL THE FIRST LANTERN.
OR THE GUARDIANS.
OR BOTH.
BUT EVEN IF HE DOES, HE'LL NEVER FILL THIS HOLE IN HIS HEART.
THAT MAKES TWO OF US.

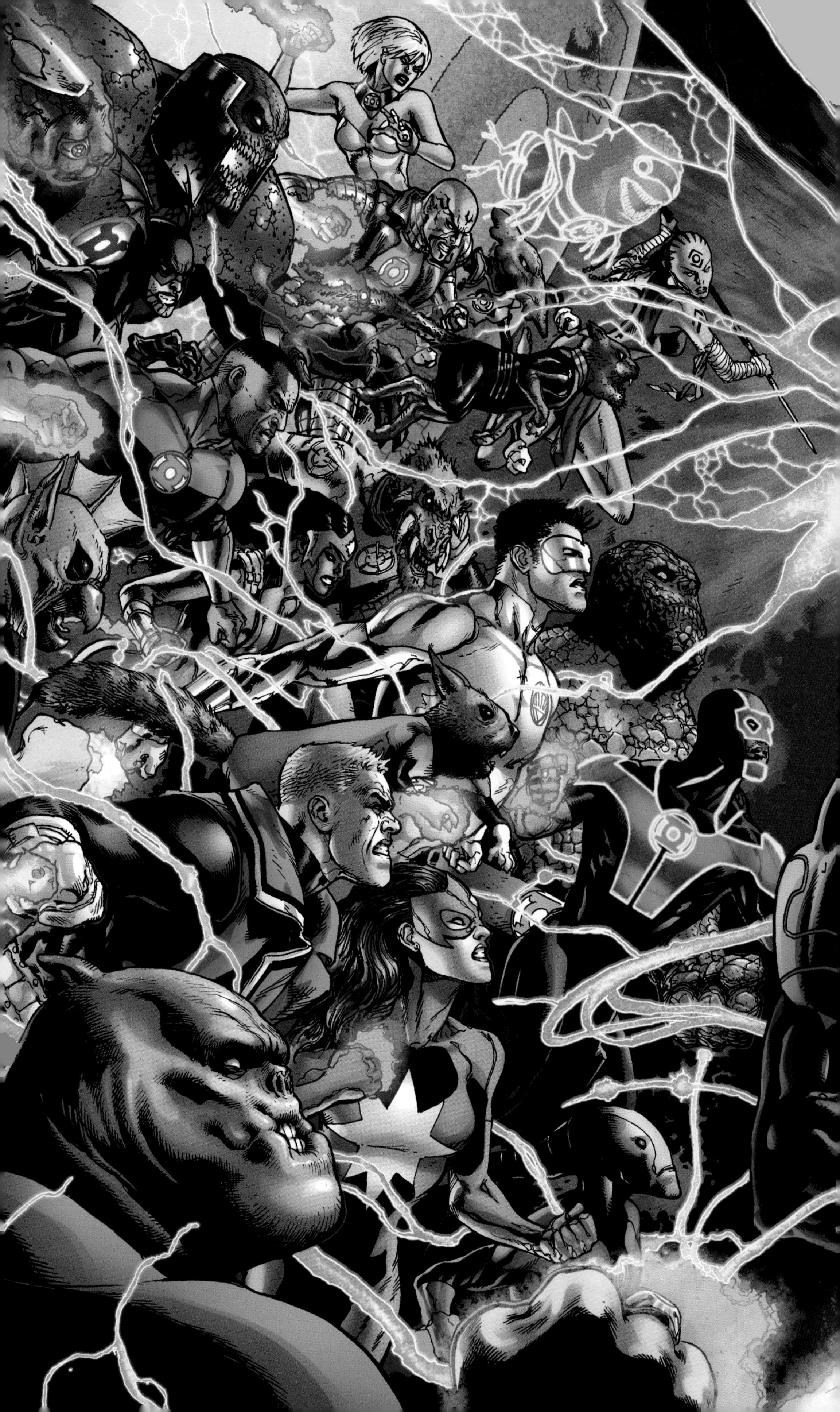

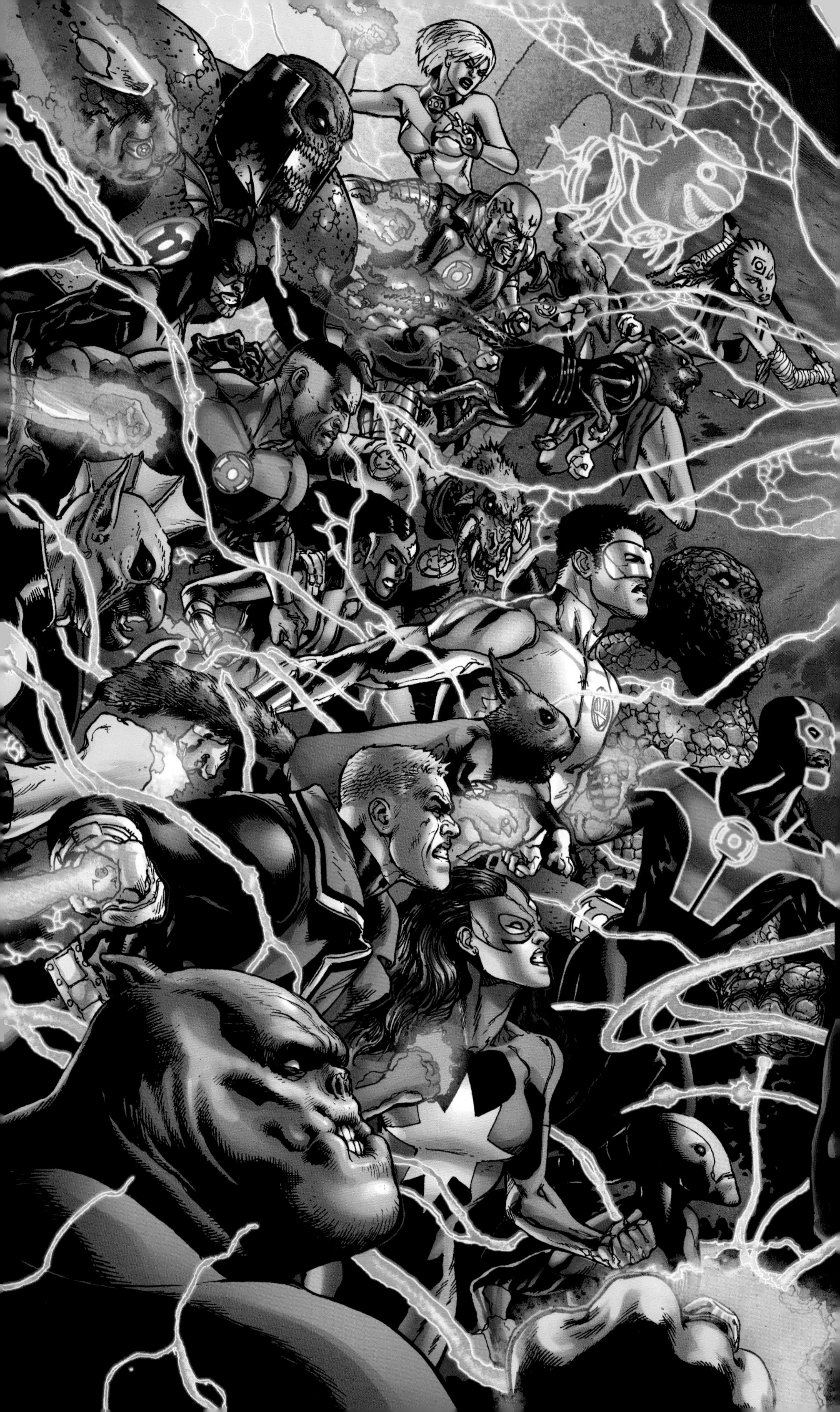

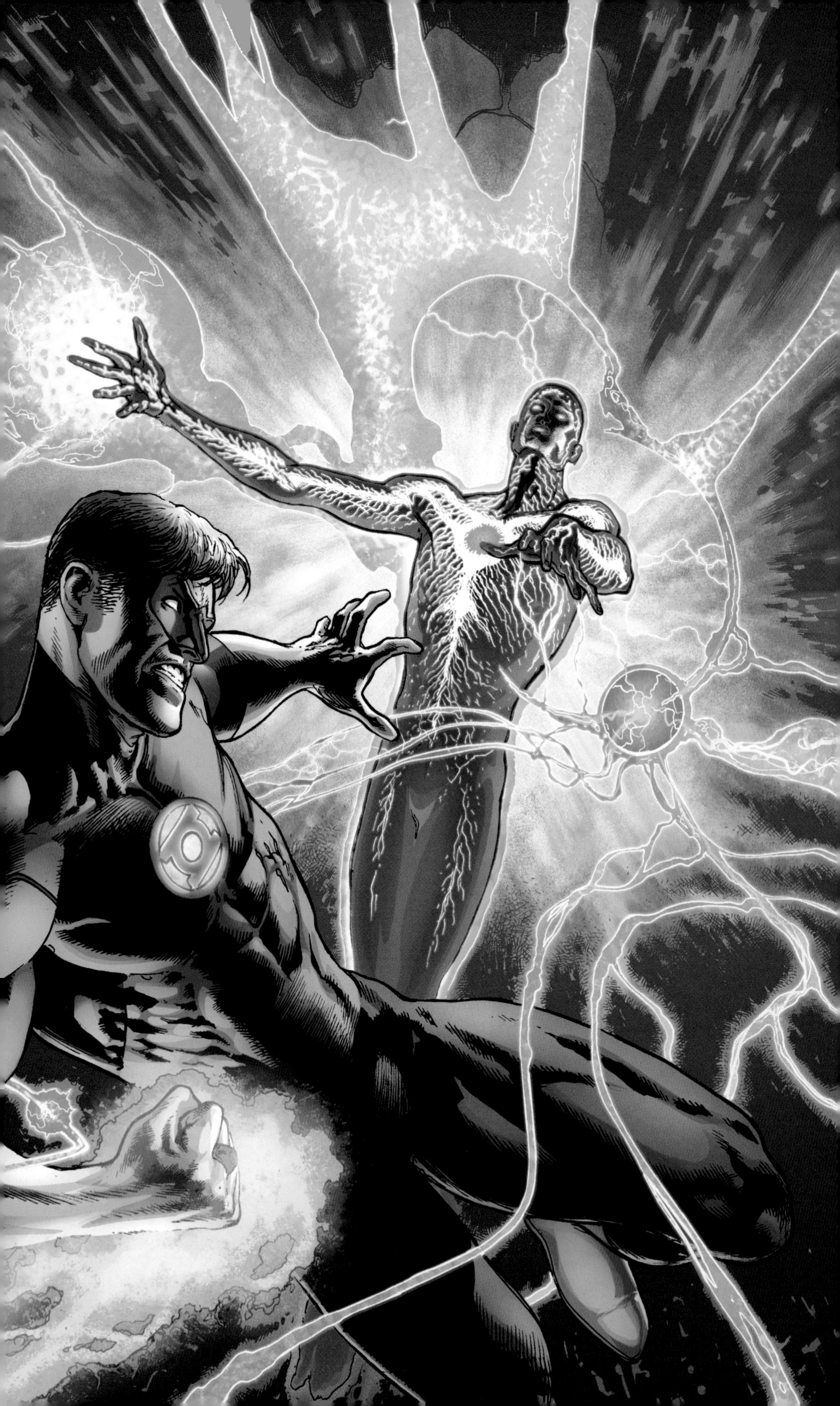

THE END

GEOFF JOHNS writer DOUG MAHNKE, PATRICK GLEASON, CULLY HAMNER, AARON KUDER, JERRY ORDWAY, ETHAN VAN SCIVER, IVAN REIS with OCLAIR ALBERT & JOE PRADO artists CHRISTIAN ALAMY, KEITH CHAMPAGNE, MARC DEERING, MARK IRWIN, WADE VON GRAWBADGER, TOM NGUYEN & DOUG MAHNKE inkers DOUG MAHNKE with ALEX SINCLAIR cover

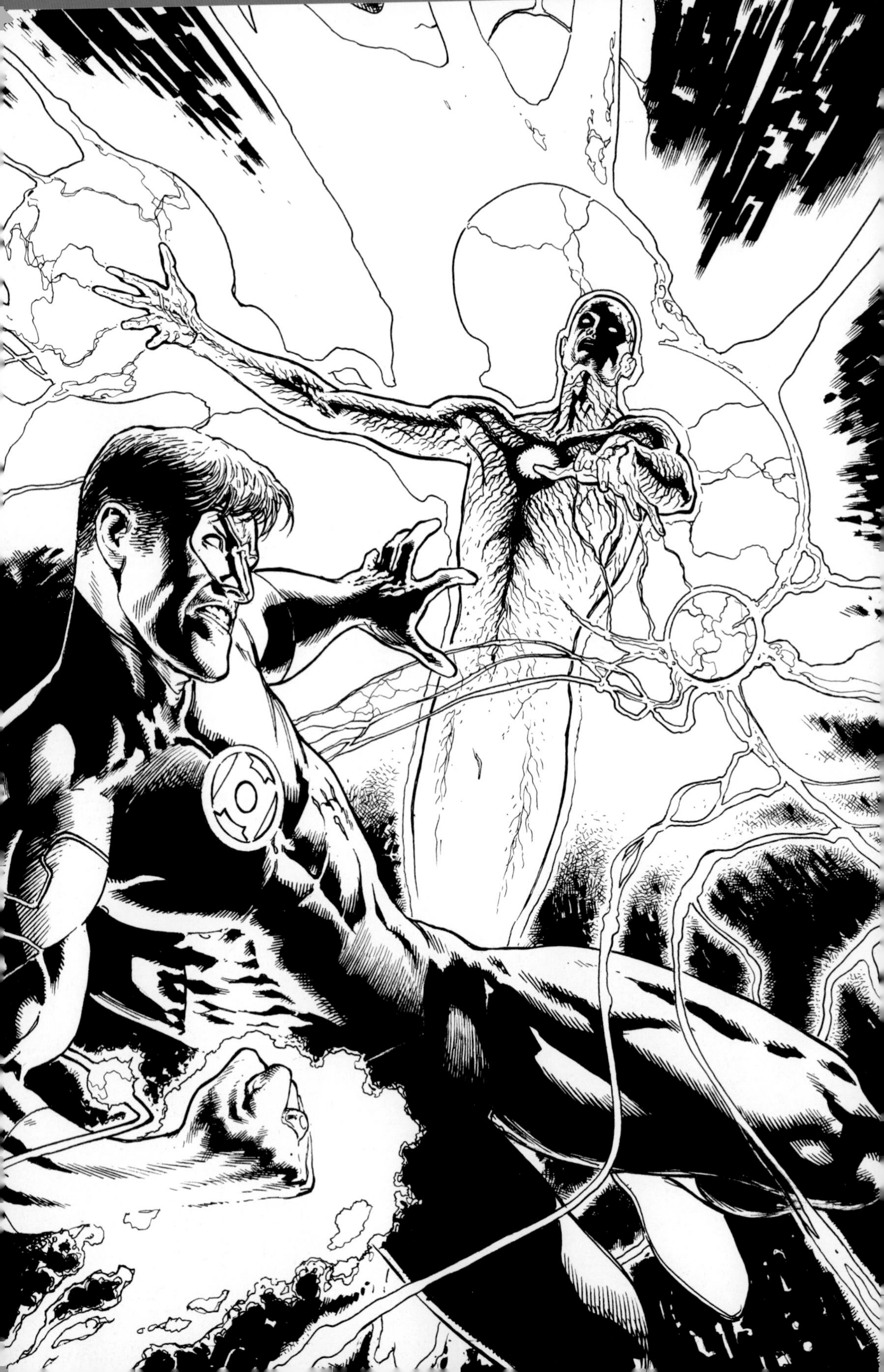

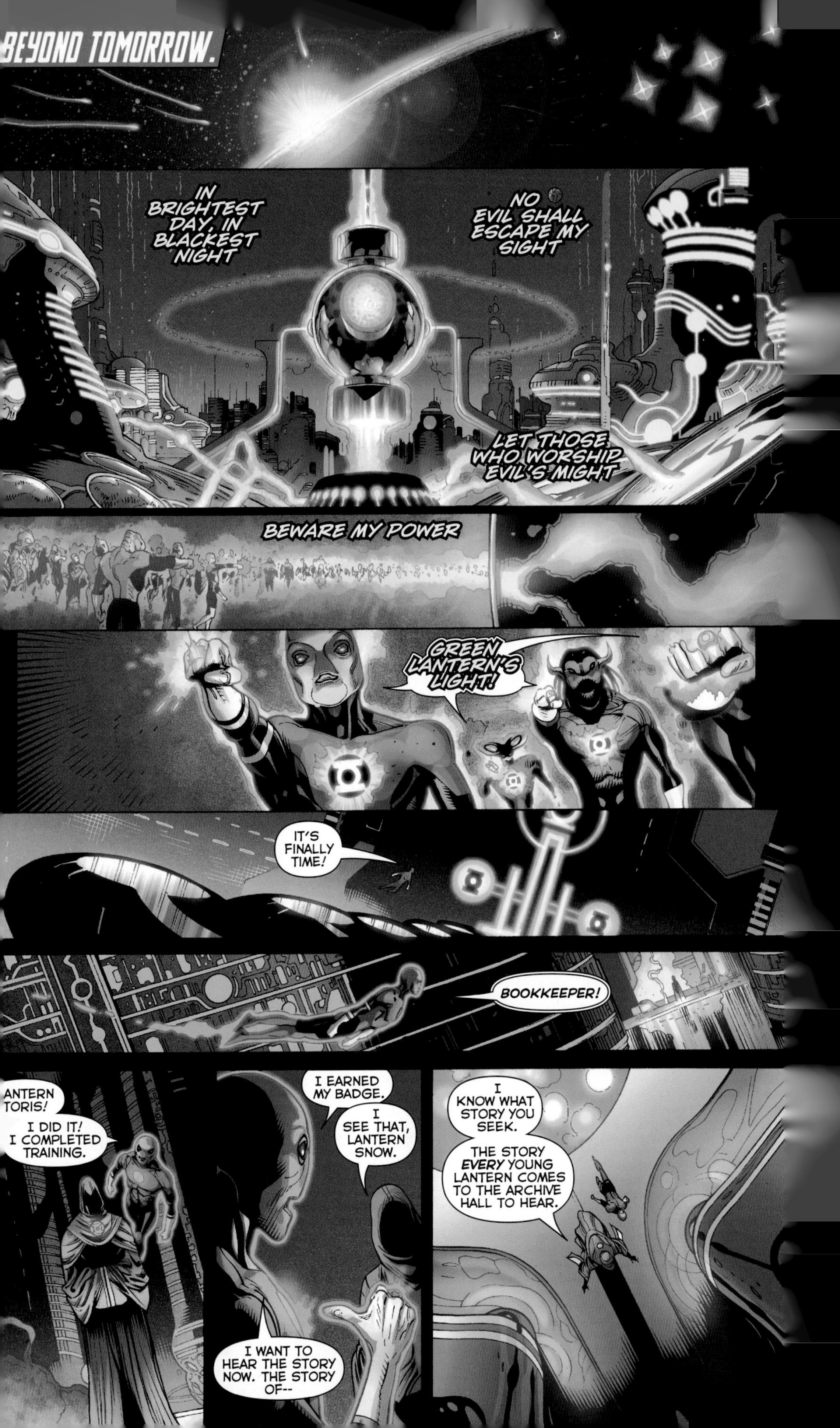

BEYOND TOMORROW.
IN BRIGHTEST DAY, IN BLACKEST NIGHT
NO EVIL SHALL ESCAPE MY SIGHT
LET THOSE WHO WORSHIP EVIL'S MIGHT
BEWARE MY POWER
GREEN LANTERN'S LIGHT!
IT'S FINALLY TIME!
BOOKKEEPER!
ANTERN TORIS!
I DID IT! I COMPLETED TRAINING.
I EARNED MY BADGE.
I SEE THAT, LANTERN SNOW.
I WANT TO HEAR THE STORY NOW. THE STORY OF--
I KNOW WHAT STORY YOU SEEK.
THE STORY EVERY YOUNG LANTERN COMES TO THE ARCHIVE HALL TO HEAR.

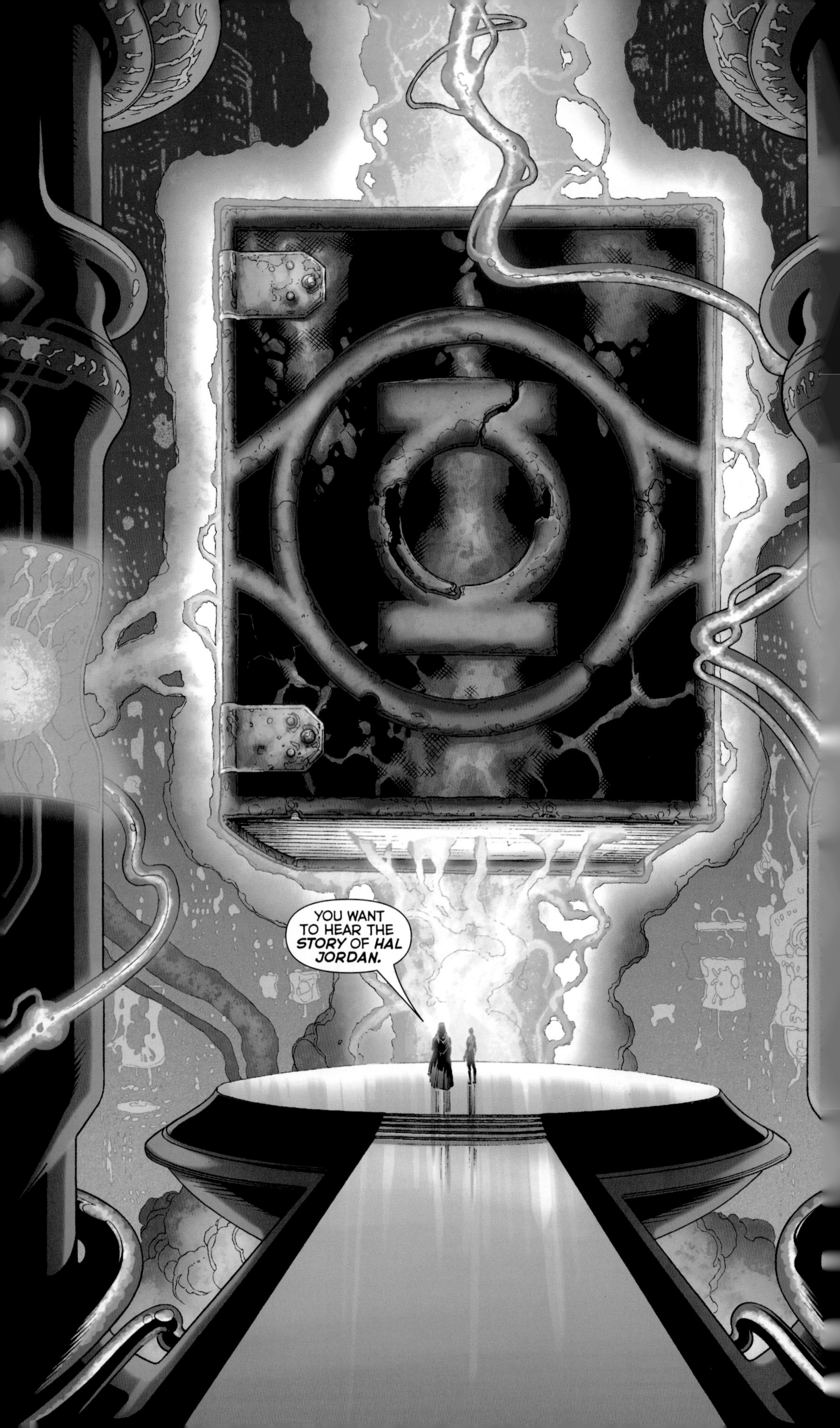
YOU WANT TO HEAR THE STORY OF HAL JORDAN.

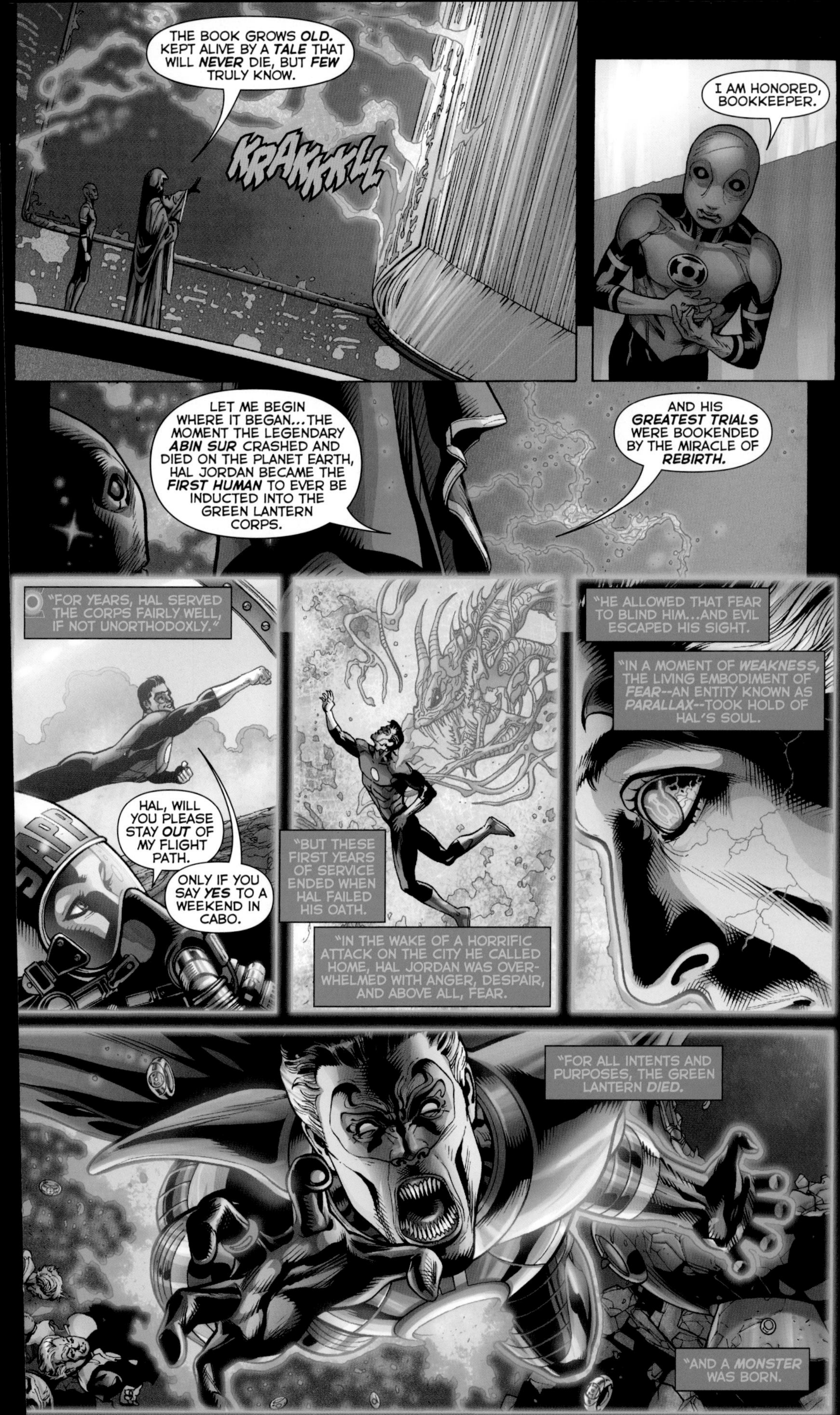
THE BOOK GROWS OLD. KEPT ALIVE BY A TALE THAT WILL NEVER DIE, BUT FEW TRULY KNOW.
KRAKKKLL
I AM HONORED, BOOKKEEPER.
LET ME BEGIN WHERE IT BEGAN...THE MOMENT THE LEGENDARY ABIN SUR CRASHED AND DIED ON THE PLANET EARTH, HAL JORDAN BECAME THE FIRST HUMAN TO EVER BE INDUCTED INTO THE GREEN LANTERN CORPS.
AND HIS GREATEST TRIALS WERE BOOKENDED BY THE MIRACLE OF REBIRTH.
"FOR YEARS, HAL SERVED THE CORPS FAIRLY WELL, IF NOT UNORTHODOXLY."
HAL, WILL YOU PLEASE STAY OUT OF MY FLIGHT PATH.
ONLY IF YOU SAY YES TO A WEEKEND IN CABO.
"BUT THESE FIRST YEARS OF SERVICE ENDED WHEN HAL FAILED HIS OATH.
"IN THE WAKE OF A HORRIFIC ATTACK ON THE CITY HE CALLED HOME, HAL JORDAN WAS OVERWHELMED WITH ANGER, DESPAIR, AND ABOVE ALL, FEAR.
"HE ALLOWED THAT FEAR TO BLIND HIM...AND EVIL ESCAPED HIS SIGHT.
"IN A MOMENT OF WEAKNESS, THE LIVING EMBODIMENT OF FEAR--AN ENTITY KNOWN AS PARALLAX--TOOK HOLD OF HAL'S SOUL.
"FOR ALL INTENTS AND PURPOSES, THE GREEN LANTERN DIED.
"AND A MONSTER WAS BORN.

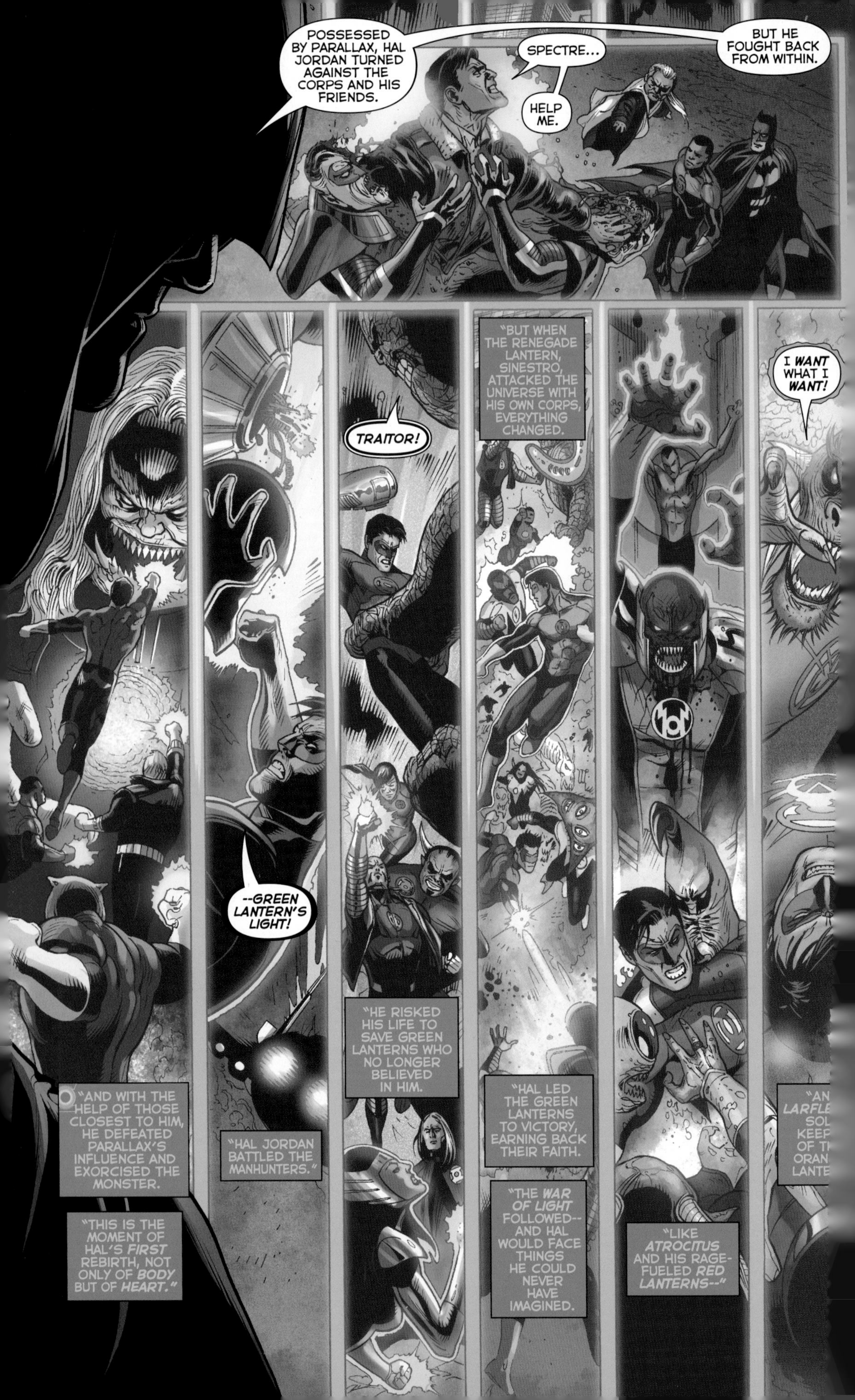

POSSESSED BY PARALLAX, HAL JORDAN TURNED AGAINST THE CORPS AND HIS FRIENDS.
BUT HE FOUGHT BACK FROM WITHIN.
SPECTRE...
HELP ME.
"AND WITH THE HELP OF THOSE CLOSEST TO HIM, HE DEFEATED PARALLAX'S INFLUENCE AND EXORCISED THE MONSTER.
"THIS IS THE MOMENT OF HAL'S *FIRST* REBIRTH, NOT ONLY OF *BODY* BUT OF *HEART*."
--GREEN LANTERN'S LIGHT!
"HAL JORDAN BATTLED THE *MANHUNTERS*."
TRAITOR!
"HE RISKED HIS LIFE TO SAVE GREEN LANTERNS WHO NO LONGER BELIEVED IN HIM.
"BUT WHEN THE RENEGADE LANTERN, SINESTRO, ATTACKED THE UNIVERSE WITH HIS OWN CORPS, EVERYTHING CHANGED.
"HAL LED THE GREEN LANTERNS TO VICTORY, EARNING BACK THEIR FAITH.
"THE *WAR OF LIGHT* FOLLOWED-- AND HAL WOULD FACE THINGS HE COULD NEVER HAVE IMAGINED.
"LIKE *ATROCITUS* AND HIS RAGE-FUELED *RED LANTERNS*--"
I *WANT* WHAT I *WANT!*

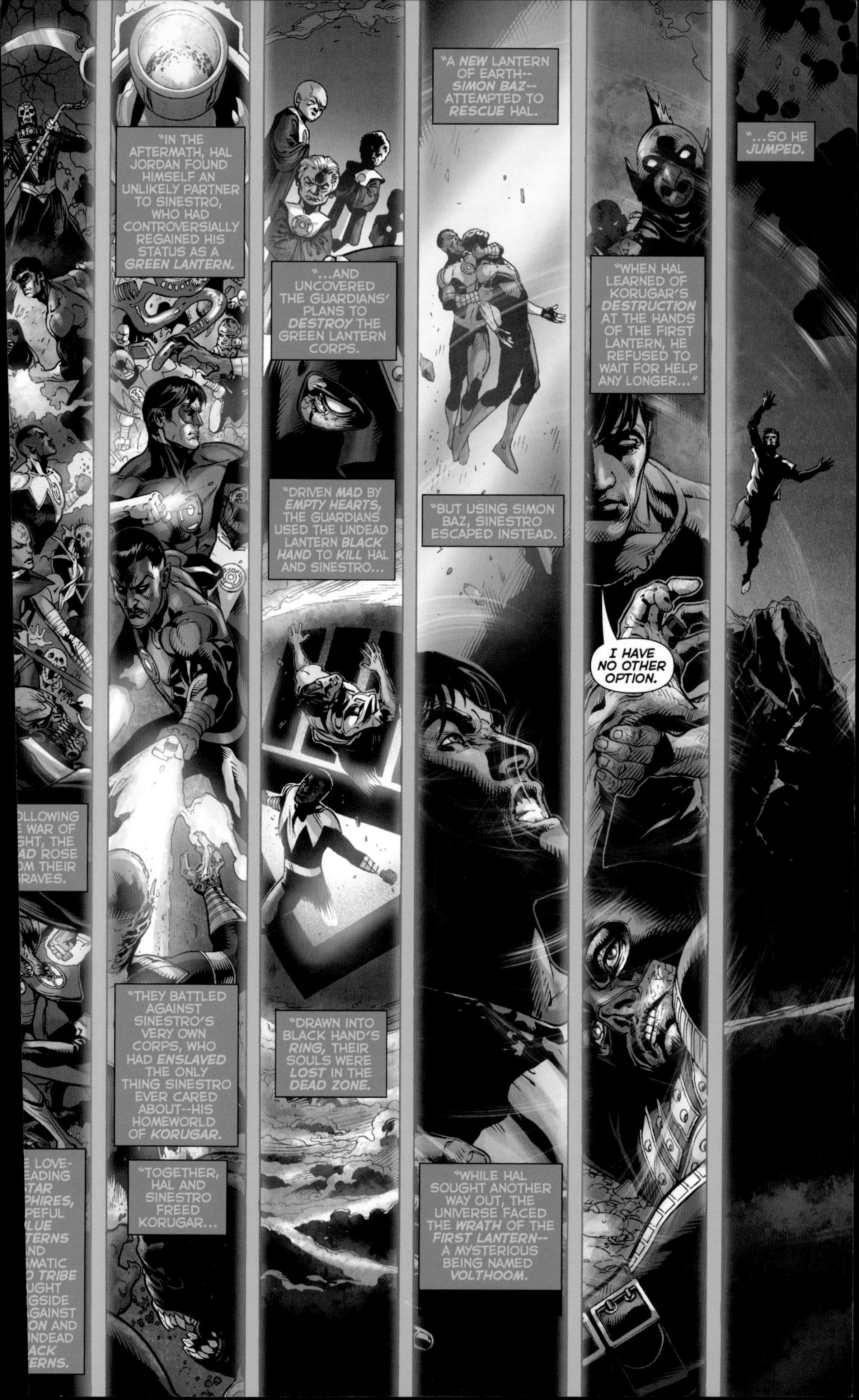
LLOWING E WAR OF GHT, THE AD ROSE OM THEIR GRAVES.
E LOVE- EADING STAR PHIRES, PEFUL LUE ANTERNS AND SMATIC O TRIBE UGHT GSIDE AGAINST ON AND UNDEAD ACK TERNS.
"IN THE AFTERMATH, HAL JORDAN FOUND HIMSELF AN UNLIKELY PARTNER TO SINESTRO, WHO HAD CONTROVERSIALLY REGAINED HIS STATUS AS A GREEN LANTERN.
"THEY BATTLED AGAINST SINESTRO'S VERY OWN CORPS, WHO HAD ENSLAVED THE ONLY THING SINESTRO EVER CARED ABOUT--HIS HOMEWORLD OF KORUGAR.
"TOGETHER, HAL AND SINESTRO FREED KORUGAR...
"...AND UNCOVERED THE GUARDIANS' PLANS TO DESTROY THE GREEN LANTERN CORPS.
"DRIVEN MAD BY EMPTY HEARTS, THE GUARDIANS USED THE UNDEAD LANTERN BLACK HAND TO KILL HAL AND SINESTRO...
"DRAWN INTO BLACK HAND'S RING, THEIR SOULS WERE LOST IN THE DEAD ZONE.
"A NEW LANTERN OF EARTH-- SIMON BAZ-- ATTEMPTED TO RESCUE HAL.
"BUT USING SIMON BAZ, SINESTRO ESCAPED INSTEAD.
"WHILE HAL SOUGHT ANOTHER WAY OUT, THE UNIVERSE FACED THE WRATH OF THE FIRST LANTERN-- A MYSTERIOUS BEING NAMED VOLTHOOM.
"WHEN HAL LEARNED OF KORUGAR'S DESTRUCTION AT THE HANDS OF THE FIRST LANTERN, HE REFUSED TO WAIT FOR HELP ANY LONGER..."
I HAVE NO OTHER OPTION.
"...SO HE JUMPED.

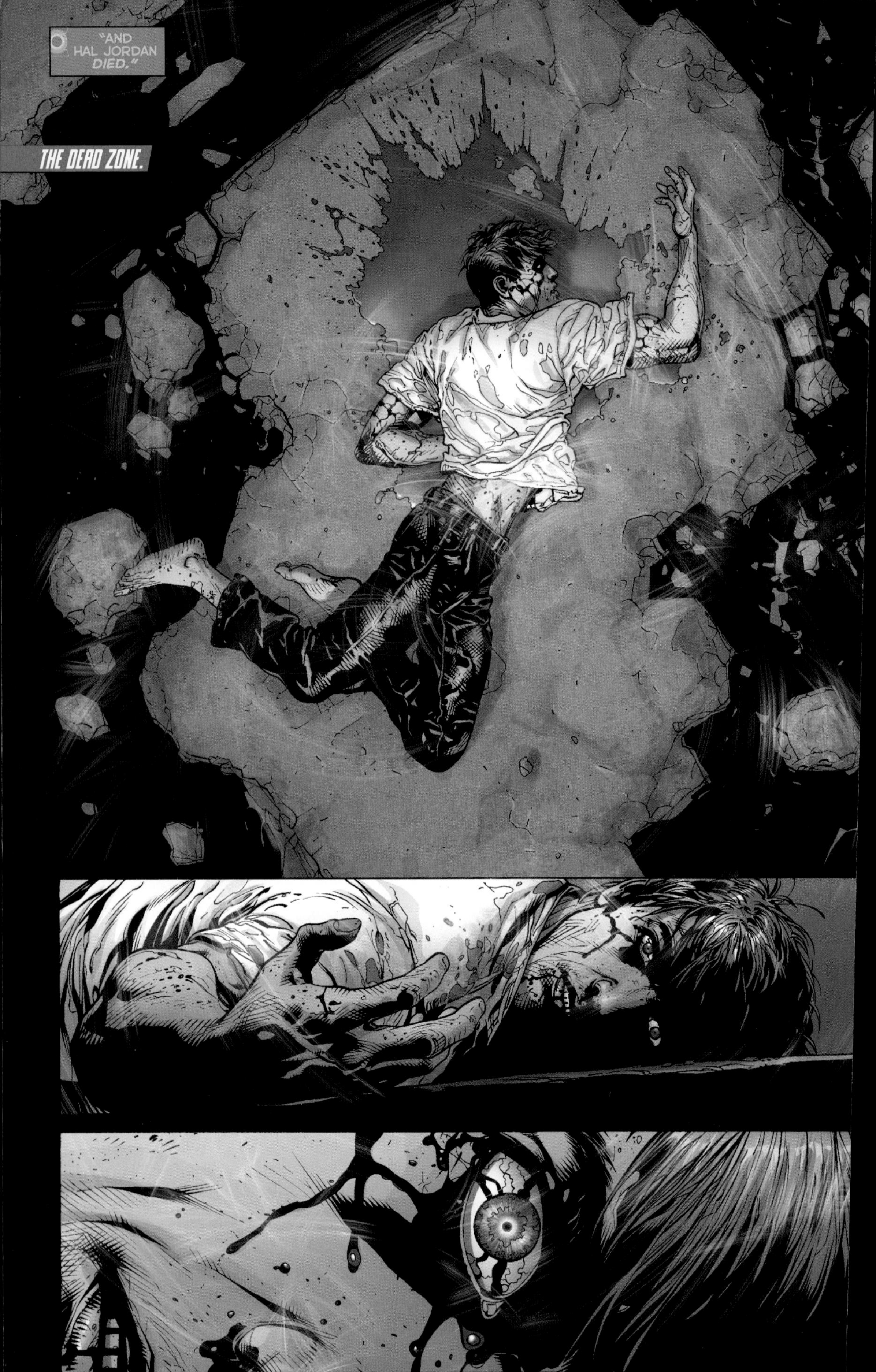
"AND HAL JORDAN DIED."
THE DEAD ZONE.

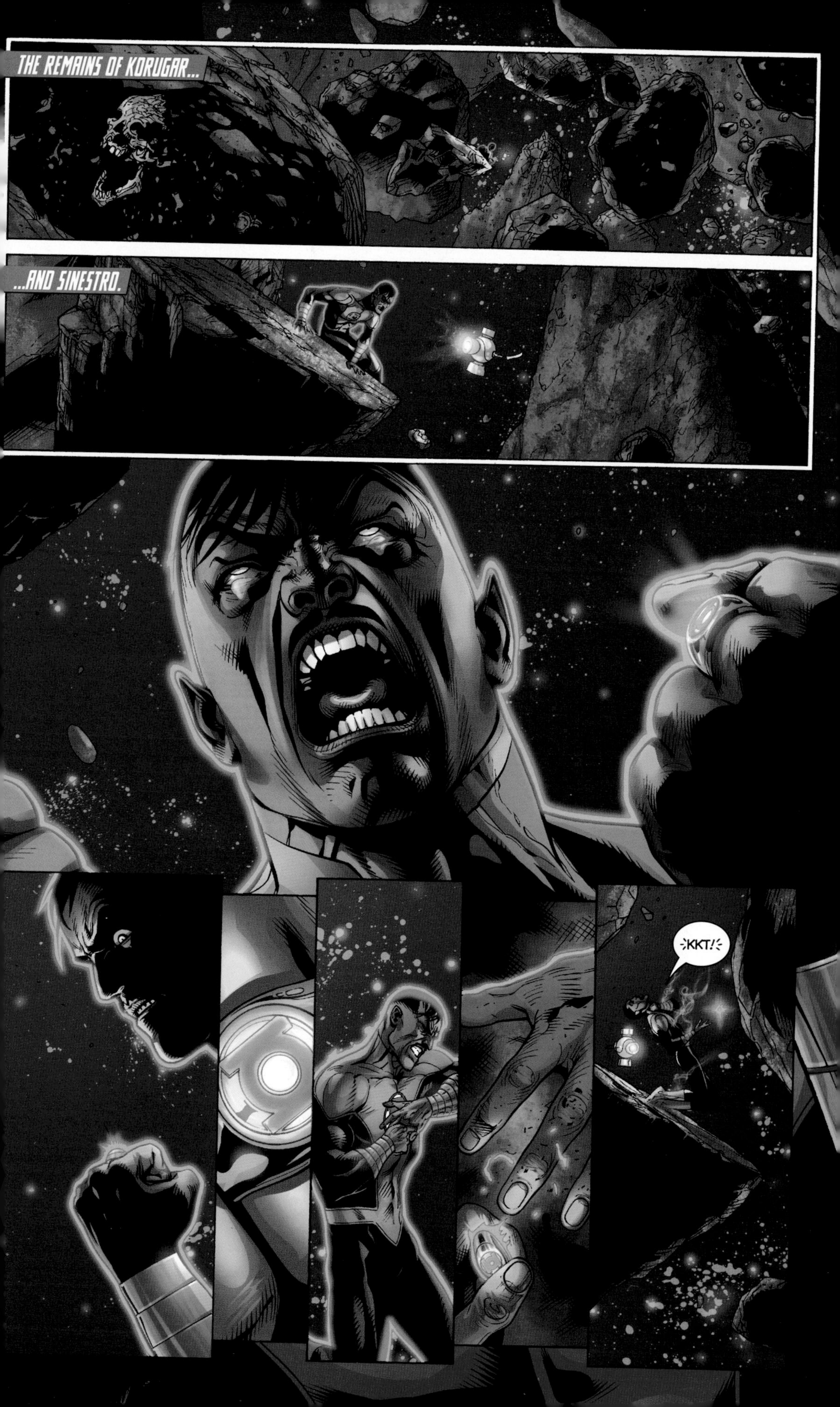
THE REMAINS OF KORUGAR...
...AND SINESTRO.
KKT!

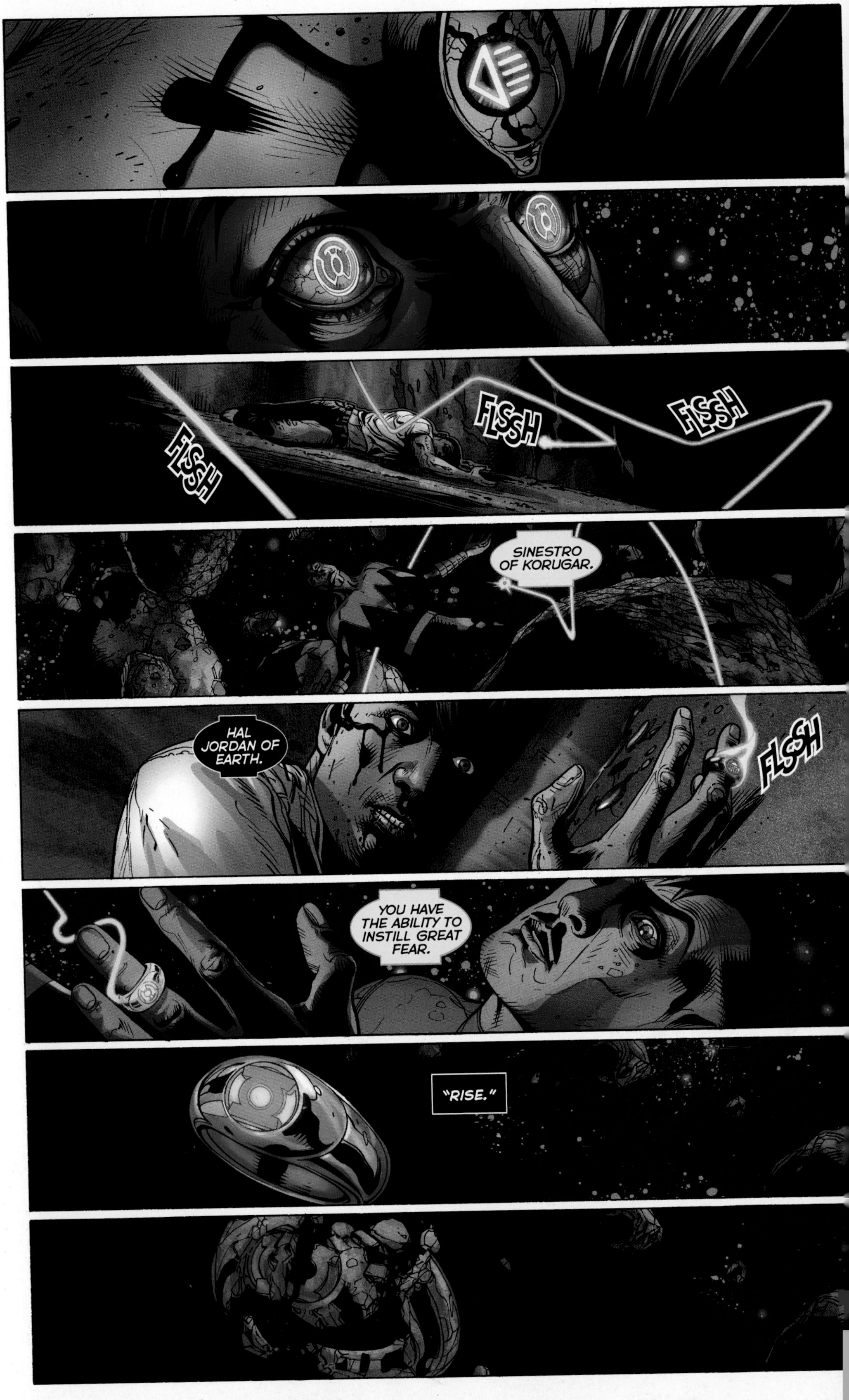
FLSSH
FLSSH
FLSSH
SINESTRO OF KORUGAR.
HAL JORDAN OF EARTH.
FLSSH
YOU HAVE THE ABILITY TO INSTILL GREAT FEAR.
"RISE."

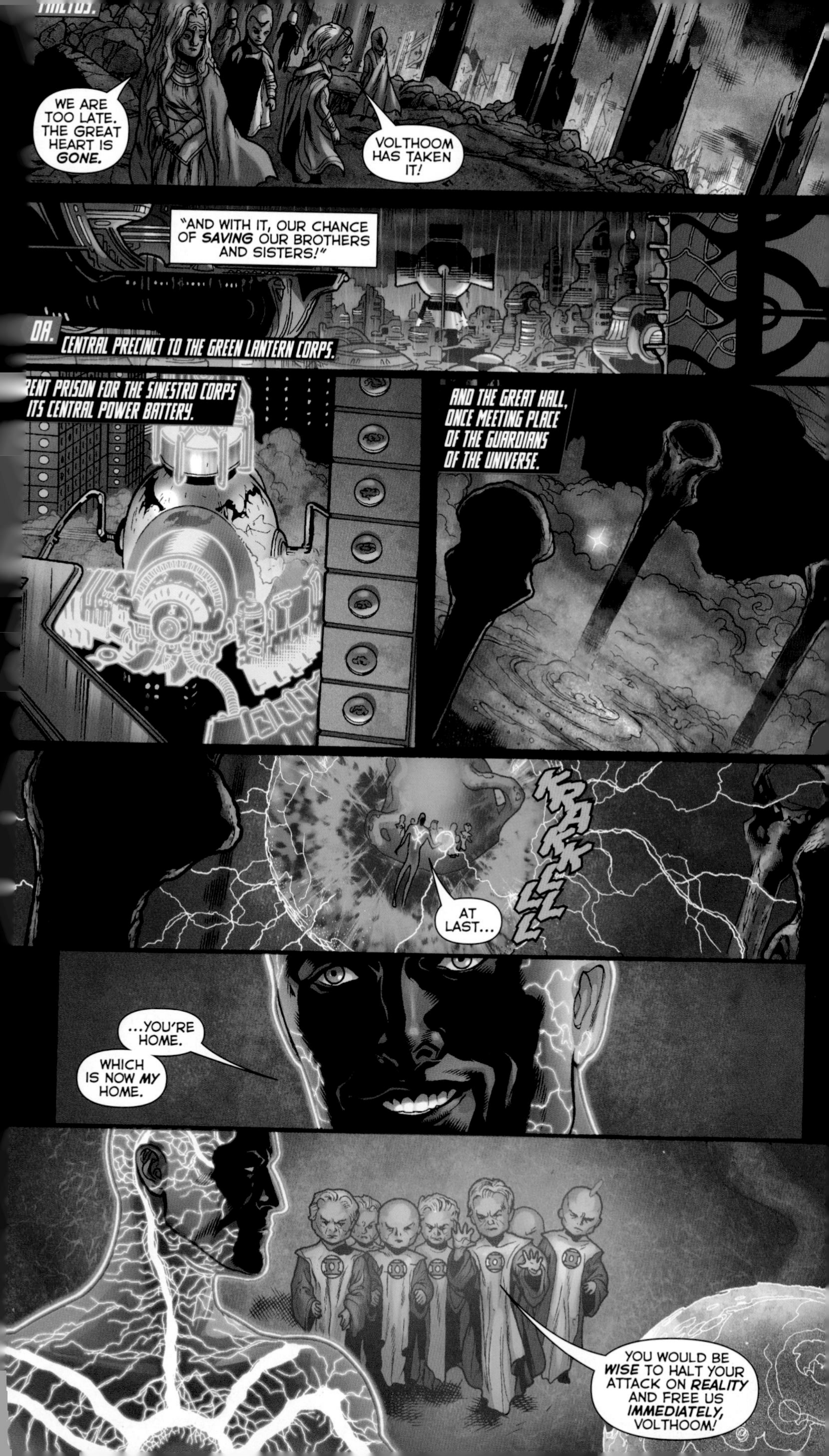
WE ARE TOO LATE. THE GREAT HEART IS GONE.
VOLTHOOM HAS TAKEN IT!
"AND WITH IT, OUR CHANCE OF SAVING OUR BROTHERS AND SISTERS!"
OA.
CENTRAL PRECINCT TO THE GREEN LANTERN CORPS.
RENT PRISON FOR THE SINESTRO CORPS
ITS CENTRAL POWER BATTERY.
AND THE GREAT HALL, ONCE MEETING PLACE OF THE GUARDIANS OF THE UNIVERSE.
KRAKKLLL
AT LAST...
...YOU'RE HOME.
WHICH IS NOW MY HOME.
YOU WOULD BE WISE TO HALT YOUR ATTACK ON REALITY AND FREE US IMMEDIATELY, VOLTHOOM!

HAVE AMASSED THE LIGHT OF THE *EMOTIONAL SPECTRUM* WITH THE INTENT TO *REACH* INTO THE FABRIC OF HISTORY AND *UNWIND* IT FOR YOUR OWN TWISTED PURPOSES.

THAT I HAVE.

BUT REMEMBER, KRONA ATTEMPTED TO LOCK THE SECRET OF THE *BEGINNING* OF *TIME* AND HE WAS *FOREVER CURSED* FOR IT.

KRONA WAS CURSED BY *YOU* FOR *DARING* TO SEEK THE ANSWER TO THE QUESTION WE *ALL* ASK: WHAT IS THE *PURPOSE* OF LIFE?

YOU WERE *AFRAID* OF WHAT THE ANSWER MIGHT BE.

NO...YOU WERE AFRAID THERE WOULD *BE* NO ANSWER AT *ALL*.

WE FEAR *NOTHING*, VOLTHOOM.

YOU FEAR NOTHING *NOW*, BUT THAT WAS NOT ALWAYS THE CASE. I WAS *THERE*, GUARDIANS.

WHAT WE FEEL IS *DANGEROUS*. THE LANTERN CAN *CONTAIN* IT.

"I WITNESSED THE *SIN* OF DIVORCING YOURSELVES FROM YOUR HEARTS."

OUR EMOTIONAL SOULS WILL BE STORED SOMEWHERE SAFE.

"I TRAVELED FROM *ACROSS* T UNIVERSES AND *BACK* IN TIME WITNESS THE *CREATION* OF TH LANTERN...THE *GREAT HEAR*

"AND AS YOUR EMOTIONS WERE SWEPT INTO THE LANTERN, A CONDUIT FOR ITS POWER WAS *MANIFESTED* IN THE STORM--*THE FIRST RING WAS BORN!*

"THE MOST *POWERFUL* OF ALL RINGS."

VOLTHOOM!

"BUT ITS POWER WAS *BEYOND* A LOWLY HUMAN."

AAIIEEE!!

I WAS FOREVER ALTERED.

I WAS *INFUSED* WITH YOUR *COMBINED EMOTIONAL AWARENESS*

THE *GREAT HEART*.

THE FIRST LANTERN.

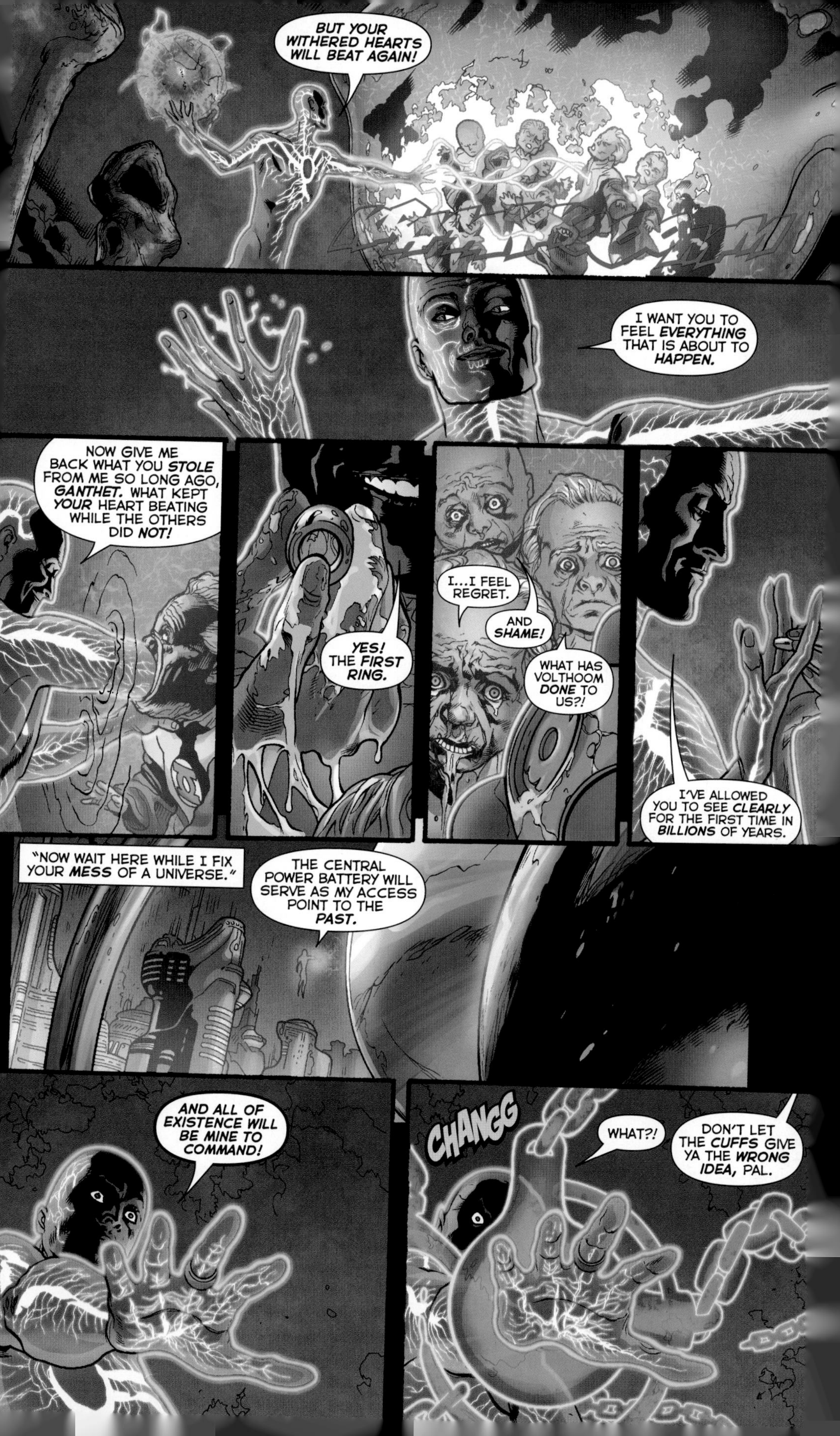

BUT YOUR WITHERED HEARTS WILL BEAT AGAIN!
I WANT YOU TO FEEL EVERYTHING THAT IS ABOUT TO HAPPEN.
NOW GIVE ME BACK WHAT YOU STOLE FROM ME SO LONG AGO, GANTHET. WHAT KEPT YOUR HEART BEATING WHILE THE OTHERS DID NOT!
YES! THE FIRST RING.
I...I FEEL REGRET.
AND SHAME!
WHAT HAS VOLTHOOM DONE TO US?!
I'VE ALLOWED YOU TO SEE CLEARLY FOR THE FIRST TIME IN BILLIONS OF YEARS.
"NOW WAIT HERE WHILE I FIX YOUR MESS OF A UNIVERSE."
THE CENTRAL POWER BATTERY WILL SERVE AS MY ACCESS POINT TO THE PAST.
AND ALL OF EXISTENCE WILL BE MINE TO COMMAND!
CHANGG
WHAT?!
DON'T LET THE CUFFS GIVE YA THE WRONG IDEA, PAL.

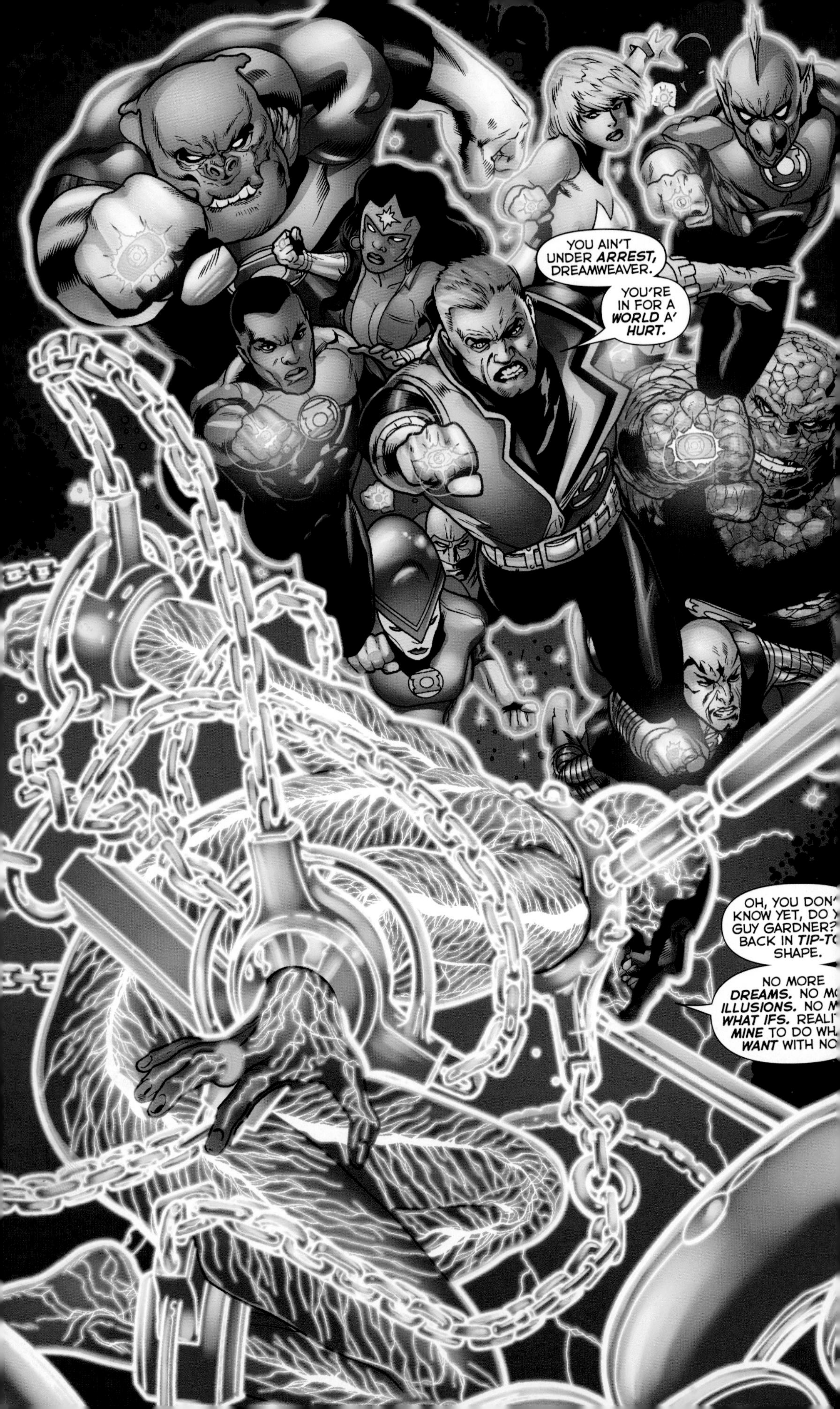

YOU AIN'T UNDER ARREST, DREAMWEAVER.
YOU'RE IN FOR A WORLD A' HURT.
OH, YOU DON' KNOW YET, DO Y GUY GARDNER? BACK IN TIP-TO SHAPE.
NO MORE DREAMS. NO MO ILLUSIONS. NO M WHAT IFS. REALI MINE TO DO WH WANT WITH NO

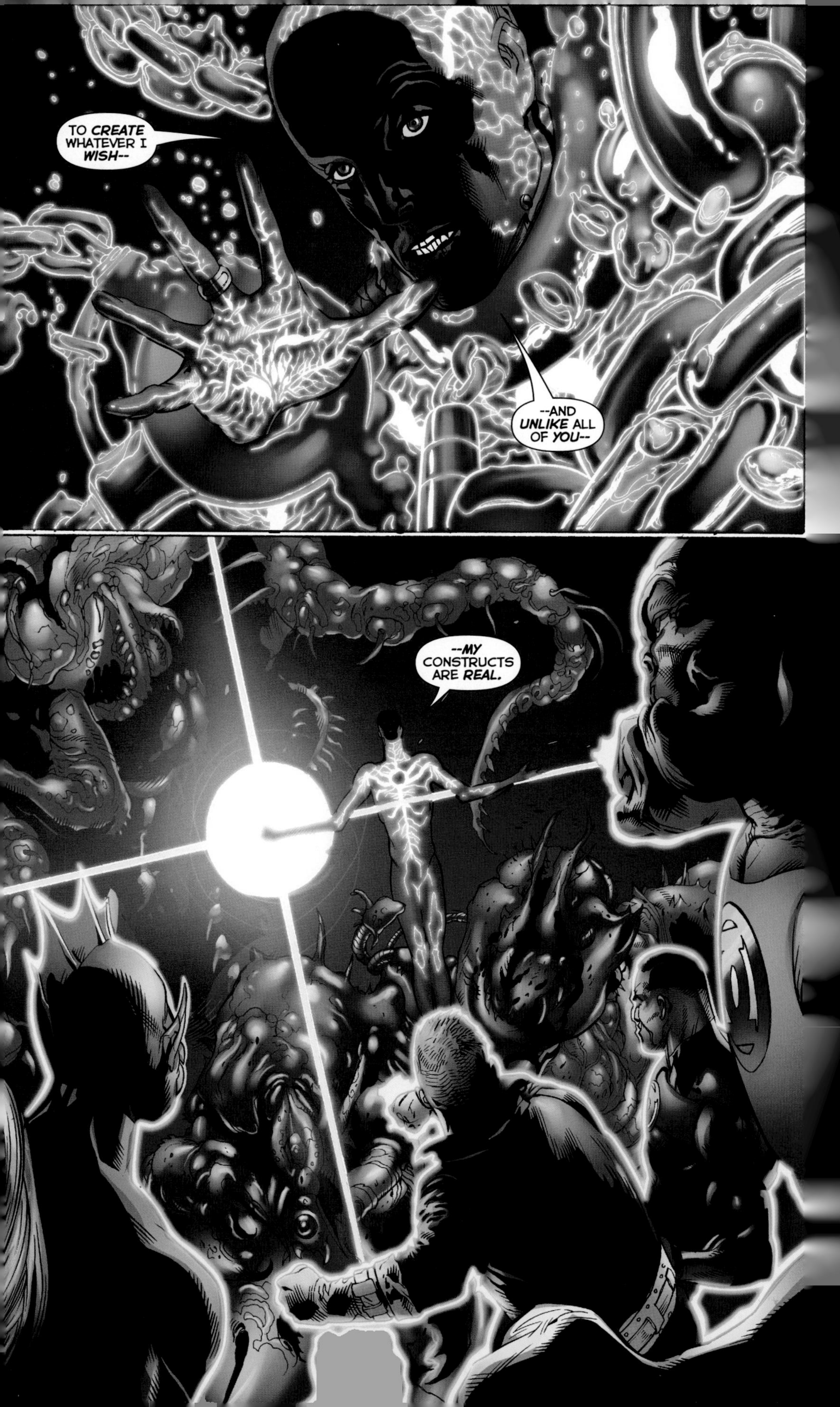
TO CREATE WHATEVER I WISH--
--AND UNLIKE ALL OF YOU--
--MY CONSTRUCTS ARE REAL.

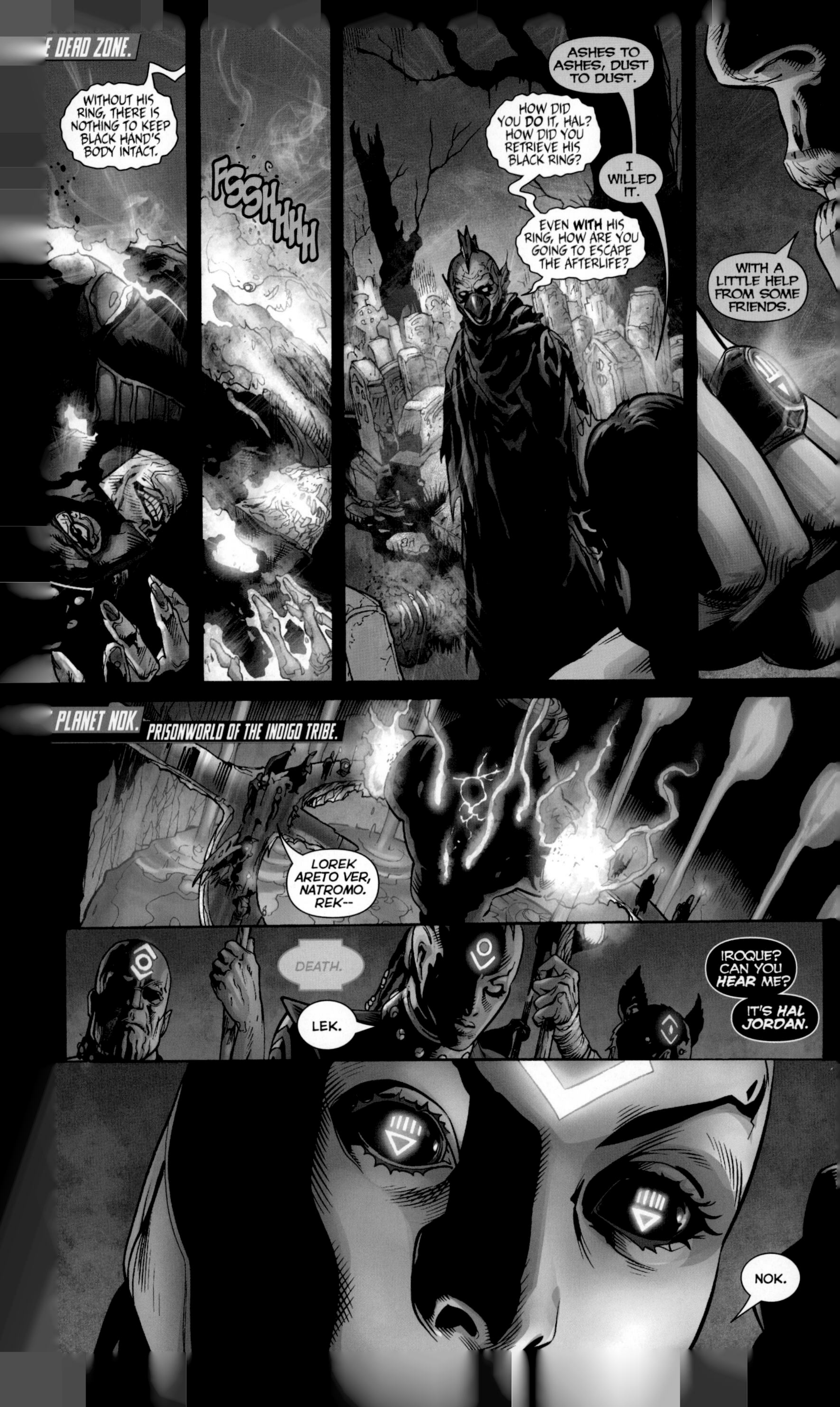

E DEAD ZONE.
WITHOUT HIS RING, THERE IS NOTHING TO KEEP BLACK HAND'S BODY INTACT.
FSSHHHHH
ASHES TO ASHES, DUST TO DUST.
HOW DID YOU DO IT, HAL? HOW DID YOU RETRIEVE HIS BLACK RING?
I WILLED IT.
EVEN WITH HIS RING, HOW ARE YOU GOING TO ESCAPE THE AFTERLIFE?
WITH A LITTLE HELP FROM SOME FRIENDS.
PLANET NOK.
PRISONWORLD OF THE INDIGO TRIBE.
LOREK ARETO VER, NATROMO. REK--
DEATH.
LEK.
!ROQUE? CAN YOU HEAR ME?
IT'S HAL JORDAN.
NOK.

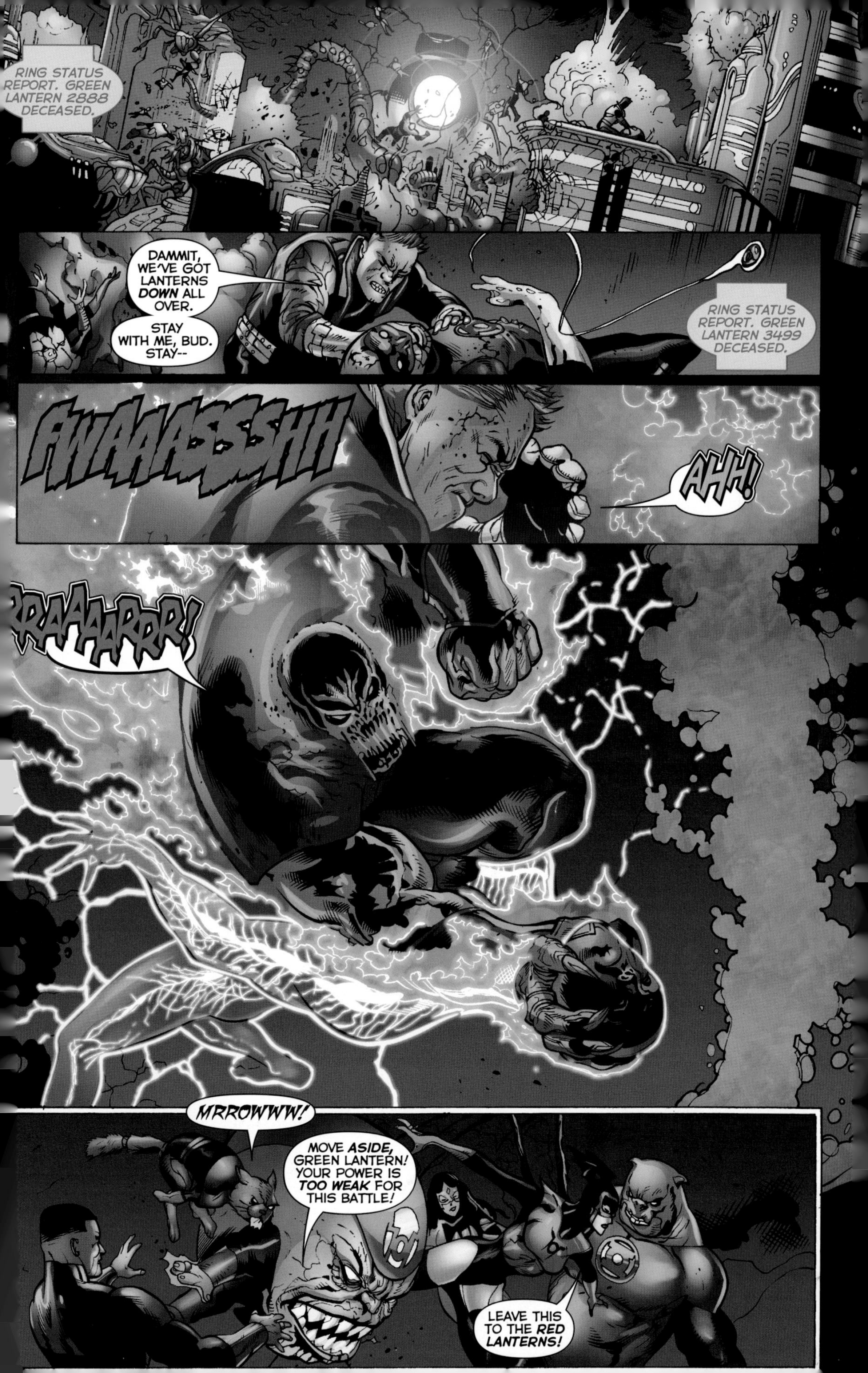
RING STATUS REPORT. GREEN LANTERN 2888 DECEASED.
DAMMIT, WE'VE GOT LANTERNS DOWN ALL OVER.
STAY WITH ME, BUD. STAY--
RING STATUS REPORT. GREEN LANTERN 3499 DECEASED.
FWAAAASSSHH
AHH!
RRAAAAARRR!
MRROWWW!
MOVE ASIDE, GREEN LANTERN! YOUR POWER IS TOO WEAK FOR THIS BATTLE!
LEAVE THIS TO THE RED LANTERNS!

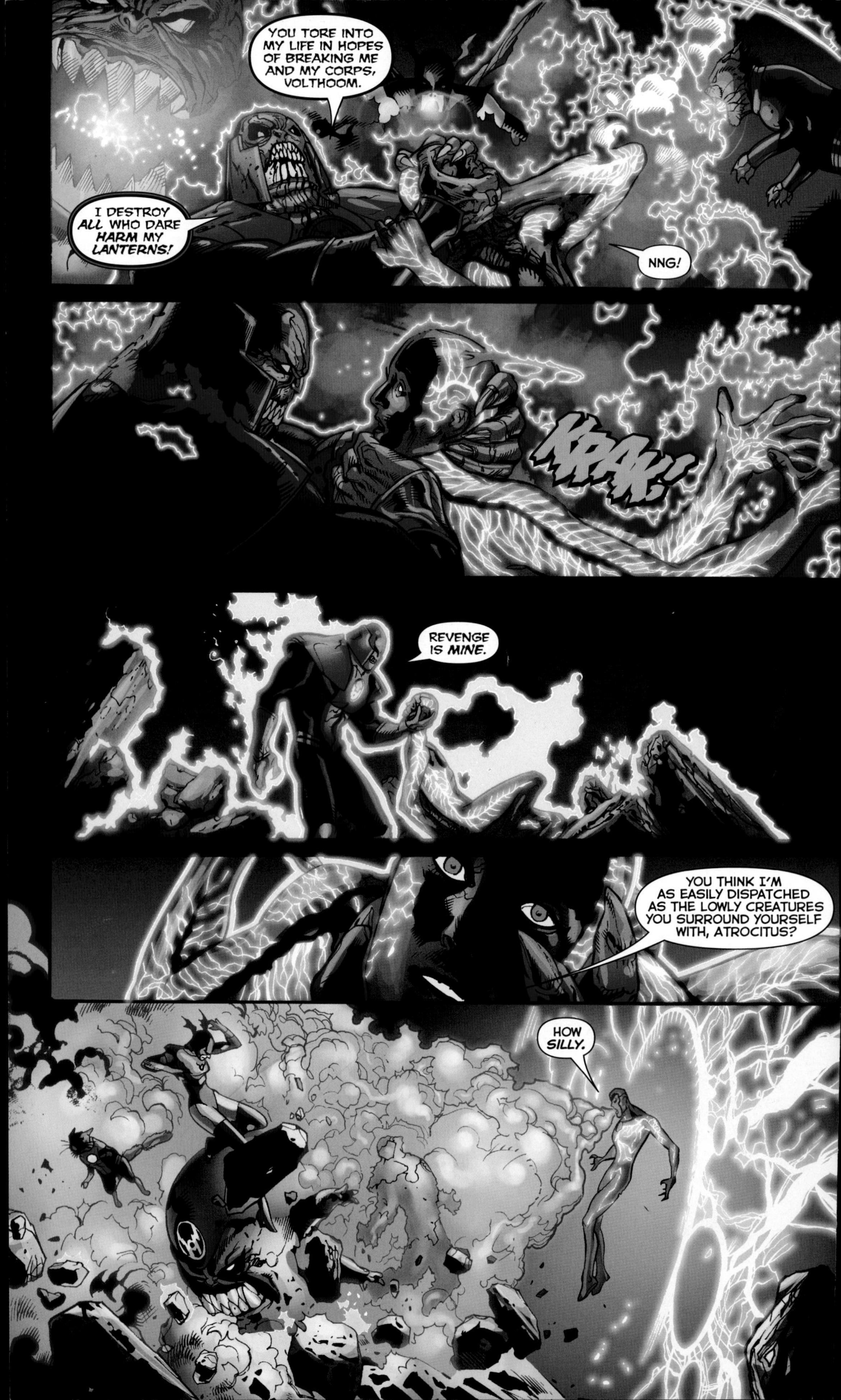
YOU TORE INTO MY LIFE IN HOPES OF BREAKING ME AND MY CORPS, VOLTHOOM.
I DESTROY ALL WHO DARE HARM MY LANTERNS!
NNG!
KRAK!
REVENGE IS MINE.
YOU THINK I'M AS EASILY DISPATCHED AS THE LOWLY CREATURES YOU SURROUND YOURSELF WITH, ATROCITUS?
HOW SILLY.

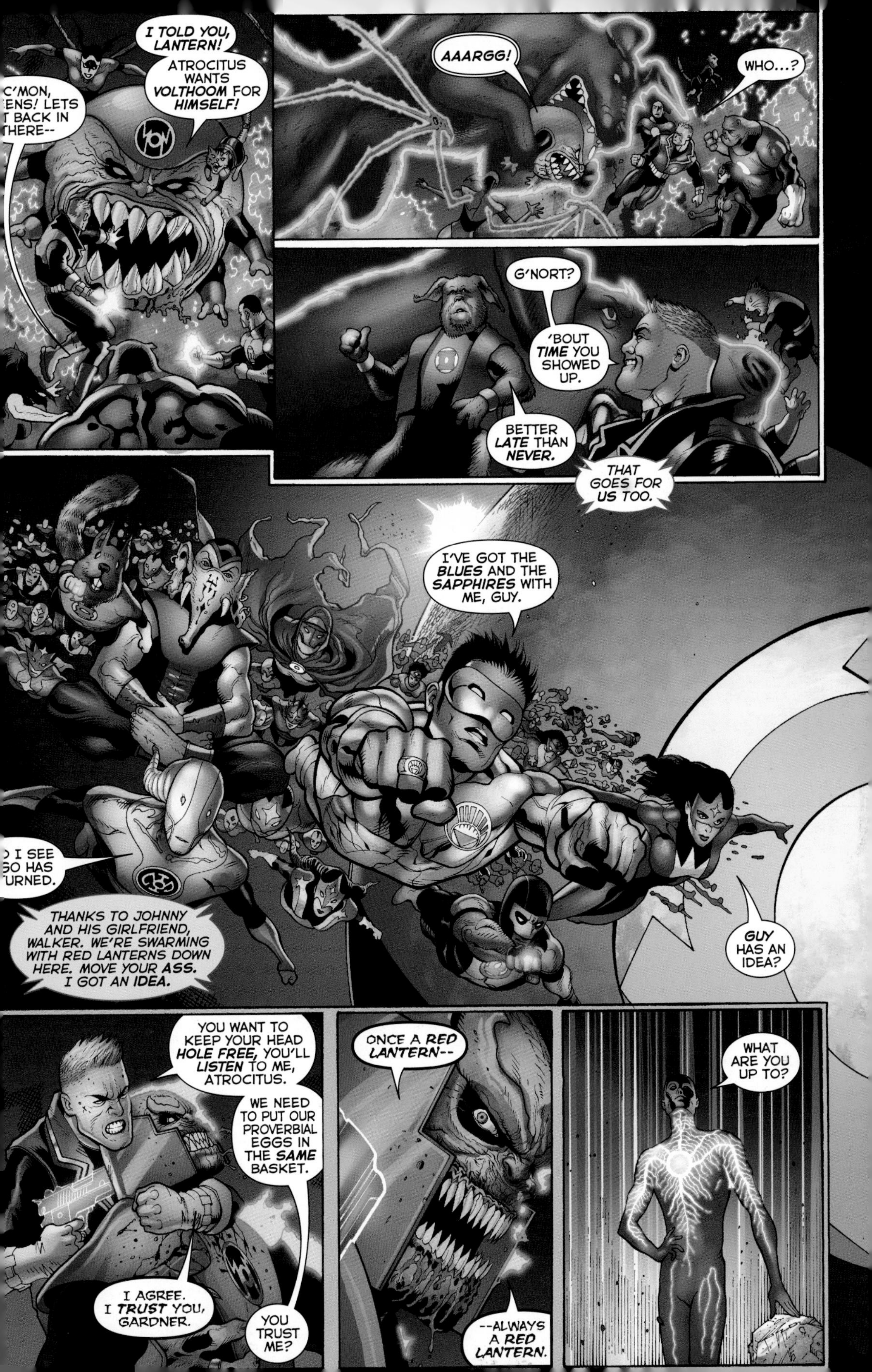
C'MON, ...ENS! LETS ...T BACK IN ...THERE--
I TOLD YOU, LANTERN!
ATROCITUS WANTS VOLTHOOM FOR HIMSELF!
AAARGG!
WHO...?
G'NORT?
'BOUT TIME YOU SHOWED UP.
BETTER LATE THAN NEVER.
THAT GOES FOR US TOO.
I'VE GOT THE BLUES AND THE SAPPHIRES WITH ME, GUY.
...D I SEE ...GO HAS ...TURNED.
THANKS TO JOHNNY AND HIS GIRLFRIEND, WALKER. WE'RE SWARMING WITH RED LANTERNS DOWN HERE. MOVE YOUR ASS. I GOT AN IDEA.
GUY HAS AN IDEA?
YOU WANT TO KEEP YOUR HEAD HOLE FREE, YOU'LL LISTEN TO ME, ATROCITUS.
WE NEED TO PUT OUR PROVERBIAL EGGS IN THE SAME BASKET.
I AGREE. I TRUST YOU, GARDNER.
YOU TRUST ME?
ONCE A RED LANTERN--
--ALWAYS A RED LANTERN.
WHAT ARE YOU UP TO?

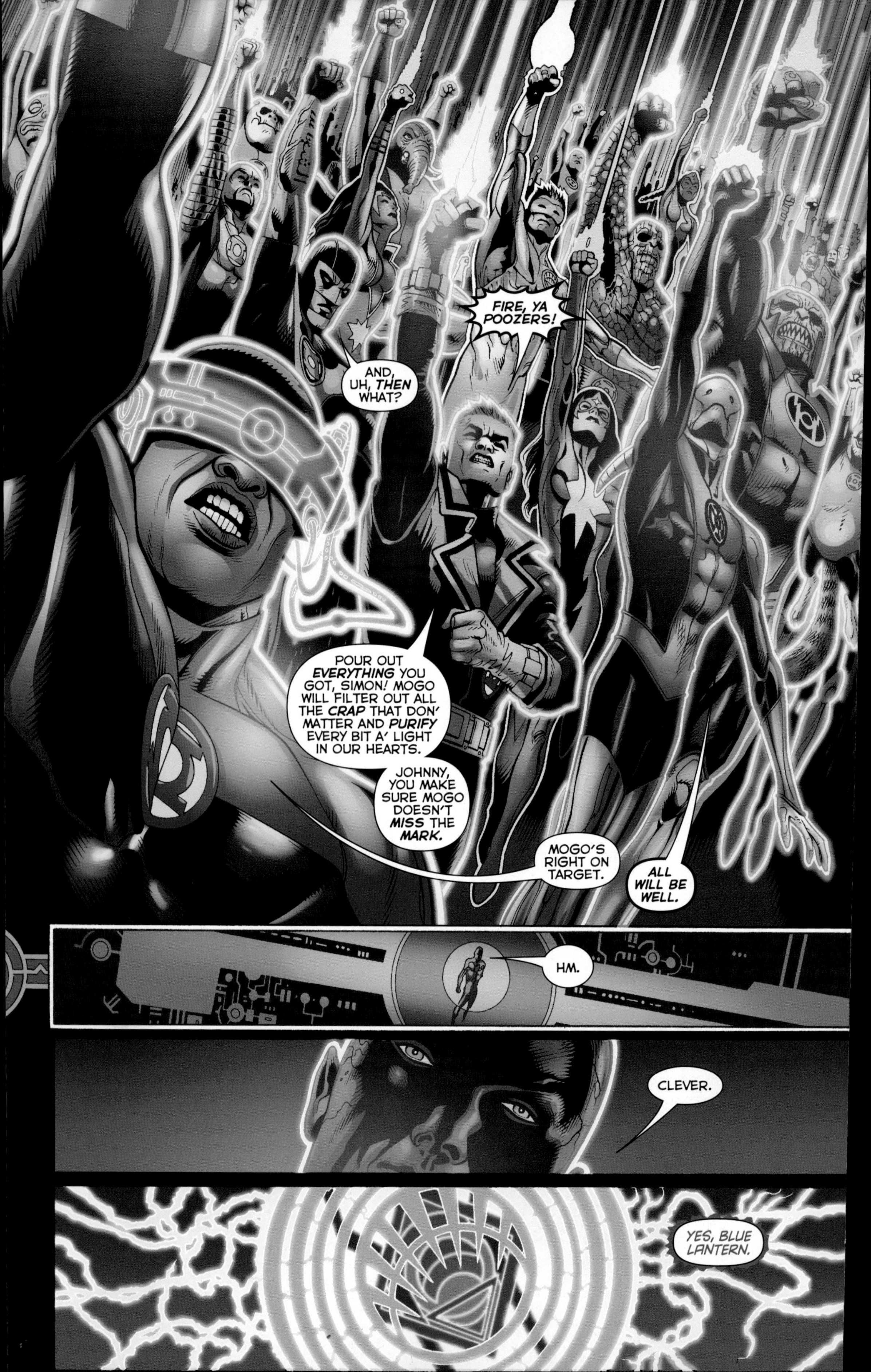
FIRE, YA POOZERS!
AND, UH, THEN WHAT?
POUR OUT EVERYTHING YOU GOT, SIMON! MOGO WILL FILTER OUT ALL THE CRAP THAT DON' MATTER AND PURIFY EVERY BIT A' LIGHT IN OUR HEARTS.
JOHNNY, YOU MAKE SURE MOGO DOESN'T MISS THE MARK.
MOGO'S RIGHT ON TARGET.
ALL WILL BE WELL.
HM.
CLEVER.
YES, BLUE LANTERN.

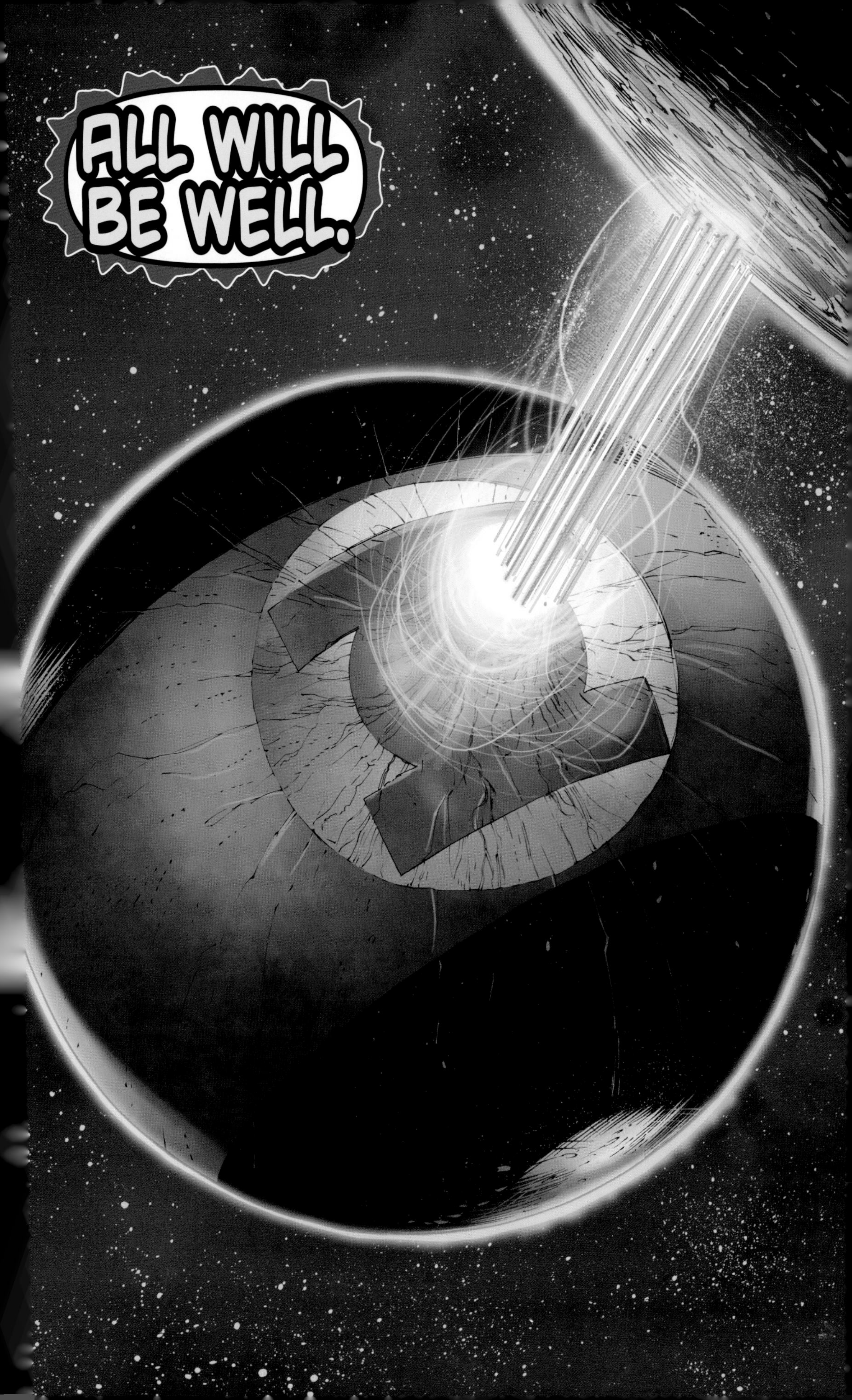
ALL WILL BE WELL.

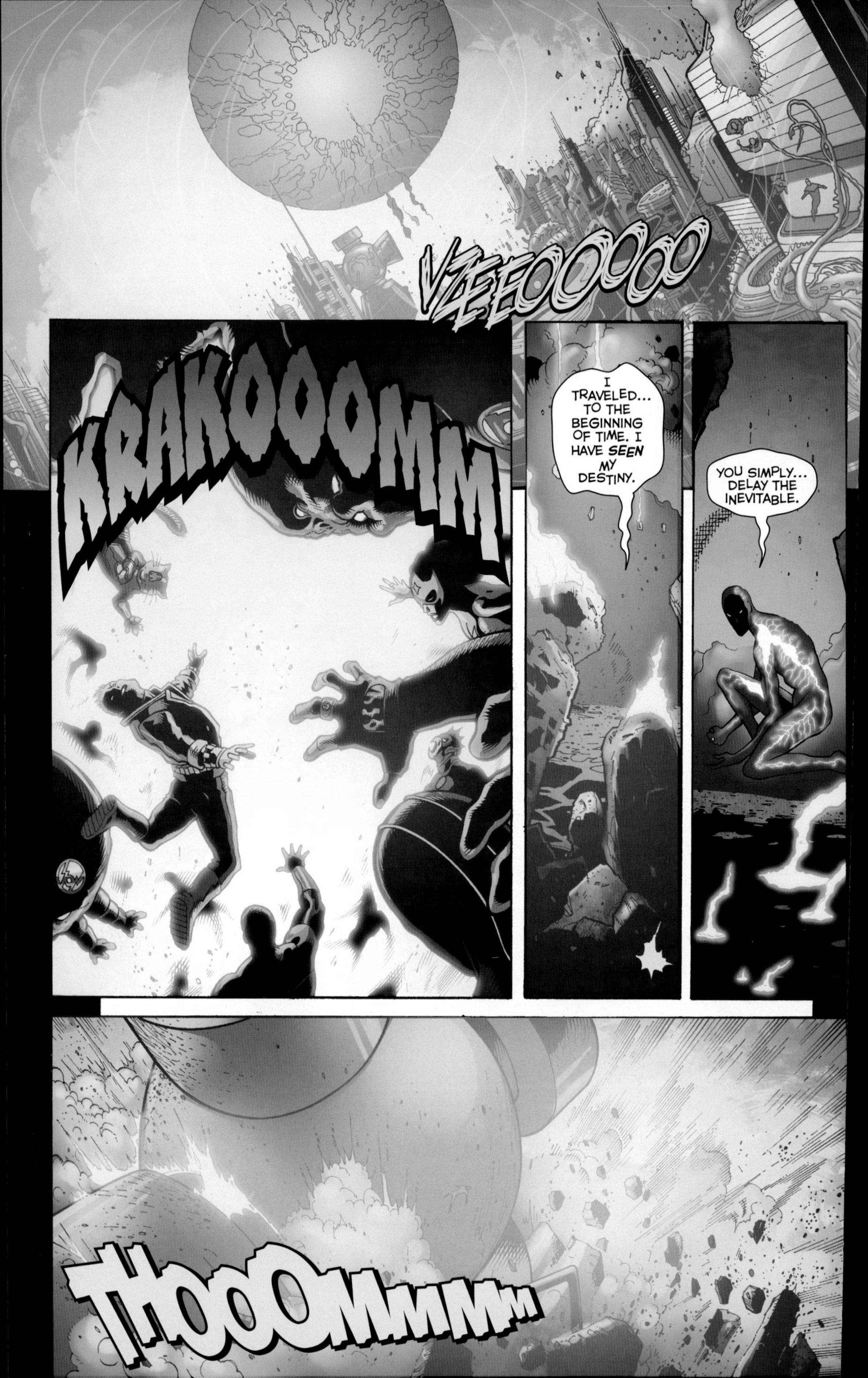
VZEEOOOOO
KRAKOOOMM
I TRAVELED... TO THE BEGINNING OF TIME. I HAVE SEEN MY DESTINY.
YOU SIMPLY... DELAY THE INEVITABLE.
THOOOMMMMM

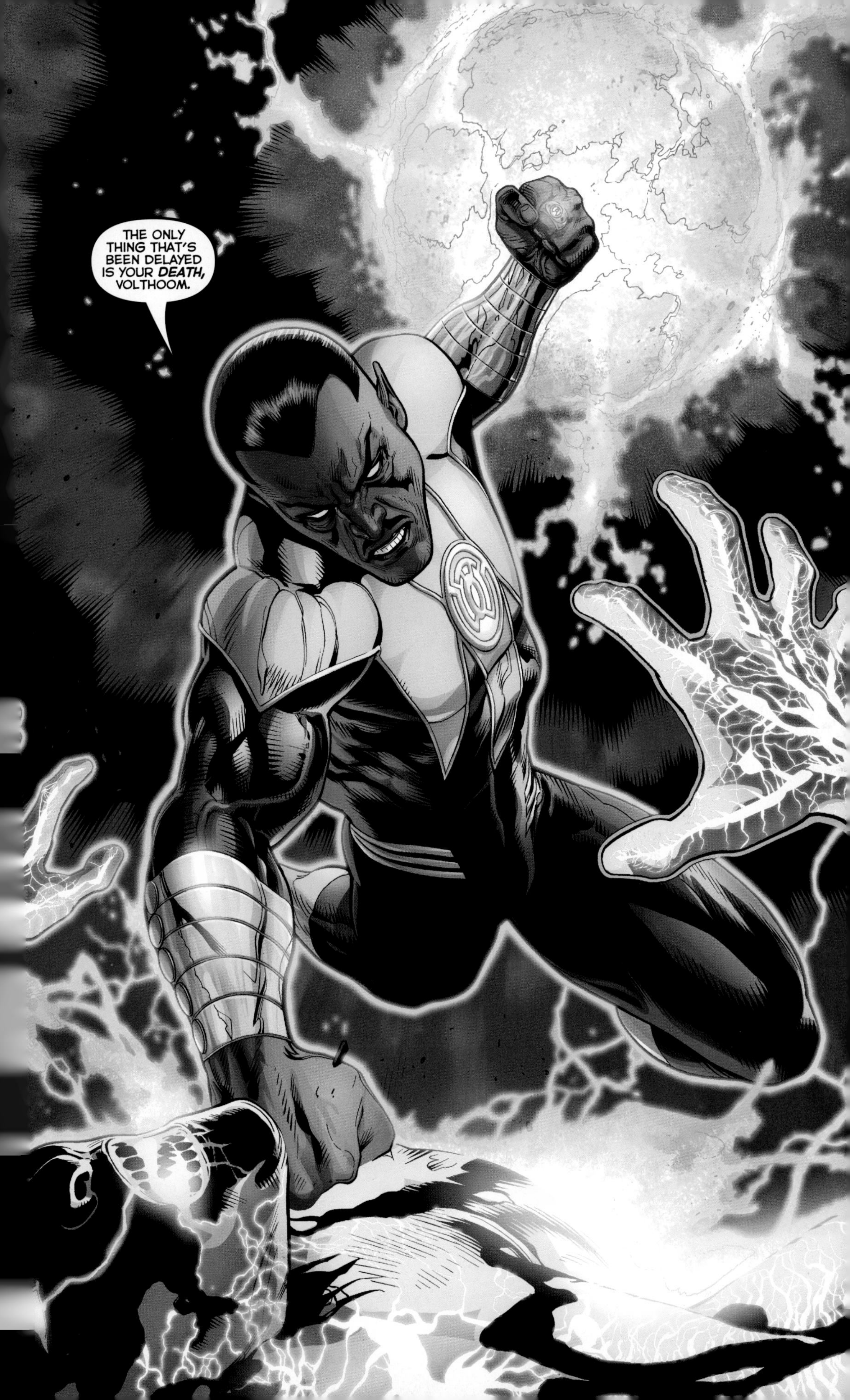
THE ONLY THING THAT'S BEEN DELAYED IS YOUR *DEATH,* VOLTHOOM.

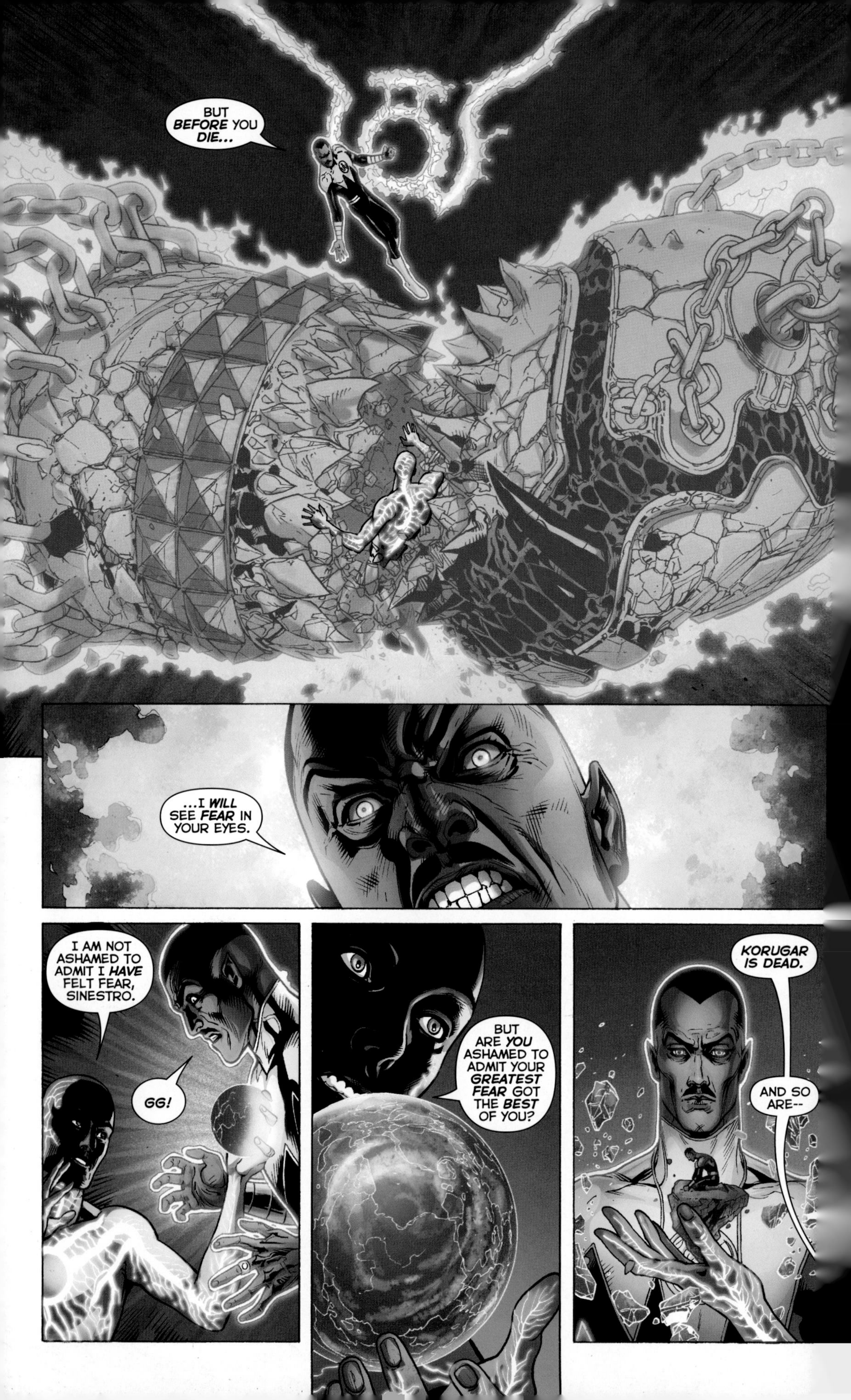
BUT BEFORE YOU DIE...
...I WILL SEE FEAR IN YOUR EYES.
I AM NOT ASHAMED TO ADMIT I HAVE FELT FEAR, SINESTRO.
GG!
BUT ARE YOU ASHAMED TO ADMIT YOUR GREATEST FEAR GOT THE BEST OF YOU?
KORUGAR IS DEAD.
AND SO ARE--

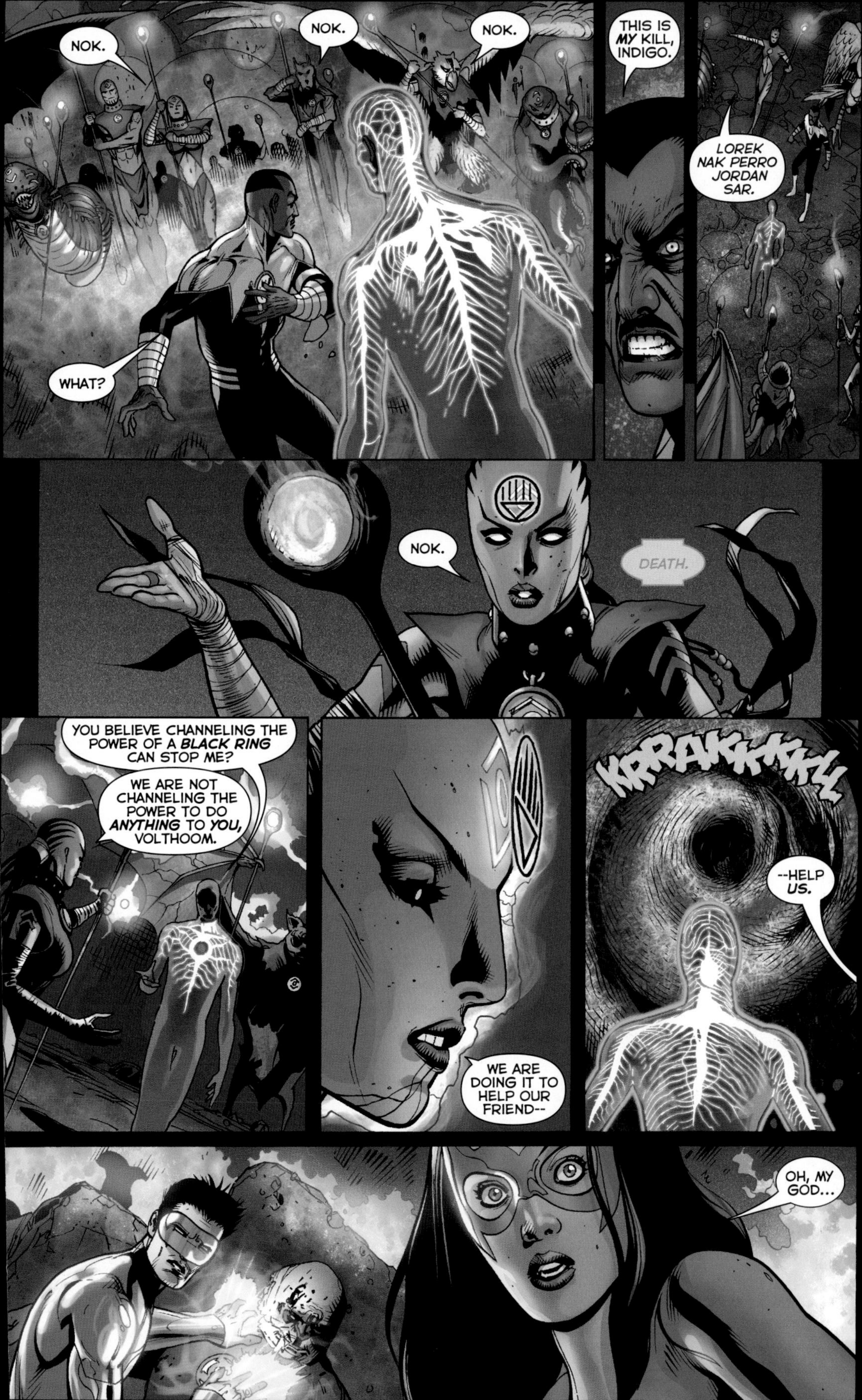
NOK.
NOK.
NOK.
WHAT?
THIS IS MY KILL, INDIGO.
LOREK NAK PERRO JORDAN SAR.
NOK.
DEATH.
YOU BELIEVE CHANNELING THE POWER OF A BLACK RING CAN STOP ME?
WE ARE NOT CHANNELING THE POWER TO DO ANYTHING TO YOU, VOLTHOOM.
WE ARE DOING IT TO HELP OUR FRIEND--
KRRAKKKKL
--HELP US.
OH, MY GOD...

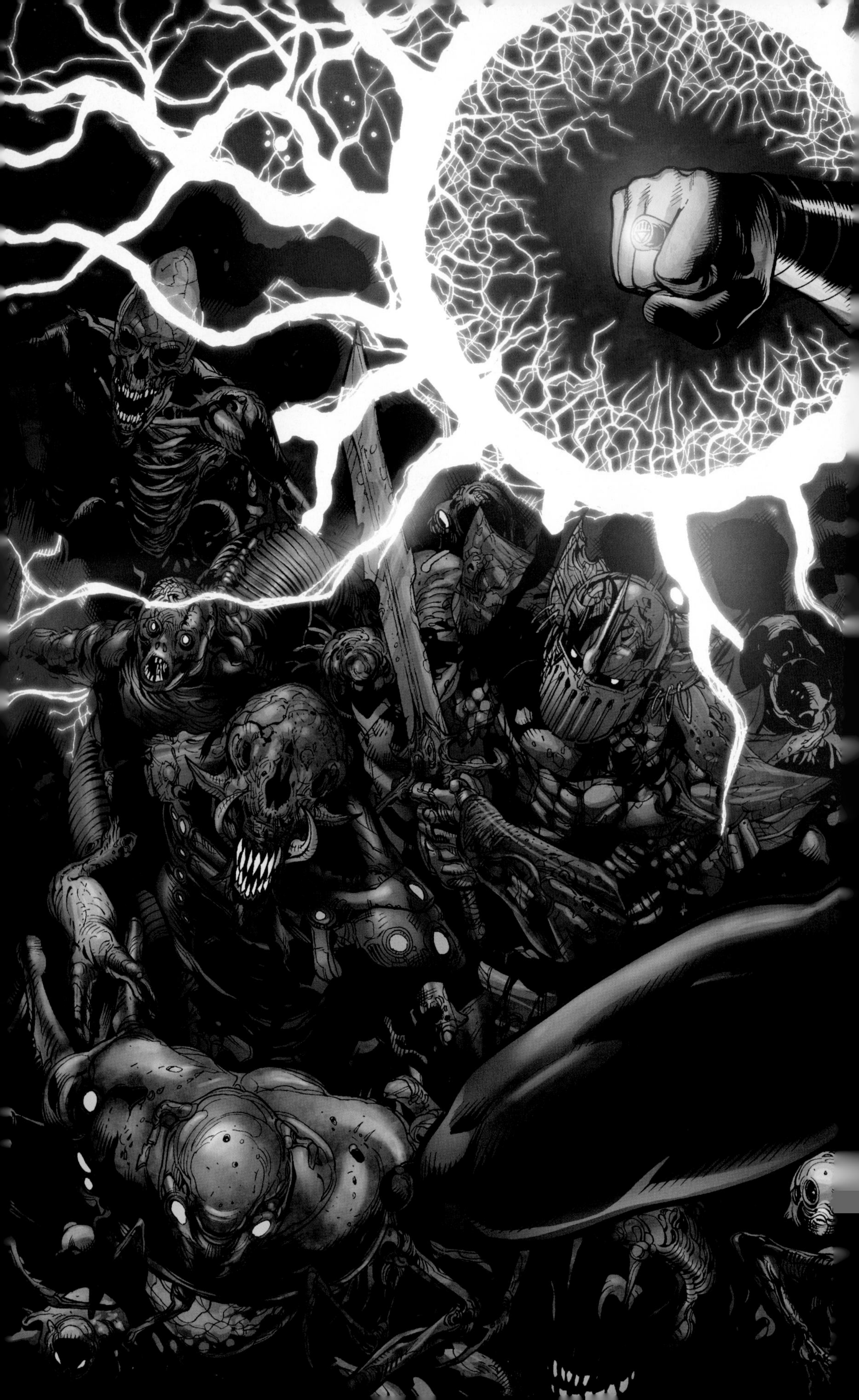

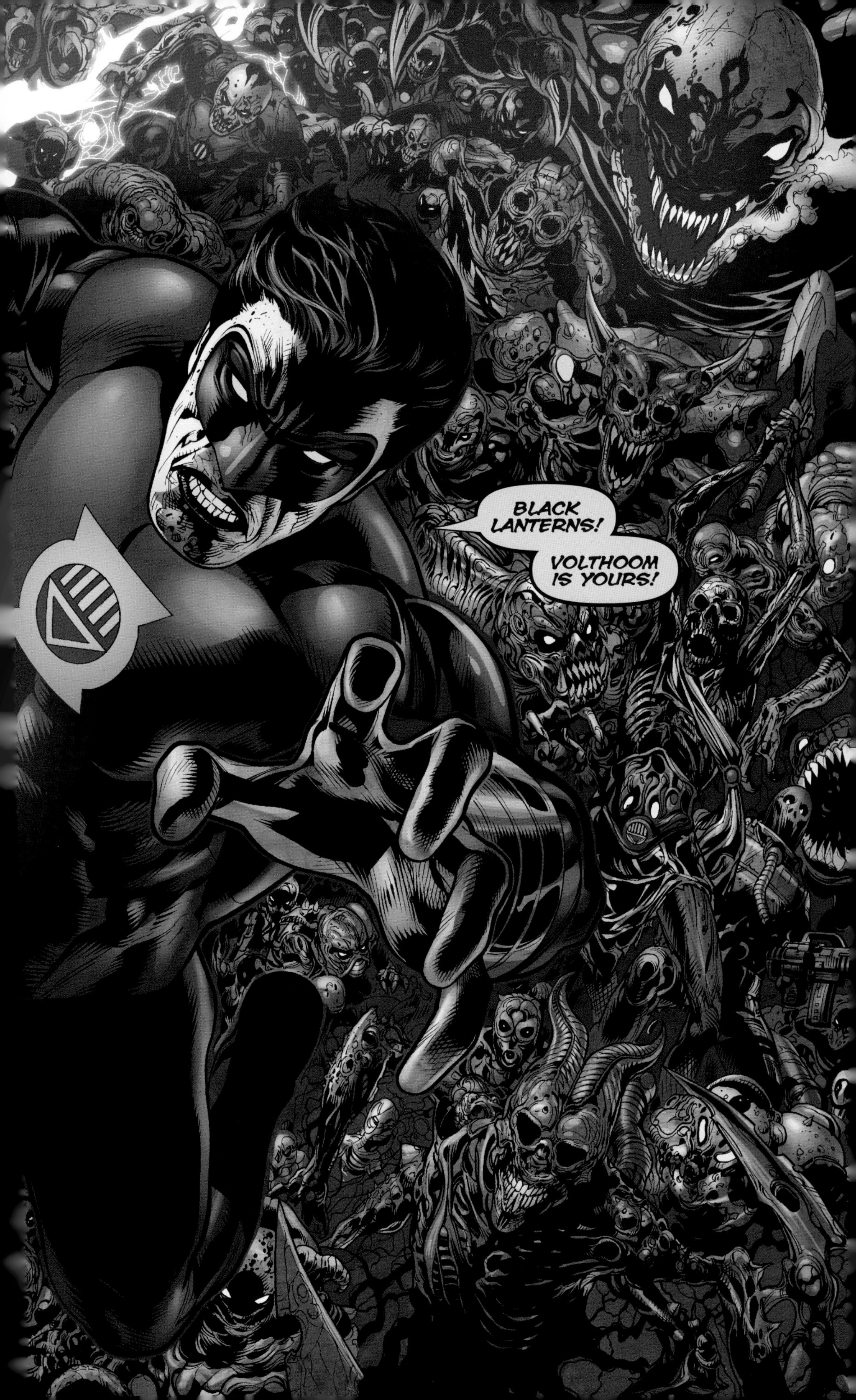
BLACK LANTERNS!
VOLTHOOM IS YOURS!

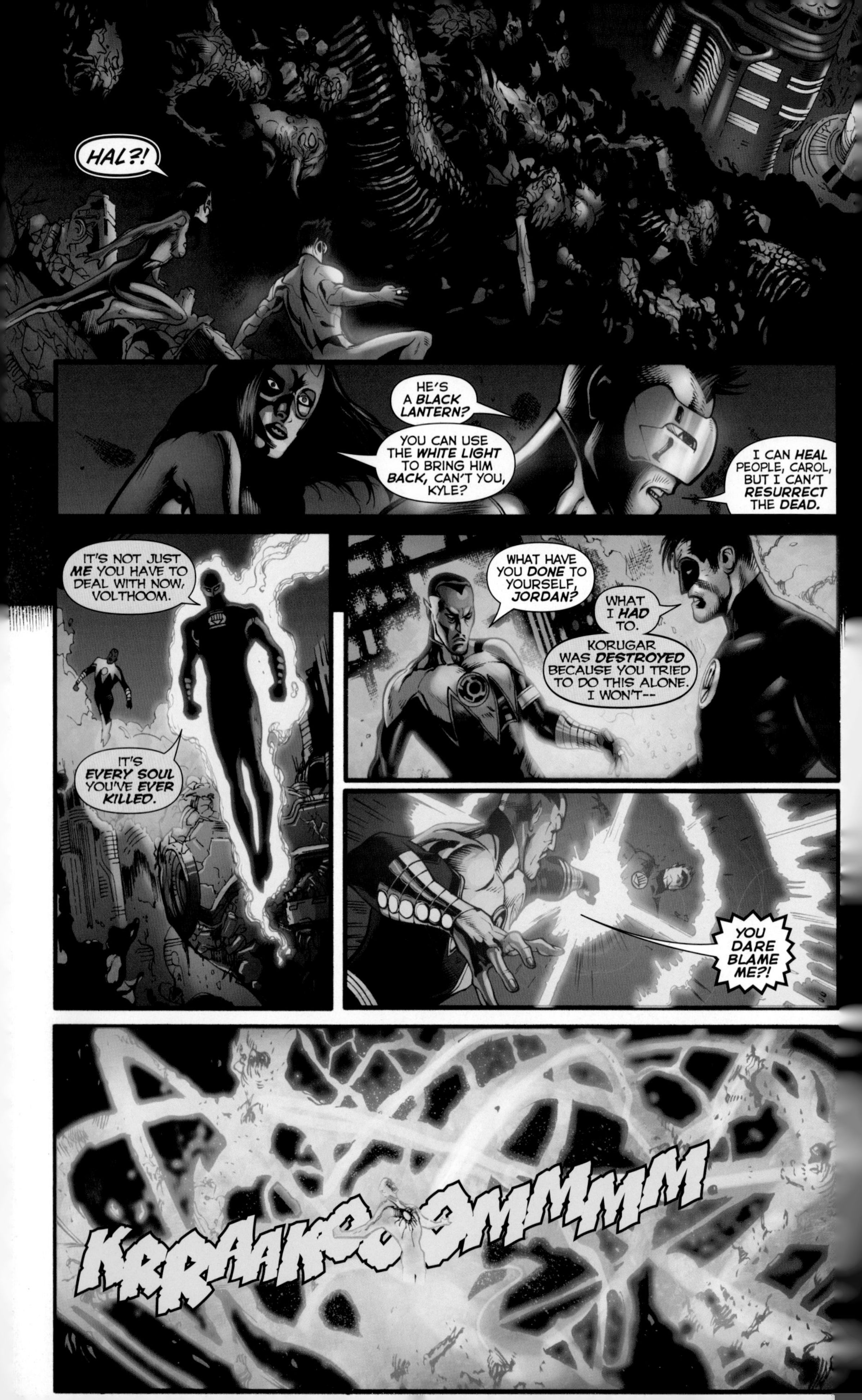

HAL?!
HE'S A BLACK LANTERN?
YOU CAN USE THE WHITE LIGHT TO BRING HIM BACK, CAN'T YOU, KYLE?
I CAN HEAL PEOPLE, CAROL, BUT I CAN'T RESURRECT THE DEAD.
IT'S NOT JUST ME YOU HAVE TO DEAL WITH NOW, VOLTHOOM.
IT'S EVERY SOUL YOU'VE EVER KILLED.
WHAT HAVE YOU DONE TO YOURSELF, JORDAN?
WHAT I HAD TO.
KORUGAR WAS DESTROYED BECAUSE YOU TRIED TO DO THIS ALONE. I WON'T--
YOU DARE BLAME ME?!

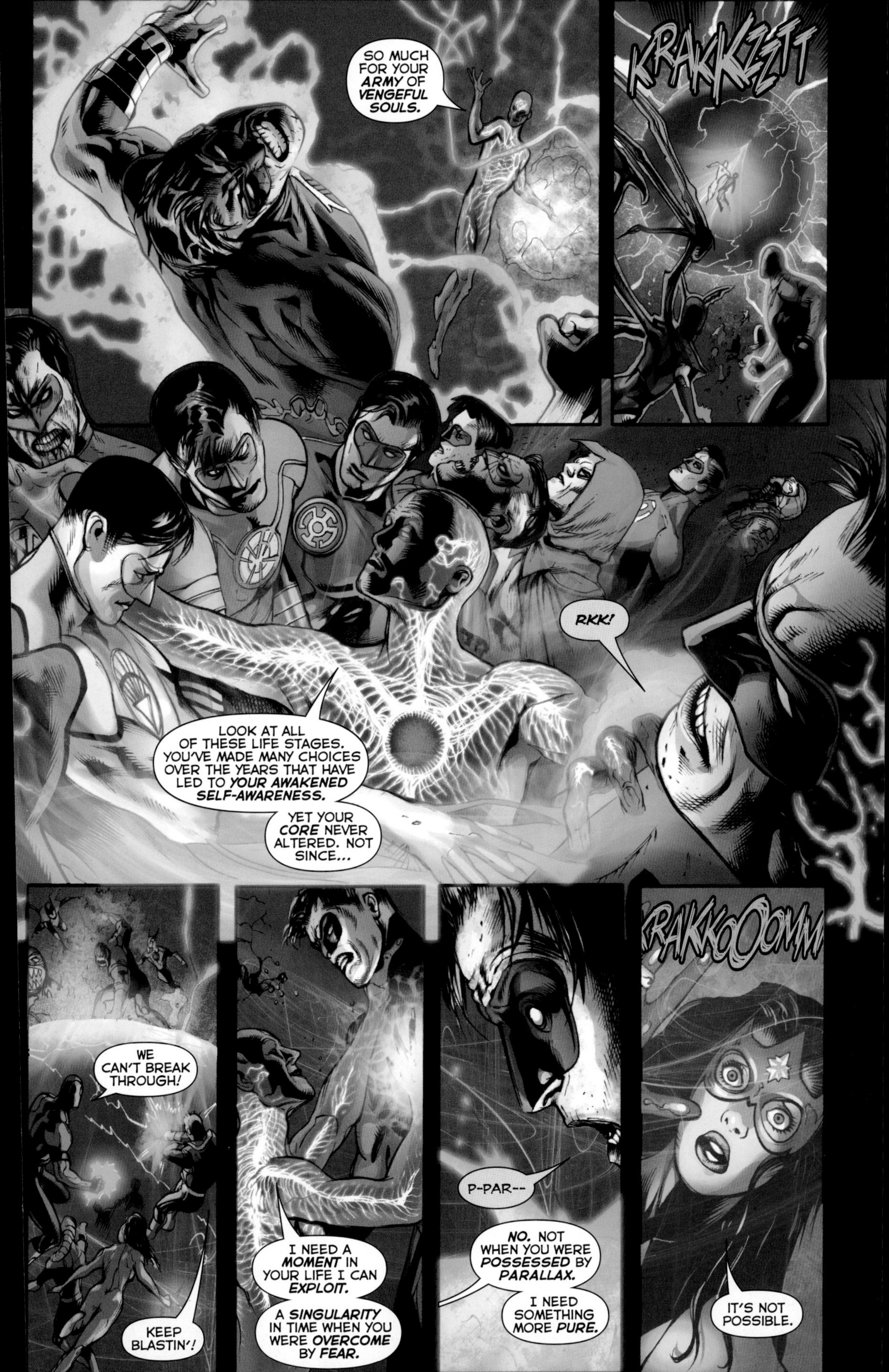
SO MUCH FOR YOUR ARMY OF VENGEFUL SOULS.
KRAKKZZTT
RKK!
LOOK AT ALL OF THESE LIFE STAGES. YOU'VE MADE MANY CHOICES OVER THE YEARS THAT HAVE LED TO YOUR AWAKENED SELF-AWARENESS.
YET YOUR CORE NEVER ALTERED. NOT SINCE...
WE CAN'T BREAK THROUGH!
KEEP BLASTIN'!
I NEED A MOMENT IN YOUR LIFE I CAN EXPLOIT.
A SINGULARITY IN TIME WHEN YOU WERE OVERCOME BY FEAR.
P-PAR--
NO. NOT WHEN YOU WERE POSSESSED BY PARALLAX.
I NEED SOMETHING MORE PURE.
KRAKKOOOMM
IT'S NOT POSSIBLE.

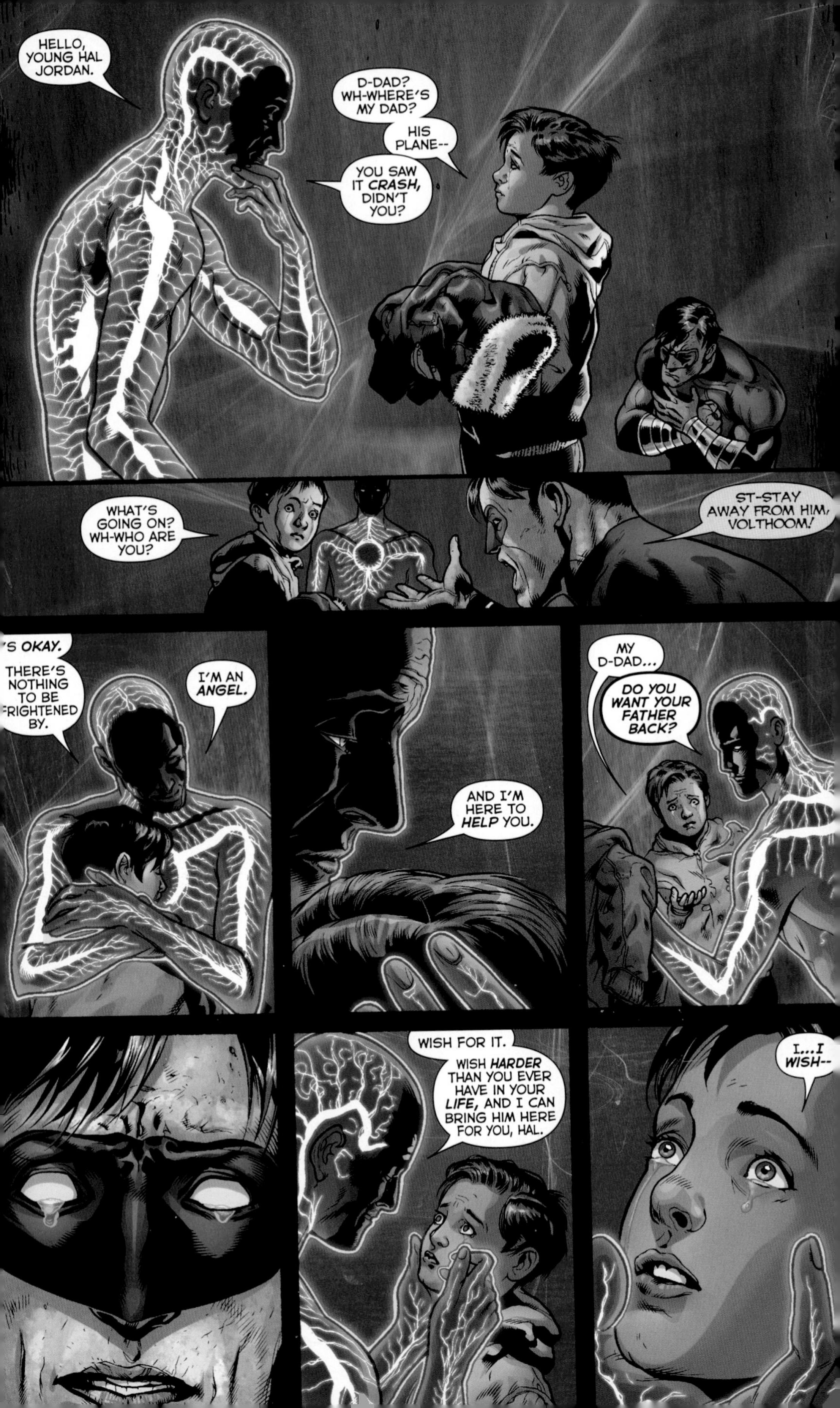
HELLO, YOUNG HAL JORDAN.
D-DAD? WH-WHERE'S MY DAD?
HIS PLANE--
YOU SAW IT CRASH, DIDN'T YOU?
WHAT'S GOING ON? WH-WHO ARE YOU?
ST-STAY AWAY FROM HIM, VOLTHOOM!
'S OKAY.
THERE'S NOTHING TO BE FRIGHTENED BY.
I'M AN ANGEL.
AND I'M HERE TO HELP YOU.
MY D-DAD...
DO YOU WANT YOUR FATHER BACK?
WISH FOR IT.
WISH HARDER THAN YOU EVER HAVE IN YOUR LIFE, AND I CAN BRING HIM HERE FOR YOU, HAL.
I...I WISH--

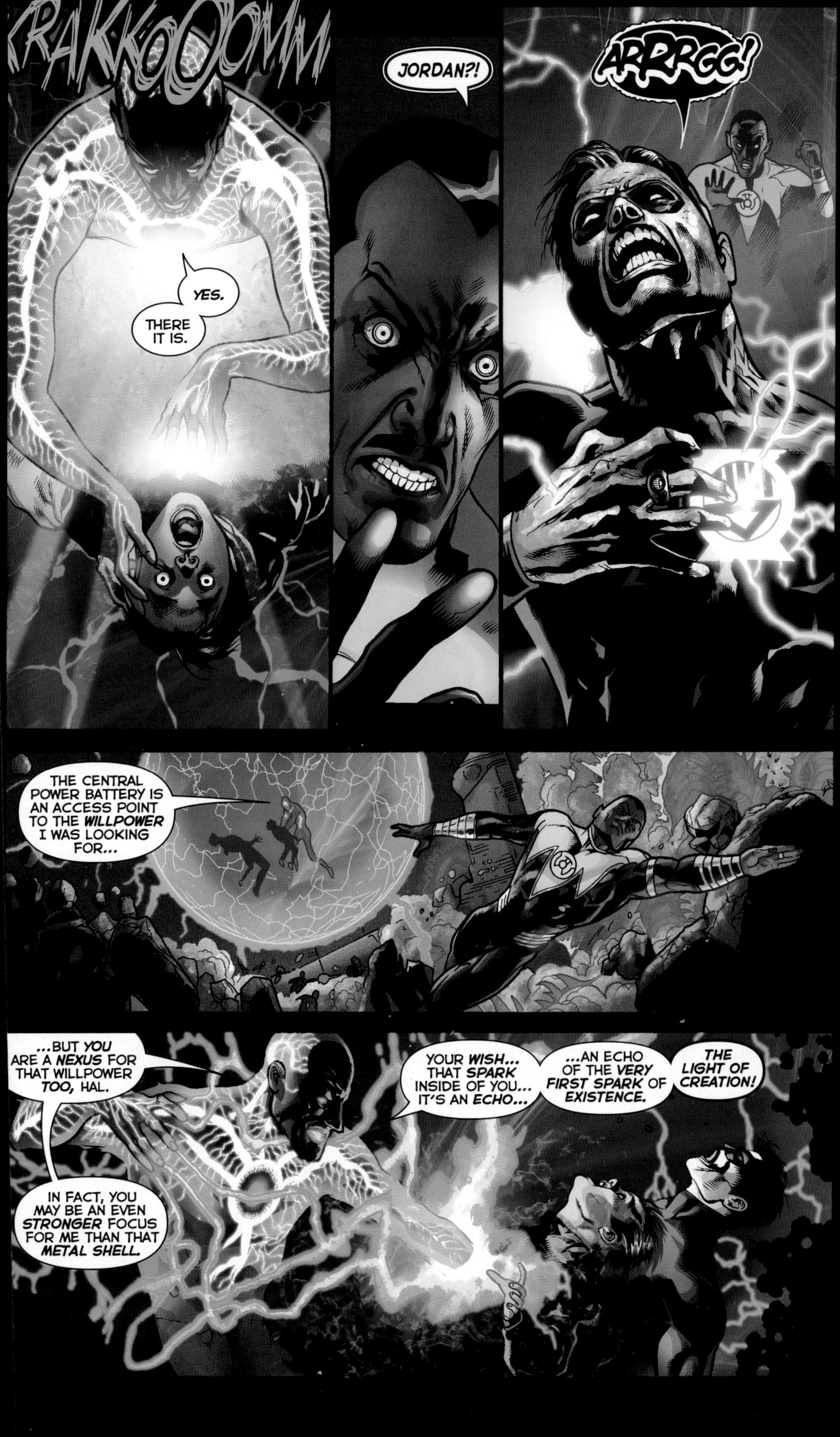

KRAKKOOOMM
YES.
THERE IT IS.
JORDAN?!
ARRRGG!
THE CENTRAL POWER BATTERY IS AN ACCESS POINT TO THE WILLPOWER I WAS LOOKING FOR...
...BUT YOU ARE A NEXUS FOR THAT WILLPOWER TOO, HAL.
IN FACT, YOU MAY BE AN EVEN STRONGER FOCUS FOR ME THAN THAT METAL SHELL.
YOUR WISH... THAT SPARK INSIDE OF YOU... IT'S AN ECHO...
...AN ECHO OF THE VERY FIRST SPARK OF EXISTENCE.
THE LIGHT OF CREATION!

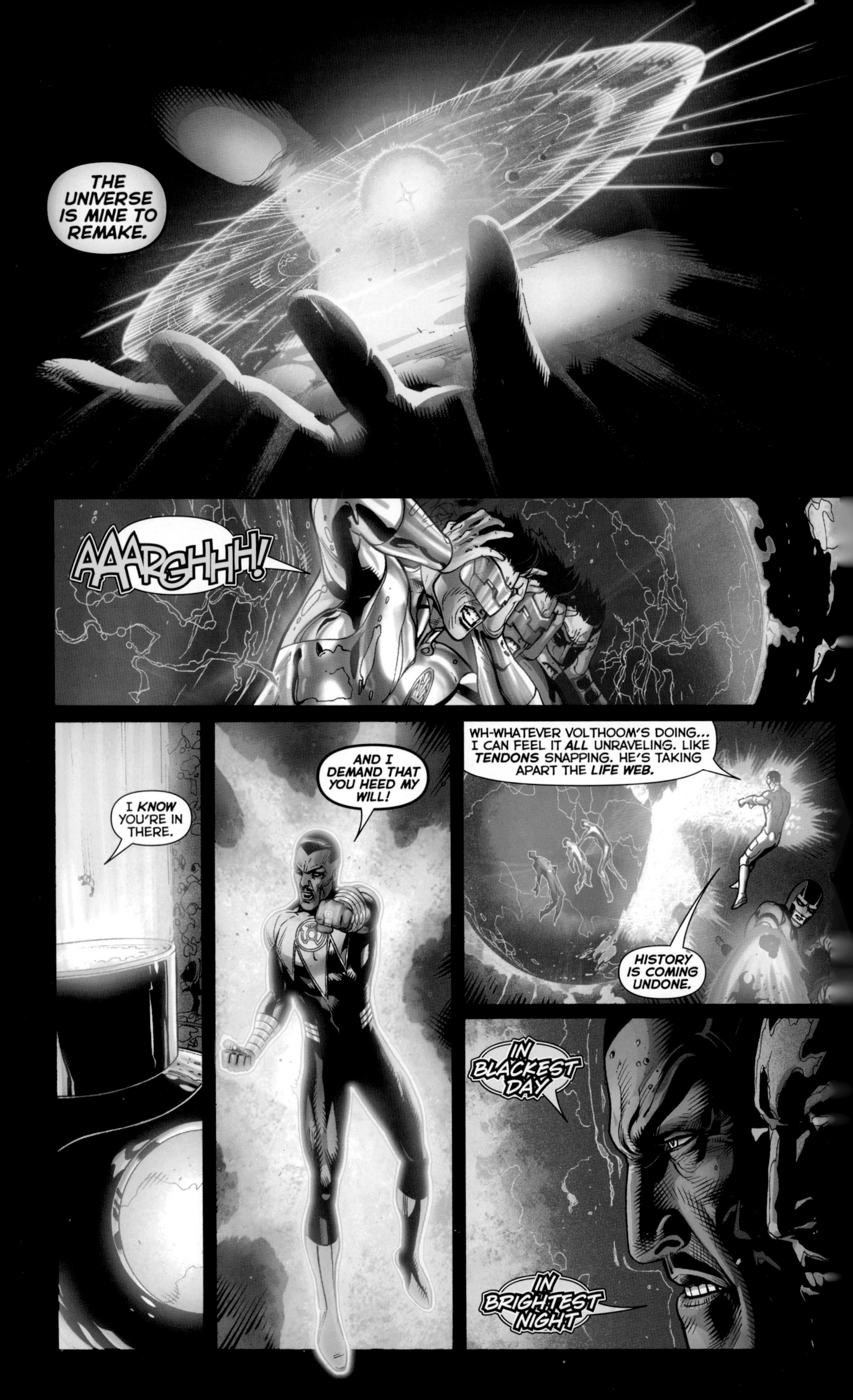
THE UNIVERSE IS MINE TO REMAKE.
AAARGHHH!
I KNOW YOU'RE IN THERE.
AND I DEMAND THAT YOU HEED MY WILL!
WH-WHATEVER VOLTHOOM'S DOING... I CAN FEEL IT ALL UNRAVELING. LIKE TENDONS SNAPPING. HE'S TAKING APART THE LIFE WEB.
HISTORY IS COMING UNDONE.
IN BLACKEST DAY
IN BRIGHTEST NIGHT

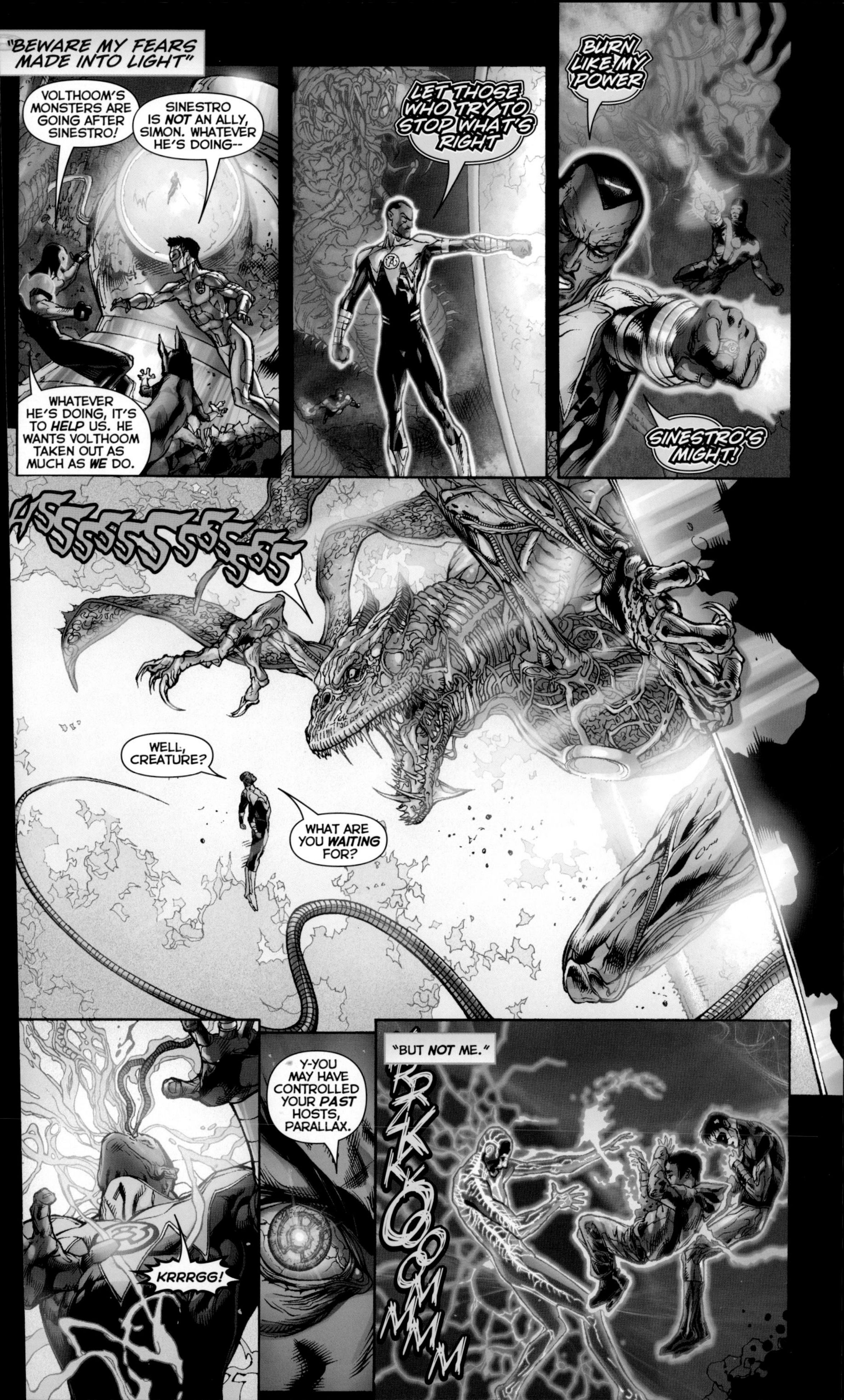
"BEWARE MY FEARS MADE INTO LIGHT"
VOLTHOOM'S MONSTERS ARE GOING AFTER SINESTRO!
SINESTRO IS NOT AN ALLY, SIMON. WHATEVER HE'S DOING--
WHATEVER HE'S DOING, IT'S TO HELP US. HE WANTS VOLTHOOM TAKEN OUT AS MUCH AS WE DO.
LET THOSE WHO TRY TO STOP WHAT'S RIGHT
BURN LIKE MY POWER
SINESTRO'S MIGHT!
HSSSSSSSSSSSS
WELL, CREATURE?
WHAT ARE YOU WAITING FOR?
KRRRGG!
Y-YOU MAY HAVE CONTROLLED YOUR PAST HOSTS, PARALLAX.
"BUT NOT ME."
KRAKOOOMMMM

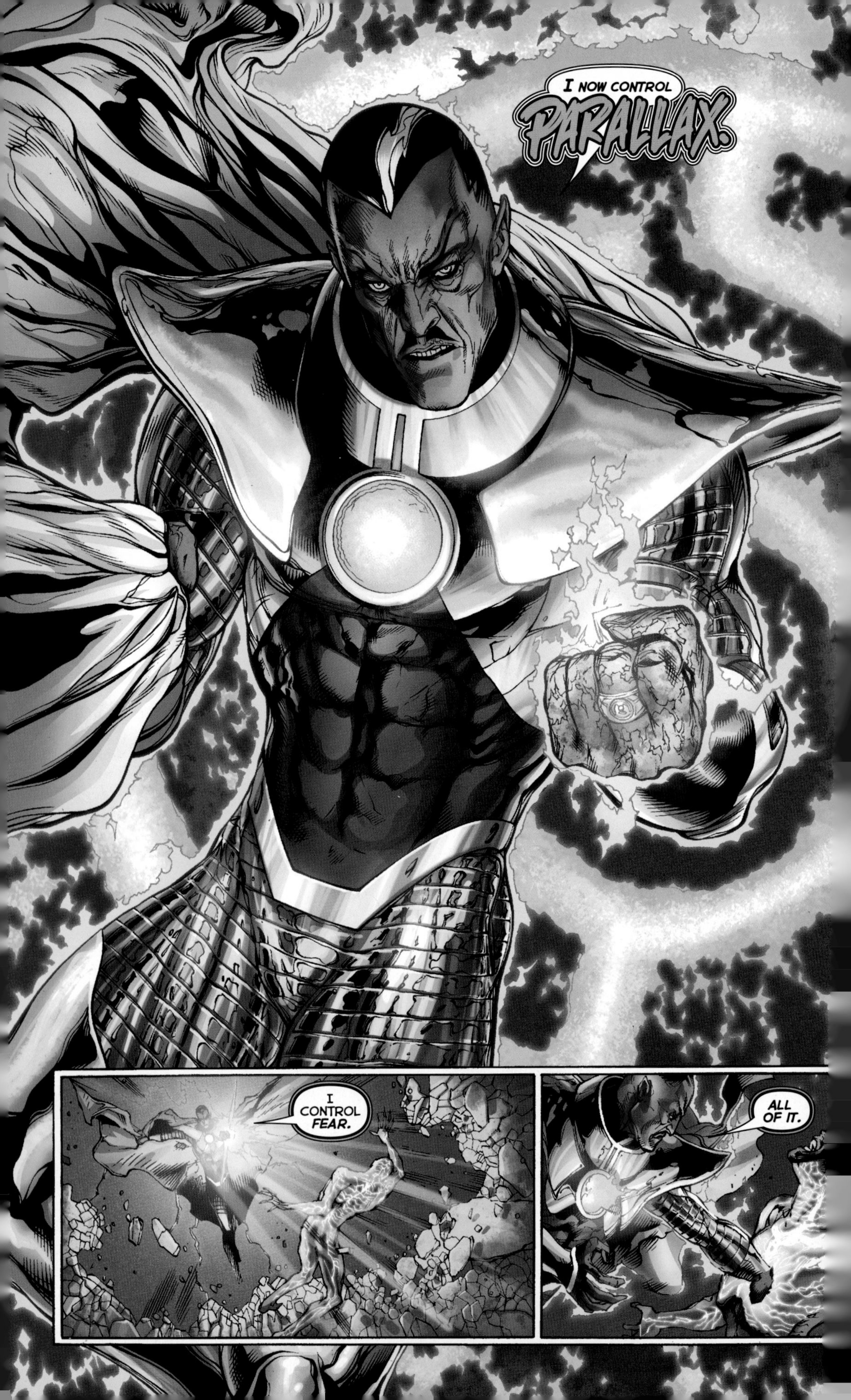
I NOW CONTROL PARALLAX.
I CONTROL FEAR.
ALL OF IT.

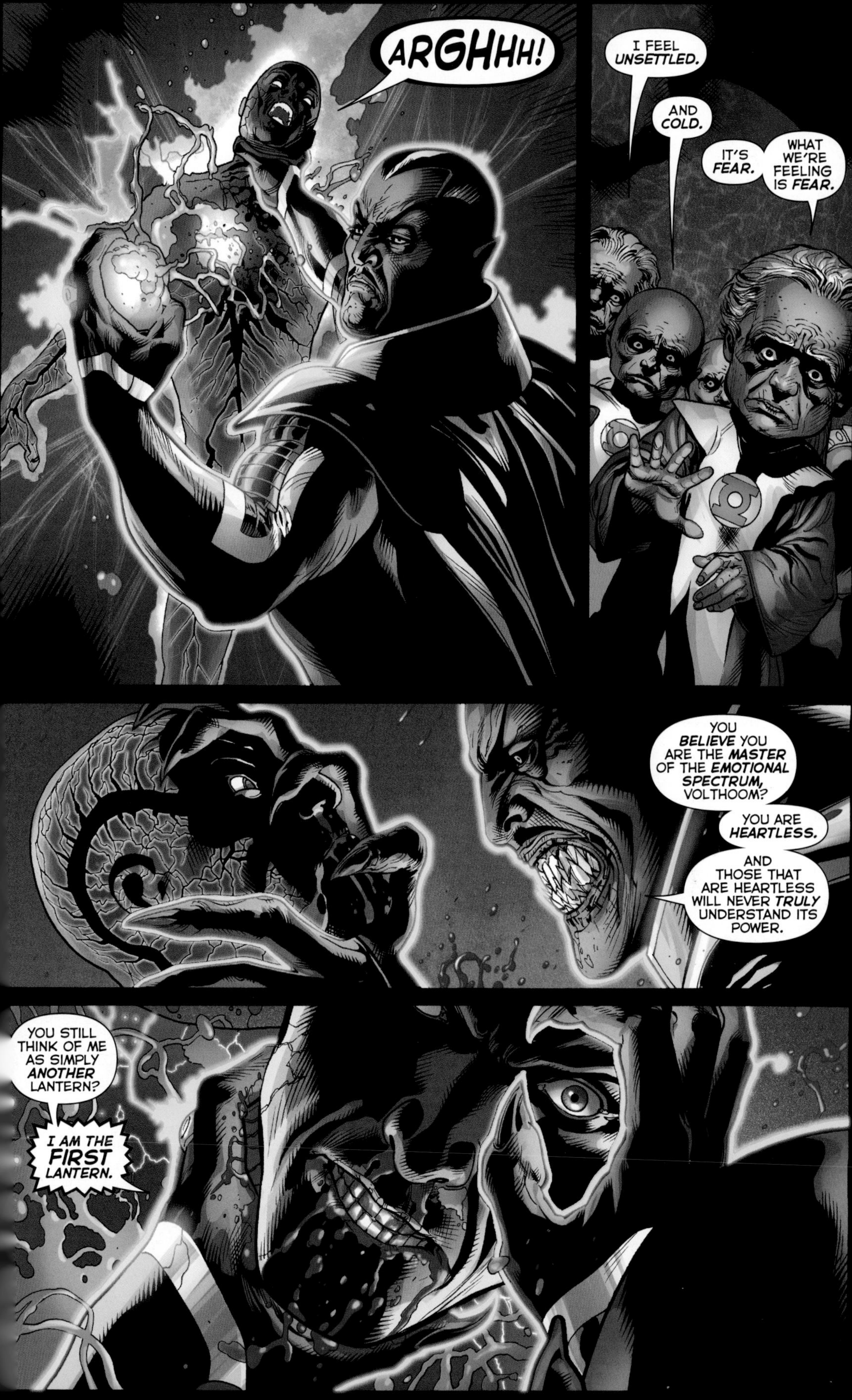
ARGHHH!
I FEEL UNSETTLED.
AND COLD.
IT'S FEAR.
WHAT WE'RE FEELING IS FEAR.
YOU BELIEVE YOU ARE THE MASTER OF THE EMOTIONAL SPECTRUM, VOLTHOOM?
YOU ARE HEARTLESS.
AND THOSE THAT ARE HEARTLESS WILL NEVER TRULY UNDERSTAND ITS POWER.
YOU STILL THINK OF ME AS SIMPLY ANOTHER LANTERN?
I AM THE FIRST LANTERN.

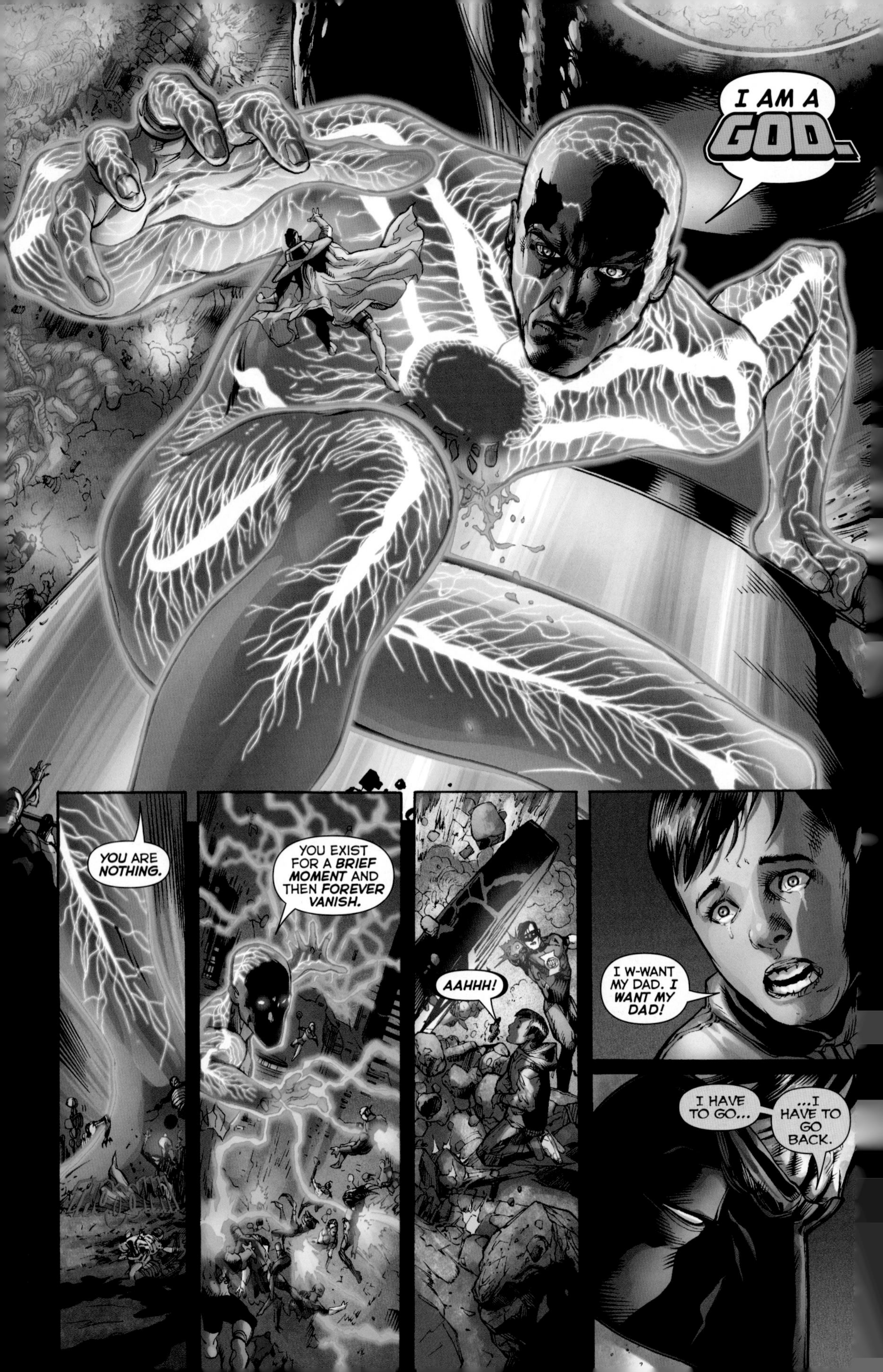

I AM A GOD.
YOU ARE NOTHING.
YOU EXIST FOR A BRIEF MOMENT AND THEN FOREVER VANISH.
AAHHH!
I W-WANT MY DAD. I WANT MY DAD!
I HAVE TO GO...
...I HAVE TO GO BACK.

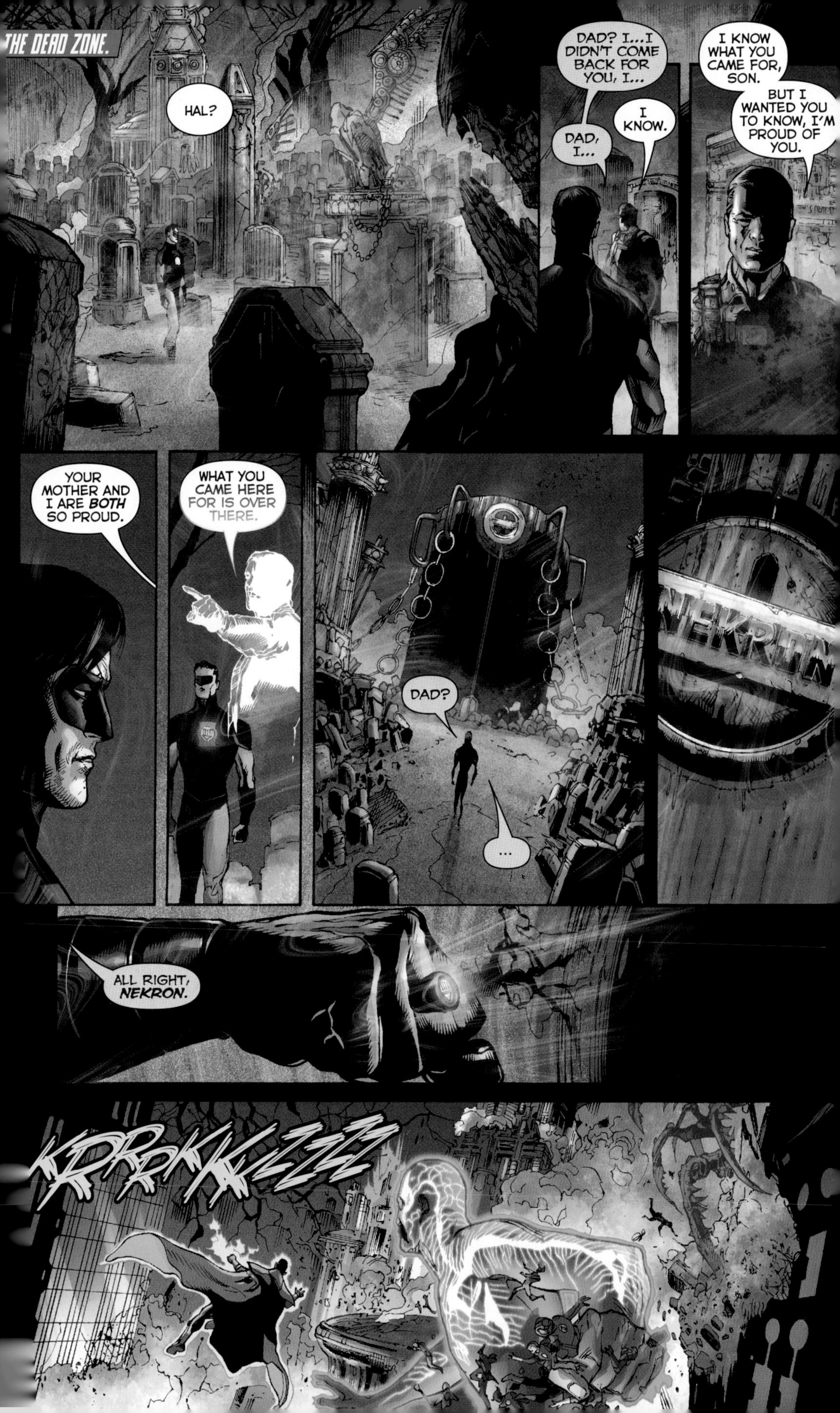
THE DEAD ZONE.
HAL?
DAD? I...I DIDN'T COME BACK FOR YOU, I...
DAD, I...
I KNOW.
I KNOW WHAT YOU CAME FOR, SON.
BUT I WANTED YOU TO KNOW, I'M PROUD OF YOU.
YOUR MOTHER AND I ARE BOTH SO PROUD.
WHAT YOU CAME HERE FOR IS OVER THERE.
DAD?
...
NEKRON
ALL RIGHT, NEKRON.
KRRKKZZZZ

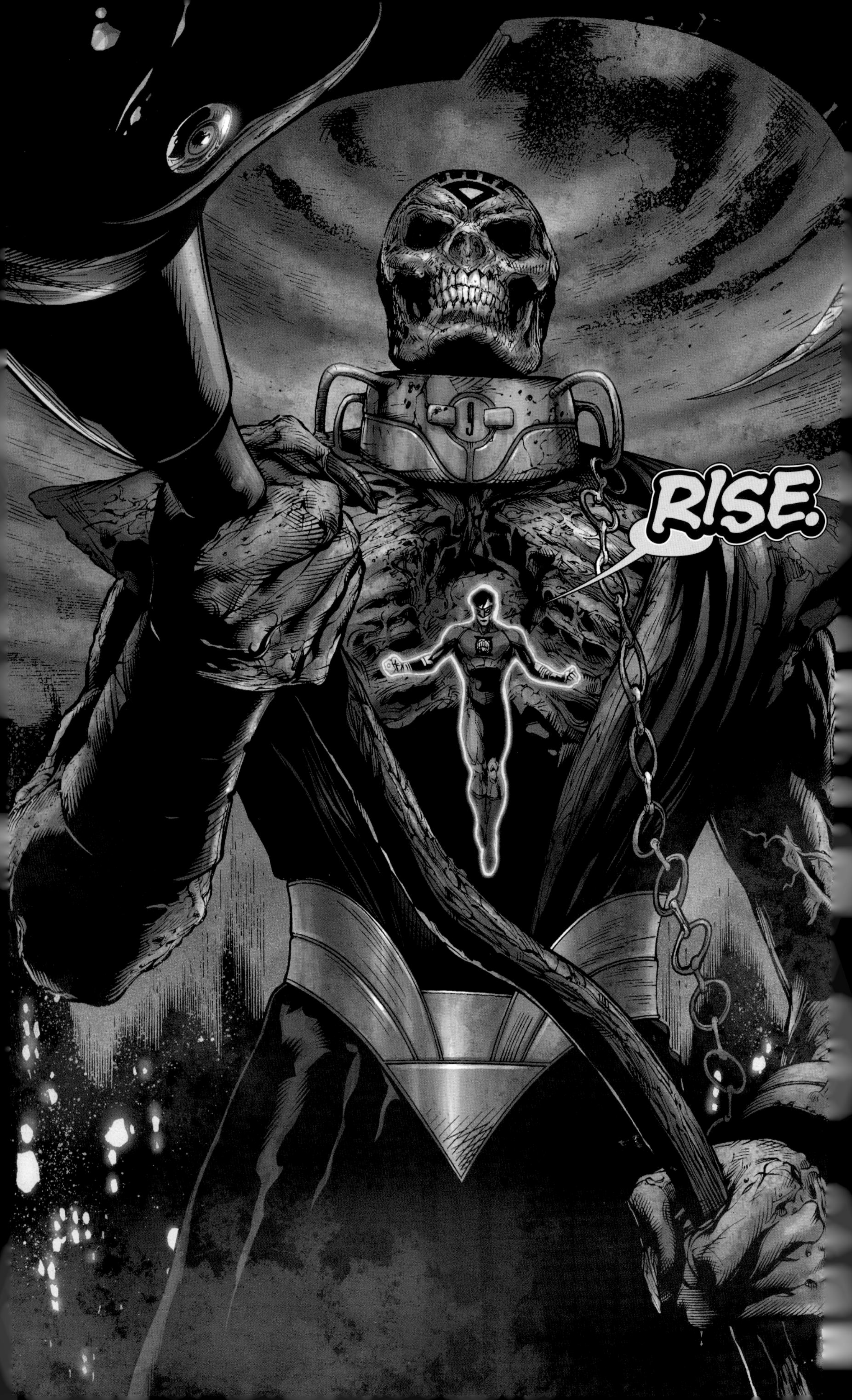
RISE.

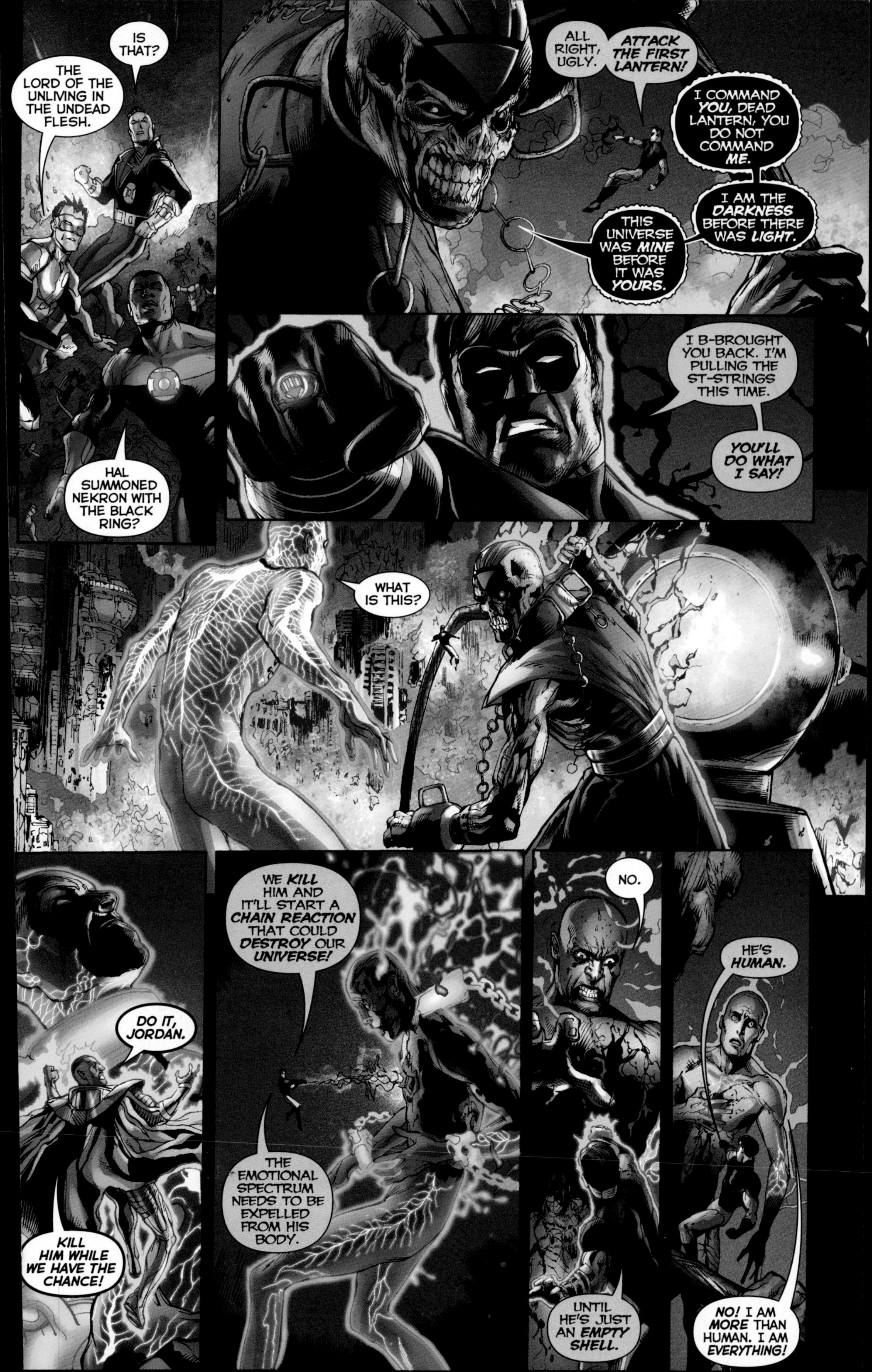
IS THAT?
THE LORD OF THE UNLIVING IN THE UNDEAD FLESH.
HAL SUMMONED NEKRON WITH THE BLACK RING?
ALL RIGHT, UGLY.
ATTACK THE FIRST LANTERN!
I COMMAND YOU, DEAD LANTERN, YOU DO NOT COMMAND ME.
I AM THE DARKNESS BEFORE THERE WAS LIGHT.
THIS UNIVERSE WAS MINE BEFORE IT WAS YOURS.
I B-BROUGHT YOU BACK. I'M PULLING THE ST-STRINGS THIS TIME.
YOU'LL DO WHAT I SAY!
WHAT IS THIS?
DO IT, JORDAN.
KILL HIM WHILE WE HAVE THE CHANCE!
WE KILL HIM AND IT'LL START A CHAIN REACTION THAT COULD DESTROY OUR UNIVERSE!
THE EMOTIONAL SPECTRUM NEEDS TO BE EXPELLED FROM HIS BODY.
NO.
UNTIL HE'S JUST AN EMPTY SHELL.
HE'S HUMAN.
NO! I AM MORE THAN HUMAN. I AM EVERYTHING!

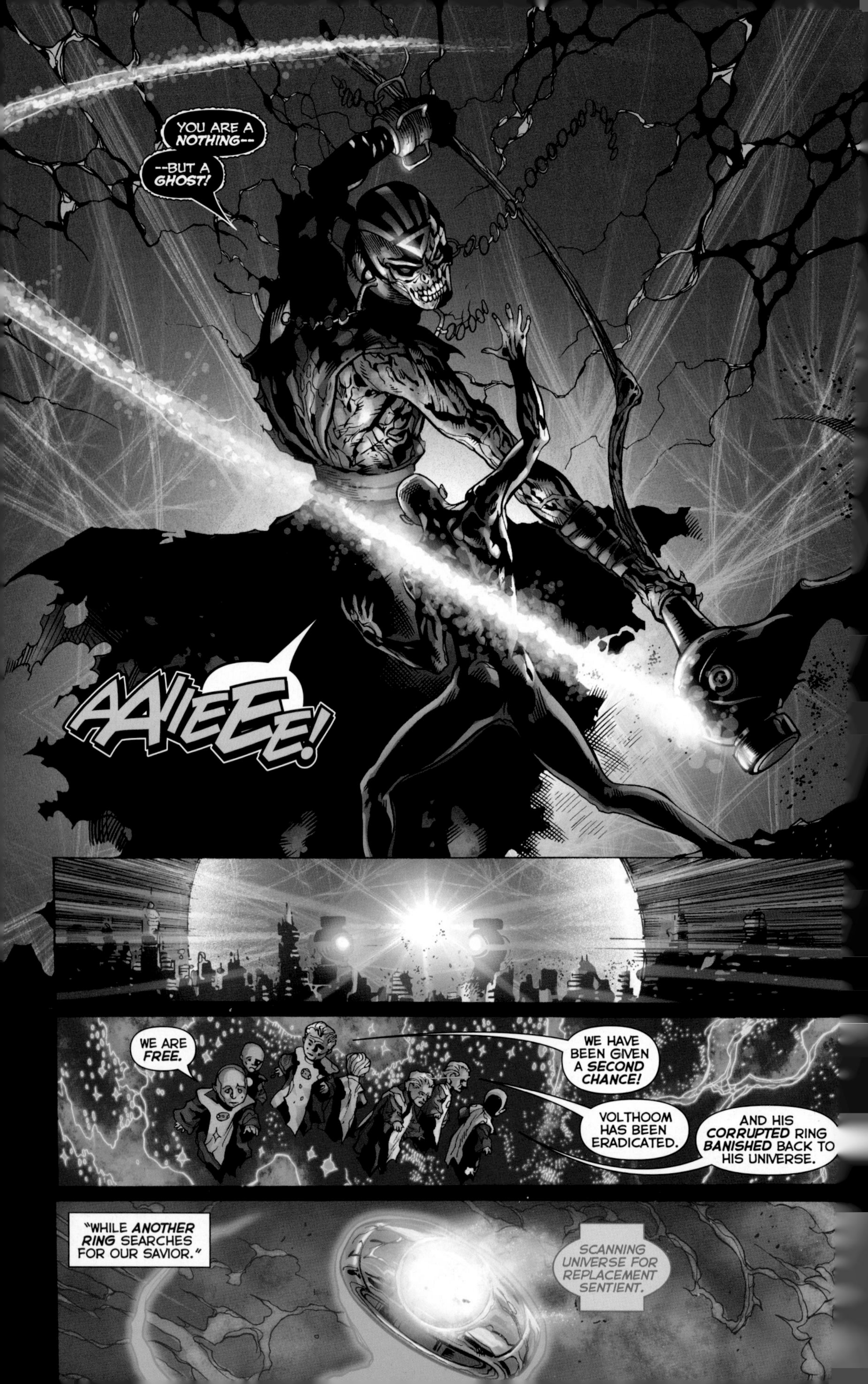
YOU ARE A NOTHING--
--BUT A GHOST!
AAIIEEEE!
WE ARE FREE.
WE HAVE BEEN GIVEN A SECOND CHANCE!
VOLTHOOM HAS BEEN ERADICATED.
AND HIS CORRUPTED RING BANISHED BACK TO HIS UNIVERSE.
"WHILE ANOTHER RING SEARCHES FOR OUR SAVIOR."
SCANNING UNIVERSE FOR REPLACEMENT SENTIENT.

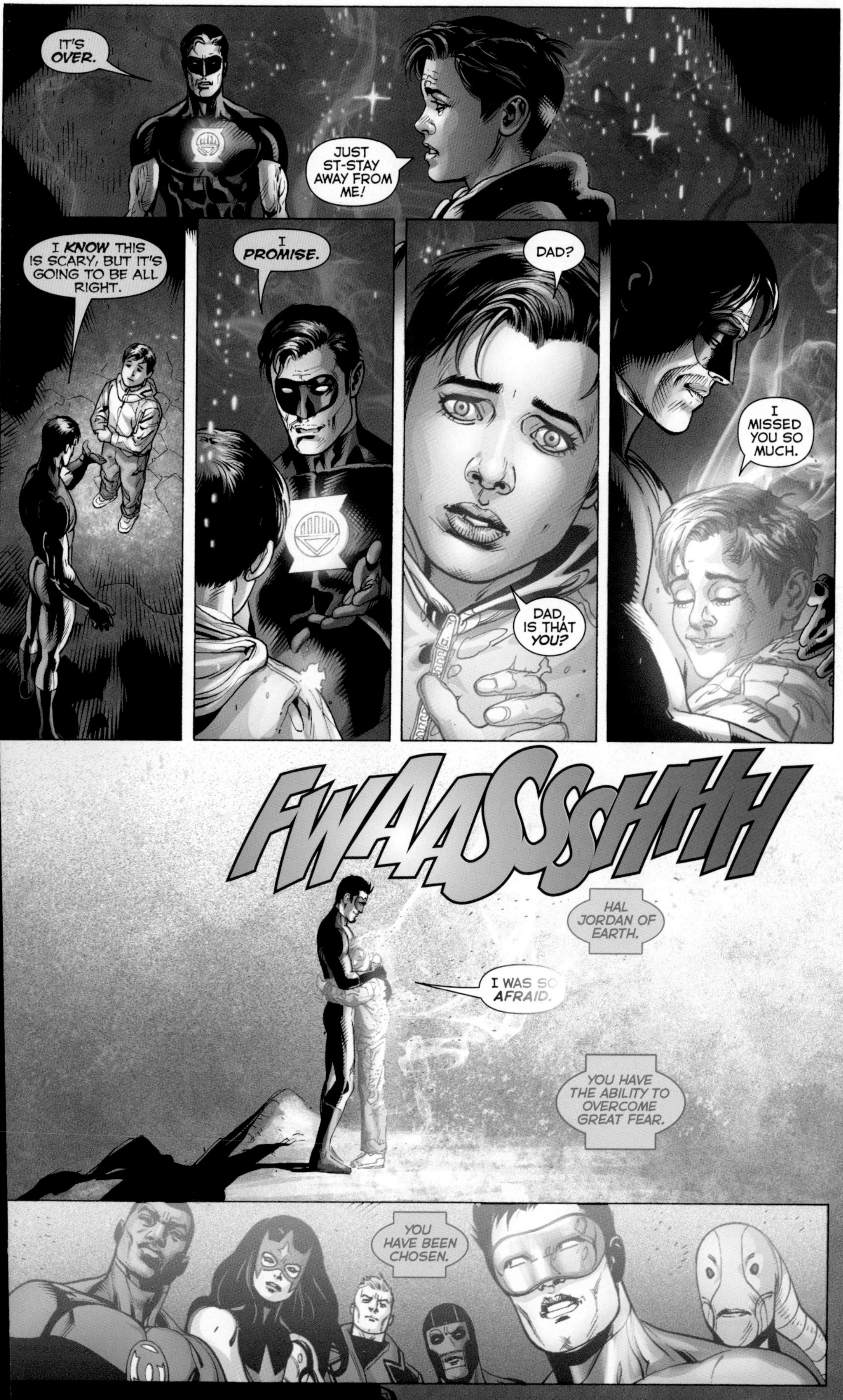
IT'S OVER.
JUST ST-STAY AWAY FROM ME!
I KNOW THIS IS SCARY, BUT IT'S GOING TO BE ALL RIGHT.
I PROMISE.
DAD?
DAD, IS THAT YOU?
I MISSED YOU SO MUCH.
FWAASSHHH
HAL JORDAN OF EARTH.
I WAS SO AFRAID.
YOU HAVE THE ABILITY TO OVERCOME GREAT FEAR.
YOU HAVE BEEN CHOSEN.

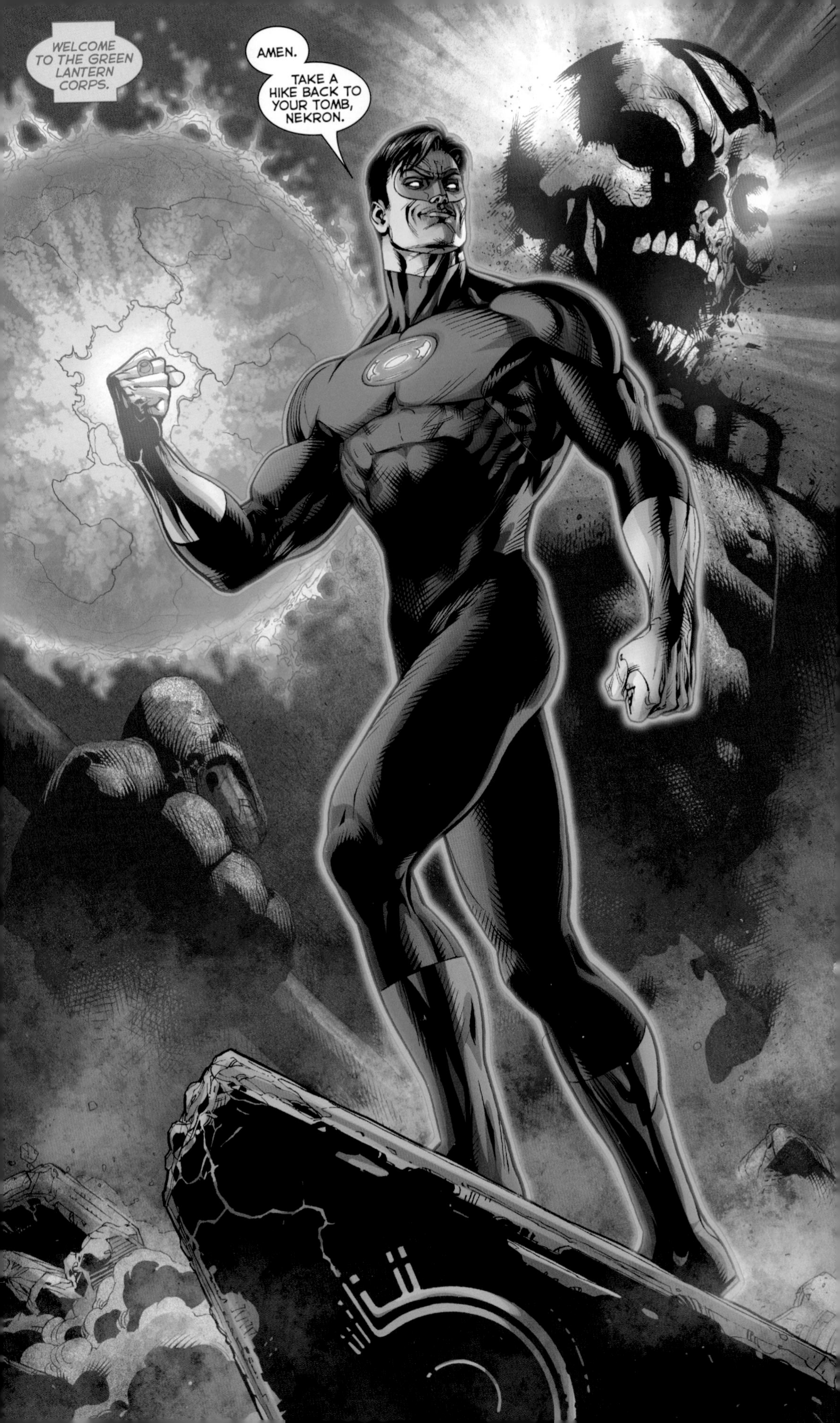
WELCOME TO THE GREEN LANTERN CORPS.
AMEN.
TAKE A HIKE BACK TO YOUR TOMB, NEKRON.

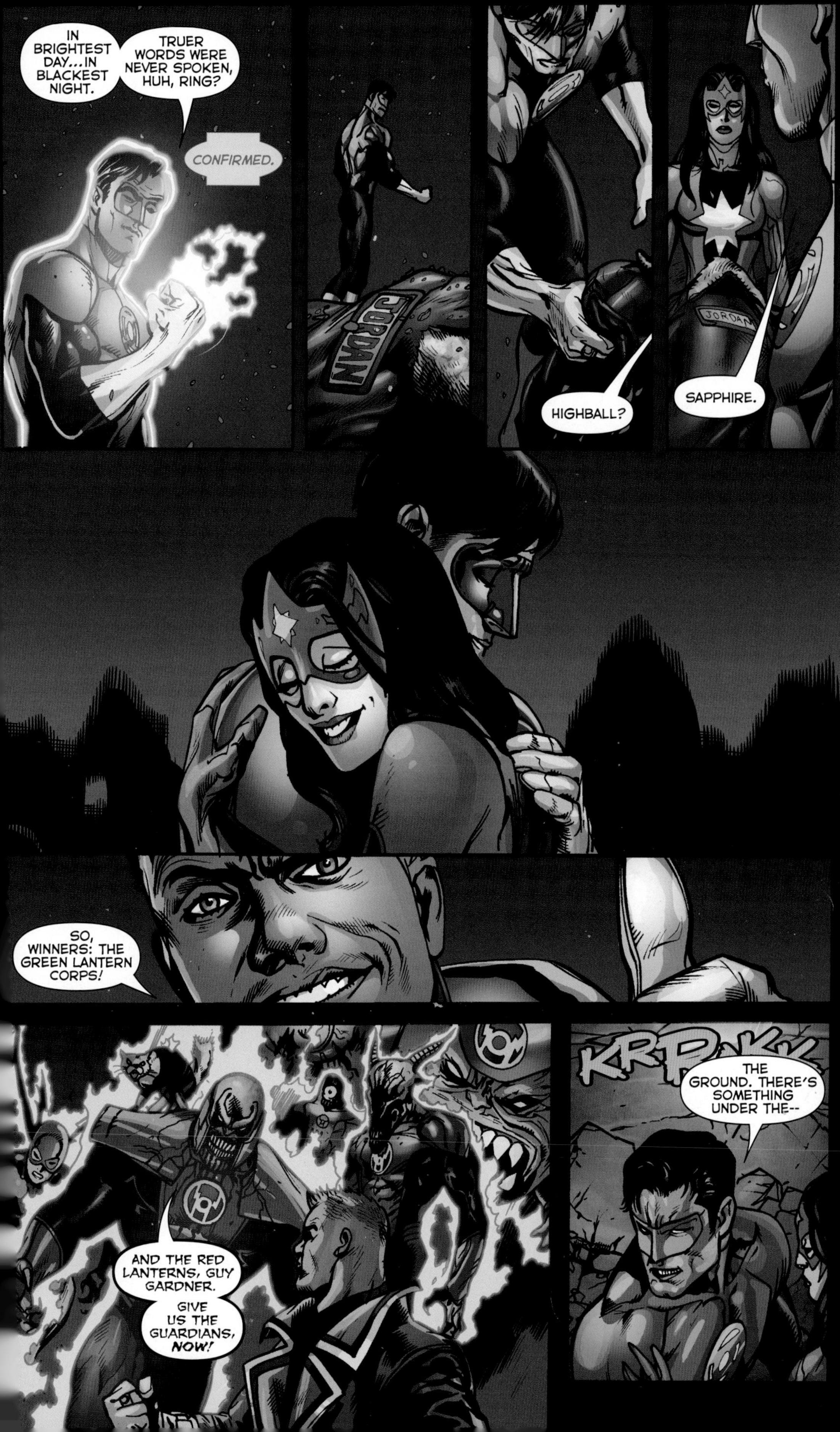
IN BRIGHTEST DAY...IN BLACKEST NIGHT.
TRUER WORDS WERE NEVER SPOKEN, HUH, RING?
CONFIRMED.
JORDAN
HIGHBALL?
JORDAN
SAPPHIRE.
SO, WINNERS: THE GREEN LANTERN CORPS!
AND THE RED LANTERNS, GUY GARDNER.
GIVE US THE GUARDIANS, NOW!
KRP KW
THE GROUND. THERE'S SOMETHING UNDER THE--

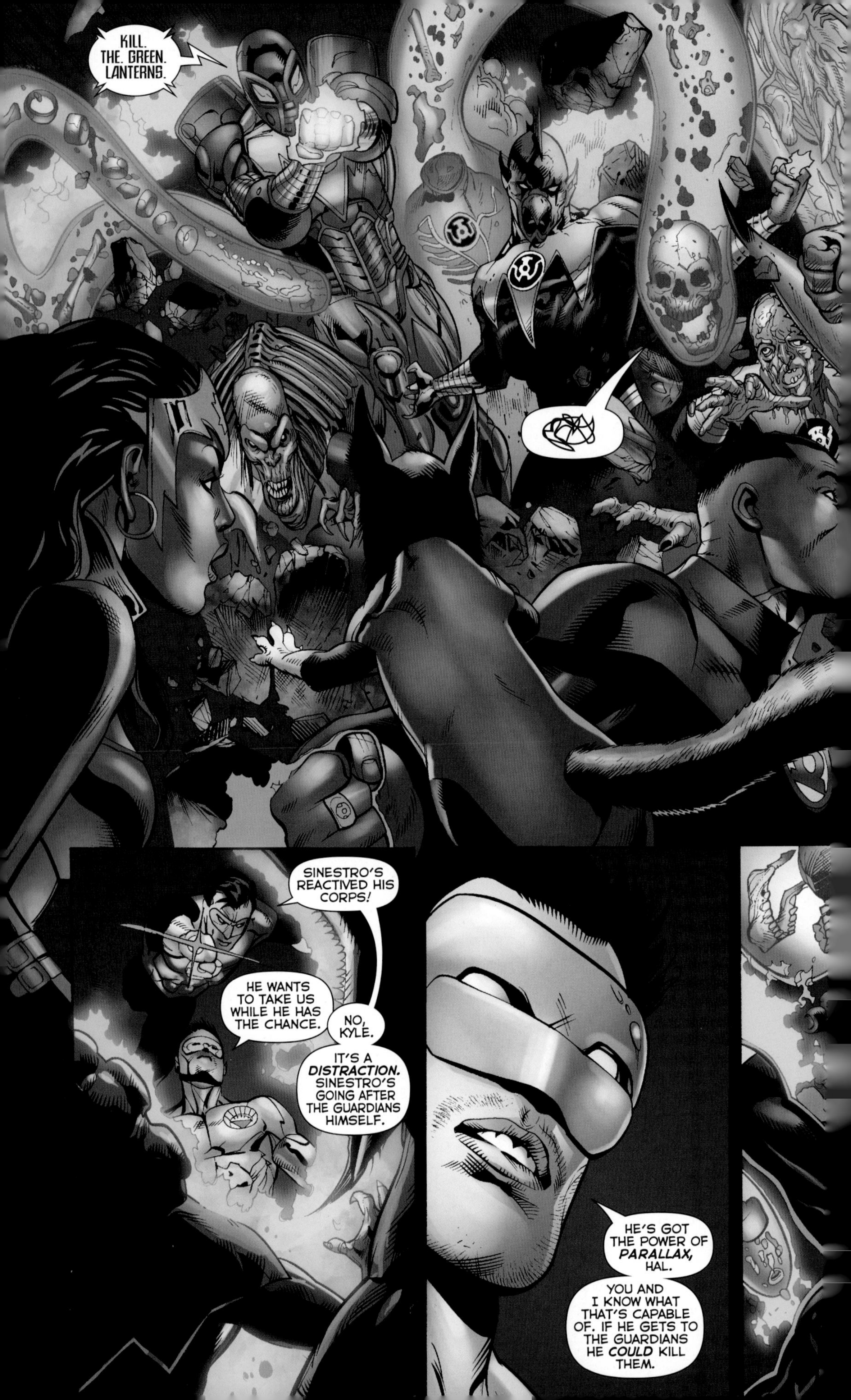
KILL. THE. GREEN. LANTERNS.
SINESTRO'S REACTIVED HIS CORPS!
HE WANTS TO TAKE US WHILE HE HAS THE CHANCE.
NO, KYLE.
IT'S A DISTRACTION. SINESTRO'S GOING AFTER THE GUARDIANS HIMSELF.
HE'S GOT THE POWER OF PARALLAX, HAL.
YOU AND I KNOW WHAT THAT'S CAPABLE OF. IF HE GETS TO THE GUARDIANS HE COULD KILL THEM.

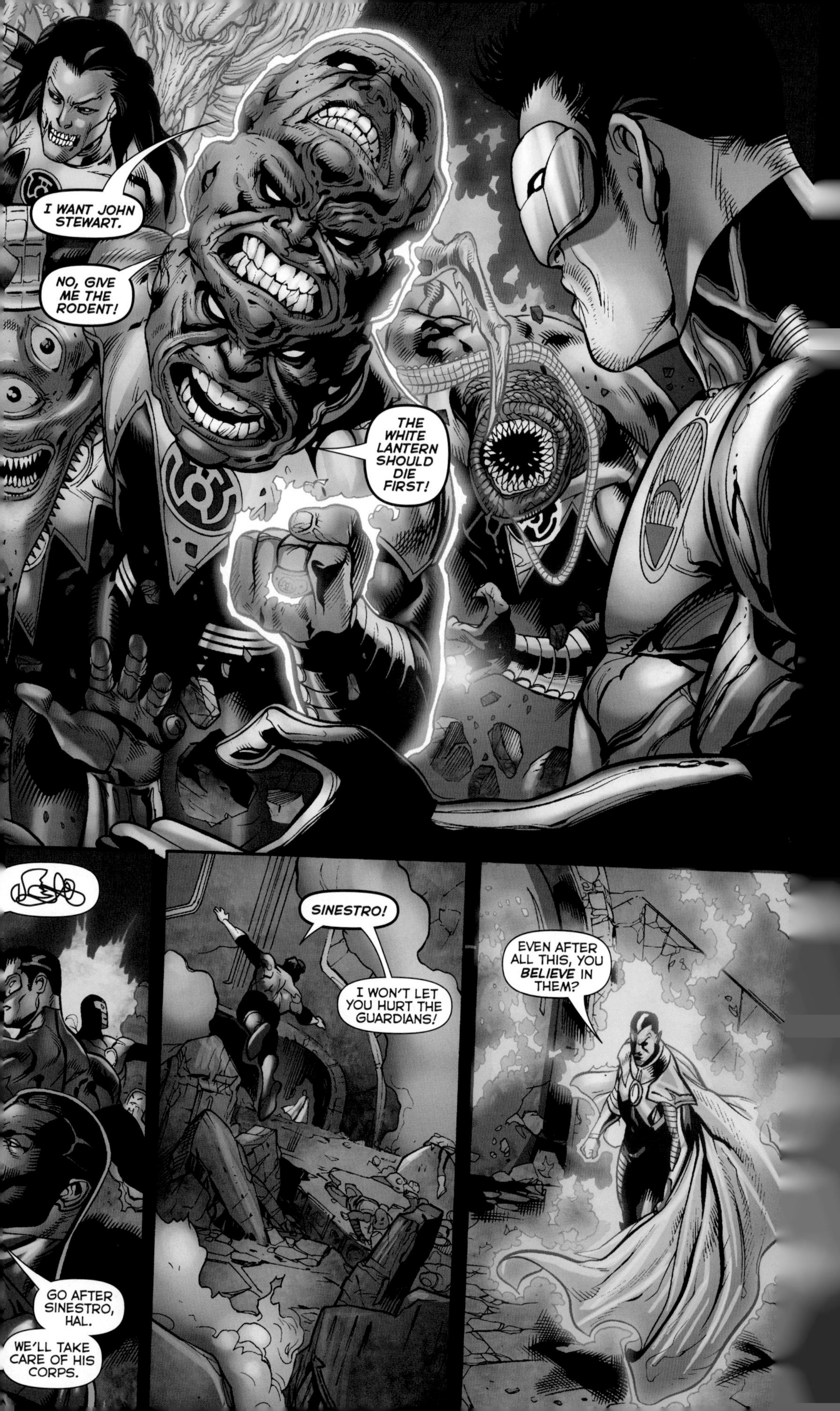
I WANT JOHN STEWART.
NO, GIVE ME THE RODENT!
THE WHITE LANTERN SHOULD DIE FIRST!
GO AFTER SINESTRO, HAL.
WE'LL TAKE CARE OF HIS CORPS.
SINESTRO!
I WON'T LET YOU HURT THE GUARDIANS!
EVEN AFTER ALL THIS, YOU BELIEVE IN THEM?

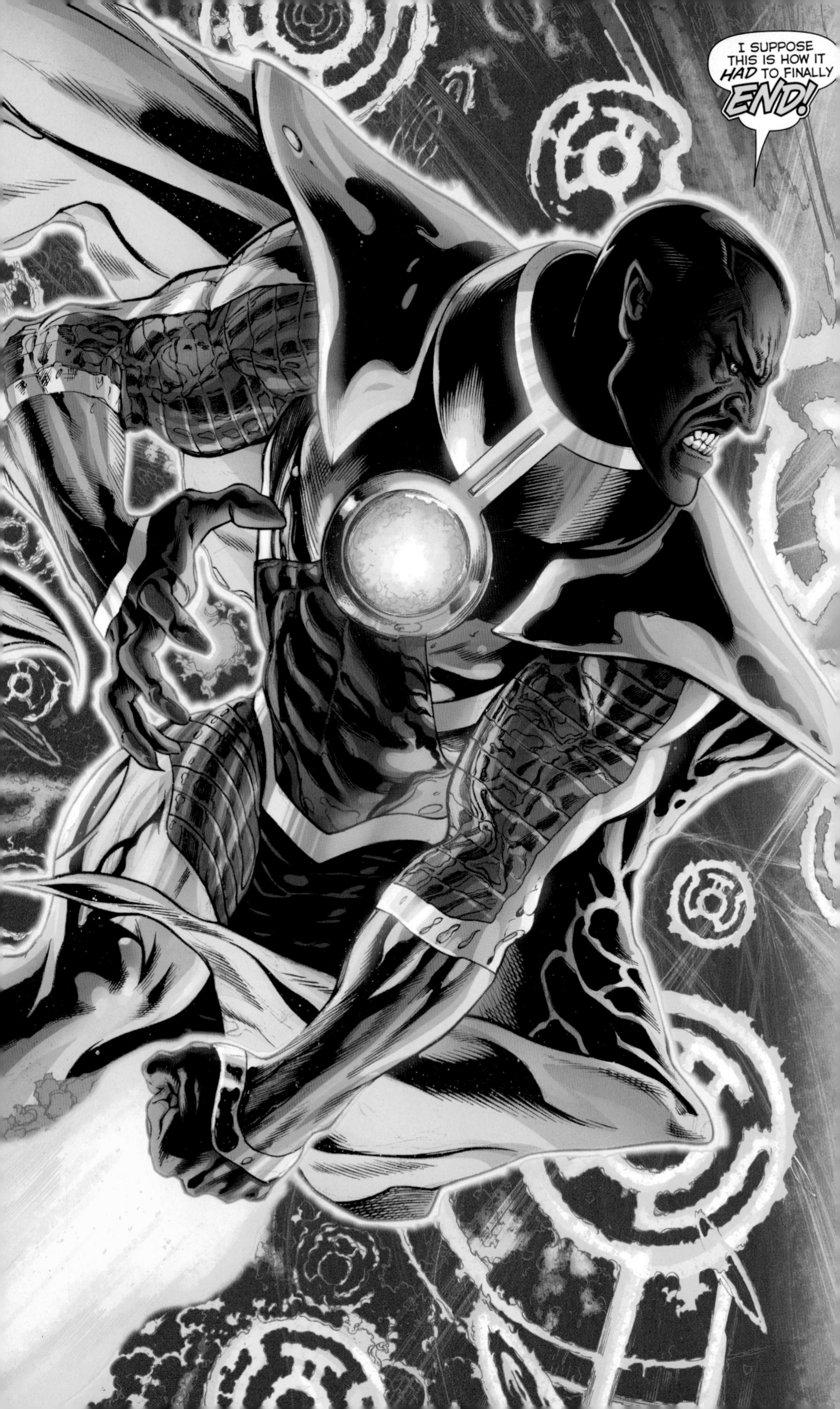
I SUPPOSE THIS IS HOW IT HAD TO FINALLY END!

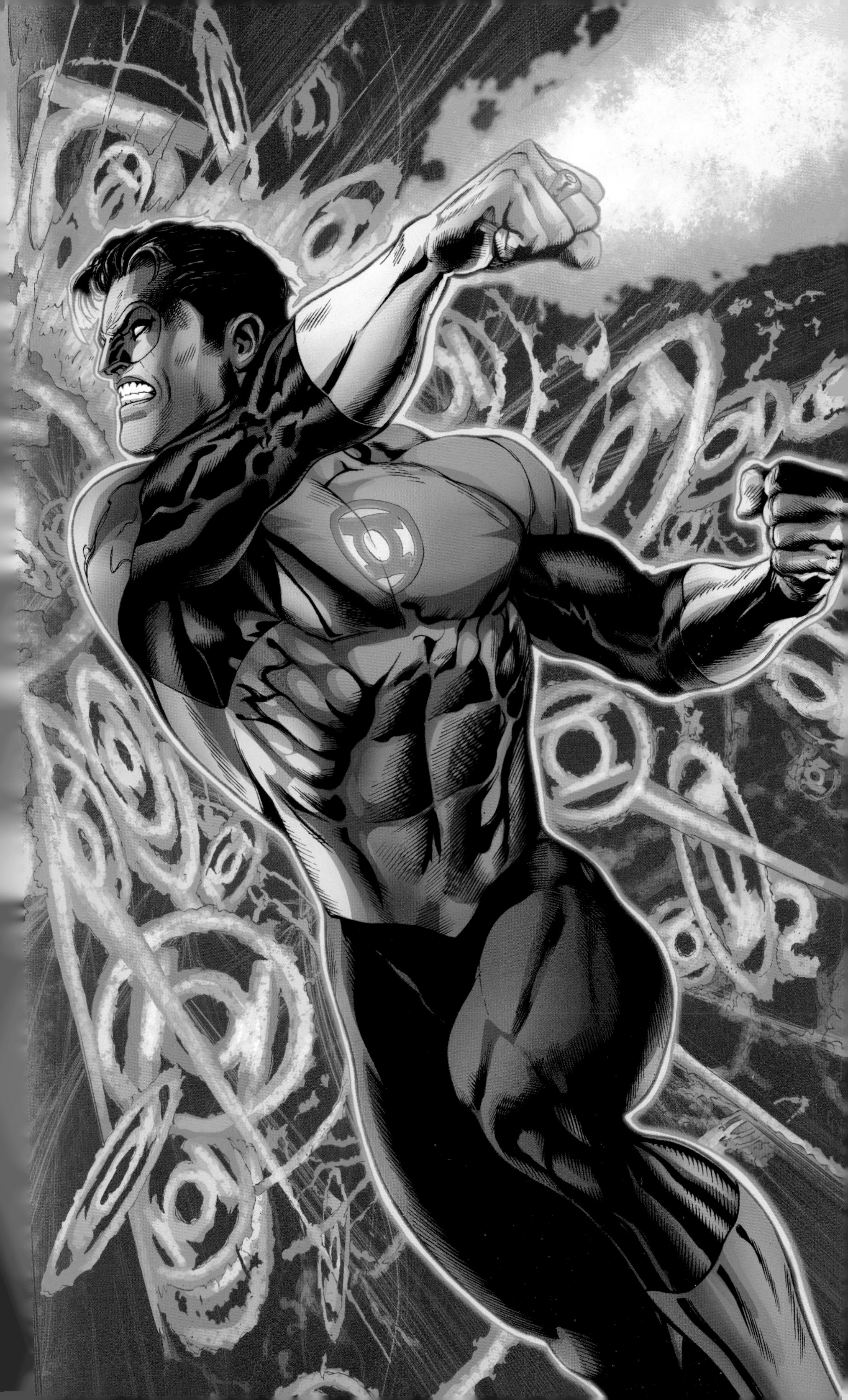

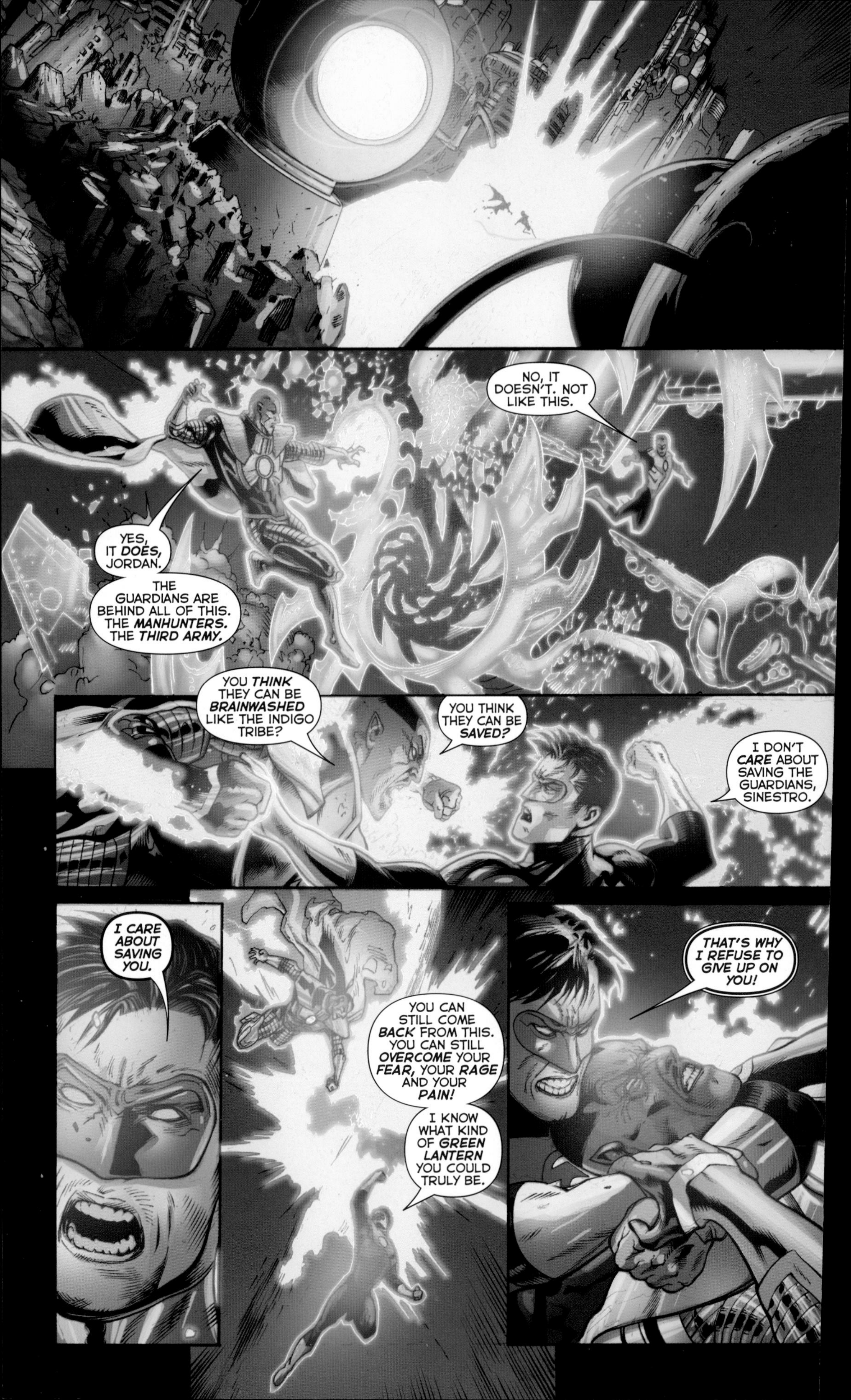
NO, IT DOESN'T. NOT LIKE THIS.
YES, IT DOES, JORDAN.
THE GUARDIANS ARE BEHIND ALL OF THIS. THE MANHUNTERS. THE THIRD ARMY.
YOU THINK THEY CAN BE BRAINWASHED LIKE THE INDIGO TRIBE?
YOU THINK THEY CAN BE SAVED?
I DON'T CARE ABOUT SAVING THE GUARDIANS, SINESTRO.
I CARE ABOUT SAVING YOU.
YOU CAN STILL COME BACK FROM THIS. YOU CAN STILL OVERCOME YOUR FEAR, YOUR RAGE AND YOUR PAIN!
I KNOW WHAT KIND OF GREEN LANTERN YOU COULD TRULY BE.
THAT'S WHY I REFUSE TO GIVE UP ON YOU!

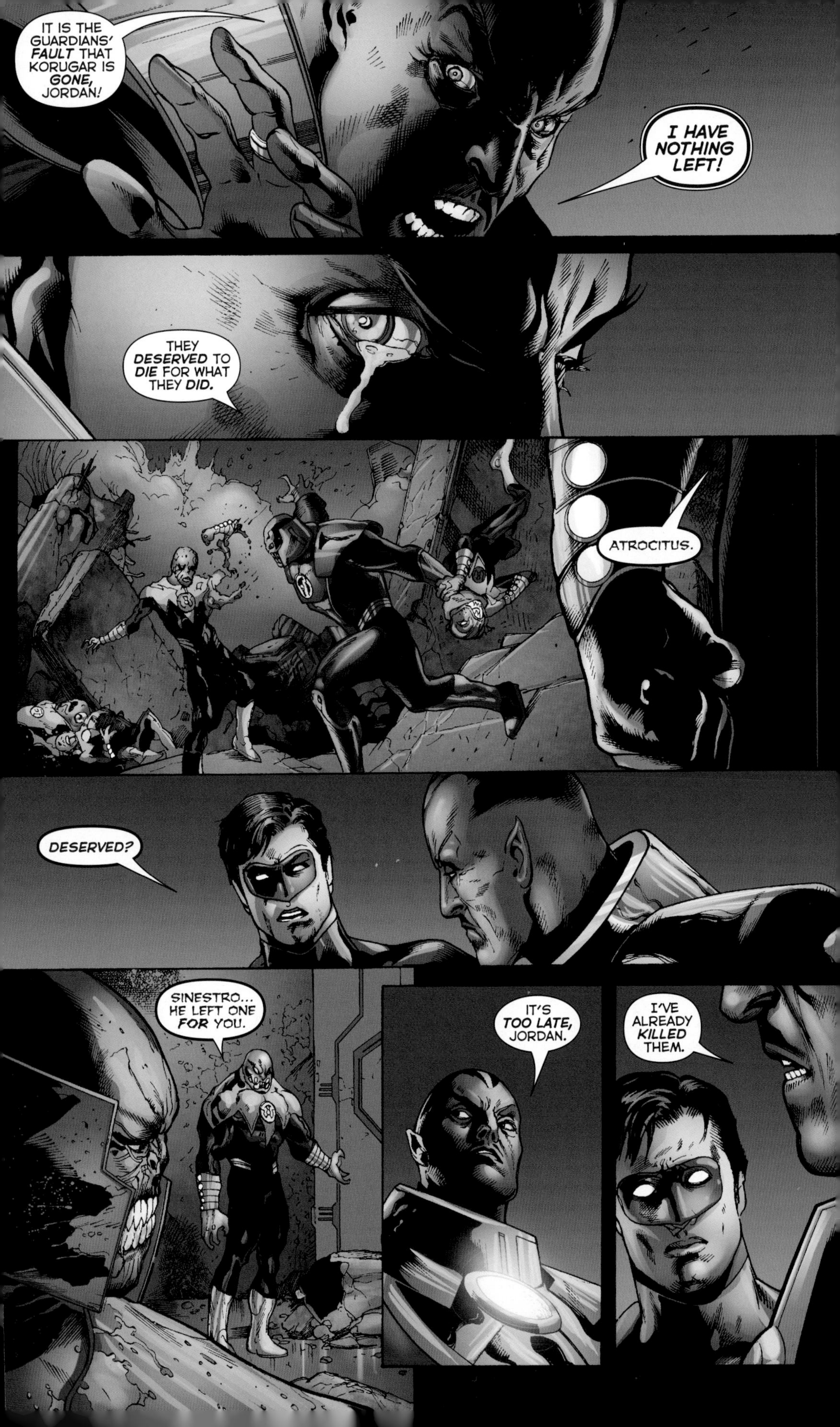
IT IS THE GUARDIANS' FAULT THAT KORUGAR IS GONE, JORDAN!
I HAVE NOTHING LEFT!
THEY DESERVED TO DIE FOR WHAT THEY DID.
ATROCITUS.
DESERVED?
SINESTRO... HE LEFT ONE FOR YOU.
IT'S TOO LATE, JORDAN.
I'VE ALREADY KILLED THEM.

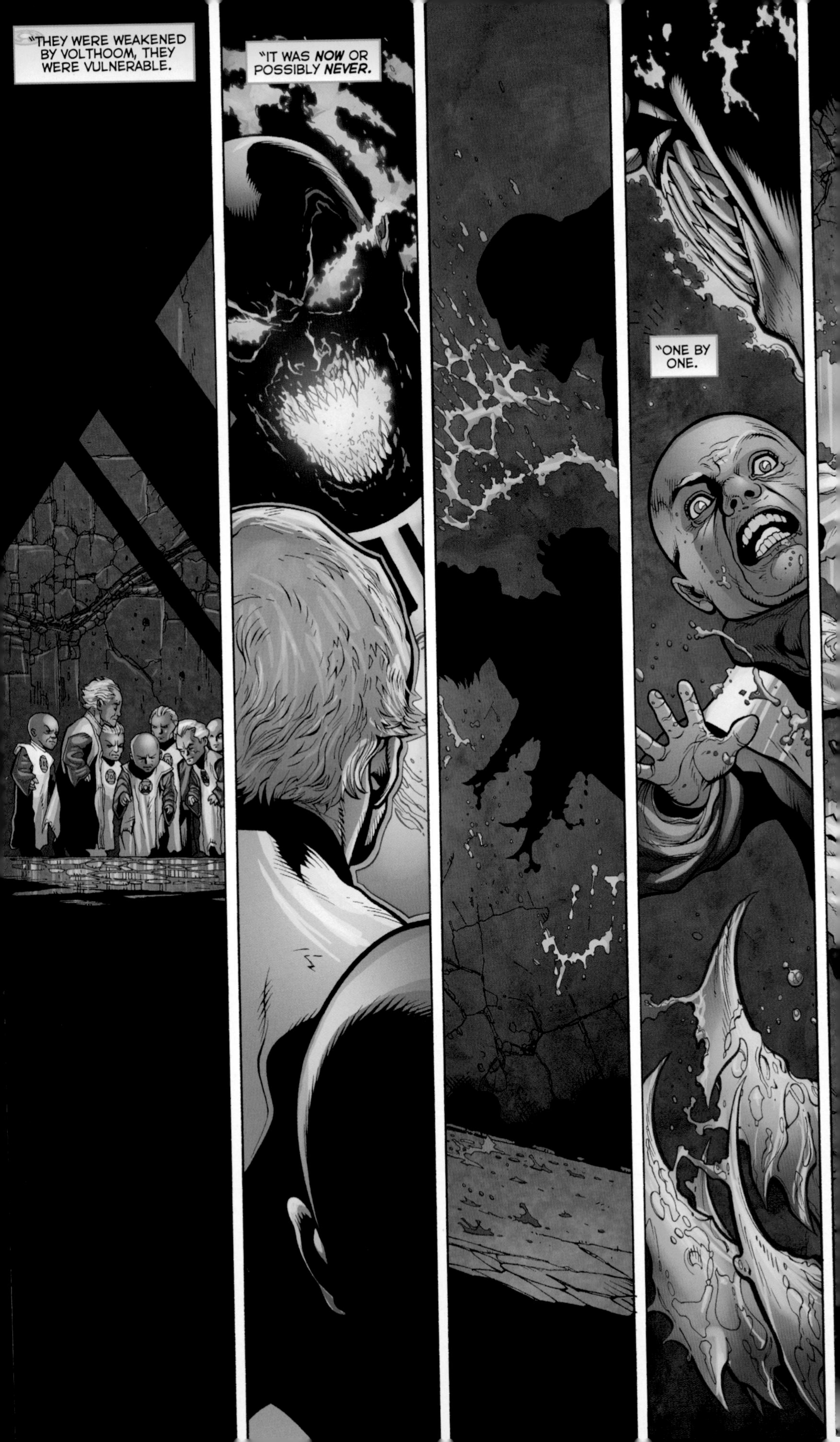
"THEY WERE WEAKENED BY VOLTHOOM, THEY WERE VULNERABLE.
"IT WAS *NOW* OR POSSIBLY *NEVER*.
"ONE BY ONE.

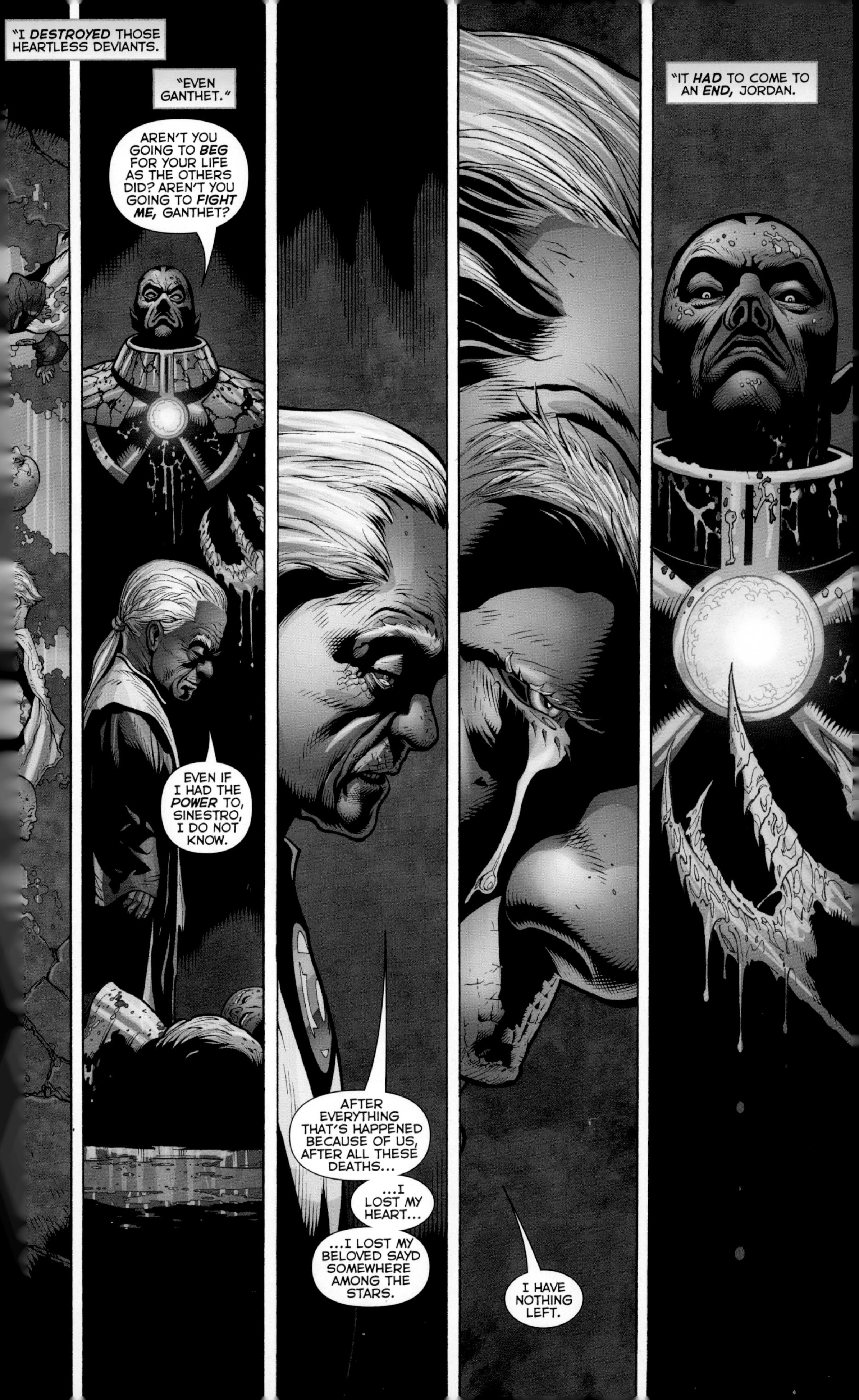
"I DESTROYED THOSE HEARTLESS DEVIANTS.
"EVEN GANTHET."
AREN'T YOU GOING TO BEG FOR YOUR LIFE AS THE OTHERS DID? AREN'T YOU GOING TO FIGHT ME, GANTHET?
EVEN IF I HAD THE POWER TO, SINESTRO, I DO NOT KNOW.
AFTER EVERYTHING THAT'S HAPPENED BECAUSE OF US, AFTER ALL THESE DEATHS...
...I LOST MY HEART...
...I LOST MY BELOVED SAYD SOMEWHERE AMONG THE STARS.
I HAVE NOTHING LEFT.
"IT HAD TO COME TO AN END, JORDAN.

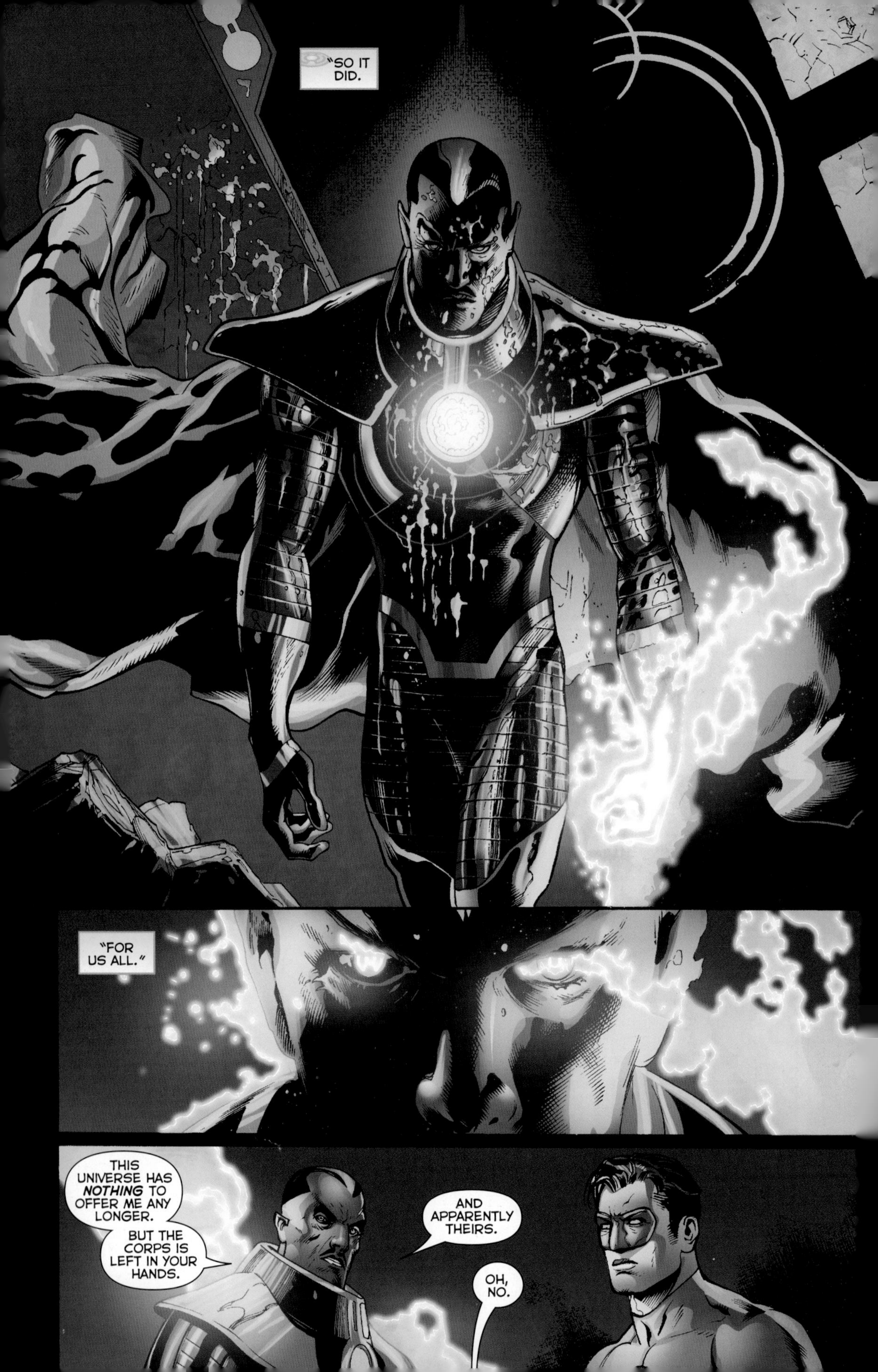
"SO IT DID.
"FOR US ALL."
THIS UNIVERSE HAS *NOTHING* TO OFFER ME ANY LONGER.
BUT THE CORPS IS LEFT IN YOUR HANDS.
AND APPARENTLY THEIRS.
OH, NO.

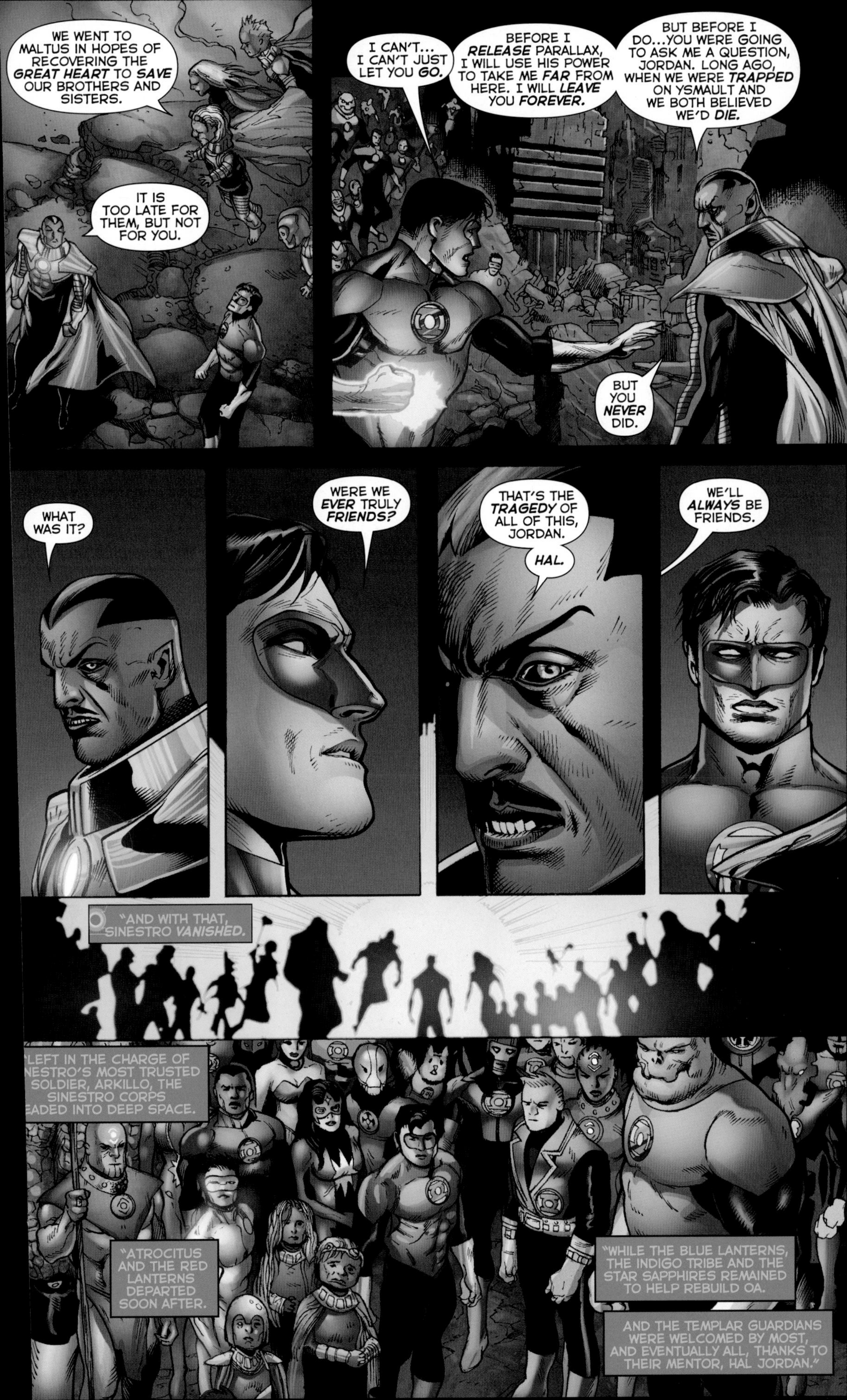
WE WENT TO MALTUS IN HOPES OF RECOVERING THE GREAT HEART TO SAVE OUR BROTHERS AND SISTERS.
IT IS TOO LATE FOR THEM, BUT NOT FOR YOU.
I CAN'T... I CAN'T JUST LET YOU GO.
BEFORE I RELEASE PARALLAX, I WILL USE HIS POWER TO TAKE ME FAR FROM HERE. I WILL LEAVE YOU FOREVER.
BUT BEFORE I DO...YOU WERE GOING TO ASK ME A QUESTION, JORDAN. LONG AGO, WHEN WE WERE TRAPPED ON YSMAULT AND WE BOTH BELIEVED WE'D DIE.
BUT YOU NEVER DID.
WHAT WAS IT?
WERE WE EVER TRULY FRIENDS?
THAT'S THE TRAGEDY OF ALL OF THIS, JORDAN.
HAL.
WE'LL ALWAYS BE FRIENDS.
"AND WITH THAT, SINESTRO VANISHED.
"LEFT IN THE CHARGE OF NESTRO'S MOST TRUSTED SOLDIER, ARKILLO, THE SINESTRO CORPS EADED INTO DEEP SPACE.
"ATROCITUS AND THE RED LANTERNS DEPARTED SOON AFTER.
"WHILE THE BLUE LANTERNS, THE INDIGO TRIBE AND THE STAR SAPPHIRES REMAINED TO HELP REBUILD OA.
AND THE TEMPLAR GUARDIANS WERE WELCOMED BY MOST, AND EVENTUALLY ALL, THANKS TO THEIR MENTOR, HAL JORDAN."

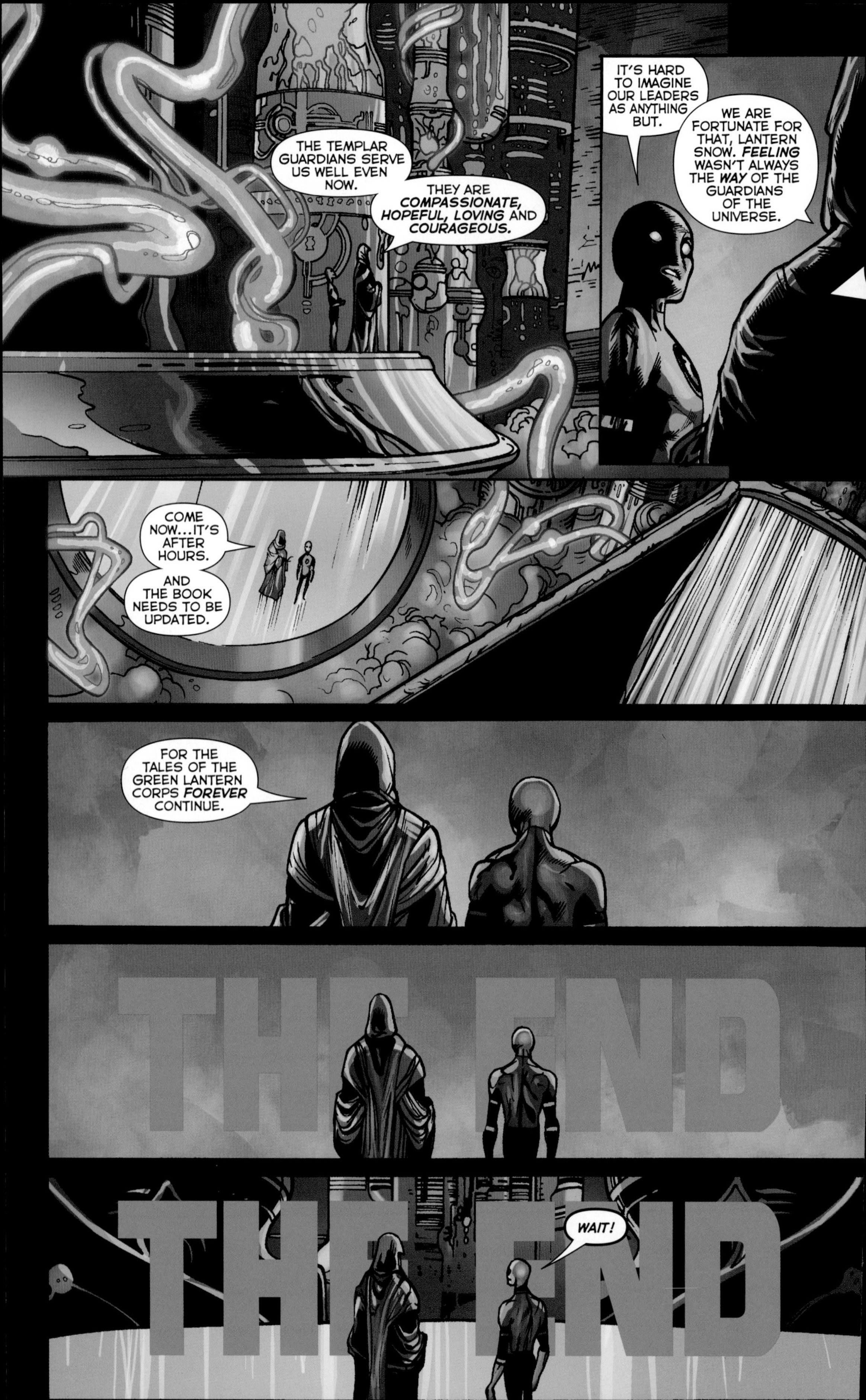
THE TEMPLAR GUARDIANS SERVE US WELL EVEN NOW.
THEY ARE *COMPASSIONATE, HOPEFUL, LOVING* AND *COURAGEOUS.*
IT'S HARD TO IMAGINE OUR LEADERS AS ANYTHING BUT.
WE ARE FORTUNATE FOR THAT, LANTERN SNOW. *FEELING* WASN'T ALWAYS THE *WAY* OF THE GUARDIANS OF THE UNIVERSE.
COME NOW...IT'S AFTER HOURS.
AND THE BOOK NEEDS TO BE UPDATED.
FOR THE TALES OF THE GREEN LANTERN CORPS *FOREVER* CONTINUE.
THE END
THE END
WAIT!

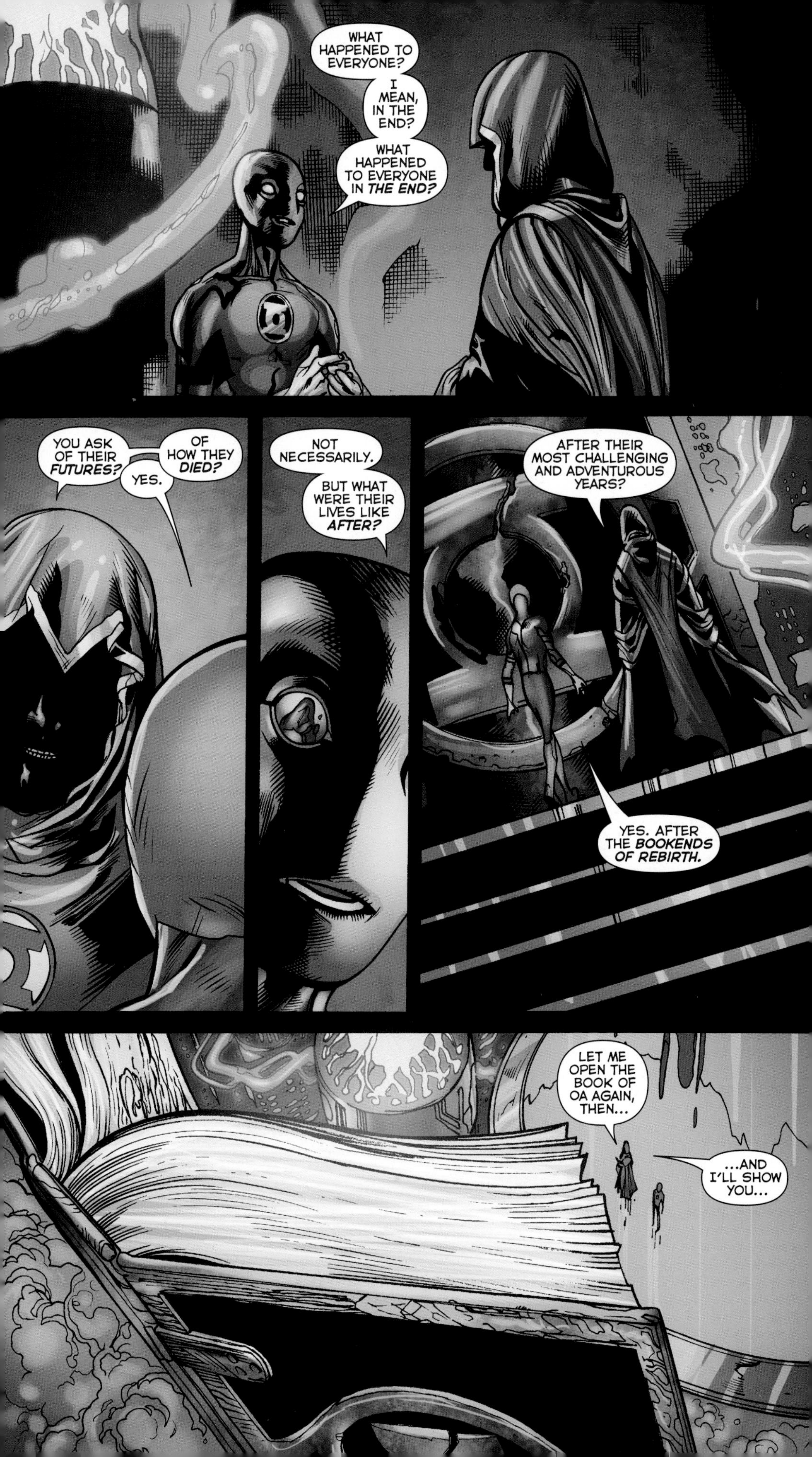
WHAT HAPPENED TO EVERYONE?
I MEAN, IN THE END?
WHAT HAPPENED TO EVERYONE IN *THE END?*
YOU ASK OF THEIR *FUTURES?*
OF HOW THEY *DIED?*
YES.
NOT NECESSARILY.
BUT WHAT WERE THEIR LIVES LIKE *AFTER?*
AFTER THEIR MOST CHALLENGING AND ADVENTUROUS YEARS?
YES. AFTER THE *BOOKENDS OF REBIRTH.*
LET ME OPEN THE BOOK OF OA AGAIN, THEN...
...AND I'LL SHOW YOU...

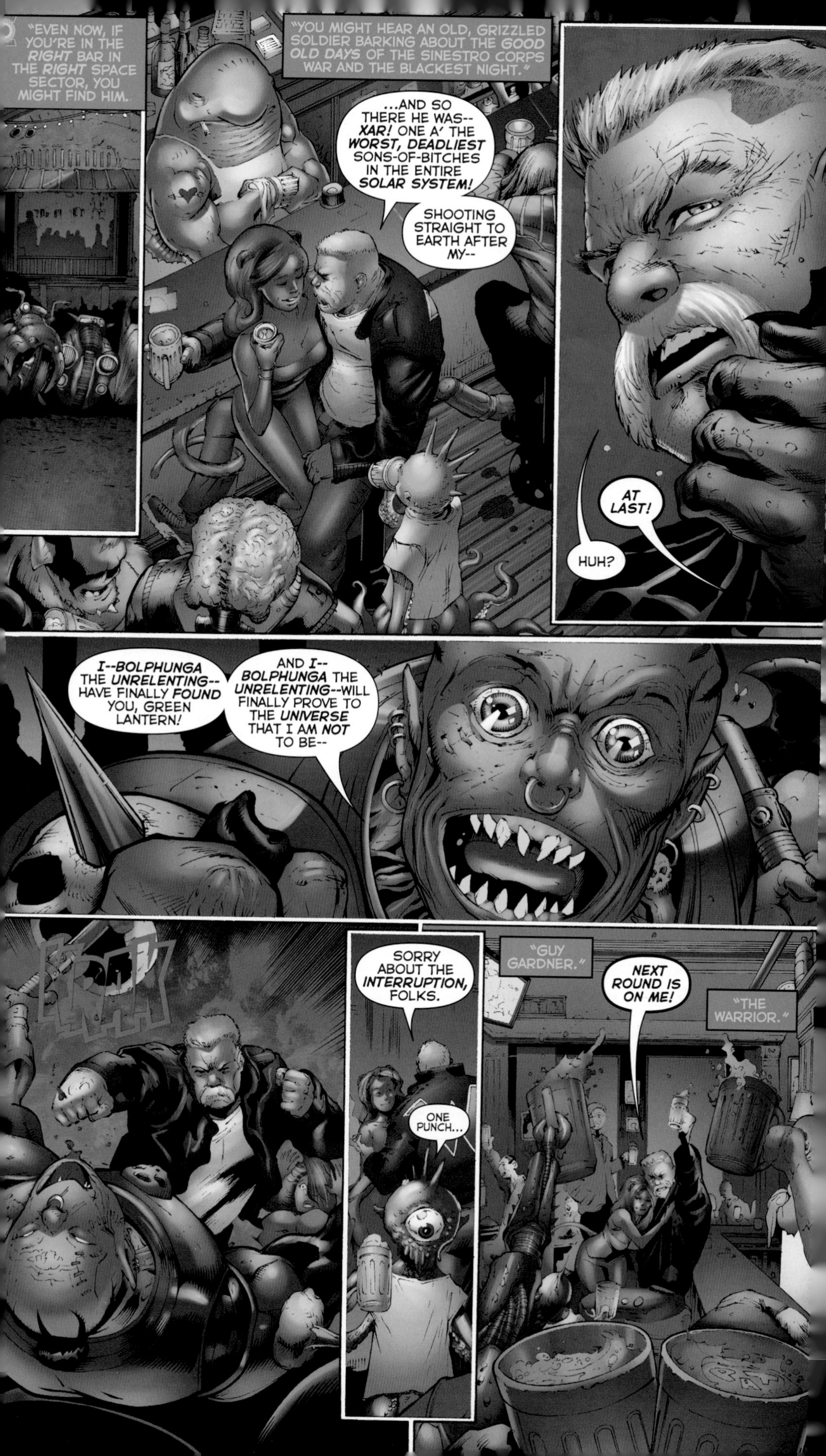
"EVEN NOW, IF YOU'RE IN THE RIGHT BAR IN THE RIGHT SPACE SECTOR, YOU MIGHT FIND HIM.
"YOU MIGHT HEAR AN OLD, GRIZZLED SOLDIER BARKING ABOUT THE GOOD OLD DAYS OF THE SINESTRO CORPS WAR AND THE BLACKEST NIGHT."
...AND SO THERE HE WAS-- XAR! ONE A' THE WORST, DEADLIEST SONS-OF-BITCHES IN THE ENTIRE SOLAR SYSTEM!
SHOOTING STRAIGHT TO EARTH AFTER MY--
AT LAST!
HUH?
I--BOLPHUNGA THE UNRELENTING--HAVE FINALLY FOUND YOU, GREEN LANTERN!
AND I--BOLPHUNGA THE UNRELENTING--WILL FINALLY PROVE TO THE UNIVERSE THAT I AM NOT TO BE--
SORRY ABOUT THE INTERRUPTION, FOLKS.
ONE PUNCH...
"GUY GARDNER."
NEXT ROUND IS ON ME!
"THE WARRIOR."

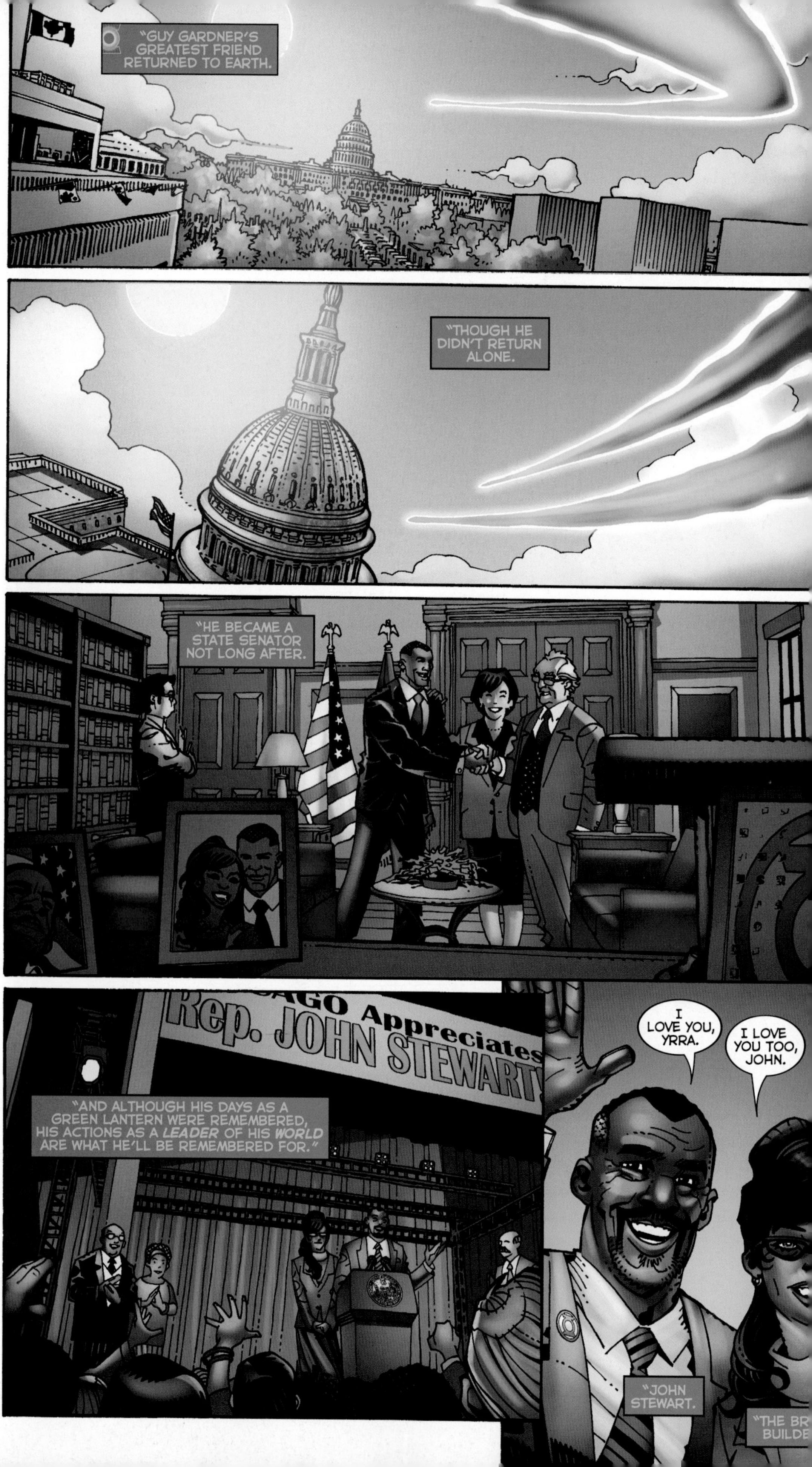
"GUY GARDNER'S GREATEST FRIEND RETURNED TO EARTH.
"THOUGH HE DIDN'T RETURN ALONE.
"HE BECAME A STATE SENATOR NOT LONG AFTER.
AGO Appreciates Rep. JOHN STEWART!
"AND ALTHOUGH HIS DAYS AS A GREEN LANTERN WERE REMEMBERED, HIS ACTIONS AS A *LEADER* OF HIS *WORLD* ARE WHAT HE'LL BE REMEMBERED FOR."
I LOVE YOU, YRRA.
I LOVE YOU TOO, JOHN.
"JOHN STEWART.

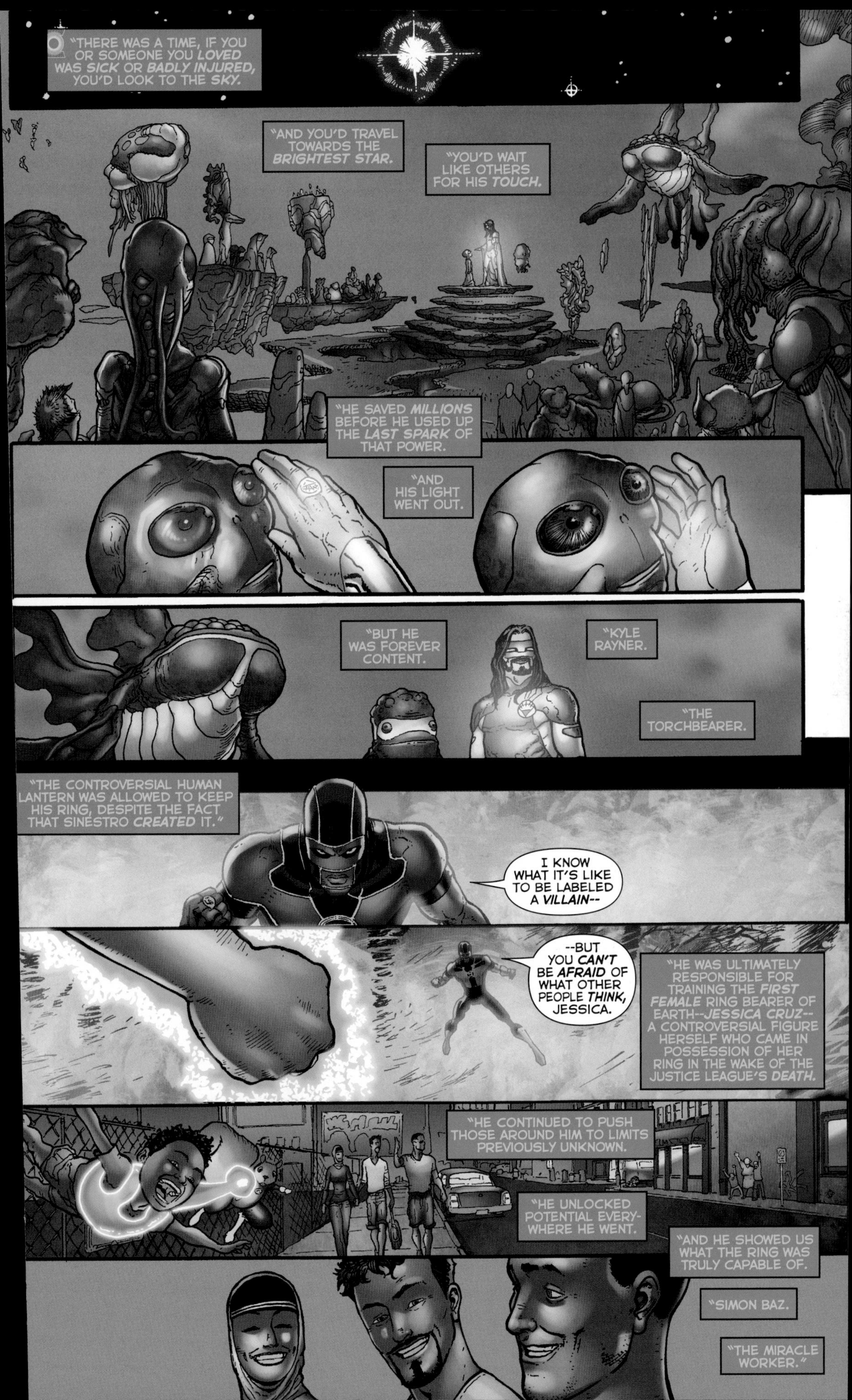

"THERE WAS A TIME, IF YOU OR SOMEONE YOU LOVED WAS SICK OR BADLY INJURED, YOU'D LOOK TO THE SKY.
"AND YOU'D TRAVEL TOWARDS THE BRIGHTEST STAR.
"YOU'D WAIT LIKE OTHERS FOR HIS TOUCH.
"HE SAVED MILLIONS BEFORE HE USED UP THE LAST SPARK OF THAT POWER.
"AND HIS LIGHT WENT OUT.
"BUT HE WAS FOREVER CONTENT.
"KYLE RAYNER.
"THE TORCHBEARER.
"THE CONTROVERSIAL HUMAN LANTERN WAS ALLOWED TO KEEP HIS RING, DESPITE THE FACT THAT SINESTRO CREATED IT."
I KNOW WHAT IT'S LIKE TO BE LABELED A VILLAIN--
--BUT YOU CAN'T BE AFRAID OF WHAT OTHER PEOPLE THINK, JESSICA.
"HE WAS ULTIMATELY RESPONSIBLE FOR TRAINING THE FIRST FEMALE RING BEARER OF EARTH--JESSICA CRUZ--A CONTROVERSIAL FIGURE HERSELF WHO CAME IN POSSESSION OF HER RING IN THE WAKE OF THE JUSTICE LEAGUE'S DEATH.
"HE CONTINUED TO PUSH THOSE AROUND HIM TO LIMITS PREVIOUSLY UNKNOWN.
"HE UNLOCKED POTENTIAL EVERY-WHERE HE WENT.
"AND HE SHOWED US WHAT THE RING WAS TRULY CAPABLE OF.
"SIMON BAZ.
"THE MIRACLE WORKER."

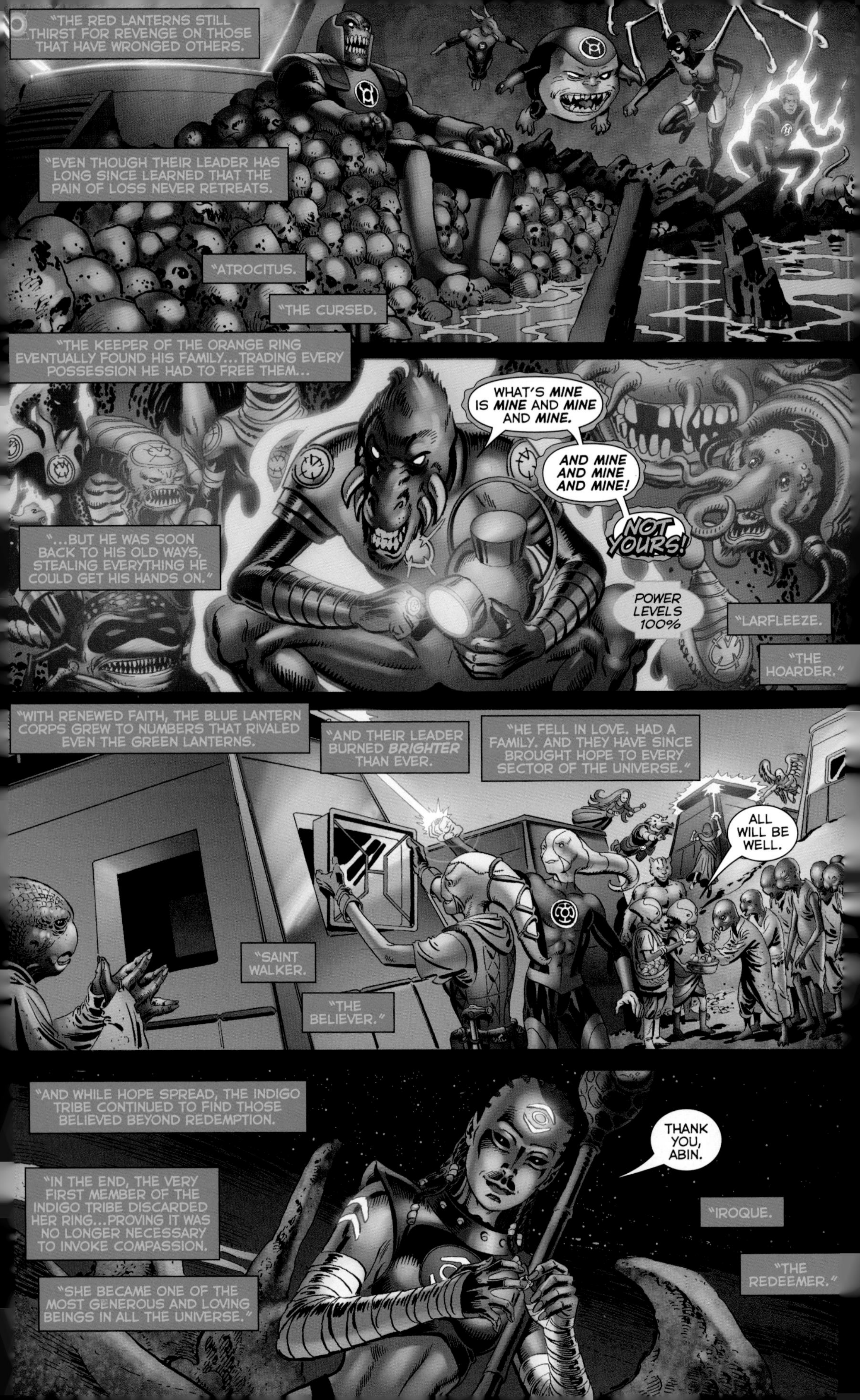
"THE RED LANTERNS STILL THIRST FOR REVENGE ON THOSE THAT HAVE WRONGED OTHERS.
"EVEN THOUGH THEIR LEADER HAS LONG SINCE LEARNED THAT THE PAIN OF LOSS NEVER RETREATS.
"ATROCITUS.
"THE CURSED.
"THE KEEPER OF THE ORANGE RING EVENTUALLY FOUND HIS FAMILY...TRADING EVERY POSSESSION HE HAD TO FREE THEM...
"...BUT HE WAS SOON BACK TO HIS OLD WAYS, STEALING EVERYTHING HE COULD GET HIS HANDS ON."
WHAT'S MINE IS MINE AND MINE AND MINE.
AND MINE AND MINE AND MINE!
NOT YOURS!
POWER LEVELS 100%
"LARFLEEZE.
"THE HOARDER."
"WITH RENEWED FAITH, THE BLUE LANTERN CORPS GREW TO NUMBERS THAT RIVALED EVEN THE GREEN LANTERNS.
"AND THEIR LEADER BURNED BRIGHTER THAN EVER.
"HE FELL IN LOVE. HAD A FAMILY. AND THEY HAVE SINCE BROUGHT HOPE TO EVERY SECTOR OF THE UNIVERSE."
ALL WILL BE WELL.
"SAINT WALKER.
"THE BELIEVER."
"AND WHILE HOPE SPREAD, THE INDIGO TRIBE CONTINUED TO FIND THOSE BELIEVED BEYOND REDEMPTION.
"IN THE END, THE VERY FIRST MEMBER OF THE INDIGO TRIBE DISCARDED HER RING...PROVING IT WAS NO LONGER NECESSARY TO INVOKE COMPASSION.
"SHE BECAME ONE OF THE MOST GENEROUS AND LOVING BEINGS IN ALL THE UNIVERSE."
THANK YOU, ABIN.
"IROQUE.
"THE REDEEMER."

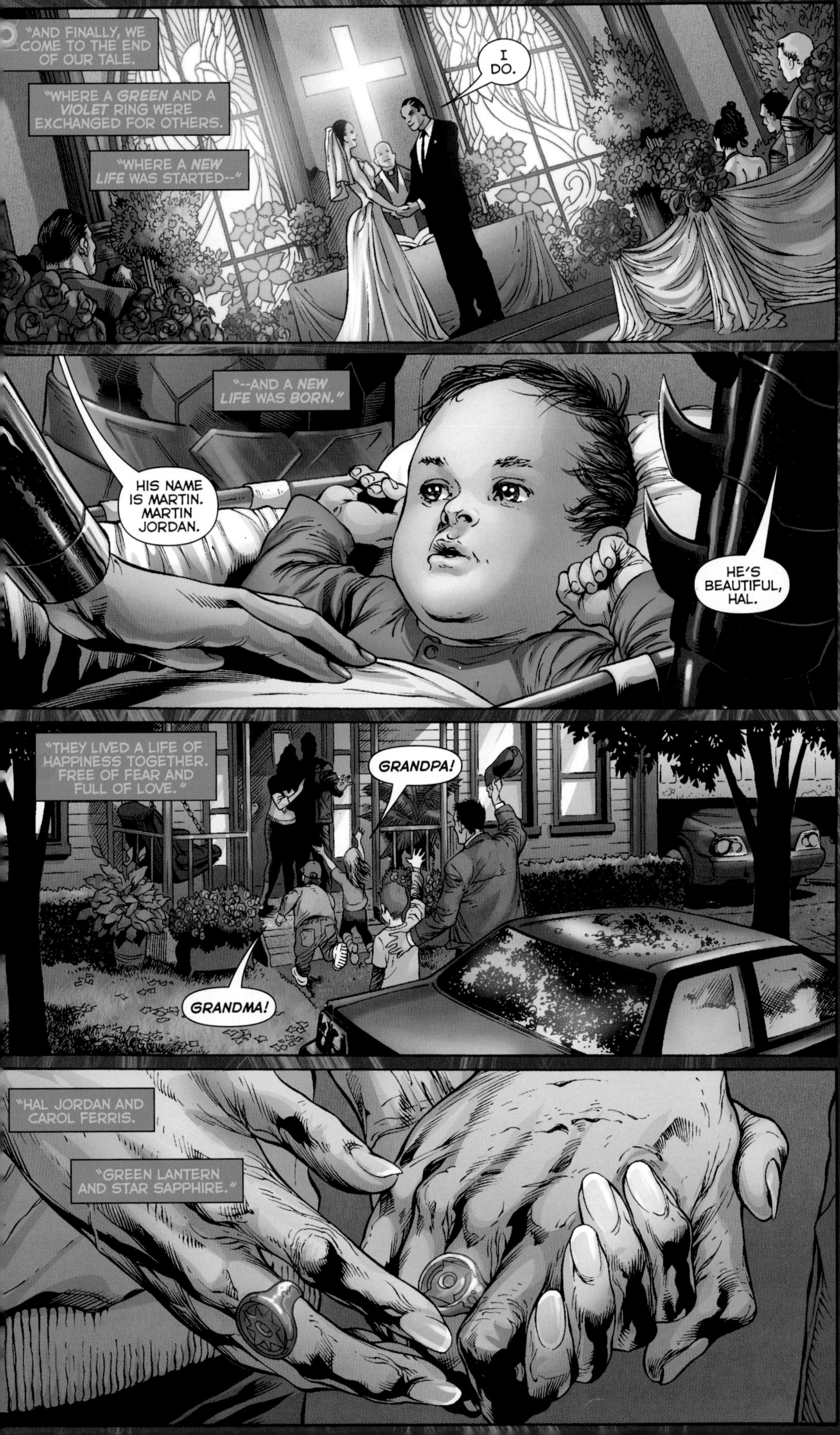
"AND FINALLY, WE COME TO THE END OF OUR TALE.
I DO.
"WHERE A GREEN AND A VIOLET RING WERE EXCHANGED FOR OTHERS.
"WHERE A NEW LIFE WAS STARTED--"
"--AND A NEW LIFE WAS BORN."
HIS NAME IS MARTIN. MARTIN JORDAN.
HE'S BEAUTIFUL, HAL.
"THEY LIVED A LIFE OF HAPPINESS TOGETHER. FREE OF FEAR AND FULL OF LOVE."
GRANDPA!
GRANDMA!
"HAL JORDAN AND CAROL FERRIS.
"GREEN LANTERN AND STAR SAPPHIRE."

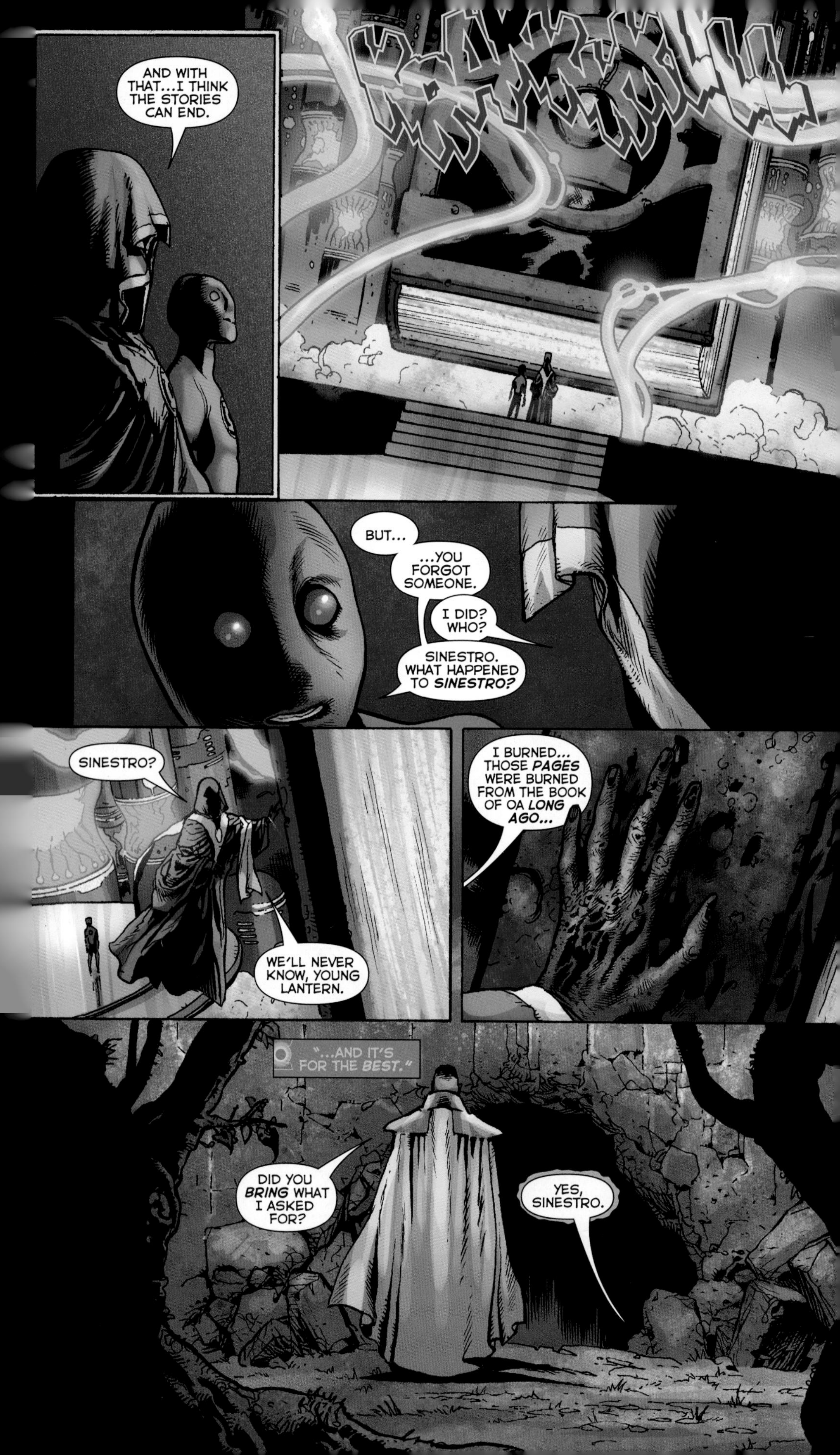
AND WITH THAT...I THINK THE STORIES CAN END.
BUT...
...YOU FORGOT SOMEONE.
I DID? WHO?
SINESTRO. WHAT HAPPENED TO SINESTRO?
SINESTRO?
WE'LL NEVER KNOW, YOUNG LANTERN.
I BURNED... THOSE PAGES WERE BURNED FROM THE BOOK OF OA LONG AGO...
"...AND IT'S FOR THE BEST."
DID YOU BRING WHAT I ASKED FOR?
YES, SINESTRO.

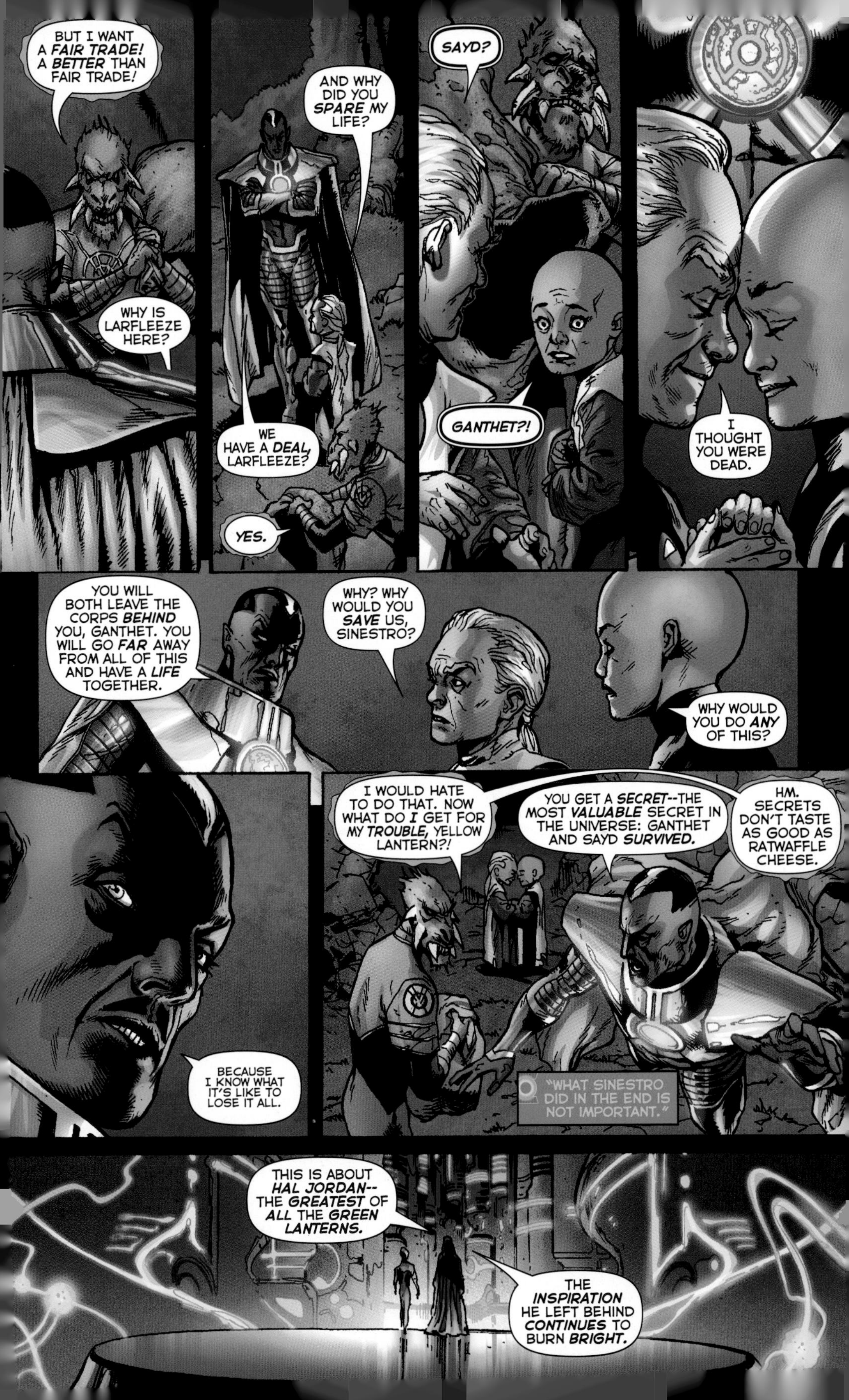
BUT I WANT A FAIR TRADE! A BETTER THAN FAIR TRADE!
WHY IS LARFLEEZE HERE?
AND WHY DID YOU SPARE MY LIFE?
WE HAVE A DEAL, LARFLEEZE?
YES.
SAYD?
GANTHET?!
I THOUGHT YOU WERE DEAD.
YOU WILL BOTH LEAVE THE CORPS BEHIND YOU, GANTHET. YOU WILL GO FAR AWAY FROM ALL OF THIS AND HAVE A LIFE TOGETHER.
WHY? WHY WOULD YOU SAVE US, SINESTRO?
WHY WOULD YOU DO ANY OF THIS?
BECAUSE I KNOW WHAT IT'S LIKE TO LOSE IT ALL.
I WOULD HATE TO DO THAT. NOW WHAT DO I GET FOR MY TROUBLE, YELLOW LANTERN?!
YOU GET A SECRET--THE MOST VALUABLE SECRET IN THE UNIVERSE: GANTHET AND SAYD SURVIVED.
HM. SECRETS DON'T TASTE AS GOOD AS RATWAFFLE CHEESE.
"WHAT SINESTRO DID IN THE END IS NOT IMPORTANT."
THIS IS ABOUT HAL JORDAN-- THE GREATEST OF ALL THE GREEN LANTERNS.
THE INSPIRATION HE LEFT BEHIND CONTINUES TO BURN BRIGHT.

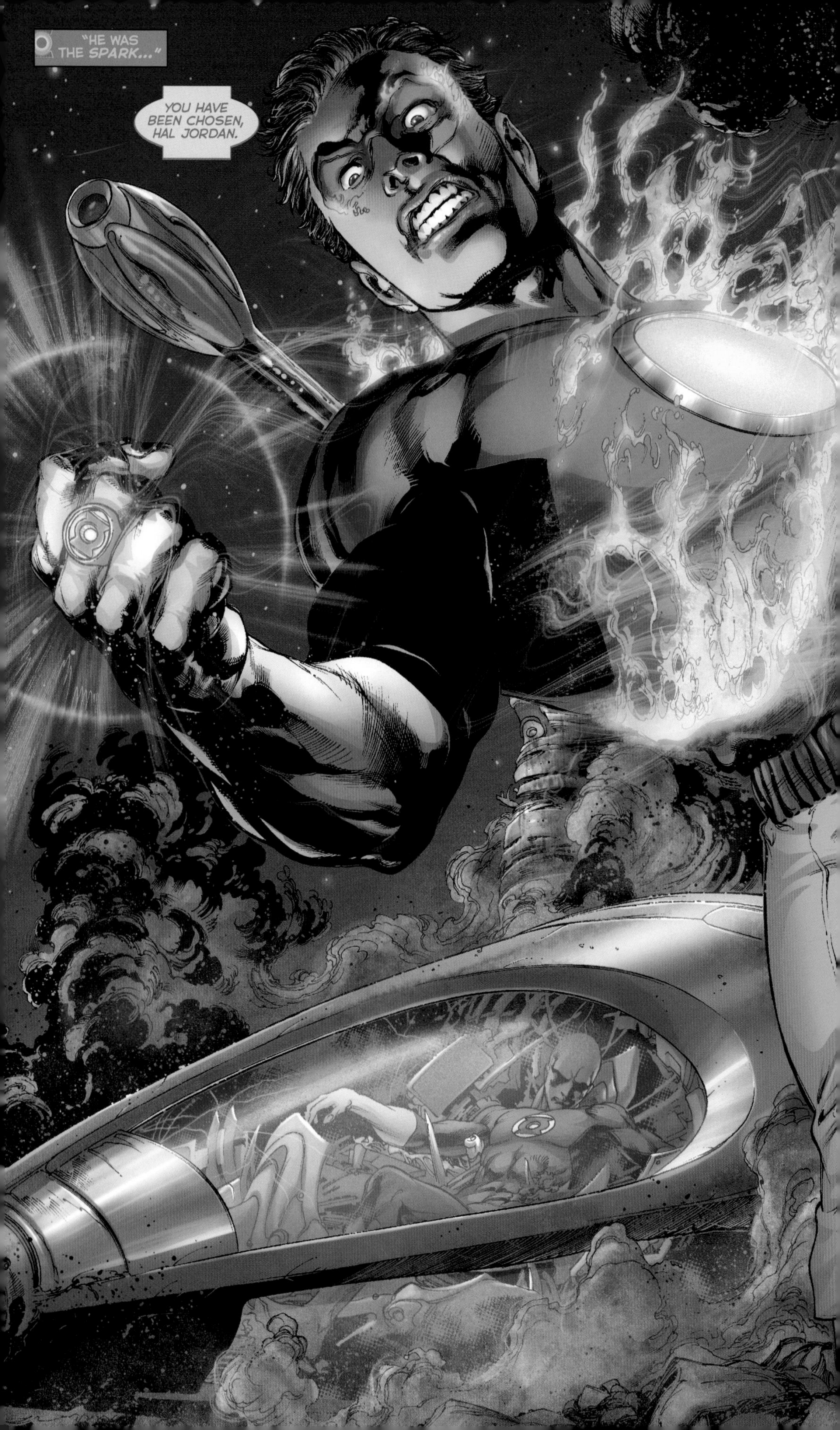
"HE WAS THE SPARK..."
YOU HAVE BEEN CHOSEN, HAL JORDAN.

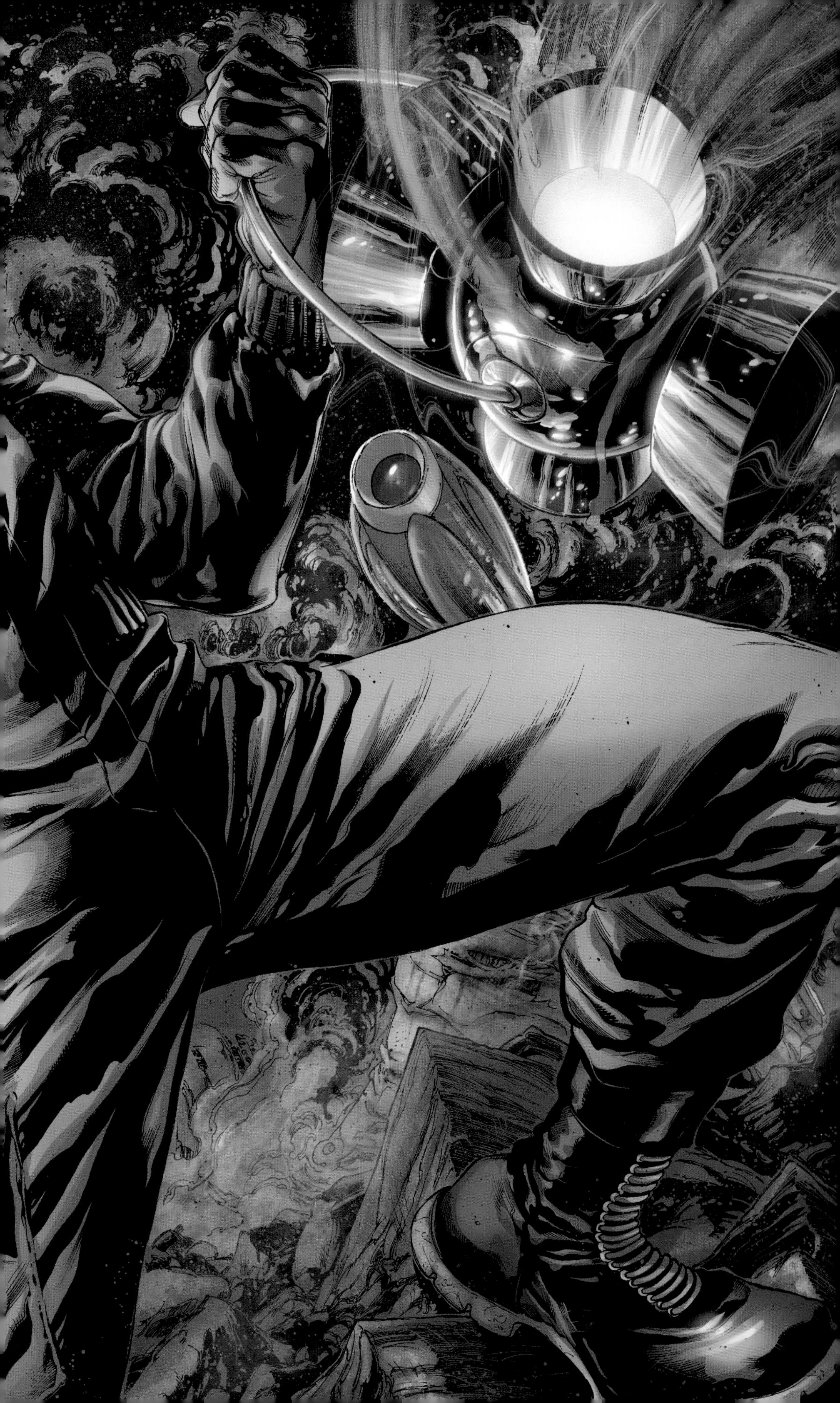

"...THAT STARTED THE *EVERLASTING FIRE.*"

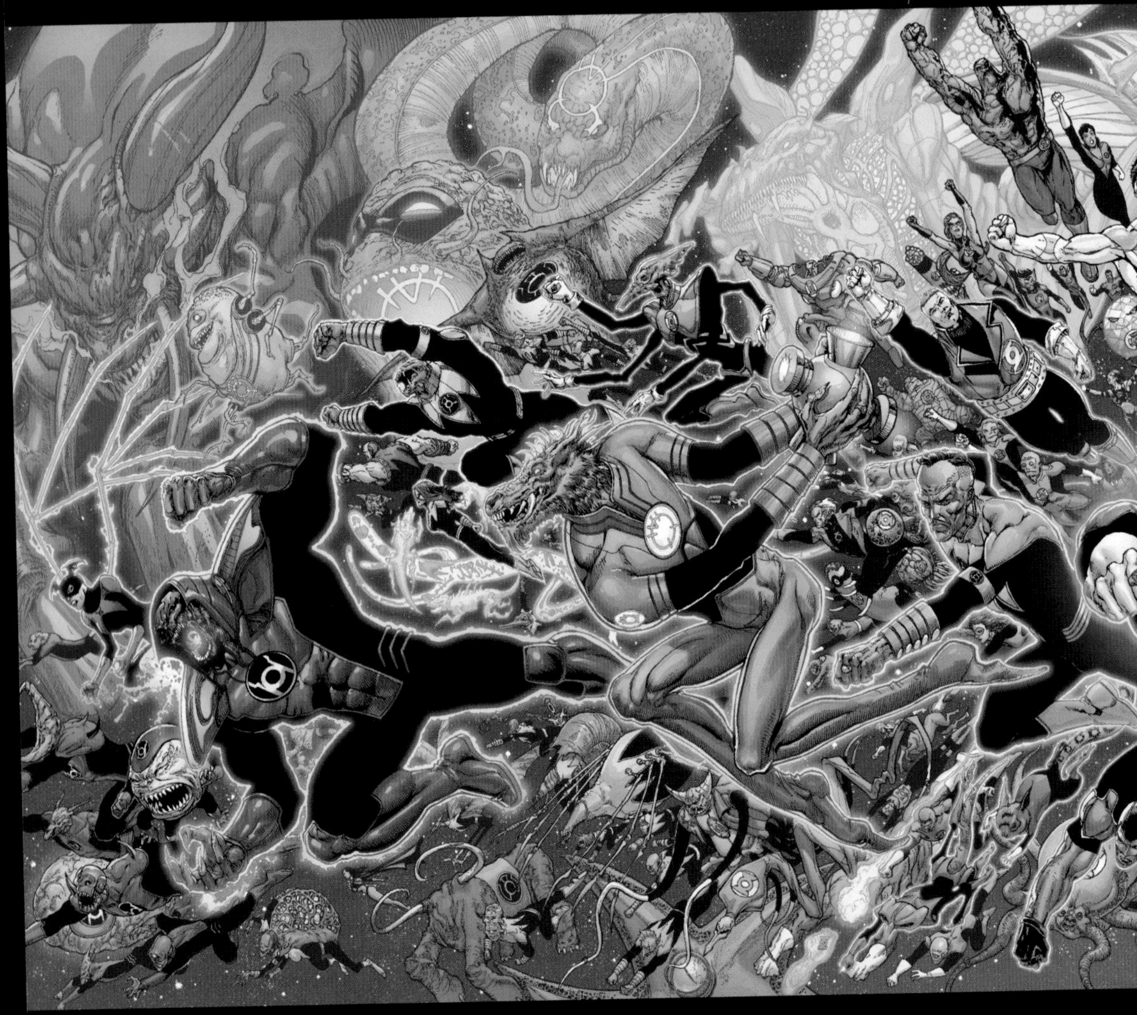

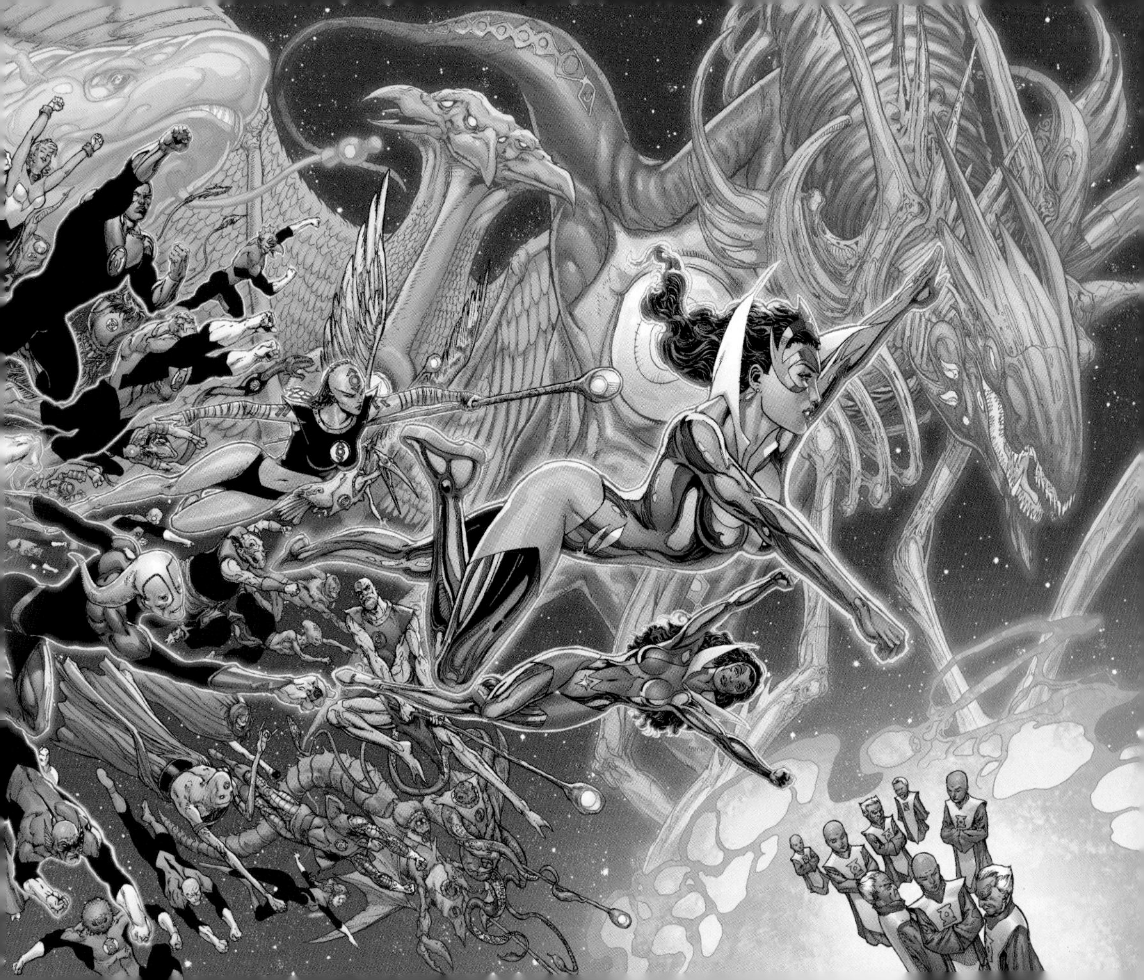

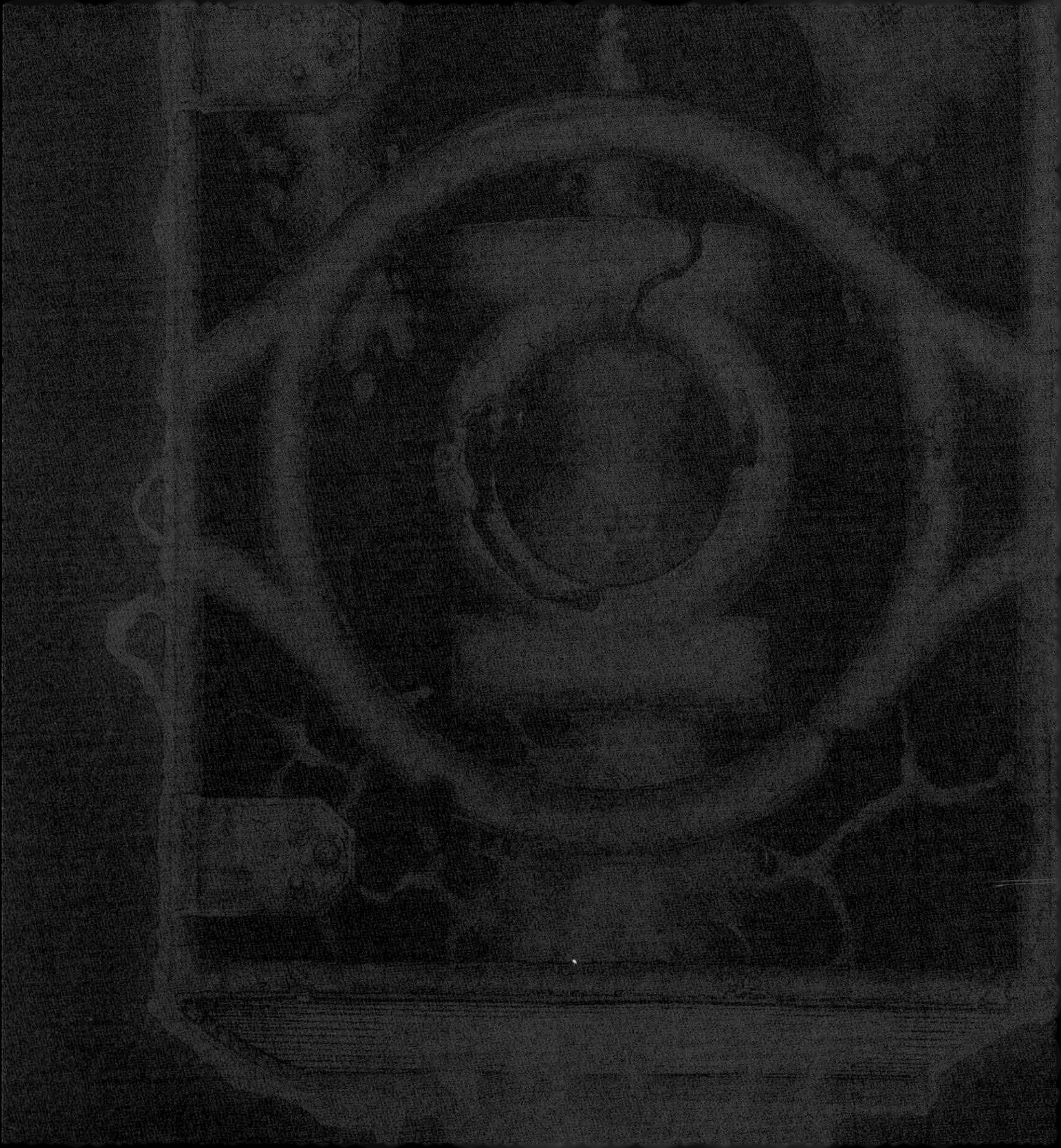

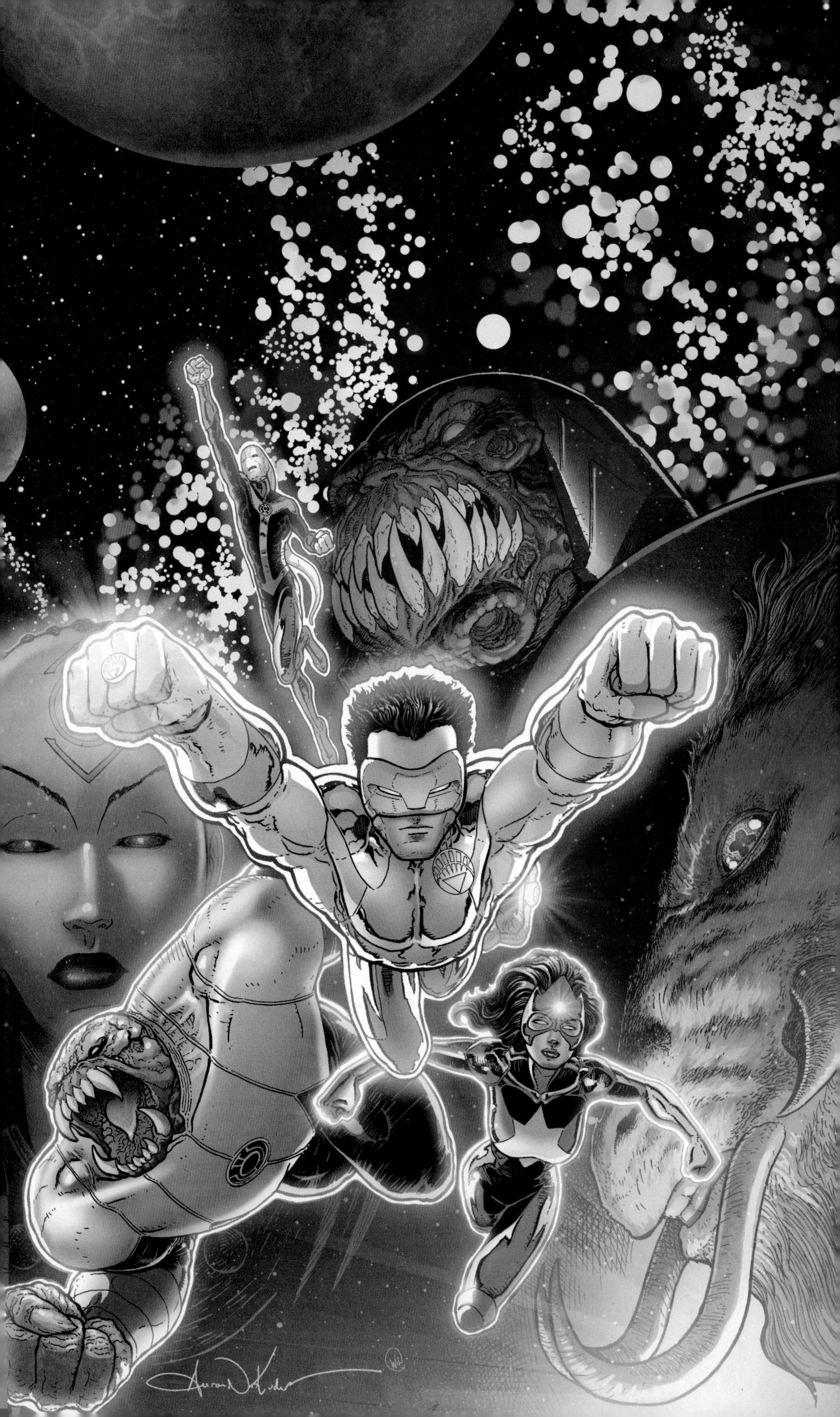

REUNION

TONY BEDARD writer ANDRES GUINALDO penciller RAUL FERNANDEZ inker
AARON KUDER & WIL QUINTANA cover

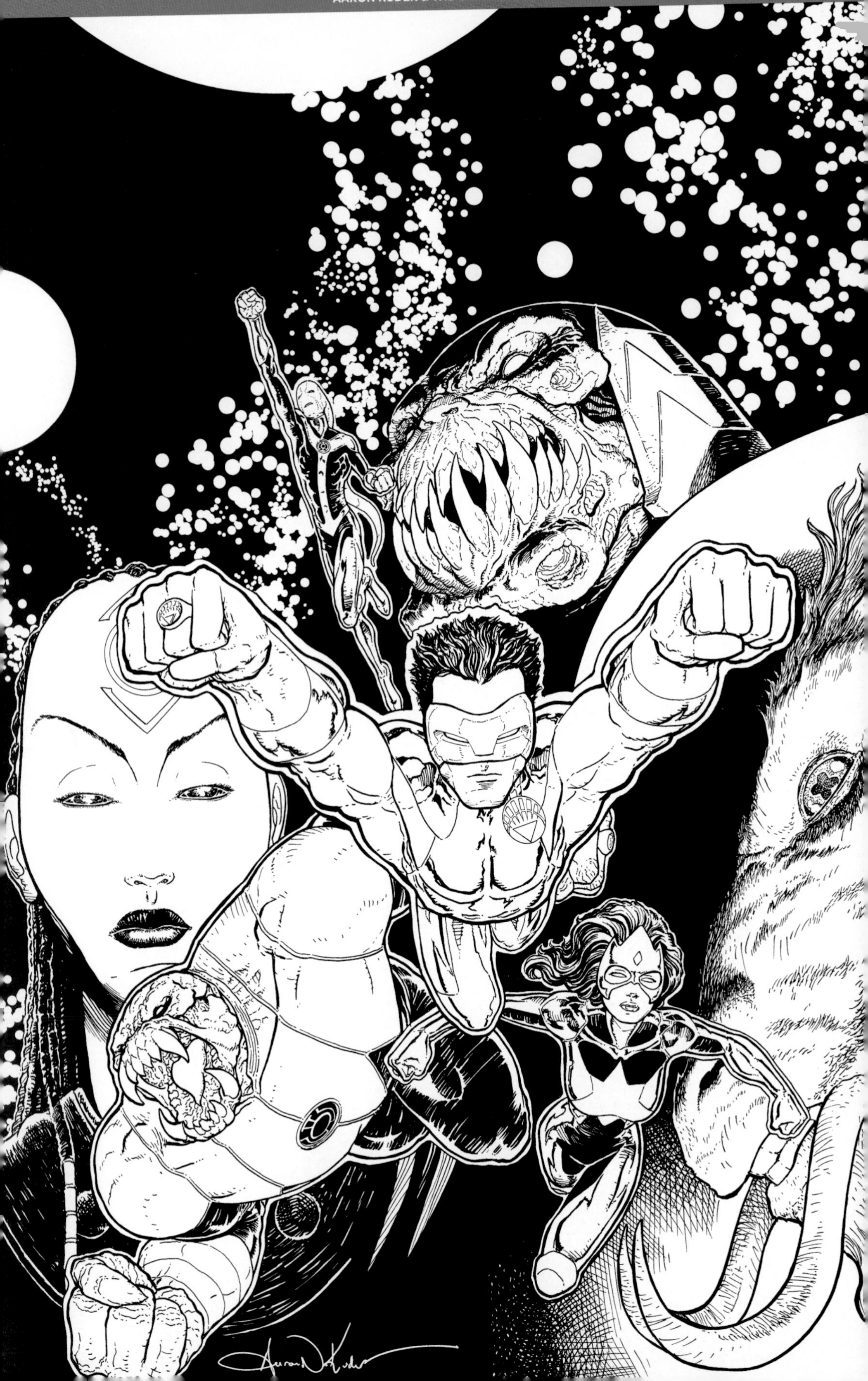

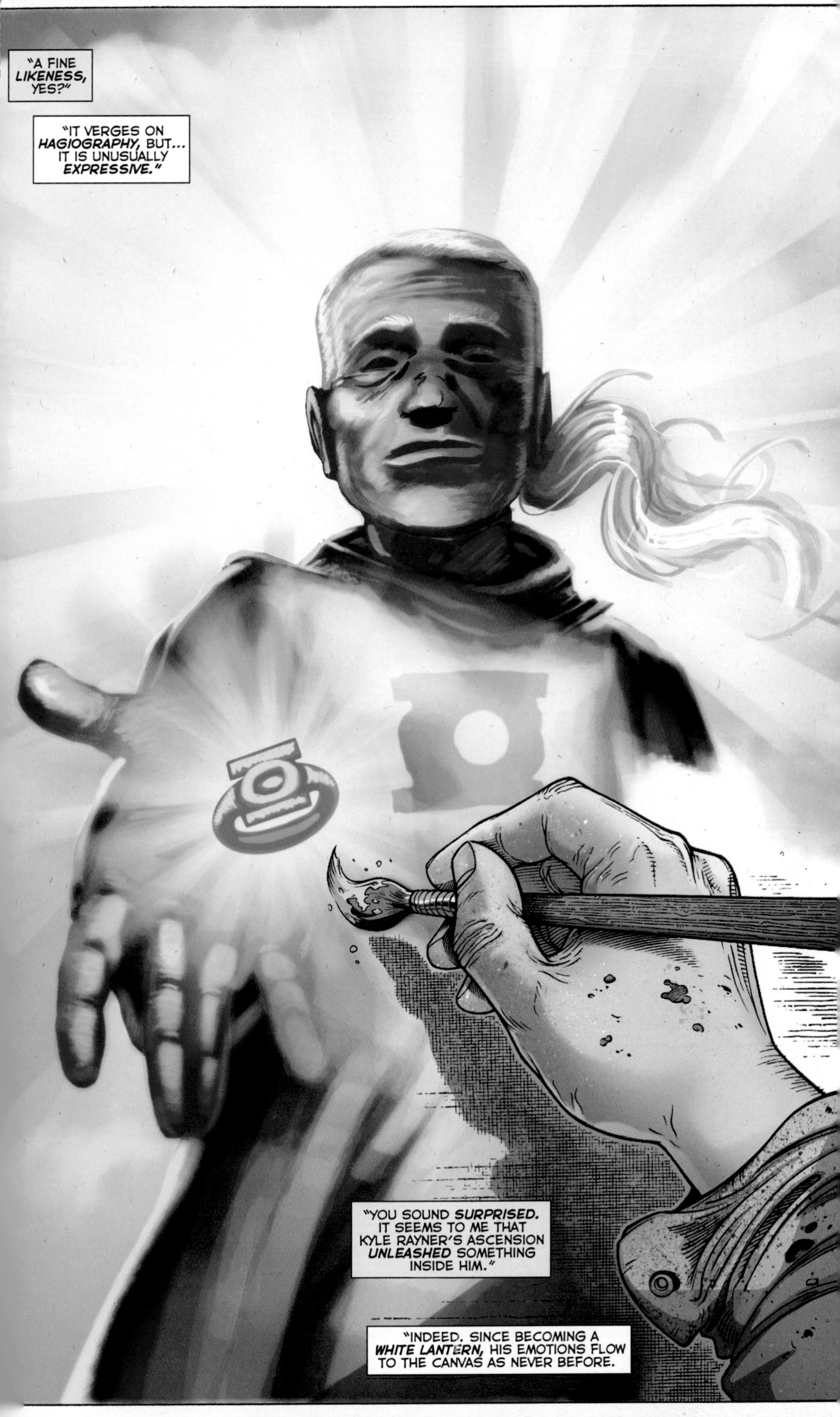
"A FINE LIKENESS, YES?"
"IT VERGES ON HAGIOGRAPHY, BUT... IT IS UNUSUALLY EXPRESSIVE."
"YOU SOUND SURPRISED. IT SEEMS TO ME THAT KYLE RAYNER'S ASCENSION UNLEASHED SOMETHING INSIDE HIM."
"INDEED. SINCE BECOMING A WHITE LANTERN, HIS EMOTIONS FLOW TO THE CANVAS AS NEVER BEFORE.

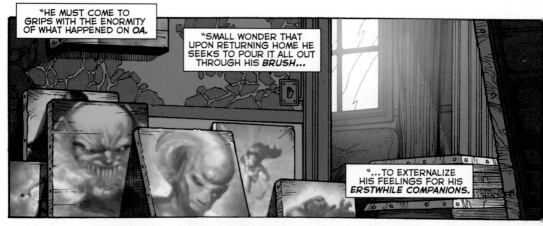

"HE MUST COME TO GRIPS WITH THE ENORMITY OF WHAT HAPPENED ON *OA.*

"SMALL WONDER THAT UPON RETURNING HOME HE SEEKS TO POUR IT ALL OUT THROUGH HIS *BRUSH...*

"*...TO EXTERNALIZE HIS FEELINGS FOR HIS ERSTWHILE COMPANIONS.*

"*SAINT WALKER,* CHAMPION OF HOPE.

"*FEARSOME ARKILLO.*

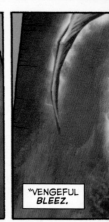

"*VENGEFUL BLEEZ.*

"*...AND HIS MISTRESS, INDIGO-1.*

"*RAGING ATROCITUS.*

"*GREEDY LARFLEE.* WHOM WE KNOW A[?] TOO WELL...

RING: *TELL ME SOMETHING.*

"GLOMULUS, PUPPET OF AVARICE.

"TACITURN MUNK...

"...AND LOVE'S HUNTRESS, FATALITY.

"CAROL FERRIS, WHO HELPED COMPLETE HIS QUEST...

"...AND SHE WHO GAVE ALL."

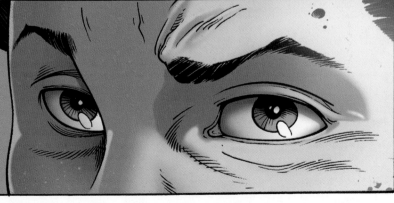

IF I'M SUCH A BIG FAT DEAL NOW, WHY DO I FEEL LIKE SOMETHING'S STILL MISSING?

INSUFFICIENT DATA.

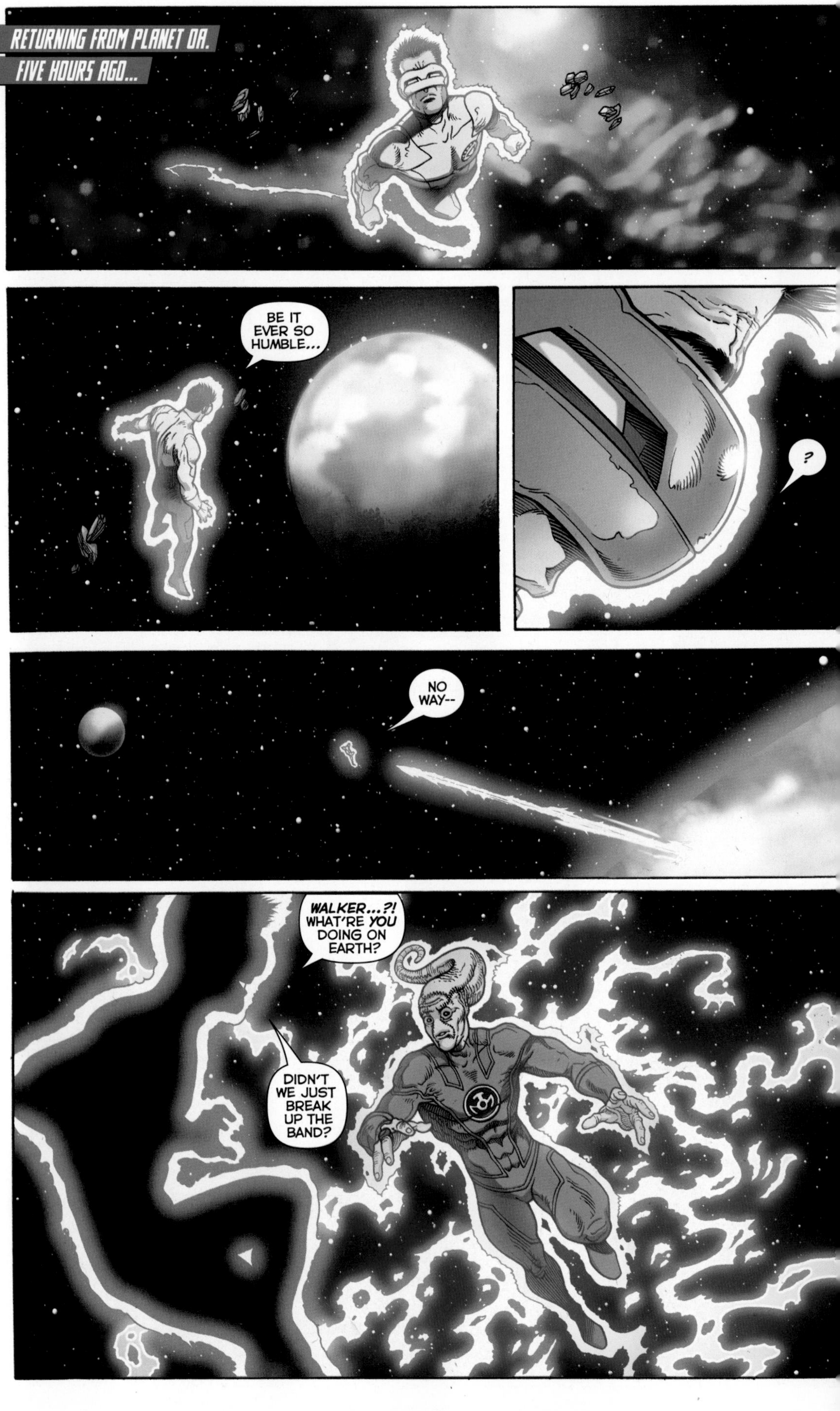

RETURNING FROM PLANET OA.
FIVE HOURS AGO...
BE IT EVER SO HUMBLE...
?
NO WAY--
WALKER...?! WHAT'RE YOU DOING ON EARTH?
DIDN'T WE JUST BREAK UP THE BAND?

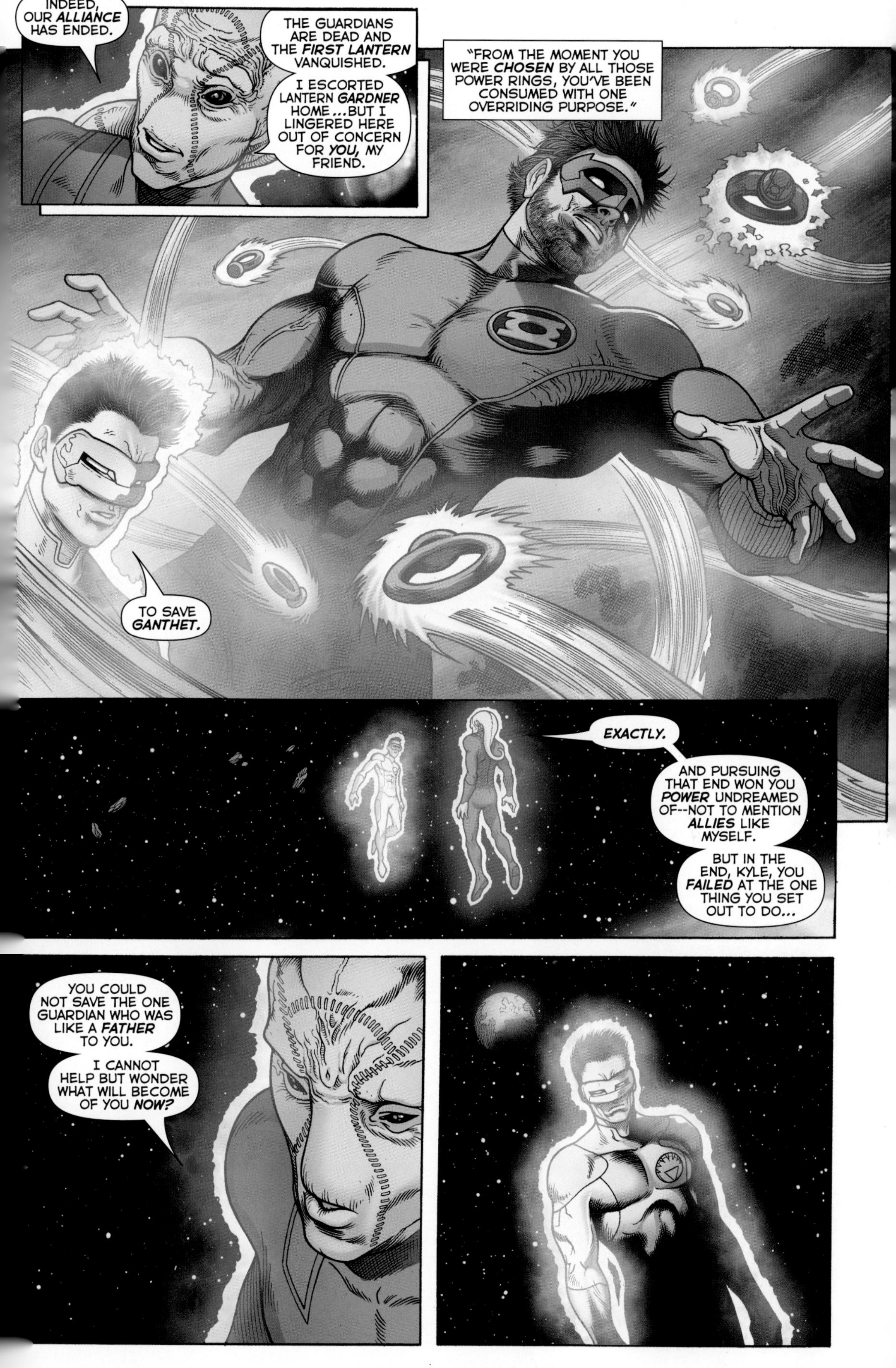
INDEED, OUR *ALLIANCE* HAS ENDED.
THE GUARDIANS ARE DEAD AND THE *FIRST LANTERN* VANQUISHED.
I ESCORTED LANTERN *GARDNER* HOME... BUT I LINGERED HERE OUT OF CONCERN FOR *YOU*, MY FRIEND.
"FROM THE MOMENT YOU WERE *CHOSEN* BY ALL THOSE POWER RINGS, YOU'VE BEEN CONSUMED WITH ONE OVERRIDING PURPOSE."
TO SAVE *GANTHET*.
EXACTLY.
AND PURSUING THAT END WON YOU *POWER* UNDREAMED OF--NOT TO MENTION *ALLIES* LIKE MYSELF.
BUT IN THE END, KYLE, YOU *FAILED* AT THE ONE THING YOU SET OUT TO DO...
YOU COULD NOT SAVE THE ONE GUARDIAN WHO WAS LIKE A *FATHER* TO YOU.
I CANNOT HELP BUT WONDER WHAT WILL BECOME OF YOU *NOW?*

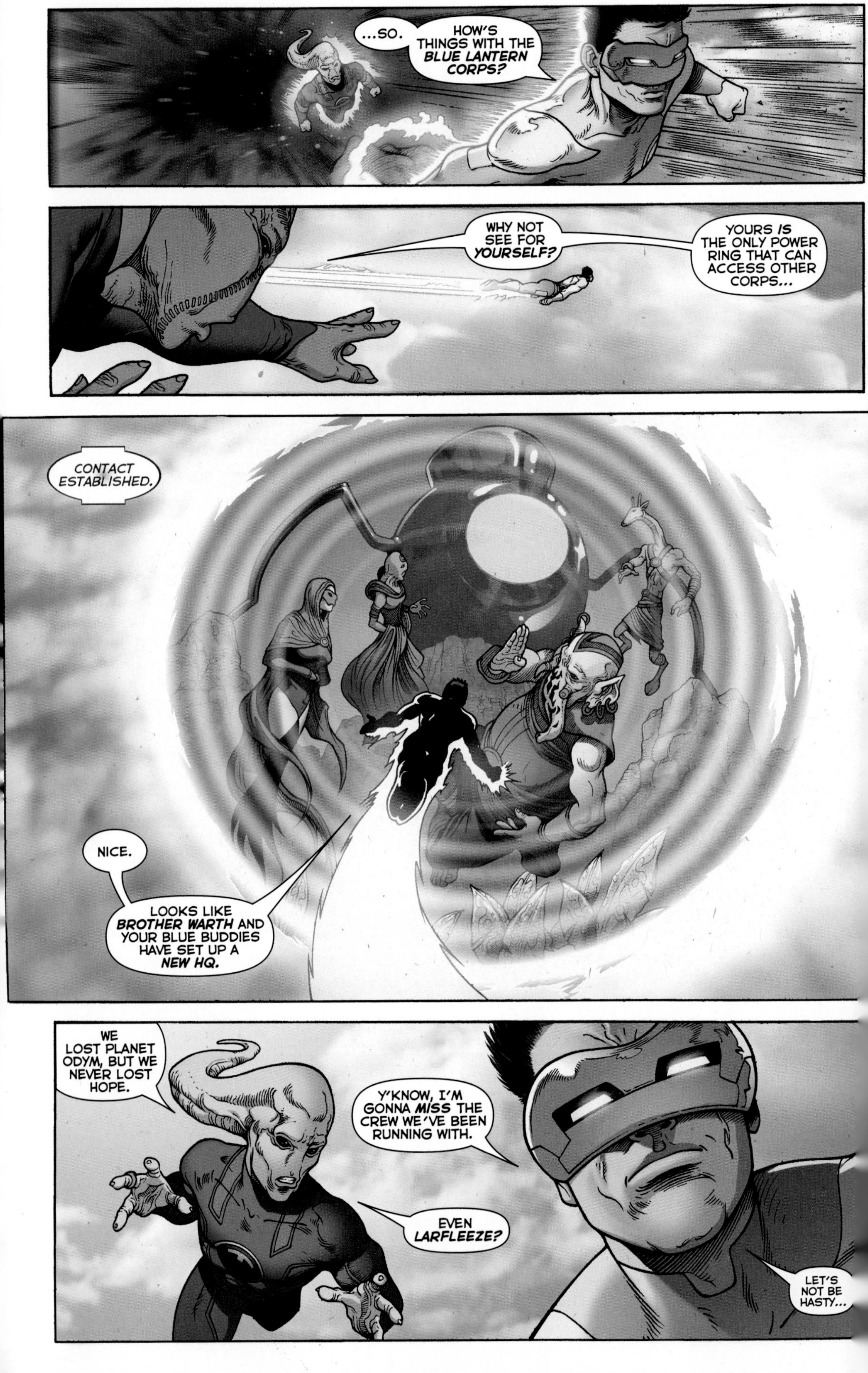
...SO.
HOW'S THINGS WITH THE *BLUE LANTERN CORPS?*
WHY NOT SEE FOR *YOURSELF?*
YOURS *IS* THE ONLY POWER RING THAT CAN ACCESS OTHER CORPS...
CONTACT ESTABLISHED.
NICE.
LOOKS LIKE *BROTHER WARTH* AND YOUR BLUE BUDDIES HAVE SET UP A *NEW HQ.*
WE LOST PLANET ODYM, BUT WE NEVER LOST HOPE.
Y'KNOW, I'M GONNA *MISS* THE CREW WE'VE BEEN RUNNING WITH.
EVEN *LARFLEEZE?*
LET'S NOT BE HASTY...

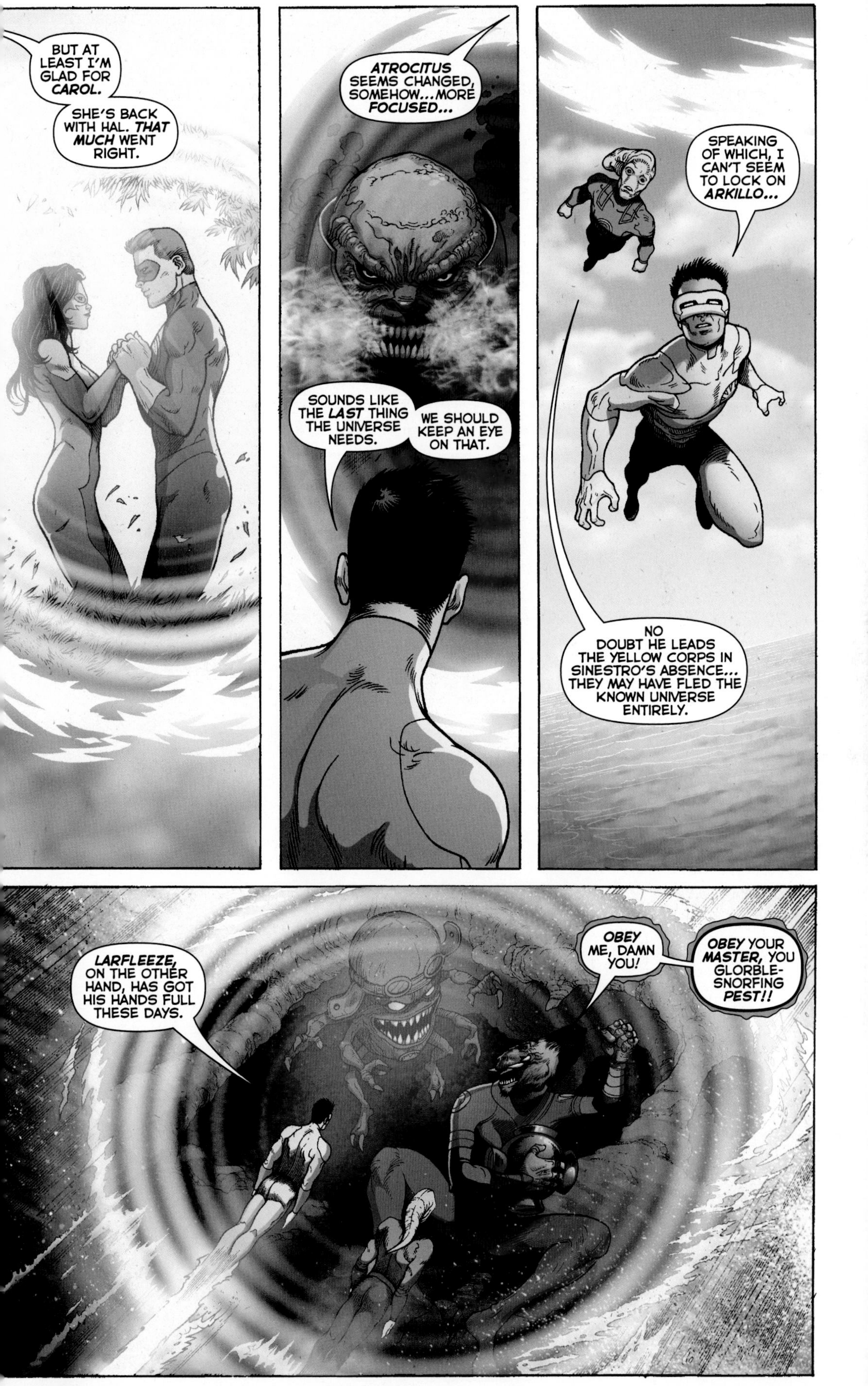
BUT AT LEAST I'M GLAD FOR CAROL.
SHE'S BACK WITH HAL. THAT MUCH WENT RIGHT.
ATROCITUS SEEMS CHANGED, SOMEHOW...MORE FOCUSED...
SOUNDS LIKE THE LAST THING THE UNIVERSE NEEDS.
WE SHOULD KEEP AN EYE ON THAT.
SPEAKING OF WHICH, I CAN'T SEEM TO LOCK ON ARKILLO...
NO DOUBT HE LEADS THE YELLOW CORPS IN SINESTRO'S ABSENCE... THEY MAY HAVE FLED THE KNOWN UNIVERSE ENTIRELY.
LARFLEEZE, ON THE OTHER HAND, HAS GOT HIS HANDS FULL THESE DAYS.
OBEY ME, DAMN YOU!
OBEY YOUR MASTER, YOU GLORBLE-SNORFING PEST!!

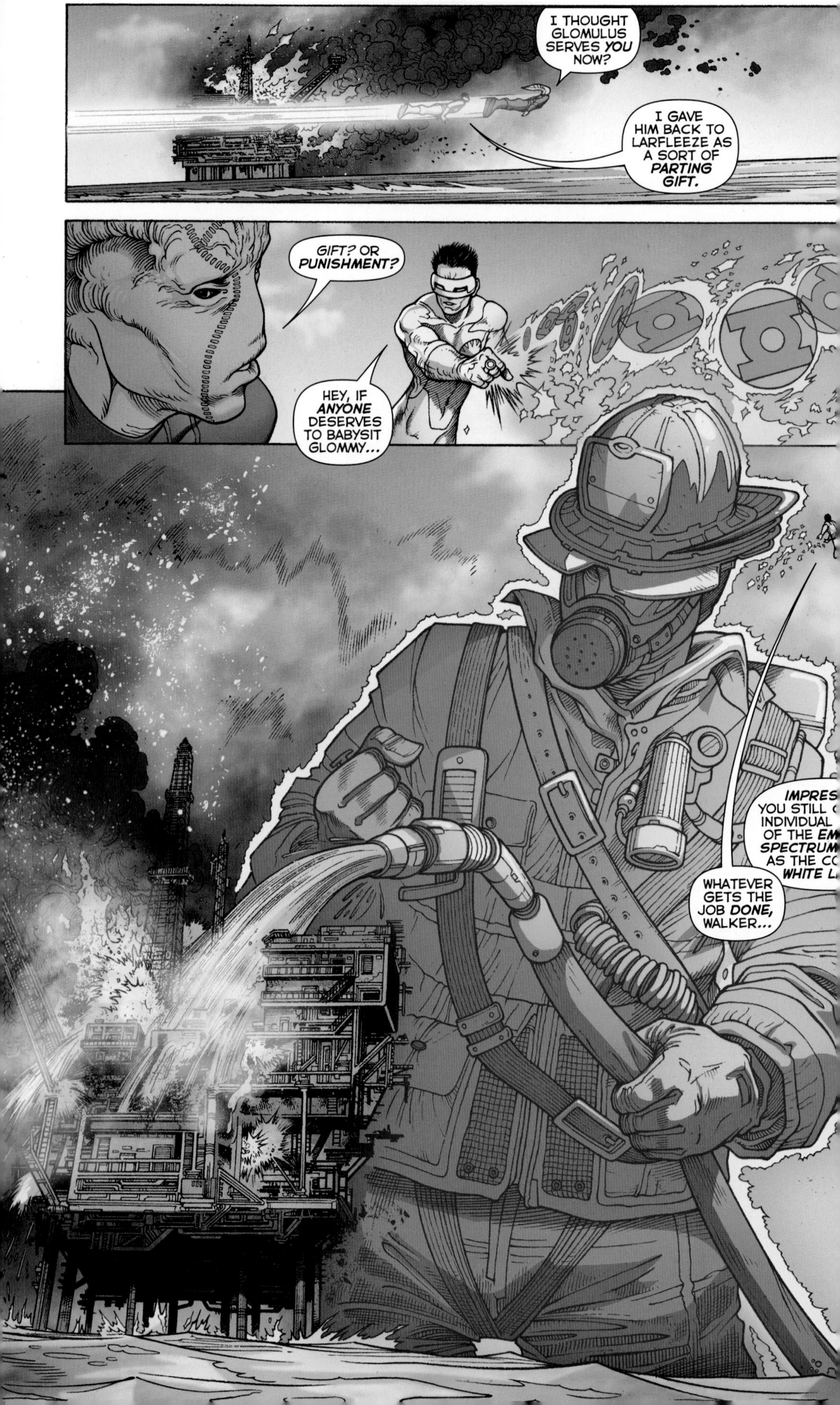

I THOUGHT GLOMULUS SERVES *YOU* NOW?
I GAVE HIM BACK TO LARFLEEZE AS A SORT OF ***PARTING GIFT.***
GIFT? OR ***PUNISHMENT?***
HEY, IF ***ANYONE*** DESERVES TO BABYSIT GLOMMY...
WHATEVER GETS THE JOB ***DONE,*** WALKER...

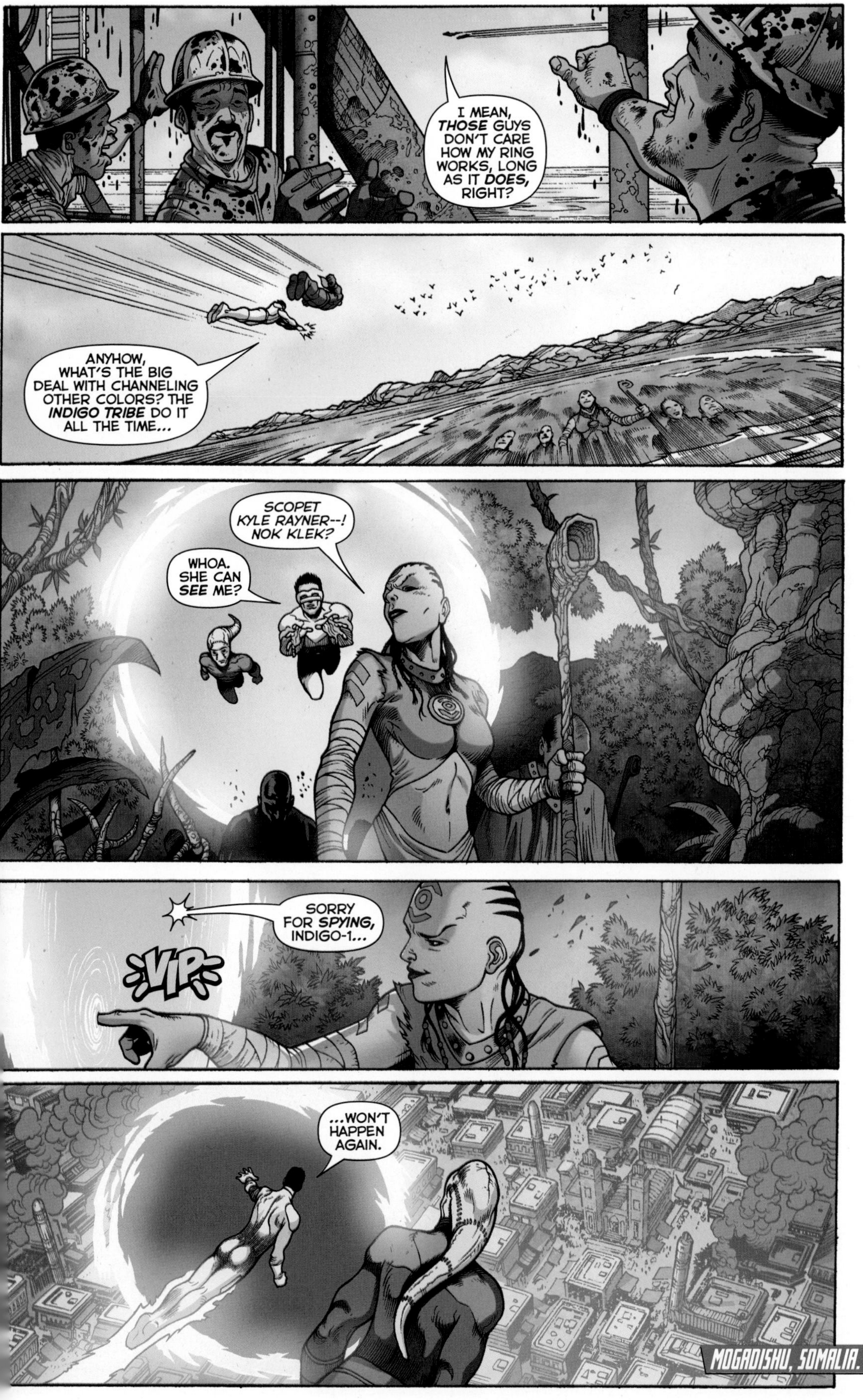
I MEAN, THOSE GUYS DON'T CARE HOW MY RING WORKS, LONG AS IT DOES, RIGHT?
ANYHOW, WHAT'S THE BIG DEAL WITH CHANNELING OTHER COLORS? THE INDIGO TRIBE DO IT ALL THE TIME...
SCOPET KYLE RAYNER--! NOK KLEK?
WHOA. SHE CAN SEE ME?
SORRY FOR SPYING, INDIGO-1...
VIP
...WON'T HAPPEN AGAIN.
MOGADISHU, SOMALIA.

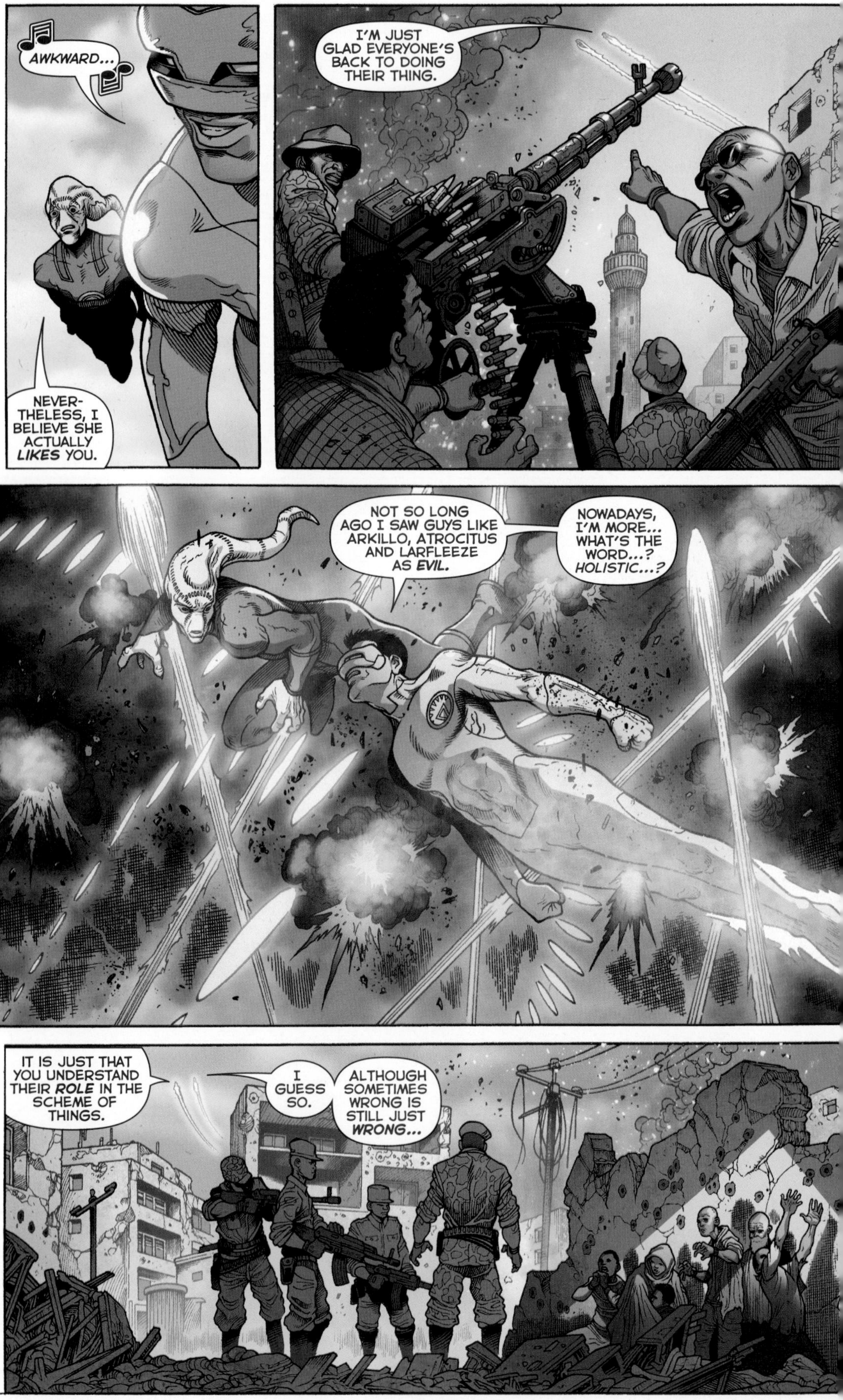
AWKWARD...
NEVER-THELESS, I BELIEVE SHE ACTUALLY LIKES YOU.
I'M JUST GLAD EVERYONE'S BACK TO DOING THEIR THING.
NOT SO LONG AGO I SAW GUYS LIKE ARKILLO, ATROCITUS AND LARFLEEZE AS EVIL.
NOWADAYS, I'M MORE... WHAT'S THE WORD...? HOLISTIC...?
IT IS JUST THAT YOU UNDERSTAND THEIR ROLE IN THE SCHEME OF THINGS.
I GUESS SO.
ALTHOUGH SOMETIMES WRONG IS STILL JUST WRONG...

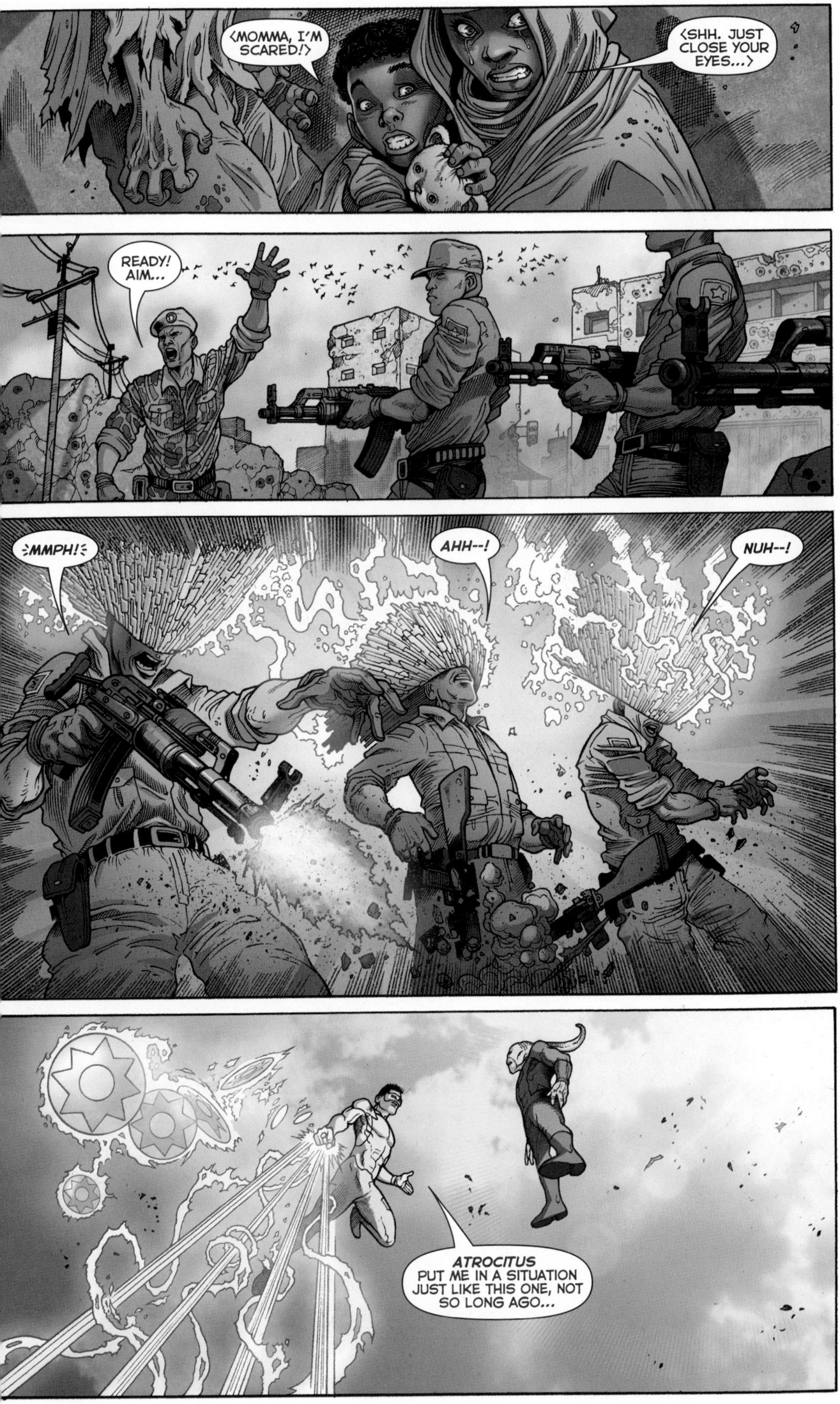
<MOMMA, I'M SCARED!>
<SHH. JUST CLOSE YOUR EYES...>
READY! AIM...
MMPH!
AHH--!
NUH--!
ATROCITUS PUT ME IN A SITUATION JUST LIKE THIS ONE, NOT SO LONG AGO...

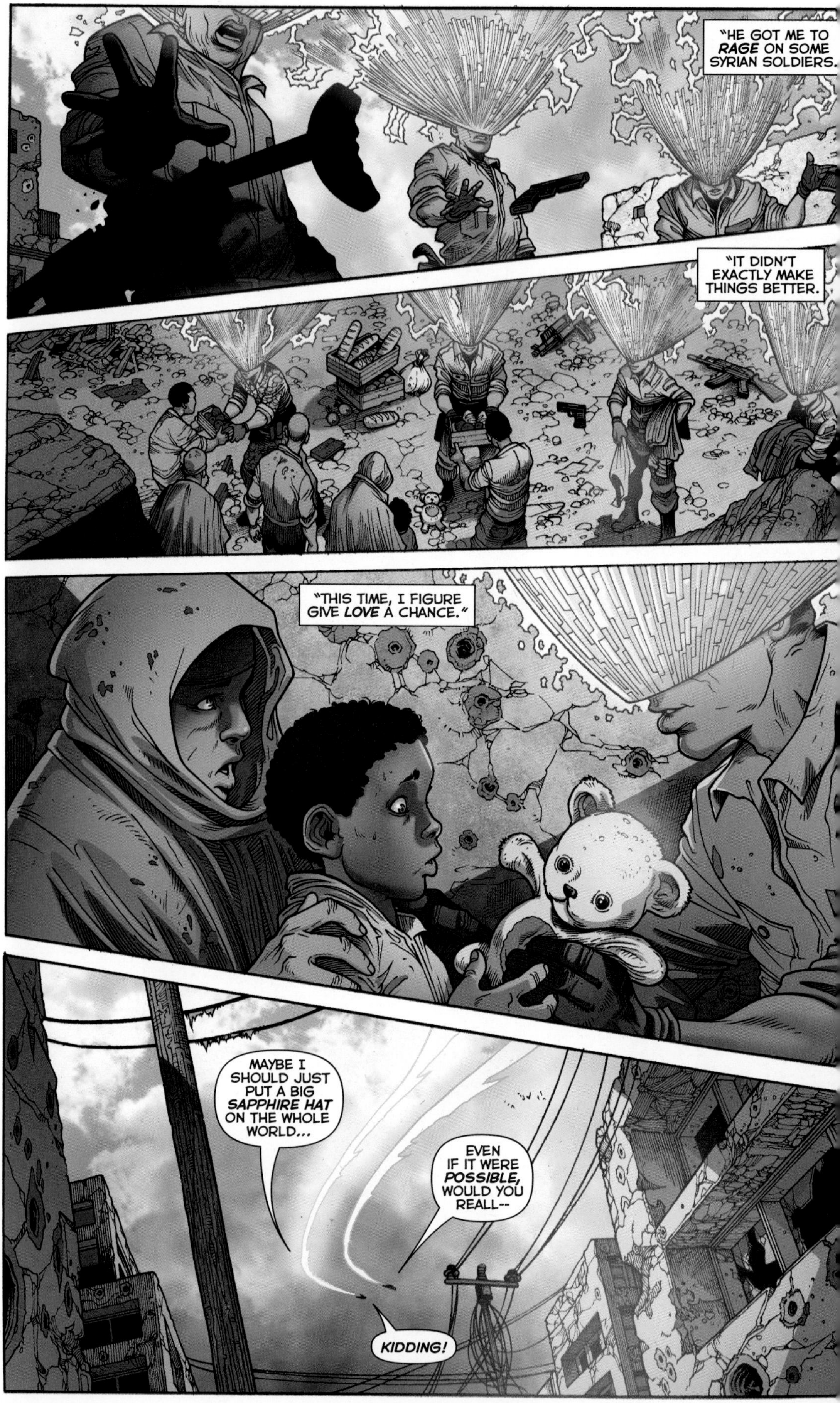
"HE GOT ME TO RAGE ON SOME SYRIAN SOLDIERS.
"IT DIDN'T EXACTLY MAKE THINGS BETTER.
"THIS TIME, I FIGURE GIVE LOVE A CHANCE."
MAYBE I SHOULD JUST PUT A BIG SAPPHIRE HAT ON THE WHOLE WORLD...
EVEN IF IT WERE POSSIBLE, WOULD YOU REALL--
KIDDING!

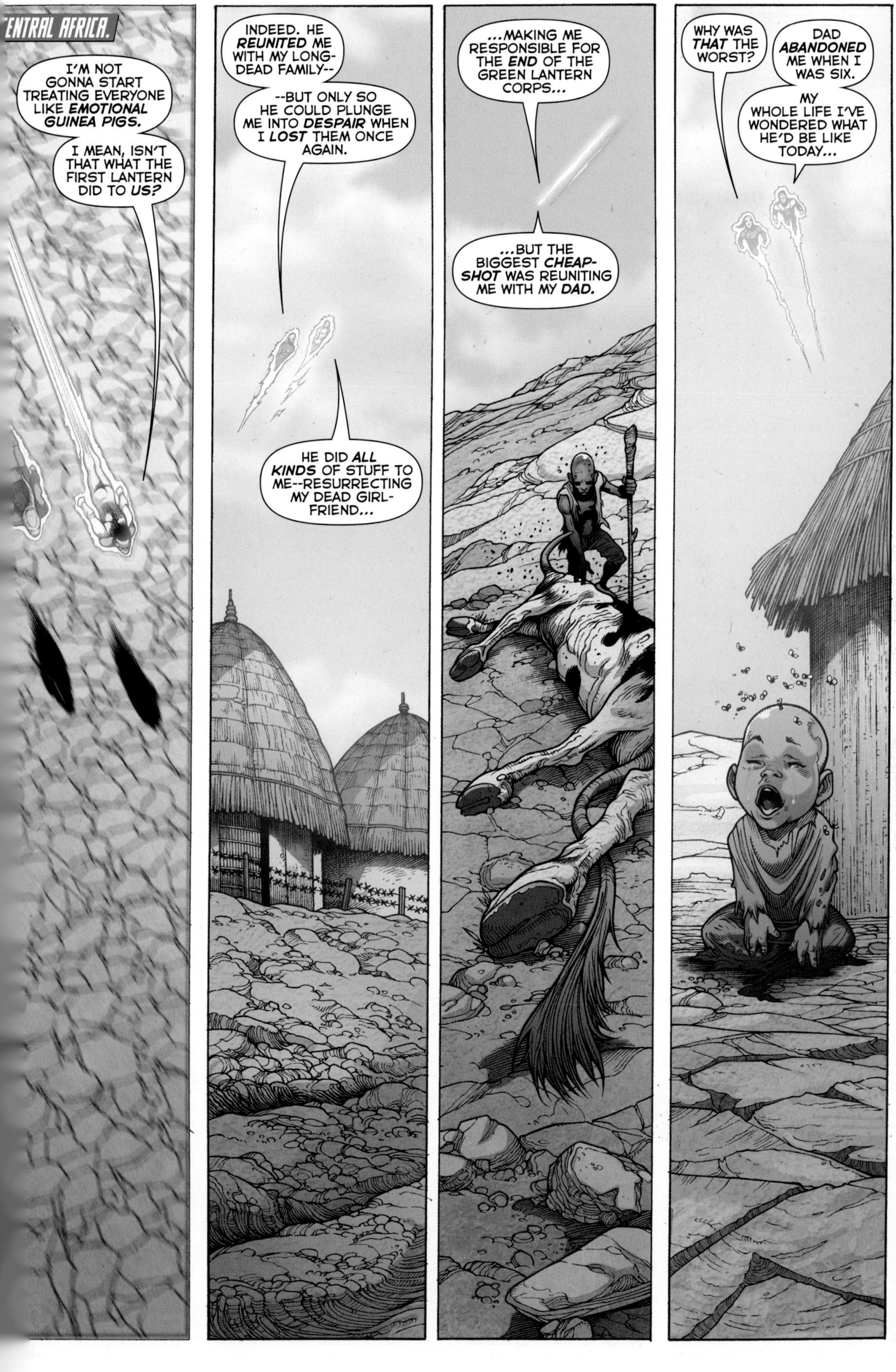

ENTRAL AFRICA.
I'M NOT GONNA START TREATING EVERYONE LIKE EMOTIONAL GUINEA PIGS.
I MEAN, ISN'T THAT WHAT THE FIRST LANTERN DID TO US?
INDEED. HE REUNITED ME WITH MY LONG-DEAD FAMILY--
--BUT ONLY SO HE COULD PLUNGE ME INTO DESPAIR WHEN I LOST THEM ONCE AGAIN.
HE DID ALL KINDS OF STUFF TO ME--RESURRECTING MY DEAD GIRL-FRIEND...
...MAKING ME RESPONSIBLE FOR THE END OF THE GREEN LANTERN CORPS...
...BUT THE BIGGEST CHEAP-SHOT WAS REUNITING ME WITH MY DAD.
WHY WAS THAT THE WORST?
DAD ABANDONED ME WHEN I WAS SIX.
MY WHOLE LIFE I'VE WONDERED WHAT HE'D BE LIKE TODAY...

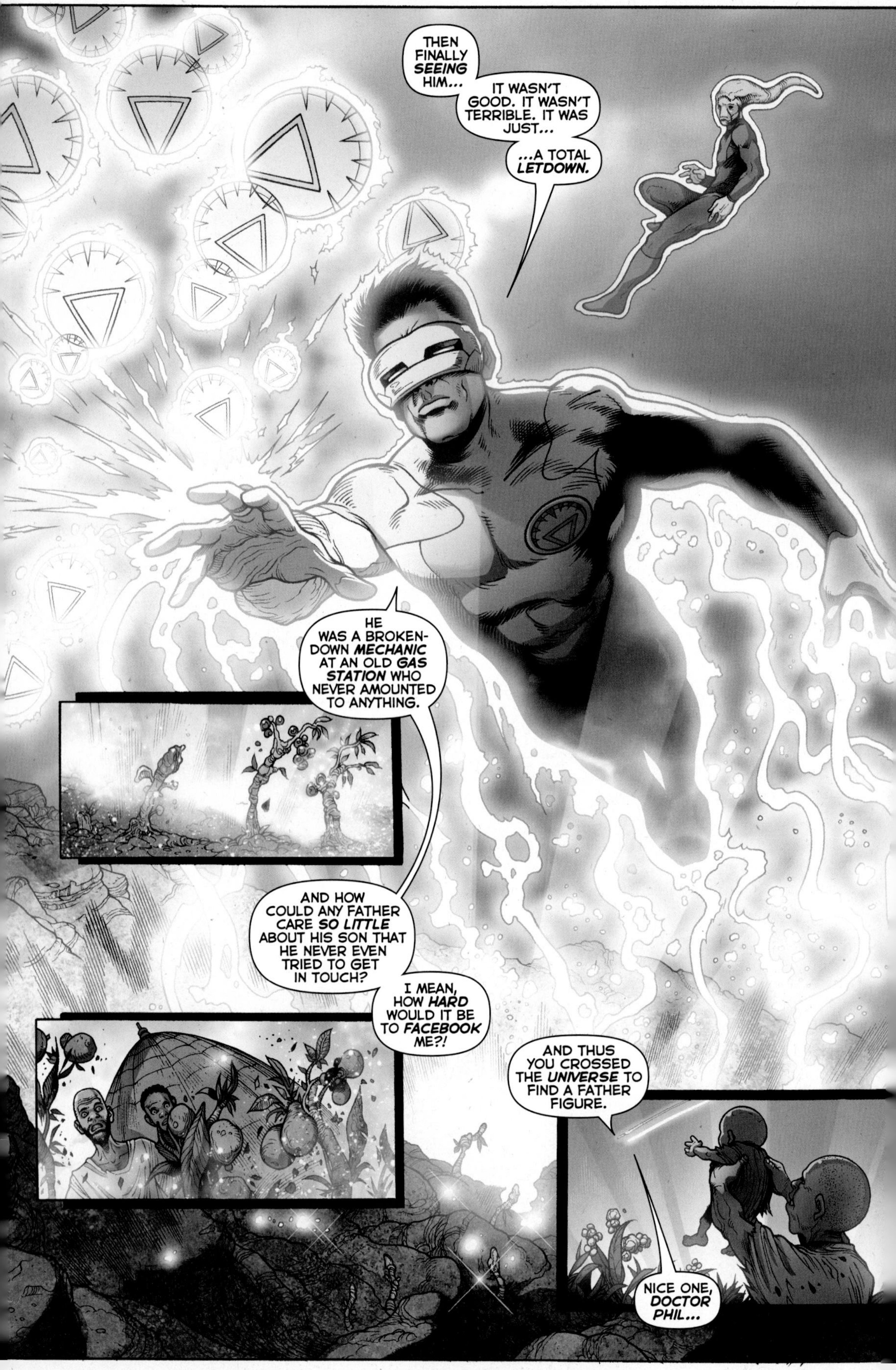
THEN FINALLY SEEING HIM...
IT WASN'T GOOD. IT WASN'T TERRIBLE. IT WAS JUST...
...A TOTAL LETDOWN.
HE WAS A BROKEN-DOWN MECHANIC AT AN OLD GAS STATION WHO NEVER AMOUNTED TO ANYTHING.
AND HOW COULD ANY FATHER CARE SO LITTLE ABOUT HIS SON THAT HE NEVER EVEN TRIED TO GET IN TOUCH?
I MEAN, HOW HARD WOULD IT BE TO FACEBOOK ME?!
AND THUS YOU CROSSED THE UNIVERSE TO FIND A FATHER FIGURE.
NICE ONE, DOCTOR PHIL...

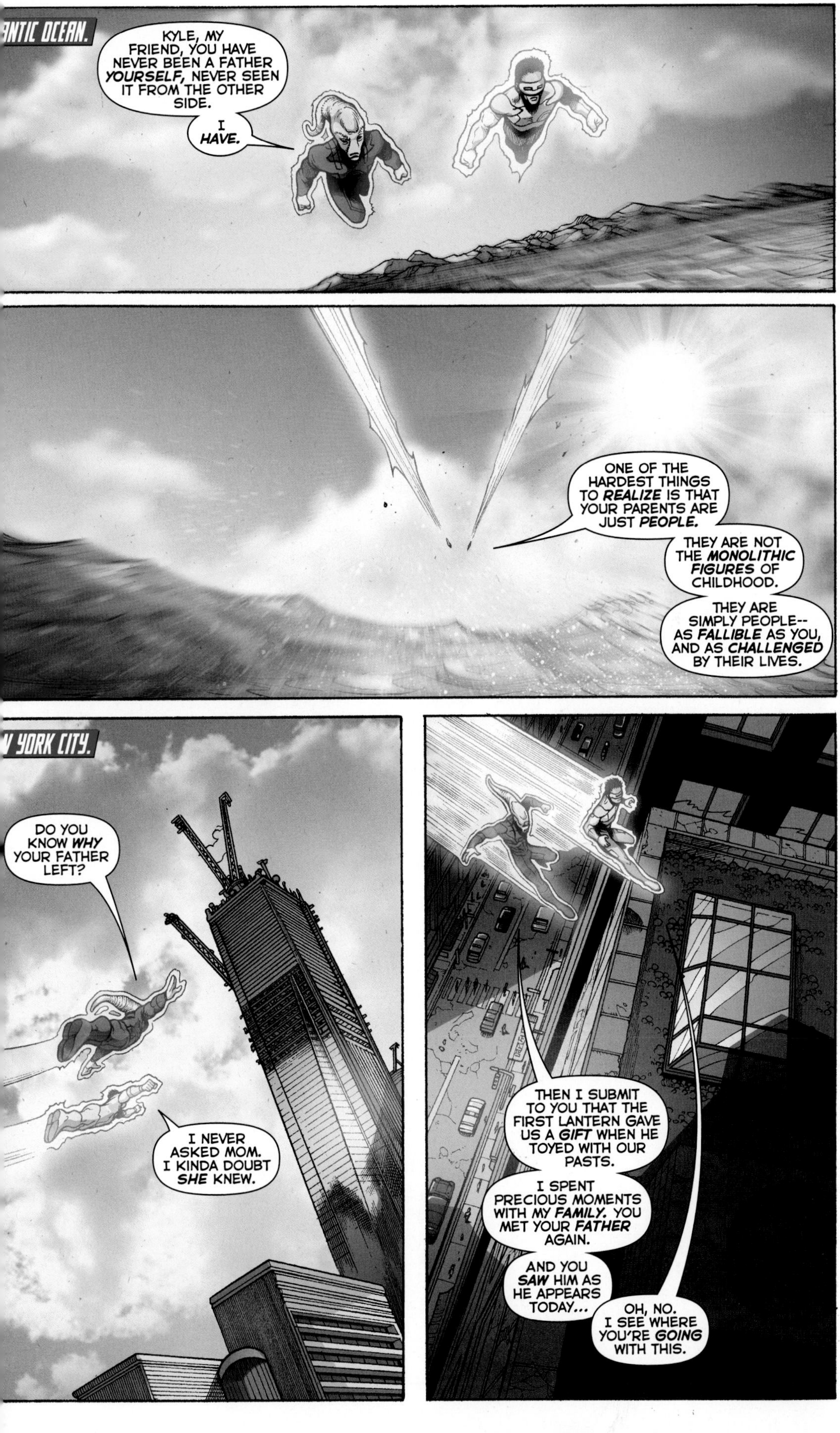
ANTIC OCEAN.
KYLE, MY FRIEND, YOU HAVE NEVER BEEN A FATHER YOURSELF, NEVER SEEN IT FROM THE OTHER SIDE.
I HAVE.
ONE OF THE HARDEST THINGS TO REALIZE IS THAT YOUR PARENTS ARE JUST PEOPLE.
THEY ARE NOT THE MONOLITHIC FIGURES OF CHILDHOOD.
THEY ARE SIMPLY PEOPLE-- AS FALLIBLE AS YOU, AND AS CHALLENGED BY THEIR LIVES.
W YORK CITY.
DO YOU KNOW WHY YOUR FATHER LEFT?
I NEVER ASKED MOM. I KINDA DOUBT SHE KNEW.
THEN I SUBMIT TO YOU THAT THE FIRST LANTERN GAVE US A GIFT WHEN HE TOYED WITH OUR PASTS.
I SPENT PRECIOUS MOMENTS WITH MY FAMILY. YOU MET YOUR FATHER AGAIN.
AND YOU SAW HIM AS HE APPEARS TODAY...
OH, NO. I SEE WHERE YOU'RE GOING WITH THIS.

I AM ONLY GOING BACK TO MY CORPS, KYLE RAYNER. WE HAVE MORE *REBUILDING* TO DO.

WHAT *YOU* DO IS UP TO YOU. BUT YOU HAVE FACED YOUR FEARS, FACED *ALL* YOUR EMOTIONS...

"WHEN WILL YOU FACE THE *UNKNOWN?*"

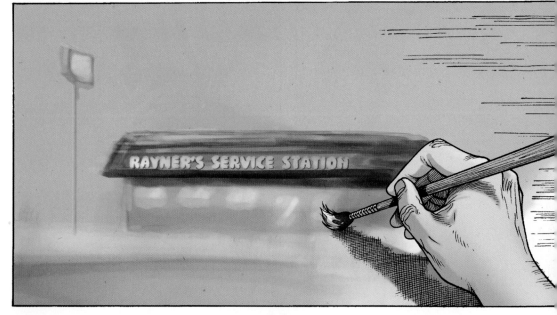

RAYNER'S SERVICE STATION

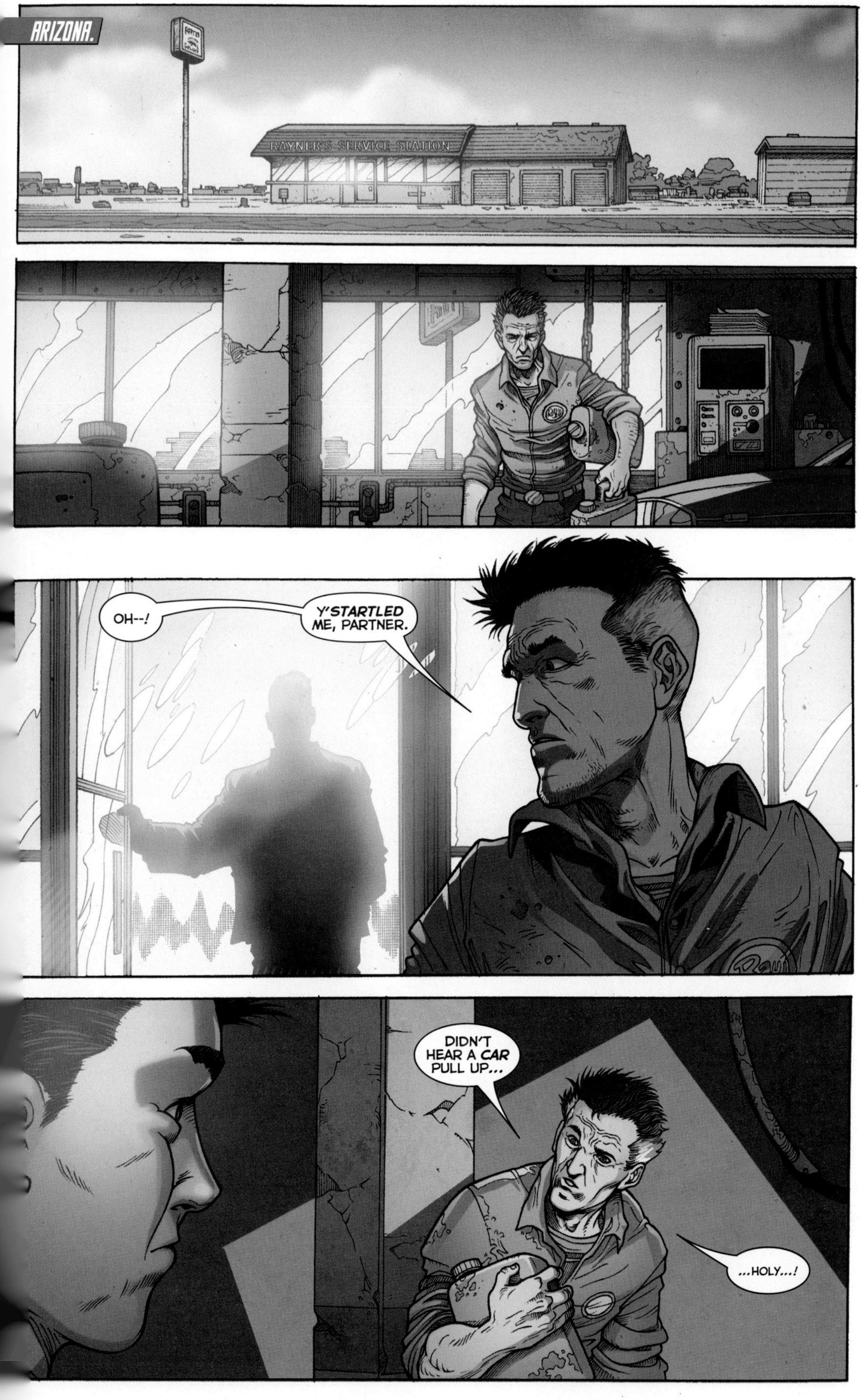
ARIZONA.
RAYNER'S SERVICE STATION
OH--!
Y'STARTLED ME, PARTNER.
DIDN'T HEAR A CAR PULL UP...
...HOLY...!

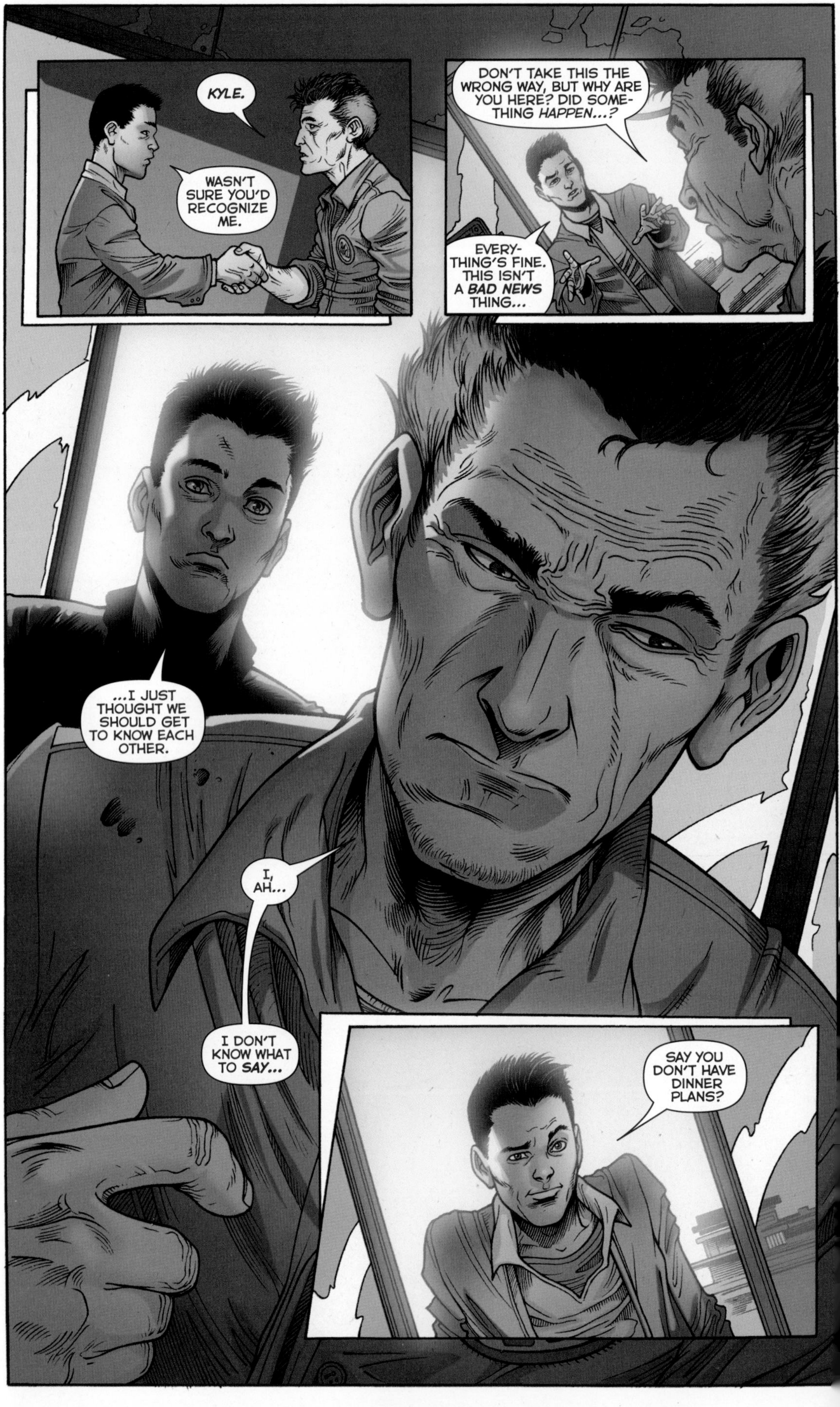
KYLE.
WASN'T SURE YOU'D RECOGNIZE ME.
DON'T TAKE THIS THE WRONG WAY, BUT WHY ARE YOU HERE? DID SOMETHING *HAPPEN...?*
EVERYTHING'S FINE. THIS ISN'T A ***BAD NEWS*** THING...
...I JUST THOUGHT WE SHOULD GET TO KNOW EACH OTHER.
I, AH...
I DON'T KNOW WHAT TO ***SAY...***
SAY YOU DON'T HAVE DINNER PLANS?

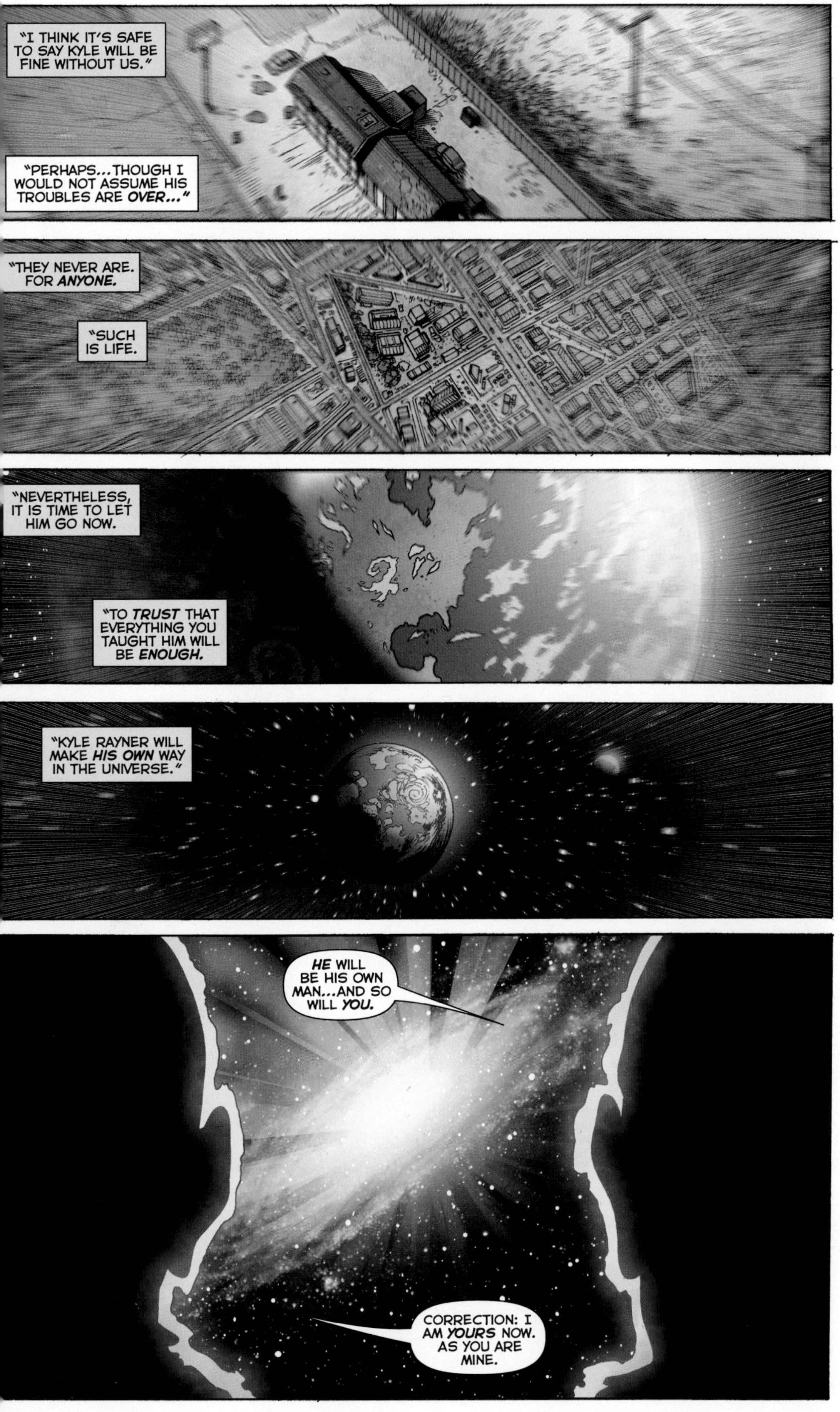
"I THINK IT'S SAFE TO SAY KYLE WILL BE FINE WITHOUT US."
"PERHAPS...THOUGH I WOULD NOT ASSUME HIS TROUBLES ARE *OVER...*"
"THEY NEVER ARE. FOR *ANYONE.*
"SUCH IS LIFE.
"NEVERTHELESS, IT IS TIME TO LET HIM GO NOW.
"TO *TRUST* THAT EVERYTHING YOU TAUGHT HIM WILL BE *ENOUGH.*
"KYLE RAYNER WILL MAKE *HIS OWN* WAY IN THE UNIVERSE."
HE WILL BE HIS OWN MAN...AND SO WILL *YOU.*
CORRECTION: I AM *YOURS* NOW. AS YOU ARE MINE.

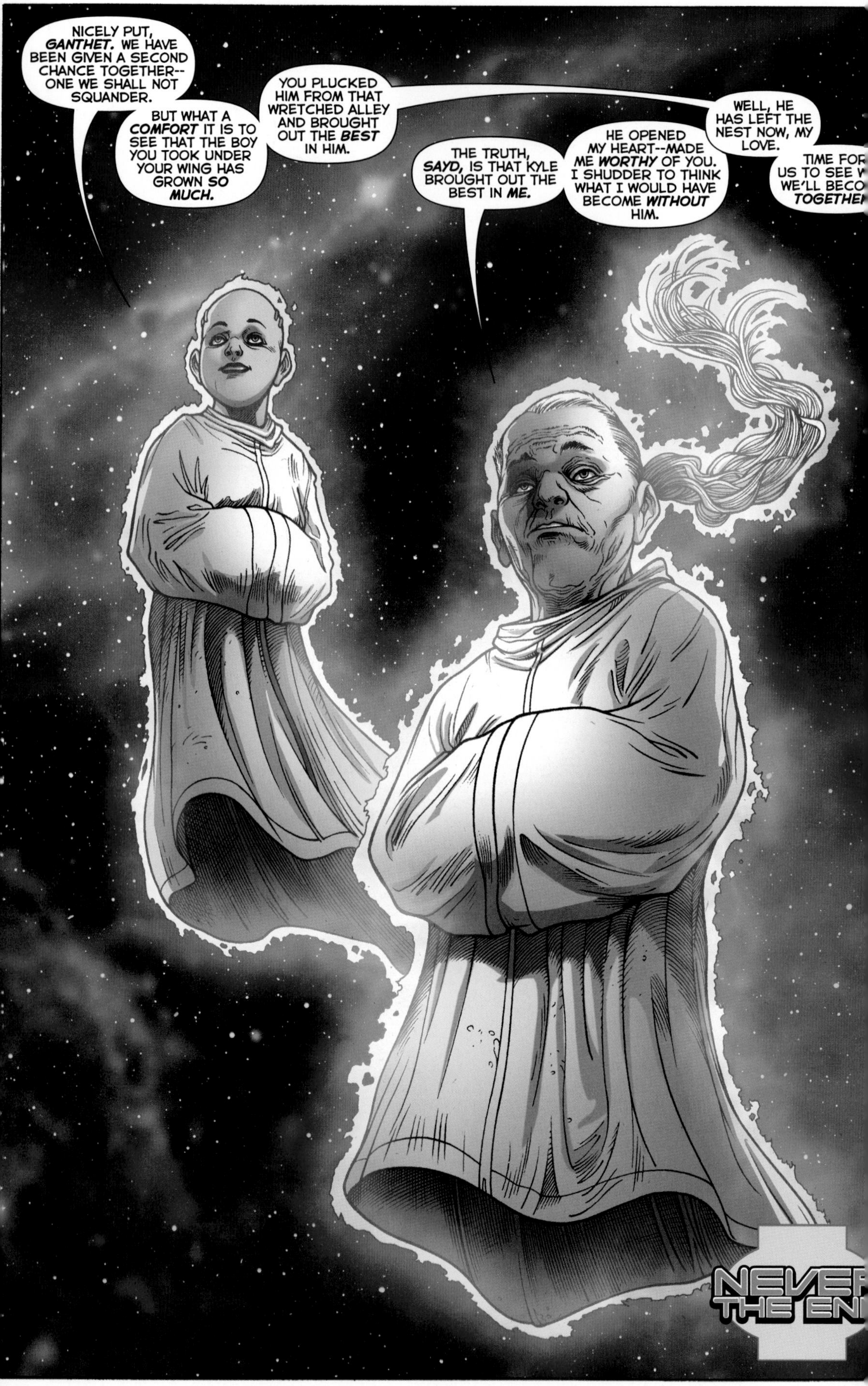
NICELY PUT, GANTHET. WE HAVE BEEN GIVEN A SECOND CHANCE TOGETHER-- ONE WE SHALL NOT SQUANDER.
BUT WHAT A COMFORT IT IS TO SEE THAT THE BOY YOU TOOK UNDER YOUR WING HAS GROWN SO MUCH.
YOU PLUCKED HIM FROM THAT WRETCHED ALLEY AND BROUGHT OUT THE BEST IN HIM.
THE TRUTH, SAYD, IS THAT KYLE BROUGHT OUT THE BEST IN ME.
HE OPENED MY HEART--MADE ME WORTHY OF YOU. I SHUDDER TO THINK WHAT I WOULD HAVE BECOME WITHOUT HIM.
WELL, HE HAS LEFT THE NEST NOW, MY LOVE.
TIME FOR US TO SEE WE'LL BECO TOGETHE
NEVE
THE EN

GREEN LANTERN: NEW GUARDIANS
DESIGNS, SKETCHES, AND LAYOUTS BY AARON KUDER

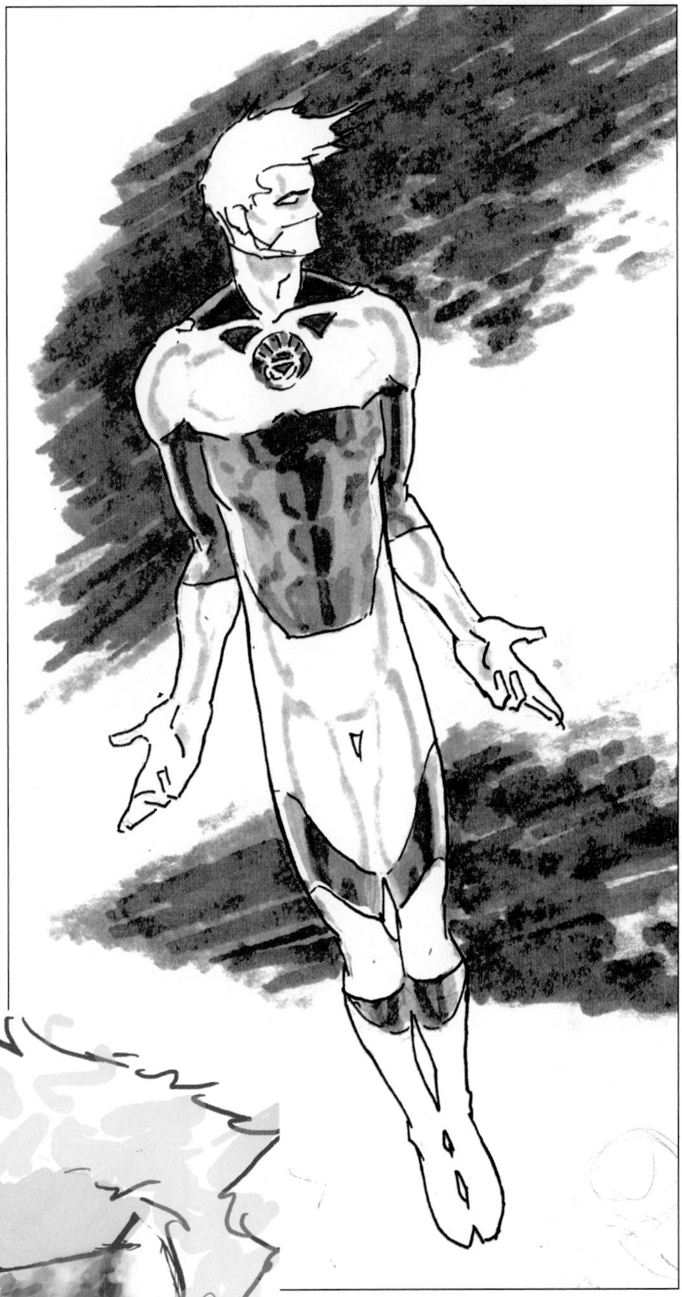

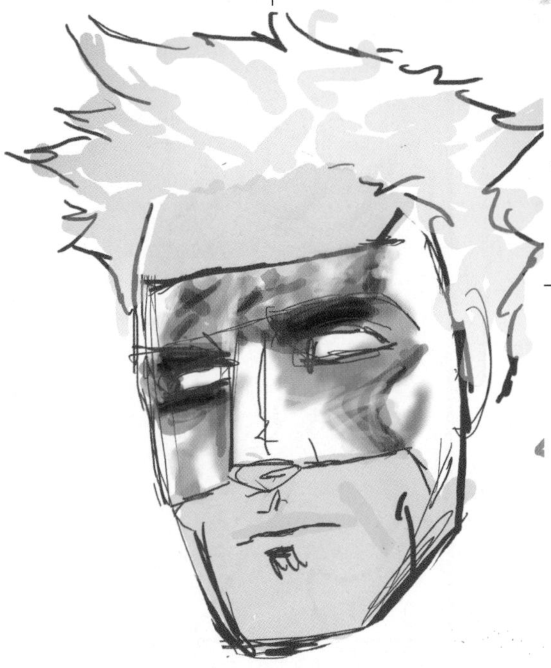

Layout for Issue #15,
Pages 2 and 3

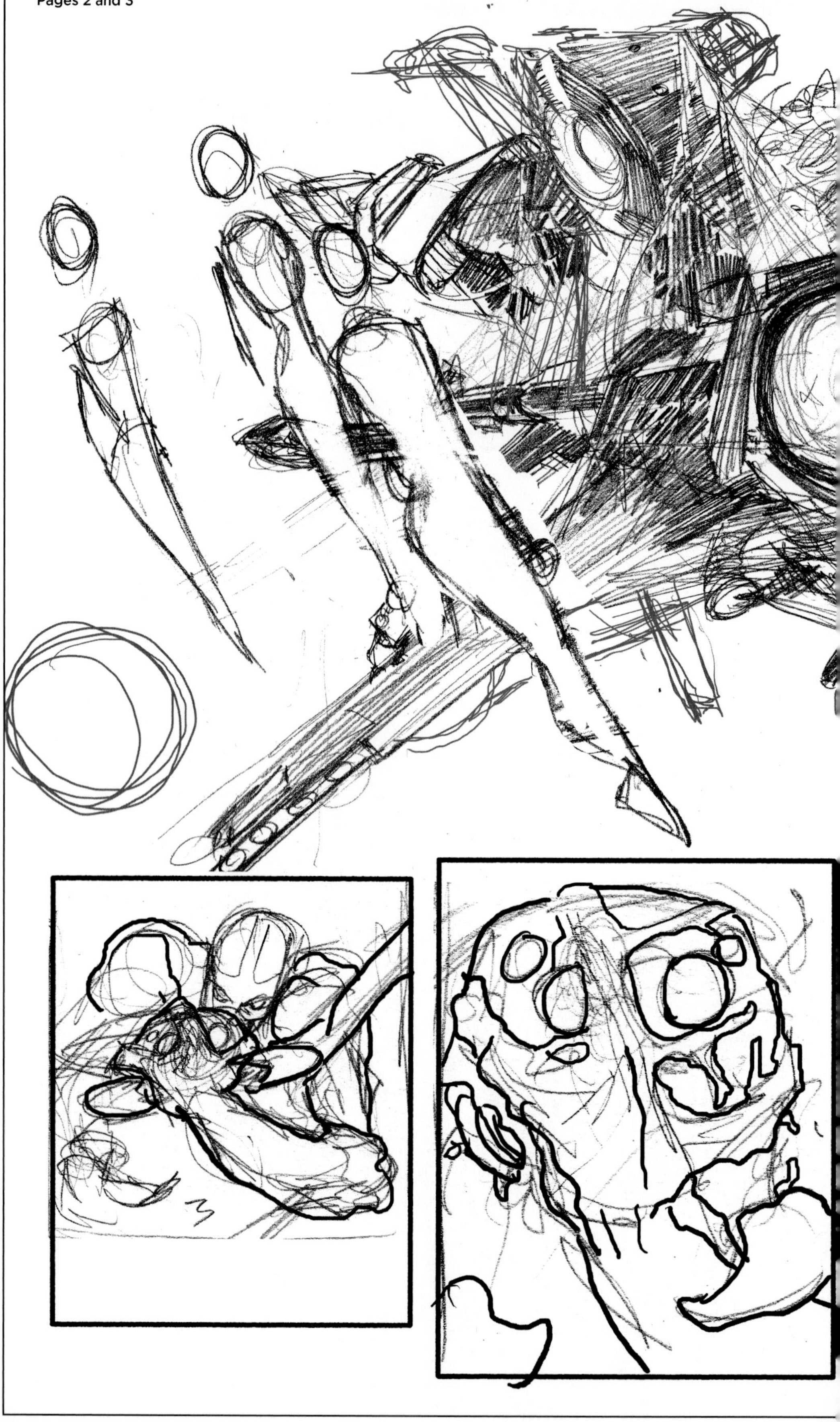

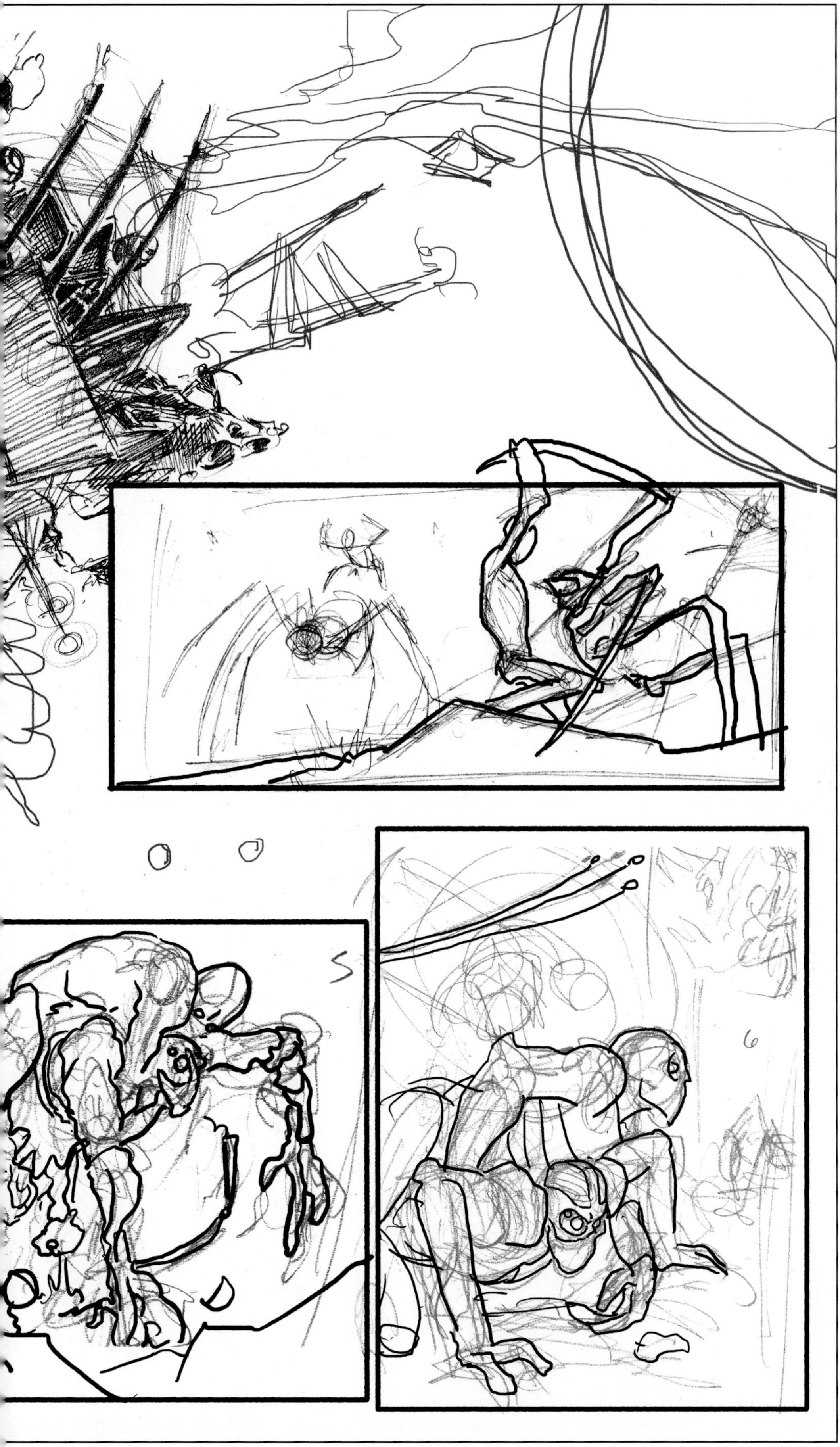
5
6

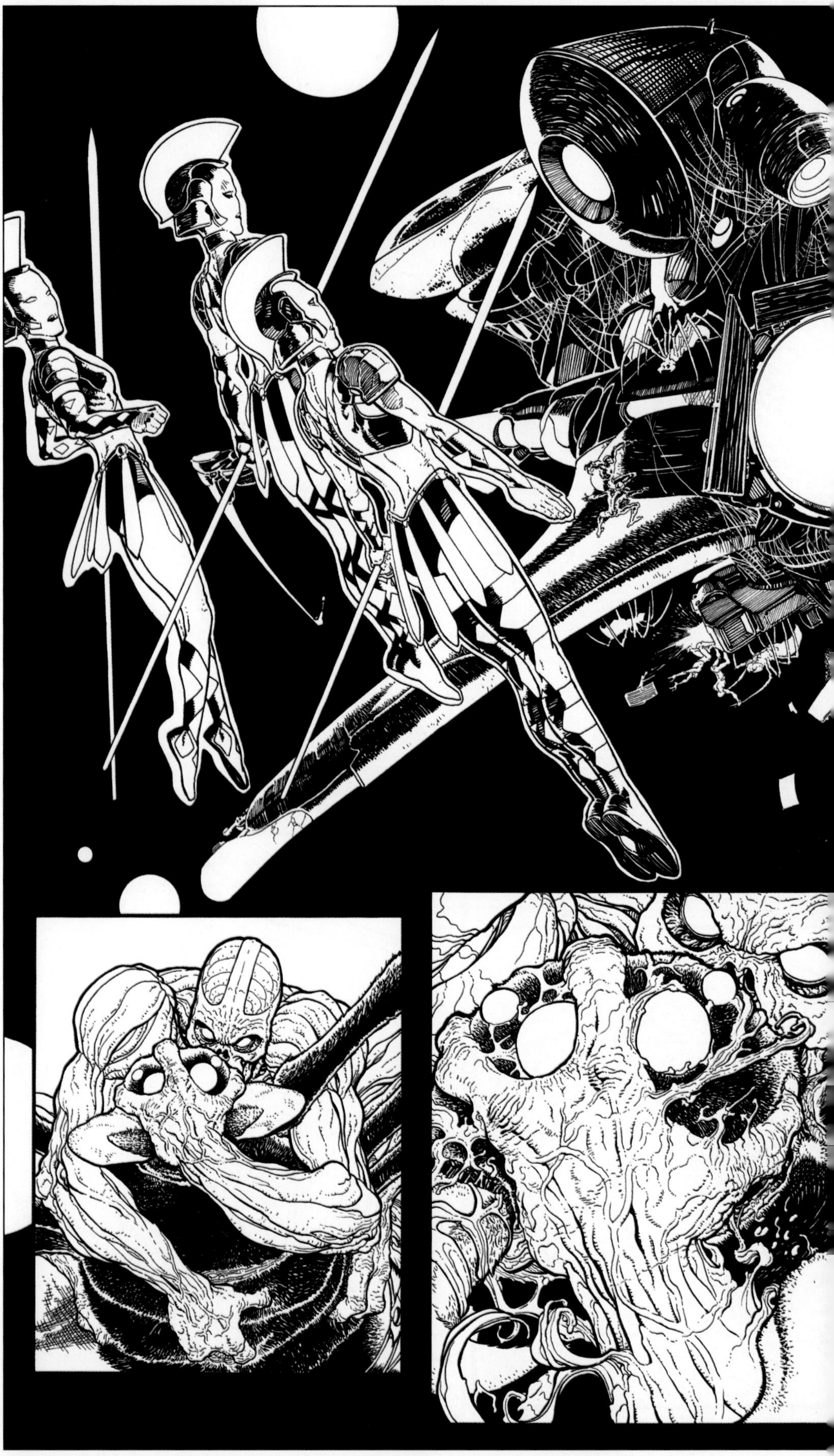

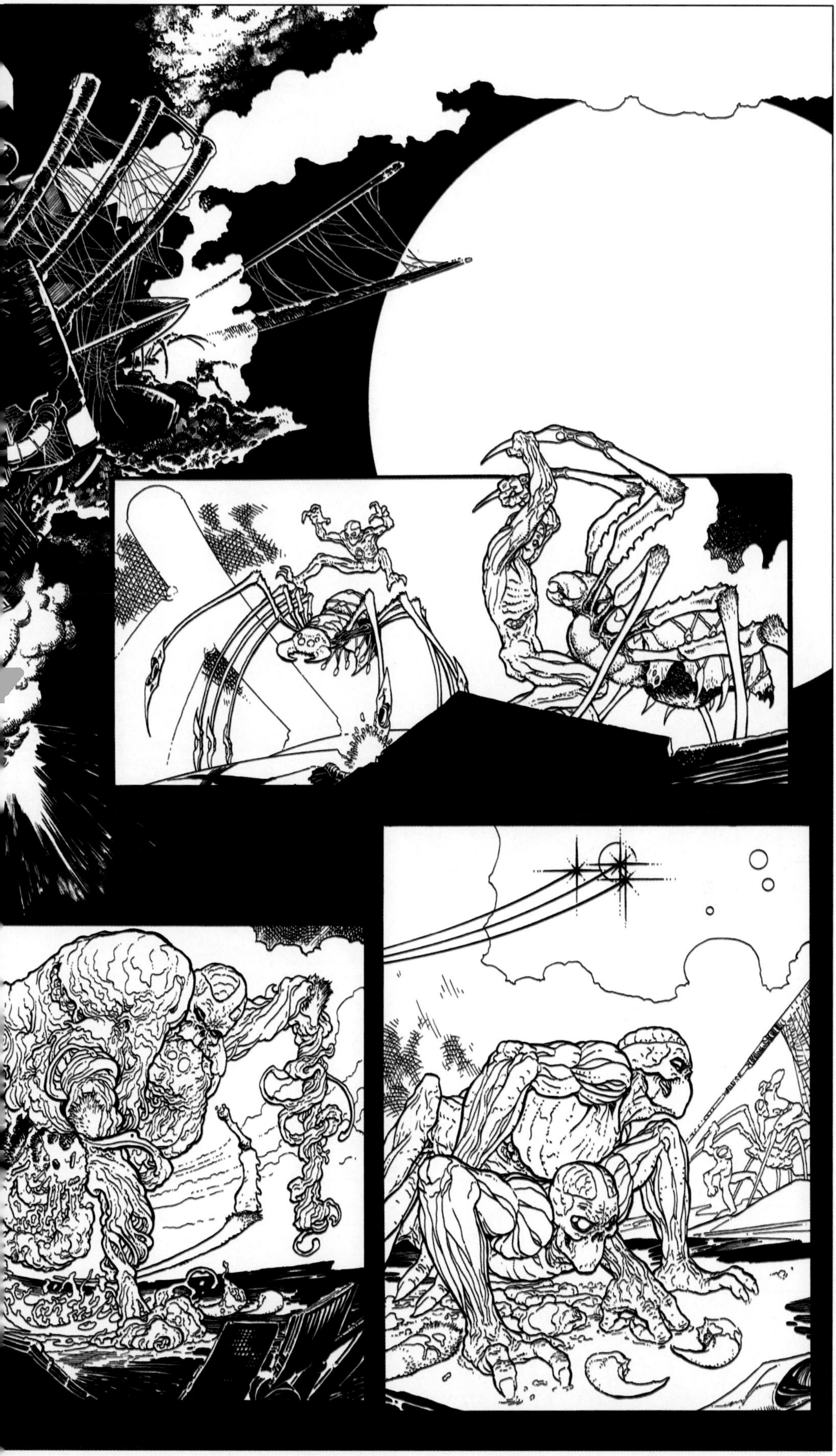

Issue #15, Page 7 inks

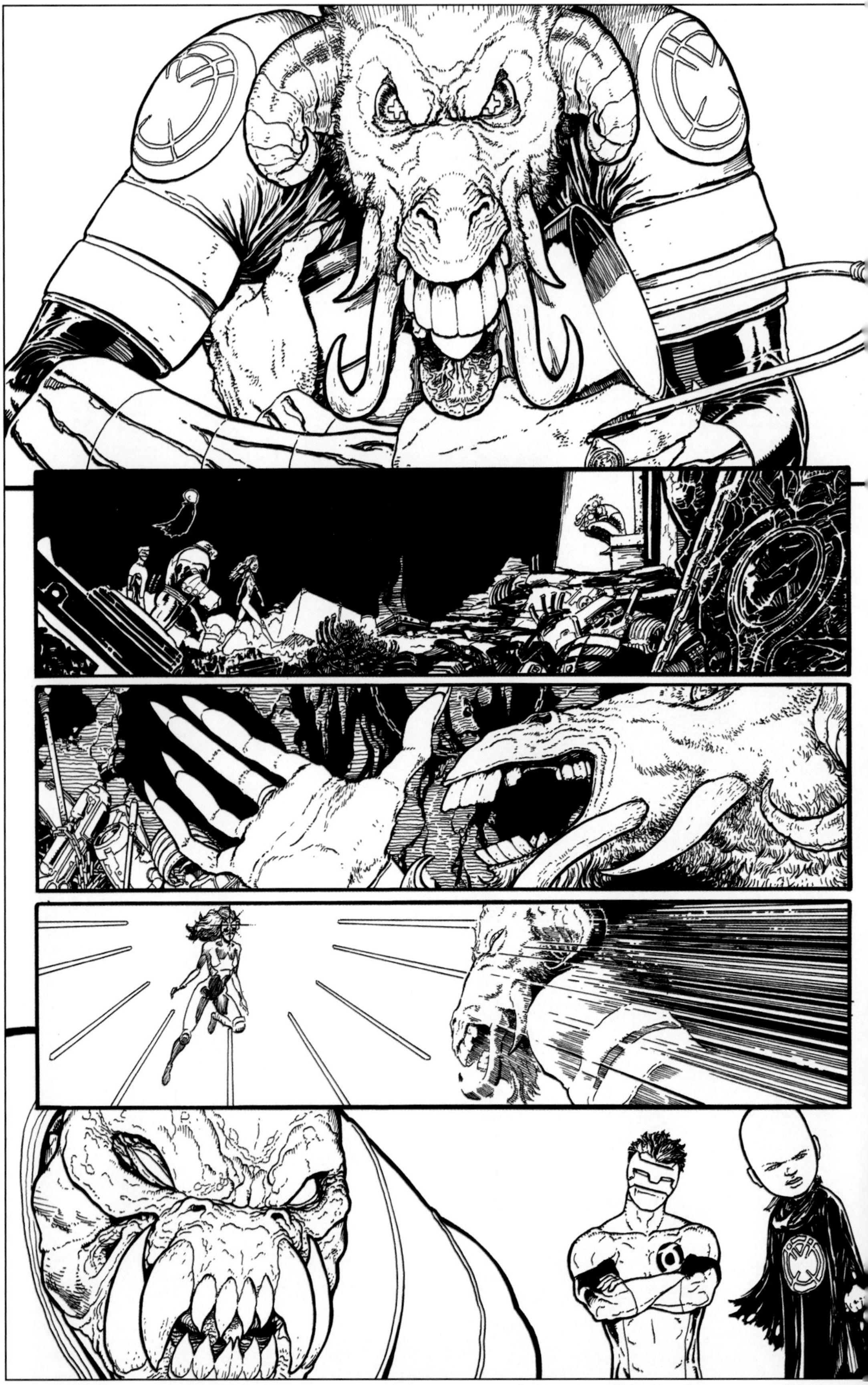

Issue #15, Page 12 inks

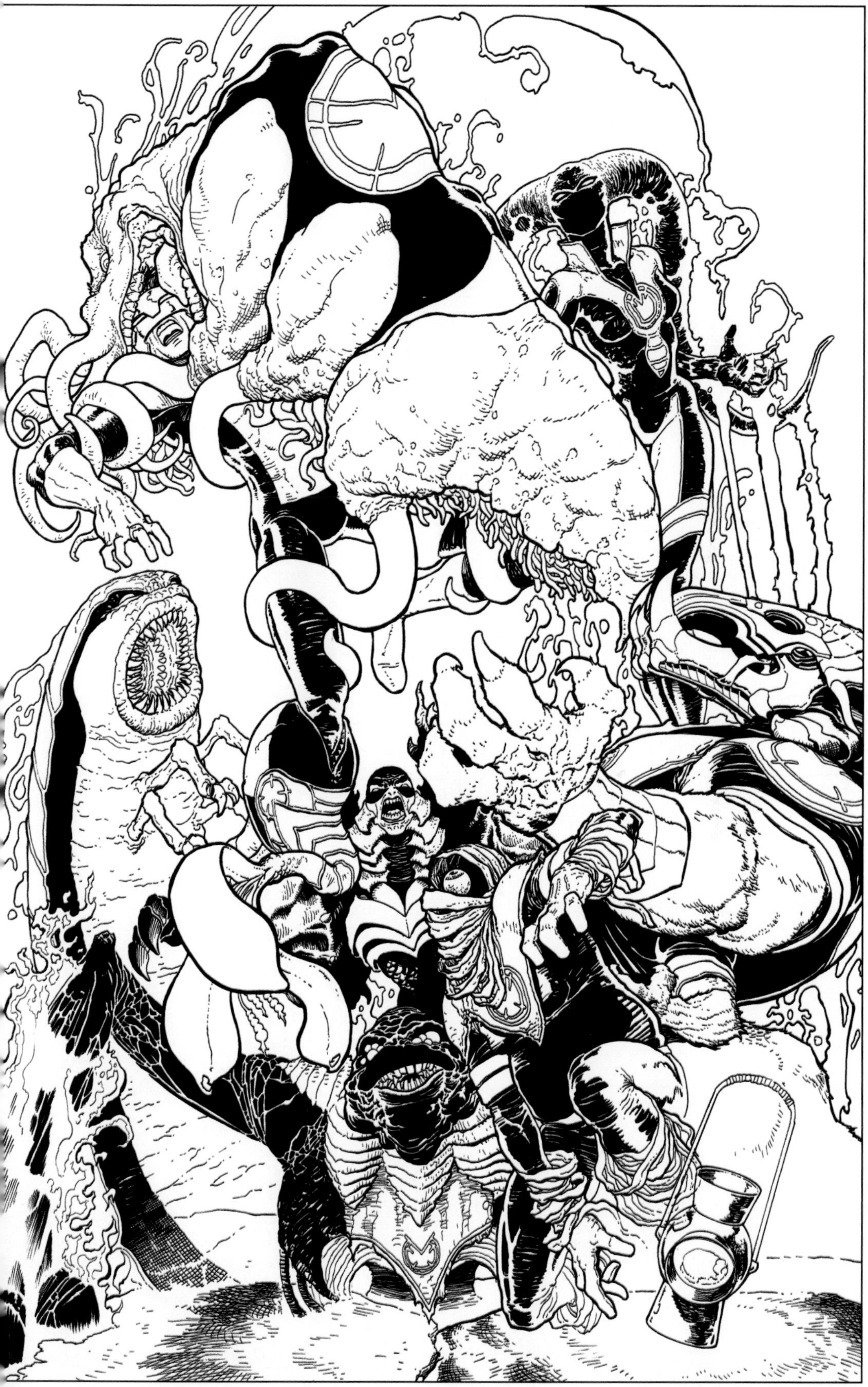

Layout for Issue #0, Page 15

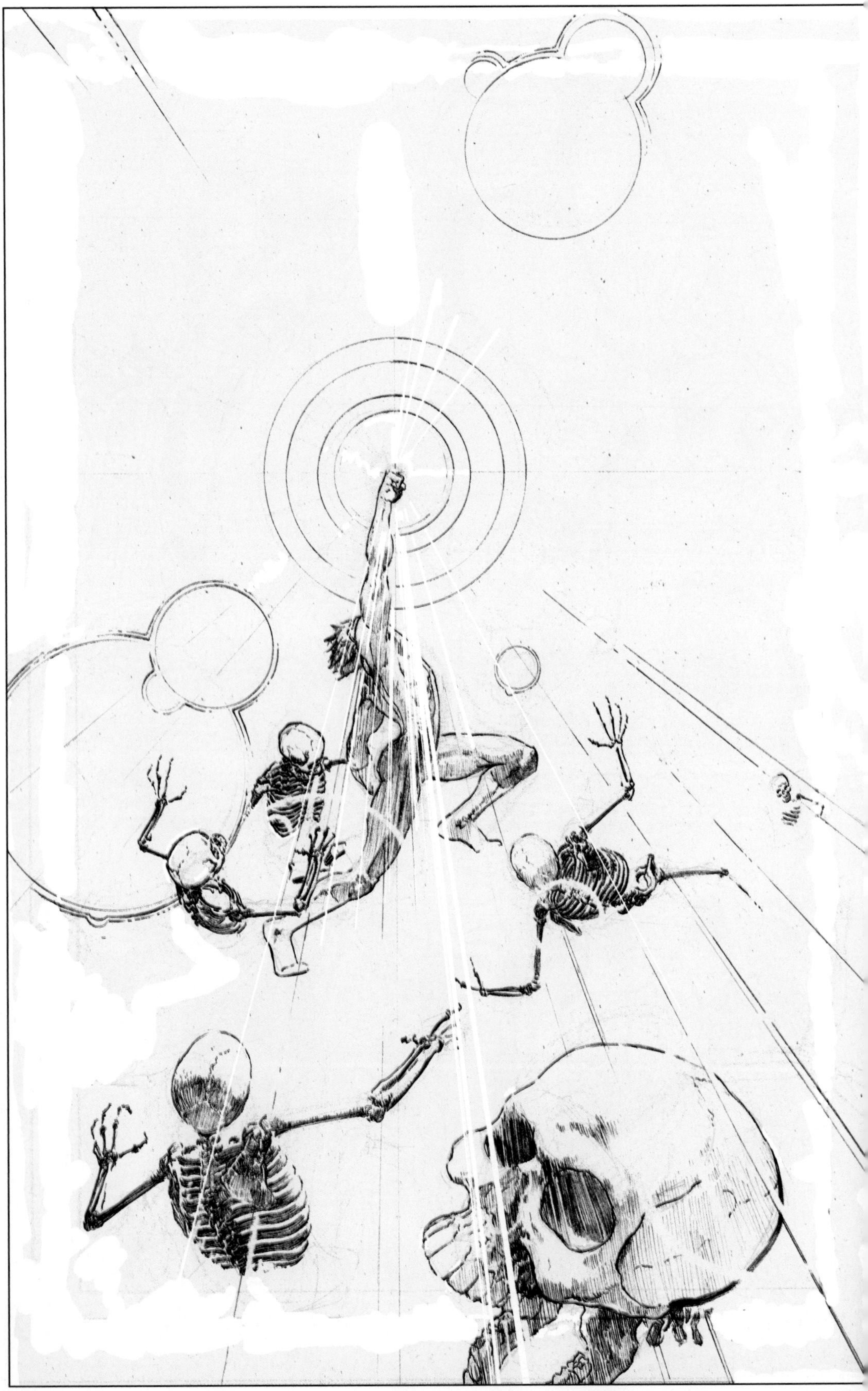

Sketch for unused
Issue #18 cover

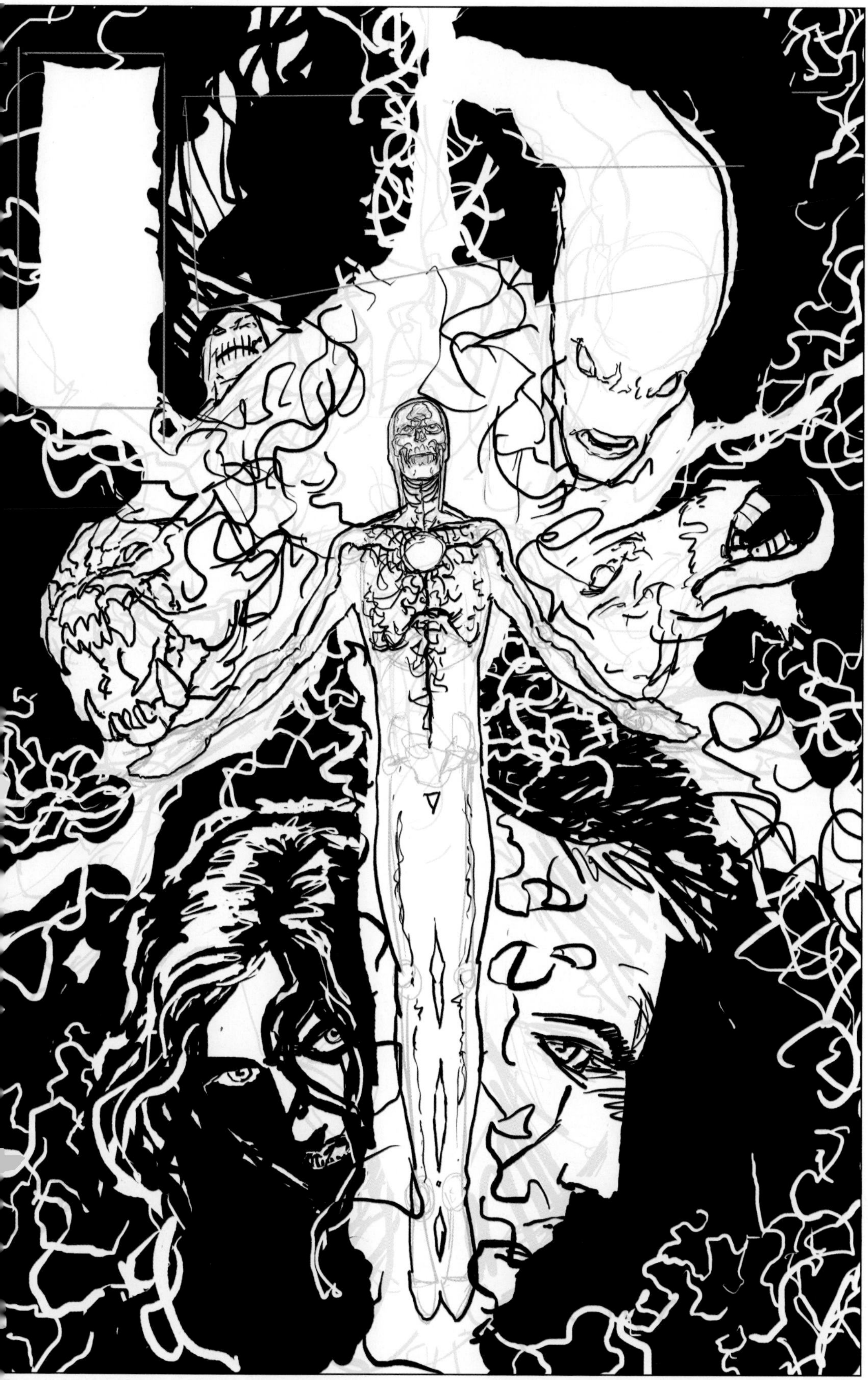

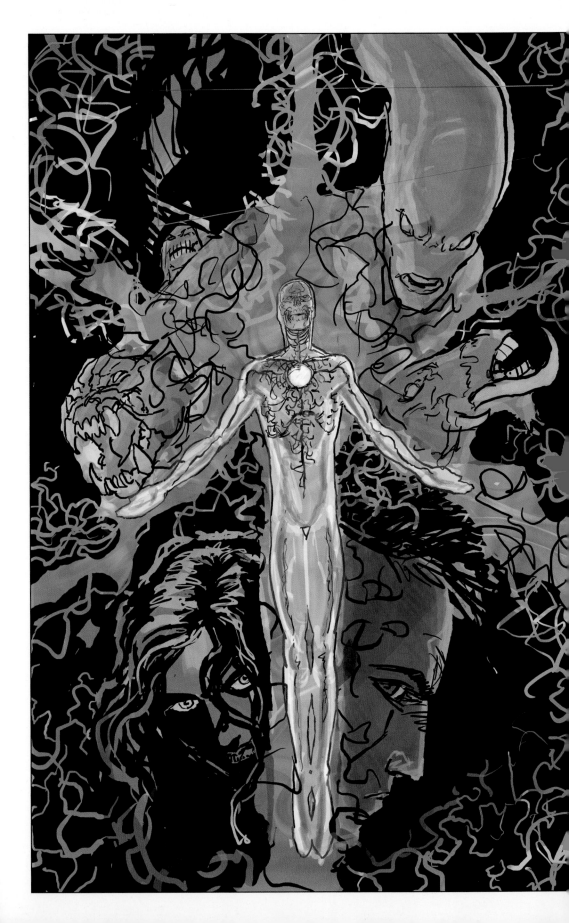

Color rough for
Issue #14 cover

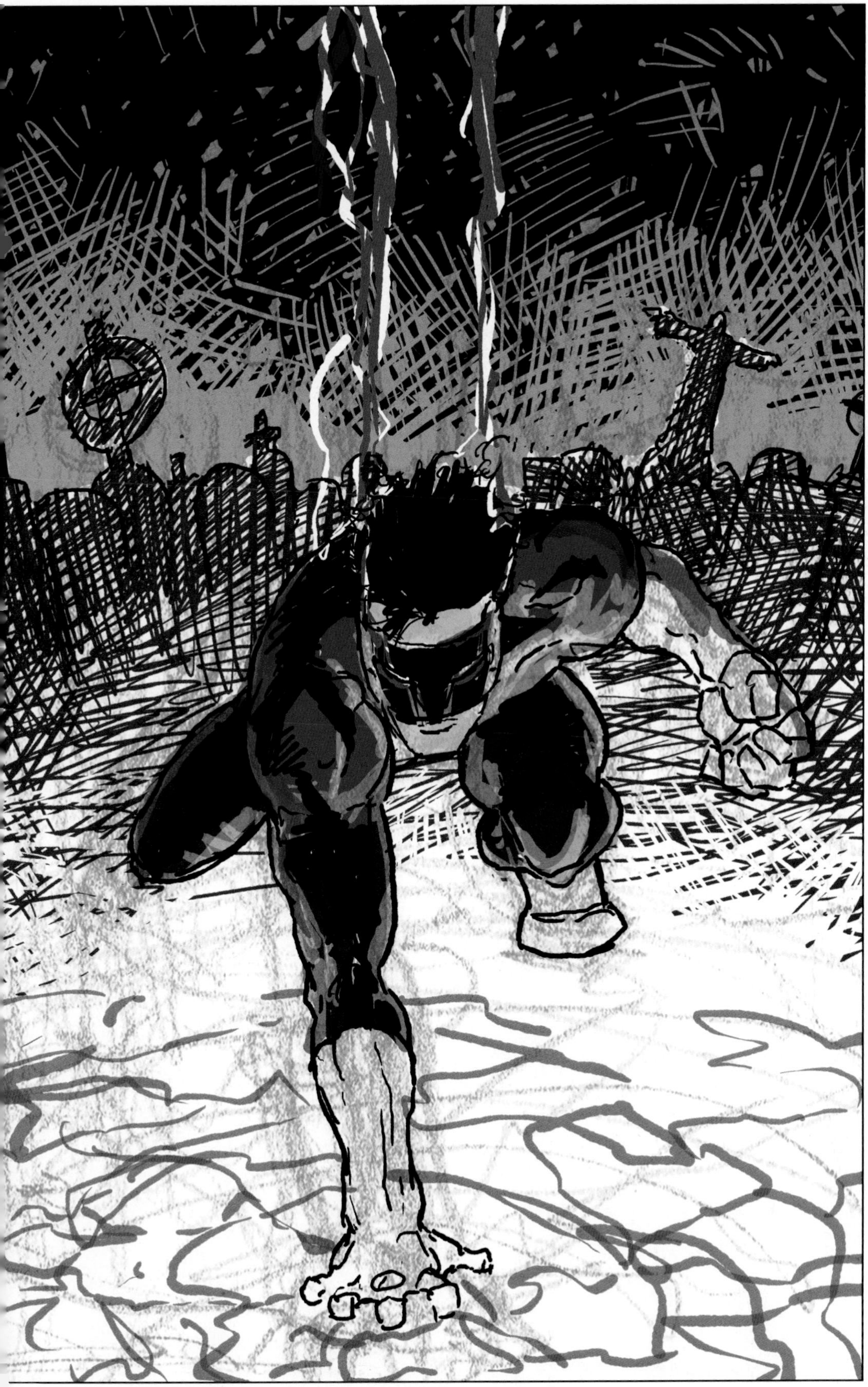

Sketch for Issue #17 cover

"This is the perfect place for people wary of the Green Lantern to start reading his adventures in order to see just how dynamic his world really is."
—COMPLEX MAGAZINE

START AT THE BEGINNING!

GREEN LANTERN
VOLUME 1: SINESTRO

GREEN LANTERN CORPS VOLUME 1: FEARSOME

RED LANTERNS VOLUME 1: BLOOD AND RAGE

GREEN LANTERN: NEW GUARDIANS VOLUME 1: THE RING BEARER

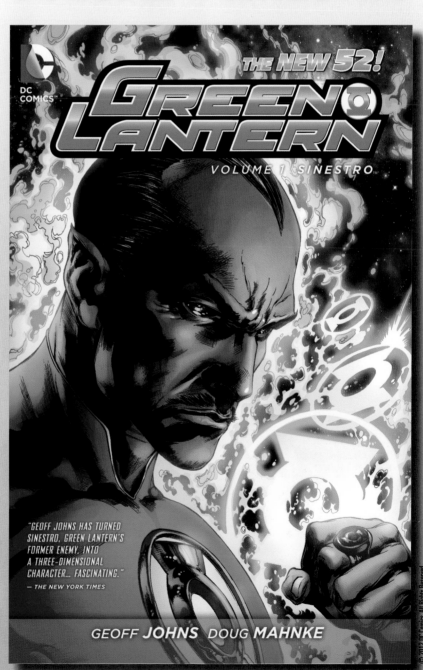

"GEOFF JOHNS HAS TURNED SINESTRO, GREEN LANTERN'S FORMER ENEMY, INTO A THREE-DIMENSIONAL CHARACTER... FASCINATING."
— THE NEW YORK TIMES

GEOFF JOHNS DOUG MAHNKE

DC COMICS™

FROM THE WRITER OF *JUSTICE LEAGUE* & *THE FLAS*

GEOFF JOHNS
GREEN LANTERN: REBIRTH

**GREEN LANTERN:
BRIGHTEST DAY**

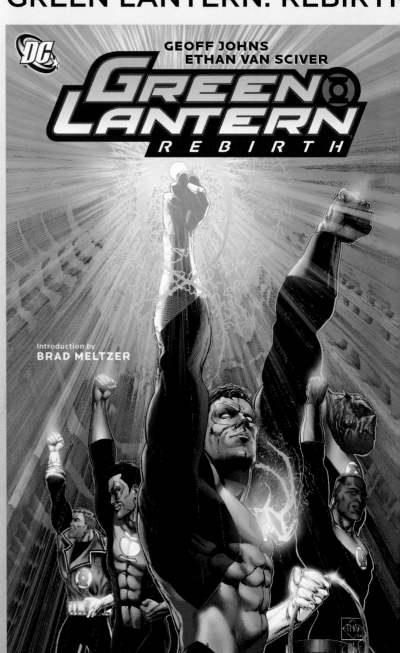

GEOFF JOHNS
ETHAN VAN SCIVER

Green Lantern
REBIRTH

Introduction by
BRAD MELTZER